Wales

THE R

There are more than sixty Rough Guide titles covering destinations from Amsterdam to Zimbabwe

Forthcoming travel titles include

Bali • Costa Rica • Goa • Hawaii • Majorca
Rhodes • Singapore • Vietnam

Rough Guide Reference Series

Classical Music • World Music

Rough Guide Phrasebooks

Czech • French • German • Greek • Italian • Spanish

Rough Guide Credits

Text editor:	Graham Parker
Series editor:	Mark Ellingham
Editorial:	Martin Dunford, Jonathan Buckley, Jo Mead, Samantha Cook, Alison Cowan, Amanda Tomlin, Annie Shaw Lemisse al-Hafidh, Catherine McHale
Production:	Susanne Hillen, Andy Hilliard, Melissa Flack, Alan Spicer Judy Pang, Link Hall, Nicola Williamson
Publicity:	Richard Trillo (UK) Jean-Marie Kelly and Jeff Kaye (US)
Finance:	John Fisher, Celia Crowley, Simon Carloss
Administration:	Tania Hummell

The Rough Guide to Wales owes a great deal to the many friends and acquaintances, Welsh or otherwise, who happily shared their knowledge, freely voiced opinions and expressed an enthusiasm for Wales which we hope is evident throughout this book. Thanks go out to all these people. **Special thanks** are due to the staff at tourist offices throughout the country and in particular to Susan Morris and Rosanne Priest and the Wales Tourist Board. Also to the Rough Guide crew, especially Jonathan Buckley for helping shape the book in its early stages, Martin Dunford and Kate Berens for judicious use of the red pen under pressure and Graham Parker for seeing the editorial process through to the end. Thanks also to Paul Gray for proofreading, Matt Welton for his inspired maps and Melissa Flack for cartographic help and advice.

Mike Parker would like to thank: Emma Clarke, Buzz magazine; Don Jones; Sion Brynach, at the Plaid Cymru office in Cardiff; Mel and Mary Ford and the members of Tylerstown working men's club; Simon Bolton; Jim Coe; Simon Lynch; Gruffudd Roland Williams; the Cox family in Brecon; Jo Griffin and Claire Hobbs for tea and sympathy.

Paul Whitfield would like to thank: James Adam, J.A. Cragg, Sarah Price and Lorna Rotbart for their generous assistance; Liz Porter and Robert Pickstone for company on the Snowdonian mountains; Annie Surtees for acting as wildlife consultant; and Andy Moorhouse and Jelly Clarke for their unending support. Also thanks to Chris Sharratt and Mick Tems for their patience and their contributions to the music section, and Jonathan Tucker for the piece of Welsh rugby.

This first edition published and reprinted in 1994 and June 1995 by Rough Guides Ltd, 1 Mercer Street, London WC2H 9QJ.

Distributed by the Penguin Group:

Penguin Books Ltd, 27 Wrights Lane, London W8 5TZ
Penguin Books USA Inc., 375 Hudson Street, New York 10014, USA
Penguin Books Australia Ltd, 487 Maroondah Highway, PO Box 257, Ringwood, Victoria 3134, Australia Penguin Books Canada Ltd, 10 Alcorn Avenue, Toronto, Ontario M4V 1E4, Canada
Penguin Books (NZ) Ltd, 182–190 Wairau Road, Auckland 10, New Zealand

Rough Guides were formerly published as Real Guides in the United States and Canada.

Typeset in Linotron Univers and Century Old Style to an original design by Andrew Oliver.
Printed in the UK by Cox & Wyman Ltd, Reading, Berks.
Illustrations in Part One and Part Three by Ed Briant.
Basics and Contexts illustrations by Henry Iles.

432pp.
Includes index

A catalogue record for this book is available from the British Library
ISBN 1-85828-096-6

Wales

THE ROUGH GUIDE

Written and researched by

Mike Parker and Paul Whitfield

THE ROUGH GUIDES

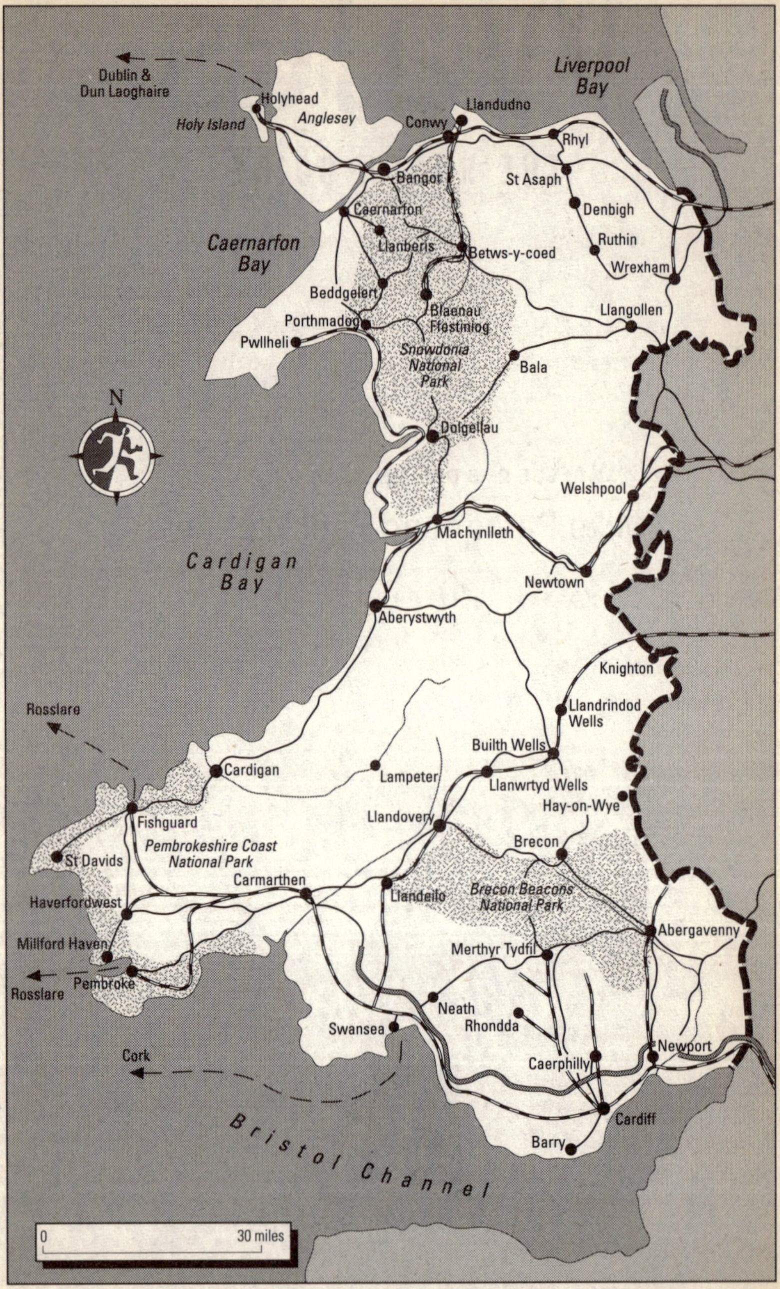
Liverpool Bay
Dublin & Dun Laoghaire
Holyhead
Holy Island
Anglesey
Llandudno
Conwy
Rhyl
Bangor
St Asaph
Denbigh
Caernarfon
Ruthin
Caernarfon Bay
Llanberis
Betws-y-coed
Wrexham
Beddgelert
Blaenau Ffestiniog
Llangollen
Porthmadog
Pwllheli
Snowdonia National Park
Bala
N
Dolgellau
Welshpool
Machynlleth
Cardigan Bay
Newtown
Aberystwyth
Knighton
Llandrindod Wells
Rosslare
Builth Wells
Cardigan
Lampeter
Llanwrtyd Wells
Hay-on-Wye
Fishguard
Llandovery
Pembrokeshire Coast National Park
Brecon
St Davids
Carmarthen
Brecon Beacons National Park
Haverfordwest
Llandeilo
Abergavenny
Millford Haven
Merthyr Tydfil
Rosslare
Pembroke
Neath
Rhondda
Swansea
Newport
Cork
Caerphilly
Cardiff
Barry
Bristol Channel
0
30 miles

CONTENTS

INTRODUCTION

Wales at its best is the most beguiling part of the British isles. Its soaring mountain ranges, plunging, battered coastline, calm, lush valleys, and old-fashioned market towns all invite long and repeated visits. The culture, too, is compelling, whether in its Welsh or English-language manifestations, in its Celtic or its industrial traditions. If all too many of the British across the border continue to regard Wales as a land of male voice choirs, rugby, and grim pit villages, more fool they – and more space to explore for the rest of us.

As you cross the border from England, you are, in fact, immediately aware of the different attitudes and cultures of the two countries. Wales shares many physical and emotional similarities with the other Celtic lands – Scotland, Ireland, Cornwall, Brittany, even Asturias and Galicia in northwest Spain. It shares, too, a desire for an individual political path, which has long been frustrated by English rulers and English-dominated governments. Even in the new, ever more devolved Europe, Wales lacks its own parliament or legislature: a situation that has led to a small but active nationalist and separatist movement. As yet, their main achievements have been in terms of culture and language, forcing the British government to honour pledges for a Welsh-language TV channel, and keeping the language alive in the schools and communities.

What Wales might lack in self-determination, though, it makes up for in its distinct cultural identity. This is expressed in a myriad of ways beyond the Welsh language as English is the predominant tongue in all but rural mid-Wales and the northwestern county of Gwynedd. The Welsh character is famously endowed with a musicality, lyricism, introspection and sentimentality that has produced bards and singers for centuries. And Welsh culture is undeniably a popular expression – a democratic impulse, as in the other Celtic lands. Anything from a rousing chorus of Welsh songs at closing time in the pub to the grandiose theatricality of an eisteddfod involve everyone in a spontaneous and class-less manner. It is unexclusive, too, on the whole, and any visitor eager to learn and join in is enthusiastically welcomed.

Where to go

Like all capital cities, **Cardiff** is atypical of the rest of the country, but as the first major stop on both rail and road routes from England into south Wales, it is a good place to start. Most national institutions are based here, including the National Museum and St Fagans Folk Museum, both of which are excellent introductions to the character of the rest of Wales. The only other centres of appreciable size are dowdy **Newport** and breezy, resurgent **Swansea**, lying respectively to the east and west of the capital. All three cities grew as ports, mainly exporting millions of tons of coal and iron from the **Valleys**, where fiercely proud industrial communities were built up in the thin strips of land between the mountains.

Much of Wales' appeal lies outside the towns, where there is ample evidence of the warmongering which has shaped the country's development. Castles are everywhere, from hard little stone keeps of the early Welsh princes to Edward I's incomparable series of thirteenth-century fortresses of **Flint**, **Conwy**,

WALES AND ITS SHIFTING COUNTY BOUNDARIES

Wales is a small and thinly populated country, and most of the 2.8 million inhabitants congregate in the southern quarter of this land, which stretches 160 miles from north to south and 50 miles from east to west. Only 8000 square miles in all, it is smaller than Massachusetts and only half the size of The Netherlands.

In 1995, after two decades of people moaning about the demise of the "true" counties, Wales is due to revert largely to the old boundaries. After Henry VIII's Acts of Union in 1536 and 1543, when the Welsh administrative system became formally linked with England's, Wales was divided into thirteen counties or shires, their borders predominantly reflecting those of the baronial domains (or Marcher lordships) they replaced. Many of the names of these shires – Brecon, Radnor and Montgomery, in particular – are still in common use today and crop up occasionally in this book.

The Local Government Act, enacted in 1974, brought wholesale reorganization, added an extra tier of bureaucracy, and left Wales with only eight counties, almost all with new names reflecting the ancient tribal divisions. North Wales is divided between Gwynedd in the west and Clwyd in the east, Dyfed encompasses a huge chunk of the southwest corner of the country, the bulk of the land bordering England falls into Powys, and the southeast got chopped into Gwent and West, Mid- and South Glamorgan. In general these county names are the ones used in the text.

With the planned axing of one bureaucratic level, Wales will have 21 counties, some with pre-1974 boundaries – the island of Anglesey will again be a county – others fanciful but self-explanatory concoctions such as Heads of the Valleys. It remains to be seen how these changes will be greeted

Beaumaris, **Caernarfon**, **Harlech** and **Rhuddlan**, and grandiose Victorian piles where grouse were the only enemy. Fortified residences formed the source of a number of the stately homes that dot the country but many castles were deserted and remain dramatically isolated on rocky knolls, most likely on spots previously occupied by prehistoric communities. Passage graves and stone circles offer a more tangible link to the pre-Roman era when the priestly order of Druids ruled over early Celtic peoples, and the great medieval monastic houses like ruined **Valle Crucis Abbey** are not that difficult to find.

Whether you are admiring castles, megaliths or Dylan Thomas's home at **Laugharne**, the experience is enhanced by the beauty of the Welsh countryside. The rigid backbone of the **Cambrian Mountains** terminates in the soaring peaks of **Snowdonia National Park** and the angular ridges of the **Brecon Beacons**, both superb walking country and both national parks. A third national park follows the **Pembrokeshire Coast** where golden strands come separated by rocky bluffs overlooking offshore bird colonies. Much of the rest of the coast remains unspoilt, though seldom undiscovered, whereas long sweeps of sand are ofter backed by traditional British seaside resorts: the north Wales coast, the **Cambrian coast** and the **Gower Peninsula** displaying a notable abundance.

When to go

The English preoccupation with the weather holds equally for the Welsh. The climate here is temperate, with Welsh summers rarely getting hot and nowhere but the tops of mountain ranges ever getting very cold, even in mid-winter. Temperatures vary little from Cardiff in the south to Llandudno in the north, but proximity to the mountains is a different matter: Llanberis, at the foot of Snowdon, gets doused with more than twice as much rainfall as Caernarfon, seven miles away, and is always a few degrees cooler. With rain never too far from the mind of any resident or visitor, it is easy to forget that throughout much of the summer, Wales – particularly the coast – can be bathed in sun. Between June and September, the Pembrokeshire coast can be as warm as anywhere in Britain.

The bottom line is that it's impossible to say with any degree of certainty that the weather will be pleasant in any given month. May might be wet and grey one year and gloriously sunny the next, and the same goes for the autumnal months – November stands an equal chance of being crisp and clear or foggy and grim. Obviously, if you're planning to lie on a beach, or camp in the dry, you'll want to go between June and September – a period when you shouldn't go anywhere without booking your accommodation well in advance. Otherwise, if you're balancing the likely fairness of the weather against the density of the crowds, the best time to get into the countryside or the towns is between April and May or in October. If outdoor pursuits are your objective, these are the best months for walking, June to October are warmest and driest for climbing, and December to March the only times you'll find enough water for kayaking.

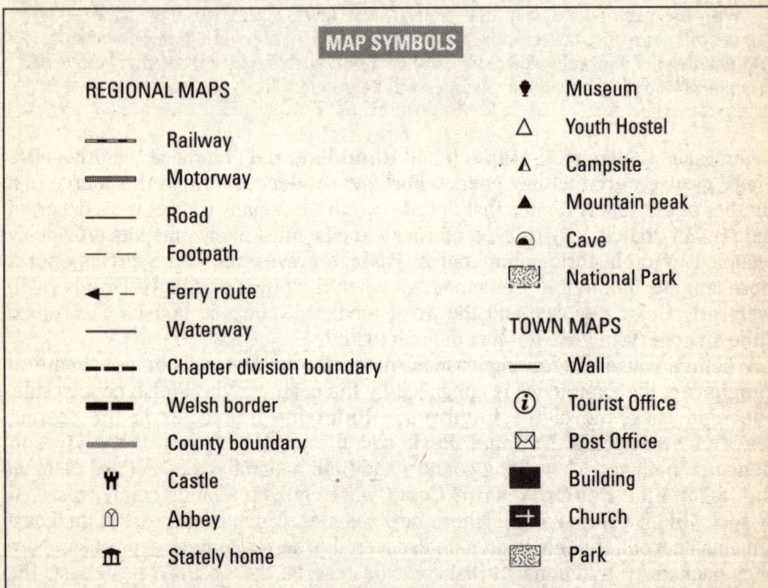

PART ONE

THE BASICS

GETTING THERE FROM THE UK AND EUROPE

Crossing the border from England into Wales is straightforward, with train and bus services forming part of the British national network. High costs and minimal time savings mean flights within Britain will be of little use, with the possible exception of those from Scotland. If you're driving from England, you'll probably be using one of the half-dozen or so roads which all run east to west through Wales. The two providing the quickest access into the heart of the country run along opposite coasts: the M4 motorway in the south, and the A55 dual carriageway in the north. These are both fast and busy roads, and minor routes are more appealing if you aren't in too much of a hurry.

Coming from Ireland ferries are definitely the cheapest and easiest way of getting to Wales. From the rest of Europe, there's the choice of flying from various destinations to Cardiff International Airport, or using either the traditional cross-Channel ferry services or the Channel Tunnel to England and making your way onwards from there.

BY PLANE

The only airport of any size in Wales is **Cardiff International Airport**, at which scheduled flights arrive from selected northern European capitals and a few British destinations. The main international carrier is *KLM* (London information on ☎081/750 9000), which flies into Cardiff from Amsterdam. The only other main carrier is *Manx Airlines* (☎0345/256256), which operates services from Paris, Dublin, Belfast and Edinburgh to Cardiff. These are mostly business flights, timed and priced accordingly, and often not operating at weekends.

In general, from Europe and Ireland you are better off flying into London or Manchester and moving on by bus or train. There are no worthwhile scheduled services from England to Wales or within Wales.

BY TRAIN

From 1995, the Channel Tunnel should be running a frequent **car-carrying train service** that crosses from Calais in northern France to Folkestone in southern England. Buses, cars and motorbikes will be loaded onto a freight train, known as *Le Shuttle*, which will take 35 minutes to get between the loading terminals at Calais and Folkestone. *Le Shuttle* is planned to run every fifteen minutes at peak periods, hourly at the quietest times of the day. For information on fares, call ☎0303/271 100. **Passenger services** will also operate through the tunnel from major European cities straight to London, and also to Cardiff; information on ☎081/784 1333.

Despite the tunnel, **car ferries** are likely to remain in business, often undercutting the trains and, in the case of the Calais–Dover service, not taking much longer (see "By Road", below, for more details).

FROM ENGLAND AND SCOTLAND

Despite the threat of rail line privatization, which may make Britain's train network a tangle of private companies, **British Rail** (BR) still runs the majority of rail services. Two main lines provide frequent, fast services **to Wales from London**: the south Wales *InterCity* line from London Paddington via Reading, Swindon and Bristol to Newport, Cardiff and Swansea; and the north Wales line to Bangor and Holyhead. Very few direct trains from England go beyond Swansea, although connections at either Cardiff or Swansea link up with trains to Carmarthen and stations in Pembrokeshire. **From other cities in England and Scotland**, you'll probably need to change en route – at Bath for the south coast line, at Crewe for the north coast – though for south Wales, a semi-fast shuttle runs between Manchester or Birmingham and Cardiff via Hereford or Gloucester.

Mid-Wales is best reached via Birmingham and Shrewsbury, with two lines plunging deep into the heart of the country. The faster route heads through Welshpool, Newtown and Machynlleth, beyond which it divides at Dyfi Junction. The southern spur goes a few miles to Borth and Aberystwyth, the northern one crawls up the coast through Tywyn, Barmouth, Harlech and Porthmadog to Pwllheli. Even slower is the second route from Shrewsbury, the **Heart of Wales line**, which limps four or five times daily into Wales, through Knighton, Llandrindod Wells, Llanwrtyd Wells, Llandovery, Llandeilo and a host of tiny halts on the way to Llanelli and Swansea.

Ordinary second-class (Standard Class in BR-speak) **fares** are high, and first-class costs an extra 33 percent, but there are six types of reduced fare ticket.

Savers are return tickets that can be used on all trains on Saturdays, Sundays and bank holidays, on most weekday trains outside the morning rush hour for the outward journey, and all trains for the return leg. If you buy a return ticket at any station outside the morning rush hour, you'll routinely be issued with a *Saver* ticket. An **Advance** ticket costs the same as a *Saver* and permits travel on most services over 150 miles, but must be bought before noon on the day before travel, and numbers are limited. **SuperSavers**, cheaper still, cannot be used on Fridays nor on half a dozen other specified days of the year, normally Saturdays in July and August. A **SuperAdvance** ticket costs the same as a *SuperSaver*, has the same limitations as the *Advance* ticket and numbers are even more limited. *Saver* and *SuperSaver* tickets are valid for one month (outward travel has to be within 2 days of the date on the ticket), and allow a break in the return (but not outward) leg of the journey.

Like the *Advance* and *SuperAdvance* tickets, the even cheaper **Apex** tickets are issued in limited numbers on certain *InterCity* journeys of 150 miles or more, but these have to be bought at least seven days before travelling and you must specify your outward and return departure times. They include a seat reservation in the price. In addition, there is a **Leisure First** ticket which is more expensive than a *Saver*, but allows travel on any train, must be booked before 4pm on the day before you travel and requires outward and return journeys to be separated by a Saturday.

In practice, you can buy *Saver*, *Supersaver* and *Leisure First* tickets to just about anywhere, but other tickets are only available in limited numbers on long, popular journeys. For Wales, that means journeys between London and the main stations on the north and south coast lines.

Children under five travel free, those aged 5–15 inclusive paying half the adult fare on most journeys – though there are no discounts on *Apex* tickets. In an apparent effort to dissuade people from using its services, *British Rail* now regards skis and large musical instruments (even a cello) as children and charges you for them accordingly. Most long-distance trains now have limited space for **bicycles** and you are required to reserve a place before you travel and pay £3 for each journey.

On Sundays, many *InterCity* services have a special deal whereby you can convert your second-class ticket to a first-class one by paying a five-pound supplement. This is seldom worthwhile within Wales, but vital if you are travelling to London after a Rugby International match at Cardiff Arms Park and don't want to stand up.

To take the **London–Cardiff** service as an example, an ordinary one-way **fare** costs £35, more than some of the reduced return fares: a *Leisure First* ticket is £52; a *Saver* is £40; a *SuperSaver* is £31; and an *Apex* is £24. For a rough idea of *Supersaver* fares from other British cities, you can expect to pay the following: from Edinburgh and Glasgow to Cardiff £61, or Holyhead £50; from Newcastle to Cardiff and Holyhead, £59 and £50 respectively; from Manchester £33 and £21; and from Birmingham £22 and £30. For all special-offer tickets, you should book as far ahead as you possibly can – many *Apex* tickets are sold out weeks before the travel date.

Journey times between main centres are remarkably short: London–Cardiff takes under 2hr and London–Swansea around 3hr. Heading for the north coast, expect the London–Holyhead service to take just over 4hr.

TRAIN INFORMATION

London Paddington ☎071/262 6767

For the numbers of **Welsh mainline stations**, see p.20.

BY BUS

Inter-town **bus** services duplicate a few of the major rail routes, often at half the price of the train or less. Buses are reasonably comfortable and often have drinks and sandwiches available on board on longer routes. By far the biggest national operator is **National Express**, whose network covers England and sends half a dozen tendrils into Wales. The chief routes are from London to Cardiff, Swansea and on to Pembroke and Milford Haven; London to Wrexham; London to Aberystwyth; London along the north coast to Holyhead and Pwllheli; Birmingham to Cardiff and Swansea; Birmingham to Haverfordwest; and Manchester along the north coast. *National Express* services are so popular that for busy routes and services during weekends and holidays, it's a good idea to buy a reserved journey ticket, guaranteeing a seat.

One-way tickets are usually little cheaper than an **economy return** ticket, which is good for travel on any day except Friday and is valid for three months. If you travel on Friday, expect to pay around 30 percent more. Typical economy return **journey costs** to Cardiff are, £45 from Edinburgh, Glasgow or Newcastle; £26 from Manchester; £16 from Birmingham; and £21 from London. Manchester–Holyhead return costs £13.

If you are planning to travel extensively throughout Britain by bus, the various *National Express* **discount passes** may save you a lot of money. UK residents under 25, in full-time education or of retirement age can buy a *National Express* **Discount Coach Card**, which is valid for one year and entitles the holder to a 30 percent discount on any fare. Two special deals are available to foreign travellers: the **Britexpress** card, which costs £12 and provides 30 percent reductions on fares over a 30-day period, or a **Tourist Trail Pass**, which offers unlimited travel on the *National Express* network. A 3-day *Tourist Trail Pass* costs £49 for adults, £39 for students and under-26s; 5 days' travel in 10 cost £79 or £65 respectively; 8 days in 16 cost £119 or £95; and 15 days in 30 will set you back £179 or £145. In Britain you can obtain both from major travel agents, at Gatwick and Heathrow airports, at the British Travel Centre in London (see p18), or at the main *National Express* office. The main Welsh offices are at Cardiff and Swansea, but tickets are available through a broad network of travel agents. In North America these passes should be available through any travel agent or direct from *British Travel International* (see box on p.11 for address).

For more bus passes for use within Wales and the rest of Britain, see "Getting Around", p.21.

BUS INFORMATION

National Express, 164 Buckingham Palace Road, London SW1 (☎071/730 0202); Wood Street, Cardiff CF1 1TR (☎0222/344751)

BY ROAD: DRIVING

Travelling to Wales by car from England, the main roads into **the north** are the upgraded coastal **A55** route, a dual carriageway all the way from Chester, and the **M56** via Holywell, St Asaph, Colwyn Bay, through a tunnel under the Conwy Estuary and on to Bangor, where it connects with the old trunk route, the A5. The **A5** is still the major road into north Wales from the Midlands and the south of England, best approached from the M6 just north of Wolverhampton, via the fast M54 and new Shrewsbury bypass. Much of the A5 has been improved in recent decades, although there are still traditional bottlenecks at Llangollen and Betws-y-Coed.

The Shrewsbury route is also the best for access into **mid-Wales** as far south as Nowtown and Aberystwyth, using the **A458** to Welshpool from the Shrewsbury bypass. Further south, the **A456** from Birmingham, via Kidderminster and Leominster, is occasionally slow when passing through towns, but generally easier than the route through Worcester and Hereford to reach the A44 in Radnorshire and, to the south, the A438/470 to Brecon. This road connects with the swift westbound A40 at the Brecon bypass, best for routes from the Midlands and north of England to southern Cardiganshire and northern Carmarthenshire. An alternative route from the Midlands is via the **M50** "Ross Spur", a quiet motorway off the M5 south of Worcester, meeting the A449 dual carriageway at Ross-on-Wye. The road continues south, dividing at Raglan into the quick A40 for Brecon and the A449 down to Newport, the M4 and all destinations west.

The **M4 from London** makes the most dramatic entry into Wales. The **Severn Bridge** (£3.40 toll) rises high over the mud flats, passing

Chepstow, Newport and Cardiff en route to Swansea and the west, and a second Severn River crossing will open in 1996. Frequently congested, and prone to enormous amounts of roadworks, the M4 is split at the turn-off for Swansea, where tailbacks will continue to be the norm until the new river crossing is opened. From here, the A48 dual carriageway connects with the excellent A40 at Carmarthen, coursing west to Haverfordwest, for connections to Pembrokeshire and southern Cardiganshire.

HITCHING

The extensive motorway network and the density of traffic makes long-distance hitching through England and Scotland to the Welsh border and along the M4 to Cardiff and Swansea relatively easy. Key junctions on the edge of metropolitan areas and motorway service stations are the favoured hitching spots, and standing with a sign at the exit produces the best results.

However, **hitching is not generally advised**, especially if you are a woman travelling alone. A way around this impasse is offered by the **lift-sharing** advertisements in the small-ads paper *Loot*, available daily in London, Manchester and Bristol, with private individuals offering and seeking lifts around Britain. *Freewheelers* (☎091/222 0090), an established England-based lift-share agency, requires passengers to pay a £5 annual registration fee, plus a £2 fee for each journey and 3.5p per mile as a contribution to the driver's costs – a fraction of the cost of any public transport service.

BY FERRY

Wales has three main ferry ports all serving boats **from Ireland** (see box). Ferries from Dublin, and both ferries and high-speed catamarans from Dun Laoghaire (six miles south of Dublin), arrive at Holyhead on the northwest tip of Wales, while Rosslare, just outside Wexford, is the departure point for ferries and catamarans to Fishguard, and ferries to Pembroke Dock, both in southwest Wales.

Stena Sealink (☎0233/647047) operates ferries and cats from Dun Laoghaire to Holyhead, and services from Rosslare to Fishguard; *B&I Line* (☎071/734 4681) runs ferries from Dublin to Holyhead and from Rosslare to Pembroke Dock. **Ferry prices** for the two companies are almost identical, whichever ports you travel between, though for cars, winter fares tend to be a little cheaper from Rosslare, as are high-summer fares to Holyhead. One-way foot passenger fares range from £18 in winter to £26 on summer sailings from Friday to Sunday. Cars with up to five people cost from £60 to £175. To save money, avoid weekend sailings from mid-July to mid-September and travel during the day rather than on night sailings. **Catamarans** cost about £5 more as a foot passenger and £10–30 more for a car depending on season. There is also a ferry from Cork to Swansea running from March to October and operated by *Swansea–Cork Ferries* (☎0792/456116). Most are ten-hour night sailings costing £18–£26 for foot passengers and £85–£180 for a car and up to four passengers.

There's a much greater choice of **ferries from Europe** to ports in England, the most convenient of which are listed in the box below. It is uncertain how the ferries crossing the English Channel will fare once the Channel Tunnel is in full operation, but competitive pricing means that unless you are in a hurry, lower prices may lure you onto a boat. There are regular crossings with *Hoverspeed*, *Stena Sealink* and *P&O* from Calais to Dover, the shortest route, for which the lowest fare for a small car and two adults is around £70. For full details of ferry routes and prices, call the ferry companies direct.

FERRY CONNECTIONS

	Company	Frequency	Duration
From Belgium			
Ostend–Dover	*P&O*	7 daily	4hr 30min
Ostend–Dover	*P&O* Jetfoil	6 daily	1hr 40min
From France			
Roscoff–Plymouth	*Brittany*	1–2 daily	6hr
Cherbourg–Southampton	*Stena Sealink*	1–2 daily	6–8hr
St Malo–Portsmouth	*Brittany*	1–7 weekly	9hr
Caen–Portsmouth	*Brittany*	2–3 daily	6hr
Cherbourg–Portsmouth	*P&O*	1–4 daily	4hr 45min
Le Havre–Portsmouth	*P&O*	2–3 daily	5hr 45min
Dieppe–Newhaven	*Stena Sealink*	2–4 daily	4hr
Boulogne–Dover	*P&O*	6 daily	1hr 15min
Calais–Dover	*Stena Sealink*	6–22 daily	1hr 30min
Calais–Dover	*P&O*	15–25 daily	1hr 15min
Calais–Dover	*Hoverspeed* SeaCat	7–20 daily	50min
Calais–Dover	*Hoverspeed* Hovercraft	12 daily	50min
Boulogne–Folkestone	*Hoverspeed* SeaCat	6 daily	55min
Dunkerque–Ramsgate	*Sally Line*	5 daily	2hr 30min
From Ireland			
Dublin–Holyhead	*Stena Sealink*	4 daily	3hr 30min
Dublin–Holyhead	*Stena Sealink* Sealynx	4 daily	1hr 50min
Dublin–Holyhead	*B&I*	2 daily	3hr 45min
Rosslare–Pembroke	*B&I*	2 daily	4hr 15min
Cork–Swansea	*Swansea–Cork Ferries*	3–6 weekly (March–Oct)	10hr
Rosslare–Fishguard	*Stena Sealink*	2 daily	3hr 30min
Rosslare–Fishguard	*Stena Sealink* Sealynx	4 daily	1hr 40min
From Spain			
Santander–Plymouth	*Brittany*	2 weekly	24hr

GETTING THERE FROM NORTH AMERICA

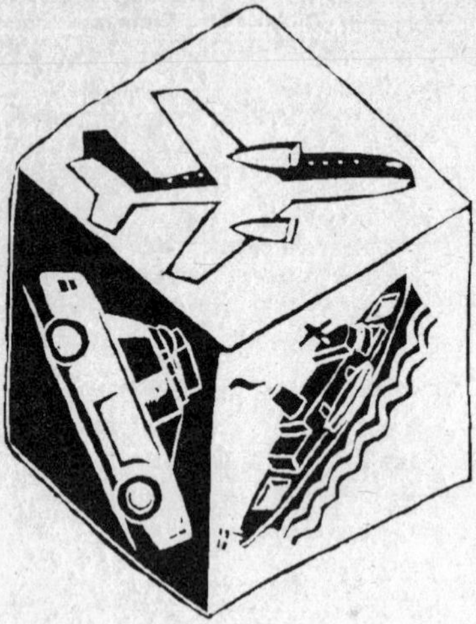

There are no direct transatlantic flights to Wales, so for visitors from the US and Canada, the usual way to get there is via one of England's main airports, covering the rest of the journey overland.

Figure on six and a half hours' **flying time** from New York to any of the British airports, eleven and a half hours from the West Coast (it's an hour extra coming the other way, due to headwinds). Most flights cross the Atlantic overnight, reaching Britain the next morning, although a few flights from the East Coast leave early in the morning and arrive late the same evening.

The range of options is always greatest – and the fares usually lowest – flying into London. Two of London's airports – Heathrow and Gatwick – handle transatlantic flights, and in terms of convenience they're about equal. There are, however, a growing number of direct flights into Manchester or Birmingham. Birmingham is the best equipped to get you on your way to Wales quickly, being directly linked to the *British Rail InterCity* network. You can rent cars on arrival at the airport, or contact one of the agencies listed on p.23 before you depart for Britain.

For details on reaching Wales by train, bus or car from the rest of Britain, see p.3 Note that *Eurail* passes are not valid in Britain, though there are specific train and bus passes that are; see below for details of train passes, and p.21 for bus passes available throughout the country.

SHOPPING FOR TICKETS

Barring special offers, the cheapest fare is usually an **APEX** (Advance Purchase Excursion) ticket, although this will carry certain restrictions: you have to book – and pay – at least 21 days before departure, spend between seven days and three months abroad, and you tend to get penalized if you change your schedule. There are also winter **Super APEX** tickets, sometimes known as "Eurosavers" – slightly less expensive than an ordinary APEX, but limiting your stay to between 7 and 21 days. Some airlines also issue **Special APEX** tickets to people under 24, often extending the maximum stay to a year. Many airlines offer youth or student fares to **under-25s**; a passport or driving licence is sufficient proof of age, though these tickets are subject to availability and can have eccentric booking conditions. It's worth remembering that most cheap return fares involve spending at least one Saturday night away and that many will only give a refund on a percentage of the price if you need to cancel or alter your journey, so make sure you check the details carefully before buying a ticket.

You can normally cut costs further by going through a **specialist flight agent** – either a **consolidator**, who buys up blocks of tickets from the airlines and sells them at a discount, or a **discount agent**, who also wheels and deals in blocks of tickets offloaded by the airlines, but tends to offer special student and youth fares and a range of other travel-related services, such as travel insurance, train passes, car rental, tours and the like. Bear in mind, though, that penalties for changing your plans can be stiff. Also remember that these companies make their money by dealing in volume – don't expect them to answer lots of questions. Some agents specialize in **charter flights**, which may be cheaper than any available scheduled flight, but again departure dates are fixed and withdrawal penalties are high – check the refund policy. If you travel a lot, **discount travel clubs** are another option: the annual membership fee may be worth it for the benefits of cut-price air tickets and car rental.

Regardless of where you buy your ticket, the **fare** will depend on the season. Fares to Britain are highest from around early June to mid-September, when the weather is best; they drop during "shoulder" seasons – mid-September to early November and mid-April to early June – and you'll get the best deals during low season, November through April (excluding Christmas and New Year, when prices are hiked up and seats at a premium). Note that flying on weekends ordinarily adds $20–60 to the round-trip fare; **prices quoted below assume midweek travel**.

FLIGHTS FROM THE USA

Transatlantic fares are very reasonable, thanks to intense competition. Any local travel agent should be able to access the airlines' up-to-the-minute fares, although in practice, they may not have time to research all the possibilities, and you might want to call airlines direct (see below).

Dozens of airlines fly from New York to London, and a few fly direct from other East Coast and Midwestern cities. The best low-season fares from **New York** to London hover around $400 round-trip, with peak-season prices likely to run $150–250 higher. To give an idea of low-season fares to London from other cities, several carriers fly from **Boston** for as little as $420, **Washington DC** from $450 or **Chicago** from $520; *Delta* flies from **Atlanta** for about $500 and from **Miami** for $540; *Virgin* from **Orlando** for $560; *TWA* from **St Louis** for $525; *American* from **Dallas/Fort Worth** for about $600; and *Continental* from **Denver** for $590.

Don't assume you'll have to change planes when flying from the **West Coast** – you might find it worth paying the extra to fly nonstop (*American*, *BA* and *United* all do so from LA). Several carriers fly or connect with flights to London from **Los Angeles** or **San Francisco**, with low-season midweek fares from both cities starting at around $500. From **Seattle** the price will be more in the region of $550. High-season travel will add at least another $200.

Aer Lingus, *American*, *BA* and *Delta* fly to **Manchester** from some of the above cities, and *Aer Lingus* and *BA* fly to **Birmingham** (see box below), from which you can make your way to Wales by road or rail (see p.3).

FLIGHTS FROM CANADA

In Canada, you'll get the best deal flying to London from the big gateway cities of **Toronto** and **Montréal**, where competition among *Air Canada*, *Canadian Airlines*, *British Airways* and other carriers drives off-season midweek fares as low as Can$550 round-trip; direct flights from **Ottawa** and **Halifax** cost only slightly more. From **Vancouver**, **Edmonton** and **Calgary**,

NORTH AMERICAN AIRLINES

Aer Lingus (☎1-800/223-6537). New York and Boston via Dublin or Shannon to London.

Air Canada (☎1-800/776-3000). Vancouver, Toronto, Montréal and Halifax to London, and seasonally to Manchester.

Air India (☎1-800/223-7776). New York and Toronto to London.

American Airlines (☎1-800/433-7300). London and Manchester from half a dozen American gateway cities.

British Airways (☎1-800/247-9297). Most major North American cities to London, with connections on to other UK destinations; from New York, nonstops to Birmingham and Manchester.

Canadian Airlines (☎1-800/426-7000). Vancouver, Edmonton, Calgary and Toronto to London, and to Manchester via Toronto.

Continental Airlines (☎1-800/231-0856). London from Newark, Houston and Denver, with other routes feeding into these gateway cities.

Delta Airlines (☎1-800/241-4141). Atlanta, Cincinnatti, Miami and Orlando to London; Atlanta to Manchester.

Kuwait Airways (☎1-800/458-9248). New York to London.

Northwest Airlines (☎1-800/225-2525). Minneapolis and Boston to London.

TWA (☎1-800/221-2000). St Louis to London.

United Airlines (☎1-800/538-2929). New York, Washington, Los Angeles, San Francisco and Seattle to London; many other routings via these gateways.

US Air (☎1-800/622-1015). New York to London.

Virgin Atlantic Airways (☎1-800/862-8621). Newark, JFK, Boston, Miami and Orlando to London.

London flights start at Can$750 off-season. High-season travel will add a premium of $300–400 to all these fares. You can pick up direct flights from many Canadian cities to **Manchester** and **Birmingham**, often at no extra cost over the fare to London.

RAIL PASSES

North Americans and other foreign visitors can invest in a **rail pass** before leaving home (see below for addresses of agents who can sell you one). The most economical short-term option is the **England/Wales Flexipass**, which costs $149 for 4 days' travel out of 30. If you're heading further afield, the standard **BritRail Pass** gives unlimited travel in Wales, England and Scotland for 8 days ($219), 15 days ($339), 22 days ($425) or a month ($495); while the **BritRail Flexipass** covers travel on 4 days out of 30 ($189), 8 days out of 30 ($269), or 15 days out of a month ($395). Note that with both these passes, there are discounts for those under 26 (*BritRail Youth* passes) or over 60 (*BritRail Senior* passes), and the Flexipass has a special 15 days out of two months rate for under-26s ($309).

PACKAGES AND ORGANIZED TOURS

Although you may want to see Wales at your own speed, you shouldn't dismiss the idea of a **package deal**. Many agents and airlines put together very flexible deals, sometimes amounting to no more than a flight plus car or rail pass and accommodation, and these can actually work out better value than the same arrangements made on arrival – especially fly-drive deals, since car rental is expensive in Britain. A package can also be great for your peace of mind, if only to ensure a worry-free first week.

DISCOUNT AGENTS, CONSOLIDATORS AND TRAVEL CLUBS

Air Brokers International, 323 Geary St, Suite 411, San Francisco, CA 94102 (☎1-800/883-3273). Consolidator.

Council Charter, 205 East 42nd St, New York, NY 10017 (☎1-800/223-7402). Youth-oriented charter broker.

Council Travel, 205 East 42nd St, New York, NY 10017 (☎1-800/743-1823 or 212/661-1450); 312 Sutter St, San Francisco, CA 94108 (☎415/421-3473); and many other regional outlets. The country's largest student and youth-oriented discount agent.

Discount Travel International, Ives Building, 114 Forrest Ave, Suite 205, Narberth, PA 19072 (☎215/668-7184). Discount travel club, membership $45.

Moment's Notice, 425 Madison Ave, New York, NY (☎212/486-0503). Travel club.

Nouvelles Frontières, 12 E 33rd St, New York, NY 10016 (☎212/779-0600); 1001 Sherbrooke Est, Suite 720, Montréal, H2L IL3 (☎514/526-8444); and other US and Canadian locations. Discount travel agent.

STA Travel, 48 East 11th St, New York, NY 10003 (☎1-800/777-0112 or 212/477-7166); 106 Geary St, San Francisco, CA 94108 (☎415/391-8407); and several other offices on the East and West coasts. Major discount agent specializing in student and youth deals.

Stand Buys, 311 W Superior St, Chicago, IL 60610 (☎1-800/548-1116). Travel club.

Travel Cuts, 187 College St, Toronto, ON, M5T 1P7 (☎416/979-2406); and outlets on most Canadian university campuses. The principal student/youth discount agency in Canada.

UniTravel, 1177 N Warson Rd, St Louis, MO 63132 (☎1-800/325-2222). Consolidator.

TRAIN OFFICES AND AGENCIES

British Rail International, 1500 Broadway, New York, NY 10036 (☎212/575-2667); 94 Cumberland St, Toronto, ON M5R 1A3 (☎416/929-3333).

CIE Tours International, 108 Ridgedale Ave, Morristown, NJ 07690 (☎201/292-3438 or 1-800/522-5258).

Rail Europe, 226–230 Westchester Ave, White Plains, NY 10604 (☎914/682-2999 or 1-800/848-7245); and branches in Santa Monica, San Francisco, Fort Lauderdale, Chicago, Dallas, Vancouver and Montréal.

A number of tour operators specialize in travel to Wales. Most can do packages of the standard highlights, and many organize walking or cycling trips through the countryside, with any number of theme tours based around the country's literary heritage, history, gardens – you name it. A few of the possibilities are listed below, and a travel agent will be able to point out others; bear in mind that bookings made through travel agents cost no more than going through the tour operator. For a full listing, contact the *British Tourist Authority* (p.18). Be sure to examine the fine print of any deal, and make sure the operator is a member of the *United States Tour Operator Association* (*USTOA*) or approved by the *American Society of Travel Agents* (*ASTA*).

For a list of **operators in Britain** who can book self-catering holidays in Wales, see p.26.

SPECIALIST TOUR OPERATORS TO WALES

British Coastal Trails, 1001 B Ave, Suite 302, Coronado, CA 92118 (☎619/437-1211). Walking trips throughout Snowdonia and central Wales, plus canal trips.

British Travel International, PO Box 299, Elkton, VA 22827 (☎1-800/327-6097). Agent for all kinds of independent arrangements including: organizing air tickets, rail and bus passes, hotel bookings, and a comprehensive B&B reservation service.

Hostelling International USA, PO Box 37613, Washington, DC 20013 (☎202/783-6161). Affiliated with the UK's Youth Hostels Association, organizes walking, cycling and general youth tours.

Lynott Tours, Empire State Bldg, 350 5th Ave, #6219, New York, NY 10118 (☎1-800/221-2474). Special-interest tours, hotel and castle stays, self-drives; agent for Ireland–Wales ferries.

Sterling Tours, 2707 Congress St, Suite 2-G, San Diego, CA 92110 (☎1-800/727-4359). Offers a variety of independent itineraries and some packages.

Travel Arrangements International, 5123 Roland Ave, Baltimore, MD 21210 (☎1-800/435-4054). Arranges independent tours of Wales, some packages.

Travel Bound, 599 Broadway, New York, NY 10012 (☎1-800/456-8656). *Virgin Atlantic*'s tour arm.

GETTING THERE FROM AUSTRALASIA

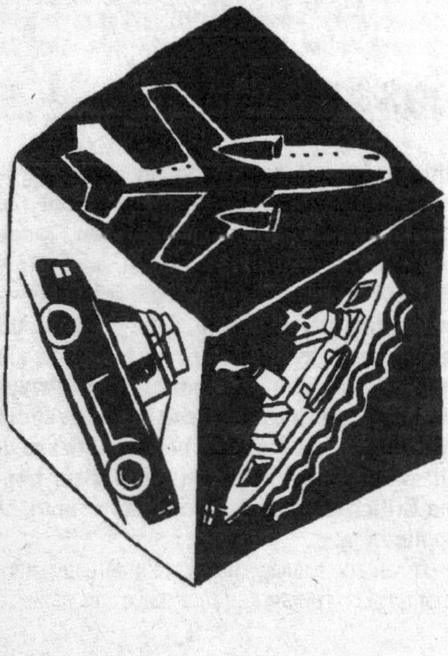

There are no direct flights to Wales from anywhere in Australia or New Zealand, so you will have to route through London and then travel onward either by connecting flight or overland. For all onward details, see "Getting There from the UK and Europe", p.3.

Daily flights connect London with **Melbourne**, **Sydney**, **Brisbane** and **Perth**, with no great difference in the fares. With *Garuda*, the least expensive airline, a return ticket from Sydney to London should cost you around Aus$1600 in the low season – mid-November to mid-December. With *British Airways*, *Thai* or *Malaysian* airlines, add at least another Aus$100. From **Auckland**, expect to pay around NZ$1170 single or NZ$2050 return in the low season – October to November – with *Qantas*.

Numerous discount agents can supply these and other low-price tickets. One of the most reliable operators is *STA* (*STS* in New Zealand), who can also advise on **visa regulations** for Australian and New Zealand citizens – and for a fee will do all the paperwork for you.

AIRLINES IN AUSTRALASIA

Air New Zealand, Air New Zealand House, Queen St, Auckland (☎09/357 3000).

British Airways, 64 Castlereagh St, Sydney (☎02/258 3300); Dilworth Building, Queen St, Auckland (☎09/367 7500).

Garuda Airlines, 175 Clarence St, Sydney (☎02/262 2011); Westpac Tower Bldg, 10th Floor, 120 Albert St, Auckland (☎09/366 1855).

Malaysian Airways, 11th Floor, Amex Tower 388, George St, Sydney (☎02/364 3590); 12th Floor, Swanson Centre, 12–26 Swanson St, Auckland (☎09/373 2741).

Qantas, Qantas International Centre, International Square, Sydney (☎02/236 3636).

Thai International Airways, Kensington Swan Bldg, 22 Fanshawe St, Auckland (☎09/377 0268).

DISCOUNT AGENTS IN AUSTRALASIA

Anywhere Travel, 345 Anzac Parade, Kingsford, Sydney (☎02/663 0411).

Brisbane Discount Travel, 360 Queen St, Brisbane (☎07/229 9211).

Budget Travel, PO Box 505, Auckland (☎09/309 4313).

Discount Travel Specialists, Shop 53, Forrest Chase, Perth (☎09/221 1400).

Flight Centres, Circular Quay, Sydney (☎02/241 2422); Bourke St, Melbourne (☎03/650 2899); plus branches nationwide except in the Northern Territory. National Bank Towers, 205–225 Queen St, Auckland (☎09/309 6171); Shop 1M, National Mutual Arcade, 152 Hereford St, Christchurch (☎03/379 7145); 50–52 Willis St, Wellington (☎04/472 8101); plus branches nationwide.

Passport Travel, 320b Glenferrie Rd, Malvern, Melbourne (☎03/824 7183).

STA, 732 Harris St, Sydney (☎02/212 1255); CAE Shop, 256 Flinders St, Melbourne (☎03/347 4711); 100 James St, Northbridge, Perth (☎09/227 7299).

STS Travel, 10 High St, Auckland (☎09/309 9995); 233 Cuba St, Wellington (☎04/385 0561); 223 High St, Christchurch (☎03/379 9098).

Topdeck Travel, 45 Grenfell St, Adelaide (☎08/410 1110).

Tymtro Travel, Suite G12, Wallaceway Shopping Centre, Chatswood, Sydney (☎02/411 1222).

VISAS, CUSTOMS REGULATIONS AND TAX

Citizens of all the European countries – except Albania, Bulgaria, Poland and the states of the former Soviet Union – and citizens of Canada, Australia and New Zealand can enter Britain with just a passport, generally for up to three months. US citizens can travel in Britain for up to six months without a visa, but for longer stays should apply to the British Embassy in Washington, DC (see box below). Citizens of all other nationalities require a visa, from the British Consular office in the country of application.

Travellers coming into Britain directly from another EU country do not have to make a declaration to **customs** at their place of entry and can effectively bring almost as much wine or beer across the Channel as they like – the limits are 90 litres of wine and 110 of beer. However, there are still restrictions on the volume of **tax- or duty-free** goods you can bring into the country, so you can't invest in a stockpile of cheap cigarettes on your flight, wherever you're coming from. The duty-free allowances are as follows:

- **Tobacco**: 200 cigarettes; or 100 cigarillos; or 50 cigars; or 250g of loose tobacco.
- **Alcohol**: 2 litres of still wine, **plus** one litre of drink over 22 percent alcohol, or 2 litres of alcoholic drink not over 22 percent, or another 2 litres of still wine.
- **Perfumes**: 60cc of perfume plus 250cc of toilet water.
- Plus **other goods** to the value of £32.

There are **import restrictions** on a variety of articles and substances, from firearms to furs derived from endangered species, none of which should concern most tourists. However, if you need any clarification on British import regulations, contact HM Customs and Excise, New Kings Beam House, 22 Upper Ground, London SE1 9PJ (☎071/620 1313). You cannot bring **pets** into Britain on holiday, as strict quarantine restrictions apply to animals brought from overseas countries (except Ireland).

Many goods in Britain, with the chief exceptions of books and food, are subject to **Value Added Tax** (VAT), which increases the cost of an item by 17.5 percent at present; it's normally already included in any given price. Visitors from non-EU countries can save some money through the Retail Export Scheme, which allows a refund of VAT on goods to be taken out of the country. Note that not all shops participate in this scheme (those who do display a sign to this effect) and that you cannot reclaim VAT charged on hotel bills or other services.

BRITISH EMBASSIES ABROAD

Australia Commonwealth Ave, Yarralumla, Canberra, ACT 2600 (☎062/270 6666).

Canada 80 Elgin St, Ottawa, ON K1P 5K7 (☎613/237-1530).

Ireland 31–33 Merrion Rd, Dublin 4 (☎01/695211).

Netherlands General Koningslaan 44, Amsterdam (☎676 43 43).

New Zealand Reserve Bank Bldg, 2 The Terrace, PO Box 1812, Wellington (☎04/726049).

USA 3100 Massachusetts Ave, NW, Washington, DC 20008 (☎202/462-1340).

OVERSEAS EMBASSIES IN BRITAIN

American Embassy, 5 Upper Grosvenor St, London W1 (☎071/499 9000).

Australian High Commission, Australia House, Strand, London WC2 (☎071/379 4334).

Canadian High Commission, 1 Grosvenor Square, London W1 (☎071/258 6600).

Irish Embassy, 17 Grosvenor Place, London SW1 (☎071/235 2171).

New Zealand High Commission, New Zealand House, 80 Haymarket, London SW1 (☎071/930 8422).

COSTS, MONEY AND BANKS

The British pound sterling (£; in Welsh, *punt*, and widely referred to as "a quid") is a decimal currency, divided into 100 pence (p; *ceiniogau* – c – in Welsh). Coins come in denominations of 1p, 2p, 5p, 10p, 20p, 50p and £1 – there's a rare £2 coin in circulation as well. Notes come in denominations of £5, £10, £20 and £50.

MONEY

There are no exchange controls in Britain, so you can bring in as much money as you like. The easiest and safest way to carry your money is in **travellers' cheques**, available for a small commission (normally one percent) from any major bank. The most widely accepted brands of travellers' cheque are *American Express*, followed by *Visa* and *Thomas Cook* – most cheques issued by banks will be one of these three. You'll usually pay commission again when you cash each cheque, normally another one percent or so, or a flat rate – though no commission is payable on *Amex* cheques exchanged at *Amex* branches (see box). Make sure to keep a record of the cheques as you cash them, so you'll be able to get the value of all uncashed cheques refunded immediately should you lose them.

You'll find that most hotels, shops and restaurants in Wales are happy to accept the major **credit cards** – *Access/MasterCard*, *Visa/Barclaycard*, *American Express* and *Diners Club* – although they're less useful in the most rural areas, and all over the country smaller establishments, such as B&B accommodation, will often accept cash only. You can get cash advances from selected banks and bureaux de change on credit cards, though there will invariably be a minimum amount you can draw. If you have a PIN, *Visa* cards can be used in *Barclays* cashpoint machines (ATMs), while *MasterCard* can be used at *Lloyds*, *Midland* and *National Westminster* banks.

BANKS AND BUREAUX DE CHANGE

Banks are almost always the best places to **change money and cheques**, and in every sizeable town in Wales you'll find a branch of at least one of the big four: *National Westminster*, *Barclays*, *Lloyds* and *Midland*. As a general rule, **opening hours** are Mon–Fri 9.30am–3.30pm, though branches in larger towns and cities are often open an hour later and on Saturday mornings. Outside banking hours, you're best advised to make your way to a **bureau de change**, found in most city centres, often at train stations or airports; try to avoid changing money or cheques in hotels, where the rates are normally very poor.

If, as a foreign visitor, you run out of money, or there is some kind of emergency, the quickest way to get **money sent out** is to get in touch with your bank at home and arrange for them to wire the cash to the nearest bank. You can do the same thing through *Thomas Cook* or *American Express* if there is a branch nearby (see box). Americans and Canadians can also have cash sent through *Western Union* (in the UK: ☎0800/833833) to a nearby bank or post office. Make sure you know when it's likely to arrive, since you won't be notified by the receiving office. Remember, too, that you'll need some form of identification when you pick up the money.

COSTS

Wales has become an expensive place to visit, though if you're coming from England, particularly London, prices will seem reasonable in comparison. The minimum expenditure, if you're camping and preparing most of your own food, would be in the region of £15 a day, rising to around £20–25 a day using the hostelling network, public transport and grabbing the odd meal out. Couples staying at budget B&Bs, eating at unpretentious restaurants and visiting a fair number of tourist attractions are looking at around £30–40 each per day – if you're renting a car, staying in comfortable B&Bs or hotels and eating well, you should reckon on at least £50 a day. Single travellers should budget on spending around 60 percent of what a couple might spend. For more detail on the cost of accommodation, transport and eating, see the relevant sections below.

AMERICAN EXPRESS OFFICES

American Express only operate one office in Wales; also listed are the most convenient English offices.

Cardiff, 3 Queen St (☎0222/668858 or 666216).

Bristol, 74 Queens Rd, Clifton (☎0272/750750 or 751751).

Chester, Apollo Travel Centre, 23 St Werburgh St (☎0244/311145).

London, 445 Oxford St (☎071/408 3644).

Shrewsbury, 27 Claremont St (☎0743/236387 or 56385).

THOMAS COOK OFFICES

Cardiff, 16 Queen St, Cardiff, CF1 4UW (☎0222/224886).

Cwmbran, 18 South Walk, Cwmbran, NP44 1PU (☎0633/869416).

Llandudno, 51 Mostyn St, Llandudno, LL30 2NN (☎0492/860957).

Newport, 144 Commercial St, Newport, NP9 1LN (☎0633/256548).

Pontypridd, 109 Taff St, Pontypridd, CF37 4UP (☎0443/486161).

Swansea, 3 Union St, Swansea, SA1 1PJ (☎0792/464311).

Wrexham, 20/21 Hope St, Wrexham, LL11 1BG (☎0978/263170).

INSURANCE AND HEALTH

Wherever you're travelling from, it's a good idea to have some kind of travel insurance to cover you for loss of possessions and money, as well as the cost of any medical and dental treatment. If you're visiting from elsewhere in Britain, you may well be covered by your existing home contents policy, but should you need extra cover, *Endsleigh* are about the cheapest British insurer, offering a month's cover for around £20. Their policies are available from most youth/student travel specialists, or direct from 97–107 Southampton Row, London WC1 (☎071/436 4451), 21 High St, Cardiff (☎0222/237977), and numerous other regional offices. Whatever your policy, if you have anything stolen, get a copy of the police report, as this is essential to substantiate your claim.

US and Canadian citizens should also carefully check their insurance policies before taking out a new one. You may discover that you're already covered for medical and other losses while abroad. Canadians especially are usually covered by their provincial health plans, and holders of ISIC cards are entitled (outside the USA) to be reimbursed for $3000-worth of accident coverage and 60 days of in-patient benefits up to $100 a day for the period the card is valid. Students may also find their health coverage extends during vacations, and many bank and charge accounts include some form of travel cover; insurance is also sometimes included if you pay for your trip with a credit card.

If you do want a specific travel insurance policy, there are numerous kinds to choose from, but short-term combination policies covering everything from baggage loss to broken legs are the best bet, costing around $50 for fifteen days, $80 for a month, $150 for two months, $190 for three months. One thing to bear in mind is that none of the currently available policies covers theft; they only cover loss while in the custody of an identifiable person – though even then you must make a report to the police and get a written statement. Two companies you might try are *Travel Guard*, 110 Centrepoint Drive, Steven Point, WI 54480 (☎1-800/826-1300 or 715/345-0505), or *Access America International*, 600 Third Ave, New York, NY 10163 (☎1-800/284-8300 or 212/949-5960).

HEALTH

No vaccinations are required for entry into Britain. Citizens of all EU countries are entitled to free medical treatment at National Health Service hospitals; citizens of other countries are charged for all medical services except those administered by accident and emergency units at National Health Service hospitals. Thus a US citizen who has been hit by a car would not be charged if the injuries simply required stitching and setting in the emergency unit, but would be if admission to a hospital ward were necessary. Health insurance is therefore strongly advised for all non-EU nationals.

Pharmacists can dispense only a limited range of drugs without a doctor's prescription. Most pharmacies are open standard shop hours, though in large towns some may stay open as late as 10pm – local newspapers carry lists of late-opening pharmacies. Doctor's surgeries tend to be open from about 9am to noon and then for a couple of hours in the evenings; outside surgery hours, you can turn up at the casualty department of the local hospital for complaints that require immediate attention – unless it's an emergency, in which case ring for an ambulance on ☎999.

EMERGENCIES AND THE POLICE

As in any other country, Wales' major towns have their dangerous spots, but these tend to be inner-city housing estates where no tourist has any reason to be. The chief risk on the streets – though still minimal – is pickpocketing, so carry only as much money as you need, and keep all bags and pockets fastened. Should you have anything stolen or be involved in an incident that requires reporting, go to the local police station; the ☎999 number should only be used in emergencies.

Although the traditional image of the friendly British "Bobby" has become tarnished by stories of corruption and crooked dealings, the **police** continue to be approachable and helpful. If you're lost in a major town, asking a police officer is generally the quickest way to get help – alternatively, you could ask a **traffic warden**, a much maligned species of law-enforcer responsible for parking restrictions and other vehicle-related matters. They're distinguishable by their flat caps with a yellow band, and by the fact that they are generally armed with a book of parking-fine tickets; police officers on street duty wear a distinctive domed hat with a silver top, and are generally armed with just a truncheon.

EMERGENCIES

For **Police** (*heddlu*), **Fire Brigade** (*brigad dan*), **Ambulance** (*ambiwlans*) and, in certain areas, **Mountain Rescue** or **Coastguard** (*gwyliwr y glaaunn*), dial **☎999**.

INFORMATION AND MAPS

If you want to do a bit of research before arriving in Britain, contact the British Tourist Authority (BTA) in your country – the addresses are given in the box below. The BTA will send you a wealth of free literature, some of it just rosy-tinted advertising copy, but much of it extremely useful – especially the maps, city guides and event calendars. If you want more hard facts on a particular area, you should approach the Wales Tourist Board offices, also listed below. In general, they are helpful and will have a few leaflets at least worth scanning.

TOURIST OFFICES

Tourist offices (usually called Tourist Information Centres) exist in virtually every Welsh town – you'll find their phone numbers and opening hours in the relevant sections of the guide. The average opening hours are much the same as standard shop hours, with the difference that in summer they'll often be open on a Sunday and for a couple of hours after the shops have

BRITISH TOURIST AUTHORITY HEAD OFFICES

Australia: 210 Clarence St, 4th Floor, Sydney, NSW 2000 (☎02/267 4555).

Canada: 111 Avenue Rd, Suite 450, Toronto, Ontario M5R 3J8 (☎416/925-6326 or 961 2175).

Ireland: BTA, 123 Lower Baggot St, Dublin 2 (☎01/661 4188).

New Zealand: BTA, Suite 305, 3rd Floor, Dilworth Building, corner of Customs and Queen streets, Auckland (☎09/303 1446).

US: Wales Representative, 551 5th Ave, Suite 701, New York, NY 10176 (☎212/986-2200); 2580 Cumberland Pkwy, Suite 470, Atlanta, GA 30339 (☎404/432-9635); 625 N Michigan Ave, Suite 1510, Chicago, IL 60611 (☎312/787-0490); World Trade Center, Suite 450, 350 S Figueroa St, Los Angeles, CA 90071 (☎213/628-3525).

WALES TOURIST BOARD OFFICES

Written requests for information should be sent to: WTB, Dept RJ3, PO Box 1, Cardiff, CF1 2XN (☎0222/227281).

Wales Tourist Board, Head Office, Brunel House, 2 Fitzalan Rd, Cardiff, CF2 1UY (☎0222/499909).

Wales Information Bureau, British Travel Centre, 12 Regent St, London, SW1Y 4PQ (☎071/409 0969).

North Wales Tourism Ltd, 77 Conway Rd, Colwyn Bay, LL29 7LN (☎0492/531731).

Mid-Wales Tourism Ltd, Canolfan Owain Glyndw^r, Machynlleth, SY20 8EE (☎0654/702653).

Tourism South Wales Ltd, Pembroke House, Phoenix Way Enterprise Park, Swansea, SA7 9DB (☎0792/781212).

closed on weekdays; opening hours are generally shorter in winter, and in more remote areas the office may well be closed altogether. All centres offer information on accommodation, local public transport, attractions and restaurants, as well as town and regional maps. In many cases all of this is free, but a growing number of offices make a small charge for their accommodation list or the town guide with accompanying street plan.

Areas designated as National Parks (the Brecon Beacons, Pembrokeshire Coast and Snowdonia) also have a fair sprinkling of **National Park Information Centres**, which are generally more expert in giving guidance on local walks and outdoor pursuits. (For information on accommodation-booking services, see p.26).

MAPS

Most bookshops will have a good selection of **maps of Wales** and Britain, but see the box below for a list of specialist travel bookshops. Of the many North American outlets, the *British Travel Bookshop* in New York, in particular, stocks a phenomenal array of maps. *Rand McNally Map and Travel* is also a good bet, with 24 stores nationwide.

Virtually every service station in Britain stocks one or more of the big **road atlases**. The best of these are the large-format ones produced by the *AA*, *RAC*, *Collins* and *Ordnance Survey*, which cover all of Britain at around 3 miles to 1 inch and include larger-scale plans of major towns. The most accurate and detailed folding map is the *Ordnance Survey* 1 inch to 4 miles Travelmaster 7, covering Wales and the West Midlands.

If you want more detail, the most comprehensive maps are produced by the **Ordnance Survey**, a series renowned for its accuracy and clarity. The 204 maps in their 1:50,000 (a little over one inch:one mile) *Landranger* series cover the whole of Britain in enough detail to be useful for most walkers. The more detailed 1:25,000 *Pathfinder* series is invaluable for serious hiking; the same-scale *Outdoor Leisure* series, though covering only the most frequently walked areas, is sensibly designed to take in a specific area on each map. There are eight *Outdoor Leisure* maps for Wales, five covering Snowdonia from the north coast down to Cadair Idris, and three spanning the Brecon Beacons and Black Mountains. *OS* maps are widely available in bookshops, but in any walking district of Wales you can be sure to find the relevant maps on sale locally.

MAP OUTLETS

NORTH AMERICA

Chicago: *Rand McNally*, 444 N Michigan Ave, IL 60611 (☎312/321-1751).

Montréal: *Ulysses Travel Bookshop*, 4176 St-Denis (☎514/289-0993).

New York: *British Travel Bookshop*, 551 5th Ave, NY 10176 (☎1-800/448-3039 or 212/490-6688); *The Complete Traveler Bookstore*, 199 Madison Ave, NY 10016 (☎212/685-9007); *Rand McNally*, 150 East 52nd St, NY 10022 (☎212/758-7488); *Traveler's Bookstore*, 22 West 52nd St, NY 10019 (☎212/664-0995).

San Francisco: *The Complete Traveler Bookstore*, 3207 Filmore St, CA 92123 (☎415/923-1511); *Rand McNally*, 595 Market St, CA 94105 (☎415/777-3131).

Seattle: *Elliot Bay Book Company*, 101 South Main St, WA 98104 (☎206/624-6600).

Toronto: *Open Air Books and Maps*, 25 Toronto St, M5R 2C1 (☎416/363-0719).

Vancouver: *World Wide Books and Maps*, 1247 Granville St (☎604/687-3320).

Washington DC: *Rand McNally*, 1201 Connecticut Ave NW, 20036 (☎202/223-6751).

Note that *Rand McNally* now have 24 stores across the US; phone ☎1-800/333-0136 (ext 2111) for the address of your nearest store, or for **direct mail** maps.

UK

London: *National Map Centre*, 22–24 Caxton St, SW1 (☎071/222 4945); *Stanfords*, 12–14 Long Acre, WC2 (☎071/836 1321); *The Travellers Bookshop*, 25 Cecil Court, WC2 (☎071/836 9132).

Edinburgh: *Thomas Nelson and Sons Ltd*, 51 York Place, EH1 3JD (☎031/557 3011).

Glasgow: *John Smith and Sons*, 57–61 St Vincent St (☎041/221 7472).

Maps by **mail or phone order** are available from *Stanfords* (☎071/836 1321).

AUSTRALIA

Adelaide: *The Map Shop*, 16a Peel St, SA 5000 (☎08/231 2033).

Brisbane: *Hema*, 239 George St, QLD 4000 (☎07/221 4330).

Melbourne: *Bowyangs*, 372 Little Bourke St, VIC 3000 (☎03/670 4383).

Perth: *Perth Map Centre*, 891 Hay St, WA 6000 (☎09/322 5733).

Sydney: *Travel Bookshop*, 20 Bridge St, NSW 2000 (☎02/241 3554).

GETTING AROUND

The large cities and densely populated valleys of south Wales support comprehensive train and bus networks, but the more thinly populated areas of mid and north Wales have to make do with skeletal services, part of the expedient governmental measures of the recession. That said, it is rare to find somewhere that isn't reached by an occasional bus, even if it also picks up the local mail. Fares are some of the highest in Europe, a product of the pro-car policies that have seen new roads carved through the countryside regardless of the environmental cost. However, this does mean that getting about by car is easy, and unless you are planning to spend all your time in Cardiff and Swansea, sheep are likely to be a more persistent problem than other road users.

As a basic rule, if you're using public transport make sure you're aware of all the passes and special deals on offer; and if

you're driving, take the more scenic back-roads unless you're in a real hurry. Cyclists should skip to the "Outdoor Pursuits" section (p.36).

TRAINS

British Rail (BR) runs the majority of services in Wales, providing coverage of the main cities and an almost random selection of rural towns and wayside halts. The two **major lines** are at opposite ends of the country and connected only by routes though England. In the north, long-distance and local services ply the coastal strip from Chester in England through Conwy, Bangor and on to Holyhead for the Irish ferries. Along the south coast, Newport, Cardiff and Swansea are joined by a fairly fast service extending to London in the east and Fishguard (where you can also pick up boats to Ireland) in the west. The remainder of the routes support an infrequent service, occasionally replaced by buses on Sunday. For all its inconveniences though, the train is one of the best ways to get around Wales: the views are superb and the engineering often impressive. In addition to the BR network, there are almost a dozen private train lines (see box) carrying these two qualities to greater heights. All run steam trains, most on narrow-gauge tracks and predominantly as tourist attractions: the best of them are exceptional.

You can buy **tickets** for BR trains at stations or from major travel agents – details of the **different types of fare** available are given on p.4, "Getting There from the UK and Europe". For busy long-distance journeys, you can **reserve a seat** for £1 – though this is seldom necessary, even on the main north and south coast routes. At many smaller stations, the ticket offices are closed at weekends, and at some rural halts they've shut for good. In these instances there's often a vending machine on the platform. If there isn't a machine, you can buy your ticket on board – but if you've boarded at a station with a machine and haven't bought a ticket, you're liable for an on-the-spot fine of £10.

BRITISH RAIL CONTACT NUMBERS

The following Welsh station information lines are listed north to south. In addition there are Credit Card ticket booking numbers in: Cardiff ☎0222/499811; Newport ☎0633/257271; and Swansea ☎0792/632410.

Holyhead	☎0407/769222
Llandudno	☎0492/585151
Machynlleth	☎0654/702311
Llandrindod Wells	☎0597/822053
Haverfordwest	☎0437/764361
Pembroke Dock	☎0646/684896
Swansea	☎0792/467777
Newport	☎0633/842222
Cardiff	☎0222/228000

RAIL PASSES

British Rail sells a number of tickets and passes that may be worth considering. If Wales is only a part of your wider British travels, you can take advantage of the **All-Line Rail Rover**, which allows unlimited travel on the whole *British Rail* network throughout Wales, England and Scotland for 7 (£215) or 15 days (£350). Three train passes cover the Welsh lines specifically, the most comprehensive being the **Freedom of Wales** ticket, allowing travel throughout Wales – and the connecting services through England – for a period of 7 days (£50 in summer; £45 in winter). Additional benefits are discounts on some of the narrow-gauge railways and a flat fare of £1 on certain long-distance buses. There's no special pass for south Wales but the **North and Mid-Wales Rail Rover**, available for 7 days (£33) or 3 days out of 7 (£20), covers Welsh routes north of Aberystwyth and the English lines linking them. Both these passes allow free travel on the Ffestiniog Railway (see below). If you are not straying far, you may have use for local **Day Ranger** tickets, valid after 9.30am on weekdays and all day at weekends. They're available in most areas but the Cambrian Coast (£15), North Wales Resorts (£7.50) and Cardiff Valleys (£5) tickets are likely to be the most useful.

Two other discount schemes are available in Britain. The **Young Persons Railcard** costs £16, is valid for a year, and gives 33 percent reductions on all standard *Saver* and *SuperSaver* fares to full-time students and those from 16 to 24 years. A **Senior Citizens Rail Card**, also £16 and offering 30 percent reductions, is available to those who have reached retirement age of 60.

For rail passes available abroad to North Americans and other foreign visitors, see p.10.

STEAM RAILWAYS

With the rising demand for quarried stone in the nineteenth century, quarry and mine owners were forced to find more economical ways than packhorses to get their products to market, but in the steep, tortuous valleys of Snowdonia standard-gauge train tracks proved too unwieldy. The solution was rails of sometimes less than a foot apart, plied by steam engines and dinky rolling stock. The charm of these railways was too much for train enthusiasts, and long after the decline of the quarries, they banded together to painstakingly restore abandoned lines and locos. Most lines are still largely run by volunteers who have also started up new services along unused sections of standard-gauge bed. All the lines run steam engines, though out of season services are sometimes diesel-hauled.

Although run primarily as tourist attractions, several of the **steam railways** operate as public transport and are detailed as such in the text. Tickets are generally sold separately, but the first eight railways listed below – *The Great Little Trains of Wales* – offer a Wanderer Ticket between late March and early November, allowing either 4 days' travel within an 8-day period (£20), or 8 days in 15 (£27). Some discounts are also available with BR rail passes (see above).

BUSES

With the skeletal nature of the train system in Wales, you're going to find yourself relying on buses which provide a much deeper penetration into the countryside. There are a limited number of inter-town buses run by **National Express** (see "Getting There from the UK and Europe"), but for travel within Wales you'll be using **local bus services** run by a bewildering array of companies. In many cases, timetables and routes are well integrated, but it is increasingly the case that private companies compete with each other on the busiest routes, leaving the far-flung spots

WALES' STEAM RAILWAYS

Bala Lake Railway, Bala (☎06784/666). Four-mile lakeside run using the bed of the former Corwen–Barmouth standard-gauge line. 24-inch gauge.

Brecon Mountain Railway, Merthyr Tydfil (☎0685/722988). Two-mile narrow-gauge line mostly on the bed of the Brecon and Merthyr Railway which closed in 1963, and which is to be extended to 3.5 miles by Easter 1995. 24-inch gauge.

Fairbourne Railway, Fairbourne (☎0341/250362). Diminutive former tramway which brought building materials for the construction of Fairbourne. Linked to the passenger ferry to Barmouth. 12-inch gauge.

Ffestiniog Railway, Porthmadog (☎0766/512340). Wonderful thirteen-mile twisting climb from Porthmadog through the Vale of Ffestiniog to the slate mining town of Blaenau Ffestiniog. Links two BR lines. 23.5-inch gauge.

Llanberis Lake Railway, Llanberis (☎0286/870549). A short waterside section of the former slate line to Port Dinorwig on the Menai Strait. 24-inch gauge.

Llangollen Railway, Llangollen (☎0978/860951). Rejuvenated four-mile section (though currently being extended) of the former Ruabon–Barmouth, running through a gorge-like section of the Dee Valley. Standard 56.5-inch gauge.

Snowdon Mountain Railway, Llanberis (☎0286/870223). Wales' only rack-and-pinion railway, climbing from Llanberis to the summit café and post office atop Snowdon. 31.5 inch gauge.

Talyllyn Railway, Tywyn (☎0654/710472). Slow-climbing one-time quarry line, revived in 1951. One of the best, running seven miles at the foot of Cadair Idris. 27-inch gauge.

Vale of Rheidol Railway, Aberystwyth (☎0970/625819). Stunning twelve-mile run intended for tourists intent on seeing Devil's Bridge. BR's only narrow-gauge line until it was sold off in 1988. 13.5-inch gauge.

Welshpool and Llanfair Railway, Llanfair Caereinion (☎0938/810441). A nine-mile-long descent to the River Banwy with locos used by the German army and a West Indian sugar plantation. 30-inch gauge.

Welsh Highland Railway, Porthmadog (☎0766/513402). Flat three-quarter-mile section of what was once the longest and one of the least profitable narrow-gauge lines in Wales. 24-inch gauge neglected. Though services are more expensive and less frequent in the rural areas, there are very few places without any service even if it is only a private minibus on market day or one of the "postbuses" that also pick up mail.

In the **northern** half of Wales, Llandudno-based *Crosville Wales* (☎0492/592111) runs the majority of local services as well as a few scenic long-distance runs. Their network is extensive enough that it might be worth buying a **rover ticket**, purchased on the bus and valid for all but the #701 or #702 services to Swansea and Cardiff. The **Day Rover** (£4.70) is good for one day's unlimited travel, or from 6pm there's an **Evening Rover** (£2.20). Greater savings can be made with the **Weekly Wide Rover**, available in Peak (all day, every day; £18) or Off-peak (not valid before 9.30am Mon–Fri; £14) versions. Lastly, there's a pass valid for ten rides over a one-year period, the **Any 10 Card** (£11).

In the **southern** half of the country the system is far less unified and only a couple of passes are likely to be of much use. Services west of Cardiff and south of Carmarthen are mostly run by the Swansea-based *SWT* (☎0492/475 511) which offers two one-day passes: the **Rover Bus** (£4), restricted to Swansea and the Gower, and the **Rover Bus Plus** (£5.20), which covers the whole *SWT* network, as does the weekly **Master Rider** (£12.40). *Bws Caerdydd* (☎0222/396521), the major company serving Cardiff and the Vale of Glamorgan, offers a wide range of day, evening and weekly tickets; prices depend on the number of zones involved. For details of more UK-wide bus passes, see "Getting There from the UK and Europe", p.5.

All regions have their own detailed local **timetable**, easily obtained from tourist offices, libraries and stations. These are usually very helpful, especially the wonderfully comprehensive *Gwynedd Public Transport Map and Timetable.*

DRIVING

If you want to cover a lot of the countryside in a short time, or just want more flexibility, you'll need your own transport. England's busy but comprehensive motorway system means that getting to Wales is fairly straighforward, but over the border you'll find there's just one **motorway**: the M4 from London, which crosses into Wales over the Severn Bridge and skirts Newport, Cardiff and Bridgend before petering out just beyond Swansea. An extensive network of dual carriageways and good quality A-roads link the major centres but in rural areas you'll often find yourself on steep, winding, single-track (but usually asphalt) lanes with passing places. In very remote areas, you sometimes still have to open gates designed to keep sheep from straying.

In order to **drive in Britain**, you must have a current **driving licence**; foreign nationals will need to supplement this with an **international driving permit**, available from national motoring organizations for a small fee. If you're bringing your own vehicle into the country you should also carry vehicle registration or ownership document at all times. Furthermore, you must be adequately **insured**, so be sure to check your existing policy.

As in the rest of the UK, you **drive on the left** in Wales, and it can lead to a few tense days of acclimatization for foreign drivers. **Speed limits** are 30–40mph (50–65kph) in built-up areas, 70mph (110kph) on motorways and dual carriageways and 50mph (80kph) on most other roads. As a rule, assume that in any area with street lighting the speed limit is 30mph (50kph) unless stated otherwise. **Fuel** is expensive in comparison with North American prices – leaded 4-star petrol costs in the region of £2.40 per English gallon (4.56 litres), unleaded and diesel slightly less. Prices are increasingly quoted by the litre (around 47–56p/litre) and are generally lowest in the suburbs of cities, where competition is fiercest, and highest at motorway service stations.

MOTORING ORGANIZATIONS

American Automobile Association, 1000 AAA Drive, Heathrow, FL 32746 (☎1-800/566-1166 or 407/444-7000).

Australian Automobile Association, 212 Northbourne Ave, Canberra, ACT 2601 (☎06/247 7311).

Automobile Association, Fanum House, Basingstoke, Hants RG21 2EA (☎0256/20123).

Canadian Automobile Association, 2 Carlton St, Toronto, ON M4B 1K4 (☎416/964 3002).

New Zealand Automobile Association, PO Box 1794, Wellington (☎064/473 8738).

Royal Automobile Club, PO Box 100, RAC House, 7 Brighton Rd, S Croydon CR2 6XW (☎081/686 0088).

The *Automobile Association*, the *Royal Automobile Club* and *National Breakdown* all operate 24-hour emergency **breakdown** services. The *AA* and *RAC* also provide many other motoring services, as well as a reciprocal arrangement for free assistance, through many overseas motoring organizations – check the situation with yours before setting out. On motorways the *AA* and *RAC* can be called from roadside booths; elsewhere ring ☎0800/887766 for the *AA*, ☎0800/828282 for the *RAC* or ☎0800/400600 for *National Breakdown* (calls are free). You can ring these emergency numbers even if you are not a member, although a substantial fee will be charged.

CAR AND MOTORBIKE RENTAL

Car rental in Britain is expensive, and, especially if you're travelling from North America, you'll probably find it cheaper to arrange in advance through one of the multinational chains. If you do rent a car when you arrive, the least you can expect to pay is around £140 a week – the rate for a small hatchback from *Holiday Autos*, the most competitive agency; reckon on paying £40 per day at one of the multinationals, £5 or so less at a local firm. There are very few automatics at the lower end of the price scale – if you want one, you should book well ahead. Most companies prefer you to pay with a credit card; otherwise you may have to leave a deposit of at least £100. You will need to show your driving licence; few companies will rent to drivers with less than one year's experience and most will only rent to people between 21 and 70 years of age.

Motorbike rental is ludicrously expensive, at around £45 a day/£200 a week for a 500cc machine, and around £80/£300 for a one-litre tourer, including everything from insurance to helmets and luggage boxes. If you are travelling to Wales via London, it may be worth trying one of the companies that rent out ex-despatch bikes; for addresses, check the weekly newspaper *Motor Cycle News*.

CAR RENTAL AGENCIES

Britain

Avis ☎081/848 8733.

Budget ☎0800/181181.

Europcar/InterRent ☎0345/222525.

Hertz ☎081/679 1799.

Holiday Autos ☎071/491 1111.

North America

Avis ☎800/331-1212.

Budget ☎800/527-0700.

Europe by Car ☎800/223-1516.

Hertz ☎800/654-3131.

Holiday Autos ☎800/442-7737.

National Car Rental ☎800/CAR-RENT.

ACCOMMODATION

Welsh tourist accommodation has changed notably in recent decades, from a stack of fearsome guest houses for English holidaymakers in the postwar years, to top-rank international hotels, farmhouse accommodation, hostels and ubiquitous Bed and Breakfast (B&B) establishments. The change has been for the better, bringing a far greater variety, and considerably better standards, than ever before.

Wales has traditionally been a holiday centre for the millions of English who live within striking distance – particularly those in Birmingham and the Midlands or Manchester, Liverpool and the northwest. This is evident at some of the more faded, tackier seaside resorts in the shape of vast and ugly caravan parks and row upon row of tawdry guest houses. However, with the lower cost of the foreign package holiday,

more English people are choosing to fly abroad for their fortnight of sun and sand, freeing up Wales – its spectacular countryside as much as its coastline – for a rapidly increasing number of international visitors.

HOTELS AND B&Bs

The **Wales Tourist Board** (WTB) operates a grading scheme for **hotels** and **B&Bs**, using crown symbols. One crown indicates a simple, reasonably cheap place with all rooms having at least a washbasin, while anywhere boasting the maximum of five crowns will be luxurious, ensuite accommodation. The crown grades are based on little more than the number of facilities and generally correspond with the price: a one- or two-crown establishment should cost £20–30 for a double room, a three-crown £30–50, four-crown £40–60 and five-crown anything above that. In addition to the crowns, however, an establishment can receive the badges of (in descending order) Highly Commended, Commended or Merit, which are a better reflection of the kind of service and general comfort you can expect.

The distinction between hotels and B&Bs is blurring all the time. A bad, fully fledged hotel (so-called because of its licensed status) can be vastly inferior to a similarly priced or even cheaper **B&B**, or **guesthouse**, as they're frequently known. This is especially the case amongst the growing army of **farmhouse B&Bs**, which quite often outstrip any hotel for the sheer warmth of welcome and quality of home cooking. B&Bs range from ordinary private houses with a couple of bedrooms set aside for paying guests and a dining room for a rudimentary breakfast, to rooms as well furnished as those in hotels costing twice as much, with delicious home-prepared breakfasts, and an informal hospitality that a larger place couldn't match.

The WTB produces a comprehensive *Farm Holidays* brochure, or consult the *Welsh Rarebits* and *Great Little Places* lists of top hotels, many of which are in rambling farmhouses. These brochures can be obtained free from *EuroWales Tour Specialists*, Pentre Bach, Montgomery, Powys SY15 6HR (☎0686/668030), and there are complete lists of accommodation throughout Wales available from the WTB (see p.18).

Official **tourist offices** will only ever give you lists of accommodation that has been "verified" by WTB inspectors, which does at least ensure that you shouldn't be short-changed. However, they can sometimes be reluctant to give information about places that haven't paid to advertise in the official local guide: if you don't see something suitable in the guide, don't be afraid to ask if there is anywhere else that matches your requirements for price and location. As far as possible we've mentioned such places in the text.

HOSTELS

The network of the **Youth Hostels Association** comprises some 45 properties in Wales, offering bunk-bed accommodation in single-sex dormitories or smaller rooms. A few of these places are spartan establishments of the sort traditionally associated with the wholesome, fresh-air ethic of the first hostels, but many have moved well away from this institutional ambience. Welsh hostels range from some remote, unheated barns in the wilds of mid-Wales and Snowdonia to more cosmopolitan, purpose-built centres in places such as Cardiff. The greatest concentration of hostels, by far, is in Snowdonia, with smaller clusters in Wales' other two National Parks, around the Pembrokeshire coast and in the Brecon Beacons. All cost under £10 a night per person. For a list of all Welsh YHA youth hostels, contact YHA Wales/Cymru, 4th floor, 1 Cathedral Rd, Cardiff CF1 9HA (☎0222/396766).

ACCOMMODATION PRICE CODES

Throughout this guide, hotel and B&B accommodation is priced on a scale of ① to ⑨. Category ① only applies to youth hostels; for the rest, the number indicates the **lowest price** you could expect to pay per night for a **double room in high season**. The prices indicated by the codes are as follows:

① under £20/$32	④ £40–50/$64–80	⑦ £70–80/$112–128
② £20–30/$32–48	⑤ £50–60/$80–96	⑧ £80–100/$128–160
③ £30–40/$48–64	⑥ £60–70/$96–112	⑨ over £100/$160

YOUTH HOSTEL ASSOCIATIONS

Australia *Australian Youth Hostels Association*, PO Box 61, Strawberry Hills, Sydney, New South Wales 2012 (☎02/212 1266).

Canada *Canadian Hostelling Association*, Room 400, 205 Catherine St, Ottawa, Ontario K2P 1C3 (☎613/237-7884).

England *Youth Hostels Association* (*YHA*), Trevelyan House, 8 St Stephen's Hill, St Alban's, Herts AL1 2DY (☎0727/855 215). London shop and information office: 14 Southampton St, London WC2E 7HY (☎071/836 1036). There are fifteen other YHA city locations throughout England.

Ireland *An Oige*, 39 Mountjoy Square, Dublin 1 (☎01/363111).

New Zealand *Youth Hostels Association of New Zealand*, PO Box 436, Christchurch 1 (☎03/799 970).

Northern Ireland *Youth Hostel Association of Northern Ireland*, 56 Bradbury Place, Belfast BT7 1RU (☎0232/324733).

Scotland *Scottish Youth Hostels Association*, 7 Glebe Crescent, Stirling FK8 2JA (☎0786/451181).

USA *American Youth Hostels*, PO Box 37613, Washington, DC 200013 (☎202/783-6161).

Membership of the YHA, which is open only to residents of England and Wales, costs £9 per year, £3 for under-18s, and can be otained either by writing to the YHA (see box above) or in person at any YHA hostel. Members are issued with a directory of all YHA hostels and gain automatic membership of the hostelling associations of the 60 countries affiliated to the International Youth Hostels Federation (IYHF). Foreign visitors who belong to any IYHF association corrrespondingly have membership of the YHA; if you aren't a member of such an organization, you can join the IYHF at any English or Welsh hostel for a £9 fee.

At any time of year it's best to **book your place** well in advance, and it's essential at Easter, Christmas and from May to August. Most hostels accept payment by *Mastercard* or *Visa*; if not, you should confirm your booking in writing, with payment, at least seven days before arrival. Bookings made less than seven days in advance will be held only until 6pm on the day of arrival. If you're tempted to turn up on the spur of the moment, bear in mind that very few hostels are open year-round, many are closed at least one day a week even in high season, and several have periods during which they take group bookings only. To give the full details of opening times within this guide would be impossibly unwieldy, so **always phone** – we've given the number for every hostel mentioned. Most hostels are closed from 10am to 5pm, with an 11pm curfew.

Independent hostels and **bunkhouses** – simple affairs close to the mountains designed for walkers, usually providing mattresses and occasionally bedding in communal dormitories – are becoming a more common feature in Wales and, where relevant, are mentioned in the text of the *Guide*.

CAMPING, CARAVANNING AND SELF-CATERING

There are hundreds of **campsites** in Wales, charging from £5 per tent per night to around £10 at the plushest sites, with amenities such as laundries, shops and sports facilities. Some YHA hostels (see above) have small campsites on their property, for which you'll pay half the indoor fee. In addition to these official sites, farmers may offer pitches for as little as £2 per night, but don't expect tiled bathrooms and hairdriers for this kind of money. Even farmers without a reserved camping area may let you pitch in a field if you ask first, and may charge you nothing for the privilege; setting up a tent without asking is an act of trespass and won't be well received. Note that **rough camping is illegal** in National Parks and nature reserves.

The problem with most accredited campsites in Wales is that tents have to share the space with **caravans**. Some of Wales' most popular areas – Pembrokeshire, the Wye Valley, the Gower, Snowdonia, the Brecon Beacons – seem to be permanently clogged with these slow-moving, low-tech mobile homes, rumbling inexorably from one park to the next.

As a hangover from the days of thousands of Midland holidaymakers decamping to the Welsh coast for a fortnight, many of the traditional seaside resorts are infested with camp upon camp of **permanently sited caravans**, rented

SELF-CATERING ACCOMMODATION COMPANIES

Brecon Beacons Holiday Cottages, Brynoyre, Talybont-on-Usk, Brecon, Powys LD3 7YS (☎0874/87446). Around 100 cottages and other buildings, some decidedly quirky, in the Brecon Beacons.

Coastal Cottages of Pembrokeshire, Abercastle, Dyfed SA62 5HJ (☎0348/837742). 350 cottages, chalets, flats and houses around or near the Pembrokeshire coast.

Gwyliau Cymreig (*Welsh Holidays*), Snowdonia Tourist Services, Ynys Tywyn, High St, Porthmadog, Gwynedd LL49 9PG (☎0766/513829). Best, and cheapest, of the many companies offering self-catering accommodation in Snowdonia and the north.

North Wales Holiday Cottages & Farmhouses, Station Rd, Deganwy, Conwy, Gwynedd LL31 9DF (☎0492/582492). Numerous cottages in Snowdonia and around the north Wales coast.

Powell's Cottage Holidays, Dolphin House, High St, Saundersfoot, Dyfed SA69 9EJ (☎0834/812791). 250 properties, mainly in south Wales and the Gower.

Quality Cottages, Cerbid, Solva, Haverfordwest, Dyfed SA62 9YE (☎0348/837871). Coastal cottages throughout Wales, largely around Pembrokeshire and Cardiganshire.

Wales Cottage Holidays, The Bank, Newtown, Powys SY16 2AA (☎0686/625267). A varied selection of 500 properties all over Wales.

out for self-catering holidays. Although these can certainly be cost-effective, with facilities such as bars, shops and discos thrown in, most discerning people prefer to take more robust self-catering holidays in self-contained **cottages, farms, town houses, apartments** or even purpose-built estates. The usual minimum rental period is a week, though long weekend breaks can often be arranged out of season. In midsummer, or over Christmas and New Year, prices start at around £300 for a place sleeping four or six, although in winter, spring or autumn they can dip below £100 for the same property.

Some companies specializing in Welsh holiday cottages are listed in the box above; the British Sunday papers generally have exhaustive lists of self-catering holiday companies in their small ads section.

Detailed annually revised **guidebooks** to Wales's camping and caravan sites include the *AA*'s *Camping and Caravanning in Britain and Ireland*, which lists their inspected and graded sites, and *Cade's Camping, Tourings and Motor Caravan Site Guide*, published by Marwain. WTB produce self-catering and camping directories, available free from their Cardiff address.

FOOD AND DRINK

For many centuries, Welsh cuisine has been considered to be little more than a poor relation of the English culinary art, itself hardly well regarded on the international scene. Restaurants were on the whole uninteresting and the pubs were strictly male-dominated and cheerless. Times have now changed to some extent, for traditional Welsh cuisine is now climbing a slope of resurgence, and this, combined with improved British fare and an eclectic range of international options, has turned eating and drinking throughout Wales into an interesting and enjoyable part of any stay in the country.

EATING

Indigenous British cuisine has taken an upturn in recent years. The pies, cheeses, puddings and meat from all of the regions are being offered in increasing numbers of establishments. Popular British dishes – steak and kidney pies, the ubiquitous fish and chips, cuts of meat with potatoes and vegetables, and stews for example – are available everywhere in Wales.

Native **Welsh cuisine** is also making something of a comeback. Not surprisingly, such food is frequently rooted in economical ingredients, although this does not mean that it is of a poor quality. Traditional dishes, such as the delicious native lamb (served at its best minted or with thyme), fresh salmon, sewin and other trout can be found on an increasing number of menus, frequently combined with the national vegetable, the leek. Specialities include laver bread (*bara lawr*), a thoroughly tasty seaweed and oatmeal cake often fried with a traditional breakfast of pork sausages, egg and bacon. Other dishes well worth investigating include Glamorgan sausages (a vegetarian combination of local cheese and spices), cawl, (a chunky mutton broth) and cockles, trawled from the estuary north of the Gower.

Dairy products, in a predominantly rural country, feature highly, especially in the range of Welsh **cheeses**. Best known is Caerphilly, a soft, crumbly white cheese that forms the basis of a true Welsh Rarebit, when mixed with beer and toasted on bread. Creamy goat cheeses can be found all over the country. Also stemming from the cheapness of their ingredients are some traditional **sweets and cakes**: Welsh Cakes are flat pancakes of sugared dough, and *bara brith* a popular accompaniment to afternoon tea, literally translated as speckled (with dried fruit) bread. Menus comprising Welsh dishes can be found in numerous restaurants, hotels and pubs, many of which are part of the **Taste of Wales** (*Blas ar Gymru*) scheme to encourage native cuisine. Such establishments generally display a sticker in their windows. The WTB can provide a leaflet about Welsh cooking, also including some of the better-known establishments where it can be found.

WHERE TO EAT

Staying in a hotel, guesthouse or B&B, it is likely that a cooked breakfast will be offered as part of the deal. These are generally served between 8–9am, with variations according to the establishment in question. A hearty breakfast is usually enough to see most people through the day, with maybe a lunchtime snack around 1pm. Lunch is generally between noon and 2pm, and evening meals from 6–10pm.

Cafés, found absolutely everywhere, are generally the cheapest places to eat, providing hearty, if cholesterol-laden, breakfasts, a solid range of snacks and full meals for lunch and, in a few instances, evening meals as well. Wales' steady influx of hippies and New Agers over the past thirty years has seen the **wholefood café** become a standard feature of most mid and west Welsh towns. Cheap and usually vegetarian, these rely extensively on fresh local produce and are also frequently an excellent resource centre for alternative and esoteric information about local groups, events, fairs, festivals and even useful things like car-sharing.

Food in **pubs** varies as much as the establishments themselves. In recent years, intense competition has required them to sharpen up their act, and many pubs now offer more imaginative dishes than standard microwaved lasagne and chips. Most places serve food at lunchtime and in the evening (usually until 8.30 or 9pm), and in many towns the local pub is the most economical place to grab a filling evening meal. Recommendations are given throughout the book.

The growth in upmarket **restaurants** has mirrored Wales' increasing sophistication and attraction to the outside world. People of all nationalities have settled in Wales and few towns are without their Indian and Chinese restaurants, joined over recent years by Japanese, French, Thai, American, Mexican, even Belgian and New Zealand establishments. In the larger, more cosmopolitan centres, **bistros** and **brasseries** have sprung up, many offering superb Welsh and international cuisine at thoroughly affordable prices.

Our restaurant listings include a mix of high-quality and good-value establishments, but if you're intent on a culinary pilgrimage, you'd do well to arm yourself with a copy of the *Good Food Guide* (Hodder), which is updated annually and includes detailed recommendations. Throughout this book, we've supplied the phone number for all restaurants where you may need to book a table. At places categorized as "**inexpensive**", you can expect to pay under £10 per head, without drinks; "**moderate**" means £10–20; "**expensive**" £20–30; and "**very expensive**" over £30.

DRINKING

As much as in any other part of the British Isles, the **pub** reigns supreme in Wales. Many people imagine that the puritanical "dry" Welsh Sunday is still commonplace: in fact, in the last seven-yearly vote on the matter, the only district to choose to remain alcohol-free on the Sabbath was Dwyfor, covering the Welsh heartland of the Llŷn peninsula – even this is likely to change.

Pubs in Wales vary as much as the landscape, from opulent Edwardian palaces of smoked glass, gleaming brass and polished mahogany in the larger towns and cities to thick-set stone barns in wild, remote countryside. Where the church has faltered as a community focal point, the pub still holds sway, with those in smaller towns and villages, in particular, functioning as a community centre as much as a place in which to drink alcohol. Live music (occasionally improvised) and, this being Wales, singing frequently round off an evening. As a rule of thumb, if the pub has both a **bar** and a **lounge**, the bar will be more basic and frequently very male-dominated, the lounge plusher, more mixed and probably a better bet for a passing tourist. **Opening times** are fairly standard: Monday to Saturday 11am–11pm (with many quieter places closed between 3 and 6pm), noon–3pm and 7–10.30pm on Sundays, with "last orders" called by the barstaff about fifteen minutes before closing time. In general, you have to be 16 to enter a pub unaccompanied, though some places have special family rooms for people with children, and beer gardens where younger kids can run free. The **legal drinking age** is 18.

Beer, sold by the pint (£1–1.80) and half-pint, is the staple drink in Wales, as it is throughout the British Isles. Many pubs are owned by large, UK-wide breweries who sell only their own **bitter** (an uncarbonated, deep-flavoured beer, best when hand-pumped from the cellar), together with a stock of **lagers**, a chilled, fizzy and light drink that corresponds with European and American ideas of beer. Despite being hard to find in England, mild, or **dark** as it is usually known in Wales, is quite common. This is a cheap, very dark and quite sweet beer that tends to pack a bit more of a punch than would be guessed from its taste. Even stronger, sweeter and darker is **porter**, making a welcome comeback in many Welsh pubs. Irish **stout** (*Guinness*, *Murphy's* or *Beamish*), although never as good as it is in Ireland, is widely available and, if well kept, very tasty.

Among beers worth looking out for are the heady brews produced by Cardiff-based **Brains**, mainly found in the southeastern corner of Wales. Their *Dark* is a superb, rich mild, whilst their *Bitter* and *SA Best Bitter* are amongst the best pints to be had anywhere in the UK. Llanelli-based **Felinfoel** covers the whole southern half of Wales, with *Double Dragon Premium* bitter the aromatic ace in their pack. **Crown Buckley**, also based in Llanelli, produces three excellent bitters and a distinctive mild. The best resource for any serious alehead is the **CAMRA** (Campaign for Real Ale) annual *Good Beer Guide*, which should steer you around the best pubs. If you see a recent CAMRA sticker in a pub window, chances are the beer will be well worth sampling.

Pubs and off-licences (liquor stores) increasingly stock the growing range of Welsh **whiskies** and other spirits. With Celtic cousins Ireland and Scotland having cornered the market in whisky, the Welsh have hit back with the standard *Swn-y-mor* and a wonderful malt, the *Prince of Wales*. Welsh gin and *Taffski* vodka can also be found, as can a number of Welsh **wines**, to be sampled more out of curiosity than anything else. Be warned that wine sold in pubs tends to be slop of the worst order, with the notable exception of pubs serving decent food. Even so, in these establishments and in dedicated **wine bars**, the cost of a bottle can be outrageous.

Pubs are gradually shedding their booze-only image, as more of them serve **tea** and **coffee**, as well as a heavily marked-up range of soft drinks. In more touristy areas, **tea shops** have sprung up like fungus, serving tea, snacks and cakes in the daytime. Less twee are the few continental-style **brasseries**, still a rarity out of the main towns, where decent coffee (rarely found in more basic cafés), other drinks and snacks are on offer.

POST AND PHONES

Virtually all post offices (*swyddfa'r post*) are open Mon–Fri 9am–5.30pm, Sat 9am–12.30 or 1pm; in small communities you'll find sub-post offices operating out of a shop, but these work to the same hours, even if the shop itself is open for longer. Stamps can be bought at post office counters, from vending machines outside, or from an increasing number of newsagents and other shops, although usually these sell only books of four or ten stamps.

Public **payphones** (*teleffon*) are operated by British Telecom (BT) or, less commonly, by its rival Mercury, and there should be one within ten minutes' walk of wherever you're standing, unless you're in the middle of a moor. Many BT payphones take all coins from 10p upwards, but an increasing proportion of BT's and all of Mercury's payphones only accept **phonecards**, available from post offices and newsagents displaying BT's green or Mercury's blue logo. These cards come in denominations of £1, £2, £4, £5 and £10; remember, though, that BT and Mercury cards are not interchangeable. All Mercury phones and some BT phones accept credit cards too, though there's a minimum charge of 50p.

Inland calls are cheapest between 6pm and 8am, and the Mercury rate is cheaper than BT's over long distances. **Reduced rate periods** for most **international calls** are 8pm–8am from Monday to Friday and all day on Saturday and Sunday, though for Australia and New Zealand it's midnight–7am & 2.30–7.30pm daily.

Within this guide, every telephone number is prefixed by the area code, followed by an oblique slash. The prefix can be omitted if dialling from within the area covered by that prefix. Any number with the prefix ☎0500 or ☎0800 is free to the caller; ☎0345 and ☎0645 numbers are charged at the local rate; while ☎0891 numbers (information services) and ☎0898 numbers (usually salacious entertainment lines) are charged at the exorbitant "premium rate".

From April 16, 1995 all telephone codes in Britain will be changed. The digit 1 will be inserted after the initial 0 in all area codes, and the code for dialling abroad will become 00 instead of 010.

OPERATOR SERVICES AND PHONE CODES

Operator ☎100

Directory assistance ☎192

Overseas directory assistance ☎153

International operator ☎155

INTERNATIONAL CALLS

To call **overseas from Wales** dial ☎010, then the appropriate country code and finally the number, including the local code minus any initial zero. Country codes include:

USA and Canada ☎1

Ireland ☎353

Australia ☎61

New Zealand ☎64

To **telephone Wales** from overseas it's ☎011 from the US and Canada, ☎0011 from Australia and ☎00 from New Zealand, followed in all cases by 44, then the area code minus its initial zero, and finally the number.

OPENING HOURS AND HOLIDAYS

General **shop hours** are Mon–Sat 9am–5.30 or 6pm, although there's an increasing amount of Sunday and late-night shopping in the larger towns, with Thursday or Friday being the favoured evenings. The big supermarkets also tend to stay open until 8 or 9pm from Monday to Saturday, as do many of the stores in the shopping complexes springing up on the outskirts of major towns. Many provincial towns still retain an "early closing day" when shops shut at 1pm – Wednesday is the favourite. Note that not all service stations are open for 24 hours although you can usually get fuel around the clock in the larger towns and cities. Also, most fee-charging sites are open on Bank Holidays, when Sunday hours usually apply.

PUBLIC HOLIDAYS IN WALES

January 1

Good Friday – late March to mid-April

Easter Monday – as above

First Monday in May

Last Monday in May

Last Monday in August

December 25

December 26

Note that if January 1, December 25 or December 26 falls on a Saturday or Sunday, the next weekday becomes a public holiday.

ADMISSION TO MUSEUMS AND MONUMENTS

Many of Wales' most treasured sites – from castles, abbeys and great houses to tracts of protected landscape – come under the control of the privately run UK-wide **National Trust**, Trinity Square, Llandudno, LL30 2DE (☎0492/860123), or the state-run **CADW, Welsh Historic Monuments**, Brunel House, 2 Fitzalan Rd, Cardiff, CF2 1UY (☎0222/465511), whose properties are denoted in the guide by "NT" and "CADW". Both organizations charge an entry fee for most places, and these can be quite high, especially for the more grandiose NT estates. If you think you'll be visiting more than half a dozen NT places or a similar number of major CADW sites, it's worth taking out **annual membership** (NT £24, under-23 £11; CADW £14, students £10), which allows free entry to their properties. NT membership covers you throughout Britain, and though CADW sites are restricted to Wales, membership allows half-price entry to sites owned by *English Heritage* and *Historic Scotland*.

A few Welsh **stately homes** remain in the hands of the landed gentry, who tend to charge in the region of £5 for edited highlights of their domain. Many other old buildings, albeit rarely the most momentous, are owned by the local authorities, and admission is often cheaper. Municipal **art galleries** and **museums** are usually free, though this doesn't hold true for either the National Museum of Wales or the Welsh Folk Museum, both in Cardiff. Although a donation is usually requested, **cathedrals** tend to be free, except for perhaps the tower, crypt, or other such highlight, for which a small charge is made. **Churches** are increasingly kept locked, except for services, but when they are open, entry is free. Wales also has a number of ventures exploiting the country's **industrial heritage**, mostly concerned with mining for coal, slate, copper or gold. A short tour supplemented by a video should cost a couple of quid while the full underground interactive "experience" can be up to £10.

The majority of the fee-charging attractions located in Wales have 25–35 percent

reductions for senior citizens, the unemployed and full-time students, and 50 percent reductions for children under 16, with under-5s admitted free almost everywhere. Proof of eligibility is required in most cases. Entry charges given in the guide are the full adult rates. Most attractions are open daily in summer and closed one or two days a week in winter, though major sites are open daily all year – full details of opening hours are given in the guide.

Finally, foreign visitors planning on seeing more than a dozen stately homes, monuments, castles or gardens might find it worthwhile to buy a **Great British Heritage Pass**, which gives free admission to over 500 sites throughout the UK. Sixty of these are in Wales, including Penhow Castle in Chepstow, Tredegar House at Newport and Cardiff Castle, as well as all National Trust and CADW properties. The pass can be purchased for periods of 15 days (£29) or 30 days (£43) through *British Airways*, major tourist offices or the British Travel Centre in London. North Americans can buy it in advance from the *British Travel Bookshop*, Box 1224 Clifton, NY 07012 (☎212/490-6688), or *Red Seal Tours*, 170 Evans Ave, Suite 210, Toronto, Ontario, M8Z 5V6 (☎416/503-2233), for $49 (Can $57) for 15 days, or $74 (Can$85) for a month.

THE MEDIA

The media that you will encounter in Wales is a predictable hybrid of Welsh and Britain-wide information. Although the London-based UK media attempts to cover life in the other corners of Britain, few people would agree that Wales, Scotland and the northern regions of England receive a fair share of coverage in any medium. Of all the solely Welsh media, newspapers are probably the weakest area and radio or TV coverage the strongest and most interesting.

NEWSPAPERS AND MAGAZINES

Of the **British daily newspapers**, all available in Wales, the vast majority are fearsomely right-wing and Londoncentric – news of Wales is not terribly well covered. The London-based **tabloid newspapers** – known otherwise, and with good reason, as the "gutter press" – are the papers you are most likely to see read in any part of Britain. Specializing in prurient gossip and scandal, the two leaders in this mucky field are the right-wing *Sun* and the damply leftish *Daily Mirror*. Slightly more upmarket, adding in a bit more news but always filtered through a severely right-wing analysis, are the *Daily Mail* and *Daily Express*. Best of the quality broadsheet papers are the vaguely left-leaning *Guardian*, the long-established *Times* and the ailing *Independent*. The only quality **Welsh daily** is the *Western Mail*, an uneasy mix of local, Welsh, British, and a token smattering of international news, with populist competitions and features on TV stars. It does, however, maintain an upbeat Welsh slant on everything, although this can sometimes be little more than a ludicrous angle given to a British story on the strength of some tenuous Welsh connection. Saturday editions include a free copy of *Sbec*, Wales' TV listings magazine. Of the **regional dailies**, north Wales' *Daily Post*, published and printed over the border in Liverpool, is best for details of local news and events and the nearby *Wrexham Evening Leader* is dependable and newsworthy. In the Cardiff area you'll come across the *South Wales Echo*, from the *Western Mail* stable; in Gwent, the evening *South Wales Argus*; and out in Swansea and the southwest, the *Swansea Evening Post*, Dylan Thomas's old sheet, endearingly old-fashioned and community centred. All areas have their own longstanding **weekly papers**, generally an entertaining mix of local news, parish gossip and events listings. Wales' national **Sunday paper**, *Wales on Sunday*, beats its weekday stablemate hands-down for quality of writing, features and coverage of news and sport.

Go into any bookshop in Wales, and you'll be surprised by the profusion of Welsh **magazines**, in both English and Welsh. For a broad overview of the arts, history and politics, it is hard to beat *Planet*, an English-language bimonthly that takes a politically irreverent line, combining Welsh interest with a wider international outlook. The more serious English-language monthly *New Welsh Review* is steeped in Wales' political, literary and economic developments. *Poetry Wales* is an excellent publication of new writing, whilst the bimonthly *Welsh Nation*, published by Plaid Cymru, is far more than a party political tract, genuinely encouraging open debate on current affairs. If you're half-proficient in Welsh, the weekly news digest *Y Cymro* is an essential read, or, if you're attempting to master the language (as many Welsh people are themselves), try *Prentis* magazine and the weekly news file *Golwg*, both aimed at learners.

For **listings** and news of arts events, pick up free copies of *Buzz* in Cardiff, *Leisure Line* in south and mid-Wales, and the quarterly *This Week Wales* in the north. The Pembrokeshire National Park also produces an excellent free newspaper, *Coast to Coast*, covering events in the region.

TELEVISION AND RADIO

It is in TV and radio that the Welsh media becomes most distinct from its London-based counterparts. Cardiff is the home of Britain's second largest concentration of TV and radio stations, both Welsh arms of devolved broadcasting organizations like the mighty BBC and indigenous Welsh operators such as S4C and HTV. The wholehearted way in which UK-wide TV and radio has moved out of southeast England is in marked contrast to the Londoncentric print media.

The state-funded British Broadcasting Corporation (BBC) operates two TV channels in Wales – the mainstream **BBC Wales on 1** and the more esoteric **BBC Wales on 2**. Although these official titles make the stations sound avowedly Welsh, the vast majority of programming is UK-wide, with Welsh programmes, principally news and sport but also features, political and education programmes, slotted into the regular schedules of documentaries, soaps, arts and music shows, quizzes, quality drama and imports. This is even more the case with **HTV** (Harlech Television), the Welsh holder of the licence to broadcast on the commercial, and determinedly populist, ITV network. The principal Welsh channel is **S4C** (*Sianel Pedwar Cymru*, verbally abbreviated to "*ess ped eck*"), whose existence is owed to the protesters (including the Plaid Cymru president) who refused to allow the government to renege on its commitment to a Welsh fourth channel alongside the planned UK-wide Channel Four. The station has grown from these shaky beginnings in the early 1980s to become a major player in the European media network and sponsor of diverse projects, including Welsh animation and feature films, notably the recent Oscar-nominated *Hedd Wyn*. It broadcasts Welsh-language programmes at lunchtime and for five or six hours every evening, although nearly all of them are subtitled in English for those with the Teletext system. In between, the output is in English, culled from the robust minority-aimed programming on the Channel 4 that broadcasts in England, Scotland and Ireland. S4C's programming is slick, confident and occasionally controversial, and includes a nightly dose of the BBC's longest-running TV soap, *Pobol y Cwm*.

Augmenting the terrestrial stations, **satellite** dishes are becoming an increasingly familiar sight on the side of houses, pubs and hotels in Wales. These tune into a vast array of European pap networks and Rupert Murdoch's **British Sky Broadcasting** (BSkyB) – numerous channels of consumer-oriented dross interspersed with expensive sports programming and a surprisingly good 24-hour news service.

The BBC is also a major player in **radio**, with five UK networks, all broadcasting in Wales: Radio One combines pop with a slightly cockeyed version of youth culture, Two is dull easy-listening, Three classical, Four a passionately loved ragbag of magazine shows, current affairs, drama, arts and highbrow quizzes, and Five Live a constant, entertaining mix of news and sport. It also operates two stations in Wales alone: **BBC Radio Wales**, an extremely competent English-language service of news, features and music, and **BBC Radio Cymru**, a Welsh-language version of much the same diet.

Of the commercial stations, the brashest is Radio One soundalike **Red Dragon Radio**, serving Cardiff and around, together with **Touch AM**, its twin for news, features and easy-listening music. **Swansea Sound**, whose reception extends west towards Pembrokeshire, is solid and frequently interesting, but the best local station is the bilingual **Radio Ceredigion**, more community-based than any of the others. In the north, **Radio Maldwyn** is the fledgling station for Montgomeryshire, whilst **BBC Radio Clwyd** and **Marcher Sound** battle it out in the north-west corner. Marcher's offshoot, the bland **Coast FM** covers the northern seaside resorts.

ANNUAL EVENTS

The most obviously unique events in Wales are the ***eisteddfodau*** (singular *eisteddfod*), a term that originally meant a meeting of bards. Nowadays it covers anything from a small village festival, where prizes of a couple of pounds are awarded for poetry and song, to two vast cultural orgies: the **International Eisteddfod**, held on a purpose-built fixed site at Llangollen in early July, and the roving **Royal National Eisteddfod**, in the first week of August, whose venue is proclaimed a year and a day in advance by the Gorsedd of Bards from within a stone circle. The similar **Urdd Eisteddfod**, for young people, takes place in early June. *Eisteddfodau* are the most Welsh of events, incorporating theatre, dance, music from rock to choirs, debate, ceremony, competitions and exhibitions. However, provision is made throughout for non-Welsh speakers, who are always welcome to what have become Europe's largest indigenous cultural festivals.

Many towns and cities now have annual **arts festivals** of some kind, mentioned throughout the guide and, in the case of the major events, in the box below. Aside from these, the old working traditions of Wales have spawned such occasions as the annual Cilgerran **coracle races** and Llanwrtyd's **drovers' runs**. Some of Wales' events have a distinctly bizarre background and appearance, for instance the snorkelling competition in peat bogs and the pilgrimages for *Prisoner* fans to the surreal village of Portmeirion. If you want to explore the odd customs and traditions of Britain in greater depth, read Martin Green's *Curious Customs* (Impact Books). Finally, New Age **fairs** and **festivals** are a common feature of summer throughout Wales; these are usually publicized by handbills, posters in wholefood shops and cafés, and by word of mouth. A few, however, have broken through to annual, and permanent, respectability.

EVENTS CALENDAR – JANUARY TO JUNE

February–March: Five Nations rugby championship. Success in 1994 has invigorated the Welsh game and tickets for home internationals are worth getting hold of.

March 1: St David's Day. *Hwyrnos* and celebrations all over Wales.

Mid-April: Swansea Beer Festival.

May–October: Festival of the Countryside, mid Wales (☎0686/625384). An assortment of events, guided walks, music and demos of rural crafts throughout the summer.

Mid-May: Tredegar House Folk Festival, Newport (☎0633/815612).

Mid-May: Pontrhydfendigaid Eisteddfod, Dyfed. One of the largest, best regional *eisteddfodau*.

Late May: Hay-on-Wye Festival of Literature (☎0497/821299). London's literati flock to the borders for a week.

Last week in May: St David's Cathedral Festival (☎0437/720804). Superb setting for classical concerts and recitals.

Early June: Gwyl Beaumaris, Anglesey (☎0248/750057 ext 110). One of the best arts festivals, combined with a regatta and fringe.

First week in June: Eisteddfod Genedlaethol Urdd (☎0269/845705). Vast and enjoyable youth eisteddfod – the largest youth festival in Europe – alternating between north and south Wales. In 1995 in Crymmych, Pembrokeshire; near Wrexham in 1996.

EVENTS CALENDAR – JUNE TO DECEMBER

Mid-June: Cardiff Singer of the World competition (☎0222/342611 ext 235 or 227). Huge, televised week-long festival of music and song, with a star-studded list of international competitors.

Mid-June: Man versus Horse Marathon, Llanwrtyd Wells, Powys (☎05913/236). A 22-mile race between runners, cyclists and horses. If a human beats a horse (it has come tantalizingly near to happening), he or she stands to pocket around £15,000.

Mid-June: Criccieth Festival (☎0766/522778). Celtic music, theatre and art.

Late June: Drovers' Walk, Llanwrtyd Wells, Powys (☎05913/236). Waymarked walks recreate the old drovers' routes, with an ex-drovers' inn reopening just for the day.

Last week in June: Gregynog Festival, near Newtown, Powys (☎0686/650224). Classical music festival in the superb country house surroundings of Gregynog Hall.

July 1: Annual commemorative march by nationalists in Abergele, Clwyd, to remember the two inept protesters who accidentally blew themselves up on the occasion of the Investiture of the Prince of Wales in 1969 (see p.345).

Mid-July: Royal Welsh Show, Builth Wells, Powys (☎0982/553683). Massive agricultural show and sales fair.

Second week in July: Llangollen International Music Eisteddfod (☎0978/860236). Over twelve thousand participants from all over the world, including choirs, dancers, folk singers, groups and instrumentalists.

Second weekend in July: Gŵyl Werin y Cnapan, Ffostrasol, near Lampeter, Dyfed (☎0239/858955 or 711374). The best folk and Celtic music festival held anywhere in the world.

Late July: Ras yr Wyddfa (☎0286/870721). A one-day race from Llanberis up Snowdon, attracting masochists from the world over.

Last week in July–first week in August: Cardiff Street Festival. Includes the Butetown Carnival, a loud, multiracial celebration and party by the bay.

First week in August: Royal National Eisteddfod (☎0222/763777). Wales' biggest single annual event: fun, very impressive and worth seeing if only for the overblown pageantry. Bardic competitions, readings, theatre, TV, debates and copious help for the Welsh language learner. At Neath in 1994, Colwyn Bay in 1995 and Llandeilo, Dinefwr in 1996.

Mid-August: Brecon Jazz Festival, Powys (☎0874/625557). Widely regarded as one of the best in Britain.

Late August: Pontardawe Music Festival, West Glamorgan (☎0792/864192). Folk, ceilidhs, international music and dance.

Late August: Cilgerran Coracle Races, Dyfed (☎0239/614204).

Late August: Llandrindod Wells Victorian Festival, Powys.

Last week in August: Gŵyl Machynlleth (☎0654/703355). Wide-ranging arts festival, with a solid programme of chamber music at its core.

August Bank Holiday Monday: World Bog Snorkelling Championships, Llanwrtyd Wells, Powys (☎059 13/236). Plus a mountain bike bog-leaping contest.

First two weeks in September: Excalibur Celtic Festival, Swansea and the Gower area (☎0792/232359). Sporting challenges, endurance tests, a triathlon and music events.

Late September–early October: Cardiff Festival (☎0222/236244). Themed annual festival that is one of the UK's largest. Incorporates music, art, drama, opera and literature.

October: Swansea Festival of Music and the Arts (☎0792/302432). Concerts, jazz, drama, opera, ballet and art events throughout the city.

December 31: 6km race in Mountain Ash, Mid Glamorgan, in memory of local eighteenth-century shepherd Guto Nyth Brân, who died after running 12 miles in 53 minutes.

December 31: Fancy dress costume night in New Quay, Dyfed.

December 31: New Year Walk-In, Llanwrtyd Wells, Powys. A boozy stagger round the town.

OUTDOOR PURSUITS

No matter where you are in Wales – even in the more populated valleys and coastline of the south – you're never far from a stretch of countryside where you can lose the crowds on a brief walk or cycle ride. For tougher specimens, there are long-distance footpaths and skyline ridge walks, as well as some of the best rock climbing and potholing (caving) in Britain. On the coast and many of the country's inland lakes, you can follow the pursuits of sailing and windsurfing, and there are plenty of fine beaches for less structured fresh-air activities.

WALKING

There's nowhere in Wales that you can't be out of a built-up area into some decent walking country in half an hour or so, but three areas are so outstanding they have been designated **national parks**. Almost the whole of the northwestern corner of Wales is taken up with the **Snowdonia National Park** (see p.278), a dozen of the country's highest peaks separated by dramatic glaciated valleys and laced with hundreds of miles of ridge and moorland paths. From Snowdonia, the Cambrian Mountains stretch south to the **Brecon Beacons National Park**, with its striking sandstone scarp at the head of the south Wales coalfield, and lush, cave-riddled limestone valleys to the south. One hundred and seventy miles of Wales' southwestern peninsula make up the third park, the **Pembrokeshire Coast National Park**, best explored by the **Pembrokeshire Coast Path** that traverses the clifftops, frequently dipping down into secluded coves. This is only one of Wales' four frequently walked **Long Distance Paths (LDPs)**. Defined as any route over twenty miles long, LDPs are waymarked at frequent intervals by an acorn symbol and are usually well supplied with youth hostels, though you may need a tent for some of the more heroic hikes. The other three LDPs are the 168-mile-long **Offa's Dyke Path** (see p.192) that traces the England–Wales border, the 274-mile **Cambrian Way**, cutting north–south over the Cambrian Mountains, and **Glyndŵr's Way**, which weaves through mid-Wales for 120 miles.

Unless you are doing your walking on weekdays out of season, don't expect to be on your own. Walking has become very popular in all the national parks and finding solitude can require some effort. This doesn't in any way reduce the **dangers**, however. Low though Welsh mountains are by world standards, the weather is fickle and you can easily find yourself disoriented in the low cloud and soaked by unexpected rain.

Many of the best day walks in the country are detailed in this guide. For more arduous mountain walks, you'll need a compass, maps and preferably a specialist walking guide, easily available in the appropriate walking area. The best are listed in *Contexts*. The *Long Distance Walkers' Association* (9 Tainters Brook, Uckfield, East Sussex, TN22 1UQ) can provide further information on all LDPs; as can *The Ramblers' Association* (1–5 Wandsworth Road, London, SW8; ☎071/582 6878), Britain's main walking and countryside campaigning organization.

RIGHTS OF ACCESS

Although they are managed by committees of local and state officials, all three Welsh national parks are in fact predominantly privately owned. There is **no general right of access**, but both the National Trust and the Forestry Commission, the principal landowners, normally allow free recreational use of their land. For how long this will be the case is currently under some doubt, as the government is considering selling off Forestry Commission land.

Access to other land is restricted to **public rights of way**: **footpaths** (pedestrians only) and **bridleways** (pedestrians, horses and bicycles) that have seen continued use over the centuries. Historically, these are often over narrow mountain passes between two hamlets, or link villages to mines or summer pasture land. Rights of way are marked on Ordnance Survey maps and are indicated with a Public Footpath (*Llwybr Cyhoeddus*) sign; any stiles and gates on the path have to be maintained by the landowner. Some less scrupulous owners have been known to block rights of way by destroying stiles – and with some walkers wilfully straying from official rights of way, some resentment is perhaps understandable. Disputes are still uncommon but your surest way of avoiding trouble is to meticulously follow the right of way on an up-to-date map. Ordnance Survey maps also indicate routes with **concessionary path** or **courtesy path** status; though these are usually open for public use they can be closed at any time.

ROCK CLIMBING AND SCRAMBLING

As well as being superb walking country, Snowdonia offers some of Britain's best **rock climbing** and some challenging **scrambles** – ascents that fall somewhere between walks and climbs, requiring some use of your hands. One or two of the tougher walks included in the text have sections of scrambling, but for the most part this is a specialist discipline, well covered in the walking books listed in *Contexts*.

There are a couple of noted climbing spots around the Pembrokeshire coast and in the Brecon Beacons, but the vast majority are in **Snowdonia**. A predominance of low-lying crags and its easy access make the area particularly popular, and on any sunny weekend you'll spot brightly coloured figures hanging off almost every cliff face. The principal areas to head for are the Llanberis Pass, the Ogwen Valley, the sea cliffs around South Stack near Holyhead, and the desperately difficult Pen Trwyn on the Great Orme at Llandudno. The best general guide for experienced climbers is *Rock Climbing in Snowdonia* by Paul Williams (Constable).

Beginners should contact *Plas-y-Brenin: The National Mountaineering Centre*, Capel Curig, LL24 0ET (☎06904/214), which runs residential courses and two-hour samplers, or the *British Mountaineering Council*, Crawford House Precinct Centre, Booth St East, Manchester M13 9RZ (☎061/273 5835).

CYCLING

Despite the recent boom in the sale of mountain bikes, **cyclists** are treated with notorious disrespect by many motorized road users and by the people who plan the country's traffic systems. There are few proper cycle routes in any of Wales' big towns, so if you're hell-bent on tackling the congestion, pollution and aggression of city traffic, get a **helmet** and a secure **lock** – cycle theft is an organized racket. Prospects are brighter in rural areas, where the backroads along river valleys or climbing mountain passes have a sufficient density of pubs and B&Bs to keep the days manageable. Steep gradients can be a problem but ascents are never long, with Wales' highest pass barely reaching 1500 feet. Your main problem is likely to be finding spare parts – for anything more complex than a tyre or inner tube, you'll need a specialist shop. The CTC (see below) lists places in their annual handbook.

Off-road cycling is becoming increasingly popular in the highland walking areas, but cyclists should remember to keep to rights of way designated on maps as bridleways, BOATs ("Byways Open To All Traffic") or RUPFs ("Roads Used As Public Footpaths"), and to pass walkers at considerate speed. Footpaths, unless otherwise marked, are for pedestrian use only. In deference to walkers, access to certain bridleways has been restricted, particularly around Snowdon: bikes are not allowed on the approaches to the summit between 10am and 5pm from June to September. With no book specifically geared to the off-roader in Wales, the best one to buy is the Britain-wide *Fifty Mountain Bike Rides* (Crowood) by Jeremy Evans, featuring ten 2–7hr rides in Wales, complete with sketch maps, riding conditions and details of pubs and cafés along the way.

Transporting your bike by **train** is a good way of getting to the interesting parts of Wales without a lot of stressful pedalling. At present, bikes are carried free on suburban trains outside the weekday rush hours of 7.30–9.30am and 3.30–6.30pm; on most other services, including *InterCity* trains, you need to pay £3 per journey. Book early, as many trains only have space for one bike. **Bike rental** is available at bike shops in most large towns and many resorts, but the specimens on offer are often pretty derelict – all right for a brief spin, but not for any serious touring. Expect to pay in the region of £8–10 per day, £40–60 per week.

Britain's biggest cycling organization is the **Cyclists' Touring Club** or CTC (Cottrell House, 69 Meadrow, Godalming, Surrey GU7 3HS; ☎0483/417217). Membership (£24 per year) entitles you to touring and technical advice, as well as insurance. Their free sheets for members cover 35 routes through Wales.

Those planning their own touring routes would do well to buy the OS 1:250,000 (4 miles to an inch) Wales and West Midlands maps. These are detailed enough to show relief and almost all tarmacked roads – and you won't find yourself cycling across a whole map in one day. The *Ordnance Survey*'s excellent series of regional *Cycle Tour* guides, though presently covering just England, is planned to extend to Welsh regions in the near future.

BEACHES

Wales is ringed by fine **beaches** and **bays**, many of the best of which are readily accessible by public transport – though of course this means they tend to get very busy in high summer. With most of the Welsh coast influenced by the currents of the North Atlantic Drift, water temperatures are higher than you might expect for this latitude, but only the hardy should consider swimming outside the warmer June–October period. For swimming and sunbathing, the best areas to head for are the Gower Peninsula, the Pembrokeshire Coast, the Llŷn and the southwest coast of Anglesey. Though it has more resorts that any other section of Wales' coastline, the north coast certainly hasn't got the most attractive beaches, nor is it a place to swim.

SURFING AND WINDSURFING

Wales' southwest-facing beaches offer the best conditions for either board or kayak **surfing**, with decent, but by no means Hawaiian-sized, waves at several key spots. In the south this means Rhossili, at the western tip of the Gower, and Whitesands Bay (Porth-mawr), near St David's. The surfing scene in north Wales centres on the long sweep of Porth Neigwl (Hell's Mouth), near Abersoch on the Llŷn, and Rhosneigr on Anglesey. As well as these major surf beaches, **windsurfers** tend to congregate at Barmouth, Borth, around the Pembrokeshire Coast and at The Mumbles. For more information, get hold of the **Welsh Surfing Federation**, 71 Fairway, Port Talbot, SA12 7HW (☎0639/886246).

KAYAKING AND RAFTING

Board riders constantly have to compete for waves with the surf ski riders and **kayakers** who

WALES' CLEAN BEACHES

With raw and partly treated effluent still being discharged off many Welsh beaches, it has to be said that they are not the cleanest in Europe. In an attempt to improve this situation, the Tidy Britain Group awards a blue flag to beaches that meet their criteria: water quality must be above EU standards and the beach must be free of litter, sewage and industrial waste. Below we list the beaches that have held a flag for the past two years, but bear in mind that a further requirement of easy access means that the idyllic cove you've just discovered, though not listed, may be perfectly acceptable. The following list runs clockwise around the coast from Cardiff.

Southerndown
Rest Bay, Porthcawl
Port Eynon
Cefn Sidan (Pembrey)
Amroth
Lydstep
Skrinkle
Manorbier
Tenby North
Tenby South
Barafundle
Broadhaven
West Angle Bay
Dale
Broadhaven (Haverfordwest)
Newgale
Caerfai, St David's
Whitesands, St David's
Abereiddy
Poppit
Mwnt
Tresaith
Penbryn
Cwmtydu
Llangrannog
Traethgwyn, Cei Newydd
Yr Harbwr, Cei Newydd
Cei Bach
Traeth y De, Aberaeron
Gilfach yr Halen
Traeth y Gogledd
Borth
Llandanwg
Morfa Dinlle
Rhosneigr
Trearddur Bay

frequent the same beaches. Paddlers, however, have the additional run of miles of superb coastline, particularly around Anglesey, the Llŷn and the Pembrokeshire coast. The northern coasts are amply detailed in Terry Storry's slightly dated *Snowdonia White Water Sea and Surf* (Cicerone), which also also contains maps and notes on Snowdonia's myriad short, steep bedrock rivers, many of which can only be paddled just after a deluge. The same author's more up-to-date *British White Water* (Constable) covers the hundred best rivers in Britain, including all those in his Snowdonia book, plus some in south Wales, though without river maps.

As equipment improves, paddlers have become more daring and Victorian tourist attractions such as Swallow and Conwy falls, both near Betws-y-Coed, are now fair game for a descent. Most of the kayaking is non-competitive but on summer weekends you might catch a slalom either on the River Dee at Llangollen or at the **National Whitewater Centre** on the River Tryweryn, near Bala, where you can also ride the rapids in rubber rafts.

Without your own kayak or canoe, it's still possible to get on the water with tour companies, who can be contacted through the **Welsh Canoeing Association**, Pen-y-Bont, Corwen, Clwyd LL21 0EL.

PONY TREKKING

Wales' scattered population and large tracts of open land make it ideal for **pony trekking**, now a major business with approaching a hundred approved riding centres and many smaller operations. Don't expect too much cantering over unfenced land: rides tend to be geared towards unhurried appreciation of the scenery from horseback and are often combined with accommodation on farms. Mid-Wales has the greatest concentration of stables but there are places all over the country, amply detailed in the brochures supplied by the *Pony Trekking & Riding Society of Wales*, Pengelli Fach, Pontsticill Vaynor, Merthyr Tydfil, CF48 2TU (☎0490/412786).

RUGBY

Few rugby fans, even Wales' biggest rivals, the English, would deny that the Welsh sides of the Seventies were some of the best ever seen.

Rugby is a passion with the Welsh – and their national game – but despite winning the 1994 **Five Nations Championship** – a tournament where Wales, England, Scotland, Ireland and France all play each other – Wales has seen some lean seasons of late.

In the Seventies, the scarlet jerseys of Wales struck fear into their opponents and won six out of the ten championships. Three of the championships were **Grand Slams**, where all four opponents were beaten individually. Players making them so formidable a side included fearless full-back J.P.R. Williams, the country's most capped player, elusive and magical outside-halves, Barry John and Phil Bennett, and the world's highest try-scoring scrum-half, Gareth Edwards.

But victories were harder to come by in the Eighties and by 1991, the national side reached its nadir with its highest-ever international loss of 63–6 at the hands of Australia. That year also saw Wales' highest point scorer, Paul Thorburn quit the international game disillusioned.

Wales' recovery to a dominant side in Rugby Union has been hampered by the loss of many players because of money. Rugby Union is strictly amateur with no players being paid, forcing a number to leave the game for professional Rugby League, which thrives in the north of England. Major losses include Jonathan Davies, Terry Holmes and, in 1994, centre Scott Gibbs.

However, many now feel a renaissance is at hand, helped along by a new spirit and the likes of Neil Jenkins – a kicker to rival Australia's Michael Lynagh at his peak.

International games are played at the impressive 58,000-capacity **Cardiff Arms Park** stadium, and as you'd expect getting tickets for the Five Nations Championship games is nigh on impossible. Most tickets are allocated months before a match, and touts will often be found selling tickets for hundreds of pounds outside the gates on the day. However, for other internationals and important games played at the Arms Park, tickets cost £22 for a seat in the stands or £7 to stand on the East Terrace.

Away from the international arena, a thriving rugby scene exists at club level, with some 178 clubs and 40,000 players taking to the field most Saturdays. It's often worth going to a match purely for the light-hearted crowd banter – if you can understand the accents.

The four top teams, which usually include a smattering of international players, are Neath, Swansea, Cardiff and Llanelli, with Pontypridd snapping at their heels. Check with individual clubs for fixtures and ticket prices, which start at well under £10.

The Rugby Union season runs from around September until soon after Easter.

FOOTBALL

Compared to rugby, football (soccer) is seen as a minority sport, but in actual fact there are just as many Welsh footballers who prefer not to pick up the ball and run with it. The three top sides in the country are Cardiff City, Swansea City and Wrexham, which all play in the English Football League Second Division (behind the Premier and First Divisions). The rest of the clubs play in the **Konica League of Wales**.

Spurred on by goal-mouth terriers such as Liverpool's Ian Rush and Manchester United's Mark Hughes, not to mention United's electrifying youngster Ryan Giggs, the national team came very close to being the only British side in the 1994 World Cup, only to be thwarted in the end by Romania.

LESBIAN AND GAY WALES

Following a high-profile campaign, Britain's age of consent for sexual relationships between men was lowered from 21 to 18 in February 1994. Although still not equal with the heterosexual and lesbian age of consent of 16, hopes are high that equality can be won in the coming few years. In a free vote in parliament (ie MPs could vote according to their conscience, not by party line), no Welsh Conservative MP (of which there are few anyway) voted for equality, and they were joined in opposition by seven Welsh Labour MPs, a disproportionately high number in the parliamentary Labour party. Plaid Cymru and Liberal Democrat MPs voted wholeheartedly for equality.

With such a rural culture, especially when compared to England, it's perhaps not surprising that Wales is less used to the lesbian and gay lifestyle than its more cosmopolitan neighbour. Although Plaid Cymru itself has always vehemently supported lesbian and gay rights, there still exists a hard strain of nationalist who believes that gay emancipation is somehow incompatible with true Welsh patriotism. At the 1993 National Eisteddfod in Llanelwedd, Powys, the stall of the national Welsh-speaking lesbian and gay organization, *Cylch*, was trashed one night – an action that was widely and wholeheartedly condemned.

The Welsh scene is muted, to say the least. The main centres of population – Cardiff, Newport and Swansea – have a number of pubs and clubs, with Cardiff especially seeing quite an increase in venues over the past couple of years; details are given in the text. Out of the southern cities, however, gay life becomes distinctly discreet, although university towns such as Lampeter, Aberystwyth and Bangor manage support groups and the odd weekly night in local bars. Cardiff's lesbian and gay **switchboard**, run by Friend, operates five evenings a week (see Cardiff listings) and is the most up-to-date source of information on places, events, accommodation and contacts throughout Wales. Alternatively, there are some informal but well-established networks, especially amongst the sometimes reclusive alternative lifestylers found in mid and west Wales. **Border Women** (who should surely have called themselves Offa's Dykes) is a well-organized network for mid-Wales, with house meetings and monthly discos. They can be contacted via PO Box 4, Builth Wells, Powys LD2 3ZZ. **Cylch** organize a variety of events – contact them at Bwlch Swyddfa Bost 23, Aberystwyth, Dyfed SY23. The UK-wide monthly *Gay Times* (£2) has thorough listings and contact information, together with the best directory of the half-dozen or so gay hotels throughout Wales.

DISABLED TRAVELLERS

Britain has numerous specialist **tour operators** catering for physically disabled travellers, and the number of non-specialist operators who welcome clients with disabilities is increasing. For more information on operators and facilities for the disabled traveller, get in touch with the **Royal Association for Disability and Rehabilitation** (RADAR), 25 Mortimer St, London W1N 8AB (☎071/637 5400); **Mobility International**, 228 Borough High St, London SE1 1JX (☎071/403 5688) and PO Box 3551, Eugene, OR 97403 (☎503/343-1284); and the **Holiday Care Service**, 2 Old Bank Chambers, Station Rd, Horley, Surrey GU9 8RW (☎0293/774535), who also run a "Holiday Helpers" service.

Should you go it alone, you'll find that Welsh attitudes towards travellers with disabilities are often begrudging and guilt-ridden; the country is years behind the advances towards independence made in North America and Australia. Access to theatres, cinemas and other public places has improved recently, but **public transport** companies rarely make any effort to help disabled people. Some British Rail *InterCity* services now accommodate wheelchair users in comfort but many stations are inaccessible and increasing numbers are unstaffed. Wheelchair users and blind or partly sighted people are automatically given 30–50 percent reductions on train fares, and people with other disabilities are eligible for the **Disabled Persons Railcard** (£14 per year), which gives a third off most tickets. There are no bus discounts for the disabled, while of the major **car rental** firms only *Hertz* offer models with hand controls at the same rate as conventional vehicles, and even these are in the more expensive categories. With **accommodation** it's much the same story: modified suites are available at the odd B&B, but mostly only at higher-priced establichments.

The most helpful **publication** is probably the *Accessible Wales* booklet (£2) published by the *Wales Council for the Disabled*, Llys Ifor, Crescent Rd, Caerphilly, Mid-Glamorgan, CF8 1XL (☎0222/887325). Packed with information covering everything from transport and restaurants to beach access and wheelchair repair, it also grades all accommodation according to accessibility. Other useful publications include the *Access* series by the *Pauline Hephaistos Survey Projects*, and RADAR's annually updated *Holidays in the British Isles – A Guide For Disabled People*. And look out for *The World Wheelchair Traveller* by Susan Abbott and Mary Ann Tyrrell (AA Publications), which includes basic hints and advice, and *Nothing Ventured: Disabled People Travel the World* by Alison Walsh (Rough Guides), which gives practical advice alongside inspiring accounts of disabled travel worldwide.

DIRECTORY

Drugs Likely-looking visitors coming to England from Holland or Spain can expect scrutiny from customs officers on the lookout for hashish (marijuana resin). Being caught in possession of a small amount of hashish or grass will lead to a fine, but possession of larger quantities or of "harder" narcotics could lead to imprisonment or deportation.

Electricity In Britain the current is 240V AC. North American applicances will need a transformer and adaptor; Australasian appliances will only need an adaptor.

Laundry Coin-operated laundries (launderettes) are to be found in Welsh towns of any size and are open about twelve hours a day from Monday to Friday, with shorter hours at weekends. A wash followed by a spin or tumble dry costs about £2, with "service washes" (your laundry done for you in a few hours) about £1 more.

Smoking The last decade has seen a dramatic change in attitudes towards smoking and a significant reduction in the consumption of cigarettes. Smoking is now outlawed on public transport and in just about all public buildings, and many restaurants and hotels have become non-smoking establishments. Smokers are advised, when booking a table or a room, to check that their vice is tolerated there.

Time Greenwich Mean Time (GMT) is in force from late October to late March, when the clocks go forward an hour for British Summer Time (BST). GMT is five hours ahead of the US Eastern Standard Time and ten hours behind Australian Eastern Standard Time.

Tipping and service charges In restaurants a service charge is usually included in the bill; if it isn't, leave a tip of 10–15 percent unless the service is unforgivably bad. Some restaurants are in the habit of leaving the total box blank on credit-card counterfoils, to encourage customers to add another few percent on top of the service charge – if you're paying by credit card, check that the total box is filled in before you sign. Taxi drivers expect a tip in the region of 10 percent. You do not tip bar staff – if you want to show your appreciation, offer to buy them a drink.

Toilets Public toilets are found at many train and bus stations and are signposted on town high streets. In urban locations a fee of 10p or 20p is usually charged.

Videos Visitors from North America planning to use their video cameras in Britain should note that Betamax cassettes are less easy to obtain in England, and VHS is the most common format.

PART TWO

THE GUIDE

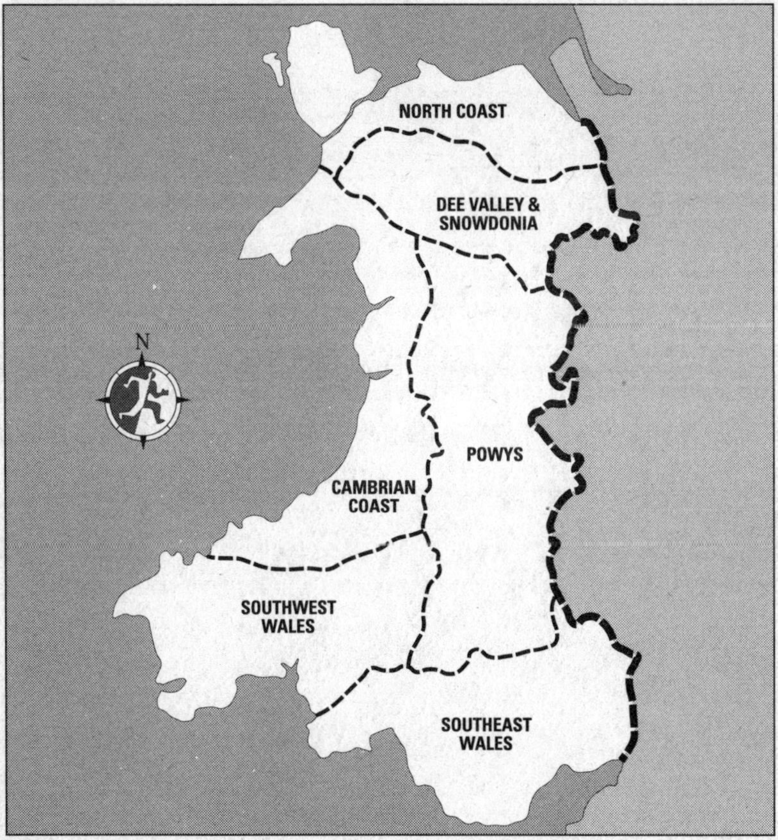

CHAPTER ONE

SOUTHEAST WALES

Home to almost 1.8 million people, 60 percent of the country's population, the southeastern corner of Wales, the counties of Gwent and Glamorgan, is also one of Britain's most industrialized regions. Both population and industry here are most heavily concentrated in the sea ports and former coal mining valleys where rivers slice through mountainous terrain.

Gwent – formerly Monmouthshire – is the easternmost county in Wales, starting at the English border in a beguilingly rural way, the **River Wye** criss-crossing between the two countries from its mouth at the fortress town of **Chepstow**; here, you'll find one of the most impressive castles in a land where few towns are without one. In the Wye's beautiful valley lie the spectacularly placed ruins of **Tintern Abbey**, downstream of the old county town of **Monmouth**. To the north, the foothills of the Black Mountains rise up out of the fertile river plains, making market towns such as **Abergavenny**, and the quieter valleys to its north, popular walking and outdoor pursuits centres.

Gwent becomes increasingly industrialized as you travel west, with the rural River Usk meandering through the middle of the county and spilling out into the Bristol Channel at **Newport**, Wales' third-largest conurbation. Although it is hardly likely to feature on a swift tour of Wales, the town has an excellent museum and the remains of an extensive Roman settlement at **Caerleon**, a northern suburb of the town.

Western Gwent and northern Glamorgan constitute the world-famous **valleys**, once the coal- and iron-rich powerhouse of the nation. This is the Wales of popular imagination: hemmed-in valley floors packed with lines of blank, grey houses, with doors and sills painted in contrasting gaudy brightness, slanted almost impossibly towards the pithead. Although nearly all of the mines have since closed, the area is still one of tight-knit towns, with a rich working-class heritage that displays itself in some excellent museums and colliery tours, such as the **Big Pit** at Blaenafon and the **Rhondda Heritage Park** in Trehafod. The valleys follow rivers coursing down towards the coast, where great ports stood to ship their products all over the world. The greatest of them all was **Cardiff**, long past its heyday as the world's busiest coal port, but bouncing back in its comparatively new status as Wales' upbeat capital. Excellent museums, a massive castle, exciting rejuvenation projects around the stolid Victorian docks and Wales' best cultural pursuits make the city an essential stop. In marked contrast to both the city and the valleys, lying to the immediate west is the lush, conservative **Vale of Glamorgan**, a world away from the industrial hangover of the valleys; stoic little market towns and chirpy seaside resorts – most notably **Barry** and **Porthcawl** – dot the area.

The west of Glamorgan is dominated by Wales' second city, **Swansea**, rougher, tougher and less anglicized than the capital. Like Cardiff, Swansea grew principally on the strength of its docks, and sits on an impressive arc of coast that

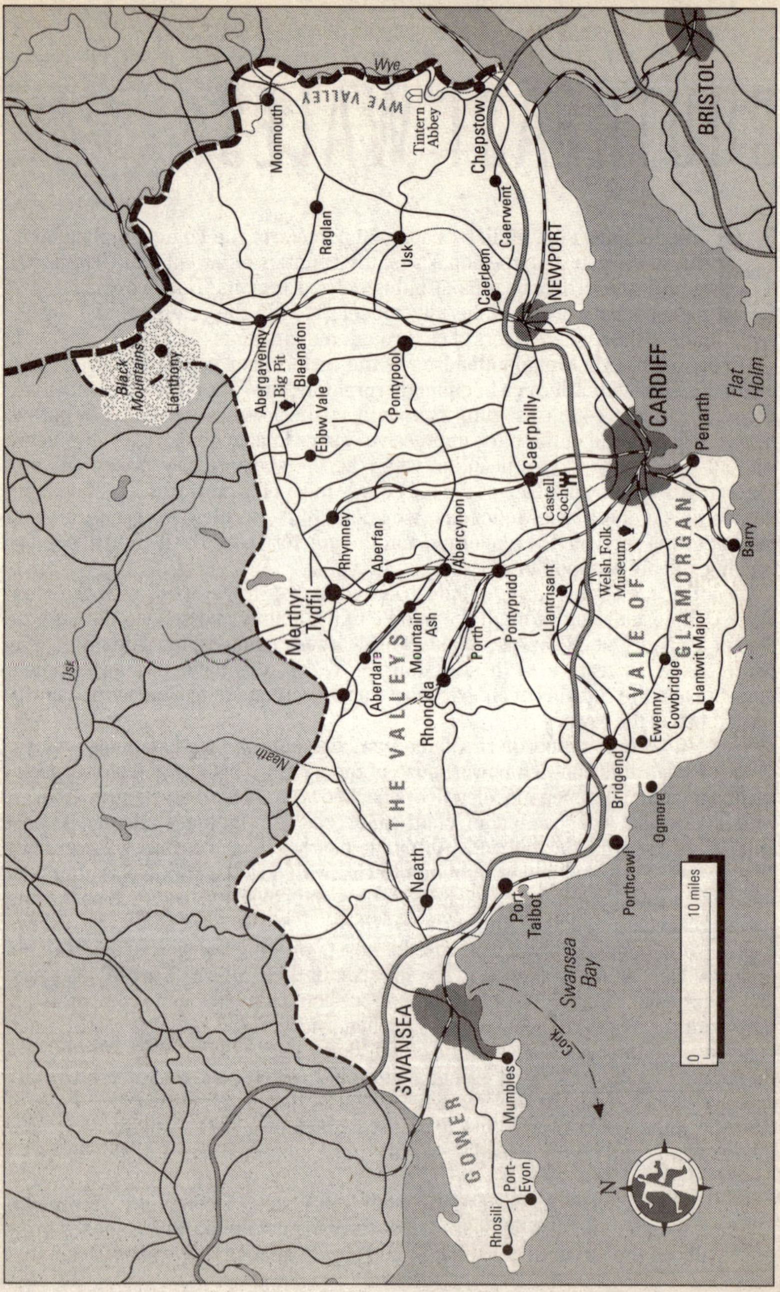
Wye
WYE VALLEY
Monmouth
Tintern Abbey
Chepstow
Raglan
Caerwent
Usk
Caerleon
NEWPORT
BRISTOL
Abergavenny
Black Mountains
Llanthony
Big Pit
Blaenafon
Pontypool
Ebbw Vale
Caerphilly
CARDIFF
Flat Holm
Penarth
Castell Coch
Rhymney
Aberfan
Abercynon
Merthyr Tydfil
Mountain Ash
Pontypridd
Llantrisant
Welsh Folk Museum
Barry
VALE OF GLAMORGAN
Aberdare
Porth
Rhondda
Cowbridge
Llantwit Major
Ewenny
Usk
Neath
THE VALLEYS
Bridgend
Ogmore
Porthcawl
Neath
Port Talbot
10 miles
0
Swansea Bay
Cork
SWANSEA
Mumbles
GOWER
Port-Eynon
Rhosili
N

ACCOMMODATION PRICE CODES

Throughout this guide, hotel and B&B accommodation is priced on a scale of ① to ⑨. Category ① only applies to youth hostels; for the rest, the number indicates the **lowest price** you could expect to pay per night for a **double room in high season**. The prices indicated by the codes are as follows:

① under £20/$32	④ £40–50/$64–80	⑦ £70–80/$112–128
② £20–30/$32–48	⑤ £50–60/$80–96	⑧ £80–100/$128–160
③ £30–40/$48–64	⑥ £60–70/$96–112	⑨ over £100/$160

shelves round from the belching steel works of **Port Talbot** in the east to **Mumbles** and **Oystermouth**, holiday towns of amusement arcades, copious pubs and chip shops, on the jaw of the delightful **Gower Peninsula** in the west. The Gower – one of the country's favourite playgrounds – juts out into the sea, a mini-Wales of grand beaches, rocky headlands, bracken heaths and ruined castles.

Getting around

Southeast Wales is by far the easiest part of the country to travel around. Swift new dual carriageways connect with the M4, bringing all corners of the region into close proximity. Public transport is similarly thorough: this is the only part of Wales with a half-decent train service, and most suburban and rural services interconnect with Cardiff, Newport and Swansea, as well as further afield to Gloucester and the Midlands; Monmouth was long ago cut off from the train network, although it is easily reached by car and bus. Bus services fill in virtually all of the gaps.

The Wye valley

Perhaps the most anglicized corner of Wales, the **Wye Valley** – along with the rest of Gwent – was only finally recognized as part of Wales in the local government reorganization of 1974, before which the county was officially included as part of neither England nor Wales, so that maps were frequently headlined "Wales and Monmouthshire". Most of the rest of Gwent is firmly and redoubtably Welsh, but the woodlands and hills by the meandering River Wye share more similarities with the landscape over the border. The two main towns – Chepstow at the Wye's mouth and Monmouth, sixteen miles upstream – are decidedly English in flavour: **Chepstow**, with its massive castle radiating an awesome strength, high above the muddy flats and waters of the river estuary; and **Monmouth**, the spruce, old-fashioned town with something of the air of an important seat of authority.

Six miles north of Chepstow lie the inspirational ruins of the Cistercian **Tintern Abbey**, worth catching first thing in the morning or into the evening when the crowds of coach-trippers have evaporated. Surrounding the abbey are some beautiful walks through bluebell woods and old oak forests on a spit of land sandwiched by the riverbend, rising high above the ruins. Running parallel to the river, albeit on the English side of the border, the southern segments of the **Offa's Dyke** earthworks are closely followed by a long distance footpath.

Chepstow

Of all the places that call themselves "the gateway to Wales", the old border town of **CHEPSTOW** (Cas-Gwent) has probably the greatest claim, being the first town on the main road into Wales on the immediate Welsh side of the border.

Situated on the western bank of the River Wye, just over a mile from where its tidal waters flow out into the muddy Severn estuary, Chepstow is a sturdy place with little of the immediate charm or quirkiness of many other Welsh market towns. This is partly due to the scale of soulless modern developments in the town centre that have combined to overwhelm the remaining buildings in streets still laid out in an identifiably medieval pattern.

The Town

Chepstow's position as a former port is evident in the thirteenth-century **Port Wall**, encasing the castle precincts and the town centre in their loop of the river. The fifteenth-century **West Gate** bisects the **High Street**, a handsome street sided by Georgian and Victorian buildings, and sloping down from the gate towards the river. Here, an elegant five-arch cast-iron bridge, built in 1816, is still in use for cross-border traffic into England today. To the southeast, a walk along the Wye leads past the **Willow Tea Room**, with its plaque commemorating the quay as the site from which the three leaders of Newport's Chartist March of 1839 were despatched to Van Diemen's Land (Tasmania). Opposite, a Union Jack flag has been provocatively painted on the English side of the river cliffs.

Bridge Street leads from the old bridge up towards the main entrance of the castle, opposite which is a crimson-painted Georgian town house containing the **Chepstow Museum** (March–Oct Mon–Sat 11am–1pm & 2–5pm, Sun 2–5pm; 70p). The displays concern themselves with local life, with nostalgic photographs and paintings of the trades supported in the past by the River Wye, and records of Chepstow's brief life in the early part of this century as a shipbuilding centre.

The main entrance to **Chepstow Castle** (April–Oct daily 9.30am–6.30pm; Nov–March Mon–Sat 9.30am–4pm, Sun 2–4pm; CADW; £2.90) is from the Bridge Street car park, but it's a good idea to get an idea of the sheer scale of the site first by taking the signposted Wye Valley Walk from Welsh Street, heading north out of the town centre to take in good views up to the battlements.

As a strategic siting, the castle can scarcely be bettered. Built tight into a loop of the River Wye, it guards one of the most important routes into Wales. Chepstow was the first stone castle to be built in Britain, with its first Norman incarnation, the Great Tower keep, rising in 1067, only one year after William the Conqueror's victory at Hastings. William had realized the importance of subduing the restless Welsh, creating borderland Marcher Lordships and encouraging the title holders to expand into Welsh territory: a succession of Chepstow's lords attempted this, necessitating renewed and increasingly powerful fortification of their castles over the ensuing two hundred years. Ownership of both title and castle passed to the earls of Norfolk and then Pembroke, who retain the fortress to this day.

The walled castle is comprised of three separate enclosures, the Lower Ward being the largest and dating mainly from the thirteenth century. Here, you'll find the **Great Hall**, the home of a wide-ranging exhibition on the history of the castle, incorporating genuine and replica armour from various stages of the castle's past, with particular emphasis on the English Civil War years, when Royalist Chepstow was twice beseiged.

Twelfth-century defences separate the Lower Ward from the Middle Ward, which is dominated by the still imposing ruins of the **Great Tower**, whose lower floors include the original Norman keep. Beyond the Great Tower is the far narrower Upper Ward which leads up to the Barbican **watch tower**, from which there are some superlative and vertiginous views looking back over the castle and down the cliff to the mudflats of the river estuary.

Practicalities

Chepstow's **train station** is five minutes' walk to the south of the High Street. Buses depart from the small **bus station** at the back of the shops on the other side of the Town (West) Gate from the High Street. *Red and White* buses leave every couple of hours for Tintern and Monmouth. The **tourist office** is located in the castle car park, off Bridge Street (Easter–Oct daily 10am–6pm; ☎0291/623772). Chepstow is well suited as a base to explore the valley by bike: **rental** is available at *Rough Riders*, 9 St Mary's St (Tues–Sat 10am–5pm; ☎0291/627056).

The town's youth hostel is now closed, although cheap B&B **accommodation** can be found along Welsh Street, north from the Town Gate, at the *Coach and Horses* pub (☎0291/622626; ③). Off Welsh Street is *Mrs Langdale's*, 71 St Kingsmark Ave (☎0291/625569; ③), and *Mrs Batchelor's*, 7 Lancaster Way (☎0291/626344; ③). A mile east of town, over the Wye in Sedbury Lane, is a wonderful and friendly B&B in an old converted jail house at *Upper Sedbury House* (☎0291/627173; ③). Pricier accommodation in town comes in the shape of stately *George Hotel* in Moor St, next to the West Gate (☎0291/625363; ④), and the small, creaky *First Hurdle Hotel*, 9 Upper Church St (☎0291/622189; ④).

The town is blessed with some good **pubs**. The riverside *Boat Inn*, along the quay walk from the old bridge, is small and enormously friendly; at the other side of the town centre, the cosy *Coach and Horses*, up near the Town Gate on Welsh Street, has a regular diet of evening live folk and rock, and real ale. In the High Street, the grimy but friendly *White Lion* boasts a bowling alley, and at the bottom of the cobbled Hawker Hill Street, leading down from the High Street, is the cheery *Five Alls*. Of these pubs, the *Coach and Horses* is the best for **food**, or try the very reasonable bar snacks in the plush *Beaufort Hotel* at the bottom of the High Street (noon–2.15pm & 6.45–8.45pm). For a more extensive meal, moderately priced *Leadon's Brasserie* is an informal underground bistro at the top of Hawker Hill Street, serving French and Italian food (☎0291/627402).

Tintern Abbey

Six miles north of Chepstow alongside some of the River Wye's most spectacular stretches, **Tintern Abbey** (April–Oct daily 9.30am–6.30pm; Nov–March Mon–Sat 9.30am–4pm, Sun 2–4pm; CADW; £2) has inspired writers and painters for over two hundred years, ever since the Reverend William Gilpin published a book in 1782 extolling the picturesque qualities of the abbey and its valley. On a quiet day, the sight of the the soft, roofless ruins beginning to fill the field of vision as you get nearer is hugely uplifting; the "tall rock/The mountain, and the deep and gloomy wood" written about by Wordsworth are still evident today. Such is the place's enormous popularity, however, that in the middle of a summer's day, the magic of the abbey can all but evaporate: it is better to go out of season or at the beginning or end of the day when the hordes of people have thinned out.

The abbey lasted as a monastic settlement from its foundation by the Cistercian order in 1131 to its dissolution in 1536, and the original order of monks was brought wholesale from Normandy, establishing themselves as major local landholders and agriculturalists. This increased the power and wealth of the abbey, attracting more monks and necessitating a massive rebuilding and expansion plan in the fourteenth century, when Tintern was at its mightiest. Most of the remaining buildings date from this time, after which the influence of the abbey and its order began to wane. Upon dissolution, many of the buildings were plundered and stripped, leaving the abbey to crumble gradually into advanced decay. Its survival is largely thanks to its remoteness, as there were no nearby villages ready to use the abbey stone for rebuilding. Travellers, searching for the picturesque rather than any religious experience, were attracted to the romantically placed, ivy-clad ruins from the eighteenth century onwards, and a trip to Tintern was essential for the Romantics – Wordsworth and Turner amongst them.

The centrepiece of the complex was the magnificent Gothic **church**, built at the turn of the fourteenth century to encase its more modest predecessor. The bulk of the building remains, with the remarkable tracery in the west window and intricate stonework of the capitals and columns firmly intact; amazingly, these details withstood plundering raiders over four hundred years, as well as the elements. Behind the great east window lie the sharply rising slopes of the wooded valley, forming a perfect backdrop.

Around the church are the less substantial ruins of the **monks' domestic quarters**, mostly reduced to one-storey rubble. Rooms are easily distinguishable, however, including an intact serving hatch in the kitchen and the square of the monks' **cloister**. The course of the abbey's waste disposal system can be seen in the **Great Drain**, an irregular channel that links kitchens, toilets and the Infirmary with the nearby Wye. The **Novices' Hall** lies handily close to the Warming House, which together with the kitchen and Infirmary, would have been the only heated parts of the abbey, suggesting that novices might have gained a falsely favourable impression of monastic life before taking their final vows. In the dining hall, you can still see the **pulpit door** that would once have led to the wall-mounted pulpit, from which a monk would read the scriptures throughout each meal.

The best way to appreciate the scale and splendour of the abbey ruins is by taking a walk on the opposite bank of the Wye. Just upstream from the abbey, a bridge crosses the river, from where a path climbs a wooded hillside. Views along the way and from the top are magnificent, framing the gaunt shell of the abbey in its sylvan setting.

Practicalities

The tiny village of **TINTERN** (Tyndyrn) is now cluttered up with tea shops and overpriced hotels, strung along the main road around the loop of the river for half a mile. The principal visitor complex is located another few hundred yards towards Monmouth at the **Old Station**. Amongst the amenities there are an interesting exhibition about the old Wye valley railway and a good selection of leaflets on local walks, including sections of the Offa's Dyke path and cliff rambles above the meandering river. B&B **accommodation** is available locally at the excellent *Wye Barn* on The Quay (☎0291/689456; ③), or slap opposite the abbey, in the sumptuous *Beaufort Hotel* (☎0291/689777; ⑥).

Monmouth

Enclosed on three sides by the rivers Wye and Monnow, **MONMOUTH** (Trefynwy) retains some of its quiet charm as an important border post and the old county town. Now bypassed by the A40 dual carriageway which shoots along the banks of the Wye, Monmouth has few reminders of the twentieth century.

The centre of the town is **Agincourt Square**, a large and handsome open space at the top of the wide, shop-lined Monnow Street, gently descending to the thirteenth-century bridge over the River Monnow. The cobbled square is dominated by old coaching inns either side of the arched Georgian **Shire Hall**, embedded in which is an eighteenth-century statue of the Monmouth-born King Henry V, victor at the 1415 Battle of Agincourt, which brought Normandy, and soon afterwards France, under the rule of the English crown. In front of the Shire Hall is the pompous statue of another local, the Honourable Charles Stewart Rolls, the first man, in 1910, to pilot a double-flight over the English Channel, and also the co-founder of the mighty Rolls-Royce empire.

Almost opposite Shire Hall is **Castle Hill**, which you can walk up to glimpse some of the ruins of the **castle**, founded in 1068, rebuilt in stone in the twelfth century and almost annihilated in the Civil War. The only notable part of the castle still to be seen is the Great Tower, in which Henry V was probably born in 1387. Next to the castle, the gracious seventeenth-century **Great Castle House**, built out of the castle bricks, now serves as the headquarters of the Royal Monmouthshire regiment, but the building is out of bounds to civilians.

Priory Street leads north from Agincourt Square to the town's **museum** (Mon–Sat 10am–1pm & 2–5pm, Sun 2–5pm; 70p), located in the market hall complex. The most comprehensive exhibit is their **Nelson Collection**, which attempts to portray the life of one of the most successful sea-going Britons through use of the Admiral's personal artefacts, such as medals, china, his sword and intimate letters, together with pictures, prints and naval equipment of the day. Charles Rolls' mother, Lady Llangattock, was an ardent admirer of Nelson and a voracious collector of any memorabilia connected with him, and it is her collection now on display in the museum.

At the very bottom of Monnow Street, a couple of hundred yards from Agincourt Square, the road narrows to squeeze into the confines of the seven-hundred-year-old **Monnow bridge**, crowned with its hulking stone gate of 1262, that served both as a means of defence for the town and a toll collection point.

Practicalities

Buses operate from the **bus station** behind *Kwik Save* at the bottom of Monnow Street, and the **tourist office** is in the Shire Hall, Agincourt Square (Easter–Oct daily 9.30am–5.30pm; ☎0600/713899). You'll find **accommodation** at the intimate and cheerful *Riverside Hotel* on Cinderhill Street, over the Monnow bridge (☎0600/715577; ⑤), or in B&Bs at *Red Lion House*, 16 Draybridge St (☎0600/713633; ③), and the welcoming *Old Gaol* on Hereford Rd (☎0600/712463; ③). The **youth hostel** is located right in the heart of town in Priory Street school (March–Oct; ☎0600/715116; ①), a converted fifteenth-century priory that was in use as a school for two hundred years until 1970. Two miles south in the village of Mitchel Troy is the excellent *Church Farm* B&B (☎0600/712176; ③). The nearest **campsite** is the *Glen Trothy Park* (☎0600/712295) at Mitchel Troy.

The main Monnow Street contains a handful of fast-food eateries; more substantial and very tasty but slightly pricy lunchtime and evening **food** is available at the *Punch House* in Agincourt Square; cheaper lunches can be had at the *Green Dragon* in St Thomas Square, down by the Monnow Bridge. Monmouth is home to a staggering number of **pubs**: worth trying are *The Bull* in Agincourt Square, the young and lively *Nag's Head*, at the bottom of Whitecross Street in St James' Square, and the *Robin Hood*, at the bottom of Monnow Street near the bridge, where Shakespeare is said to have drunk.

If transport is no problem, a superb pub lies three miles south of Monmouth off the A466 in the Wye valley: *The Boat*, in the hamlet of Redbrook, must be reached by stumbling over the River Wye and the English border, courtesy of a dizzying footbridge stapled to the side of the disused rail bridge. The bizarre journey is worth it, for the pub is home to some amazing characters, liable to strike up a live jazz or folk session at the drop of a woolly hat.

Mid-Gwent

The confrontational past of the middle tranche of Gwent, long-disputed border country, can be gleaned from the castles that dot the landscape with dependable regularity. This section of the county is noticeably more "Welsh" than the border country of the Wye valley. Stretching up from the wide-skied marshland that falls gently into the Severn estuary, the land reaches the flat, ugly settlement of **Caldicot**, only notable for its over-restored castle. The A48 runs from the border into south Wales, connecting **Caerwent**, a near-deserted village that was once a great Roman town, and **Penhow**, crowned by a homely fortified manor that guarded the quiet valley.

To the north is an undulating land of forests and tiny villages, criss-crossed by winding lanes that offer unexpectedly delightful views around each corner. The contours shelve down in the west to the valley of the **River Usk**, the former border of Wales as decreed in the sixteenth century by Henry VIII. Today, the A449 road roars through the valley, bypassing lanes, villages and the peaceful small town of **Usk**, home of the excellent Gwent Rural Life Museum.

Caldicot

Sandwiched between the main motorway and rail links between south Wales and London, **CALDICOT** is a sprawling, overgrown village of modern housing and little interest. The only possible exception is the heavily restored **castle** (March–Oct Mon–Fri 10.30am–1pm & 2–5pm, Sat 10.30am–1pm & 1.30–5pm, Sun 1.30–5pm; £1), on the eastern side of the village. Built in the twelfth century as one of the Norman Marcher castles, constructed to keep a wary eye on the Welsh, the buildings crumbled in the years leading up to the 1800s, before being rebuilt by a wealthy Victorian barrister, Joseph Cobb. The only original parts are a large fourteenth-century round tower and elaborate gatehouse, situated either side of a grassy courtyard, whose centrepiece is one of Nelson's battle cannon from his *Foudroyant* flagship. The castle buildings contain exhibitions of local history, together with an impressive furniture collection from the seventeenth to the nineteenth centuries. Rather pricy medieval banquets (☎0291/421425) take place throughout the summer. Caldicot is the first sight of Wales that train travellers using the main line from London have. As can be seen by the extensive building work on the edge of the town, it will, by 1996, also be the first sight for those using the second Severn road crossing, currently under construction to ease pressure on the M4 Severn Bridge.

Caerwent

Two miles northwest of Caldicot lies the apparently unremarkable village of **CAERWENT**, from which the county of Gwent takes its name. Almost two thousand years ago, the village was known by the Romans as *Venta Silurum*, the "market town of the Silures", a local tribe forcibly relocated here from a nearby hillfort by the conquering Romans in around 75 AD, after 25 years of battle between them.

Venta Silurum is an unusual Roman remain, for this was a domestic market town, not, as was far more common, a military base. The most complete remnant of the Roman town is the crumbling **walls** which form a large rectangle around the modern village. Access is easiest from the steps next to the *Coach and Horses* inn, leading you up onto stone ramparts that still command melancholic views around the quiet valley. The South Wall is the most complete, still maintaining its fourth-century bastions, and it continues around to the old West Gate. Half way along, a lane cuts up towards the rather ugly tower of the village **church**, in whose porch are maps and diagrams explaining the site of the village, as well as examples of artefacts that have been dug up. Here, you can also see two inscribed stones, one a dedication from the Siluri tribe to their Roman overlord, Paulinus, and another, dedicated to Ocelus Mars, demonstrating the odd merging of Roman and Celtic gods for worship. Opposite the church, on the village's main street, the remains of a Roman temple are currently being excavated. Nowadays, Caerwent sits on top of an altogether more contemporary military occupation, as the home of Europe's largest American rocket base at the neighbouring RAF station.

Penhow

There's another castle three miles west of Caerwent in the hamlet of **PENHOW**, whose neat church sits next to a fortified moated manor house on top of a grassy hillock. The manor house is known as **Penhow Castle** (Easter–Sept Wed–Sun 10am–5.15pm; Oct–Easter Wed 10am–5.15pm; £2.95), and its buildings are an accumulation of styles from the twelfth to the fourteenth centuries. The house is privately owned and claims to be the oldest lived-in castle in Wales, and you can tour it with a headset commentary. It was originally built for the St Maur family, a name later corrupted to Seymour. The oldest section is the impressive, thick-set Norman keep, the family's private apartments from 1129, now filled with period trimmings such as rush lights and sporting clubs to give a credibly authentic feel. The tour continues through a tiny, narrow defile into the fifteenth-century Great Hall, complete with a minstrel gallery decorated with the Seymour family wings. Steps lead up to the Seymour bedchamber, with one step deliberately built an inch higher than the others, a common ploy in medieval days to trip up intruders. The tour concludes chronologically, passing through some of the Regency-style lodging rooms and finally through into a cluttered Victorian kitchen and child's nursery.

Usk

Bypassed by the main A449 is the orderly little town of **USK** (Brynbuga), astride the river of the same name. Pastel-painted houses, shops and some great pubs and restaurants line narrow Bridge Street, which leads up from the river and crosses towards the castle, looming up on a hilltop to the left. Opposite the ivy-clad ruins is the hub of the town, **Twyn Square**, where the buses stop amongst the copious amounts of garish flower boxes that surround the twee restored clock tower. At the top of the square is a thirteenth-century **gatehouse**, once part of a Benedictine nunnery, and now guarding the passage to the impressive twelfth- and thirteenth-century church. There are surviving features from its days as a nunnery in the 1200s, including the nave and the slightly later tower.

Forking to the right off Bridge Street near the river is New Market Street, which runs past the **Gwent Rural Life Museum** (April–Oct Mon–Fri 10am–5pm, Sat & Sun 2–5pm; £2), housed in a converted eighteenth-century malt barn and specializing in the period from the early 1800s up until the end of World War II. Recreated old farmhouse interiors illustrate life in a rural Welsh county, and include examples of the exquisite local japanning trade (a means of ornamental decoration, using a glossy black lacquer), specimens of the back-breaking machinery used by bygone farm labourers, and themed groups of implements (eg dairy, wheelwrighting, woodland crafts, saddling, cobbling and smocking).

Practicalities

Usk is a quietly enjoyable place to **stay**, with good pubs for evening entertainment. For central **accommodation**, try the upmarket *Nag's Head* in Twyn Square (☎0291/672820; ④), the lively and friendly *Inn Between*, 53 Bridge St (☎0291/672838; ③), or the smart, spacious *King's Head* on Old Market St (☎0291/672963; ③). Cheapest accommodation is the hostel-style *Usk Centre of Agriculture* (☎0291/672311, ext 25; ①), a mile from town on the Pontypool Road. There are **campsites** at *Cwm Farm*, at Bettws Newydd (☎0873/840263), four miles north, and nearer Usk, two miles southeast at the *Grass Ski Centre* in Llanllowell (☎0291/672652).

Most of the town pubs serve **food** – the best being the *Royal Hotel* up by the Italianate Town Hall on New Market Street. Otherwise, Bridge Street is lined with small cafés, delicatessens and the excellent, moderately priced Italian bistro *Caro Vino* at no. 7 (☎0291/672459; closed Sun), and the reasonable *Bush House* at no. 15 (☎0291/672929), serving French, Mediterranean and Welsh dishes, with an extensive choice for vegetarians. For down-to-earth **drinking**, try the *Inn Between*, or the genial *White Hart*, on the corner of Bridge and Maryport streets.

Raglan

Numerous buses leave Usk every day for **RAGLAN** (Rhaglan), seven miles to the north. An unassuming village wallowing in the folds of the hills, Raglan is worth visiting for its glorious **castle** (April–Oct daily 9am–6.30pm; Nov–March Mon–Sat 9.30am–4pm, Sun 2–4pm; CADW; £1.80), whose fussy, and comparatively intact, style make it stand out from so many other crumbling Welsh fortresses. The last medieval fortification built in Britain, Raglan was begun on the site of a Norman motte in 1435 by Sir William ap Thomas, whose design combines practical strength with ostentatious style. Various descendants added to the castle after his father's death, and building carried on into the late sixteenth century.

The **gatehouse** is still used as the main entrance, and houses the best examples of the castle's showy decoration in its heraldic shields, intricate stonework edging and gargoyles. Inside, stonemasons' marks, used to identify how much work each man had done, can be seen on the walls. Ap Thomas' grandson, William Herbert II, was responsible in the mid-fifteenth century for the two inner courts, built around his grandfather's original gatehouse, hall and keep. The first court is the cobbled **Pitched Stone Court**, designed to house the functional rooms like the kitchen (with two vast double-flued chimneys) and the servants' quarters. To the left is **Fountain Court**, a well-proportioned grassy space surrounded by opulent residences that included grand apartments and state rooms. Separating the two are the original 1435 **Hall**, the **Buttery**, the remains of the **chapel** and the dank, cold **cellars** below.

Off Fountain Court, through the South Gate, is the pristine **bowling green**, standing on twelve-foot-high walls above the Moat Walk, and reached by a flight of stone steps from the green. The moated yellow ashlar **Great Tower**, off Fountain Court, demonstrates continental influences in its construction, and gives it a surprisingly contemporary appearance. Two sides of the hexagonal tower were blown up by Cromwell's sidekick Fairfax after an eleven-week onslaught against the Royalist castle in 1646. The tower can still be climbed, however, right to its peak, giving phenomenal views over the green water of the moat, the intricate masonic detail of the castle and the smooth hills beyond.

Abergavenny and North Gwent

Of all the towns in Gwent, **Abergavenny** is the best base for a holiday. As well as a fine range of places to eat, drink and stay, the lively market town has a delightfully whimsical Museum of Childhood and a town museum in the ugly keep of the castle. Abergavenny is surrounded by commanding hills, a magnet for cyclists and walkers, of which the **Sugar Loaf** and the legend-infused **Skirrid** are deservedly the most popular.

The town is also a good base for the pastoral border country to the east, most commonly visited to see **White**, **Skenfrith** and **Grosmont** castles, known collectively, if unimaginatively, as the **Three Castles**, and first built in the later Norman years as William the Conqueror's field marshals battled continuously to impose their authority on the rebellious Welsh. Of the three, White Castle is the most imposing, although all three are in sufficiently good repair to warrant a visit.

A pointing finger of the north of the county stretches from Abergavenny along the **Vale of Ewyas** and the Honddu River at the bottom of the stark **Black Mountains**. Lost in rural isolation are the astounding churches at **Partrishow** and **Cwmyoy**, a couple of miles below **Llanthony Priory**, which has many features in common with Tintern Abbey, although with a fraction of the crowds. The road twists up to **Capel-y-ffin**, whose crumbling monastery was colonized in the 1920s by Eric Gill's artistic commune, and on through the **Gospel Pass** to some of Wales' most invigorating mountain scenery, before dropping once more down to the Wye valley and the border town of Hay (see p.179).

Getting around in this largely rural patch of Gwent can be difficult. Abergavenny is easy to reach from all destinations by train or bus, but, once up into the mountains of the north, public transport completely dries up; with bike and car rental available in Abergavenny, this need not be too much of a problem.

Abergavenny

Although only a couple of miles and a few hills from the iron and coal towns of Gwent's northern valleys, **ABERGAVENNY** (Y Fenni) grew because of its weaving trades and markets, giving it an entirely different feel. Despite Neolithic finds and the certainty that a small Roman outpost was situated here, the first main settlement in the town was around the Norman castle, which was built by the English king Henry I's local appointee, Hameline de Ballon, with the express aim of securing enough power to evict local Welsh tribes from the area, an important through route into Wales. Hostility to the Welsh reached its peak at Christmas 1175, when William de Braose, then lord of the town, invited Gwent chieftains to the castle, only to to murder them all. The town grew, shaken badly by the Black Death (1341–51) and a routing by Owain Glyndŵr in 1404, but continued to prosper, thanks largely to the weaving and tanning trades that developed from the sixteenth century. The industries of Abergavenny prospered alongside its flourishing market, still the focal point for a wide area, drawing many people up from the valleys every Tuesday. In World War II, Hitler's deputy, Rudolf Hess, was kept in the town's mental asylum as a prisoner after his plane crash-landed in Scotland in 1941. He was allowed a weekly walk in the nearby hills, growing, it is said, to love the Welsh countryside. This combination of urban amenities in a thriving market town and vastly rewarding upland scenery nearby is Abergavenny's main attraction today, making the town the best base in Gwent.

Arrival and information

Abergavenny is well connected by train to the national network, its **train station** (☎0873/852393) lying on the well-used line between Newport and Hereford. Buses depart from Swan Meadow **bus station** in all directions. The **tourist office** (Easter–Oct daily 10am–6pm; ☎0873/857588) and **Brecon Beacons National Park office** (Easter–Oct daily 9.30am–5.30pm) are in the same building in the Swan Meadow car park. The National Park office is especially good for planned walking routes and leaflets on local wildlife, flora and fauna. *Brook Bikes*, 9 Brecon Rd (☎0873/857066), **rents cycles**, and *Castle Narrowboats* (☎0873/830001) on the Church Road wharf in Gilwern, four miles west of Abergavenny, rents out **boats** for self-drive day trips and longer along the Monmouthshire and Brecon Canal. **Concerts** and **theatre** take place in the spiky Victorian Town Hall, Cross St (☎0873/852721).

Accommodation

Apart from those listed below, there are numerous cheap B&Bs on the Monmouth Road, between the town centre and the station, and the Brecon Road, on the western side of town.

Angel, Cross St (☎0873/857121). Smart and quiet town centre hotel. ⑤.

Great George, 49 Cross St (☎0873/854230). Opposite the *Angel*, although more animated, and hosting regular live music. ④.

Guest House, 2 Oxford St (☎0873/854823). Friendly town centre B&B, adjoining the popular local *Mansel Restaurant*. ③.

Halidon House, 63 Monmouth Rd (☎0873/857855). Best of the many B&Bs along the Monmouth Road towards the station. ③.

King's Arms, Neville St (☎0873/855074). A surprisingly cheap and well-appointed town centre pub, situated between Castle and High streets. ③.

Park Guest House, 36 Hereford Rd (☎0873/853715). Plush B&B in a beautiful Georgian town house, near the station and town centre. ③.

Pentre Court, Brecon Rd (☎0873/853545). Cheerful B&B a mile out of town, which comes complete with outdoor swimming pool. ②.

Pentre House, Brecon Rd (☎0873/853435). Roomy, friendly guesthouse at the turning for Sugar Loaf mountain. ②.

The Town

From the train station, Monmouth Road rises gently into the town centre, becoming Cross Street and, finally, the High Street. Running off to the right are Monk Street and, next to the blue-turreted Victorian Gothic Town Hall, Market Street, running down past the sites of the frenetic Tuesday (livestock) and Friday (produce) markets to the austere redbrick chapel that now houses the **Museum of Childhood and the Home** (Mon–Sat 10am–5pm, Sun 1–5pm; £2), an unashamed wallow in nostalgia, from Victorian dolls (and an Edwardian one saved from the *Titanic*) and a reputedly haunted doll's house to cigarette cards, rocking horses, needlework samplers, clockwork toys and cribs. Well-to-do children's playrooms from the Edwardian and Victorian eras have been recreated, contrasting with the far less sophisticated interior of a contemporary Welsh farmhouse. Underneath the chapel is an excellent small coffee shop.

Any street heading left off Cross or High streets leads to Castle Street, where the dark, fragmented remains of the medieval **castle** moulder. The castle's keep was entirely remodelled in the nineteenth century, and left to sit in the middle of the shabby ruins like an incongruously ugly Lego model. The only real saving features of Abergavenny Castle are its serene position near the River Usk, at the bottom of the bowl of surrounding hills, and the mildly interesting **town museum** in the keep (March–Oct Mon–Sat 11am–1pm & 2–5pm, Sun 2–5pm; Nov–Feb Mon–Sat 11am–1pm & 2–4pm; £1). Displays cover the town's history, using photographs and billboards, and recreated interiors including a saddlery and a sanitized Border farmhouse kitchen of 1890.

Abergavenny's parish **church of St Mary**, behind the Swan Meadow car park, contains some superb effigies and tombs that span the entire medieval period. Originally built as the chapel of a small twelfth-century Benedictine priory, the existing building goes back only as far as the fourteenth century, although some of the monuments within predate the building. There are effigies of members of the notorious de Braose family, along with the tomb and figure of Sir William ap Thomas, founder of Raglan Castle and Dr David Lewis (died 1584), the first Principal of Jesus College, Oxford.

Eating and drinking

There are places to eat everywhere in Abergavenny – from the legion of takeaways in Cross Street, Market Street and along the Brecon Road, to excellent lunchtime and evening food in virtually all of the town's pubs.

Ant and Rubber Plant, 7 Market St (☎0873/855905). Enormously – and deservedly – popular brasserie, with highly imaginative dishes, including Welsh specialities. Closed Sun. Moderate.

Great George, 49 Cross St. Young and lively pub, especially for the weekend discos and live music on Sunday evenings.

Great Western, Station Rd. Nostalgia-soaked railway pub next to the station, offering cheap and dependable food. Inexpensive.

Greyhound Vaults, Market St (☎0873/858549). Opposite the Museum of Childhood, this is great for a wide range of tasty Welsh and English specialities, including the best vegetarian dishes in town. Moderate.

Hen and Chickens, Flannel St, off the High St. The best beer in town is to be found in this staunchly traditional pub, with a separate dining room for food. Inexpensive.

Incredible Edible Brasserie, 22 Cross St (☎0873/859379). Popular, informal eatery, with a varied menu from steak to light snacks, even if the rustic decor is a little overplayed. Closed Sun. Moderate.

Somerset Arms, Victoria St. Soothingly old-fashioned locals' pub with hearty food, up by the junction of Merthyr Road. Inexpensive.

Swan, Cross St. Endearingly shabby town centre hotel pub, behind the tourist office. Good bar menu. Inexpensive.

Walnut Tree Inn, on the B4521 at Llanddewi Sgyrrid, 2 miles north of town (☎0873/852797). Legendary foodies' paradise, drawing diners from all over Britain, just for the evening. It's exorbitantly expensive (especially in the evening), but the food, from the owner's native Italy, is astounding. Expensive.

Blorenge, Sugar Loaf and The Skirrid

Standing in the quiet grounds of Abergavenny Castle, the surrounding skyline is dominated by three southern outposts of the Black Mountains climbing out of the river plain. To the southwest is **Blorenge** (1834ft), a corruption of Blue Ridge, accessible from the road that strikes off the B4246 a mile short of Blaenafon. The open road climbs the shale- and sheep-covered slopes to the car parks near the radio masts. An easy walk from here leads across boggy heathland to the long cairn at the summit, from which there are some glorious views south over the old mining region and north over the Usk valley, Abergavenny and the Black Mountains. Clinging to the lower contours of Blorenge is the **Monmouthshire and Brecon canal**, built into its own ridge as it glides through beech woods above the Usk valley. The canal, built around the turn of the nineteenth century to support coal mining, iron ore and limestone quarrying, is a marvellous feat of engineering, successfully steering a 25-mile lock-free stretch (the longest in Britain) through some of the most mountainous terrain. There is a steeper ascent of the Blorenge from **LLANFOIST**, a mile southwest of Abergavenny, which cuts past the church and under the canal before zigzagging up the mountain.

The broad and smooth cone of **Sugar Loaf** (1955ft) commands the Black Mountains foothills to the northwest of Abergavenny (see p.56). Falling away from its summit are paths scouring the windswept slopes before descending to tiny villages in the valleys of the Usk, the Grwyne Fawr and the Grwyne Fechan. The easiest ascent is from the south, taking the right fork of Pentre Lane off the A40, half a mile west of Abergavenny, and following the road to Mynydd Llanwenarth. A longer, but fairly easy climb goes from the Rholben of Den Spurs, to the immediate east of the Mynydd Llanwenarth; but perhaps the most glorious ascent is the longest, on the north side of the mountain, from the Fforest Coal Pit, down by the Grwyne Fawr.

The Skirrid (Ysgyryd Fawr), at 1595ft, is the most eye-catching and mysterious mountain in the area. Shooting up from the Gavenny valley, three miles northeast of Abergavenny, the hill almost seems man-made, as the gentle green fields climb about halfway up before stopping suddenly in favour of purple scrub and bracken. The best path, although it is still a steep ascent, leads from the lay-by on the B4521 just short of the *Walnut Tree Inn*. The almighty chasm that splits the peak is said to have occurred by the force of God's will when Christ died, drawing Saint Michael and legions of ensuing pilgrims to the bleak spot. A few boulders lean on the summit, sole remains of the forbidden chapel built by persecuted Catholics in this most inhospitable but breathtaking spot.

The Three Castles

The fertile, low-lying land between the Monnow and Usk rivers was important as an easy access route into the agricultural lands of south Wales, and the Norman invaders built a trio of strongholds here to protect their interests. Skenfrith, Grosmont and White castles (April–Oct daily 9.30am–6pm; Nov–March Mon–Sat 9.30am–4pm, Sun 2–4pm; CADW; £1 each) were founded in the eleventh century, and lie within an eight-mile radius of each other.

The size and splendour of the castles demonstrates their significance in protecting the border lands from both the restless English and disgruntled Welsh, who first attacked nearby Abergavenny Castle in 1182, prompting King Ralph of Grosmont to rebuild the three castles in stone. In July 1201, the three were presented as a unit by King John to Hubert de Burgh, who fought extensively on the continent and brought back sophisticated new ideas on castle design to replace earlier castles with square keeps. He rebuilt Skenfrith and Grosmont, and his successor as overlord, Walerund Teutonicus ("the German"), worked on White Castle. In 1260, the advancing army of Llywelyn ap Gruffydd began to threaten the king's supremacy in south Wales, and the three castles were refortified in readiness.

Gradually, the castles were adapted more as living quarters and royal administrative centres than military bases, as the Welsh began to adapt to English rule. The only return to military usage came in 1404–5, when Owain Glyndŵr's army pressed down to Grosmont, only to be defeated by the future King Henry V. The castles slipped into disrepair, and were finally sold by the Duchy of Lancaster to the Duke of Beaufort in 1825. The Beauforts sold the three castles off separately in 1902, the first time since 1138 that the three had fallen out of single ownership.

White Castle

White Castle (Castell Gwyn) lies about eight miles north of Raglan and six miles east of Abergavenny, just north of the village of Llantilio Crossenny. This most awesome of the three is sited in open, rolling countryside with some superb views over to the Skirrid mountain and the hills surrounding the River Monnow. A few patches of the white rendering that gave the castle its name can be seen on the exterior walls. Entering the grassy Outer Ward, enclosed by a curtain wall with four towers, gives an excellent view over to the brooding mass of the castle, situated neatly in a moat on the Inner Ward. A bridge leads over the moat into the dual-towered Inner Gatehouse, where the western tower, on the right, can be climbed for its sublime vantage point. Here, you can appreciate the scale of the tall twelfth-century curtain walls in the Inner Ward. The arrowslits in the walls are unusually cross-shaped, a distinctive feature of the castle's thirteenth-century rebuilding. Of the domestic buildings within the walls, only the foundations and a few inches of wall remain. At the back of the ward, there are massive foundations of the Norman keep, demolished in about 1260 and unearthed once more in the early part of this century. The southern wall that took the place of the keep was once the main entrance to the castle, as can be seen in the postern gate in the centre, on the other side of which a bridge leads over to the Hornwork, one of the castle's three original enclosures, although now no more than a grassy mound.

Skenfrith Castle

Seven miles northeast of White Castle, alongside the River Monnow, is the thirteenth-century **castle** in the centre of the tiny border village of **SKENFRITH** (Ynysgynwraidd), dominated by the circular keep that replaced an earlier Norman incarnation. Whilst not as impressive as White Castle, Skenfrith is in a pretty riverside setting on the main street of an attractive village.

The castle's walls are built of a sturdy red sandstone in an irregular rectangle. In the centre of the ward is the 21-foot-high round keep, raised slightly on an earth mound to give archers a greater firing range, and containing the vestiges of the private apartments of the castle's lord on the upper floors; most notable are the huge fireplace and private latrine. Along the west curtain of the wall are the excavated remains of the Hall Range of domestic buildings, including an intact thirteenth-century window, complete with its original iron bars.

Grosmont Castle

Five miles upstream of Skenfrith, right on the English border, the most dilapidated of the Three Castles, **Grosmont Castle** (Castell y Grysmwnt), sits on a small hill above the village. Entering over the wooden bridge above the dry moat, the first ruins you pass through are those of the two-stage gatehouse. This leads into the small central courtyard, dominated on the right-hand side by the ruins of a large Great Hall, dating from the first decade of the thirteenth century. The ground floor rooms were lit by lancet windows with widening stepped sills, as can still be seen.

Practicalities

The Three Castles can only reached by walking, cycling (bike rental is available in Abergavenny) or driving. A circular route of all three castles is described in a *Green Guide* leaflet (35p) available from Abergavenny tourist office, and a more detailed 18-mile walk leaflet (£1) is also available.

Accommodation in the area is largely in farmhouse B&Bs, many of which are excellent. Half a mile north of White Castle is the immensely friendly *Great Tre-Rhew Farm* (☎0873/821268; ②). One mile the other side of White Castle is the slightly posher *Mrs Ford's* at Little Treadam (☎0600/85326; ③), just north of Llantilio Crossenny. Of the village pubs, pride of place goes to the *Hostry Inn* in Llantilio Crossenny (☎060 085/278; ③) for B&B and bunkhouse accommodation, excellent food, and regular folk and rock music nights. For other nearby accommodation and amenities, see "Abergavenny" (p.56).

The Vale of Ewyas

In total contrast to the urban blights in the north valleys just a handful of miles away, the northern finger of Gwent, stretching along the English border, is one of the most enchanting and reclusive parts of Wales. The main A465 Hereford road leads north out of Abergavenny, passing the surreal mound of The Skirrid on the right-hand side. Six miles out of town, the road bypasses the village of

Llanfihangel Crucorney, where the B4423 diverges off to weave along the bank of the Honddu River past the remote village of **Cwmyoy**, with its wonky, subsided church, and on to the crumbling old religious institutions of **Llanthony Priory** and **Capel-y-ffin**. Parallel to the Honddu, a couple of miles and some impressive mountains to the west, is the **Gwyrne Fawr**, a sparkling river that flows through the heart of some of Wales' most peaceful and gentle countryside, a patchwork of lush fields moulded along improbably shaped hills. Folded amongst the contours is one of the country's most perfect small churches at **Partrishow**.

Llanfihangel Crucorney, Partrishow and Cwmyoy

The place most geared up to suck in the tourists around these parts is the graceless village of **LLANFIHANGEL CRUCORNEY** (*Llanfihangel Crucornau*, the Holy Place of Michael at the Corner of the Rock), named after the tales of Saint Michael and The Skirrid (see above). On the main village street, quietened by the new bypass, are the odd fifteenth-century **church**, whose tower is divided from the nave by an abandoned roofless section, and the less-than-hospitable **Skirrid Inn**, which makes great play to be the "oldest pub in Wales", a fact singularly difficult to prove.

On the southern outskirts of Llanfihangel Crucorney, the exquisite *Penyclawdd Court* (☎0873/890719; ③) is a rambling Tudor manor house where meals can be taken by candlelight in the ponderous oak dining room. Just north of the village, the Georgian *Great Llwyn Farm* (☎0873/890418; ③) overlooks the river valley.

From here, the B4423 heads north into the beautiful **Vale of Ewyas**, along the banks of the Honddu River. After a mile, a lane heads west towards the enchanting valley of the **Gwyrne Fawr**, lost deep in the middle of quiet hills. The road is well worth following, if only for the discovery of the hamlet of **PARTRISHOW**, where a bubbling tributary of the Gwyrne Fawr trickles past the delightful **church** and **well** of St Issui. First founded in the eleventh century, the tiny church was refashioned in the thirteenth and fourteenth centuries, with major restoration work needed in 1908 to prevent it collapsing. The church interior's finest feature is the lacy fifteenth-century rood screen carved out of solid Irish oak, and adorned with crude symbols of good and evil – most notably in the corner, where an evil dragon consumes a vine, a symbol of hope and well-being; the rest of the whitewashed church breathes simplicity by comparison. Of special note are the wall texts painted over the doom picture of a skeleton and scythe – before the Reformation, such pictures were widely used in the hope of teaching an illiterate population about the scriptures, until King James I ordered that such "Popish devices" should be whitewashed over and repainted with scripture texts. Here, the ghostly figure of doom is once again seeping through the whitewash. Encased in glass by the pulpit is a rare example of a 1620 bible in Welsh.

Back on the main B4423, the road winds its way on the valley's western side, past the fork at the *Queen's Head* inn (☎0873/890241; ②), excellent for B&B and pony trekking, as well as a place to **camp**. It's well worth taking the little lane that peels off the main road, as it dips down over the river and into the village of **CWMYOY**, where all eyes are drawn to the amazing spectacle of the parish **church of St Martin**, whose age and history are shrouded in uncertainty, and which has substantially subsided due to geological twists in the underlying rock. Nothing squares up: the tower leans at a severe angle from the bulging body of the church and, the view inside from the back of the nave towards the sloping altar, askew roof and straining windows is unforgettable.

Llanthony

Four miles further up this most remote of valleys is the hamlet of **LLANTHONY**, nothing more than a small cluster of houses, an inn and a few outlying farms around the wide open ruins of **Llanthony Priory** – a grander setting, and certainly a quieter one than Tintern. With origins swaddled in myth and hearsay, the priory is believed to have been founded around 1100 on the site of a ruined chapel by Norman knight, William de Lacy, who, it is said, was so captivated by the spiritual beauty of the site that he renounced worldly living and founded a hermitage, attracting like-minded recluses and forming Wales' first Augustine priory. The church and outbuildings still standing today were constructed in the latter half of the twelfth century. Roving episcopal envoy, Giraldus Cambrensis visited the emerging priory church in 1188, noting that "here the monks, sitting in their cloisters, enjoying the fresh air, when they happen to look up at the horizon behold the tops of mountains, as it were touching the heavens". Now that this same church, with its row of wide, pointed transitional arches and squat tower, is roofless, the heavens and the sheep-speckled Black Mountains (see p.177) are even nearer. The *Abbey Hotel* here, fashioned out of part of the tumbledown priory, was built in the eighteenth century as a hunting lodge.

Sometimes compared with the riverside setting and mountainous backdrop of Tintern Abbey, Llanthony, although on a far more modest scale, has the edge over Tintern in many respects. Whereas Tintern has grown into a mini-industry, supporting garish restaurants and shops around the abbey, Llanthony remains much as it has been for 800 years, retaining a real sense of spirituality and peace, in a far grander setting. A hundred yards along the road from the priory is the thick-set *Half Moon Inn* (☎0873/890611; ②), home of superb beer, good-value food and accommodation.

Capel-y-ffin and the Gospel Pass

From Llanthony, the road climbs slowly along side the narrowing Honddu River before coasting gently along by ruined farmhouses for four miles to the isolated hamlet of **CAPEL-Y-FFIN**, just yards over the Gwent border in Powys. Locked in the middle of sheer hills, Capel-y-ffin has a strangely devotional feel, due principally to the fact that the village is made up of little more than two chapels and a curious ruined monastery. The minute whitewashed eighteenth-century chapel on the main road has the aptest text inscribed into one of its windows: "I will lift up mine eyes unto the hills from whence cometh my help" – at Capel-y-ffin, you can barely help doing anything else. A lane forks off by the phone box, leading up to the ruins of the privately owned (and confusingly named) **Llanthony Monastery**, founded in 1870 by the Reverend Joseph Lyne. The religious order failed to survive his death in 1908, but the place later became a self-sufficient outpost of the art world when, in 1924, it was bought by English sculptor, typeface designer and mild eccentric, Eric Gill, whose commune, a motley collection of artists and their families, drew much of their artistic inspiration from the tiny valley of Nant y Bwch, the stream that runs by the lane, which can be followed all the way to its source underneath the commanding heights of **Rhiw Wen**.

From here, the road narrows as it weaves a tortuous route up into the **Gospel Pass** and onto the glorious roof of the Black Mountains (see p.177). A howling, windy moor by **Hay Bluff**, five miles up from Capel-y-ffin, affords vast views and terrific walking over spongy hills, punctuated by bleak crags and the distant view of minuscule villages. The road drops just as suddenly as it climbed, descending five miles into Hay-on-Wye (see p.179).

Facilities are scarce around here; *The Grange* (☎0873/890215; ③) is a comfortable B&B in whose extensive grounds (including a portion of Offa's Dyke) you can pitch a tent. Capel-y-ffin **youth hostel** (closed Dec & Jan; ☎0873/890650; ①), where you can camp, lies a mile up the valley from the hamlet itself.

Newport and around

The westernmost slice of Gwent is the most stark in terms of contrast, from the lofty and windswept peaks of the northern segment around Abergavenny to the grit and industry of the valley towns in the south. Dominating the latter is **NEWPORT** (Casnewydd-ar-Wysg), Wales' third largest town, a downbeat, working-class place that grew up around the docks at the mouth of the Usk.

Its rich history has been largely swept away by the twentieth century, but isolated nuggets remain, whether in the scant ruins of the riverside **castle**, or the church of St Woolos, high on a hill over the town and elevated to cathedral status in 1921. The superb municipal museum draws together the strings of the town's vibrant past, including a memorable and informative section on the nineteenth-century **Chartist movement**, formed to fight for universal franchise. **Caerleon** – the "old port" on the River Usk – has become little more than a northern suburb of the town, although it predates Newport by about a thousand years as one of the most important Roman military bases in Britain.

The Town

Scything the town in two is the River Usk, foul and muddy as the tidal waters flow down to the Severn estuary, three miles away. Wedged in between the rail and main road bridges are the pathetic remains of the town's **castle**, first built in 1191, rebuilt in the fourteenth century, sacked by Owain Glyndŵr in 1402 and refortified later in the same century. Apart from its remarkably uncongenial position, the castle is notable for the sheer drop down to the mud flats of the estuary and the vaulted ceiling still retained in the central tower.

On the other side of the Newport Bridge, a walkway leads along the river bank past Peter Fink's giant red 1990 sculpture, **Steel Wave**, a nod to one of Newport's great industries. The main route into the town centre proper is up the pedestrianized High Street, which shortly meets up at the main crossroads of Newport and Westgate squares. Here stands the **Westgate Hotel**, an ornate Victorian successor to the hotel where soldiers sprayed a crowd of Chartist protesters with gunfire in 1839, killing at least a dozen. The hotel's original pillars still show bullet marks.

Commercial Street, leading south from Westgate Square, is Newport's main shopping thoroughfare, lined with tatty shops, but beautifully framing the town's famous Transporter Bridge (see below). One hundred yards along Commercial Street, the pedestrianized **John Frost Square** (named after a former mayor and one of the 1839 Chartist leaders) lies to the left. Although no more than an ugly 1960s precinct, the square does contain the distinctly quirky **Newport clock**. Every hour, the silver mock-temple shudders, shakes, splits, spits smoke, and

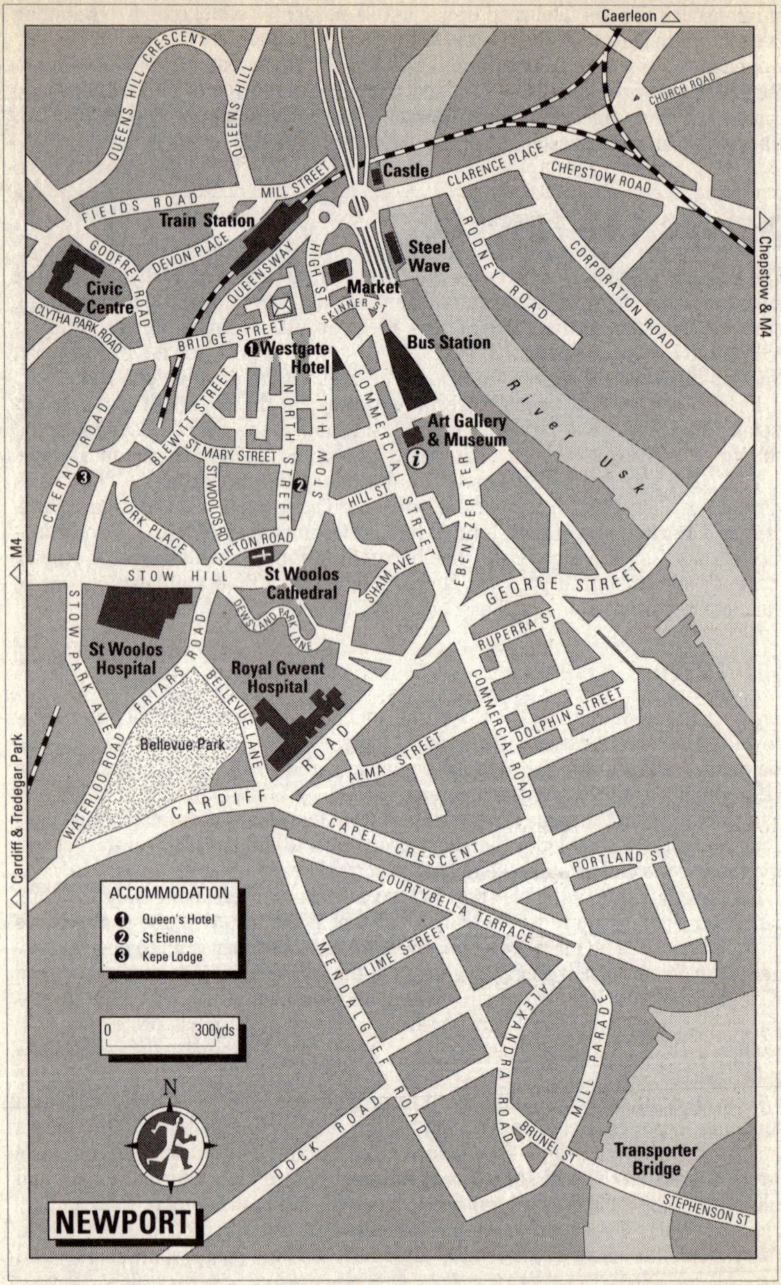

NEWPORT
Caerleon
Chepstow & M4
M4
Cardiff & Tredegar Park
Castle
Train Station
Steel Wave
Civic Centre
Market
Westgate Hotel
Bus Station
Art Gallery & Museum
St Woolos Cathedral
St Woolos Hospital
Royal Gwent Hospital
Bellevue Park
Transporter Bridge
River Usk
QUEENS HILL CRESCENT
QUEENS HILL
MILL STREET
FIELDS ROAD
DEVON PLACE
GODFREY ROAD
CLYTHA PARK ROAD
QUEENSWAY
HIGH ST
SKINNER ST
BRIDGE STREET
NORTH STREET
STOW HILL
COMMERCIAL STREET
BLEWITT STREET
ST MARY STREET
CAERAU ROAD
YORK PLACE
ST WOOLOS RD
CLIFTON ROAD
HILL ST
SHAM AVE
EBENEZER TER
STOW HILL
STOW PARK AVE
DEWSLAND PARK LANE
FRIARS ROAD
BELLEVUE LANE
WATERLOO ROAD
CARDIFF ROAD
GEORGE STREET
RUPERRA ST
DOLPHIN STREET
COMMERCIAL ROAD
ALMA STREET
CAPEL CRESCENT
PORTLAND ST
COURTYBELLA TERRACE
LIME STREET
MENDALGIEF ROAD
ALEXANDRA ROAD
MILL PARADE
BRUNEL ST
DOCK ROAD
STEPHENSON ST
CLARENCE PLACE
CHEPSTOW ROAD
CHURCH ROAD
RODNEY ROAD
CORPORATION ROAD
ACCOMMODATION
1 Queen's Hotel
2 St Etienne
3 Kepe Lodge
0 300yds
N

comes near to apparent collapse, usually drawing an appreciative crowd to watch. In front of the clock is the town's library, tourist office and imaginative civic **museum** (Mon–Thurs 9.30am–5pm, Fri 9.30am–4.30pm, Sat 9.30am–4pm; free). Starting with the origins of Gwent, the displays look at the county's original occupations and early lifestyles, and includes a section on mining with a roll call of those killed in local pit accidents – 3,508 men between 1837 and 1927. Newport's spectacular growth from a small Uskside dock in 1801 with a population of 1000 to a grimy port town of 70,000 people by the turn of this century is well charted, through the use of photographs, paintings and contemporary documents. The two most interesting sections deal with the Chartist uprising and the Roman mosaic remains excavated at Caerwent, and on the top floor, the **Wait Collection** of Edwardian kitsch is most noted for its three hundred-plus teapots.

The other road that heads south from Westgate Square is **Stow Hill**, one of Newport's few handsome thoroughfares of Victorian and Georgian townhouses. A ten-minute walk up the hill leads to **St Woolos Cathedral**, a curious jigsaw of architectural styles and periods. The tiny, whitewashed twelfth-century Lady Chapel leads through a superb Norman arched doorway – supported by columns reputedly of Roman origin from Caerleon – into the Norman nave, notable for its clerestory windows, bounded by two fifteenth-century aisles. The modern east end of the cathedral harmonizes well, with a circular east window in a swirl of autumn colours locked in a marbled round-headed arch that harks back to the Norman features.

Dominating the Newport skyline is the 1906 **Transporter Bridge**, built to enable cars and people to cross the river without disturbing the shipping channel, as they had to be hoisted high above the Usk on a dangling platform. Its comical, spidery legs flare out to the ground, connecting the aptly named Brunel Street on the west bank (reached down Commercial Street and its continuation, Commercial Road) and Stephenson Street opposite. At the time of writing, the bridge is closed for renovation, but will reopen in 1995.

Tredegar House

Buses #3, #15 and #30 go out to the westerly suburbs of Newport and **Tredegar House** (house April–June & Sept Wed–Sun noon–6pm; July & Aug Tues–Sun noon–6pm; Oct Sat & Sun noon–6pm; park daily 9am–dusk; house tour & gardens £3.40, walled gardens & park £1), just off junction 28 of the M4. The

THE CHARTISTS

During an era when wealthy landowners bought votes from the enfranchised few, the struggles of the Chartists were an historical inevitability. Thousands gathered around the 1838 People's Charter that called for universal male franchise, a secret (and annual) ballot for Parliament and the abolition of property qualifications for the vote. Demonstrations in support of these principles were held all over the country, with some of the most vociferous and bloodiest taking place in the radical heartlands of industrial south Wales. On November 4, 1839, Chartists from all over Monmouthshire marched on Newport and descended Stow Hill, whereupon they were gunned at by soldiers hiding in the Westgate Hotel, killing around 22 protesters. The leaders of the rebellion were sentenced to death, which was commuted to transportation, by the self-righteous and wealthy leaders of the town. Queen Victoria even knighted the mayor who ordered the random execution.

home of wealthy local landowners, the Morgan family, from 1402 until 1951, Tredegar and its grounds have been transformed into a recreation park that includes a boating and fishing lake, craft workshops and donkey rides. The house itself is an unassuming seventeenth-century pile in warm red brick, built to replace the Morgans' earlier home, and its interior is in the process of restoration to an approximation of its Regency heyday, when Tredegar was one of Wales' most fashionable and exclusive mansions, where royalty and politicians mingled right up to the years preceding World War II. Of the rooms in the tour, the first-floor Gilt Room is the most memorable: an explosion of glittering fruit bosses, an intricate gilded marble fireplace, mock-walnut panelling and an elaborate painted stucco gold ceiling. The formal walled gardens are behind the housekeeper's shop and are in the process of being re-laid in patterns culled from eighteenth-century designs.

Practicalities

Newport's **tourist office** is in the museum complex in John Frost Square (Mon–Thurs 9.30am–5pm, Fri 9.30am–4.30pm, Sat 9.30am–4pm; ☎0633/842962), a hundred yards from Kingsway **bus station** (town enquiries ☎0633/263600, trans-Gwent services ☎0633/265100), and a quarter-mile from the **train station** (☎0633/842222).

If you stay, **accommodation** is abundant and generally reasonable. For hotels, try the informal, pink *Queen's Hotel*, 19 Bridge St (☎0633/262992; ③), the central, if starchy *Westgate Hotel*, at the bottom of Commercial Street and Stow Hill (☎0633/244444; ⑤), or the genteel *St Etienne*, 162 Stow Hill (☎0633/262341; ④). At the western end of Bridge Street, Caerau Road rises up sharply to the south, passing the relaxed, hospitable *Kepe Lodge* at no. 46a (☎0633/262351; ③). There is a **campsite** at *Tredegar House* (☎0633/815880); see above for bus services.

There are plenty of chain **food** outlets along Bridge and Commercial streets, and nearby *Rocky's* serves individualistic burgers on the tiny Baneswell Road, off Bridge Street (closed Sun eve). Up by the cathedral, the *Ristorante Vittorio*, 113 Stow Hill (☎0633/840261), is a popular and traditional Italian trattoria. The *Westgate Hotel* has a reasonable daytime café-bar open in the small alley alongside in Commercial Street, next to the *Scrum Half* café, excellent for cheap and filling breakfasts and lunches.

Despite the profusion of **pubs**, none is terribly special: the 1530 *Olde Murenger House*, High St, has a beautiful Tudor frontage spoiled by a tatty interior, the *Queen's Hotel*, Bridge St, is large and unremarkable, and the cosy *Lamb* just down the road at no. 6 is popular. The most spirited pub in the town centre has to be the *Hornblower*, 127 Commercial St, though it's not a place for the faint-hearted, a raucous biker's pub with some heavy choices of music.

Caerleon

Half-hourly buses wind their way along the three-mile journey north of Newport to **CAERLEON** (Caerllion), whose compact town centre is situated to the immediate northwest of the town bridge over the River Usk. The remnants of the Roman town lie scattered throughout the present-day centre.

It was the Usk (Wysg) that gave Caerleon its old Roman name of Isca, a major administrative and legionary centre built by the Romans to provide ancillary and military services for the smaller, outlying camps in the rest of south Wales. Its only near equivalents in Roman Britain were Chester, servicing north Wales and northwest England, and York, dealing with the Roman outposts up towards Hadrian's Wall and beyond. Founded in 74 AD, lasting until its abandonment late in the fourth century, Isca was a garrison housing up to six thousand members of the Second Augustan Legion in a neat, rectangular walled town. Although the town fell gradually into decay after the Romans had left, there were still some massive remains standing when itinerant churchman and chronicler Giraldus Cambrensis visited in 1188. In his effusive writing about the remains, he noted with evident relish the "immense palaces, which, with the gilded gables of their roofs, once rivalled the magnificence of ancient Rome". Although time has had an inevitable corrosive effect on the remains since Giraldus' time, the excavated bath house and preserved amphitheatre still maintain a powerful sense of ancient history.

At the back of the *Bull Inn* car park are the Roman **fortress baths** (April–Oct daily 9.30am–6.30pm; Nov–March Mon–Sat 9.30am–4pm, Sun 2–4pm; CADW; £1.25). The bathing houses, cold hall, drain (in which teeth, buttons and food remnants were found) and communal pool area are remarkably intact and beautifully presented, with highly imaginative uses of audio-visual equipment, sound commentary and models. On the High Street, the Victorian neo-classical portico is the sole survivor of the original **Legionary Museum** (April–Sept Mon–Sat 10am–6pm, Sun 2–6pm; Oct–March Mon–Sat 10am–4.30pm, Sun 2–4.30pm; £1.25), now housed in a modern building behind. The bulk of the collection is of artefacts, such as tools, ornaments, dental equipment, lamps and even a bronze finger from an emperor's statue, that have been unearthed both at Caerleon and the smaller fortress at Burrium (Usk).

Opposite the Legionary Museum, Fosse Lane leads down to the hugely atmospheric Roman **amphitheatre** (same times as the baths; free), the only one of its kind preserved in Britain. Hidden under a grassy mound called King Arthur's Round Table until excavation work brought it to light in the 1920s, the amphitheatre was built around 80 AD, the same time as the Colosseum in Rome; legions of up to six thousand would take seats to watch the gory combat of gladiators, animal baiting or military exercises. The oval shape of the amphitheatre is backed by grassy stepped walls, on which the members of the legion would sit, tightly packed in, to watch activities in the middle. Over the road, alongside the school playing fields, are the scant foundations of the legion's **barracks**.

Practicalities

Fifty yards up the High Street is the **Ffwrrwm** arcade, home to a collection of oddball curiosity shops and the delightfully informal **tourist office** (daily 10am–1pm & 2–5pm; ☎0633/430777); in the courtyard of the Ffwrrwm is a statue of the golden-horned Welsh fertility bull that is reputed to invest anyone who clasps its horns with untold powers of procreation.

Staying in Caerleon is a more amenable option than nearby Newport. You can follow in the footsteps of Lord Tennyson, who came here to investigate the town's claim to be Arthur's seat of Camelot, by staying at the comfortable *Hanbury Arms* (☎0633/420361; ④), at the bottom of the High Street above the river. Alternatively, there's a wonderful B&B at *Clawdd Farm* on Bullmoor Road (☎0633/423250; ②). The best place for **food** and **drink** is *Tabards* on the High Street, a hospitable bistro, where you can also drink without eating.

The Valleys

No other part of Wales is as instantly recognizable as **the Valleys**, a generic name for the string of settlements packed into the narrow cracks in the mountainous terrain to the north of Newport and Cardiff.

Coming through Gwent, the change from rolling countryside to sharp contours and a post-industrial landscape is almost instantaneous. Each of the valleys depended almost solely on coal mining which, although nearly defunct as an industry, has left its mark in the staunchly working-class towns, where row upon row of brightly painted terraced housing, tipped along the slopes at some incredible angles, are broken only by austere chapels, the occasional remaining pithead or the miners' old institutes and drinking clubs.

This is not traditional tourist country, and yet is doubtless one of the most interesting and distinctive corners of Wales. Some of the former mines have reopened as gutsy and hard-hitting museums – **Big Pit** at Blaenafon and the **Rhondda Heritage Park** at Trehafod being the best. Other civic museums, at **Pontypool**, **Pontypridd** and **Merthyr Tydfil**, have grown up over decades, chronicling the lives (and, all too frequently, the deaths) of miners and their families. A few older sites, such as vast **Caerphilly castle** and the sixteenth-century manor house of **Llancaiach Fawr**, have been attracting visitors for hundreds of years. But it is beyond the mainstream sights that the visitor can gain a more rounded impression of Valleys life, whether in the Utopian workers' village at **Butetown**, the roundhouses at **Nantyglo**, fortified against an anticipated workers' uprising, the iron gravestones of **Blaenafon**, the dignified memorials found in almost every community to those who died underground or, in the heart-rending case of **Aberfan**, when a loose slag tip buried a primary school, and nearly 150 people, in 1966. South Wales, perhaps more than any other part of Britain, demonstrates the true cost of being the world's first industrialized nation.

Now much cleaned up, the Valleys combine unique sociological and human interest with staggering beauty in the sheer hills that rise behind each community. As a result of the formidable terrain, each valley was almost entirely isolated. Canals, roads and train lines competed for space along the valley floor, petering out as the contours became untameable at the upper end. Not until the 1920s were any roads connecting the valleys built, and even today, transport is frequently restricted to the valley bottoms, with roads and train lines radiating out through the south Wales coalfield like spokes on a giant wheel.

Some history

The land beneath the inhospitable hills of the south Wales valleys had some of the most abundant and accessible natural seams of coal and iron ore to be found, readily milked in the boom years of the nineteenth and early twentieth centuries. In many instances, wealthy English capitalists came to Wales and ruthlessly stripped the land of its natural assets, while simultaneously exploiting those that were paid lowly amounts to risk life and limb in the mines. The mine owners were in a formidably strong position – thousands of Welsh peasants, bolstered by their Irish, Scottish and Italian peers, flocked to the Valleys in search of work and some sort of sustainable life. The Valleys – virtually unpopulated at the turn of the nineteenth century – became blackened, packed with people, pits and chapels by the turn of the twentieth.

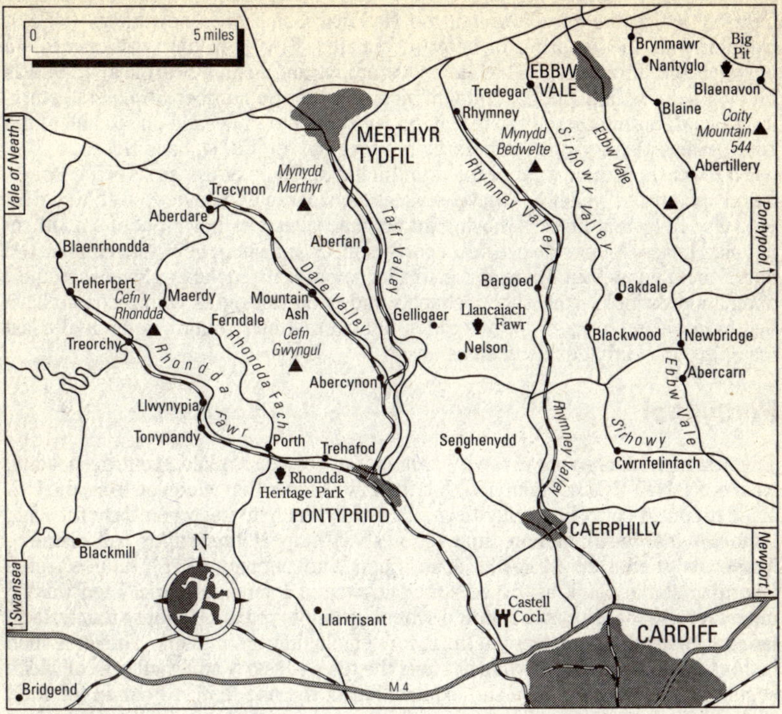

In 1920, there were 256,000 men working in the 620 mines of the south Wales coalfield, providing one-third of the world's coal resources. Vast Miners' Institutes, paid for out of a wages' levy, jostled for position with the Nonconformist chapels, whose fervent brand of Christianity was matched by the zeal of the region's politics, trade-union-led and avowedly left-wing. Great socialist orators rose to national prominence, cementing the Valleys' reputation as a world apart from the rest of Britain, let alone Wales. Even Britain's pioneering National Health Service, founded by a radical Labour government in the years following World War II, was based on a Valleys' community scheme by locally born Aneurin Bevan.

The Valleys' decline has taken place in rapid bursts, with over half of the original pits closing in the harsh economic climate of the 1930s. A Welsh cabinet secretary proposed in the mid-1930s that losses could be cut by the wholesale flooding of the Rhondda valleys as part of a massive hydro-electricity scheme. World War II saw a brief respite in the closure programme, which continued even more swiftly in the years immediately after. As coal seams have been exhausted and the political climate changed, the number of men employed in the industry has dipped down into four figures, precipitated by the aftermath of the 1984–85 miners' strike. No coalfield was as solidly behind the strike as south Wales, whose workers and families responded wholeheartedly to the call to defend the industry which their trade union, the National Union of Mineworkers (NUM), claimed was on the brink of being decimated. The year-long war of attrition between the intransigent Thatcher government and Arthur Scargill's NUM was bitter, finally seeing the government victorious as the number of miners returning to work outnumbered those staying out on strike. A decade on, and all of the south Wales pits, bar one temporarily reprieved in April 1994, have closed.

The Valleys without coal seemed unthinkable. Some of the areas – the larger, better populated valleys – have staged considerable recovery, with units of Japanese hi-tech industries moving into industrial estates hewn out of smoothed-out slag heaps. Alongside are new sports centres and shiny new museums honed out of the old pits. But many of the smaller, more isolated valleys have seen their population dwindle, with shops, chapels and pubs closing as young people have fled to leave an older, ex-pit generation behind that may well prove to be the last major group of inhabitants in some towns.

Pontypool

The first identifiably Valleys town – although never a coal mining centre – heading west is **PONTYPOOL** (Pontypŵl), on the Llwyd River that winds up from the Usk at Caerleon. A sprawling, hilly town, it's hardly likely to keep you busy for long, although it's worth finding time for a short stop at the **Valley Inheritance Museum** (Feb–Dec Mon–Sat 10am–5pm, Sun 2–5pm; £1.20), housed in a Georgian stable block at the western entrance of Pontypool Park. The building once served a mansion and is now a school, belonging to the Hanbury family, local landowners and the pioneers of the town's staple tinplate industry. The exhibition inside the museum casts a wide net over the town's history and trades, all of which seems to have sprung from the exploitation of the one family. Founding father, Richard Hanbury (1538–1608), the exhibition drily notes, was a true entrepreneur, "but on occasion his enterprise led to prison sentences for fraud". The Hanburys established Pontypool's tinplate-making industry which led, in turn, to elaborate japanning decoration and thence to ironworking.

A rare surviving feature of Valleys towns can be found in Pontypool, in the shape of the steamy *Mario's Café* at the bottom of Broad Street. Italian emigrants flocked to south Wales in the nineteenth century, many shunning mining and opening quite grand chrome-plated coffee houses. As successive generations have abandoned the family business, cafés have closed all over the Valleys.

The **train station** is inconveniently sited over a mile to the east of the town centre, making **buses**, which stop by the handsome Victorian Town Hall, a far easier option.

Blaenafon and around

Road and river continue six miles north from Pontypool to the iron and coal town of **BLAENAFON**, at the source of the Llwyd River. It has a very different feel to many valley towns, lying in a lofty hillside position that makes it feel far less claustrophobic, but its decline is testified by a shrinking population of little more than 5000, a quarter of its nineteenth-century size. The town's Victorian boom can be seen in its architecture, none more so than the impressively florid **Working Men's Hall** that dominates the town centre, and where miners would pay a halfpenny a week for the use of the library and other recreational and educational facilities. The parish **church of St Peter** is a good example of what became known as Enginehouse Churches – an enginehouse being the sole type of building familiar to local masons. The church door, font and some of the gravestones are all constructed from iron.

Blaenafon's **ironworks**, just off the Brynmawr Road (May–Sept Mon–Sat 11am–5pm, Sun 2–5pm; CADW; £1; group tours all year; ☎04955/52036), were founded in 1788, although iron smelting in this area dates from the sixteenth century. Limestone, coal and iron ore – ingredients for successful iron smelting – were abundant locally, and the Blaenafon works grew to become one of the largest in Britain in the early nineteenth century, finally closing in 1900. The remains on the site offer a thorough picture both of the process to produce iron, and the workers' lifestyles that went with it. At the **museum**, housed in the Stack Square cottages (built for the foremen and craftsmen between 1789 and 1792), there are exhibitions on the history of iron and steel making in the Llwyd Valley. Unless you're on a pre-booked guided tour, you'll have to content yourself with staring from the viewing platform at the awesome sight of the line of late Georgian blast furnaces and the adjoining water-balance lift, used to collect water from a diverted stream to lift the iron from the site on to tramlines and thence to the canal.

Big Pit

Just as it is now possible to visit the scene of Blaenafon's iron industry, the town's defunct coal trade has also been transformed smoothly into a tourist attraction: **Big Pit** (March–Dec daily 10am–5pm, last underground tour 3.30pm; £4.75, surface tour only £1.75) lies three-quarters of a mile west of the town in wide, open countryside; a half-hourly shuttle bus runs from Blaenafon. The colliery closed exactly a century after its 1880 opening. Of all the mining museums in south Wales, Big Pit brings the visitor closest to the experience of a miner's work and life, as you descend 300 feet, kitted out with lamp, helmet and very heavy battery pack, into the labyrinth of shafts and coal faces for a guided tour. The guides – most of whom are ex-miners – lead you through explanations and examples of the different types of coal mining, from the old stack-and-pillar operation, where miners would manually hack into the coal face before propping up the ceiling with a wooden beam, to more modern mechanically worked seams. Constant streams of rust-coloured water flow by, adding to the dank and chilly atmosphere that must have terrified the small children who were once paid twopence for a six-day week (of which one penny was taken out for the cost of their candles) pulling the coal wagons along the tracks. Back on the surface, the old pithead baths, blacksmiths, miners' canteen and winding engine house have all been preserved and filled with some fascinating displays about the local and south Wales mining industries, including a series of characteristically feisty testimonies from the miners made redundant here in 1980.

Out on the rolling moorland by the entrance of the pit, the old mine train line has been brought partly back into use and is now known as the **Pontypool and Blaenafon steam railway** (April–Sept Sun & bank holiday Mon only), worth taking for the couple of hundred yards to the evocative **Whistle Inn**, once the main pub for the miners, but now dependent on tourists. The atmosphere is unashamedly nostalgic, with a vast collection of miners' tin lamps hanging from the ceiling.

The Rhymney Valley

Travelling west, the first valley you come across is the **Rhymney valley**, gathered around a river that reaches its first major settlement at **CAERPHILLY** (Caerffili), seven miles north of Cardiff. A flattened and colourless town, the only feature of any interest is its **castle** (April–Oct daily 9.30am–6.30pm; Nov–March Mon–Sat 9.30am–4pm, Sun 2–4pm; CADW; £2), notable for its sheer bulk and for being the first castle in Britain built concentrically, with an inner system of defences overlooking the outer ring. Looming out of its vast surrounding moat, the medieval fortress with its cock-eyed tower occupies over thirty acres, presenting an awesome promise not entirely fulfilled inside. On the site of a Roman fort and an earlier Norman fortification, the castle was begun in 1268 by Gilbert de Clare, who wanted to protect the vulnerable coastal plains around Cardiff from the warring of Llywelyn the Last. Two years later, Llywelyn largely destroyed the castle, which was swiftly rebuilt, but for the next few hundred years, Caerphilly was little more than a decaying toy, given at whim by kings to their favourites – most notably by Edward II to his minion, or perhaps even lover, Hugh le Despenser, in 1317. The Civil War necessitated the building of an armoury within the castle, which prompted Cromwell to seize it, drain the moat and blow up the towers. By the turn of the twentieth century, Caerphilly Castle was in a sorry state, sitting amidst a growing industrial town that saw fit to build in the moat and the castle precincts. Houses and shops were demolished to allow the moat to be reflooded in 1958.

You enter the castle through a great **gatehouse** that punctuates the barbican wall by a lake, much restored and now housing an exhibition about the castle's history. A platform behind the barbican wall exhibits medieval war and siege engines, pointing ominously across the lake. From here, a bridge crosses the moat, part of the wider lake, to the outer wall of the castle itself, behind which sits the hulking inner ward. On the left is the southeastern tower, outleaning its rival in Pisa, a great cleft buried deep in its walls where Cromwell's men attempted to blow it sky high. With the exception of the ruined northeastern tower, the other corner turrets have been blandly restored since the Civil War, with the northwestern tower housing a reasonably interesting exhibition designed to give a thorough overview of Welsh castles, their methods of construction and some speculative facts and figures about the day-to-day life of their medieval inhabitants. More interesting is the massive eastern gatehouse, which includes an impressive upper hall and oratory and, to its left, the wholly restored and reroofed **Great Hall**, largely built around 1317 by Hugh le Despenser.

Butetown

The Rhymney becomes increasingly industrialized as it steers through the contours to the north of Caerphilly, past a seamless succession of small towns and rotting industry. At the very head of the valley, a mile beyond **RHYMNEY** town and just short of the A465 Heads of the Valleys road, is **BUTETOWN**, a tiny settlement utterly different from any other in the area. Built as a model workers' estate in 1802–3 by the Marquess of Bute, of Wales' richest land and resource-owning family, the town was originally conceived as the beginning of a whole new, airy workers' community. His idealism was unusual amongst the ironmasters and coal owners of the day and sadly, only the central grid of houses was built. Two ironworkers' cottages in the main street have been converted into a small local **museum** (April–Sept daily 2–5pm; £1), detailing life for nineteenth-century employees, still arduous in such uplifting surroundings.

The Taff and Cynon valleys

Like the Rhymney, the River Taff also flows out into the Bristol Channel at Cardiff, after passing through a condensed couple of dozen miles of industry and population. The first town in the Taff vale is **Pontypridd**, one of the most cheerful in the Valleys, and where the Rhondda River (see p.76) hives off west. Continuing north, the river splits again at **Abercynon**, where the Cynon River flows in from Aberdare, site of Wales' only remaining deep mine. Just outside Abercynon is the enjoyable sixteenth-century **Llancaiach Fawr** manor house. To the north, the Taff is packed into one of the tightest of all the Valleys, passing **Aberfan** five miles short of the imposing valley head town of **Merthyr Tydfil**.

Pontypridd

PONTYPRIDD's quirky arched **bridge** of 1775 was once the largest single-span stone bridge in the world. It was built by local amateur stonemason, William Edwards, whose previous attempts had crumbled into the river below. His final effort stands to this day, its three holes either side designed to lessen the bridge's overall weight and allow gusty winds through.

On the other side of the river is **Ynysangharad Park**, where Sir W. Goscombe John's gooey double statue in honour of Pontypridd weaver Evan James and his son, represents allegorical figures of music and poetry. In 1856, James composed the stirringly nationalistic *Mae Hen wlad fy nhadau* (*Land of My Fathers*) that has become the Welsh national anthem.

By the bridge at the end of Taff Street, the **Pontypridd Historical and Cultural Centre** (Mon–Sat 10am–5pm; June–Aug also Sun 2–5pm; 25p) is honed out of the town's typically austere 1861 chapel. This is one of the best museums in the Valleys – a real treasure trove of photographs, video, models and exhibits that succeed in painting a warm and human picture of the town and its outlying valleys. The interior of the old *tabernacl* itself has been lovingly restored, with ornate ceiling bosses, pillars, pulpit, stained glass window and tinny organ, all contributing to the atmosphere. There are exhibitions of old Pontypridd in photographs and paintings, transport in the area, and records from the nearby Albion colliery, at which 290 men and boys died in an underground explosion in 1894. Pontypridd is the home town of crooner Tom Jones and opera star and actor Sir Geraint Evans, both celebrated amongst the exhibitions here.

Near the elegant and impressive train station, **John Hughes' Grogg Shop** on Broadway caricatures legions of rugby stars and Welsh celebrities in oddball sculpture, and a short walk past the pubs at the bottom of Taff Street brings you out parallel to Market Street and the chaotic bustle of the old-fashioned market spilling out into the surrounding streets and squares.

Pontypridd is one of the best bases in the valleys, as it is well connected to bus, train and road networks. The **tourist office** (Mon–Sat 10am–5pm, plus June–Aug Sat & Sun 2–5pm; ☎0443/402077) is in the Historical and Cultural Centre on Bridge Street. **Accommodation** is rather scarce: in the town centre, try the lively *Millfield Hotel* in Mill Street, near the station (☎0443/480111; ④), or, right in the thick of the action, the bustling *Market Tavern* in Market Street (☎0443/485331; ③). On the other side of the Taff is *Y Ddraig Goch*, 53 West St (☎0443/409934; ③), a quiet and friendly B&B. The **youth hostel** at Llwynypia (see p.78) is only four short stops up the valley rail line. **Food** options are fairly basic: from the Italian coffee house atmosphere of *Merengi's* in the Taff Vale precinct, and the hearty café in the *Muni Arts Centre* on Gelliwastad Road, above Taff Street, to a huddle of cheap take-aways and restaurants opposite the station. **Pubs** are more Pontypridd's style, with the musical *Globe* up on Graig High Street, behind Pontypridd station, the lively *New Inn* on Market Street and, just over the bridge from the Heritage Centre, the *Llanover Arms* on Bridge Street.

Llancaiach Fawr

The river divides at **ABERCYNON**, four miles up the Taff valley, with the Cynon River flowing in from Aberdare in the northwest. Abercynon is a stark, typical valley town of punishingly steep streets lined with blank, grey houses, fading out into a coniferous hillside. Two miles east of Abercynon, just north of the village of Nelson, is the sixteenth-century **Llancaiach Fawr** (Mon–Fri 10am–5pm, Sat & Sun 10am–6pm; £3.30), a Tudor house, built around 1530, that has been transformed into a living history museum set in 1645, the time of the Civil War, with all of the guides dressed as house servants, speaking the language of seventeenth-century Britain. Although there is great opportunity for the whole experience to be nightmarishly tacky, it is quite deftly done, with well-researched period authenticity and numerous fascinating anecdotes from the staff; visitors are even encouraged to try on the master of the household's armour. Special tours – candlelit, murder mystery and seventeenth-century evenings – are also available. Regular buses from Pontypridd, Cardiff and Ystrad Mynach station pass the entrance.

Aberfan

North of Abercynon, the Taff valley contains one sight that is hard to forget: the two neat lines of distant arches that mark the graves of the 144 people killed in October 1966 by an unsecured slag heap sliding down a hill and on to the Pantglas primary school in the village of **ABERFAN**. Thousands of people still make the pilgrimage to the village graveyard, to stand silent and bemused by the enormity of the cost of coal, while the human cost – including 116 children that died huddled in panic at the beginning of their school day – is beyond comprehension. Amongst the gravestones that strive so hard to rationalize the tragedy, one of the most humbling and beautiful valedictions to be seen is to a ten-year-old boy, who, it simply records, "loved light, freedom and animals". Official enquiries all told the sorry tale that this disaster was an almost inevitable eventuality, given the cavalier approach to safety so often displayed by the coal bosses. Gwynfor Evans, then the newly-elected first *Plaid Cymru* MP in Westminster, spoke with well-founded bitterness when he said "let us suppose that such a monstrous mountain had been built above Hampstead or Eton, where the children of the men of power and wealth are at school . . .". That, of course, could never have happened.

Merthyr Tydfil

MERTHYR TYDFIL sits at the top of the Taff valley, on the cusp of the industrial Valleys to the south and the grand, windy heights of the Brecon Beacons to the north. Merthyr's strategic site was first exploited by Romans as an outpost of their base at Caerleon (see p.66), then in 480 AD, Tydfil, Welsh princess and daughter of Brychan, Prince of Brychianog, was captured as she rode through the area, and murdered for her Christian beliefs. She became St Tydfil the Martyr, and her name was bestowed on the scattered population of the area.

In the seventeenth century, the village became a focal point for Dissenters and Radicals, movements which, through poverty and crass inequality, gained momentum in the eighteenth century as the town's massive ironworks were founded to exploit the abundant seams of iron ore and limestone. Merthyr became the largest iron producing town in the world, as well as by far the most populous town in Wales – in 1831, the town had a population of 60,000, more than Cardiff, Swansea and Newport combined. By the turn of the eighteenth century, Merthyr's four monumental iron works had all been founded, and workers flocked from all over the Britain and beyond, finding themselves crammed into squalid housing whilst the ironmasters built themselves great houses and palaces on the better side of town. Merthyr's radicalism bubbled furiously, breaking out into occasional riots and prompting the election of Britain's first socialist MP, Keir Hardie, in 1900.

Although the twentieth century has been a story of decline for Merthyr, with the big works closing in the century's early years, the haphazard streets and towering hills of the town are now far cleaner and better placed to exploit the town's natural position as a well-connected light industrial and touring centre.

The Town

The town centre is wedged in between the High Street and, running parallel to the west, the River Taff, but the sights listed here are all around the Taff to the immediate northwest of the town centre. The **Ynysfach Engine House** (March–Oct Mon–Fri 11am–5pm, Sat–Sun 2–5pm; Nov–Feb Mon–Fri 10am–4pm, Sat–Sun 1–4pm; £1) was once the powerhouse behind the mighty ironworks. Costumed models portray scenes from Merthyr's past as a centre of iron and steel making, coupled with an entertaining video about the town's industrial history. The overall effect is gritty, with a special look at the social conditions in the urban chaos of the nineteenth century.

Half a mile further up the River Taff, just off Nant-y-Gwenith Street, the lower end of the Neath Road, is **Chapel Row**, a line of skilled ironworkers' cottages built in the 1820s, one of which holds composer **Joseph Parry's Birthplace** (March–Oct daily 2–5pm; free), though this is most interesting as a social record of slightly better-than-average workers' domestic conditions of the nineteenth century. Parry's music, including the national favourite *Myfanwy*, is piped between rooms, and the upstairs section of the house is given over to a display of his life and music.

Back across the other side of the river, just beyond the Brecon Road, is a home in absolute contrast to Parry's humble and cramped birthplace: **Cyfartha Castle** (April–Sept Mon–Sat 10am–6pm, Sun 2–5pm; Oct–Mar closes 5pm; £1), built in 1825 as an ostentatious mock-Gothic castle for William Crawshay II, boss of the town's original iron works. The castle is set within a vast, attractive parkland which slopes down to the river and afforded Crawshay a permanent view over his iron empire. The old wine cellars contain a varied and enjoyable walk through the history of Merthyr, with the political turmoil and massive exploitation of the past couple of centuries picked over in gory detail. The museum's modern art **gallery** houses an impressive collection of Welsh pieces, including offerings by Augustus John, Cedric Morris, Vanessa Bell, Jack Yeats, Vanessa Bell and Kyffin Williams, as well as those of local nineteenth-century artist Penry Williams. The castle grounds include public boating, bowling, tennis and crazy golf.

Practicalities

The **train station** is on the east of the town centre, a minute's walk from the High Street. North up the High Street from here is Glebeland Street and the bus station, where services depart for all points of south and mid Wales. The **tourist office**, 15 Glebeland St (Easter–Sept daily 9.30am–5.30pm; Oct–Easter closed Sun; ☎0685/379884), is behind the bus station.

Accommodation is varied, including the smart *Arlington Castle Hotel*, Castle St (☎0685/722327; ④), and the unpretentious *Tregenna Hotel* in Park Terrace, next to Penydarren Park (☎0685/723627; ③); there are humbler surroundings at the *Hanover Guest House*, 31 Hanover St (☎0685/379303; ②), the *San Marie*, 24 Lancaster Villas (☎0685/373408; ②), or the *Penylan*, 12 Courtland Terrace (☎0685/723179; ②). There is a **campsite** four miles north of town in the beautiful surroundings of *Glawen Farm*, Cwmtaff, near Cefn-Coed (☎0685/723740).

There are plenty of daytime **food** outlets in the main shopping area of the town centre, with a few cafés, Chinese and Indian restaurants open into the evening along the High Street. Pubs serving food include the *Harp Inn* on Swansea Road, the *Tregenna Hotel* in Park Terrace, or the historic *Three Horseshoes Inn*, Dynevor St (☎0685/722523), where up to three hundred Chartists used to cram into the small bar. Any of these will also prove amenable for a night's **drinking**, as will the downbeat *Belle Vue* and lively *Narrow Gauge*, both on Glebeland Street.

The Rhondda

The most famous of all the Welsh valleys, **The Rhondda** is, in fact, two valleys: the great **Rhondda Fawr** (the Big Rhondda), stretching from the outskirts of Pontypridd to Blaenrhondda – sixteen miles long and never as much as a mile wide – and the frequently forgotten little sibling, the **Rhondda Fach** (the Small Rhondda), parallel to it and swerving around the contours from Porth to Maerdy. The name of the Rhondda is synonymous with the Valleys for many people, partly due to Richard Llewellyn's 1939 book *How Green Was My Valley*, which was based on the author's life in Ton Pentre, Rhondda Fawr, and partly because it was the heart of the massive south Wales coal industry, an industry that, at its peak, provided around one third of the entire world's consumption.

By 1860, tentative mining explorations had taken place in Rhondda's quiet, fertile land, and the two valleys housed around 3000 people. In 1910 nearly 160,000 were squeezed into the available land, in ranks of houses grouped around sixty or so pit heads. The Rhondda, more than any other of the Valleys, became a self-reliant, hard-drinking, chapel-going, deeply poor and terrifically spirited breeding ground for radical religion and firebrand politics. The Communist Party ran the town of Maerdy (nicknamed "Little Moscow" by Fleet Street in the 1930s) for decades. The 1984 miners' strike saw solidarity in the Welsh pits on a greater scale than any other part of Britain. But the last pit in the Rhondda, the epicentre of the coal mining industry, closed four days short of Christmas in 1990. Left behind is not some dispiriting ragbag of depressing towns, but a range of new attractions, cleaned-up hillsides and some of the friendliest pubs and working

MALE VOICE CHOIRS

Fiercely protective of its reputation as a land of song, the voice of Wales is most commonly heard amongst the ranks of male voice choirs. Although they can be found all over the country, it is in the southern, industrial heartland that they are loudest and strongest. The roots of these choirs lie in the Nonconformist religious traditions of the seventeenth and eighteenth centuries, when Methodism in particular swept the country, and singing was a free and potent way of cherishing the frequently persecuted faith. Throughout the breakneck industrialization of the nineteenth century in the Glamorgan valleys, choirs of coal miners came together to praise God in the fervently religious way that was typical of the packed, poor communities. Classic hymns like *Cwm Rhondda* and the Welsh national anthem, *Mae Hen Wlad Fy Nhadau* (*Land of My Fathers*), are synonymous with the choirs, whose full-blooded interpretation of them continues to render all others insipid.

The collapse of coal mining in the twentieth century has left a few choirs perilously short of members, although most continue to practise with almost religious devotion, performing in Wales and abroad with regularity. Each small valleys town has its own choir, most of whom happily accept visitors to sit in on rehearsals. The Wales Tourist Board issue a leaflet, available from tourist offices, which gives contact phone numbers for each choir's secretary. Contact them directly, and take the chance to hear one of the world's most distinctive choral traditions in full, roof-raising splendour.

men's clubs to be found anywhere in Britain. Hillwalking, with astounding views over the tight little towns, is now serious business.

The Lower Rhondda

The Lower Rhondda starts just outside Pontypridd, winding through the mountains alongside train line, road and river for a few miles to Trehafod and the colliery museum of the **Rhondda Heritage Park** (daily 10am–6pm, last admission 4.30pm; £3.50), formed by locals when the Lewis Merthyr pit closed in 1983. You can explore the engine winding houses, lamp room, fan house and a new trip underground, with stunning visuals and sound effects, recreating 1950s and late nineteenth-century life (and death) through the eyes of colliers. A chilling roll call of pit deaths and a final narration by Neil Kinnock about the human cost – especially for the valley women – of mining are stirringly moving. Nearby, in Warwick House on Trehafod Road, is the **Kingmaker Coal Craft** studio and shop, where the "black gold" of the Rhondda is fashioned into amazing figurines and models.

The Upper Rhondda

A mile beyond the museum is the solid town of **PORTH**, where – as its name, which means "gateway" suggests – the two Rhondda valleys divide. The Rhondda Fach River twists its way northwards through the smaller valley, past the quintessential valleys towns of Ynyshir, Pontygwaith, Tylerstown, Ferndale and into **MAERDY**, an endless line of impossibly perched rows of houses clinging tightly to the sheer valley walls. The major Rhondda Fawr valley heads northwest from Porth, blessed still with a train line and a decent, swift road. The first notable settlement is **TONYPANDY**, birthplace of Lord George Thomas, former honey-toned Speaker of the House of Commons, a mile short of **LLWYNYPIA**, now wedged in by forested hillsides and home of the Rhondda's excellent **youth**

hostel (see below). The road, river and train line wind tortuously past the endless stream of towns to **TREORCHY** (Treorchi), one of the most famous mining towns in Wales, largely due to the international status of their **Royal Male Voice Choir**, the oldest in Wales. Visitors are welcome to rehearsals, which take place each Sunday, Tuesday and Thursday (Mr Morgan on ☎0443/435852) at the Treorchi Primary School in Glynocli Road. Treorchy is also home of the splendid **Parc and Dare Hall** and theatre.

From Treorchy, the A4601 branches off the valley road and heads west up the mountainside, twisting its way around Mynydd Maendy and Mynydd Llangeinwyr. One of the most spectacular roads in Wales, it divides to head west down the Cwm Afan and south for the Cwm Ogwr Fawr. At the top of the Rhondda Fawr is **TREHERBERT**, its straggle of houses continuing up the valley at **BLAENCWM** and **BLAENRHONDDA**, two communities effectively bypassed since the new road was built in the 1930s by unemployed miners, connecting Treherbert to the forests and lakes of Hirwaun Common en route to Brecon.

Spectacular walks, with views both into the dark valley and over the mountains, can be found almost anywhere in the Rhondda, with many of them now signposted from the valley floor. Climbing west from Ton Pentre train station, the roads peter out into a stiff walk rising over the wooded hillside and to some good views from Mynydd Maendy. Signposted walks from Llwynypia youth hostel lead up into the forests behind and, on the far bank of the river, sheer paths veer up to the grotty Catholic shrine at Penrhys, better as a viewpoint over the huddled towns below.

Practicalities

A **train** line, punctuated with stops every mile or so, runs from Pontypridd to its terminus at Treherbert, the entire length of the Rhondda Fawr. Buses also cover the route, continuing up into the mountains and the Brecon Beacons. The Llwynypia **youth hostel**, in the Glynocornel Centre opposite the station (closed Nov & mid-Dec to mid-Feb; ☎0443/430859), is well placed for residential environmental studies and walking. Other **accommodation** includes the chintzy *Heritage Park Hotel*, next to the Rhondda Heritage Park at Trehafod (☎0443/687057; ④), and, just opposite, the *Village Inn* (☎0443/688204; ③). In Porth itself is the scruffy but friendly *G&T's*, 64–66 Pontypridd Rd (☎0443/685775; ③), which also serves winning French **food**. Nearly a mile up from Llwynypia is Ystrad, where the cosy *Greenfield* pub in William Street serves good food and beer. Although, for the most part, eating options in the Rhondda towns mean a range of chip shops, Chinese takeaways and pickled eggs in the pubs, some of the **pubs** and **working men's clubs** (which you'll generally need to be invited into, although there are many people more than happy to do this for you) serve food.

Cardiff

Official capital of Wales since only 1955, the buoyant city of **CARDIFF** (Caerdydd) has swiftly grown into its new status, and although the country is still without any directly elected government or assembly of its own, the increasing number of Welsh Office subsections in Cardiff, together with new, progressive developments, are beginning to give the city the true feel of an international capital.

Many of the city's rivals – amongst them Machynlleth, seat of Glyndŵr's parliament, Swansea, a large, sprawling and unmistakably Welsh city and even Ludlow, an English border town that was once the seat of the Council of the Marches – dismissed Cardiff as a young upstart. True, the civic charter incorporating Cardiff dates only from 1905 and, before the coal exporting explosion during the nineteenth century, Cardiff was an insignificant fishing village. The "not very Welsh" charge is also frequently levelled at the city: in some ways, this is perhaps justified – if compared with Swansea, Cardiff is very anglicized, and you will, for example, rarely hear *Cymraeg* on the city's streets. But, Cardiff's standard-bearers argue, what sort of snobbery is it that decrees a young and vibrant city should *not* be the nation's capital? Cardiff is an exciting city that is still developing, and unlike Edinburgh or London, which rest on their wistful and long histories, Cardiff pushes on, as one of Europe's largest regeneration projects transforms the old dock land around Tiger Bay into a vast freshwater marina bounded by a new opera house, spruce waterfront buildings, new museums and transport systems.

Some history

It is known that some of the Roman tribes from Isca settled in Cardiff, building a small civilian village alongside the military fort. The fort is thought to have been uninhabited from the Romans' departure until the Norman invasion, when William the Conqueror offered Welsh land to his knights if they could subdue the local tribes. In 1093, Robert FitzHamon built a simple fort on a moated hillock that still stands today in the grounds of the castle. A town grew up in the lee of the fortress, becoming a small community of fishermen and farmers that remained a quiet backwater until the end of the eighteenth century. The Bute family, lords of the manor of Cardiff, instigated new developments on their land, starting with the construction of a canal from Merthyr Tydfil (then Wales' largest town) to Cardiff in 1794. The second Marquis of Bute built the first dock in 1839, opening others in swift succession. The Butes, who owned massive swathes of the rapidly industrializing south Wales valleys, insisted that all coal and iron exports used the family docks in Cardiff, and it became one of the busiest ports in the world. By the turn of twentieth century, Cardiff's population had soared to 170,000 from its 1801 figure of around 1000, and the spacious and ambitious new civic centre in Cathays Park was well under way.

The twentieth century has seen the city's fortunes rise and plummet. The dock trade slumped in the 1930s, and the city suffered heavy bombing in World War II, but with the creation of Cardiff as capital in 1955 – widely felt to be long overdue – optimism and confidence in the city have blossomed. Many large governmental and media institutions have moved here from London, and the development of the dock areas has provided a positive boost to a flagging cityscape. Unlike so many British cities, there is an almost tangible feeling here of optimism.

Arrival, information and getting around

Cardiff-Wales international **airport** is ten miles southwest of the city on the other side of Barry. Hourly buses #X91 (Mon–Sat) and #145 (Sun) operate from the main terminal into the city **bus station** on the southwestern side of the city centre, which serves all *National Express* buses, local and trans-Wales bus routes. Across the forecourt is Cardiff Central **train station**, for all *InterCity* services (including a speedy hourly shuttle to London), as well as many suburban and *Valley Line* services. **Queen Street station**, at the eastern edge of the centre, is for local services only.

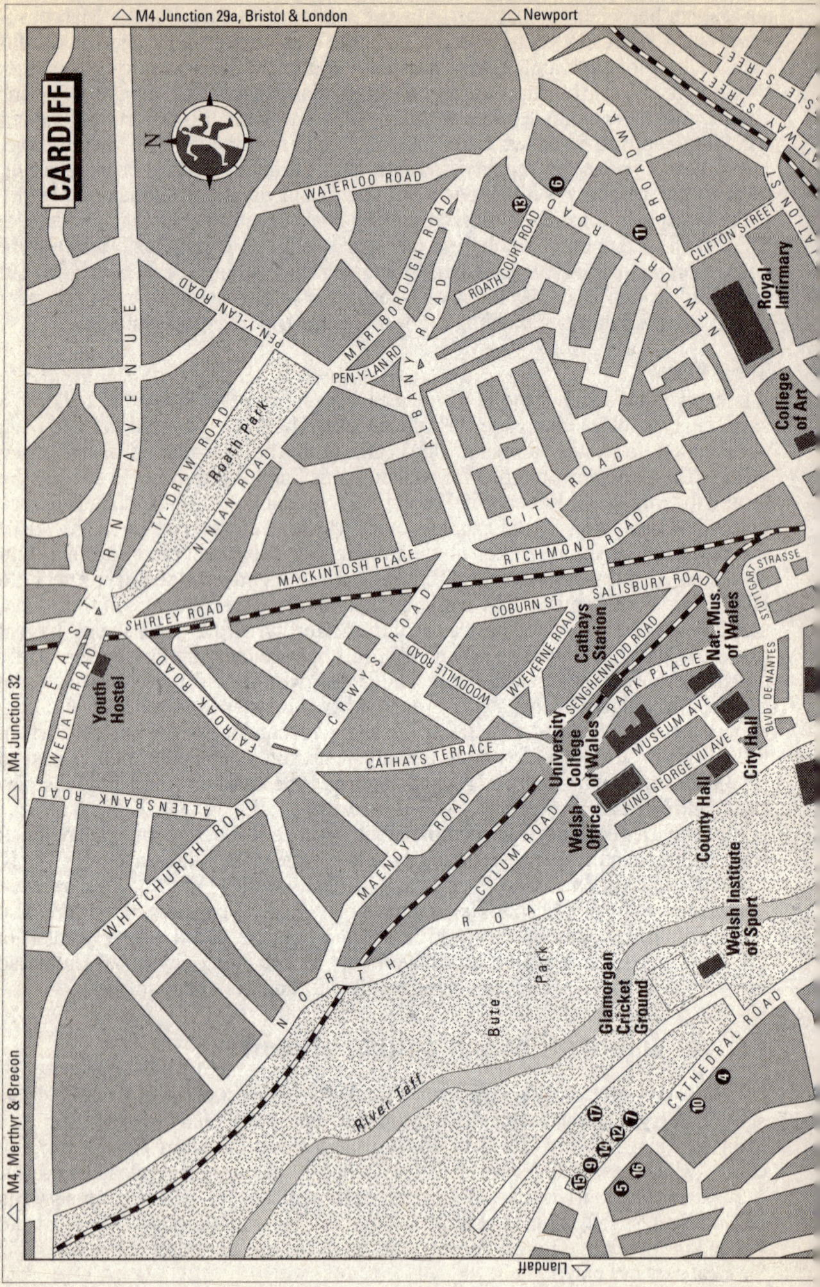
CARDIFF
M4 Junction 29a, Bristol & London
Newport
M4 Junction 32
M4, Merthyr & Brecon
Llandaff
Roath Park
Youth Hostel
Cathays Station
University College of Wales
Welsh Office
County Hall
City Hall
Nat. Mus. of Wales
Royal Infirmary
College of Art
Welsh Institute of Sport
Glamorgan Cricket Ground
Bute Park
River Taff
WATERLOO ROAD
PEN-Y-LAN ROAD
PEN-Y-LAN RD
MARLBOROUGH ROAD
ALBANY ROAD
ROATH COURT ROAD
NEWPORT ROAD
BROADWAY
CLIFTON STREET
TY-DRAW ROAD
NINIAN ROAD
EASTERN AVENUE
WEDAL ROAD
FAIROAK ROAD
SHIRLEY ROAD
MACKINTOSH PLACE
CITY ROAD
RICHMOND ROAD
SALISBURY ROAD
COBURN ST
CRWYS ROAD
WOODVILLE ROAD
WYEVERNE ROAD
SENGHENNYDD ROAD
PARK PLACE
MUSEUM AVE
KING GEORGE VII AVE
STUTTGART STRASSE
BLVD. DE NANTES
CATHAYS TERRACE
ALLENSBANK ROAD
WHITCHURCH ROAD
MAENDY ROAD
COLUM ROAD
NORTH ROAD
CATHEDRAL ROAD

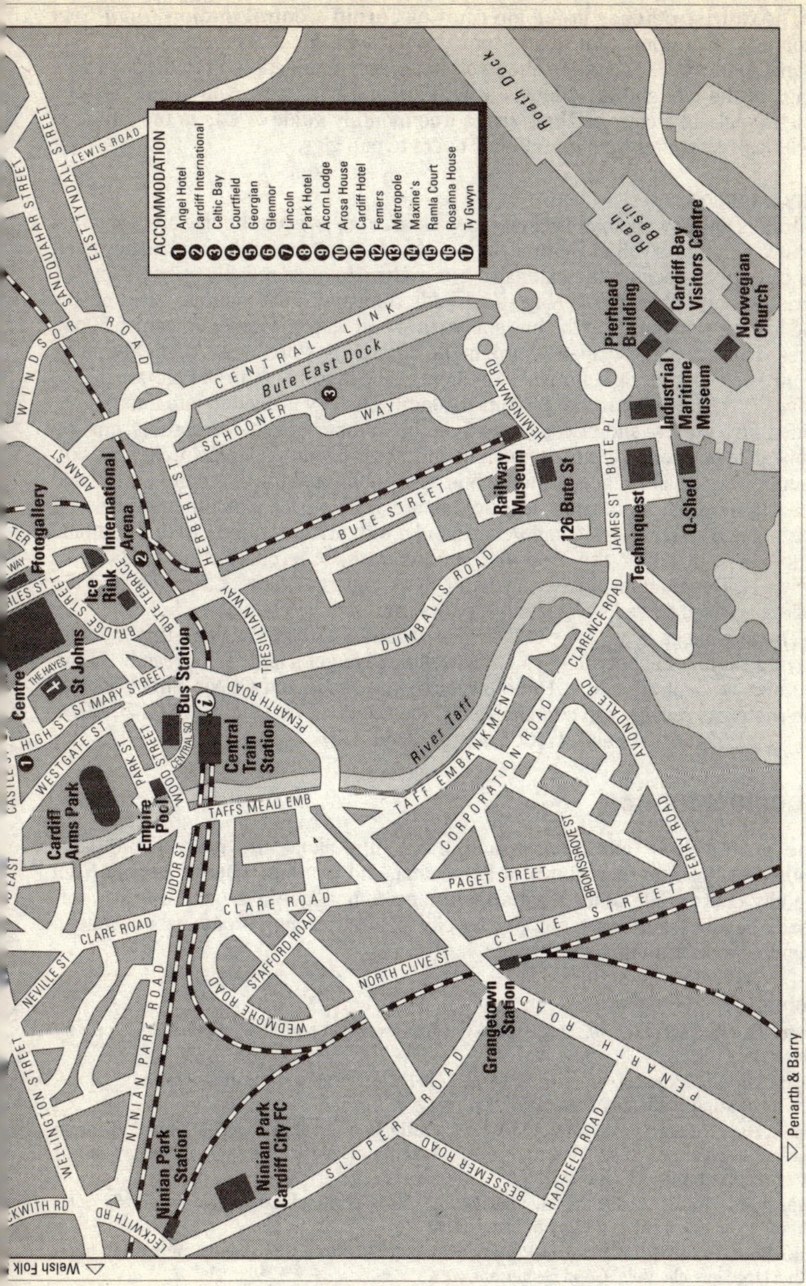
ACCOMMODATION
1 Angel Hotel
2 Cardiff International
3 Celtic Bay
4 Courtfield
5 Georgian
6 Glenmor
7 Lincoln
8 Park Hotel
9 Acorn Lodge
10 Arosa House
11 Cardiff Hotel
12 Femers
13 Metropole
14 Maxine's
15 Ramla Court
16 Rosanna House
17 Ty Gwyn
Roath Dock
Roath Basin
Cardiff Bay Visitors Centre
Norwegian Church
Pierhead Building
Industrial Maritime Museum
Q-Shed
Techniquest
126 Bute St
Railway Museum
Bute East Dock
CENTRAL LINK
SCHOONER WAY
HEMINGWAY RD
BUTE PL
JAMES ST
BUTE STREET
DUMBALLS ROAD
CLARENCE ROAD
HERBERT ST
TRESILLIAN WAY
WINDSOR ROAD
SANDQUAHAR STREET
EAST TYNDALL STREET
LEWIS ROAD
ADAM ST
International Arena
Ice Rink
Photogallery
BUTE TERRACE
BRIDGE STREET
THE HAYES
St Johns
Centre
HIGH ST
ST MARY STREET
Bus Station
Central Train Station
PENARTH ROAD
River Taff
TAFF EMBANKMENT
CORPORATION ROAD
AVONDALE RD
FERRY ROAD
BROMSGROVE ST
PAGET STREET
CLIVE STREET
NORTH CLIVE ST
Grangetown Station
PENARTH ROAD
Penarth & Barry
TAFFS MEAD EMB
WESTGATE ST
PARK ST
WOOD STREET
CENTRAL SQ
Cardiff Arms Park
Empire Pool
TUDOR ST
CLARE ROAD
STAFFORD ROAD
WEDMORE ROAD
NEVILLE ST
WELLINGTON STREET
NINIAN PARK ROAD
Ninian Park Station
Ninian Park Cardiff City FC
SLOPER ROAD
BESSEMER ROAD
HADFIELD ROAD
LECKWITH RD
Welsh Folk

The **tourist office** is in the forecourt of **Cardiff Central station** (April–Sept Mon–Sat 9am–8pm, Sun 10am–4pm; Oct–March Mon–Sat 9am–6.30pm, Sun 10am–3pm; ☎0222/227281). They will book accommodation, provide good free maps of the city and give details of walking and bus tours. You should also be able to pick up a copy of *The Buzz!*, a free monthly guide to arts in the city, that includes everything from grand-scale opera to pub gigs.

City transport

Cardiff is an easy and compact city to walk around, as even the bay area is within twenty minutes' stroll of Central station. Once you're out of the centre, however, it's best to fall back on the extensive **bus network**, most reliably operated by the garish orange *Cardiff Bus* (*Bws Caerdydd*) company. They operate sales offices and information kiosks at the bus station in Wood Street (Mon & Fri 8am–5.30pm, Tues–Thurs & Sat 8.30am–5.30pm), in the *Littlewoods* store in St David's Shopping Centre on Working Street (open store hours) and in front of the Old Library in The Hayes (Fri 8am–5.30pm, Sat 8.30am–4.30pm). The city is divided into four colour-coded **fare zones**, and prices depend on the number of zones crossed, from 30p off-peak in one zone to £1 in the rush hour across all four. A **Capital ticket** (£2.65), bought from a sales office or on the bus, gives unlimited travel around Cardiff and Penarth for a day, and **multiride tickets** are available for a minimum of a week, starting at £7.50 for Cardiff and Penarth only, with prices around £10 that combine this area with either the Vale of Glamorgan, the Caerphilly district, Barry or Newport. Destinations further afield, such as Penarth, Barry, Caerphilly and the valleys are well served by local rail services, with regular connecting buses.

The last buses leave the city centre at around 11.20pm, meaning that if you're staying slightly further afield you may well need to get a **taxi**. These can be found in ranks at Central station, Duke Street by the castle and Queen Street station. Alternatively, reliable cab companies include *Capital Cars* (☎0222/777777), *Metro Cabs* (☎0222/464646) and *West Cars* (☎0222/487171).

Accommodation

The main belt of guesthouses and hotels lies along the genteel and leafy Cathedral Road, in the suburb of Pontcanna, and is easily reached by foot from the city centre. The other main area for accommodation is around the Newport Road, heading northeast out of the city centre through Roath, about fifteen minutes' walk from the centre.

Hotels

Angel Hotel, Castle St (☎0222/232633). Cardiff's grandest and best-known hotel, opposite the castle. ⑧.

Cardiff International, Mary Ann St (☎0222/464141). Large and plush modern hotel opposite the new International Arena. ⑥.

Celtic Bay, Schooner Way, Atlantic Wharf, Cardiff Bay (☎0222/465888). Grand Victorian building transformed into a smart hotel in an area that is slowly coming together as part of the great plan for the old docks. ⑦.

Churchills Hotel, Cardiff Rd, Llandaff (☎0222/562372). Mock-Edwardian hotel in a quiet part of the city near the cathedral of Llandaff. ⑥.

Courtfield Hotel, 101 Cathedral Rd, Pontcanna (☎0222/227701). Popular and lively hotel with a large gay clientele. Good restaurant. ④.

Georgian Hotel, 179 Cathedral Rd, Pontcanna (☎0222/232594). Good value in a comfortable small hotel. ④.

Glenmor Hotel, 150–152 Newport Rd, Roath (☎0222/489545). Peaceful, moderately priced hotel; all rooms have en suite facilities. ④.

Lincoln Hotel, 118 Cathedral Road, Pontcanna (☎0222/395558). One of the nicest hotels along Cathedral Road, housed in two comfortable Victorian houses. ⑤.

Park Hotel, Park Place (☎0222/399309). Just off Queen Street in the centre, the *Park Hotel* is large and formal, with all rooms swathed in floral designs. ⑧.

Guesthouses

Acorn Lodge, 182 Cathedral Rd, Pontcanna (☎0222/221373). Pleasant and quiet B&B near Pontcanna Fields, fifteen minutes' walk from the city centre. ③.

Arosa House, 24 Plasturton Gardens, Pontcanna (☎0222/395342). Lying next to the city centre, the *Arosa* is very friendly and reasonably priced. ③.

Cardiff Hotel, 138 Newport Rd, Roath (☎0222/491964). Informal and well-placed small licensed hotel. ③.

Ferriers, 130 Cathedral Rd, Pontcanna (☎0222/383413). Best value B&B in Cardiff, welcoming, inexpensive and with excellent service. ③.

Hotel Metropole, 175 Newport Rd, Roath (☎0222/464642). Downbeat, but reasonable, large guesthouse. ③.

Maxine's, 150 Cathedral Rd, Pontcanna (☎0222/220288). Cosy low-cost B&B. ③.

Ramla Court, 188 Cathedral Rd, Pontcanna (☎0222/221187). Good-value, welcoming guesthouse with a few en suite rooms. ③.

Rosanna House, 175 Cathedral Rd, Pontcanna (☎0222/229780). Very cheap, reflected, to some extent, in the decor of the place. Handy for the city and the river. ②.

Ty Gwyn, 7 Dyfrig St, off Cathedral Rd, Pontcanna (☎0222/239784). Close to the city centre and well placed for Pontcanna Fields and the River Taff. Friendly and quiet. ③.

Hostel and campsites

Cardiff youth hostel, 2 Wedal Rd, Roath Park (☎0222/462303). Large, purpose-built redbrick building, situated just underneath the A48 Eastern Avenue flyover at the top of Roath Park, almost two miles from the city centre. Buses #78, #80 or #82 go from the central bus station. Closed Dec.

Lavernock Point Holiday Estate, Fort Rd, Lavernock, near Penarth (☎0222/707310). Buses #P4, #P5 and #P8 pass within a mile of Lavernock Point, a sadly rundown piece of coast just south of Penarth. It has a campsite and also caters for touring caravans.

Pontcanna Fields campsite, off Cathedral Rd, Pontcanna (☎0222/398362). Limited tent spaces, so booking advised in high season.

The City

Cardiff's sights are clustered around fairly small, distinct districts. The **commercial centre**, compact and easily walked around, is bounded by the River Taff, the nickname of generations of ex-patriate Welsh, on the western side. The Taff flows past the walls of Cardiff's extraordinary **castle**, an amalgam of Roman remains, Norman keep and Victorian fantasy. Nearby is the great ribbed stadium of **Cardiff Arms Park**, home of Welsh rugby and the nation's soccer team. By the southeast tip of the castle walls is the crossroads of Cardiff, where great Edwardian shopping boulevards Queen Street and High Street conceal a world of arcades, great stores and predictably bland malls. North of the castle are a series of white Edwardian buildings – the spacious **civic centre** around **Cathays Park**, home of the **National Museum**, **City Hall** and **University College**.

A mile south of the commercial centre is the area around **Cardiff Bay**, once the city's liveliest district. With the construction of the barrage to form a vast freshwater lake, the Bay has been spruced up considerably, and now houses the various sites of the excellent **Welsh Industrial and Maritime Museum**.

The other city area that is most likely to detain you is the elegant suburb of **Llandaff**, two miles northwest of the city centre above the banks of the Taff, and still feeling like a closely knit village built around the city's patchwork **cathedral**.

The commercial centre

The commercial centre of Cardiff is roughly square-shaped, bordered by the castle, Queen Street station, the International Arena and Central station, making a surprisingly compact city.

Between Central station and Castle Street is the fat bowl of **Cardiff Arms Park**, the mecca of Welsh rugby that sits on the banks of the Taff. With its giant ribs and curving sides, the Arms Park is as obvious a Cardiff landmark as any, even if the national team's performance slipped into the doldrums before the unexpectedly successful 1994 Five Nations Championship. Even so, the atmosphere in the Park, or in the pubs and streets of the city, when Wales have a home match – particularly against old enemy England – is charged with good-natured beery fervour.

Running up from Central station to the castle walls is **St Mary's Street**, one of the city's grandest boulevards of ornate Victorian and Edwardian shop frontages, leading north to become the **High Street**, off which the elegant turn-of-the-century **indoor market** leads. Along both streets, Edwardian arcades, cleaned up and with some of the city centre's most interesting shops inside, lead off between the buildings. Amongst them, nearest the station, the glorious Morgan Arcade and its near neighbour, the Royal Arcade, run east to the bottom of **The Hayes**, a pedestrianized street of disparate restaurants and some great pubs. A few yards to the south, the Hayes meets up at a junction of five streets by the belching towers of the **Brains brewery**, opposite the **Wales National Ice Rink**, home to one of Britain's top ice hockey teams, the Cardiff Devils. At the junction, Bridge Street runs away to the east and into the elegant Regency part of the city centre around David and Charles streets. At 31 Charles Street is **Ffotogallery** (times variable), the country's foremost galleries for bold and often hard-hitting photographic exhibitions.

The Hayes leads north to the beautifully sandblasted and colonnaded frontage of the **Old Library** (Tues–Sat 10am–5.30pm; free), which contains a craft centre and is used as a venue for touring art exhibitions, frequently with a Welsh theme. Here the road divides, with both left and right prongs leading past either side of the fifteenth-century grey limestone parish **church of St John**. The most notable feature – the slender tower – is difficult to appreciate with the cluster of buildings around it, although the light and graceful interior is worth seeing, especially for the floridly pompous altar in the south aisle by prolific Victorian sculptor, Goscombe John. The right turn at the Old Library is **Working Street**, a very busy shopping area, especially around the entrances to the gargantuan **St David's Centre** and the **St David's Hall** complex, which, between them, have succeeded in obliterating a huge section of the old city centre, although St David's Hall serves as a much-needed concert and entertainment venue.

Queen Street is Cardiff's most impressive shopping thoroughfare, now pedestrianized with many of the fine nineteenth-century buildings spruced up. At its western end, a typically pugnacious statue of **Aneurin Bevan**, post-war Labour politician and classic Welsh firebrand, stands aloof from the bustle. First left off Queen Street is the Friary, at the end of which is **Oriel** (Mon–Sat 9am–5.30pm), Cardiff's best selection of modern art and sculpture exhibitions, culled from the international circuit, as well as reflecting Welsh identity and interest (*Oriel* is Welsh for "gallery"). The showpiece oval glass and brick mound at the bottom of Churchill Way is the **Cardiff International Arena**, host of massive concerts, trade fairs and conferences.

Cardiff Castle

The political, geographical and historical heart of the city is **Cardiff Castle** (daily May–Sept 10am–6pm with tours every 20min; March–April & Oct 10am–5pm with tours every 30min; Nov–Feb 10am–4.30pm with tours at 10.30am, 11.45am, 2pm & 3.15pm; £3 full tour, £2.50 shorter tour, £2 self-guided), an intriguing, appealing hotch-potch of remnants of the city's history. The fortress hides inside a vast walled yard, each side measuring well over 200 yards long and corresponding roughly to the outline of the original fort built by the Romans, Cardiff's first inhabitants. A few dozen yards of **Roman wall**, the sole reminder of their presence, has been unearthed to the immediate right of the entrance in the thirteenth-century Black Tower on Castle Street, and is now lit and labelled, along with some excellent three-dimensional murals depicting life in a Roman fort. Tucked into the southeastern corner wall beyond the Roman segment are the dry **regimental museums** of the Welsh Regiment and the Queen's Dragoon Guards, filled with a starchy collection of military memorabilia. From here, walkways lead along the **battlements**, offering some excellent views over the city and the gracious Portland stone buildings of Cathays Park.

Occupying the northwestern corner of the castle grounds is a neat Norman motte crowned with the eleventh-century **keep**, with views down onto the turrets and towers of the **domestic buildings**, dating in part from the fourteenth and fifteenth centuries, but much extended in Tudor times, when residential needs began to overtake military safety in terms of priority. Ultimately, it was the third Marquis of Bute (1847–1900), one of the richest men on the globe, who lavished a fortune on upgrading his pile, commissioning architect and decorator William Burges (1827–81) to aid him. With their passion for the religious art and the symbolism of the Middle Ages, they systematically overhauled the buildings, adding a spire to the octagonal tower and erecting a clock tower; but it was inside that their imaginations ran free, and they radically transformed the crumbling interiors into palaces of vivid colour and intricate, high-camp design. These buildings can only be seen as part of the guided tour, making the extra fee well worth while.

The tour starts in the square corner **clock tower**, running through the Winter Smoking Room at the bottom, up to the Batchelor's Bedroom and bathroom and, above that, the Summer Smoking Room. All are decorated in rich patterns of gold, maroon and cobalt, with many of the images culled from medieval myths and beliefs. From here, the tour goes through the 1878 **Nursery**, with hand-painted tiles and silhouette lanterns depicting contemporary nursery rhymes, the 1881 **Arab Room**, decorated by imported craftsmen, and into the grand **Banqueting Hall**, which dates orginally from 1428, but was transformed by Bute and Burges with the installation of a riotously kitsch fireplace to commemorate Robert the Consul, Earl of Gloucester and late Norman lord of the castle. In all the rooms, fantastically rich trimmings complement the dizzily gaudy style so beloved of two nineteenth-century eccentrics, and it's worth remembering that as one of over 60 residences owned by the Butes in Britain alone, Cardiff was only lived in for six weeks of the year.

The last point of note in Cardiff Castle can only be seen from outside the precincts. The **Animal Wall**, where stone creatures are frozen in cheeky poses was another tongue-in-cheek nineteenth-century creation, running all along the route of Castle Street west to the river bridge.

Cathays Park and the civic centre

On the north side of the city centre, only a hundred yards from the northeastern wall of the castle precinct, is the area known most commonly as **Cathays Park**. The park itself is really the large rectangle of grass that forms the centrepiece for the impressive Edwardian buildings of the **civic centre**, but the term Cathays Park is generally used for the whole complex. Dating from the first couple of decades of this century, the gleaming white buildings arranged with pompous Edwardian precision speak volumes about Cardiff's self-assertion, even half a century before it was officially declared capital of Wales. The processional **Boulevard de Nantes**, named after Cardiff's twin city in Brittany, fronts the complex on the city centre side.

Centrepiece of the complex is the magnificent dragon-topped domed **City Hall** (1905), an exercise in every cliché about ostentatious civic self-glory, none more so than in the first-floor Marble Hall, swathed in columns of Sienese marble amongst the roll call of (all male) Welsh heroes, frozen for eternity as statues.

Amongst the figures are twelfth-century chronicler Giraldus Cambrensis, thirteenth-century native prince of Wales, Llywelyn ap Gruffydd, fifteenth-century national insurgent and perpetual hero, Owain Glyndŵr, Welsh king Henry Tudor and Hywel Dda (Howell the Good), tenth-century architect of Wales' progressive codified laws. Overseeing them all is the figure of Dewi Sant himself, the national patron saint, St David.

The low-key **Law Courts** (1906), stand to the left of the City Hall, with the **National Museum of Wales** (see below) balancing the view on the right-hand side. Behind them, two ruler-straight boulevards, evidently designed with ceremonial splendour uppermost in mind, run through the rest of the civic centre, arranged in symmetrical precision around **Alexandra Gardens** in the middle. At the very centre of the park is the colonnaded circular **National War Memorial** (1928), a popular and surprisingly quiet place to sit and contemplate the rush of civic and governmental duty all around. At the north end of the western boulevard, **King Edward VII Avenue**, is the **Temple of Peace** (1938), dedicated just before the outbreak of World War II to Welsh men and women the world over who were fighting for peace and relief of poverty. The eastern road, **Museum Avenue**, runs past an assortment of buildings belonging to the University of Wales College of Cardiff. At the northern head of Cathays Park is the ugliest and most foreboding building of them all: ironically, the principal Cardiff departments of the **Welsh Office**.

National Museum of Wales

The **National Museum of Wales** (Tues–Sat 10am–5pm, Sun 2.30–5pm; £2) is one of Britain's finest. Housed in a large, white, domed Portland-stone building that was built in sections from 1912 through to 1992, the museum manages to carry off the illusion of a singular *grand projet*. As a national museum, the displays attempt both to tell the story of Wales, as well as reflect the nation's place in the wider, international sphere.

You enter underneath the vast dome, into the main hall that houses the principal **sculpture collection** of Welsh notables alongside international luminaries, such as an assortment by prolific nineteenth-century sculptor W. Goscombe John – his spirited evocation of *David Lloyd George* and an uncharacteristically tender sculpture of John's own wife. John's only Welsh rival was John Evan Thomas, whose *Death of Tewdric, King of Gwent* is his masterpiece here. Amongst the wider stars of sculpture are representations from Henry Moore and, best of all, Auguste Rodin's sublime *The Kiss*, drawing passing strollers instantly to its side.

Just off the main hall is the **dinosaur gallery**, whose highlight is a collection of giant footprints of the beasts. To the left of the main hall is the West Wing and the **science collection**, on both the ground floor and the upper gallery. This includes a themed set of recreated environments, conveying a good deal of well-presented information about different coastal settings, inland bogs, natural lakes, glacial features and woodlands: some are a little tatty, although many have imaginative sound and light effects. The **zoology section** next door largely consists of an assortment of pallid stuffed animals and the world's largest leatherback turtle.

On the other side of the dome is the **botany** collection, which covers a huge spectrum of subjects from simple classifications of some of Wales' major species of flower, to quite detailed analysis of the place the conservation movement and the National Parks have in combatting pollution and encouraging responsible tourism in the ecologically delicate countryside and coastland of Wales.

The remaining sections of the West Wing, the museum's restaurant excluded, cover a rich display of **archeology**, telling the story of Wales' development chronologically. Starting with prehistoric finds, the collection courses through the Stone Age, with models and excavated examples of weapons and the conditions in which they were built, and into the comparatively sophisticated Bronze Age, most spectacularly represented in the **Caergwrle Bowl**, a wonderfully delicate, gold-leafed ornament that's around 3000 years old. The first Celts arrived in Wales around 200 BC from La Tène in Switzerland, bringing with them new styles of wrought ironwork, of which a handful of exceptional examples from Wales have been unearthed. The Roman period is cursorily examined, and the long period of the Dark Ages up to the Norman Conquest of 1066 is best seen in the developing styles of the stone crosses into some recognizable Celtic designs.

THE ART COLLECTIONS

The bulk of the East Wing is given over to fine art, with ten galleries on the first floor containing the majority of the museum's extraordinary art collection. The oldest part of the collection starts with a gathering from the fifteenth- and sixteenth-century **Italian schools** of religious art, including a typically sickly altarpiece by Allori and the sumptuous marble *Nynehead Tabernacle*, built for a Florentine church in the mid-fifteenth century. The **seventeenth-century** galleries are rich in Flemish and Dutch work, including Rembrandt's coolly aloof portrait of *Catrina Hooghsaet* and Jacob van Ruisdael's mesmerizing *Waterfall*. The most famous, or perhaps infamous, pieces here are the **Cardiff Cartoons**, four monumental tapestries bought at great expense in 1979, and presumed to be the work of Rubens. This fact seems increasingly unlikely, and other artists, especially Jan van Boeckhurst, have been aired as possible creators of what remain remarkable works, whose themes are taken from Virgil's *Aeneid*.

The first of the great Welsh artists is shown to maximum effect in the **eighteenth-century** galleries. Richard Wilson (1714–82), one of Wales' greatest landscapists, drew inspiration from the luminescent beauty of the Welsh scenery; take a look at the semi-formal paintings of *Caernarfon Castle* and *Dolbadarn Castle*, and more emotionally intense pieces such as the beautiful *Pistyll Cain*. One of Wilson's proteges, William Hodges, is also shown, most effectively in his beautiful evocation of *Llanthony Priory*.

The **nineteenth-century** galleries include a round-up of some of the century's greatest painters, such as J. M. W. Turner, whose *Thames Backwater, with Windsor Castle* is gently diffused with a characteristic wash of colour and light. There is also a thorough collection of work by the **Pre-Raphaelites** and half a dozen sentimental pieces by Jean-François Millet.

The artistic pride of the National Museum, however, is the Davies collection of **Impressionist paintings**, housed in a new gallery, amassed by sisters Gwendoline and Margaret Davies who were left a fortune by their grandfather, David Davies, incidentally the first man to challenge Cardiff's coal carrying monopoly by building a rival port at Barry. Among many canvases, the work of Cézanne, the sisters' favourite, figures predominantly, including still life and landscapes, Corot's legendary *Distant view of Corbeil, Morning*, Pissaro's classic views of Rouen and Paris, Renoir's chirpy portrait of *La Parisienne*, numerous paintings by Monet that include three serene studies of water lilies, winsome scuplture and painting by Degas, Van Gogh's *Rain at Auvers*, and pieces by Manet, Rodin, Boudin and Sisley.

The **contemporary galleries**, also in the new section, contain the work of some of Wales' greatest twentieth-century artists: Augustus and Gwen John's delicate portraits, vivid still lifes and gentle landscapes, especially Augustus' captivating portrait of a belligerent, but fragile, *Dylan Thomas*. Ceri Richards' meaty, almost cubist portrayals of industrial and rural Welsh life are amongst the most arresting pictures in the entire gallery, the perfect foil to some of the more fantastical and allegorical landscapes of David Jones, devotee of Eric Gill and his Capel-y-ffin commune in the Black Mountains, and the Arts and Crafts-inspired sweeping canvases of Frank Brangwyn. Other European twentieth-century art schools are well depicted, including Cubist sculpture, abstract painting, surrealism from Magritte and Expressionism from Heckel.

Cardiff Bay

A thirty-minute walk from the city centre (or a short ride on half-hourly bus #8) through endearingly tatty Butetown is the **Cardiff Bay** area. Names are rather indiscriminately used around this area: Butetown is the solidly Victorian area immediately north of the docks, with Grangetown to the west, on the far bank of the Taff. Both are part of what is most commonly known as Cardiff Bay, the spicier tag of Tiger Bay (immortalized by Cardiff-born Shirley Bassey) being rarely used these days.

The first impression of the area is one of immense and rapid change. New roads and roundabouts are being cut through rusted wasteland, riotous Victorian and Edwardian frontages have been swabbed clean, and soulless new buildings are spreading like advanced fungus. Cardiff Bay has become one of the world's biggest regeneration projects, aiming to transform the seedy (but quite appealing) dereliction of the old docks into a designer heaven. Transformation of the docks area is well underway, and will become unstoppable once the Cardiff Bay

Barrage – one of the largest in the world – is constructed, creating a vast freshwater marina. All involved in the project want to make clear that Cardiff Bay will not become a Welsh version of London's yuppified white elephant, Docklands.

Central to the whole project is the controversial **Cardiff Bay Barrage**, due to be built right across the Ely and Taff estuaries, transforming a vast mudflat into a freshwater lake. Opponents say that this will have serious ecological implications in disturbing one of Britain's most important habitats for wading birds and that the rise in the water table could well destabilize the foundations of buildings and homes around the bay. Supporters claim that the project is essential to provide the single biggest catalyst in the total transformation of the area, creating a vast marina as a centrepiece. You are unlikely to be in Cardiff long before hearing one side or other of this ferocious and long-running argument. Central to the new proposals is the creation of a brand new waterfront opera house, currently in the design stages and due to be begun over the next year or two. Butetown and the docks are among the most fascinating parts of Cardiff, where ostentatious Victorian shipping company headquarters rub shoulders with spruced-up dockers' housing and the four excellent sites of the **Welsh Industrial and Maritime Museum** (WIMM) (Tues–Sat 10am–5pm, Sun 2.30–5pm; £1 covers all sites), part of the National Museum of Wales. The architectural highlights of the whole area are detailed in a free leaflet, *Butetown Walkabout*, which can be picked up in the tourist office or any of the local museums.

Bute Street runs straight alongside the disused train line that terminates at the old Bute Road station. This elegant, white Victorian station has recently been converted into the **Railway Gallery** of WIMM and now houses display boards and photographs of the history of Welsh railways, together with working models of trains and locomotive works. Bang opposite is **126 Bute Street**, another branch of WIMM, in the old Frazer's Ship Chandlery shop. Old pub and house interiors mingle with a well-documented display that focuses on the people who lived in Tiger Bay, having come from all over the world, and created a multiracial community in the first half of this century.

At the bottom of Bute Street you'll find the main site of the **Welsh Industrial and Maritime Museum** (see above), mainly made up of a series of modern buildings purpose-built around the giant engines and boats that form a major part of the exhibition. Wales' great industries, particularly coal and iron ore mining, are explained through the use of video, photographs and exhibits, including some entertaining facts and photos about the pit ponies that were once such a feature of the coalfield. Cardiff's nautical heritage is represented in exhibits like the transplanted bridge of an ocean-going steamship and buxom figureheads that once ruled the waves. The Hall of Power contains working models of the methods of power that drove south Wales into massive industrialization, right from the waterwheel to up-to-date contemporary exhibitions about energy conservation. Outside in the yard are numerous railway locomotives, including an impressive replica of Richard Trevithick's engine that made the world's first train journey in 1804 up the Taff valley. Other forms of transport on display include a steam tugboat and an air-sea rescue helicopter. On a reconstructed rail bridge, telescopes enable superb viewing across the marshes and the bay.

The museum's temporary exhibition space, **Q-shed**, was converted out of a Victorian shipping warehouse facing the bay; behind it is Stuart Street and **Techniquest** (Tues–Fri 9.30am–4.30pm, Sat & Sun 10.30am–5pm; £3), a fun, "hands-on" science gallery. Experiments confusing all five senses mingle with basic scientific theory put into entertaining practice, such as in the pneumatic red dragon whose different joints are activated through the use of air-driven pulleys.

On the other side of the main site of WIMM is the **Pierhead Building**, that has beckoned ships into Cardiff port since its construction in 1896. Typically rich Victorian neo-Gothic terracotta pile, it was built for the Bute Dock Company and perfectly embodies the wealth and optimism of the Bute family and their docks. A hundred yards east of the Pierhead, the altogether different style of architecture of the modern tubular **Cardiff Bay Visitor Centre** (Mon–Fri 9.30am–4.30pm, Sat & Sun 10.30am–5pm; free), looks like a giant eye out on to the bay. Although it's a thinly disguised PR job for the controversial developments in the bay, the centre contains a fabulous scale model of the entire docks area, illuminated to show different infrastructure projects at the touch of a button.

From the visitor centre, a path leads down along the waterfront past a park and to the rebuilt **Norwegian church**, an old seamen's chapel and now a café. The gleaming white board exterior and stumpy black Nordic spire act as an unusual focus for the Bay.

From Bute Park to Llandaff

Between Cardiff Castle and the River Taff lies **Bute Park**, once the private estate of the castle, and now containing an **arboretum** and some pleasant walks along the Taff banks. The main road crosses over the river at Cardiff Bridge, with a right turn leading up into the coolly formal **Sophia Gardens**. A quarter of a mile along the river is the multi-purpose **Welsh Institute of Sport**, the national sports centre and, beyond that, the home of Wales' sole first-class cricket team, and the less formal open spaces of **Pontcanna Fields**, which lead along the Taff for a couple of miles to the suburb of Llandaff.

Llandaff is a small, quiet ecclesiastical village two miles northwest of the city centre along Cathedral Road. The church that has now grown up into the city's **cathedral** is believed to have been founded in the sixth century by Saint Teilo, but was rebuilt in Norman style from 1120 and well into the thirteenth century. From the late fourteenth century, the cathedral fell into an advanced state of disrepair, hurried along by the adverse attention of Cromwell's soldiers during the Civil War. In the early eighteenth century, one of the twin towers and the nave roof collapsed. Restoration only began in earnest in the early 1840s, and Pre-Raphaelite artists such as Edward Burne-Jones, Dante Gabriel Rossetti and the firm of William Morris were commissioned for colourful new windows and decorative panels. Llandaff is evidently not a lucky cathedral, however, for in January 1941 a German landmine destroyed whole sections of it. Faithful and painstaking restoration was finally completed in 1960.

The fusion of different styles and ages is evident from outside, especially in the mismatched western towers. The northwest tower is by Jasper Tudor, a largely fifteenth-century work with modern embellishments, whilst the adjoining tower and spire were rebuilt from nineteenth-century designs. Inside, Jacob Epstein's overwhelming *Christ in Majesty* sculpture, a concrete parabola topped with a circular organ case on which sits a soaring Christ figure, was the only entirely new feature added in the postwar reconstruction, and dominates the nave today. At the west end of the north aisle, the **St Illtyd Chapel** features Rossetti's cloying triptych *The Seed of David*, whose figures – David the shepherd boy, David the King and the Virgin Mary – are modelled on Rossetti's Pre-Raphaelite friends. Most of the windows along the south aisle came from similar sources, namely

William Morris' stained glass company and Edward Burne-Jones. Along a little further, in the south presbytery, is the tenth-century Celtic cross that is the cathedral's only pre-Norman survivor.

At the far end of the cathedral is the elegantly vaulted and beautifully painted **Lady Chapel**, notable for its gaudy fifteenth-century reredos on the back wall that contains, surrounded by golden twigs and blackthorn in each niche, bronze panels with named flowers (in Welsh) in honour of Our Lady. Over two dozen flowers take their Welsh names from the Virgin Mary.

Eating

The city's longstanding internationalism has paid handsome dividends in the range of **restaurants**. One of the largest and best-established communities in south Wales is Italian, still evident in the range of cafés, bistros and restaurants. Most places are within easy walking distance of the city centre, although a few of the better cafés and restaurants are in the cheaper corners of Cathays and Roath (particularly the curry houses along Crwys, Albany and City roads), a stone's throw from the centre beyond the University, and some of the old docker's haunts around Cardiff Bay. The speed of change and gentrification here means that many have undergone metamorphosis into expensive showpiece bars and restaurants.

For bargain-priced **takeaways** in the city centre, your best bet is Caroline Street, between St Mary Street, and the bottom of the Hayes. St Mary Street, especially the lower end towards the station, is the home of numerous reliable pizza and pasta chains.

Welsh

Armless Dragon, 97 Wyverne Rd, Cathays (☎0222/382357). Unusual and enjoyable restaurant, with a good range of Welsh dishes amongst a wider bill of fresh fish and game. Closed Sun. Moderate to expensive.

Blas ar Gymru, 48 Crwys Rd, Cathays (☎0222/382132). Meaning "taste of Wales", this is a comfortable restaurant with a highly imaginative menu culled from delicious traditional recipes of every corner of Wales. Leave room for the selection of Welsh cheeses. Closed Sun. Moderate.

Celtic Cauldron, Castle Arcade. Right opposite the castle's main entrance is this friendly daytime café, dedicated to bringing a range of simple Welsh food – soups, stews, laver bread, cakes – to an appreciative audience. Inexpensive.

Yesterdays, The Lodge, Sophia Close, off Cathedral Rd, Pontcanna (☎0222/371420). Slightly pretentious Victorian decor, but the food – a strange combination of Welsh and Japanese cuisine – is excellent. Moderate to expensive.

British

Babs' Bistro, 14 West Bute St, Cardiff Bay. Legendary licensed café, serving great piles of Italian and British food (usually laced with a mountain of chips) until 7.30pm in the week and right through the small hours between Thursday and Saturday. Popular after-club haunt at the weekend. Inexpensive.

Louis Restaurant, 32 St Mary St. Wonderful old-fashioned tea rooms with an eclectic mix of genteel old ladies and bargain-hungry students. Food is basic, cheap, lavish in quantity and superb in quality. Last orders 7.45pm Mon–Sat; closed Sun. Inexpensive.

New Harvesters, 5 Pontcanna St, Canton (☎0222/549866). Small restaurant with a limited menu of fresh and extremely well-cooked British food. Closed Sun. Moderate.

Italian

Da Giovanni Ciao Ciao, The Hayes (☎0222/220077). One of Cardiff's best-reputed Italian restaurants, Giovanni's is lively and enormously friendly, with a wide menu of old favourites and some unusual house specialities. Closed Sun. Moderate.

Saverio, 110–112 Caerphilly Rd, Heath (☎0222/623344). Busy and friendly traditional Italian trattoria in the north of the city. Inexpensive.

International

Bombay Brasserie, 175 City Rd, Roath (☎0222/494779). One of the better Indian restaurants amongst the many in the area. Inexpensive.

Bo Zan, 78 Albany Rd, Roath (☎0222/493617). Functional Chinese restaurant, serving a fairly standard range of dishes which belie their place at the lower end of the price range. Popular with students. Closed Sun, and Mon lunch. Inexpensive.

La Brasserie, 60 St Mary St (☎0222/372164). Extremely loud and lively, with beautifully prepared French food and a speciality of sublime charcoal grills. Moderate.

Noble House, 9–10 St David's House, Wood St (☎0222/388317). The best Chinese restaurant in town, with an excellent range of Peking and Szechuan dishes. Moderate.

Taste of India, 103–105 Woodville Rd, Cathays (☎0222/228863). Well-priced Indian restaurant, frequented by students. Inexpensive.

Drinking

Cardiff's pub life has expanded exponentially over recent years, and includes some wonderful Edwardian palaces of etched smoky glass and deep red wood. Don't forget Cardiff's own beer, Brains, whose Bitter is pale and refreshing and whose Dark is a deep mild that should not be missed on a visit to its home city.

Chapter, Market Road, Canton. Three bars in the arts complex, far better than the traditional rather downmarket arts centre bar. Good choice of real ale and whisky.

Duke of Wellington, corner of Caroline St and The Hayes. Over-restored Edwardian city pub, serving excellent beer, piped all the way from the brewery next door.

Four Bars Inn, Castle St. Basic and smoky jazz (and occasional folk) pub-cum-club with few fripperies but a great atmosphere. Nightly music.

Golden Cross, 283 Hayes Bridge Rd. A few hundred yards from the Duke of Wellington, but a far better bet for an unhurried pint of beer in a more laid-back restored Victorian atmosphere. Has some beautiful tiled pictures of yesteryear Cardiff.

Mulligan's, corner of St Mary's and Caroline streets. Packed Irish pub with regular live music sessions.

Old Arcade, Church St. Small, old-fashioned arcade bar next to the market, opening its lounge bar on busy nights only. Popular with rugby enthusiasts for its game memorabilia.

Rummer Tavern, 14 Duke St. Opposite the castle entrance is a dark, wooden city pub with a varied clientele of shoppers in the day and young people in the evening.

Nightlife

Top-flight **concert venues** such as *St David's Hall* and the *Cardiff International Arena* have brought internationally acclaimed orchestras and performers to the city, although these sterile environments are no match for the sweatier gigs and traditional rock found in some of Cardiff's earthier pubs and clubs. The burgeoning Welsh rock scene, both English and Welsh language, breaks out regularly in the capital. Cardiff is also used as the home of the magnificent *Welsh National Opera* – the only major British company to have grown organically from long-established amateur roots – and a significant number of touring Welsh theatre companies.

Venues and clubs

Club Mix, High St (☎0222/529127). Trendy rave and indie club, standing way out from the dross of many city centre clubs.

Clwb Ifor Bach, Womanby St (☎0222/232199). A sweaty and massively fun live music club with nightly gigs and sessions, many by Welsh language bands.

Dog and Duck, Womanby St (☎0222/224754). Late-night beer-swilling music club.

Faces, 7 High St (☎0222/226468). Guest DJs and Happy House nights in a much revamped club.

Gassey Jacks, 39–41 Salisbury Rd, Cathays (☎0222/239388). Loud, boisterous and enjoyable pub and club, with nightly live RnB, blues, soul and jazz in a studenty environment.

Sam's Bar, 63 St Mary St (☎0222/345189). Lively mixed bar, with regular folk, stand-up comedy, rock and indie music.

Student Union, Park Place (☎0222/396421). Big name live bands in an impressive club complex, open to non-students.

The lesbian and gay scene

Although the scene in the city is far from massive, it has grown in both size and confidence over the last couple of years. The best source for current information and advice is **Friend** (Tues–Sat 8–10pm; ☎0222/340101) or **Lesbian Line** (Tues 8–10pm; ☎0222/374051). All venues are for men and women.

Charlie's, Wesley Lane. Tucked away in a small side street near *Club X* and the *Exit*, *Charlie's* is a quiet but highly enjoyable gay restaurant. Inexpensive to moderate.

Club X, 39 Charles St. Stylish and popular gay club, open until 2am between Wednesday and Saturday.

Exit Bar, 48 Charles St. Opposite *Club X*, this is where most people have their pre-club drinks. Late-opening (until midnight) disco bar, with loud music and frantic atmosphere.

King's Cross, Hayes Bridge Rd/Caroline St. Large and long-established gay pub, with few frills but a friendly atmosphere.

Theatre, cinema and classical music

Theatre in Cardiff encompasses everything from the radical and alternative at the *Sherman* and the *Chapter* to big, blowzy productions at the *New Theatre*, home of the *Welsh National Opera*. Classical music is best heard at *St David's Hall*, although the newly opened *Cardiff International Arena* is likely to siphon off some of the more prestigious shows.

Theatre

Chapter Arts Centre, Market Rd, Canton (☎0222/399666). Home of fine British and touring theatre and dance companies in a multi-use arts complex.

New Theatre, Park Place (☎0222/394844). Splendid Edwardian city centre theatre that plays host to big London shows. Currently the home of the *Welsh National Opera*, at least until their shiny new opera house is built in Cardiff Bay.

St Stephen's Theatre, West Bute St, Cardiff Bay (☎0222/498885). Experimental theatre from the resident *Moving Being* company, as well as visiting performers.

Sherman Theatre, Senghenydd Rd, Cathays (☎0222/230451). An excellent two-auditorium repertory theatre hosting a mixed bag of new and translated classic Welsh language pieces, stand-up comedy, children's entertainment, drama classics, music and dance. Many plays on Welsh themes in both English and Welsh.

Cinema

Capitol Odeon, Capitol Shopping Centre, Queen St (☎0222/227058).

Chapter, Market Rd, Canton (☎0222/399666). Cardiff's main arthouse and alternative film centre, with two screens.

MGM, 63 Queen St (☎0222/231715).

Odeon, 55 Queen St (☎0222/227058).

Classical music

Cardiff International Arena, Harlech Court, Bute Terrace (☎0222/464141). Mighty impressive new development, rising high over the city centre's southern streets. Occasional venue for visiting international orchestras and operas.

Cardiff Male Voice Choir, c/o 577 Cowbridge Rd East (☎0222/563488). Regular perfomances in the city and twice weekly rehearsal nights (Wed and Fri), to which members of the public are welcome. Phone first for details.

St David's Hall, The Hayes (☎0222/371236). Part of the massive St David's shopping centre, this large and glamorous venue is possibly the most architecturally exciting building in town. Home to visiting orchestras and musicians from jazz to opera, it's frequently used by the excellent *BBC Welsh Symphony Orchestra and Chorus*.

University Concert Hall, Corbett Rd, Cathays Park (☎0222/874816). Home of public concerts by university and local orchestras, jazz groups and easy listening ensembles.

Welsh National Opera – see *New Theatre* above.

Listings

Airlines *Cardiff Air Travel* for general information (☎0446/711777); *Manx Airlines* (☎0222/342797).

Airport Cardiff-Wales, out at Rhoose, near Barry (☎0446/711111).

Bike rental *Taff Trail Cycle Hire*, Forest Farm Country Park, Whitchurch (Easter–Oct daily 10am–6pm; ☎0222/751235). Located on the other side of the river footbridge from Radyr station.

Books *Lear's* at 37 St Mary St, and in the Cardiff Students' Union in Senghennydd Rd, Cathays; *Dillons* at 1–2 St David's Link, The Hayes.

Bus enquiries *Cardiff Bus* (☎0222/396521); *National Express* (☎0222/344751).

Car rental *Avis*, 4 Saunders Rd, Station Approach (☎0222/342111); *Crwys Auto Service*, 59 Crwys Rd (☎0222/225789); *Hertz*, 9 Central Square (☎0222/224548).

Dentist Emergency dental work at *Riverside Health Centre*, Wellington St, Canton (☎0222/371221).

Exchange *American Express*, 3 Queen St (☎0222/665843); *Commercial Bank of Wales*, 114 St Mary St (☎0222/396131); *Thomas Cook*, 56 Queen St (☎0222/343044).

Football Cardiff City, Ninian Park, Sloper Rd (☎0222/398636).

Hospital *Cardiff Royal Infirmary*, Newport Rd (☎0222/492233).

Laundries *Launderama*, 60 Lower Cathedral Rd; *GP*, 244 Cowbridge Rd, Canton; *Drift Inn*, 104 Salisbury Rd, Cathays Park.

Left luggage At Central station (Mon–Fri 10am–9pm, Sat 10am–8.30pm).

Newspapers and magazines The Cardiff-based daily *South Wales Echo* is a fairly uninspiring read, although it does have some good listings, especially for films in the city. For a wider overview of arts and events, pick up a free copy of *The Buzz!*, a monthly listings magazine.

Pharmacy *Boots*, 5 Wood St (Mon–Sat 8am–8pm, Sun 6–7pm; ☎0222/234043).

Police *Cardiff Central Police Station*, King Edward VII Ave, Cathays Park (☎0222/222111).

Post office The Hayes (Mon–Fri 9am–5.30pm, Sat 9am–12.30pm; ☎0222/227363).

Rugby International games at Cardiff Arms Park (☎0222/390111) and club matches next door on the Arms Park smaller pitch (☎0222/383546).

Swimming pools *Wales Empire Pool*, Wood St (☎0222/382296); *Welsh Institute of Sport*, Sophia Gardens (☎0222/397571).

Train enquiries ☎0222/228000 (daily 8am–10pm).

Travel agencies *Campus Travel* in the YHA shop, 13 Castle St (☎0222/220744); *John Cory Travel*, Park Place (☎0222/371878); *Welsh Travel Centre*, 240 Whitchurch Rd, Cathays (☎0222/621479).

Women's Cardiff *Cardiff Women's Centre*, 2 Coburn St, Cathays Park (☎0222/383024) for advice and information about local groups and events.

Around Cardiff

On the edge of the Cardiff suburbs, the thirteenth-century fairytale castle of **Castell Coch** stands on a hillside in woods. West of the city, the massively popular **Welsh Folk Museum** tells the country's history with bricks and mortar, with a sundry collection of buildings salvaged from all over Wales. The museum lies in the grounds of the rambling Elizabethan country house of **St Fagans Castle**, restored over the centuries by its various owners.

Castell Coch

Four miles north of Llandaff is the plain village of **TONGWYNLAIS**, above which the coned turrets of **Castell Coch** (April to mid-Oct daily 9.30am–6.30pm; mid-Oct to March Mon–Sat 9.30am–4pm, Sun 2–4pm; CADW; £2) rise mysteriously out of the steep wooded hillside, a ruined thirteenth-century fortress that was rebuilt and transformed into a fantasy castle in the late 1870s by William Burges for the third Marquess of Bute. With its working portcullis and drawbridge, Castell Coch is the ultimate wealthy man's medieval fantasy, isolated on its almost Alpine hillside, yet only a few hundred yards from the motorway and Cardiff suburbs. Many similarities with their joint work on Cardiff Castle can be seen here, notably the outrageously lavish decor, culled from religious and moral fables, that dazzle in each room. Lady Bute's bedroom, at the top of one of the three towers, comes complete with a fabulously painted double dome, around which are 28 panels depicting frolicking monkeys, some of which were considered to be far too lascivious for their day. Bus #136 from Central station turns round at the castle gates, or the #26 drops in Tongwynlais village, from where it's a ten-minute climb.

The Welsh Folk Museum and St Fagans Castle

Separated from Cardiff by only a sliver of greenery, the village of **ST FAGANS** (Sain Ffagan), four miles west of the city centre, none the less has a rural feel that is only partially disturbed by the busloads of tourists that roll in regularly to visit the **Welsh Folk Museum** (daily 10am–5pm; Nov–March closed Sun; £3.50), a branch of the excellent National Museum of Wales built around **St Fagans Castle**, a country house built in 1580 on the site of a ruined Norman castle and furnished in early nineteenth-century style, complete with heavy oak furniture and gloomy portraits. The mansion's formal gardens and eighteenth-century fishponds have also been restored to something akin to their original design.

The collection of buildings from all corners of Wales have been carefully dismantled and rebuilt on this site since the museum's inception in 1946. The most impressive part of the museum is the fifty-acre **outdoor collection** of buildings, which were saved from extinction and re-erected on this site. There are particular highlights, like the diminutive whitewashed 1777 **Pen-Rhiw Chapel** from Dyfed, the pristine and evocative Victorian **St Mary's Board School** from Lampeter and the ordered mini-fortress of a 1772 **Tollhouse** that once guarded the southern approach to Aberystwyth. Many of the domestic buildings are farmhouses of different ages and styles – compare, for example, the grandeur of the seventeenth-century red-painted **Kennixton Farmhouse** from the Gower or the homely Edwardian comforts of **Llwyn-yr-Eos Farm** with the paucity of luxury in the Gwynedd farmworkers' **Llainfadyn Cottage**.

The best demonstration of how life changed over the years for a section of the Welsh population comes in the superlative **Rhyd-y-car** ironworkers' cottages from Merthyr Tydfil. Built originally around 1800, each of the six houses, with their accompanying strip of garden, has been furnished in the style of a different era – stretching from 1805 to 1985. Even the frontages and roofs are true to their age, offering a wade through working-class Welsh life over the past century. Next door are the Victorian **Gwalia Stores** from the mining community of Ogmore Vale, whose deep smell of polished mahogany is as evocative as the starchy-aproned assistants and jars of boiled sweets on sale. A large and interesting variety of workplaces, including a stinking **tannery**, a **pottery**, three **mills**, a **bakehouse** and a **smithy**, most of which house people demonstrating the original methods, make up a large number of the remaining buildings. Hourly bus #32 (and the irregular #C1) leaves Central station for the village.

The Vale of Glamorgan

The bowl of land at the very bottom of Wales is known as the **Vale of Glamorgan**, a rich, pastoral land of gentle countryside shelving down to a cliff-ridden coastline, punctuated by long, sandy beaches. The Vale does not feature on many visitors' itineraries, as they speed through from Cardiff to Swansea, the Gower and the west. This really is their loss, for the quiet and pretty towns, together with the sheer profusion of excellent beaches and tumbledown castles warrant a good couple of days' exploration. Public transport is easy and, being so close to Cardiff, thorough. Brash seaside resorts at **Porthcawl** in the west and **Barry** to the east contrast with the far more refined, breezy atmosphere of **Penarth**, a crusty seaside town clinging on to the coat tails of Cardiff. In between lie yawning wide bays, bracing cliff walks and spectacular ruins of castles and priories. At the western tip of the Vale coast is **Kenfig**, a vast grass-spotted desert of coastal dunes and nature reserves.

Inland, the lower parts of the Vale are a curious mix of urban reminders such as Wales' major **airport** at Rhoose and occasional looming factories, set against rolling green pastureland sprinkled with charming, if scarcely thrilling, market towns like **Cowbridge**, **Llantrisant** and, most pleasing of all, **Llantwit Major**.

Barry and Penarth, almost suburbs of Cardiff, are easily reached by bus and train. Further west, the only mainline train route through the Vale has a stop at Bridgend, a useful interchange for bus services to the coast and some of the larger inland settlements. Alternatively, buses from Cardiff reach most places.

Penarth and around

Considering itself to be a cut above the boisterous capital of Cardiff and the down-beat resort of Barry, **PENARTH** is a quietly enjoyable town wedged between the two. The Cardiff Bay developments over on the other side of the Ely estuary are lending benefits to the town, and new roads are drawing Penarth ever more inexorably into Cardiff, despite the actions of staunch denizens of the town to ensure the independence of this half plush suburb, half seaside resort. In any event, it's an easy, enjoyable day out from Cardiff, if not really a place to stay.

The Town

Penarth is the end of the train line from Cardiff, receiving half-hourly shuttle trains that ply their way from here, through the capital, and out into the valleys. From the train station, a path on the right leads up to Stanwell Road, which continues into the clean-cut Edwardian shopping streets of the town centre.

The redbrick **Turner House Art Gallery** (opening times and prices variable; ☎0222/708870) is on the Plymouth Road, and houses temporary exhibitions, usually brought out from the National Museum of Wales' vast collection.

The Dingle path runs down the left-hand side of the Turner House, leading into the showy civic **Alexandra Park**, from which it is easy to glean Penarth's character from the oceans of flower beds, elderly inhabitants on the many benches and bandstand. This picture only intensifies on continuing down the hill on to the charmingly fusty **Esplanade**, with the amusement arcade in the green bubble of a hall on the pier, which also houses the seasonal tourist office and a few fish-and-chip stands. The overall effect, even in the garishly painted wrought-iron seafront, is sedately pleasing.

Flat Holm and Lavernock Point

Two miles due south of Penarth is **Lavernock Point**, jutting out into the Bristol Channel, a forlorn setting for campsites and pubs, but notable as the place in which conversation was first heard by means of radio waves. This – as a plaque on the wall of the dismal Victorian chapel notes – took place on 11 May 1897, when Guglielmo Marconi sent the immortal words "Are you ready?" over to his assistant George Kemp on the island of **Flat Holm**, three miles out in the Bristol Channel. From Penarth or Lavernock, it is easy to see that Flat Holm (Welsh) and its near neighbour, Steep Holm (English) live up to their names, with Steep Holm jutting proudly out of the water like a great whale and Flat Holm, by contrast, looking like a large dirty plate tipping gently into the waves, crowned with a lighthouse.

Flat Holm has been used as a Viking anchorage, a cholera hospital, a lighthouse and a look-out point. Today it's an interesting and beautifully remote nature reserve, the nest of thousands of gulls and shelduck. **Boats** depart daily in season, and irregularly in the winter, from Barry Harbour. Overnight stays are possible in the small **hostel** on the island. Both the boats and the hostel are operated by the Flat Holm Project in the Old Police Station on Harbour Road in Barry (☎0446/747661; ①).

Lavernock Point is a fifteen-minute walk from the bus stop on the B4267. Half-hourly bus #P4 operates from Cardiff and Penarth, dropping just near the dreadful **Comeston Medieval Village**, a tourist board excuse for an attraction that should be avoided.

Practicalities

Penarth's **tourist office** kiosk (April–June & Sept Fri–Sun 10am–6pm; July–Aug daily 10am–6pm; ☎0222/708849) is at the head of the pier on the Esplanade. For those wishing to see Cardiff without the bustle of city life, staying in Penarth is a good option – **accommodation** ranges from the well-placed *Croeso* guesthouse, 13 Plymouth Rd, near the station (☎0222/709167; ②), and the *Alandale* at no. 17 (☎0222/709226; ②), to the frillier surrounds of the Victorian *Raisdale House Hotel* on Raisdale Road, off the Plymouth Road (☎0222/707317; ③). The dingy *Lavernock Point Holiday Estate* (☎0222/707310) has tent pitches. Along Penarth Esplanade are a number of pricy **restaurants**. Cheapest for hearty English and Italian snacks is *Rabaiotti's*. Pizza and pastas are available at *Villa Napoli* in the *Glendale Hotel*, 10 Plymouth Rd, or there's the *Prince of India* (closed Sun) at 13 Ludlow Lane, tucked behind the main shops on Windsor Road. For **pubs**, try the enjoyably scruffy and youngish *Railway*, behind the station on Plymouth Road.

Barry and Barry Island

Good only as a day trip, the brashest seaside resort in south Wales is **BARRY** (Barri), whose speciality of loud, chip-swallowing, beer-swilling seaside fun is a million miles from the effete coastal charms of Penarth, or any of the small villages further along the Vale coast. Barry was, until the 1880s, a small fishing village and was developed as a rival port to the Bute family's Cardiff, and line upon line of neat, genteel avenues – many with cheap B&Bs – still run down to the town's quieter, stonier beach at **The Knap**; here, you'll find an old-fashioned open air **lido pool** (Easter–Sept school holidays, Sat & Sun 10am–6pm; term time daily noon–6pm, weather permitting).

Most of the resort's activity centres on **BARRY ISLAND** (Ynys y Barri), an odd-shaped stump of land that sticks out from the town along Harbour Road, a riotous sprawl of fun fairs, promenades and chip shops. Bang opposite is the **Pleasure Park** (daily Easter–June & Sept–Oct 1–10pm; July–Aug 11am–10pm), a fairly shabby collection of rides, arcades and fairground attractions. To the left is the enormous residential **Barry Island Resort** (Easter–Oct daily 10am–11.30pm; £5 for non-residents for the day), an ex-Butlin's holiday camp that has all of the allure and architectural appeal of a prison camp, but which is stuffed to the gunwales with rides (free after you've paid the entrance fee), tacky end-of-the-pier entertainment by small-time TV personalities, pools with slides and glitzy theme bars around every corner.

The Resort stretches out behind barbed-wire fences along one headland that frames the eastern end of the main beach, **Whitmore Bay**. Running behind the sands is a dowdy old promenade, the focal point for legions of fun pubs, cheap cafés and bleeping, flashing amusement arcades. At the back of the Prom is the **tourist office** (April–Sept daily 10am–6pm; ☎0446/747171). Trains rattle through Barry Docks and Barry stations before terminating at Barry Island.

The Vale coast

West of Barry, the coast of the Vale of Glamorgan alternates between craggy cliffs and wide, white sand beaches. Arriving at **LLANTWIT MAJOR** (Llanilltud Fawr) is deceptively mundane, as the rickety winding streets of the village centre have been surrounded by modern housing estates and rows of ugly shops. Despite this, the town has an ancient pedigree, and is most noted as the centre of Saint Illtud's ministry around 500 AD. Here, the scholarly Illtud educated a succession of young men at his monastery, giving the town the chance to claim the title of Britain's earliest centre of learning. Amongst Illtud's pupils were Saint David himself and Saint Patrick, who was abducted from the monastery by Irish pirates to become their patron saint.

Buses decant their passengers behind the 1960s Napolean Way precinct, from where it's a short walk down East Street or Station Road into the town centre. A miniature Italianate **town hall** sits just before the main town square and was built in the fifteenth century as the replacement of one destroyed by Owain Glyndŵr; it now serves as council offices and a **tourist office** (Mon–Fri 9am–1pm & 2–4pm; Easter–Sept also Sat 9am–5pm, Sun 2–5pm; ☎0446/796086). From here, Burial Lane winds its way past the triangular pub-lined village square and down to the front of the magnificent **parish church**, sheltering in a hollow next to the trickle of the Col Huw River.

The first thing that strikes you about the church is its size: it is, in fact, two churches joined at the tower. The older west church, nearer the stream, dates from around 1100, and in the twelfth and thirteenth centuries, aisles were added to transform it into the nave of a new church. The west church is notable for the collection of decorative Celtic crosses and stones arranged haphazardly inside. Prize amongst these is the exquisitely carved eighth-century boulder at the back of the church, on which the letters ILT and half of a U (remains of ILTUD) can still be made out. A guidebook (£2) about the church and its history is available from *Harvest Pottery*, opposite the front entrance on Church Street.

At the junction at the top of Burial Lane, Colhugh Street descends for a little over a mile along the scrubby valley of the Col Huw River to the partially sandy **beach**, starting-point for some wonderful walks along the caves and inlets of the stratified cliffs and back into the rolling countryside. The best route to take is the path that runs west along the cliff tops for two miles to **St Donat's Bay**, dominated by a mock Gothic castle, now an American college. Halfway along, a path dips down to the beach at **Tresilian Bay**, from where you can return to Col Huw cove along the beach. In the other direction, you can climb wooden steps at the side of the Col Huw car park and walk along the precarious cliffs to Stout Point, a mile away.

Llantwit Major is well blessed with good pubs and recreational facilities, making it pleasant enough to stay. For **accommodation**, try the quiet *West House Country Hotel* (☎0446/792406; ③), between the parish church and the castle ruins; for B&B there's the friendly *Curriers Guest House* in the main square (☎0446/793506; ③), peaceful *Mrs Plested's*, 2 Anchor Cottages on Colhugh Street (☎0446/792727; ②), or *Kenilworth House* on Station Road (☎0446/796900; ③). Rose Dew Farm on Ham Lane South has the *Acorn* **campsite** (☎0446/794024).

For **food**, there are cheap takeaways along East Street and its continuation, Boverton Road, or, in the old town centre, try the daytime *Truffles* café in Church Street, where you should leave plenty of room for their sublime homemade chocolates. The best restaurant in town is fairly pricy *Italian Joe's* on Colhugh Street (☎0446/792321), or, for something cheaper, most of the town centre **pubs** do food at lunchtime and in the evening. Of them all, the *Old White Hart* on the Square is best for food and has a pleasant enough atmosphere, although the nearby *Tudor Tavern* is more of an earthy drinking hole.

Southerndown and Ogmore

West of Llantwit Major, the coast ducks and dives past remote, sandy beaches and cliffs, punctuated by small streams trickling in from the lush farmland behind. **SOUTHERNDOWN** is a diffuse holiday village of touristy pubs and one excellent restaurant – the fairly expensive *Frolics* on Beach Road (☎0656/880127; closed Sun & Mon), with a creative and wholesome menu dictated entirely by seasonal specialities – but the real reason for coming here is **Dunraven Bay**, a beautiful, wide beach backed by the jagged cliffs whose different layers of limestone and shale are perfectly defined. In the busy car park by Dunraven Beach is the **Heritage Coast Centre** (☎0656/880157), a small information point about walks and drives you can do along this splendid part of the south Wales coastline. This is the western end of a magnificent five-mile **coastal walk**, dipping down into tiny, wooded valleys and up across wide stretches of cliff and sand.

The village of **OGMORE** (Ogwr) is a straggling, windswept sort of place, but lies close to the remains of **Ogmore Castle**, situated about a mile north along the coast from Southerndown. The castle's position is stunning, in the very bottom of a flat valley, sided by tree-clad hillsides and peaks of dunes behind them. The castle dates from the Norman Conquest in around 1100, and its solid central stone keep, in which a few original windows are still intact, was added later in the twelfth century.

Ewenny Priory

Two miles further up the B4524 is **EWENNY**, a village whose main drawcard is the towering remains of Benedictine **Ewenny Priory**, tucked away down leafy lanes, three-quarters of a mile to the east of the village. Founded in 1141, the priory's formidable fortress-like walls were intended to protect against the hostile Welsh, who saw the Benedictines as little more than lapdogs of the Norman invaders. The walls, strengthened continuously throughout the thirteenth century, are still very much intact today, broken only by the two huge gateways in which the portcullis holes can still be seen. The priory was dissolved during the Dissolution of the monasteries, shortly after which a private house was built in the precincts, and it is not possible to visit.

The priory **church**, on the other side of the mansion, is squat and powerful, brooding over the ecclesiastical remains scattered around it. It is divided into two sections by a plain early medieval rood screen. On the western side (nearest to the rest of the priory) is the nave, whose damp, cold interior includes some splendid Norman windows. This nave served as the parish church, as opposed to the eastern chancel, which housed the monastic chapel.

Merthyr Mawr

On the banks of the Ogmore River two miles west of Ewenny, the small village of **MERTHYR MAWR** seems a rural haven of unexpected beauty. A narrow lane steers around into the village of neat thatched and whitewashed cottages. The lane continues along a wooded glen to its end on the edge of the great dune desert of Merthyr Mawr, stretching over miles to the distant sea. By the car park is the gaunt ruin of **Candleston Castle**, a fifteenth-century fortified manor house that was abandoned last century as the shifting sands came too close. There is a **campsite** (☎0656/652038) for those seeking solitude.

Porthcawl

Once one of Wales' most popular seaside resorts, **PORTHCAWL** has been on a downward slide for years. Tatty bungalows and depressing caravan parks announce entry into the town, now little more than a retirement centre. Recent years have seen concerted attempts to re-ignite the spark of the town with limited success: half-decent entertainment tends to bypass the place and, apart from the usual clutch of tacky seaside shops, cheap B&Bs and pubs alongside some safe, sandy beaches, there is little here to excite the adventurous visitor.

Half-hourly buses connect Bridgend with Porthcawl, depositing travellers at the top of John Street in the town centre. A two-minute walk straight down leads along the pedestrianized John Street, where the Old Police Station houses the less-than-friendly **tourist office** (April–Sept Mon–Sat 9.30am–5.30pm; ☎0656/782211), who give away a fairly useful free town guide, and there's a sporadically open local history **museum** in the police station. John Street continues down to the Esplanade, a typical line of Victorian and Edwardian hotels along a rocky beach, and where you'll find the domed **Grand Pavilion**, home to assorted seaside entertainment shows, pantomimes and the like. East, the Esplanade runs to a lifeboat station at the harbour before veering north with the coast as Eastern Promenade. Here are the solid seaside attractions: the **Coney Beach amusement park** behind whelk stalls and candy floss shops that look out over the donkey rides on Sandy Bay, and two vast caravan parks perched over this cove and neighbouring Trecco Bay. On the northwest side of town, a 20-minute walk from the centre, is the far quieter and more beautiful **Rest Bay**.

Accommodation in Porthcawl is plentiful, cheap and mostly concentrated around Mary Street, Gordon Road and Esplananade Avenue: right in the centre are the *Collingwood Hotel*, 40 Mary St (☎0656/782899; ③), the slightly plusher *Minerva Hotel*, 52 Esplanade Ave (☎0656/782428; ③), *Rossett House*, 1 Esplanade Ave (☎0656/771664; ②), and the welcoming *Rosedale Guest House*, 48 Esplanade Ave (☎0656/785356; ②). There are dozens of places to **eat** in the hotels, pubs and cafés strewn around the town centre; one of the best, surprisingly, is *Pizza R Us*, 108 John St (☎0656/773900), serving a sturdy range of good pizzas. Of the many **pubs**, the *Rock Hotel*, 98 John St, has decent beer and generous food.

Kenfig

The cliffs and beaches north of Porthcawl stop at the one-time fishing port of **KENFIG** (Cynffig), two miles along the coast, where a thriving community founded in the Bronze Age was finally overwhelmed by the shifting sand dunes in the sixteenth century – they have obliterated whole swathes of land, burying houses and the church in its path; the only surviving remains of the town are the miserable stumps of the **castle**. Today, the dunes of Kenfig Burrows have been stabilized by marram grass plantations, and the whole site is open as a **nature reserve** (summer daily 10am–5pm; winter Sat & Sun 2–5pm), with a small display about local wildlife and advice for those who want to go walking or birdwatching at the hide by the freshwater **Kenfig Pool**. Apart from the inevitable gulls, frequent visitors here are oystercatchers, ringed plovers and redshanks. Most remarkable is the reserve's backdrop: firstly the smoking stacks of the Port Talbot steel works and secondly, the great, hazy curve of Swansea Bay stretching for dozens of miles to the Gower. When in Kenfig, don't miss the historic *Prince of Wales* inn over the road from the nature reserve, the main survivor of the old port.

The inland Vale

Although the scenery is not as startling as the coast, the rural land of the Vale of Glamorgan is speckled with some interesting towns, villages and ruined castles, connected by small, high-hedged lanes. **Llantrisant**, a hilltop market town just off the M4, sits astride the border of mountainous valley and rural vale, while **Cowbridge**, seven miles south, nestles firmly in a green patchwork of countryside, secure in its quiet charms as the unofficial capital of the Vale.

Llantrisant

LLANTRISANT perches dramatically between two peaks that rise suddenly out of the flattened valley of the rivers Ely and Clun, ten miles west of Cardiff, and was once encircled by fortifications to exploit its natural position as a watching post over the Vale of Glamorgan.

The centre of the small town is the **Bull Ring**, where there's a suitably wild-eyed statue (donated by the Cremation Society) of **Dr William Price** (1800–93), dressed in his favoured druid's outfit of moons, stars and a fox fur on his head. Dr Price subscribed to some wonderful beliefs – vegetarianism, nudity, republicanism, the unhealthiness of socks, anti-smoking, free love and the potential environmental disasters from mass industrialization; many have since passed into common parlance. He is best remembered for cremating his dead infant son, Iesu Grist (Welsh for Jesus Christ), in a makeshift service on Llantrisant Common in January 1884, burning the small body in an oil drum. He was arrested and, in a sensational trial at Cardiff, acquitted, after which cremation was made legal.

Overlooking the Bull Ring is the **Model House Craft and Design Centre** (closed Jan–April Mon & Tues), which serves as one of the region's best centres for exhibitions, workshops and conventions. It also houses a shop where local crafts are sold, the excellent *Workshouse* café and a permanent display on the work of the **Royal Mint**, moved here from London in 1967. All British coins are now minted at Llantrisant, and the small display runs through some of the historical background that produced one national mint, including examples of coins from the eighteenth and nineteenth centuries and some of the heavy old machinery that once had to be employed.

Cowbridge

The A48 now bypasses **COWBRIDGE** (Y Bont Faen) – and you might want to do the same – although the smugly prosperous town boasts an interesting range of architectural styles and numerous good pubs and restaurants. The town's Norman street pattern, focusing on the main street, is still evident, stretching for almost a mile in a virtual straight line. On the south side of the High Street, Church Street leads under the narrow gatehouse that is the sole remainder of the town's fourteenth-century walls. One third of a mile further east along the High Street is *Basil's Brasserie* if you have to stop for a bite to eat.

A little more than a mile out of town, down a quiet lane fringed with high hedges, there is a tiny layby opposite the Regency finery of Howe Mill. A path opposite leads along the bank of the River Thaw for quarter of a mile to the gauntly impressive ruins of **Beaupre Castle**, largely an Elizabethan manor house. Built by the local noble family, the Bassetts, Beaupre is a huge shell of ruined Italianate doorways and vast mullioned windows in the middle of a quiet Glamorgan field.

Vale of Neath

The **Vale of Neath** likes to think of itself as a world apart from the Valleys, looking more towards Cymric Swansea than anglicized Cardiff. **Neath**, the focal point of the Vale, is a curious town with antiquities dating from the Roman, Norman and medieval periods, all set in grim industrial surroundings that somehow make them all the more remarkable. The River Neath flows in from the northeast, past **Aberdulais**, where the waterfalls are now having their accompanying industrial buildings that date from sixteenth-century copper workings restored. The falls are on the Dulais River, which heads north to the **Cefn Coed Colliery Museum**.

Winding east from Neath is the B4287, climbing into the conifer forests around the village of **Pontrhydyfen**, the birthplace of one of Wales' greatest-known exports, Richard Burton, whose quiet village sits on the Afan River in a valley that is a spectacular montage of crisp mountains, forests and clear streams. A couple of miles down the track is the **Afan Argoed Country Park**, including the excellent **colliery museum**.

Neath

Recently cleaned up, the town of **NEATH** (Castell-Nedd) has overcome its past as a centre of copper smelting to become a spacious, pleasantly ordinary place that is much overshadowed by near neighbour Swansea. The tumbledown **castle** ruins (closed to the public) sit unhappily in a corner of the *Safeway* car park, and the most picturesque corner of town is Church Place, where the borough **museum** (Tues–Sat 10am–4pm; free), a mildly interesting ramble through Neath's history over the past six thousand years, is housed in the splendid surroundings of the Old Mechanics' Institution. Just outside of town on the A465 are the remains of **Neath Abbey** (April–Oct Mon–Sat 9.30am–6.30pm, Sun 2–6.30pm; Nov–March Mon–Sat 9.30am–4pm, Sun 2–4pm; CADW; £1). The ghostly, dark silhouette of the abbey, founded in the early twelfth century, is wedged in amongst an industrial estate and oily canal. In the sixteenth century, a chunk of the abbey was converted into a mansion, which later metamorphosed into a copper smelting works.

Aberdulais and around

Two miles further up the River Neath (accessible by hourly bus from Station Square in Neath) is the village of **ABERDULAIS**, where the River Dulais tumbles over the scoops and platforms of the **Aberdulais Falls** (April–Oct Mon–Fri 10am–5pm, Sat–Sun 11am–6pm; Nov–March daily 11am–4pm; NT; £2.50). The natural power of the site was first harnessed in 1584 for a copper works that developed into a corn mill, ironworks and, a tin-plating unit in the nineteenth century. One hundred and sixty million litres of deep green water course over the rocks every day, gouging out bowls of rock and pouring over precarious lips jutting out over the spume below. In the old stable block, an excellent **interpretive centre** contains a glass-fronted window onto one of the falls' subterranean channels, where pounding water can be seen rushing by, inches away. It also contains replicas of some of the many paintings of the falls, a venue beloved of eighteenth- and nineteenth-century landscapists, including Turner.

On the other side of the main road, beyond the Falls' car park, is the **canal basin** of the restored Neath canal, fed by a curious low-slung aqueduct over the wide River Dulais. The walk from here through the woods to the basin at **RESOLVEN**, four miles northeast, is beautiful as it criss-crosses the route of the river at the bottom of the Vale of Neath.

The main A465 heads up the Vale from Aberdulais, with the A4109 branching off north to the **Cefn Coed Colliery Museum** (April–Sept daily 10.30am–6pm; Oct–March daily 10.30am–4pm; £1.50), four miles away. Although not as impressive as the Rhondda Heritage Park or Big Pit, Cefn Coed includes a huge working winding engine, and some well-presented exhibitions about the site, once the deepest anthracite mine in the world. There are also some glorious signposted walks from the museum up into the surrounding wooded hills.

Pontrhydyfen

Winding east from Neath town centre, the B4287 climbs five miles into the starkly beautiful village of **PONTRHYDYFEN**, dominated by its redundant viaduct. In a small house at its foot, the actor Richard Burton was born. The viaduct passes over the confluence of the rivers Pelenna and Afan, the latter disgorging into the sea at Port Talbot, five miles to the south. The Afan meanders its way east from Pontrhydyfen through some of the most delightful scenery in the valleys, a steep, wooded gorge spattered with paths and bridleways. Two miles up the valley is **Afan Argoed Country Park**, complete with an an excellent **visitor centre** (April–Sept daily 10.30am–6pm; Oct Sat & Sun and half-term week 10.30am–6pm; Nov–March Sat & Sun 10am–5pm; ☎0639/850564), where bikes can be rented, and from which Land Rover tours across the mountains operate in the summer. The park is also home to the immensely enjoyable **Welsh Miners' Museum** (same times as above; 50p), where miners themselves tell of their lives. There is a particularly poignant section dedicated to the story of children that were sent underground. Regular buses operate from Neath and Port Talbot to Pontrhydyfen and Afan Argoed, en route to Cymmer and Glyncorrwg.

Swansea

An "ugly, lovely town" is the description applied by Dylan Thomas as summing up his birthplace, and it still seems true today. Large, sprawling and boisterous, **SWANSEA** (Abertawe) is the second city of Wales, with great aspirations to be the first. It's far more of a Welsh town than Cardiff, and you'll hear *yr iaith*, the Welsh language, spoken daily on the city's streets.

At first sight, Swansea seems summed up by Thomas' scathing epithet. A jumble of tower blocks and factory units dot the sloping horizons, gathered around the concrete city centre, massively rebuilt after devastating bomb attacks in World War II. But Swansea's multifarious charms appear on closer inspection: some intact old corners of the city centre, the spacious and graceful suburb of Uplands, a wide seafront overlooking the huge sweep of Swansea Bay and a bold marina development around the old docks. Spread throughout are some of the best funded museums in Wales. Another great bonus is the city's position on the fringe of the ever-popular Gower, with the seaside resorts of **Mumbles** and **Oystermouth** (for both, see p.111), now little more than salty suburbs.

Some history

The city's Welsh name, Abertawe, refers to the settlement at the mouth of the River Tawe, a grimy ditch that is slowly being teased back to life after centuries of usage as a sewer for Swansea's metal trades. The English name is believed to have been prompted from Viking sources, suggesting that a pre-Norman settlement existed in the area. The first reliable origins of Swansea came in 1099, when a Norman castle was built here as an outpost of William the Conqueror's empire. A small settlement grew near the coalfields and the sea, developing into a mining and shipbuilding centre that, by 1700, was the largest coal port in Wales.

Copper smelting became the area's dominant industry in the eighteenth century, soon attracting other metal trades to pack out the lower Tawe valley, which gradually became a five-mile stretch of rusting, stagnant land and water that has only recently begun to be re-landscaped. With the town's flourishing metal trades, a swiftly growing port and the arrival of the Swansea Canal, thousands of emigrants moved to the city from all over Ireland and Britain. By the nineteenth century, the town became one of the world's most prolific metal-bashing centres.

Smelting was already on the wane by the turn of the twentieth century, although Swansea's port continued to flourish. Britain's first oil refinery was opened on the edge of the city in 1918, with dock developments growing in its wake. Civic zeal, demonstrated best in the graceful 1930s Guildhall dominating the west of the city, was reawakened after the establishment of an important branch of the University of Wales here in 1920, but World War II had a devastating effect on Swansea, with thirty thousand bombs raining down in three nights in 1941. The rebuilding of the centre has left a series of soulless concrete streets and underpasses weaving between shopping centres, although now, with a population of around 200,000, Swansea is undergoing something of a renaissance. Partly as a nod to its enduring popularity as the birthplace of Dylan Thomas, it has been granted the title of UK City of Literature for 1995, which it will celebrate with the opening of a new literary museum and cultural centre.

Arrival, information and getting around

Swansea is the main interchange station for services out to the west of Wales and for the slow line across the middle of the country to Shrewsbury in Shropshire. The **train station** is at the top end of the High Street, a ten-minute hike from the bus station, from where local and national services fan out to all corners of south Wales and beyond. The **bus station**, complete with a highly efficient information office, is sandwiched between the Quadrant shopping centre and the *Grand Theatre*. On the northern side of the Quadrant is Singleton Street, where you'll find the municipal **tourist office** (Mon–Sat 9.30am–5.30pm; ☎0792/468321).

Getting around Swansea is easy: most of the sights are within walking distance of each other. Popular suburbs, such as Uplands and Sketty, near the University, are a bracing half-hour walk from the centre, although SWT buses cover the suburbs extremely thoroughly, and run out into Mumbles and the Gower.

Accommodation

As a lively city on the edge of some of Wales' most popular and inspirational coast and rural scenery, Swansea makes a logical base. Transport is good out into the surrounding areas and **beds** tend to be less expensive in the city than in the

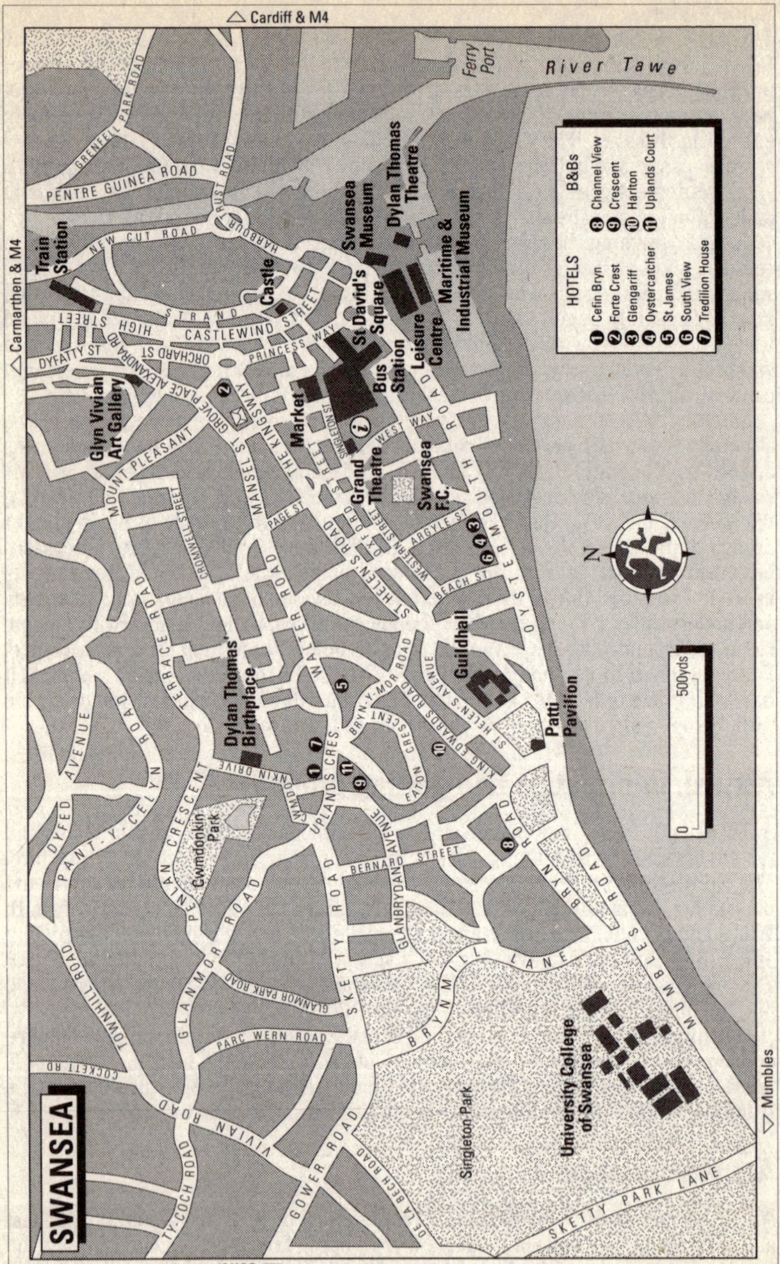
SWANSEA
Cardiff & M4
Carmarthen & M4
Mumbles
Gower
River Tawe
Ferry Port
HOTELS
1 Cefn Bryn
2 Forte Crest
3 Glengariff
4 Oystercatcher
5 St James
6 South View
7 Tredilion House
B&Bs
8 Channel View
9 Crescent
10 Harlton
11 Uplands Court
Train Station
Castle
Swansea Museum
Dylan Thomas Theatre
Maritime & Industrial Museum
St David's Square
Leisure Centre
Bus Station
Market
Glyn Vivian Art Gallery
Grand Theatre
Swansea F.C.
Guildhall
Patti Pavilion
Dylan Thomas' Birthplace
Cwmdonkin Park
Singleton Park
University College of Swansea
500yds
PENTRE GUINEA ROAD
GRENFELL PARK ROAD
NEW CUT ROAD
RUST ROAD
HARBOUR
STRAND
HIGH STREET
CASTLEWIND STREET
DYFATTY ST
ORCHARD ST
ALEXANDRA RD
PRINCESS WAY
GROVE PLACE
THE KINGSWAY
MOUNT PLEASANT
MANSEL ST
CROMWELL STREET
PAGE ST
WEST WAY
SINGLETON ST
OYSTERMOUTH ROAD
ARGYLE ST
WESTERN STREET
OXFORD STREET
ST HELEN'S ROAD
BEACH ST
WALTER ROAD
TERRACE ROAD
BRYN-Y-MOR ROAD
ST HELEN'S AVENUE
KING EDWARDS ROAD
EATON CRESCENT
UPLANDS CRES
CWMDONKIN DRIVE
PENLAN CRESCENT
GLANMOR ROAD
GLANMOR PARK ROAD
PARC WERN ROAD
BERNARD STREET
GLANBRYDAN AVENUE
SKETTY ROAD
BRYN ROAD
BRYNMILL LANE
MUMBLES ROAD
SKETTY PARK LANE
DE LA BECHE ROAD
GOWER ROAD
VIVIAN ROAD
TY-COCH ROAD
COCKETT RD
TOWNHILL ROAD
PANT-Y-CELYN ROAD
DYFED AVENUE

more picturesque parts of the Gower. There are dozens of dirt-cheap hotels and B&Bs stretched out along the seafront Oystermouth Road, whose trade is particularly pitched at those catching the Swansea–Cork ferry. There are no campsites or hostels in the city itself, although nearby Gower places are easily reached (see pp.111–115).

Hotels

Cefn Bryn, 6 Uplands Crescent, Uplands (☎0792/466687). Cheery enough, family-run hotel in Swansea's most elegant suburb. ③.

Forte Crest, Kingsway (☎0792/651074). In the city centre, overlooking the Kingsway traffic island, with all of the usual *Forte* attributes and facilities. ④.

Glengariff, 372 Oystermouth Rd (☎0792/458137). Pleasant, if fairly basic seafront hotel. ②.

Oystercatcher, 386 Oystermouth Rd (☎0792/456574). Cheap and cheerful seafront hotel with a slightly wider range of facilities than many others in this price band. ②.

Parkway, 253 Gower Rd, Sketty (☎0792/201632). Quiet and extremely comfortable hotel in a comparatively salubrious area. ③.

St James, 76B Walter Rd, Uplands (☎0792/649984). Small and friendly hotel in airy Victorian house. ③.

Southview, 392 Oystermouth Rd (☎0792/651720). Agreeable hotel overlooking the bay. ②.

Tredilion House, 26 Uplands Crescent, Uplands (☎0792/470766). One of the city's best reasonably priced hotels, set in a large Victorian house. ③.

Guesthouses

Channel View, 17 Bryn Rd, Brynmill (☎0792/466834). Friendly and unpretentious guesthouse almost next to the St Helens cricket and rugby ground. ②.

Crescent, 132 Eaton Crescent, Uplands (☎0792/466814). Large and pleasant well-converted Edwardian guesthouse with sublime views over the city and the bay. ②.

Harlton, 89 King Edward Rd, Brynmill (☎0792/466938). Budget guesthouse near to the university and cricket/rugby ground. ②.

Uplands Court, 134 Eaton Crescent, Uplands (☎0792/473046). Welcoming and enjoyable guesthouse within a gracious Victorian villa in a pleasant area. ②.

The City

Swansea's train station faces out on to the morose **High Street**, which heads south into Castle Street and past the remains of the **castle**, sitting awkwardly amidst modern shopping developments. The most obvious landmark of the ruins are the semi-circular arcades, built into the wall between 1330 and 1332 by Bishop Gower to replace a Norman predecessor.

Alexandra Road forks right off the High Street immediately south of the station, leading down to the **Glynn Vivian Art Gallery** (Tues–Sun 10.30am–5.30pm; free), on the corner of Clifton Hill, a road so steep that the pavement gives way to steps every few yards. This delightful Edwardian gallery houses an inspiring collection of Welsh art including works by Gwen John, her brother Augustus, whose mesmerizing portrait of *Caitlin Thomas*, Dylan's wife, is a real highlight, and Kyffin Williams; the grimy mining portraits of Josef Herman; and a whole room of the huge, frantic canvases of Ceri Richards, Wales' most respected twentieth-century painter. In the early nineteenth century, Swansea was a noted centre of fine porcelain production, of which the gallery houses a large collection, together with pieces of contemporary works from Nantgarw, near Cardiff.

Belle View Way, off Alexandra Road just south of the gallery, leads to the ugly traffic island that acts as a focus for Swansea's shopping districts, with Orchard Street, a pedestrian link to the High Street, the Kingsway and Princess Way all converging on the same gloomy spot. The main shopping streets lie to the southwest, bounded by Kingsway and Princess Way. Sheltering underneath the Quadrant Centre, the curving-roofed **market** makes a lively sight, with plenty of bustle, colourful stalls and the smells of flowers, fresh baking and food. Traditional and long-standing stalls here sell local delicacies such as laver bread, a delicious savoury made from seaweed, as well as cockles trawled from the nearby Loughor estuary, typical Welsh cakes, fish and cheeses.

The Maritime Quarter

The spit of land between the Oystermouth Road, sea and the Tawe estuary has been christened the Maritime Quarter – tourist board-speak for the tarted-up old docks – and the centrepiece is a vast marina surrounded by legions of unsold modern flats.

The city's old South Dock, now cleaned and spruced up, features the **Swansea Museum** (Tues–Sun 10.30am–5.30pm; free), or more properly the Royal Institution of South Wales, on Victoria Road. Wales' oldest public museum was founded in 1835, and is still enticingly old-fashioned, with dusty exhibits of local Roman remains annotated in copper-plate handwriting, and a stroll through the history of the heavily industrialized Lower Swansea valley. A small grid of nineteenth-century streets around the museum has been thoughtfully cleaned up and now houses some enjoyable cafés, pubs and restaurants.

Behind the museum, Burrows Place leads down to the marina and the superb new **Maritime and Industrial Museum** (Tues–Sun 10.30am–5.30pm; free). Taking Swansea's seaside position as its starting point, the museum presents a lively history of the city, with an especially compulsive section on the horrors of the Blitz. A large number of vehicles include an old tram that once rattled along the seafront to Mumbles and a rare example of Gilbern cars, Wales' principal (and long-dead) contribution to the motor industry.

The Maritime Museum faces out on to a flotilla of yachts bobbing in the marina. Close by stands John Doubleday's statue of Dylan Thomas, dubbed "A Portrait of the Artist as Someone Else", due to its remarkable lack of resemblance to the poet. Just behind the statue, on Gloucester Place, is the mural-splattered warehouse that has now become the **Dylan Thomas Theatre**, which intersperses productions of his work with visiting and local companies' offerings. Slap opposite is the **Swansea Arts Workshop**, used as a live venue for contemporary music, exhibitions, theatre and workshops.

West Swansea

West of the city centre, St Helen's Road dips down to the seafront near the tall white tower of the **Guildhall** and Walter Road, staying inland until the airy suburb of **Uplands**. The Guildhall, a typically soaring example of 1930s civic architecture, contains **Brangwyn Hall** (☎0792/301301 for access), named after painter Sir Frank Brangwyn (who painted the eighteen enormous British Empire Panels that line the hall), and a frequent venue for some excellent live classical concerts. Immediately behind the Guildhall, down by the coast road, is **Victoria Park**, home of the **Patti Pavilion**, imported from opera singer Adelina Patti's home at Craig-y-nos and now used for variety shows and concerts.

The drab postwar achitecture of **Swansea University**, three quarters of a mile further, enjoys a commanding position over the bay stretching to Mumbles Head. Within the complex is the eclectic **Taliesin Arts Centre**, Swansea's most imaginative performance space, together with the **Ceri Richards Gallery** (Mon 11am–5pm, Tues–Fri 11am–6pm, Sat noon–6pm; free), specializing in touring exhibitions, frequently by contemporary Welsh and Celtic artists.

Hourly buses leave the Quadrant depot to trundle along Walter Road in the direction of Uplands, which is otherwise a half-hour walk from the city centre. North of the main road, leafy avenues rise up the slopes past the sharp terraces of **Cwmdonkin Park**, at the centre of which is a memorial to Dylan Thomas inscribed with lines from *Fern Hill*, one of his best-known poems. From the park, the views over huddles of houses down to the curving shoreline is breathtaking. On the eastern side of Cwmdonkin Park is Cwmdonkin Drive (reached from the main road via The Grove), a sharply rising set of solid Victorian semis, notable only for the blue plaque on no. 5, birthplace in 1914 of Dylan Thomas.

Eating, drinking and nightlife

Swansea's metamorphosis from a sturdily working-class, industrial city into a would-be tourist centre is well demonstrated in the pubs, restaurants and entertainment centres of the city. Many of the grittier, older establishments survive, although increasing numbers are being steadily gentrified. This leaves a fairly stark choice between grotty, if more interesting, places and some rather sterile newer developments. For nightlife, the city is well placed as a major centre in Wales, with most passing theatre, opera and music of all sorts being obliged to make a stop here.

Cafés and restaurants

Bengal Brasserie, 47 Walter Rd (☎0792/643747). Best of the many Indian restaurants in Swansea, well worth the ten-minute hike from the city centre. Moderate.

Bizzie Lizzie's, 55 Walter Rd (☎0792/473379). Relaxed and informal cellar bar bistro, with a good range of cheapish Welsh, international and vegetarian dishes. Inexpensive.

Casa Reba, 8 Craddock St, off Kingsway (☎0792/643526). Spanish eatery with a reasonable lunch menu and a more extensive, expensive, evening selection. Moderate to expensive.

Eleo's Brasserie, 33 The Kingsway (☎0792/648609). Gloriously tacky mock olde-worlde bistro, with pub classics and pasta dishes in large quantities at reasonable rates. Moderate.

Footlights Coffee Bar, Grand Theatre, Singleton St. Good daytime meeting space with a delicious lunch menu, including some imaginative vegetarian options. Inexpensive.

Hwyrnos, Green Dragon Lane, off Wind St (☎0792/641437). Fixed Welsh evening menu plus harp-twanging entertainment in an extremely convivial, bordering on boozy, atmosphere. More sedate lunchtime menu also available. Moderate.

New Capriccio, 89 St Helen's Rd (☎0792/648804). Popular Italian restaurant, with bargain lunch menu. Closed Mon and Sun eve. Inexpensive.

The Schooner, 4 Prospect Place (☎0792/649321). Excellent fish restaurant, with a speciality of locally caught dishes. Closed Sun eve. Moderate.

Steak by Night, 10 Craddock St, off The Kingsway (☎0792/466810). Late-opening, standard priced and lively steakhouse, with a dependable menu. Moderate.

Bars, pubs and clubs

Adam and Eve, 207 High St. Traditional pub, with a great atmosphere and varied clientele. Well known for the excellence of its beer.

Bush Inn, High St. Only worth mentioning as a warning not to be deceived by the charmingly olde-worlde exterior: inside, it's a loud, video-filled nightmare.

Cardiff Arms, 53 The Strand. Boisterous and packed live rock pub, with visiting bands and a laid-back atmosphere. Saturday afternoon blues sessions.

Champers, 210 High St. Soulless wine bar, serving as the city's early evening gay venue.

Duke of York, Princess Way. Swansea's best venue for jazz and blues music, as their *Ellington's* club (small fee payable) hosts nightly gigs.

DV8 at the *Palace*, High St. Spruced-up gay club, open until 2.30am from Wednesday to Saturday.

Mothers, 3–4 Kingsway, next to the YMCA. Open nightly until 2am, for regular live music sessions and club nights.

No Sign Bar, 56 Wind St. A narrow frontage on the street leads into a long, warm pub interior with a rather soulless restaurant at the back. The etymology of the pub's name is explained in depth in the window.

Queen's Hotel, Gloucester Place, near the marina. Large old seafaring hotel and pub, with good snack lunches and Sunday roasts. Regular evening live music and quizzes.

Theatre, cinema and classical music

Brangwyn Hall, Civic Centre, South Rd (☎0792/302432). Vastly impressive music hall in the Art Deco Civic Centre. Hosts regular concerts by the *BBC Welsh Symphony Orchestra* and others. It also administers the **Patti Pavilion** in Victoria Park.

Dylan Thomas Theatre, Gloucester Place, by the marina (☎0792/473238). Re-runs of Thomas' classics, intertwined with other modern works.

Grand Theatre, Singleton St (☎0792/475715). One of Britain's best provincial theatres, with a wide-ranging diet of visiting high culture, comedy, farce and music.

Taliesin Arts Centre, Swansea University (☎0792/296883). Welsh, English and international visiting theatre, music and film, including offbeat and alternative fare.

Listings

Bike rental See "The Gower: Getting around", below.

Books *Uplands Bookshop*, 27 Uplands Crescent (☎0792/470195).

Bus enquiries *SWT* office in the Quadrant Centre bus station, Plymouth St (Mon–Fri 8.30am–5.30pm, Sat 8.30am–5pm) or telephone enquiries (Mon–Sat 8.30am–6pm, Sun 10am–6pm; ☎0792/475511).

Car rental *Brisco*, Dyfatty St (☎0792/457338); *Century*, 304 Carmarthen Rd (☎0792/645711); *Europcar*, 187–9 Lower Oxford St (☎0792/650526).

Ferry enquiries *Swansea–Cork Ferries* (☎0792/456116) run daily crossings of the Irish Sea.

Festivals *Swansea Festival* of music and the arts takes place around October every year, and the city's *Beer Festival* occupies the Patti Pavilion in mid-April; details of both from the tourist office.

Hospital *Singleton Hospital*, Sketty Park Lane, Singleton, West Swansea (☎0792/205666).

Laundries *Lendart*, 71 Uplands Crescent, Uplands; *Brynmill Launderette*, 121 Rhyddings Terrace, Brynmill.

Pharmacies *Evans Taylor*, 56 The Kingsway, and *Dragon Pharmacy*, 13 Orchard St (Mon–Sat 10am–6pm).

Police Main station is near the train station on Orchard St (☎0792/456999).

Post office 35 The Kingsway (☎0792/655759).

Rugby Swansea Rugby Club, one of Wales' premier sides, play at St Helens Park in Uplands (☎0792/648654).

Soccer Swansea City FC at the Vetch Field (☎0792/474114).

Train enquiries ☎0792/467777.

The Gower

A fifteen-mile-long peninsula of undulating limestone, the **GOWER** (Gwyr) points down into the Bristol Channel to the west of Swansea. The area is fringed by sweeping yellow bays and precipitous cliffs, caves and blowholes to the south, and wide, flat marshes and cockle beds to the north; brackened heaths with prehistoric remains and tiny villages lie between, and castle ruins and curious churches are spread evenly around. Out of season, the winding Gower lanes afford opportunities for exploration; but in the height of the summer, they are congested with caravans shuffling between one overpriced car park and the next.

The Gower can be said to start in Swansea's western suburbs, along the coast of Swansea Bay that curves round to a point in the pleasantly old-fashioned resort of **Mumbles** and Mumbles Head, which marks the boundary between the sandy excesses of Swansea Bay and the rocky inlets that dip and tuck along the serrated coastline of the southern Gower. This southern coast is punctuated by sites exploited for their defensive capacity, best seen in the eerie isolation of the sandbound **Pennard Castle**, high above **Three Cliffs Bay**. West, the wide sands of **Oxwich Bay** sit next to inland reedy marshes, beyond which is the glorious village of **Port Eynon**, home to an excellent youth hostel and a beautiful beach. West of Port Eynon, the coast becomes a wild, frilly series of inlets and cliffs, topped by a five-mile path that stretches all the way to the peninsula's glorious westernmost point, **Worms Head**.

Rhossili Bay, a spectacular four-mile yawn of sand backed by the village of Rhossili, occupies the entire western end of the Gower from Worms Head to the islet of **Burry Holms**. The northern coast merges into the tidal flats of the estuary, running past the salted marsh of **Llanrhidian**, overlooked by the gaunt ruins of **Weobley Castle**, and on to the famous cockle beds at **Pen-clawdd**.

Getting around

Apart from the coastal track to Mumbles, no train line has been built on the Gower. With its proximity to urban Swansea, however, **bus** transport is fairly comprehensive, with at least hourly connections from Swansea to Mumbles, Pennard, Oxwich, Port Eynon, Rhossili, Pen-clawdd and regular journeys to the northwestern corner around Llanrhidian, Weobley Castle and Llangennith. Driving around the Gower in peak season can be frustratingly slow and parking chronically pricy. Cycling, together with walking, are ideal ways to tour the area, as the peninsula's attractions are all within a short distance of each other and, in many cases, are well off-road. **Bike rental** is available at *Clyne Valley Cycles* in Walters Row, Dunvant (☎0792/208889), five miles west of Swansea city centre, and in Mumbles from *Swansea Bay Cycle Hire* on Village Lane (☎0792/814290 or 818248), at the front of the *Antelope Hotel*.

The Mumbles and Oystermouth

At the far westernmost end of Swansea Bay, **The Mumbles** (Mwmbwls) derives its name from the French *mamelles*, or breasts, a reference to the twin islets off the end of Mumbles Head, and is now used as the name for all of the loose sprawl around **OYSTERMOUTH** (Ystumllwynarth). Here, the seafront is an unbroken curve of budget hotels, breezy pubs and cafés leading down to the old-fashioned pier and funfair towards the rocky plug of Mumbles Head. Behind the promenade, a busy warren of streets climb the hills, lined with souvenir shops and department stores. Around the headland, reached either by the longer barren coast road or a short walk over the hill, is the district of **Langland Bay**, with a sandy beach, fairly popular with surfers.

The small seasonal **tourist office** on the seafront lies opposite Newton Road, which leads up to the hilltop ruins of **Oystermouth Castle** (April–Oct daily 11am–5.30pm; £1). Founded as a Norman watchtower, the castle was strengthened to withstand attacks by the Welsh, before being converted for more amenable residential purposes during the fourteenth century. Today you can see the remains of a late thirteenth-century keep next to a more ornate three-storey ruin incorporating an impressive banqueting hall and state rooms.

Practicalities

Mumbles is a lively and enjoyable base for the southern Gower coast, with a good clutch of typically tacky seaside entertainment on offer. **Accommodation** is plentiful: try the shorefront *Tides Reach*, 388 Mumbles Rd (☎0792/404877; ②), the brassy *Carlton Hotel* at 654–656 Mumbles Rd (☎0792/360450; ③), or the *Osborne Hotel*, high on a clifftop in Rotherslade Road, Langland Bay (☎0792/366274; ③). There are dozens of **eating places** along and behind the seafront, most notably the Welsh specialities of *Easterbrooks*, 590 Mumbles Rd (closed Sun eve & Mon; ☎0792/362338), the earthy vegetarian and vegan food of *Roots*, 2 Woodville Rd, off Queens Road (closed Sun & Mon; ☎0792/366006), and the cosy Italian atmosphere of *Quo Vadis*, 614–616 Mumbles Rd (☎0792/360706).

Scores of seafront pubs constitute the **Mumbles Mile**, one of Wales' most notorious pub crawls. Of them all, *The Antelope*, the *Oystercatcher* and the *White Rose* are the most enjoyable, if most touristy alternatives. Most tourists feel that they have to have a pint in *Dylan's Tavern*, which, when it was known as the *Mermaid*, was the young writer's most regular haunt. Unsurprisingly, it's now packed full of Dylan Thomas kitsch and memorabilia.

The south and west Gower coasts

From Mumbles Head, the limestone crags of the **southern Gower coast** twist and delve the fifteen miles or so to Worms Head, at the bottom of Rhossili Bay. Many of the sandy bays that rupture the cliffs are easily accessible by car, although they tend to be crowded in peak season.

From Mumbles Head to Three Cliffs Bay

The first few miles of the Gower coastline are disappointingly developed, and the first truly remote spot you reach is the National Trust-owned **Pwlldu Bay**, reached by a spectacular one-mile cliff walk from nearby **Caswell Bay**, or by a walk along the cliffs from the other direction, via the lane that snakes its way around the villages from Pennard church. The wooded ravine behind Pwlldu Bay offers many stunning walks.

The main A4118 courses along the southern side of Gower through the touristy hamlet of **PARKMILL**, where the twee charms of the **Y Felin Ddwr** craft centre (daily 10am–6pm; £1.50) are forced on passing visitors. Far more interesting are the paths that fan out from the bridge, leading up into the unearthly landscape of the Penard Pill valley, which follows a stream winding its way to the sea at glorious **Three Cliffs Bay**, a mile from Parkmill. The silent valley comprises vast dunes, tufted grass and the ruins of eerie **Pennard Castle** high up on the windy sand bank. A shorter walk to Three Cliffs Bay is via the tiny lane that heads off the A4118 at Penmaen, a mile beyond Parkmill.

A mile north of Parkmill (reached by the lane that heads past Y Felin Ddwr) is the Neolithic (3000–1900 BC) burial chamber known, in honour of the thirteenth-century lords of Oystermouth Castle, as **Parc le Breos**. Although not intrinsically fascinating, as it has been much restored, the roofless chamber is impressive, if only when you consider its age and sheer size – seventy foot long and divided into four separate chambers. In 1869, the skeletons of two dozen people were found in it. Just beyond the chamber and to the right, a deep fissure in a limestone outcrop marks the position of the dank and musty **Cathole Rock Cave**, in which flint tools, dated at over 12,000 years old, have been found.

The best local **B&B** is *Lunnon Farm* (March–Oct; ☎0792/371205; ②), a welcoming farmhouse just north of Parkmill. Otherwise, the rather dismal *Langrove Lodge* (☎0792/232410; ③) lies just off the A4118, two miles nearer Swansea from Parkmill, near the city's airport. **Camping** is possible at *North Hills Farm*, overlooking Three Cliffs Bay and the Penard Pill valley between Parkmill and Penmaen (April–Oct; ☎0792/371218).

Oxwich

One of the most curious landscapes in the Gower is the reedy **nature reserve** around **Oxwich Burrows**, a flatland of salt and freshwater marshes reached via the lane that forks left off the A4118 at the ruined gatehouse of the privately owned **Penrice Castle**. The marshes are dotted with pools and bounded by ancient woodland and, down by the coast, sweeping dunes. Close by on the coast, the scattered village of **OXWICH** is grouped next to the gaping sands of Oxwich Bay. This is one of the Gower's most popular resorts, as the host of caravan parks, campsites, hotels and B&Bs testify. The squat church of St Illtud sits alone, away from the village, at the top of the beach. A quieter beach can be found just over a mile away at **Slade Sands**, reached along the lane that climbs from the Oxwich crossroads past the ruins of a Tudor manor, known as **Oxwich Castle** (currently under restoration).

Accommodation is plentiful in and around Oxwich: for B&Bs on the main street, try the *Little Haven* (☎0792/390940; ②), and *Woodside* (☎0792/390791; ②), or the *Oxwich Bay Hotel* (☎0792/390329; ③), in splendid isolation by the sands near the parish church. The *Oxwich Camping Park* on the Penrice road (closed Oct–March; ☎0792/390777), includes a swimming pool and laundry on site.

Horton and Port Eynon

The rocky cliffs from Oxwich Point fade into wide stony bays towards the quiet village of **HORTON**, with a decent beach, and its brasher neighbour, **PORT EYNON**, busy and touristy by comparison, with a clutch of seafood restaurants, chip shops and the laid-back *Ship Inn*. The village's sands and dunes are sheltered by a prominent headland, easily reached by a series of paths that wind their way along the shore from the car park, past the Victorian lifeboat station, now the youth hostel, and above the bleak ruins of the old shoreline salt house and oyster pools. The headland, owned by the National Trust, is a wild and windy spot, where tufted grass gives way to sharp limestone crags. A natural cave at the tip can be seen from above, a great dome-shaped chasm that plummets into the hillside. Around the headland to the west is the more ordered and accessible **Culver**

Hole, built into the cliffs. A man-made cave, it may originally have been a stronghold for the long-gone Port Eynon castle, and has served its time subsequently as a smugglers' retreat, dovecot and armoury.

The lichen-spattered limestone headland casts good views over the curve of Port Eynon Bay and the cliffs round to Rhossili, five miles west. This **coastal path** is the most spectacular walk on the Gower, veering along crags above thundering waves for five miles, and the only real beach in this stretch is the secluded **Mewslade Bay**, just short of Rhossili, accessible by the path from Pitton. Along the coast walk, about midway between the two villages, is **Paviland Cave**, the site of an astonishing find in 1823: the skeleton of a Stone Age hunter, dated at least 19,000 years old. At **Thurba Head**, on the eastern side of Mewslade Bay, there are a few scant remains of an Iron Age hillfort sited magnificently a few hundred feet above the waves.

Port Eynon **youth hostel** (mid-Feb to Nov; ☎0792/390706; ①) is welcoming, with the warden passionately knowledgeable about the area. Otherwise, there's the *Culver House Hotel* in Port Eynon (☎0792/390755; ③), or **camping** at *Carreglwyd Park*, Port Eynon (☎0792/390795), and *Bank Farm*, off the A4118 between Horton and Port Eynon (☎0792/390228).

Rhossili and Worms Head

The village of **RHOSSILI** (Rhosili), at the western end of the Gower, is a centre for walkers and beach loungers alike. Dylan Thomas described the terrain to the west of the village as "rubbery, gull-limed grass, the sheep-pilled stones, the pieces of bones and feathers", and you can tread in his footsteps to **Worms Head**, an isolated string of rocks, accessible for only five hours at low tide. At the head of the road, near the village, is a well-stocked, helpful **National Trust information centre** (April–Oct daily 10.30am–5.30pm; Nov–Dec Sat & Sun 11am–4pm; ☎0792/390707). They post the tide times outside for those heading for Worms Head, and hold details of local companies renting surfing and hang-gliding equipment.

Below the village, a great curve of white sand stretches away into the distance, a dazzling coastline vast enough to absorb the crowds, especially if you are prepared to head north along it towards **Burry Holms**, an islet that is cut off at high tide. The northern end of the beach can also be reached along the small lane from Reynoldston, in the middle of the peninsula, to Llangennith, on the other side of the towering sandstone **Rhossili Down**, rising up to 633 feet. **Surf instruction** and rental are available from *PJ's* at Llangennith (☎0792/872686).

In Rhossili village, there are reasonable **B&Bs** in *Broadpark* (☎0792/390515; ②), and *Sunnyside* (☎0792/390596; ②). **Campsites** can be found at *Pitton Cross Park* (☎0792/390593), a mile short of Rhossili off the B4247 and, at the foot of the northern slopes of Rhossili Down, *Hillend* (☎0792/386204), at the end of the southern lane from Llangennith, behind the dunes that bump down to the glorious beach. Evening **drinking** and **food** in Rhossili is largely down to the bar of the rather dingy, but friendly, hotel in the middle of the village.

Mid and north Gower

The great sweep of land that rises to the north of the main Gower road tends to be more overlooked by visitors than the congested villages and packed beaches of the south and west, due solely to the lack of comparable coastline: the northern fringe of the Gower is a flattened series of marshes and mud flats merging indistinguishably with the sands of the Loughor estuary. Wading birds, gulls and bedded cockles can all be found amongst the flats, dunes and inlets burrowing into the land from the estuary.

The Gower's central plateau is often ignored, with much of the countryside nothing more than a pleasant patchwork of pastoral farm land. The great ridge, Cefn Bryn, stretched across the centre of the peninsula, is savage and impressive, its wiry peat and grass dotted with hardy sheep, ancient stone cairns and holy wells. From the road brushing over its roof are the best views over the peninsula.

From Llanrhidian to Llanmadoc

The small and unremarkable village of **LLANRHIDIAN** sits above the great marsh of the same name, a largely inaccessible goo of mud and water virtually indistinguishable from the sands of the Loughor estuary. Views from the village pub, the *Welcome to Town*, are superb in its direction. An unclassified road weaves west for two miles towards **Weobley Castle** (April–Oct Mon–Sat 9.30am–6.30pm, Sun 2–6.30pm; Nov–Dec Sat & Sun 11am–4pm; CADW; £1.50). Gaunt against the backdrop of the marsh and the estuary, the castle was built as a fortified manor in the latter part of the thirteenth century.

The lane continues for two miles to the village of **CHERITON**, with its charming thirteenth-century church, and then on to **LLANMADOC**, where you can use the car park and venture onto the land spit of **Whitford Burrows**, a soft patch of dunes now open as a nature reserve. Paths lead from Llanmadoc village up the steep hump of **Llanmadoc Hill** to the south. **The Bulwark**, a lonely and windy hillfort, can be seen at the eastern end of Llanmadoc Hill's summit ridge.

The **Cefn Bryn** ridge of sandstone, stretched out across the middle of the Gower, climbs over five hundred feet to give some astounding views to both coasts of the peninsula. It is most easily explored from the quiet village of **REYNOLDSTON**, grouped around its sheep-filled village green. The village's pub, the *King Arthur Hotel*, hosts live folk and rock music nights. From Reynoldston, a dramatic road rises up the slope of Cefn Bryn before skating across its summit in a perfect, straight line. A small car park lies next to a path across the boggy moor to **King Arthur's Stone**, a massive and isolated burial chamber capstone dating from at least 4000 BC and weighing over 25 tons. The rest of the chamber has long since disappeared, giving the remaining boulder a powerful sense of windswept presence on one of the ridge's natural peaks. Paths lead off the road in all directions, giving clear views to both Gower coasts.

B&Bs in the area include the *Britannia Inn* in Llanmadoc (☎0792/386624; ③), the smoke-free and vegetarian-friendly *Bryn-y-Mor* in the same village (☎0792/386603; ②), and the *Greenways Hills Farm* in Reynoldston (☎0792/390125; ②). There is an excellent **campsite** in Llanmadoc (☎0792/386202).

travel details

Trains

Cardiff to: Abergavenny (hourly; 40min); Barry Island (every 20min; 25min); Birmingham (8 daily; 2hr 20min); Bridgend (every 30min; 20min); Bristol (every 30min; 45min); Caerphilly (every 30min; 20min); Carmarthen (8 daily; 2hr); Chepstow (hourly; 30min); Crewe (hourly; 2hr 40min); Haverfordwest (6 daily; 2hr 40min); Llwynypia (every 30min; 45min); London (hourly; 2hr); Maesteg (hourly Mon–Sat; 50min); Manchester (8 daily; 3hr 20min); Merthyr Tydfil (hourly; 1hr); Neath (hourly; 40min); Newport (every 15–30min;

12min); Penarth (every 20min; 15min); Pontypool (every 2hr; 30min); Pontypridd (every 15min; 30min); Swansea (hourly; 50min); Trehafod (every 30min; 35min); Ystrad Rhondda (every 30min; 50min).

Newport to: Abergavenny (hourly; 25min); Birmingham (8 daily; 2hr 10min); Bristol (every 30min; 35min); Caldicot (hourly; 13min); Cardiff (every 15–30min; 12min); Chepstow (hourly; 20min); Hereford (hourly; 50min); London (hourly; 1hr 50min); Pontypool (every 2hr; 15min); Swansea (hourly; 1hr 5min).

Swansea to: Cardiff (hourly; 50 min); Carmarthen (hourly; 45min); Ferryside (10 daily; 40min); Fishguard (3 daily; 2hr 30min); Haverfordwest (9 daily; 1hr 45min); Kidwelly (10 daily; 30min); Knighton (5 daily; 3hr); Llandeilo (5 daily; 1hr); Llandovery (5 daily; 1hr 20min); Llandrindod Wells (5 daily; 2hr 30min); Llanelli (hourly; 20min); Llanwrtyd Wells (5 daily; 1hr 45min); London (hourly; 2hr 50min); Milford Haven (9 daily; 2hr); Narberth (every 2hr; 1hr 15min); Newport (hourly; 1hr 5min); Pembroke (every 2hr; 2hr); Tenby (every 2hr; 1hr 35min); Whitland (hourly; 1hr 5min).

Buses

Abergavenny to: Brecon (hourly; 1hr); Cardiff (hourly; 2hr); Clydach (hourly Mon–Sat; 25min); Crickhowell (hourly; 20min); Llanfihangel Crucorney (6 daily Mon–Sat; 15min); Merthyr Tydfil (hourly; 1hr 20min); Newport (hourly; 1hr 10min); Pontypool (hourly; 25min).

Bridgend to: Cardiff (hourly; 50min); Cowbridge (every 30min; 20 min); Cymmer (every 30min Mon–Sat; 1hr); Kenfig (every 30min; 40min); Llantrisant (hourly; 50min); Llantwit Major (9 daily; 40min); Margam Park (hourly; 15min); Ogmore (9 daily; 15min); Pontypridd (hourly; 1hr 20min); Porthcawl (every 30min; 25min); Southerndown (9 daily; 20min); Swansea (hourly; 50min).

Cardiff to: Abergavenny (hourly; 2hr); Aberystwyth (2 daily; 4hr); Bangor (3 daily; 8hr); Barry Island (hourly; 50min); Birmingham (5 daily; 2hr 30min); Blaenafon (hourly Mon–Sat; 1hr 40min); Caernarfon (1 daily; 7hr 40min); Caerphilly (every 30min; 40min); Cardiff youth hostel (every 30min; 15min); Cardiff-Wales Airport (hourly; 30min); Cowbridge (every 30min; 35min); Heathrow Airport (8 daily; 2hr 45min); Lampeter (2 daily; 3hr 10min); Llandrindod Wells (1 daily; 2hr 30min); Llantwit Major (hourly; 1hr); London (6 daily; 3hr 10min); Machynlleth (1 daily; 5hr 30min); Merthyr Tydfil (every 30min; 45min); Nelson (hourly Mon–Sat; 35min); Newport (every 20min; 45min); Penarth (every 30min; 30min); Pontypridd (hourly Mon–Sat; 25 min); Senghenydd (hourly Mon–Sat; 50min); Swansea (hourly; 1hr); Welshpool (1 daily; 4hr 30min).

Chepstow to: Caerwent (hourly Mon–Sat; 25min); Monmouth (11 daily Mon–Sat; 55min); Newport (hourly; 1hr); Penhow (hourly; 35min); Pontypool (every 2hr Mon–Sat; 1hr 30min); Tintern (8 daily Mon–Sat; 20min); Usk (every 2hr Mon–Sat; 45min).

Merthyr Tydfil to: Abergavenny (hourly Mon–Sat; 1hr 20min); Brecon (7 daily; 40min); Cardiff (every 30min; 45min).

Monmouth to: Chepstow (11 daily Mon–Sat; 55min); Newport (every 2hr Mon–Sat; 1hr); Raglan (every 2hr Mon–Sat; 20min); Ross-on-Wye (8 daily Mon–Sat; 40min); Tintern (9 daily Mon–Sat; 30min); Usk (every 2hr Mon–Sat; 30min).

Neath to: Aberdulais (hourly; 15min); Cymmer (hourly Mon–Sat; 35min); Pontrhydyfen (hourly; 25min).

Newport to: Abergavenny (hourly; 1hr 10min); Abertillery (every 30min; 55min); Birmingham (5 daily; 2hr); Blaenafon (every 30min; 1hr 10min); Brecon (every 2hr; 2hr); Caerphilly (every 30min; 40min); Caerwent (hourly; 40min); Cardiff (every 20min; 45min); Chepstow (hourly; 1hr); Holyhead (1 daily; 8hr 30min); London (5 daily; 2hr 45min); Monmouth (every 2hr Mon–Sat; 1hr); Pontypool (every 30min; 45min); Pwllheli (1 daily; 9hr); Raglan (every 2hr Mon–Sat; 45min); Usk (every 2hr Mon–Sat; 30min).

Swansea to: Aberdulais (hourly; 45min); Brecon (3 daily; 1hr 30min); Cardiff (hourly; 1hr); Dan-yr-ogof (3 daily; 55min); Llangennith (3 daily; 1hr 20min); Mumbles (every 10min; 15min); Neath (every 30min; 30min); Oxwich (every 2hr; 1hr); Pennard (hourly; 35min); Port Eynon (every 2hr; 1hr 10min); Rhossili (every 2hr; 1hr 15min); Uplands (hourly; 10min).

CHAPTER TWO

SOUTHWEST WALES

The most westerly outpost of Wales, the counties of **Carmarthenshire** and, in particular, **Pembrokeshire** attract thousands of visitors. The principal draw is the glorious coastline, sweeping and flat around **Carmarthen Bay** and rocky, indented and spectacular around the **Pembrokeshire Coast National Park** walk.

The last remnants of industrial south Wales peter out at **Llanelli**, before the undistinguished county town of **Carmarthen**. Of all the routes that converge on the town, the most glorious is the winding road along the Tywi Valley, past ruined hilltop forts on the way to **Llandeilo** and Wales' most impressively sited castle at **Carreg Cennen**, high up on the dizzy plug of rock of the Black Mountain. Burrowing further into the sparsely populated countryside, broken only by endearing small market towns such as **Llandovery**, leads to remote hills and tiny valleys, home to the gloomy ruins of **Talley Abbey** and the Roman gold mines at **Dolaucothi**.

The wide sands of southern Carmarthenshire, just beyond Dylan Thomas' adopted home town of **Laugharne**, merge into the popular south Pembrokeshire bucket-and-spade seaside resorts of **Tenby** and **Saundersfoot**. Tenby sits at the entrance to the south Pembrokeshire peninsula, divided from the rest of the county by the Milford Haven and Daugleddau Estuary, which brings its tidal waters deep into the heart of the pastoral county. The peninsula's turbulent, rocky coast is ruptured by some remote historical sites, including the Norman baronial castle at **Manorbier** and **St Govan's chapel**, a minute place of worship wedged into the rocks of a sea cliff near Bosherston. At the top of the peninsula is the old county town of **Pembroke**, dominated by its fearsome castle, across the Milford Haven Estuary from small seaside villages and tiny islands along the rugged curve of **St Bride's Bay**, inland of which is the market town and transport interchange of **Haverfordwest**, dull but seemingly difficult to avoid. St Bride's Bay's rutted coastline is the most glorious part of the coastal walk, leading north to brush past the impeccable village of **St David's**, whose exquisite cathedral shelters from the town in its own protective hollow. St David's, founded by Wales' patron saint in the sixth century, is a magnet for visitors; aside from its own charms, there are opportunities locally for spectacular coast and hill walks, hair-raising dinghy crossings to local islands and numerous other outdoor activities.

The coast turns towards the north at St David's, becoming the southern stretch of Cardigan Bay. Sixteen miles away by road, and well over thirty by rugged nips and tucks of the coastal walk, is the pretty port of **Fishguard**, terminus for ferries to Rosslare in Ireland. To the south and southeast lies some of Pembrokeshire's best inland scenery: mile upon mile of undulating, deserted lanes interspersed with windswept plateaux of heathland and scattered villages, with the barren **Mynydd Preseli** (Preseli Hills) rising sharply to dominate the eastern side of the county.

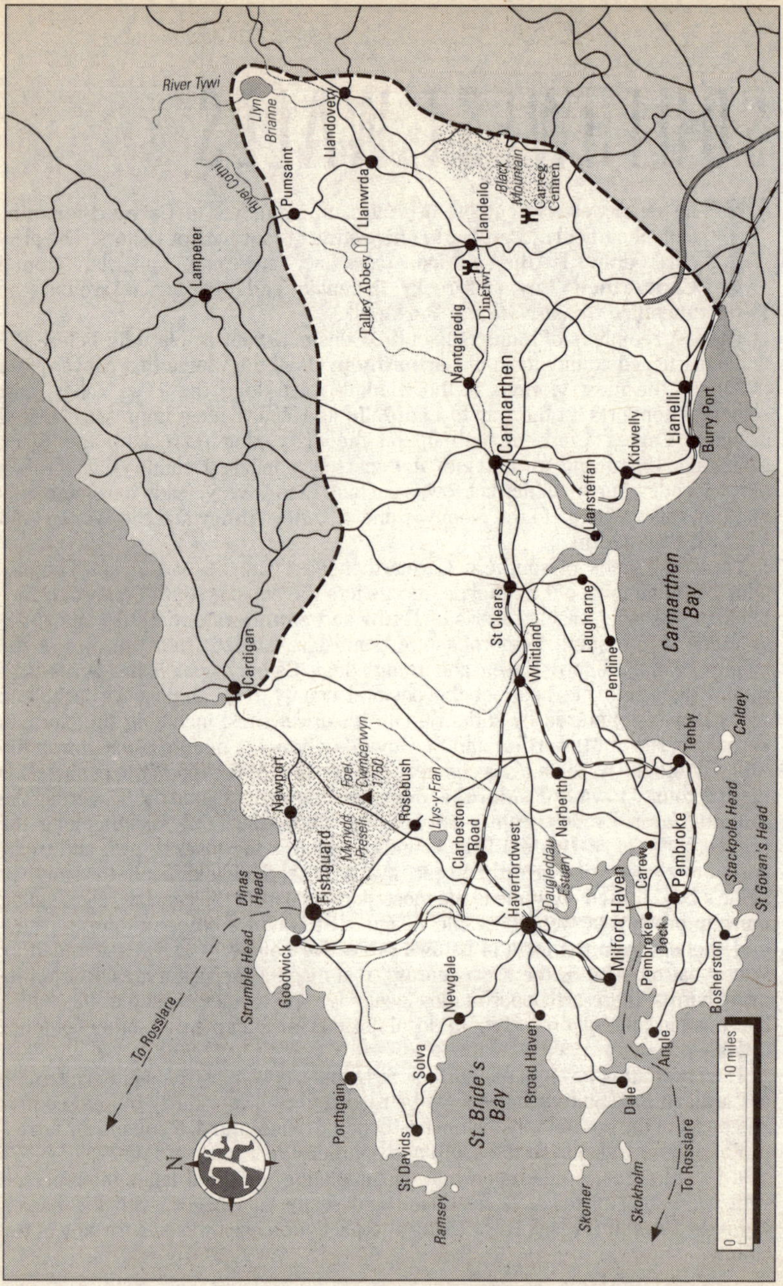

River Tywi
Llyn Brianne
River Cothi
Llandovery
Pumsaint
Llanwrda
Lampeter
Black Mountain
Carreg Cennen
Llandeilo
Talley Abbey
Dinefwr
Nantgaredig
Carmarthen
Llanelli
Burry Port
Kidwelly
Llansteffan
St Clears
Laugharne
Pendine
Whitland
Carmarthen Bay
Cardigan
Newport
Foel Cwmcerwyn 1760
Mynydd Preseli
Rosebush
Llys-y-Fran
Clarbeston Road
Narberth
Tenby
Caldey
Fishguard
Dinas Head
Strumble Head
Goodwick
Haverfordwest
Daugleddau Estuary
Milford Haven
Carew
Pembroke
Pembroke Dock
Stackpole Head
St Govan's Head
Bosherston
Angle
Newgale
Solva
Porthgain
St Davids
St. Bride's Bay
Broad Haven
Dale
Ramsey
Skomer
Skokholm
To Rosslare
To Rosslare
N
0
10 miles

ACCOMMODATION PRICE CODES

Throughout this guide, hotel and B&B accommodation is priced on a scale of ① to ⑨. Category ① only applies to youth hostels; for the rest, the number indicates the **lowest price** you could expect to pay per night for a **double room in high season**. The prices indicated by the codes are as follows:

① under £20/$32	④ £40–50/$64–80	⑦ £70–80/$112–128
② £20–30/$32–48	⑤ £50–60/$80–96	⑧ £80–100/$128–160
③ £30–40/$48–64	⑥ £60–70/$96–112	⑨ over £100/$160

Getting around

Despite the remoteness of much of the southwestern part of Wales, public transport is surprisingly efficient and comprehensive. Direct **train** services connect Cardiff and Swansea with Llanelli, Carmarthen, Tenby, Haverfordwest, Milford Haven and Fishguard. The Heart of Wales line shuffles out of Swansea and Llanelli to Llandeilo and Llandovery, before delving into Powys. Connecting bus services out to the smaller towns and villages are regular and dependable, especially to the more popular destinations of Laugharne, Saundersfoot, Broad Haven and Dale on St Bride's Bay, and St David's.

Bus services are more thorough in peak tourist season, when most coastal villages have a fairly regular operation. Carmarthen and Haverfordwest are the principal bus terminuses, with services radiating out from Tenby, Pembroke and Fishguard. There are ample places to rent **bikes** throughout the area. Off the mainland, most of the islands are connected by regular (seasonal) **boat** services, although few of these allow for overnight stops.

From Llanelli to Carmarthen

A dour town of refineries and the dominant *Felinfoel* and *Buckley* breweries, **LLANELLI** marks the informal border between anglicized southeast Wales and the part of the country where the Welsh language can frequently be heard in everyday conversation. You're not missing much by not coming here, and in any case, it's a good half-mile walk from Llanelli station into the town centre, a standard collection of newly pedestrianized streets flanked by chain stores. Half a mile northwest of the town centre, off the Felinfoel Road, **Parc Howard** is a large, rambling park around a Victorian tinplate merchant's mansion, now a well-presented **museum and art gallery** (Mon–Fri 11am–1pm & 2–4pm, Sat & Sun 2–4pm; free), with a small collection of local metal goods, Welsh art and rare examples of Llanelli pottery that was manufactured in the eighteenth and nineteenth centuries. There's also Llanelli **rugby club** (☎0554/774060), known as the Scarlets, one of the country's most famous and successful teams, who play at Stradey Park out on the A484 to Burry Port. And that's about it as far as the town goes.

The most notable **accommodation** here is at the *Hotel Miramar*, 158 Station Rd (☎0554/754726; ③), whose speciality Portuguese restaurant is excellent. The *Awel y Mor* guesthouse, 86 Queen Victoria Rd (☎0554/755357; ②), is also very good. For **food**, there are a few cheap Indian and Chinese restaurants on Station Road.

Burry Port and Pembrey

Four miles west, along the sands of the Loughor Estuary, is the undistinguished town of **BURRY PORT**, whose harbour, a ten-minute walk south of the station, is a pleasant surprise, as the town shows no sign of any nautical connection – a few theme pubs notwithstanding. On the eastern side of the town, the skyline is dominated by the hundred-foot turbines of the **Carmarthen Bay Wind Energy Centre** (☎055 46/4989), where a small, irregularly open exhibition about wind energy is housed in a site Portakabin.

The village of **PEMBREY**, a mile to the west along the A484, is now virtually indistinguishable from Burry Port. To the east of the village, the flat expanse of **Pembrey Burrows** forms an area of alternating wetland and dunes, now featuring a family-oriented **country park** (☎05546/3913, ski slope ☎4443), with a short dry ski slope, adventure playground, miniature train, pony trekking and nature trails. The country park leads down to the seven-mile **Cefn Sidan** sands, a gentle slope of beautiful beach curving around the end of the Burrows. At the northern end of the Burrows, an old airfield has been recently converted into the **Welsh Motor Sports Centre** (☎0554/891042), a venue for Formula Three racing, a rally school and numerous motorcycling and driving events.

Kidwelly

The next stop up the train line from Llanelli is **KIDWELLY** (Cydweli), a sleepy little town stretched along its main street, dominated by an imposing **castle** (April–Oct daily 9.30am–6.30pm; Nov–March Mon–Sat 9.30am–4pm, Sun 2–4pm; CADW; £1.50), on a steep knoll over the River Gwendraeth. The castle, and an accompanying priory – since demolished – were established around 1106 by the Bishop of Salisbury as a satellite of Sherborne Abbey in Dorset. Kidwelly's strategic position, overlooking vast tracts of coast, was the main reason for its construction. On entering through the massive fourteenth-century gatehouse, you can still see portcullis slats and murder holes, through which noxious substances could be tipped onto unwelcome visitors. The **gatehouse** forms the centrepiece of the impressively intact semicircular outer ward walls, which can be climbed for some great views over the grassy courtyard and rectangular inner ward above the river. This is the oldest surviving part of the castle, dating from around 1275, with the upper stories added in the fourteenth century by warlord Edward I's nephew. Views from the musty solar and hall, packed in to the easternmost wall of the inner ward, show the castle's defensive position at its best, with the river directly below. Although the whole castle is long since roofless, the remains are some of the most intact of any medieval Welsh castle that has not been extensively restored. As well as climbing the walls of the outer ward, stairs in the inner ward also lead into the upstairs rooms, largely domestic quarters.

A fourteenth-century town **gate**, just above the medieval bridge of the same age, shields the castle approach from the main through road, and in the shadow of the gatehouse is the tiny whitewashed local **museum**, an irregularly opened collection of artefacts from the medieval town. More entertaining, the small-scale **Industrial Museum** up Priory Street (Easter–Sept Mon–Fri 10am–5pm, Sat & Sun 2–5pm; £1) is housed in an old tinplate works on the northwest edge of the town. Many of the works' old features have been preserved, including the rolling mills where long lines of tin were rolled and spun into wafer-thin slices.

On the other side of the train station from the town is the old **Quay**, cleaned up and restored into an appealingly remote and forlorn picnic area and nature reserve. From here, there are views of wading birds skimming over the nearby mudflats and old saltings of the Gwendraeth Estuary, once an important port for the medieval town.

In Kidwelly, there's decent pub **accommodation** at the *Old Malthouse*, by the castle (☎0554/891091; ③), and B&B at 21 Ferry Rd (☎0554/891368; ②), off the main street towards the Carmarthen Bay **campsite** at *Tanylan Farm* (☎0267/267306), which perches alongside the estuary between Kidwelly and Ferryside. Good **food** and drink are available at the cosy *Boot and Shoe*, 2 Castle St.

St Ishmael and Ferryside

As the train leaves Kidwelly and hugs the side of the River Towy's estuary, the views out across the water are magnificent. You'll pass by a tiny chapel at **ST ISHMAEL** that served a medieval village completely destroyed in a storm three hundred years ago, and now buried deep beneath the flats; another storm in 1896 briefly revealed the remains of houses. A mile further on, **FERRYSIDE** (Glanyfferi) is a tranquil village that grew as a daytrip destination by train for Valley miners. Although the station still remains, Ferryside is far quieter today, its narrow streets facing Llansteffan Castle across the calm waters and circling sea birds. A yacht club, fishing centre and sandy beach make up the village facilities, together with a handful of pubs and restaurants. **Accommodation** can be found at *Beach Cottage* on Foreshore (☎0267/267507; ②), and there's good food and drink in the main square at the *White Lion Hotel* and the earthier *Ship Inn*.

Carmarthen

The unquestioned capital of its region, **CARMARTHEN** (Caerfyrddin) does not live up to the promise of its status. Although it's a useful transport interchange and lively market town, with a few excellent shops and some sixty pubs for fifteen thousand inhabitants, there's little of great interest here, and the predominantly dull architecture and shabby streets hardly entice a visitor to stay long. Added to that, many of the town's pubs are dowdy, and can even feel slightly threatening to an outsider. It's the first major town in west Wales, where the native language is heard at all times, and was once – in the early eighteenth century – the largest town in the principality.

Founded as a Roman fort, Carmarthen's most popular moment of mythological history dates from the Dark Ages and the supposed birth of the wizard Merlin (Myrddin in Welsh gives the town its name) just outside the town. In the late eleventh century, the Normans began a castle near the remains of a Roman fort, extending its walls to encompass a growing village. In 1313, Carmarthen was granted its first charter by Edward I, helping the town to flourish as an important wool centre, and was taken by Owain Glyndŵr in the early years of the fifteenth century. An eisteddfod was founded in the mid-fifteenth century, and is still used as the basis for today's National Eisteddfod. The importance of the town grew, attracting trade and new commerce, industrial works, a key port and a position as a seat of local government, a status still held by Carmarthen as the county town of Dyfed.

Arrival, information and accommodation

The **train station** (☎0267/235803) lies over the Carmathen Bridge on the south side of the river. All **buses** terminate at the bus station on Blue Street, and many connect with trains at the station. The town's **tourist office** is located in Lammas Street, close to the Crimea Monument (Sept–June Mon–Sat 9.30am–5.30pm; July & Aug daily 9.30am–6pm; ☎0267/231557), although more esoteric information on the alternative scene in the area – book and record fairs, gigs, meetings and festivals – can be found in *Aardvark Wholefoods* in Mansel Street or *Zac's*, selling hippy gear, opposite the Neuadd Ddinerig San Pedr Civic Hall at the Nott Square end of King Street. There's a **laundry** opposite the *Golden Lion* on Lammas Street.

There's lots of **accommodation** in town, especially on Lammas Street, where you'll find the *Boar's Head* (☎0267/222789; ④), one of the town's grandest old coaching inns, the rather anodyne *Falcon Hotel* (☎0267/237152; ④), and the cheerier *New Park Hotel* (☎0267/235175; ③). B&B accommodation is best at *Y Dderwen Fach*, 98 Priory St (☎0267/234193; ②), and the *Old Priory* guesthouse, 20 Priory St (☎0267/237471; ②), both out along the main road to Lampeter and Llandeilo.

The Town

The stern facade of the early twentieth-century **County Hall** shields the rambling streets of the town centre when you approach from the train station, and largely swallows up the uninspiring remains of Edward I's **castle** off Nott Square. The most picturesque eighteenth- and nineteenth-century part of town lies spread out at the base of the castle, around King Street and Nott Square, the town's main shopping hub.

Lying just off Nott Square is the town's handsome eighteenth-century **Guildhall**, the other side of which leads you out on to Darkgate and Lammas Street, a wide Georgian thoroughfare flanked by coaching inns, some interesting local shops and branches of all the main banks. Mansel Street leads north off Lammas Street to the indoor **market**, a great centre for local produce, secondhand books, endearingly useless tat and cheap cafés. On the main market days – Wednesday, Friday and Saturday – stalls spill outside into a slate grey modern square.

From Nott Square, King Street heads northeast towards the sturdy tower of **St Peter's church**, architecturally undistingished but well placed amongst the trees and surrounding town houses. Inside, Carmarthen's status as one of the most important Roman towns in Wales is evident from the altar in the western porch. Opposite is the Victorian School of Art that has now metamorphosed into the **Oriel Myrddin** (Mon–Sat 10.30am–4.45pm; free), a craft centre and excellent art gallery that acts as an imaginative showcase for many local artists. The gallery also plays host to a varied diet of exhibitions culled from contemporary arts and crafts, as well as a tantalizing shop of designer crafts.

Half a mile further east, just off Priory Street, lie the tawdry and insubstantial remains of a **Roman amphitheatre**, excavated in the late 1960s. In contrast with the atmospheric bowl at Caerleon, Carmarthen's remnants, surrounded by modern housing, are no more than a few grass humps.

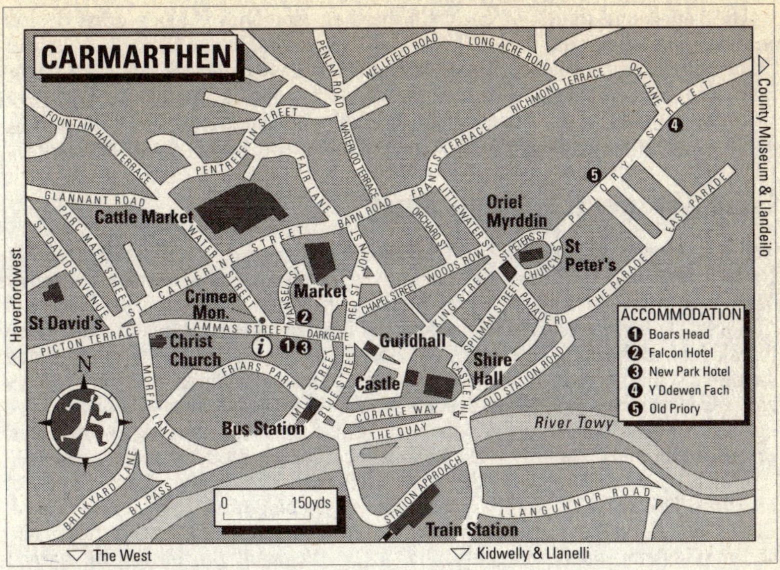

Eating and drinking

For **food**, daytime snacks are great at the old-fashioned *Morris Tea Rooms*, almost opposite the Lyric Theatre in King Street, and the vegetarian café in the *Waverley Stores* health food shop, 23 Lammas St. Most of the busy town centre pubs offer reasonable lunches – for evening food, try the smartish but inexpensive *Hamilton's Wine Bar*, 11–12 Queen St (☎0267/235631), or, right next door, *The Queens*, a friendly, oak-panelled pub. Slightly scruffier, although excellent value, is the *Blue Boar* in Water Street, off Lammas Street, and, in the same street, *Morgan's* excellent chip shop and pizzeria, which closes at 8pm. The best-value pub food can be found at the *Boar's Head* on Lammas Street. Just off Nott Square, *MP's Pizzeria*, 20b Bridge St, is unremarkable, but offers a huge range of different pizzas every evening until just after pub closing time.

Of the town's profusion of **pubs**, some can get a little raucous at times. The *Drovers' Arms* in Lammas Street is an unpretentious place with some superb beers on offer, while the *Granby* in King Street is a quiet, friendly place with some good characters willing to spin a yarn or two.

The Tywi Valley

The **River Tywi** curves and darts its way east from Carmarthen through some of the most magical scenery in south Wales. The thirty-mile trip to Llandovery is punctuated by gentle, impossibly green hills topped with ruined castles. It's not hard to see why the Merlin legend has taken such a hold in these parts – the landscape does seem infused with some kind of eerie splendour.

The year-round tourist office in Carmarthen (see above) has a great deal of **information** about the Tywi Valley and surrounding area. There's a smaller office in the Crescent Road car park at Llandeilo (Easter week & May–Sept Mon–Sat 10am–5pm). There is a regular **bus** service from Carmarthen to Llandeilo, with the majority of the buses using the A40 via Nantgaredig and Pontarcothi, and a couple daily heading off at Nantgaredig down the B4300 via Llanarthny.

From Abergwili to Llanarthney

The severe grey Bishop's Palace at **ABERGWILI** was the seat of the Bishop of St David's between 1542 and 1974, and now houses the **Carmarthen County Museum** (Mon–Sat 10am–4.30pm; 50p), a spirited amble through the history of the area. This surprisingly interesting exhibition covers the history of Welsh translations of the New Testament and Book of Common Prayer – both translated for the first time here in 1567. Local pottery, archeological finds, wooden dressers and a lively history of local castles are presented in well-annotated displays. The upstairs section looks at local police and crime, geology, the origins of Wales' first eisteddfod in Carmarthen in 1450, the local coracle industry and education.

A mile east of Abergwili, the main A40 road passes the sharp slopes of **Merlin's Hill** (Bryn Myrddin), reputedly the sleeping place of the great wizard. Close by, the quiet roadside hamlet of **WHITEMILL** (Felinwen) has value accommodation and decent pub food at the *Whitemill Inn* on the main road (☎0267/290239; ②). In the hamlet of **NANTGAREDIG**, just over three miles from Abergwili, there's little apart from the welcoming *Cwmtwrch Hotel* (☎0267/290238; ③), complete with swimming pool and leisure club; a good mile north is the superb and beautifully remote *Pantgwyn Farm* (☎0267/290247; ②), justifiably famous for its lavish breakfasts. Nearby **PONTARGOTHI** has the slightly touristy *Cresselly Arms* and the chintzier, but more locally frequented, *Cothi Hotel* (☎0267/290251; ③); a few miles north of the village is *Plâs Alltyferin* (☎0267/290662; ②), a cosy B&B in a Georgian farmhouse that does excellent food.

The village of **LLANARTHNEY** (Llanarthne) lies south of the main A40, and has two superb pubs: the *Golden Grove Arms* (☎0558/668551; ③), which serves up hearty food and has extremely comfortable accommodation, and the delightfully wacky *Paxton Inn*, home of live jazz, other music and innumerable guest beers.

High above the village, accessible by a steep twenty-minute walk or a more leisurely drive around the lanes, is **Paxton's Folly**, a castellated tower, providing an exhilarating viewpoint over the rural patchwork below. Sir William Paxton, a London banker, built the folly after trying to bribe the electors of Carmarthen to make him MP with one of the most expensive campaigns in history, and the promise to pay for a bridge over the Tywi at Dryslwyn if successful. When the electors rejected him, he refused to build the bridge and constructed his folly overlooking the proposed site.

Dryslwyn and Dinefwr castles

There is now a bridge over the Tywi from below the tower over to **DRYSLWYN** and its forlorn **castle** (open all hours), straddling the top of a mound next to the river. Dryslwyn was built by Rhys ap Rhys Gryg, one of the Welsh princes of Deheubarth, in the thirteenth century, overlooking an important crossing point of the river. He had originally sided with Edward I before turning against him, incurring the king's wrath and an 11,000-strong army to beseige him in the castle in 1287. The collapsed stone walls surround a desolate inner courtyard, currently being restored as part of the castle's renaissance. Although the remains of the castle are barely worth the climb, the views are delightful.

The strategic importance of the Tywi valley is underlined by the presence of the tumbledown ruins of **Dinefwr Old Castle**, reached through the extensive parkland of Plas Dinefwr, which forms a spectacular isolated spot on a wooded bluff over the river. Currently under restoration, the castle was built in the twelfth century by Lord Rhys, who successfully united the warring Welsh princes against the Normans. The vital site had been used for a previous castle, built as a royal fortress in the ninth century and used by Hywel Dda, Hywel the Good, king of Deheubarth and codifier of Welsh laws (see Whitland, p.131).

By 1523, the old castle had become ill-suited to the needs of the descendants of Lord Rhys, who aspired to something a little more luxurious. The "new" castle, now named **Plas Dinefwr** (April–Oct daily 10am–5pm; £1.60), was built in 1660 half a mile north of the old castle, added to over the ensuing centuries and given a new limestone facade in the 1860s. The National Trust is currently restoring the house, in which you can see an informative display about the history of Dinefwr, although no period rooms are yet open. The spectacular parkland (open all year) was landscaped mainly in the 1770s by George Rhys, whose work was much admired and slightly enhanced – by Capability Brown, following a visit in 1775. It now contains rare white cattle, fallow deer and a woodland nature reserve.

Llandeilo and Carreg Cennen Castle

A mile further on from the Dinefwr castles, the main street – Rhosmaen Street – of the handsome small market town of **LLANDEILO** climbs up from the Tywi bridge, behind which are the tourist office and the train station. Although there is little in the way of actual sights in the town, Llandeilo is brilliantly situated in a bowl of hills amidst the Tywi Valley and on the edge of the magnificent uplands of the Black Mountain (see p.173). It's a quiet, rustic little place, whose few streets cluster around the main thoroughfare and the unusual raised graveyard of the parish **church of St Teilo**. Down by the river bridge, a waterside path leads into Dinefwr Park and to the isolated **Llandyfeisant chapel** (April–Sept Sat & Sun 1.30–6.30pm), now a Dyfed Wildlife Trust information centre. They provide leaflets and information on walks in the district, notably the stroll from the church to the old Dinefwr castle, along the wooded escarpment tumbling down to the Tywi.

There are numerous places in Llandeilo to **stay**, including inexpensive B&B accommodation with *Mrs Denton*, 7 Thomas St (☎0558/822950; ②), or slightly more upmarket at *Brynawel*, 19 New Rd (☎0558/822925; ③), or town pubs such as the supposedly haunted *Three Tuns Inn* in Market Street and the *Cawdor Arms* on Rhosmaen Street. Rhosmaen Street and New Road are home to numerous small **cafés** and **pubs**, the best of which are the *Farmers Arms* and the old coaching inn, the *White Horse*.

Carreg Cennen Castle

Isolated in the rural hinterland four miles southeast of Llandeilo is one of the most magnificently sited castles in the whole of Wales: **Carreg Cennen Castle** (daily 9.30am–4.30pm; £1.50), just beyond the tiny hamlet of Trapp. It was first constructed on its fearsome rocky outcrop in 1248, although Sir Urien, one of

King Arthur's knights, is said to have built his fortress here first. Built primarily as a Welsh stronghold, Carreg Cennen fell to the English in 1277 during Edward I's initial invasion of Wales. The castle lasted as an inhabited fortress until 1462, when it was partially destroyed by the Earl of Pembroke, William Herbert, who believed it to be the base of a group of lawless rebels.

The most astounding aspect of the castle is its commanding position, three hundred feet above a sheer drop down into the green valley of the small Cennen River. The car park and **rare breeds farm**, catering primarily for children with rare species of cows, sheep and goats, are at the bottom of a long path that climbs sharply up, opening out quite astounding views towards the uncompromising purple lines of the Black Mountains in utter contrast to the velvet greenery of the Tywi and Cennen valleys. The castle seems impenetrable, its crumbling walls merging with the limestone on which it defiantly sits. The highlights of a visit are the views down the sheer drop into the river valley and the long descent down into a watery, pitch-black cave that is said to have served as a well. Torches are essential (50p rental from the excellent tea room near the car park), although it is worth continuing as far as possible and then turning them off to experience absolute darkness. The tea room near the car park has a superb selection of home-cooked Welsh dishes, and you'll find B&B in the nearby hamlet of Trapp at *Tŷ Isaf* (☎0558/822002; ③), in a farmhouse and its outlying cottages.

The A40 and train line trail one another to the northeast of Llandeilo, through a pastoral landscape, in which Biblical reminders, testimony of the Welsh fervour in their Christian faith, can be seen in the hamlets of Bethlehem (whose main industry is postmarking Christmas mail) and Salem, either side of the main road. **LLANGADOG**, halfway between Llandeilo and Llandovery, is a pretty little town under the glowering bluff of the Black Mountain. Three miles southwest of the town is **Garn Goch**, a massive Iron Age hillfort spread over fifteen acres, as impressive for its bleak position of isolation as for the remaining earthworks and stone rampart.

Llandovery and around

Twelve miles beyond Llandeilo, the town of **LLANDOVERY** (Llanymddyfri) has architecture and a layout that have changed little for centuries. Like so many other mid-Wales settlements, an influx of New Agers from the 1960s has had discernible effect on the town: there's a thriving independent theatre, and bookshops and wholefood stores abound. Alongside this more alternative flavour, Llandovery is still a major centre for cattle markets every other Tuesday.

Arrival and accommodation

Llandovery is a natural base for exploring the Tywi Valley, being well connected by bus and train, and containing numerous good pubs, guesthouses and eating places. The **train station** sits on the main A40 just before Broad Street, and **buses** leave from Broad Street and Market Square. The **tourist office** in Broad Street (Easter–Sept Mon–Sat 9.30am–5.30pm; ☎0550/20693) is combined with an excellent Brecon Beacons National Park office, stocking numerous leaflets on local walks and natural history. Local guides and books are stocked in the *Old Printing Office*, near the war memorial on Broad Street. Information on more esoteric events can be found at the Llandovery Theatre on Stone Street (☎0550/20113), or in the *Iechyd Da* health food shop in Broad Street.

The best **accommodation** is at the *King's Head Inn* in the Market Square (☎0550/20393; ③), a friendly, popular pub-cum-restaurant. Slightly more expensive is the colonnaded *Castle Hotel*, Broad St (☎0550/20343; ④), where the eighteenth-century travelling writer George Borrow lodged for a night. Cheap B&Bs include *Mrs Billingham's*, Pencerrig New Rd (☎0550/21259; ②), *Cwm Gwyn Farm*, Llangarreg Rd (☎0550/20410; ②), and *Ashgrove*, Llangadog Rd (☎0550/20136; ②). For a more isolated stay, the *Royal Oak Inn* (☎055 06/201; ③) in the old lead mining hamlet of Rhandirmwyn, midway between Llandovery and Llyn Brianne reservoir, has a superb restaurant. The nearest **campsite**, a mile east of Llandovery off the A40, is the *Erwlon* (☎0550/203321). There is also an excellent site on the way to Llyn Brianne by the river at Rhandirmwyn (☎055 06/257). A gas-lit **youth hostel** lies a mile above Rhandirmwyn (☎055 05/235).

The Town

On the south side of the main Broad Street, a grassy mound holds the scant remains of the town's **castle**. There are good views from the ruins over the shallow waters of the Bran River, which splits from the Tywi a mile short of the town, and the huddled grey buildings that make up Llandovery itself.

Broad Street has been the main through route for years, as can be seen from the solid early nineteenth-century town houses and earlier inns that line it; the road widens up towards the cobbled, rectangular Market Square, crowned by a clock tower. This thoroughfare has changed little since George Borrow visited the town in 1854 as part of his grand tour of Wales, remembering it as the "pleasantest little town in which I have halted in the course of my wanderings". The imposing, colonnaded cream *Castle Inn*, where Borrow stayed, betrays its eighteenth-century status as an important coaching inn. Stone Street heads north from the square, past some slightly tattier pubs and up to the redoubtable **Llandovery Theatre**, home of part of the theatre bookselling operation of Hay-on-Wye's Richard Booth, as well as a coffee shop – an excellent place in which to pick up an update on events in the area.

Eating and drinking

The best places to **eat** in Llandovery are the numerous pubs. The *King's Head* in the Market Square offers delicious lunchtime and evening food, as do the *Castle Hotel* on Broad Street (slightly more expensive) and the *White Swan* in the High Street. The town has a number of daytime cafés and tea rooms, mainly around the Market Square, together with a chip shop in Water Street. Out of Llandovery, the *Royal Oak Inn* in Rhandirmwyn (see above), is well worth the hike for its imaginative menu of well-cooked classics.

For **drinking**, the eccentric and bizarrely old-fashioned *Red Lion*, tucked away in an easy-to-miss corner at 2 Market Square, can't be beaten. If you can't find it, or if – as frequently happens – the landlord has chosen to close early, try the nearby *King's Head*, or, round the corner, the young and sporty *Greyhound/Y Milgi* in Stone Street.

The Dolaucothi Gold Mine, Talley Abbey and Llyn Brianne

The countryside to the west of Llandovery is blissfully quiet, with just a handful of main roads and lanes rarely containing traffic of any volume. The principal route off the A40 between Llandeilo and Llandovery, the A482 heads towards the straggling village of **PUMSAINT** (Five Saints), whose etymology is explained in the stone seen near the entrance of the **Dolaucothi Gold Mine** (site visit daily April–May & Sept–Oct 11am–5pm; June–Aug closes 6pm; £2.50; site visit & underground tour £4.50; NT), half a mile off the main road: the indentations in the rock are said to be the marks left by five sleeping saints, who rested here one night.

Pumsaint is the only place in Britain that the Romans definitely mined gold, laying complicated and astoundingly advanced systems to extract the precious metal from the rock, and remains of Roman workings – a few water channels and an open cast mine – can still be seen from the self-guided walk around the site. After they left in 140 AD, the mine lay abandoned until 1888, when the promise of gold opened the mine once more; further probes unearthed gold, but not enough to justify costs, and the mines closed once again. Today, the underground tour goes deep into the mine workings and usually allows visitors, equipped with the mine's panning dishes, to prospect for gold themselves.

A mile to the north of Pumsaint, a characteristically straight road heads north above the valley of the Twrch River. This is a segment of **Sarn Helen** (Sarn y Lleng), a trans-Wales Roman road built between forts at Caernarfon and Carmarthen, often crossing some of the country's bleakest terrain. Its whimsical name may be a corruption of the Welsh, meaning Causeway of the Legion, although it is more popularly held to refer to Helen, the Welsh wife of a Roman chieftain in Britain.

Southwest of Pumsaint is the village of **TALLEY** and the landmark crumbling tower of its twelfth-century **abbey**, sited spectacularly alongside the reeds and lily pads of two gloomily dark lakes. Established in the late 1100s, Talley was Wales' only Premonstratensian abbey, lasting as such only into the next century. Adjoining the distinctly unimpressive ruins is the serene **church of St Michael**, intact from its foundation in 1773 and still including its original box pews.

An unclassified road winds north from Llandovery, at first right on the bank of the Tywi, before heading down to the car park by the dam at the southern tip of **Llyn Brianne**, a remote reservoir built for the city of Swansea in the 1970s, but which has adapted itself to the scenery with surprising harmony. The new road clinging to the eastern shore of the lake winds its way up through desolate, incomparably grand highland scenery to meet the Abergwesyn Pass (see p.184).

Just before Llyn Brianne, a car park by the chapel at Ystradffin Farm leads on to a riverside nature trail that ambles around the side of Dinas Hill to **Twm Siôn Cati's Cave**, where the notorious sixteenth-century bandit and folk hero successfully evaded the Sheriff of Carmarthen by hiding within it.

South Carmarthenshire

Frequently overlooked in the stampede towards the resorts of Pembrokeshire, **southern Carmarthenshire** is a quiet part of the world, with few of the problems of mass tourism suffered by more popular parts of Wales. The coastline is broken by the triple estuary of the Tywi, Taf and Gwendreath rivers, forking off at right angles to each other; between the Tywi and Taf is a knotted landscape of hills and tiny, winding lanes. One decent, dead-end road penetrates this slip of land, petering out at **Llansteffan**, a village cowering below the hilltop ruins of its castle.

On the other side of the Taf Estuary, the village of **Laugharne** is the area's sole big tourist attraction, on the strength of its position as a place of pilgrimage for Dylan Thomas devotees. A curious and insular village, Laugharne was the last home of the Thomases, whose boathouse has been turned into a loving museum to the writer, and whose regular drinking hole is as much a part of the pilgrimage as the house.

The A40 continues into **Whitland**, an architecturally unremarkable town, but historically significant as the site of the first parliament in Wales. Roads descend south from Whitland to the coast at **Pendine**, a popular resort due to its seemingly endless sweep of sand, venue for an assortment of land speed record attempts.

Regular trains connect Carmarthen with Whitland and the west. Buses fill in the gaps, with a service from Carmarthen and St Clears to Laugharne and Pendine. Another service also leaves Carmarthen for Llansteffan.

Llansteffan

The impressive ruins of a **castle** (free entry) loom above the seemingly forgotten village of **LLANSTEFFAN** (sometimes anglicized to Llanstephan), on the opposite bank of the Tywi Estuary from Ferryside. It's a ten-minute walk up from the tawdry beach car park to the solid castle gatehouse, the most interesting survivor of this Norman ruin, which was built between the eleventh and thirteenth centuries by the Anglo-Norman de Camille family, attracting the occasional wrath and warring tactics of the Welsh as a result.

The entrance used today is not the original gatehouse, which was converted into living quarters in the fourteenth century: the bricked up entrance is obvious from outside. In both gatehouses, however, the portcullis and murder holes can still be seen. A couple of other towers, in considerably more advanced states of dereliction, punctuate the crumbling walls that surround the D-shaped grassy courtyard in the middle. From the top of the towers, it's easy to appreciate the importance of this site as a defensive position, with far-reaching views in all directions. It's no surprise that, before the present castle, there was an Iron Age promontory fort here, known to have been occupied from 600 BC.

From the castle, descend the path down towards Wharley Point, past *Parc Glas*, formerly a milk-and-rum tavern, and continue down the lane towards the beach. The door in the wall on the right conceals **St Anthony's Well**, with its supposed powers of healing for lovesickness.

Informal **tourist information** for the Llansteffan area is available at the friendly post office in the village of Llangain (☎0267/83487), halfway between Carmarthen and Llansteffan. They produce **accommodation** lists for the area. In Llansteffan, there are **B&Bs** at *Brig y Don* on The Green (☎026 783/349; ②), and, two miles short of the village from Carmathen and with superb views over the estuary, at *Pantyrarthro Manor* (☎026 783/226; ②). There's a **campsite** at *Church House Farm* in Llangain (☎026 783/274). The best source of reliable budget **food** are the *Sticks Inn* on Main Street, and the *Wern Inn* in Llangynog, five miles north of the town.

Laugharne

The village of **LAUGHARNE**, on the other side of the Taf Estuary from Llansteffan, is being increasingly taken over by the legend of Dylan Thomas, the nearest thing that Wales has to a national poet. Along an excruciatingly narrow lane (not suitable for cars) bumping along the estuary, you'll stumble across the **Dylan Thomas Boathouse** (Easter–Oct daily 10am–5.15pm; Nov–Easter daily except Sat 10.30am–3pm; £1.50), the simple home of Dylan, his wife Caitlin and their three children from 1949 until he died from "a massive insult to the brain" (spurred by numerous whiskies) on a lecture tour in New York four years later. It's an enchanting museum with a feeling of inspirational peace above the ever-changing water and light of the estuary and its "heron-priested shore". The upstairs is given over to a selection of local artists' views of the estuary and the village – none so rewarding as the one from the windows. Downstairs, the family's living room has been preserved intact, with the rich tones of the man himself reading his work via a period wireless set. Numerous artefacts are encased or on display, and contemporary newspaper reports of his demise show how he was, while alive, a fairly minor literary figure: the *Daily Mirror* manages a small obituary on page 5, while even the *Carmarthen Journal* relegates the story to second place behind the tale of a missing local farmer. A small tea room and outdoor terrace give views over the water and a welcome chance for refreshment. Back along the narrow lane, you can peer into the blue garage where he wrote: a gas stove, curling photographs of literary heroes, pen collection and numerous scrunched-up balls of paper on the cheap desk suggest quite effectively that he is about to return at any minute. The poet is buried in the graveyard of the parish church in the village centre, marked by a simple white cross.

Laugharne is probably the closest to the original of Llareggub, Thomas' fictional town of darkly rich characters in *Under Milk Wood* – an honour, it is claimed, that is shared with New Quay in Cardiganshire. Whichever village he really meant, Laugharne has numerous Thomas connections and plays them with curiously disgruntled aplomb – none more so than the great alcoholic's old boozing hole, **Brown's Hotel** on the main street where, in the nicotine-crusted front bar, Dylan's cast-iron table still sits in a window alcove, although the brusque landlord is loathe to discuss the poet and his work. *Brown's* is a tight, secretive, locals' pub, but one that is on the receiving end of thousands of visitors.

Back in the village, the main street courses down to the ornate ruins of Laugharne **castle** (currently under restoration). Built in the twelfth and thirteenth centuries, most of the original buildings were obliterated in Tudor times when Sir John Perrot transformed it into a splendid gentleman's mansion. Opposite the castle entrance is the tiny toytown **Town Hall**, topped by a white-washed Italianate bell tower, which served as a one-cell prison.

Practicalities

Laugharne has surprisingly very little B&B **accommodation**: try *Brook House Farm* on Pendine Road (☎0994/427239; ③), the *Cors* (☎0994/427219; ③), just off the main street as you come into the village from St Clears, or the very comfortable *New Three Mariners* pub on Victoria Street (☎0994/427426; ③). Alternatively, there are numerous cheap places down the road in Pendine (see p.132), or a **campsite** at *Waunygroes* in Llanybri (☎026 783/250). On the Pendine side of Laugharne is the *Ants Hill* camping park (☎0994/427293).

For **eating**, the choice is a little wider, although not a great deal better. *Brown's Hotel* (see above) serves large, stodgy lunches and early evening meals (until 8.30pm) guaranteed to fill anyone. The *Mill House Diner* on Wogan Street takes food orders until 10pm (Tues–Sat; 9pm Sun & Mon), but offers an uninspiring menu. Unless you're prepared to eat in *Dylan's Diner* (né the *Rose and Crown* pub), just across the road, there isn't much option. The best drinking hole in Laugharne is the effortlessly cheery *New Three Mariners* pub on Victoria Street.

DYLAN THOMAS

Dylan Thomas (1914–53) was the quintessential Celt – fiery, verbose, richly talented and habitually drunk. Born into a snugly middle-class family in Swansea's Uplands district (see p.108), Dylan's first glimmers of literary greatness came when he was posted, as a young reporter, on the *South Wales Evening Post* in Swansea, from which some of his most popular tales in the *Portrait of the Artist as a Young Dog* were inspired. Thomas' wordy enthusiasm is well demonstrated in a passage describing his gulping down a pint of beer, waiting for the senior reporter to join him for a pub crawl: "I liked the taste of beer, its live, white lather, its brass-bright depths, the sudden world through the wet brown walls of the glass, the tilted rush to the lips and the slow swallowing down to the lapping belly, the salt on the tongue, the foam at the corners".

Rejecting the coarse provincialism of Swansea and Welsh life, Thomas arrived in London as a broke twenty-year-old in 1934, weeks before the appearance of his first volume of poetry, which was published as the first prize in a *Sunday Referee* competition. Another volume followed shortly afterwards, cementing the engaging young Welshman's reputation in the British literary establishment. He married in 1937, and the newlyweds returned to Wales, settling in the hushed, provincial backwater of Laugharne. Short stories – crackling with rich and melancholy humour – tumbled out as swiftly as poems, further widening his base of admirers, although they remained numerically small until well after his death and, like so many other writers, Thomas has only gained star status posthumously. Despite his evident streak of hedonism and his long days in Laugharne's *Brown's Hotel*, Thomas was a surprisingly self-disciplined writer, honing his work into some of the most instantly recognizable poetry written this century, mastering both lyrical ballads of astounding simplicity and rhythmic metre, as well as more turgid, difficult poetry of numerous dense layers. Perhaps better than anyone, he writes in an identifiably Celtic, rhythmic wallow in the language. Although Thomas knew little Welsh – he was educated in the time when the native language was stridently discouraged – his English usage is definitively Welsh in its cadence and bold use of words.

Thomas, especially in public, liked to adopt the persona of what he perceived to be an archetypal stage Welshman: sonorous tones, loquacious, romantic and inclined towards a stiff tipple. Playing this role was particularly popular in the United States, where he journeyed on lucrative lecture tours. It was on one of these, in 1953, that he died, poisoned by a massive whisky overdose. Just one month earlier, he had put the finishing touches to what many regard as his masterpiece: *Under Milk Wood*, the "play for voices". Describing the dreams, thoughts and lives of a straggling Welsh seaside community over a twenty-four-hour span, the play has never dipped out of fashion and has lured Wales' greatest stars, including Richard Burton and Anthony Hopkins, into the role of chief narrator. The small town of Llareggub (mis-spelt Llaregyb by the po-faced BBC, who couldn't sanction the usage of the expression "bugger all" backwards) is loosely based on Laugharne, New Quay in Cardiganshire and a vast dose of Thomas' own imagination.

Whitland and Pendine

Heading west down the A40 from Laugharne, you soon come across **WHITLAND** (Y Hendy Gwyn), a small town dominated by a hulking dairy complex, an important place in the history of Wales. It was here – in 930 – that Hywel Dda (Hywel the Good), king of Deheubarth, called together representatives from all the other Welsh kingdoms to the first all-Wales assembly, designed to pull together disparate bands of legislation in order to codify common laws between them for the whole of Wales. There, they set up an elaborate and exhaustive code of egalitarian laws for their kingdoms, including the right of bastard children to be equal to legitimate siblings, the ending of marriage by common consent, the equal division of land between man and wife upon separation, and the equal division amongst all children of land upon the death of the parents. Many of these customs survived until the Tudors conquered Wales, and Welsh people today still hold great pride in the fairness and lack of oppression in a once independent Wales. The tales of Hywel Dda are told at a **commemorative centre** (Easter–Sept Mon–Sat 10am–5.30pm), where Hywel Dda's laws are inscribed (in Welsh) on stone tablets around the walls. It's located two minutes from the station on St Mary Street.

Due south of Whitland, the tatty seaside resort of **PENDINE** is home to a mass of caravan parks, souvenir shops and cheap cafés, but the crowning glory is the six-mile-long stretch of sand that sweeps away to the east. In 1927, Malcolm Campbell set a new world land speed record of 174.88mph here; Welsh rival J.G. Parry-Thomas tried to better Campbell's record a month later, dying gruesomely when he was decapitated by a loose part of the car. The *Beach Hotel* displays photographs and mementoes of the record attempts.

Tenby and around

On a natural promontory of great strategic importance, the beguilingly old-fashioned resort of **TENBY** (Dynbych-y-Pysgod) has a long pedigree. First mentioned in a ninth-century bardic poem, the town grew under the twelfth-century Normans, who erected a castle on the headland in their attempt to colonize south Pembrokeshire and create a "Little England beyond Wales" – an appellation by which the area is still known today.

Three times in the twelfth and thirteenth centuries the town was ransacked by the Welsh; the last time, in 1260, by Prince Llewellyn himself. In response, the castle was refortified and the stout town walls that largely still exist were built. Tenby prospered as a major port for a wide variety of foodstuffs and fine goods between the fourteenth and sixteenth centuries, but decline followed, and, with the arrival of the train in the mid-nineteenth century, the town became a fashionable resort. Lines of neat, prosperous hotels and expensive shops still stand haughtily along the seafront.

Although the town is extremely conservative, with a large population of retired people, there is plenty of entertainment and a huge number of pubs and restaurants to attract visitors of any age. In the middle of summer, it can seem full to bursting point, with heavy traffic restrictions and a considerable rush on decent accommodation.

Tenby is also one of the major stopping-off points along the **Pembrokeshire Coast Path**, a welcome burst of glitter and excitement amidst mile upon mile of undulating cliff scenery. The **National Park** boundary skirts around the edge of the town, and further along the coast are the two picturesque sandy stop-offs of **Amroth** and **Saundersfoot**. A couple of miles offshore from Tenby, the old monastic ruins of **Caldey Island** make for a pleasant day trip.

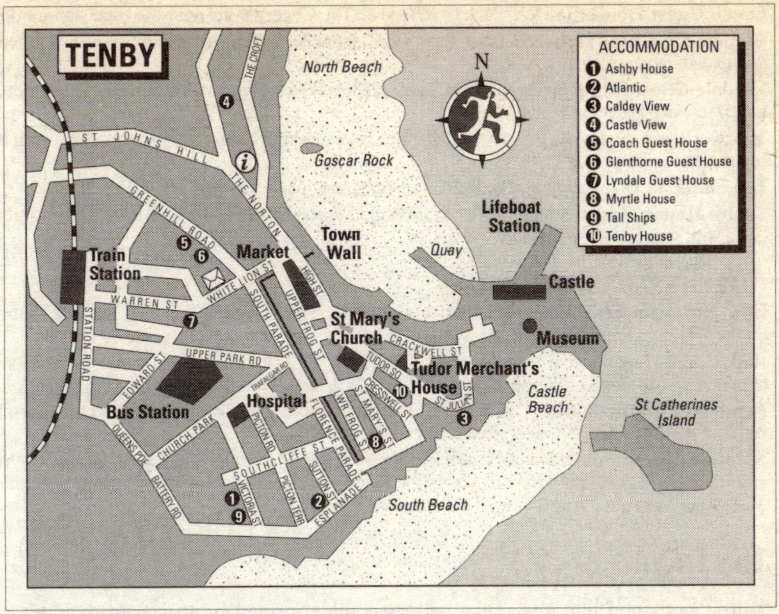

Arrival, information and accommodation

The **train station** (☎0834/842248) is at the western end of the town centre, at the bottom of Warren Street. Some **buses** stop at South Parade, at the end of Warren Street, although most (including *National Express* coaches) call at The bus station on Upper Park Road. The **tourist office** faces the North Beach on The Croft (daily July & Aug 10am–9pm; Easter–June & Sept–Oct 10am–6pm; Nov–March 10am–4pm; ☎0834/842189). It has details of day trips by bus to St David's that cannot be done on public transport. *Equinox* on St Julian Street sells a curious combination of hippy ephemera alongside painfully twee gifts; posters on the walls also detail local gigs and festivals.

Accommodation

As a major resort, there are dozens of hotels and B&Bs in Tenby, and although prices are a little higher than you might expect, decent and reasonable accommodation is not hard to find.

HOTELS AND GUESTHOUSES

Ashby House, 24 Victoria St (☎0834/842867). A comfortable, low-key hotel next to the Esplanade and the South Beach. ③.

Atlantic, The Esplanade (☎0834/842881). One of the better hotels along the South Beach, with a high standard of rooms and even a small indoor pool. ④.

Caldey View, St Julian St (☎0834/842126). Good value B&B, with showers in all rooms. ②.

Castle View, The Norton (☎0834/842666). Well located, staring out over Castle Hill and the harbour, a friendly hotel with all en suite rooms. ③.

Coach Guest House, 11 Deer Park (☎0834/842210). Cheery hotel near the train station. ③.

Glenthorne Guest House, 9 Deer Park (☎0834/842300). Large guesthouse, well reputed and excellent value. ②.

Lyndale Guest House, Warren St (☎0834/842836). Welcoming small B&B near the station, happy to cater for vegetarians. ②.

Myrtle House, St Mary's St (☎0834/842508). Non-smoking hotel in the town centre with a reputation for fine food. ③.

Tall Ships, 34 Victoria St (☎0834/842055). Bright, airy place near the South Beach. ②.

Tenby House, Tudor Square (☎0834/842000). Pleasantly old-fashioned town centre pub-hotel with well-appointed en suite rooms. ④.

CAMPSITES AND YOUTH HOTELS

Kiln Park campsite, Marsh Road (☎0834/844121). This campsite is a mile west of Tenby off the A4139 to Pembroke. Closed Nov–Feb.

Red House Farm, New Hedges (☎0834/813918). Pleasant and cheap campsite midway between Tenby and Saundersfoot, just off the A478. Closed Oct–March.

Pentlepoir youth hostel, Old School, Pentlepoir (☎0834/812333). A YHA youth hostel right on the A478 near Saundersfoot station; take bus #350. ①.

Skrinkle Haven youth hostel, Skrinkle Haven, near Manorbier (☎0834/871803). Bright and modern YHA hostel four miles west of Tenby overlooking the cliffs. Situated near the Manorbier bus route from Tenby. Tent spaces available. ①.

The Town

Tenby is shaped like a triangle, with two sides formed by the coast meeting at Castle Hill. The third side is formed by the remaining town **walls**, which are reached from the train station after a ten-minute walk straight up Warren Street. South Parade runs alongside the massive twenty-foot-high wall, first built in the late thirteenth century and massively strengthened by Jasper Tudor, Earl of Pembroke and uncle of the future king, Henry VII, in 1457. Further refortification came in the 1580s, when Tenby was considered to be in the frontline against a possible attack by the Spanish Armada. In the middle of the remaining stretch is the only town gate still standing at **Five Arches**, a semicircular barbican that combined practical day-to-day usage as an entrance for the town's citizens and peacetime visitors, with hidden look-outs and angles acute enough to surprise invaders. The wall continues south to the Esplanade, with a long line of snooty hotels facing out over the smarter and far less commercialized South Beach.

The centrepiece, and most notable landmark, of the town centre is the 152-foot spire of the largely fifteenth-century **St Mary's church**, between St George's Street and Tudor Square. A pleasantly light interior shows the elaborate ceiling bosses in the chancel to good effect, and fifteenth-century tombs of local barons demonstrate Tenby's important mercantile tradition. On the western side of St Mary's runs Frog Street, home of numerous craft shops and an indoor **arcade market**, containing craft stalls and gift shops.

Wedged between the town walls and the two bays, the **old town** makes a thoroughly enjoyable place to wander, with many interesting and unusual shops tucked away down small alleyways and steps. Many of the original medieval lanes are still intact in the immediate area around the parish church. **Sun Alley** is a tiny crack between overhanging whitewashed stone houses that connects Crackwell and High streets. Due east, on the other side of the church, **Quay Hill** runs parallel, a narrow set of steps and cobbles tumbling down past some of the town's oldest houses to the top of the harbour. Wedged in a corner of Quay Hill is the **Tudor Merchant's House** (April–Oct Mon–Fri 11am–6pm, Sun 2–6pm; NT £1.60), built in the late fifteenth century for a wealthy local merchant at the time when Tenby was second only to Bristol as an important west coast port. The rambling house is on three floors, packed with period furniture from the sixteenth century (with later additions), although more notable are the examples of a prominent local weakness, tapering Flemish-style chimney pieces. The walls are adorned with three surviving Tudor religious frescoes.

Crackwell and Bridge streets run down to the picturesque **harbour**, which can look idyllic if it's not too crowded. Sheltered by the curving headland and fringed by handsome pastel-shaded Georgian and Victorian town houses, it is a great place to stroll around on a warm evening. During the day, it's the scene of considerable activity as the departure point for numerous excursion boats, the most popular being the short trip over to Caldey Island (see below). Above the harbour is the headland and **Castle Hill**, where paths and flower beds have been planted around the sparse ruins of the Norman **castle**. A surviving gatehouse is the most impressive remain, although fragments of walls, an archway and windswept tower are scattered around the site, impressive if only for the all-round views that it offers. Now, the breezy grass slopes are covered with a proud collection of rampant Victoriana in the form of ornate benches, vast beds of bright flowers (notably Tenby's indigenous small daffodil in springtime), a pompous memorial to Prince Albert, a bandstand, and the town **museum** (Easter–Oct daily 10am–6pm; Nov–Easter Mon–Fri 10am–noon & 2–4pm; 70p), founded in 1878. Doubling up as a small art gallery (most notably including work by locals Nina Hamnett, and Gwen and Augustus John), the museum is typical of Tenby: slightly ponderous and municipally minded, but still interesting. The maritime exhibition, looking at the town's relationship with the sea, is absorbing, especially in the grainy photographs of old fishermen and the records of wrecks around the coast. From the top of Castle Hill, there are great views over the more sedate South Beach and to the tiny **St Catherine's Island**, cut off at high tide but otherwise reached by way of the beach. The remains of the **fort** that can be seen on the islet date only from 1869, when Lord Palmerston constructed a chain of similar defences to be built as a protection for the Admiralty docks at Pembroke.

Caldey Island

Looming large over Tenby's seascape is **Caldey Island** (Ynys Pyr), a couple of miles offshore due south of the Esplanade. Celtic monks first settled here in the sixth century, perhaps establishing an offshoot of St Illtud's monastery at Llantwit Major (see p.98). The exact duration of this Celtic settlement is unclear, although the ninth-century Latin inscription on the island's sixth-century Ogham stone would indicate that the community was still thriving then. Nothing is then known of the island until 1113, when English king Henry I gave it to Norman nobleman, Robert Fitzmartin, who in turn gave it to his mother. In 1136, it was given to the Benedictine monks of St Dogmael's at Cardigan, who founded their priory here. Upon the Dissolution of the monasteries in 1536, the Benedictine monks left the island and a fanciful succession of owners bought and sold it on a whim, until it was, once again, sold to a Benedictine monastic order in 1906 and subsequently to an order of Reformed Cistercians. The island has been a monastic home almost constantly ever since.

Boats leave Tenby Harbour every fifteen minutes in season (mid-May to mid-Sept Mon–Fri 9.45am–4pm; Easter–mid May & mid-Sept to early Oct occasional sailings; school summer holidays also Sat 1–4pm; ☎0834/842404; £4.50). Tickets (not tied to any specific sailing) are sold at the kiosk in Castle Square, directly above the harbour. On landing at Caldey's jetty, a short walk leads through the woods to the island's main settlement. Just before the village is reached, a fuchsia-soaked lane cuts up to the right in the direction of a tiny **chapel**, built out of an original watch tower constructed by the first Benedictines in the early part of the twelfth century.

The village itself is the main hub of Caldey life. As well as a tiny post office and popular tea room, there's a **perfume shop** selling the herbal fragrances distilled by the monks from Caldey's abundant flora. The narrow road going to the left leads down to the heavily restored **chapel of St David**, whose most impressive feature is the round-arched Norman door. Opposite is the gathering point for daily (men only) tours of the garish twentieth-century **monastery**, a white, turreted heap that resembles a Disney castle. In peak season, tours take place every couple of hours.

A lane leads south from the village to the old **priory**, abandoned at the Dissolution and restored at the turn of this century. Centrepiece of the complex is the remarkable twelfth-century **St Illtud's church**, marked out by its curiously blunt (and leaning) steeple. This houses one of the most significant pre-Norman finds in Wales, the sandstone **Ogham Cross**, carved with an inscription from the sixth century and added to, in Latin, during the ninth, found under the stained glass window on the south side of the nave. The church's rough flooring is largely comprised of pebbles from the island's beaches. The lane continues south from the site, climbing up to the gleaming white island **lighthouse**, built in 1828. Views from here are memorable.

Eating and drinking

There are dozens of **cafés** and **restaurants** around the town – in high season, the beaches (especially the North Beach) are packed in by cheap places. Many of the restaurants in the narrow streets of the town centre are tourist traps, over-priced and less than memorable – once again, pub food is often far better value.

Cafés and restaurants

Charney's, High St (☎0834/842024). Popular café, with some imaginative menu choices. Inexpensive.

Chortles, High St. Informal bistro, with some unusual local dishes amongst the more pedestrian fare. Good for grills and Sunday lunches. Inexpensive.

Fecci and Sons, Upper Frog St. Genuine Italian snackery and ice cream parlour, with over sixty speciality ice creams. Inexpensive.

La Cave, Upper Frog St (☎0834/843038). Relaxed and impressive restaurant, with well-cooked local specialities. Moderate.

Munchies, Crackwell St. Daytime wholefood takeaway. Inexpensive.

Pam Pam, Tudor Square. Just about the best of the avowedly "family" restaurants, serving good value portions of everyone's favourite dishes. Inexpensive.

Plantagenate, Quay Hill (☎0834/842350). Cosy and thoroughly enjoyable restaurant serving local specialities, tucked in next to the Tudor Merchant's House. Apparently, it's the oldest house in Tenby – you can see a thirteenth-century Flemish chimney en route to the loo. Moderate.

Pubs

Coach and Horses, Upper Frog St. Lively and with a young crowd who appreciate the good beer and reasonable bar snacks.

Five Arches Tavern, St George's St. Snooty and upmarket, but pleasant enough, and with good food.

Lamb, High St. Reasonably priced bar food makes up for the slightly pricy drinks in this convivial, mixed-age pub.

Lifeboat Tavern, Tudor Square. Popular and enjoyable young people's pub.

Normandie Hotel, Upper Frog St. Old-fashioned pub, which suffers from being too bright and loud. Good food available at all times.

Tenby House, Tudor Square. Another young favourite, which borders on the rowdy of a weekend evening.

Three Mariners, St George's St. Home of good beer and regular live music.

Listings

Bike rental *Broadmoor Garage*, Kilgetty (☎0834/813266).

Car rental *Five Arches Garage*, South Parade (☎0834/842244).

Cinema The elegant *Royal Playhouse*, White Lion St (☎0834/844809).

Exchange The main banks are on Tudor Square and have currency-changing facilities.

Festivals The fairly highbrow *Tenby Arts Festival* takes place in the latter half of September – details from the tourist office.

Hospital Trafalgar Rd (☎0834/842040).

Laundry Broadwell Hayes, near the viaduct.

Leisure centre Marsh Rd (☎0834/843574), including a swimming pool.

Pharmacies *Boots*, High St; *Craven*, White Lion St.

Police Warren St (☎0834/842303).

Post office Warren St.

Taxis *Dai's* (☎0834/843096) and *Tudor* (☎0834/844301).

Amroth and Saundersfoot

AMROTH marks the easterly end of the 170-mile **Pembrokeshire Coast Path**, which winds and darts its way around every cove and cliff in the county, right the way around to St Dogmael's, just outside Cardigan. It's a pleasant village, without being especially exciting; the beach is good, with south-facing sands ensuring maximum sunshine. For those starting or finishing the path at Amroth, a bed for the night might be a welcome necessity: the best places in the village are the *Ashdale* (☎0834/813853; ②) and *Beach Haven* (☎0834/813310; ②). The *New Inn* is right next to the beach and is an enjoyable place to eat and drink, if generally packed come the summer.

The coast between Amroth and Tenby is one long line of caravan parks, broken only by the picturesque harbour of **SAUNDERSFOOT**, built originally for the export of local anthracite and coal. The town has been attracting visitors for centuries, and is a lively, good-natured place, and now all the industry has folded, the harbour and the wide yawn of sand are used purely for recreational purposes. The main focus of activity is the large **harbour** area, where there are a predictable clutch of cafés, tawdry shops, a faded crazy golf course and boisterously fun pubs. You can also rent a power boat for either a day (starting at £34) or a week (£170), or try out waterskiing: the best starting point is *Jones & Teague*, on the far end of the harbour wall (☎0834/813429).

Saundersfoot's **train station** is located a mile outside town, a journey up a winding wooded hillside road. The excellent Pembrokeshire National Park **information office** (Easter–Sept Mon–Sat 9.30am–1pm & 2–5.15pm) is in a small, white building on the harbour, although it doesn't book **accommodation**. If you want to stay in the village, try the airily pleasant *Harbour Light Hotel*, 2 High St (☎0834/813496; ③), the small *Hurst Lea* B&B on St Bride's Lane (☎0834/812339; ③), or the incredibly cheap *Rose Cottage*, Sandyhill Road (☎0834/812544; ②), off the main Tenby Road. A mile south of Saundersfoot, the best **campsite** in the area is at *Trevayne Farm* (April–Aug; ☎0834/813402), just short of Monkstone Point, which has excellent views over Saundersfoot and the great arc of sand that sweeps round to Amroth and Pendine. There's a **youth hostel** in the Old School at Pentlepoir (☎0834/812333; ①), on the A478 near Saundersfoot station.

Saundersfoot contains copious numbers of **places to eat**, with numerous cafés and pubs vying for your business: the best bets are the charming *Old Chemist Inn* on The Strand and, around the main harbour square, the *Royal Oak* on Wogan Terrace.

South Pembrokeshire coast

The southern zigzag of coast that darts west from Tenby is a strange mix of caravan parks and Ministry of Defence shooting ranges, above some spectacularly beautiful bays and gull-covered cliffs. From Tenby, the A4139 passes through **Penally**, little more than an extended suburb of the town, before delving down past the **Lydstep Haven** beach. A road dips south, past **Skrinkle Haven** and into the winding streets of **Manorbier**, whose ghostly castle sits above a small bay. Three miles inland from here is the quintessentially pretty village of **St Florence**, its narrow lanes crowned by a profusion of Flemish chimneys.

The coast nips and tucks in past some excellent, and comparatively quiet, beaches, passing the tourist magnet of **Freshwater East** before rising up to some impressive cliffs en route to the beautiful **Barafundle Bay** and the National Trust's **Stackpole Head**. Behind Stackpole, and the neighbouring **Broad Haven** beach, is the picturesque village of **Bosherston** and its lily lakes. Between Bosherston and the coast is the first MoD artillery range, which has to be crossed if you want to see the remarkable and ancient **St Govan's chapel**, squeezed into a rock cleft above the crashing waves.

On foot, you can get closer to the best of the scenery, by way of the Pembrokeshire Coast Path's four-mile walk west, brushing along the top of some of Wales' most dramatic cliffs, with the **Stack rocks** and limestone arch that mark the last point of access on this part of the coast. All around, and to the west, are artillery ranges, forcing the Coast Path inland to avoid snipers. The next point of access on the coast is the west-facing **Freshwater West**, a wide beach popular with surfers, reached across windy grass dunes and heathland. The peninsula tapers out to the west, a long finger of rugged coastline pointing out towards the main part of the county. The westernmost village is **Angle**, sitting on the edge of its bay that faces out across the Milford Haven towards the grim reminders of industrialization in the shape of a vast oil refinery.

THE PEMBROKESHIRE NATIONAL PARK AND COAST PATH

Of the ten National Parks in England and Wales, the **Pembrokeshire Coast** is the only one that is predominantly sea-based, hugging the rippled coast around the entire western section of Wales. Established in 1952, the park is not one easily identifiable mass, rather a series of occasionally unconnected patches of coast and inland scenery. Starting at its southeastern corner, the first segment clings to the coast from Amroth through to the Milford Haven waterway, an area of sweeping limestone cliffs and some fabulous beaches. The second, and by far the quietest, part courses around the inland pastoral landscape of the Daugleddau Estuary, which plunges deep into the rural heart of Pembrokeshire southeast of Haverfordwest. Best for cliff walking and scenery is the third part, around the beaches and resorts of St Bride's Bay, where the sea scoops a great chunk out of Wales' westernmost land. In the north of the county, the boundary of the park runs deep inland to encompass the Mynydd Preseli, a barren but invigoratingly beautiful range of hills dotted with ancient relics.

Crawling around almost every wriggle of the coast, the **Pembrokeshire Coast Path** winds 186 miles from St Dogmaels near Cardigan in the north to its southern point at Amroth. For the vast majority of the time, the path clings precariously to clifftop routes, overlooking seal-basking rocks, craggy offshore islands, unexpected gashes of sand and shrieking clouds of sea birds. Only on the southwestern end of the Castlemartin peninsula does it veer inland for any major length, as the coast is given over to army training camps and rifle ranges; the path also ducks inland along the Milford Haven Estuary, where the close proximity of belching great oil refineries and the huge expanse of hill-backed water provide one of the many surprises around the route.

The most popular, and ruggedly inspiring, segments of the coast path are around St David's Head and the Marloes Peninsula, either side of St Bride's Bay, the stretch from the castle at Manorbier to the tiny cliff chapel at Bosherston along the southern coast and, generally quieter, the undulating contours, massive cliffs, bays and old ports along the northern coast, either side of Fishguard. These offer miles of windswept walking amongst great flashes of gorse, heather and seasonal plants, as well as the opportunity to study thousands of sea birds at close quarter. Basking seals are frequent visitors to some of the more inaccessible beaches, particularly around the time when pups are born in the autumn. This is reckoned to be one of the major causes of accidents along the route, as people try to gain better views of the creatures and consequently tip over the edge.

Few walkers appreciate the danger of the path, on which there is a grim annual death toll, mainly through those falling over the cliffs. Of all the seasons, perhaps spring is the finest for walking as the crowds are yet to arrive and the clifftop flora is at its most vivid. There are numerous publications available about the coast path, of which the best is Brian John's *National Trail Guide*, which includes section 1:25,000 maps of the route. The National Park publishes a handy *Coast Path Accommodation* guide, detailing B&Bs and campsites the entire length of the route, available from tourist and National Park offices and bookshops. It also publishes the excellent free newspaper, *Coast to Coast*, which contains exhaustive listings of special walks, boat trips and other events, and which you can pick up from the various National Park offices listed throughout this chapter. A further path has been created around the haunting Daugleddau estuaries, inland from the Milford Haven. For details of both the National Park and the coast path, contact the National Park offices at County Offices, Haverfordwest, Dyfed SA61 1QZ (☎0437/764591).

Penally, Manorbier and St Florence

Just over a mile down the A4139 from Tenby, the dormitory village of **PENALLY** is unremarkable save for the vast beach, a wide and sunny sprawl of sand that runs right up to become Tenby's South Beach a mile further up. The coastal path hugs the clifftop from the viewpoint at Giltar Point, just below Penally, reaching the glorious privately owned beach at the 54-acre headland of **Lydstep Haven** after two miles (a fee being charged for the sands); it's a beautiful spot, with limestone caverns to explore in the craggy Lydstep Point. Although some of the caverns are only accessible at low tide, the Smuggler's Cave is safe at all times. A mile further west is the cove of **Skrinkle Haven**, reached via steep steps from the car park at the end of the little lane off the Manorbier road. Above the beach is an excellent **youth hostel** (☎0834/871803; ①), where you can also camp, or you can find B&B at *Myrtle House*, near the Penally train station (☎0834/843623; ②), or the slightly superior *Hillgarth*, in Skrinkle village (☎0834/871266; ③). There's another campsite at *Whitewell Farm* (☎0834/871569), sandwiched between the main road and train line just west of the town. Of the pubs, the lively *Cross Inn*, near the station, is best.

Manorbier

The next part of the coast path heads inland to avoid the artillery range that occupies the beautiful outcrop of **Old Castle Head**, then leads straight into the quaint village of **MANORBIER**, pronounced "Manner-beer" (Maenorbŷr), birthplace in 1146 of Giraldus Cambrensis, Gerald of Wales (see p.249), who described the castle here as "excellently well defended by turrets and bulwarks, and . . . situated on the summit of a hill extending on the western side towards the sea". Founded in the early twelfth century as an impressive baronial residence, the **castle** (April–Sept daily 10.30am–5.30pm; £1.50) sits above the village and its beach on a hill of wild gorse. The Norman walls are in a very decent state of repair, surrounding an inner grass courtyard in which the extensive remains of the castle's chapel and state rooms jostle for position with the nineteenth-century domestic residence, whose TV aerial strikes a note of contemporary discord. Views from the ramparts are wonderful: you can see the corrugated coastline, bushy dunes, deep green fields, and smoking chimneys of the tinted village houses. In the walls and buildings are a warren of dark passageways to explore, occasionally opening out into little cells with lacklustre wax figures, purporting to illustrate the castle's history. Needless to say, prime position goes to a waxwork of Gerald himself.

The lane below the castle leads past the curious, elongated tower of the parish church down to Manorbier's shell-shaped **cove**, a sandy break in the red sandstone cliffs. For a more secluded bathe, follow the path on the left of the beach (as you face the sea) up over the headland known as the Priest's Nose, past the Neolithic cromlech (burial chamber) known as the **King's Quoit**, with its lopsided capstone, and round for just over half a mile to the steep steps down to often deserted **Precipe Beach**. At high tide, the beach is entirely flooded, so check times carefully.

In Manorbier, you'll find **accommodation** at the smart and comfortable *Old Vicarage* (☎0834/871452; ③), or camp at *Park Farm* (☎0834/871273) near the village centre. The *Castle Inn* hosts live music on Saturdays.

Swanlake Bay and Freshwater East

The lanes and coast path wriggle ever westwards, the path skirting across the top of the beautifully remote, and always quiet, **Swanlake Bay**, a mile from Manorbier; car drivers will find it almost impossible to find a place to park, although just off the small lane from Manorbier to Hodgeston, the farmers at East Moor Farm and *West Moor Farm* (☎0834/871204; ③), where you are also able to stay, usually allow a few people to park and walk the remaining distance. Swanlake is a far better option than the next beach along, close to the garish village of **FRESHWATER EAST**, whose magnificent sheltered beach is spoiled by the profusion of hideous sprawling holiday developments in the village that backs it.

St Florence

Three miles north of Manorbier is the delightful little village of **ST FLORENCE**, whose whitewashed stone cottages, many with their original medieval Flemish chimney stacks, are huddled around the tiny lanes. The Ritec stream, along whose banks there is a beautiful walk which takes you east of the village, was once an inlet, and St Florence an important port during the Middle Ages before the stream retreated. If you want to **stay** here, the country house atmosphere of *Elm Grove* (☎0834/871255; ③) comes at a very reasonable price. The village pubs are also excellent: the wonderful *New Inn* is the first amongst equals in this village of great pubs.

From Stackpole Quay to Angle

The rocky little harbour at **Stackpole Quay**, reached via the small lane from Freshwater East through East Trewent, is a good starting point for walks along the breathtaking cliffs to the north, or half a mile south to the finest beach in Pembrokeshire: **Barafundle Bay**. Idyllically clear water and a soft beach are fringed by wooded cliffs at either end; south of the beach is an isolated stretch of path with an amazing number of sea birds circling around the cliffs and their arched limestone outcrops.

The path continues around the coast, through the dunes of **Stackpole Warren**, to **BROAD HAVEN**, where a pleasant small beach overlooks several rocky islets, now managed by the National Trust. Basing yourself here gives good access inland to the nearby **Bosherston Lakes**, three fingers of water artificially created in the late eighteenth century, but beautifully landscaped. The westernmost lake is the most scenic, especially in late spring and early summer when the lilies that form a carpet across its surface are in full bloom.

Another lane dips south from the village of **BOSHERSTON**, a mile inland from Broad Haven, across the MoD training grounds peppered with warning signs reminding that "military debris may explode and kill you", and at times access to the land is altogether banned, as indicated at National Park information offices and other points like Bosherston post office. Persevere through the series of unwelcoming gates down the lane running for just over a mile to a spot overlooking the cliffs where **St Govan's chapel** is wedged: it's a remarkable tiny, grey chapel, known to be at least eight hundred years old (and could be as much as fourteen hundred). Legend has it that Saint Govan chose this spot to be buried when a gang of hoodlums was attacking him on the clifftop, and the cliffs opened up and folded gently around him, protecting him from certain death. The steps descend straight into the sandy-floored chapel, now devoid of any furnishings, save for the simple stone altar. At its side steps lead into a small cell honed from the rock, containing the fissure that is supposed to have sheltered St Govan. Steps continue down to the spume of the sea hurtling at the rocks. Here, you get a magnificent close-up of the precarious crags, caves and arches, deep turquoise water, rigidly straight rock strata and limestone worn and washed by the sea. Good value **accommodation** is found at the enjoyable *St Govan's Inn* in Bosherston village (☎0646/661311; ③), which also has reasonably priced food.

All the land to the west of St Govan's is dominated by the dugouts and abandoned shells and tanks of the army and, apart from the narrow strip of clifftop land on which the coast path runs, is entirely out of bounds. The path skirts along the top of the cliffs to the west for four miles, past the striking cleft in the rocks known as **Huntsman's Leap**, two isolated beaches at **Bull's Laughter** and **Flimston Bay** to the **Stack Rocks**. Alternatively, a lane – with restrictive times of opening – runs down to the Stacks from near Merrion on the B4319, passing the mourning little chapel of **FLIMSTON** village en route, a hamlet forcibly abandoned to the army.

The Stack Rocks jut out of the sea like a series of tall, lichen-spattered stepping stones. A few hundred yards further west (and as far as you're allowed to go) is a graceful, curving limestone arch rising out of a wave-flattened platform of rock, known as the **Green Bridge of Wales**. On a quiet day, the only company you will have are the shrieking gulls, guillemots and kittiwakes swooping around before perching on the limestone ledges.

Castlemartin, Freshwater West and Angle

Forced to turn inland here, the coast path continues back up the lane to Merrion and follows the B4319 through the village of **CASTLEMARTIN** – whose church houses an organ once owned by Mendelssohn. Here you'll find a few places to **stay**: the *Court Farm* (May–Sept; ☎0646/661228; ②), and *West Farm*, Castlemartin's old vicarage (April–Sept; ☎0646/661227; ③), where you can also camp; another campsite, *Gupton Farm* (☎0646/661268), lies between Castlemartin and **FRESHWATER WEST**, a west-facing beach resort that's excellent for surfers, although the currents can be too strong for swimming. The desolation of the wind-battered dunes behind the beach make for interesting walking.

The B4319 meets the B4320 from Pembroke near the **Devil's Quoit**, a Neolithic burial chamber topped by an impressive capstone. The road continues west into the last finger of the peninsula, reaching the remote village of **ANGLE**, at the western end of a wide curve of mud, known as **Angle Bay**. Angle consists of one long street, bounded by old, coloured cottages and some impressive pubs. Better for swimming is **West Angle Bay**, a secluded spot a mile to the west of the main village, overlooking another of the Lord Palmerston protective forts on **Thorn Island**, now converted into the most secluded of **hotels**, the *Thorn Island Hotel* (June–Aug; ☎0646/641225; ④). You can stay at the *Timothy Lodge* (☎0646/641342; ②) in the middle of Angle, or camp at *Castle Farm* (☎0646/641220). For **eating and drinking**, try the *Point House*, a charming old inn with a fire that is said to have burned continuously for 300 years, or the nearby *Hibernia Inn*, noted for its excellent meals.

Pembroke and around

The old county town of **PEMBROKE** (Penfro) and its fearsome **castle** sit on the southern side of the Pembroke River, a continuation of the massive Milford Haven waterway, described by Nelson as the greatest natural harbour in the world. The slightly over-restored castle is nonetheless an essential sight, dominated by its vast 75-foot Norman keep. But aside from that, and the town's wonderful **Museum of the Home**, Pembroke is surprisingly dull, with one long main street of attractive Georgian and Victorian houses, some intact stretches of medieval town wall and little else to catch the eye.

The town grew up solely to serve the castle, the mightiest link in the chain of Norman strongholds built across southern Wales. The walled town, drawn out along a hilltop ridge, flourished as a port for Pembrokeshire goods to be exported throughout Britain and to Ireland, France and Spain. The main quay was situated alongside the waters below the imposing walls of the castle.

Cromwell attacked the town in 1648 during the English Civil War. By this stage, the castle was partially derelict and it was only the strength of the recently repaired town walls that enabled the citizens to withstand the worst of the onslaught. They were beaten, however, by a 48-day seige and by the Parliamentarian troops seizing the water supply, after which Cromwell ordered the continued demolition of the castle and walls.

Pembroke developed as a centre of leather making, weaving, dyeing and tailoring, never really regaining its former importance. In the twentieth century, the small town was on a serious slope of decline, its port long since overtaken by neighbouring sites. One fortunate result of this is that the town is mercifully free of postwar development in the centre, although the fringes around the main street are largely modern and bland.

Around the town are several noteworthy sights, the most interesting being the ruined Bishop's Palace in **Lamphey**, a country residence for the bishops of St David's in the thirteenth century, and a couple of miles further on, the attractive town of **Carew**, with its Celtic cross and castle. **Pembroke Dock**, a couple of miles north of Pembroke, grew up in a grid pattern during the nineteenth century to serve its parent town as a naval dockyard.

The Town

The **Pembroke River**, a tidal mass of mud, flows in from the Daugleddau to frame the northern side of Pembroke town centre. Running parallel to the southern bank is the long **Main Street**, which stretches from the train station (as Station Road) in the east to the mighty lines of the castle.

Opposite the castle walls at 7 Westgate Hill (the continuation north of the Main Street) is the delightfully eccentric **Museum of the Home** (May–Sept Mon–Thurs 11am–5pm; £1.20), an all-encompassing name for the thousands of objects packed into a steep town house. It's a collection of utterly ordinary items from the eighteenth to the twentieth centuries, loosely gathered into themes – the dairy, toiletries, personal and smoking accessories, kitchen equipment, bedroom accessories and children's games. The enthusiasm of the owners, who show people around with illuminating conversation and great interest, makes the sensation somewhat akin to being let loose in a small stately home.

From the museum and the castle gates, Main Street widens out past multi-coloured shop frontages of eighteenth- and nineteenth-century construction, dipping down for over half a mile towards the towered **St Michael's church**, heavily, and unsympathetically, restored by the Victorians. Blackhorse Walk turns north, running down to the Mill Pond and the most impressive remnants of the thirteenth-century town **walls** running between the demolished East Gate and Barnard's Tower, a medieval towered house attached to the walls.

The castle

Pembroke's history is inextricably bound up with that of the **castle** (April–Sept daily 9.30am–6pm; March & Oct daily 10am–5pm; Nov–Feb daily 10am–4pm; £2), founded as the strongest link in the chain of fortresses built by the Normans across south Wales to tame and subjugate the people. In the early years following the Norman invasion, the people of Deheubarth (west Wales) avoided the conquest, thanks to a tacit agreement between Rhys ap Tewdwr and the Norman victors. Upon his death in 1093, however, Norman lord Roger de Montgomery didn't hesitate for a moment in charging into the area and capturing it by force from the surprised natives. Pembroke's powerful bulk, protected by a hill on its southern side and water on the other three, proved impregnable to the Welsh, who attempted to besiege it. But to no avail, it has never been under the control of the Welsh. The earldom of Pembroke, created in 1138, was passed down to the Marshals, or local landowners awarded an earldom, who almost entirely rebuilt the castle between 1189 and 1245, and over the ensuing three centuries, enforced the feudal rule of "Little England beyond Wales", a primitive (but successful) way of ensuring Welsh subservience to the English in the farthest flung corner of the country, by establishing firm English military rule from the chain of powerful castles built in a string across Pembrokeshire. In 1452, Henry VI granted the title and castle to Jasper Tudor, whose nephew Harri (or Henry) was born here and became king, as the Lancastrian heir to the throne, after defeating Yorkist Richard III at Bosworth Field in 1485. During the Civil War, Pembroke was a Parliamentarian stronghold until the town's military governor suddenly switched allegiance to the King. Cromwell's troops sacked the castle after besieging it for 48 days.

Despite Cromwell's incessant battering and centuries of subsequent neglect, Pembroke still inspires feelings of awe at its sheer, bloody-minded bulk, even if it is largely due to extensive restoration over the last century. Entering through the soaring gatehouse brings the visitor into the large, grassy courtyard, around which the battlements are broken up by great hulking towers. These marked the positions where the town walls formerly attached themselves to the fortress.

At the back of the courtyard is the inner ward, grouped around the castle's most eye-catching feature: the vast, round Norman **keep**, 75 foot high and with walls 18 feet thick, crowned by a dome. The intact towers and battlements contain many heavily restored communal rooms, now empty of furniture, and to a large extent, atmosphere too, although the walkways and dark roofed passages that connect them give the visitor ample chance to chase around spiral stairways into great oak-beamed halls. Some of the rooms, mainly in the gatehouse, are used to house some excellent displays on the history of the castle and the Tudor empire.

The view of the dank, dripping interior is quite disorientating, as the tower seems to taper upwards. Even better is the eerie view into the yawning innards from the top, which can be reached via steps in the massive walls. The tower was probably built at the beginning of the thirteenth century by William Marshal. One clue to its age comes in the two contrasting windows in its side – one round-headed and Norman, the other pointed and Perpendicular – suggesting that the construction spanned the transitional period between the two architectural ages.

Alongside the keep is a cluster of domestic buildings, largely ruined and unrestored, and seeming insignificant in comparison with the sheer bulk of the rest of the castle. Apart from a dungeon tower – complete with grille to peer through into the gloomy cell below – there's a Norman Hall, where the period arch has been disappointingly over-restored and reinforced, next to the Oriel or Northern Hall, a Tudor recreation of an earlier antechamber. A set of steps at the side of the Northern Hall leads down and down into a huge natural cavern, dank and slimy, way below the castle, where light is beamed in through a barred hole in the wall that looks out over the waterside path.

Practicalities

Pembroke's **train station** (☎0646/684896) is on the easternmost side of the town centre on Station Road. From there, head left out of Station Drive, over the roundabout and down the Main Street into the town centre. A new **tourist office** is on Commons Road (Easter–Sept daily 10am–5.30pm; Oct–Easter Sat & Sun only; ☎0646/622388), parallel to Main Street, and provides a useful free town booklet guide. At the entrance to the castle is a small **National Park information centre** (Easter–Sept Mon–Sat 9.30am–1pm & 2–5.30pm; ☎0646/682148).

Accommodation ranges from cheap B&Bs such as the *Connaught*, 123 Main St (☎0646/684655; ②), and rooms at the real ale *Old Cross Saws* pub (☎0646/682475; ②) on Hamilton Terrace, just before it becomes the Main Street, to slightly plusher hotels like the *King's Arms*, near the castle on the Main Street (☎0646/683611; ④), and the *Moat House* on The Commons (☎0646/684557; ⑤).

Food is easy to find in Pembroke: try *The Pantry*, 4 Main St, near the castle, for stodgy and cheap daytime and early evening snacks, the excellent *Woodhouse* restaurant (☎0646/687140), which specializes in a limited, but beautifully cooked, menu of local produce, or the bar food at the *King's Arms Hotel*, also on Main Street. In Pembroke Dock, the food at the *Welshman's Arms* on London Road is excellent, as is the pricier continental *La Brasseria* in Law Street (☎0646/686966).

There are dozens of **pubs** – the best in Pembroke is the *Old Cross Saws* on Hamilton Terrace (see "Accommodation" above), although it's hard to beat a summer evening on the verandah, overlooking the Mill Pond, at the *Waterman's Arms*, over the bridge on Northgate Street. The *Castle Inn*, 17 Main St, is dowdy, but friendly and entertaining enough. Near the ferry terminal in Pembroke Dock on Pembroke Street, the friendly *White Hart* is good value all round.

Pembroke Dock

Built as a result of a local argument that developed when Milford Haven refused to provide a home for a naval dockyard, the town of **PEMBROKE DOCK**, a couple of miles north of its parental city, grew up almost instantaneously in the nineteenth century. Constructed on a rigid grid plan with some handsome Victorian buildings flanking the wide streets, its fortunes have fluctuated severely between recession and boom, but today, thanks to the oil refineries and the development of a deep-water dock, the town is on a firmer footing than it has been for decades.

Pembroke Dock's train station leads out on to Water Street. To the right, Pier Road heads down to Hobbs Point, a spectacular viewpoint over the boats and smoking stacks of the Daugleddau River, and the departure point for *Tudor Line* **leisure cruises** along the waterway (☎0646/685627). The **ferry terminal**, for *B&I* trips to Rosslare in Ireland (☎0646/684161), is to the west of the station (p.6).

Carew

A tiny village that can become unbearably packed in high season, **CAREW**, four miles east of Pembroke by the Carew River, is a pretty place. Just south of the river crossing, by the main road, is the village's **Celtic cross**, erected as a memorial to Maredydd, ruler of Deheubarth, who died in 1035. The graceful, remarkably intact taper of the shaft is covered in fine tracery of ancient Welsh designs.

A small hut beyond the cross serves as the ticket office for **Carew Castle** and **Mill** (Easter–Oct daily 9.30am–5pm; £1.40 castle only, £2 castle & mill). The castle, a hybrid of Elizabethan fancy and earlier defensive necessity, is reached across a field. Explanatory models illustrate the development of the site, which is an excellent example of the organic nature by which castles grew, from the Norman tower believed to be the original gatehouse, through the thirteenth-century front battlements, to the newer Tudor gatehouse and the Elizabethan mansion grafted on to them all. A few hundred yards west of the castle is the **Carew French Mill**, the only mill powered by the shifting tides in Wales. The impressive eighteenth-century exterior belies the pedestrian exhibitions and self-guided audio-visual displays of the milling process at different stages.

Lamphey

The humdrum village of **LAMPHEY**, two miles east of Pembroke, is best known for the ruined **Bishop's Palace** (May–Sept daily 10am–5pm; £1.50; Oct–April free entry at all times; CADW), off a quiet lane to the north of the village. This was a country retreat for the bishops of St David's, dating from at least the thirteenth century and abandoned at the Reformation in the mid-sixteenth century, although it was in use as Crown apartments for a few decades afterwards.

Stout walls surround the palace ruins, scattered over a large area, with many of the palace buildings having long been lost under the grassy banks. Most impressive are the remains of the Great Hall across the entire eastern end of the complex, with fourteenth-century Bishop Gower's hallmark arcaded parapets on its top, similar to those that he built in the Bishop's Palace of St David's. The gloomy hall beneath the Great Hall has the feeling of a crypt, lit as it is only by narrow slits.

Mid-Pembrokeshire

Pembroke Dock lies on the southern banks of the magnificent **Daugleddau** river estuary, the continuation of one of the world's greatest natural harbours, the **Milford Haven**. This spawned an eponymous Quaker community on the northern bank, which now seems, rather sadly, to be searching for a new post-industrial identity by ploughing vast sums into the development of some dubious tourist features. Seven miles to the north, the chief town of the region, **Haverfordwest**, makes an important market and transport centre that, despite some handsome architecture, remains rather soulless.

The A40 arrives in Haverfordwest from the east, brushing through an unspectacular, but effortlessly pleasant, rural landscape on the way. Just south of the road, five miles from the town, **Picton Castle** houses the notable **Graham Sutherland Art Gallery**, a branch of the National Museum of Wales. The lanes around here descend gently to the wide, tidal waters of the Daugleddau, a river estuary flooding the valleys of inland Pembrokeshire and providing a surprisingly maritime feel in the middle of such impressively rolling countryside. The main road roars on, bypassing the stout little town of **Narberth**, self-appointed capital of the **Landsker borderlands**, a revived name for the imaginary, but effectively real, line that divides the anglicized corner of south Pembrokeshire from its Welsh-speaking neighbour.

A branch train line leaves the *InterCity* Fishguard route at Whitland, calling at Narberth en route to Pembroke and Pembroke Dock. The train line divides again at Clarbeston Road, with the Milford Haven-bound branch calling at Haverfordwest. A reasonable bus service throughout the area has most routes starting at either Pembroke or Haverfordwest.

Milford Haven

One of the most impressive sights in this part of Wales is the view from the 1970s **Cleddau Bridge** (car toll 75p), which curves out of Pembroke Dock over to **NEYLAND** on the opposite bank. Pedestrians can also try it: the views over the jutting headlands are magical, the masts of boats far below and the full skies reflected in the clear water. Even the refineries look attractive from this far up. Even better, try to synchronize your journey over the bridge with a decent sunset, when the glowing sun dips perfectly into the estuary mouth.

Four miles west of Neyland, **MILFORD HAVEN** (Aberdaugleddau) was founded in the late eighteenth century by a group of early American settlers from Nantucket, who were imported as whalers. The grid pattern they imposed survives today – principally three streets rising sharply parallel to the waterway – when new civic and religious buildings were founded. Despite a magnificent site and interesting heritage, Milford Haven has a deadbeat atmosphere, due largely to the town attractions being relocated around a horribly sterile dock development, now given the misnomer of the Marina. The waterside is impressive though, with tugs and steamers ploughing up the glittering waters of the Haven, stretching out below the pleasant gardens.

The waterside road is Hamilton Terrace, which skirts around to the tarted-up **docks**, home of an assortment of museums – the child-oriented **discovery centre**, *Kaleidoscope* (daily 10am–6pm; £4), a tawdry **Dockside Gallery**, some unpleasant cafés and restaurants, and the genuinely interesting town **museum** (Easter–Oct Tues–Sun 11am–5pm; £1), housed in an eighteenth-century warehouse, built to store whale oil. Exhibits include photographs and mementoes from the fishing trade, an explanation of the modern oil industry, details of the Quaker beginnings of the town and some fascinating archive material of Milford Haven in wartime.

Practicalities

Milford Haven **train station** is located under the Hakin road bridge, next to the docks. The docks **information office** (daily 10am–6pm) is not an official one, but sells an all-in-one ticket to the town's sights, apart from the museum (£5) – for the official information office, head up to 94 Charles St (April–Sept Mon–Sat 10am–5pm; ☎0646/690866). The town is home to west Wales' only professional **theatre**: the *Torch* on St Peter's Road, at the end of Charles Street (☎0646/695267).

Accommodation includes the classy *Belhaven House Hotel*, 29 Hamilton Terrace (☎0646/695983; ③), the *Pebbles Guest House*, 15–18 Pill Fold (☎0646/698155; ②), and in the western suburb of Hakin, the *Cleddau Villa*, 21 St Anne's Rd (☎0646/690313; ②); there's a **campsite** at *Sandy Haven*, near Herbrandston, two miles west of town (☎0646/693180). For **food** and **drink**, the *Wanderer Bistro* in Hamilton Terrace (☎0646/697594) serves an excellent range of local and continental dishes.

Haverfordwest and Picton Castle

In the seventeenth century, the town of **HAVERFORDWEST** (Hwlffordd), lying in the valley of the Western Cleddau seven miles northeast of Milford Haven, was created as the county town of Pembrokeshire, replacing the old settlement of Pembroke. Haverfordwest itself is an old town, having grown up around one of Gilbert de Clare's castles, the remains of which dominate the town to this day. The town prospered as a port and trading centre in the seventeenth and eighteenth centuries, its homely architecture reflecting the richness of the age. Despite all the natural advantages, Haverfordwest's half-empty modern shopping centre seems to reflect the lack of pride in the place these days, and it's scarcely a place to linger.

Castle Square is the epicentre of the town, and it's from here that a small alleyway to the right of *Woolworths* ascends to the **castle**, unfortunately failing to live up to the expectations created by views of it from down below; all there is to see is a dingy shell of the thirteenth-century inner ward. Adjoining the castle is the old prison, now the less-than-exciting **district museum** (April–Sept Mon–Sat 10am–5.15pm; Oct–March Mon–Sat 11am–4pm; 50p). Back down below, the Riverside Shopping Centre follows the river from Castle Square up to the Old Bridge, next to the bus terminus and tourist office, and adjoining the centre is a lively indoor **market** (Mon–Sat).

The **tourist office** is next to the bus terminus at the end of the Old Bridge (Mon–Sat 10am–5pm; ☎0437/763110), and there is also an excellent **National Park office** at 48 High St. Haverfordwest offers **accommodation** at the solidly Georgian *Castle Hotel* in Castle Square (☎0437/769322; ⑤), or, a little cheaper, the *College Guest House*, 93 Hill St (☎0437/763710; ③), and the *Villa House*, St Thomas Green (☎0437/762977; ③). There's a **campsite** two miles northwest on the A487, at the *Rising Sun Inn* in Pelcomb Bridge (☎0437/765171). The *Hotel*

Mariners is an old coaching inn in Mariners' Square, and offers the best bar snacks in the town, along with a pricier **restaurant**. The *Carmarthen Arms*, near the station, is low-key, but enjoyable enough and with a good bar menu.

Picton Castle

The main A40 heads east out of Haverfordwest, past the train station. After two or three miles, signs point south towards **Picton Castle** (castle mid-July to mid-Sept Thurs & Sun noon–5pm; £2 includes grounds), a graceless building, something of a hybrid of architectural styles from the fourteenth to the eighteenth centuries, but sited in glorious **grounds** (April–Sept Tues–Sun 10.30am–5pm; £1) with views over the Eastern Cleddau and its valleys. The English artist Graham Sutherland (1903–80) loved Pembrokeshire, describing the landscape as if it were always "poised on the brink of some drama", and bequeathed a collection of his work to the county, now housed in a **gallery** in the castle's stables (March–Oct Tues–Sun 10.30am–12.30pm, 1.30–5pm; £1). The collection well reflects the diversity of Sutherland's skills: elemental landscapes, many of them inspired locally, and semi-abstract dramas on canvas stand side-by-side with etchings, aquatints and jowly portraits. Another gallery hosts travelling exhibitions of contemporary work.

Having visited the Sutherland collection, it's a good idea to tour the quiet lanes around Picton that wind and open out, suddenly and unexpectedly, onto the great tidal waters of the estuaries, cutting an incongruous gash through the lush rural landscape. This was the land that inspired Sutherland – as he noted, after his first visit in 1934, "I came here, I was hooked and obsessed".

Narberth and the Landsker Borderlands

In contrast to Milford Haven and Haverfordwest, the area now known as the **Landsker Borderlands** forms a quiet, charming part of mid-Pembrokeshire, broken by some beautiful villages that are still well off the beaten tourist track. Landsker is a Norse word meaning "frontier", here used as a definition of the division between Cymric north Pembrokeshire and the anglicized south. Although the division is ancient, going back to the Norman colonization of the south of the county, the name, despite sounding sufficiently archaic, is a comparatively recent soubriquet – first mentioned, in this context, in the 1930s.

The "capital" of the borderlands is **NARBERTH** (Arberth), a pleasing little town on the train line to Tenby, just off the main A40; this is supposed to be the court of Pwyll in the *Mabinogion*, a collection of pre-Norman Welsh folk tales and legends, and in reality, its ruined **castle** was the old home of the Welsh princes.

At the far eastern end of the town is the **train station**, at the top of Station Road, which runs down to St James Street, and connects with the market square and the bottom of the town's neat High Street. Dividing the High Street is the curious, spiky **town hall**, built in the 1830s to mask the municipal water tank underneath. Upstairs is the **tourist office** (see below), and the **Landsker Visitor Centre**, which aims to illustrate local history interwoven with the lurid tales of the *Mabinogion*, which it describes as a "window on the Iron Age".

Water Street runs down from behind the town hall to the **Wilson Museum** (Easter–Sept Mon–Sat 10.30am–5pm; 60p), housed in an old town pub – the entrance lobby is the barely altered front parlour. Much of the collection comes from local people, the net result being a beguiling slice of Narbeth life over the past couple of centuries. There are themes, such as local transport, religion and education, but these are soon forgotten in the pursuit of yet more trivia. Completely unrelated to Narberth, but interesting nonetheless, the museum also has a rare 1925 stuffed velvet Mickey Mouse, complete with his early rat-like features. The museum opens out into a great little bookshop and coffee shop, giving onto the market square.

Narberth lies to the east of the most impressive scenery around the Daugleddau Estuary. The tidal reach of the Eastern Cleddau River goes as far as **Blackpool Mill** (Easter–Oct daily 11am–6pm; £2), four miles west of Narberth. An elegant four-storey stone block, the mill was built in 1813 to grind wheat using water power, although this source was replaced at the beginning of this century by turbines. Much of the machinery has been restored and can be seen throughout the building, alongside replica workshops filled with bland wax models. Below the mill, a series of caves have also been filled with models, this time replica brown bears, cavemen, wolves and a huge Welsh dragon in a fanciful attempt to depict life in prehistoric Wales.

Landshipping, Lawrenny and Llawhaden

Far more interesting are the walks and lanes that fan out to the west of the mill, along the southern bank of the Eastern Cleddau. The best place to oversee the muddy flats and skimming birds is from the creaky *Stanley Arms* in the lonesome hamlet of **LANDSHIPPING**, whose desolate **quay**, a mile to the south, was once a ferry point and place from where coal was exported. Here, the two Cleddau rivers diverge, with the main estuary plunging southwards through wooded hillsides. The best walk, less than two miles long, hugs the river banks between **Garron** and **Lawrenny Quay**, passing through ancient oak woodlands. To the north of the quay is the peaceful village of **LAWRENNY** (Lawrenni), dominated by the four-storey tower of the magnificent twelfth-century **St Caradoc's church**. Just as breathtaking is **Oakwood Leisure Park** (April–Sept daily 10am–5pm; £6.95; ☎0834/891376), where a mini-railway whisks you from the ticket kiosk into a park filled with rides, an adventure playground, go-karting, tobogganing and family-pitched theatre shows; all the attractions are pre-paid in the cost of entrance. Oakwood is just outside the village of Cross Hands on the A4075, two miles south of the junction with the A4075 at Canaston Bridge.

North of Narberth, the most spectacular scenery is along the rich, non-tidal valley of the Eastern Cleddau, especially in the idyllic and steep village of **LLAWHADEN**, whose ghostly **castle** (free access, collect key from post office if locked) sits on a bluff above the river. Once a residence of the Bishop of St David's, the castle's remains reflect its later role more as a luxurious home than as a defensive fort. Most impressive is the decorative square fourteenth-century gatehouse, dating from the castle's major transformation into a bishop's palace.

Practicalities

The **tourist office** in Narberth is open at the same times as the Landsker Visitor Centre (April–Oct Mon–Sat 10am–5pm; summer school holidays also Sun; Nov–March Thurs–Sat 10am–1pm; free; ☎0834/860061). They stock a wide selection of free leaflets that give intricate details about local villages and walks. There are a couple of occasional **B&Bs** along Station Road, Spring Gardens and St James Street, with the town's only real hotel being the splendid *Plas Hyfryd* on Moorfield Road, off the top end of the High Street (☎0834/860653; ④).

Neighbouring **ROBESTON WATHEN** contains the *Traethgwyn* (☎0834/860598; ③) and *Canton* guesthouses, down towards Canaston Bridge (☎0834/860620; ③). There is a peaceful **campsite** near the village of Landshipping, at *New Park Farm* (☎0834/891284), a mile from the village and the estuary.

Drinking is easy in Narberth, with a multitude of pubs, although **eating** presents fewer choices. The restaurant at the *Plas Hyfryd* hotel (see above) is excellent, if costly. Alternatives for evening food are the fresh and reasonable food at *Gregory's* on the Market Square (☎0834/861511) or standard pub fare at the *Angel Inn* on the High Street. The creaky *Stanley Arms* in Landshipping is excellent for food at all times. For unadulterated drinking, there's the earthy *Ivy Bush* at the top of Narberth High Street and, further down by the Town Hall, the young and lively *Dragon*. Most "local" of all the town's pubs is the *Kirkland Arms*, at the top of St James Street where it meets Station Road. The *Bridge Inn* at Robeston Wathen plays host to regular **jazz nights** (information ☎0834/861408).

St Bride's Bay

The most western point of Wales – and the very furthest you can get from England – is one of the country's most enchanting areas. The coast around **St Bride's Bay** is broken into rocky crops, islands and broad, sweeping beaches curving around between two headlands that sit like giant crab pincers facing out into the warm Gulf Stream amidst the crashing Atlantic. The southernmost headland winds around every conceivable angle, offering calm, east-facing sands at **Dale**, sunny expanses of south-facing beach at **Marloes** and wilder west-facing sands at **Musselwick**. Between the latter two, the peninsula descends to its dramatic end at the **Deer Park**, just beyond **Martin's Haven**, where boats for the offshore islands of **Skomer**, **Skokholm** and **Grassholm** depart.

The middle scoop of the Bay combines the typical ruggedness with a little more in the way of golden sands, backed by teeming, popular holiday villages such as **Little Haven**, **Broad Haven** and **Newgale**. From here, the spectacularly lacerated coast veers to the left and the **St David's peninsula**, along stunning cliffs interrupted only by occasional gashes of sand. Just north of **St Non's Bay**, the tiny cathedral city of **St David's**, founded in the sixth century by Wales' patron saint, is a justified highlight. Rooks and crows circle above the impressive ruins of the huge **Bishop's Palace**, sitting beneath the delicate bulk of the **cathedral**, the most impressive in Wales. The St David's peninsula, more windswept and elemental than any other part of Pembrokeshire, tapers out just west of the city at the popular **Whitesands Bay** and the hamlet of **St Justinian**, staring out over the crags of **Ramsey Island**.

Bus transport to most corners of the peninsula radiates out from Haverfordwest: a twice weekly service to Dale and Marloes, a daily service to Broad and Little Haven and an hourly service to Newgale, Solva and St David's.

Marloes and Dale peninsula

DALE is a popular yachting and windsurfing centre, fourteen miles from Haverfordwest. In the peak season, it can become unbearably crowded, the village car park at the top of the shingle beach filling up with alarming speed.

Although not an especially attractive village, its east-facing shore makes it excellent for watersports in the lighter seas. Equipment and instruction for windsurfing, sailing, surfing and even mountain biking are available on the seafront from *West Wales Windsurfing & Sailing* (☎0646/636642).

The calm waters of Dale are deceptive, and as soon as you head down further towards **St Ann's Head**, one of the most invigoratingly desolate places in the county, the wind speed whips up, with waves and tides to match. The coast path sticks tight to the undulating coastline, passing tiny bays en route to the St Ann's lighthouse. Tucked in the eastern lee of St Ann's Head is **Mill Bay**, where Henry VII landed in 1485, marching the breadth of his native Wales and gathering a loyal army to face Richard III at Bosworth Field.

Marloes and around

The coast turns and heads north from St Ann's Head, reaching the sandstone-backed **West Dale Bay**, less than a mile from Dale on the opposite side of the peninsula. Warnings are usually given about the unpredictability of the currents and hidden rocks in the sea here, and you may find the broad sands of **MARLOES**, a mile from the village, a safer place to swim – a rarely crowded sandy spread dissected by rocky spills and looking out into the clear sky towards the island of Skokholm. From here, the coast path continues for two miles to the National Trust-owned **Deer Park** (which incidentally has no deer), the name given to the far tip of the southern peninsula of St Bride's Bay, from where some of Pembrokeshire's best sunsets can be seen. Alternatively, take the narrow lane across the wind-battered heights from Marloes to the Deer Park car park at **MARTINS HAVEN**, from where you can make crossings out to the islands of Skomer, Skokholm and Grassholm.

Skomer Island (boats April–Sept Tues–Sun 10am, 11am & noon; £5; ☎0646/601636) is a 722-acre flat-topped island rich in seabirds and spectacular carpets of wild flowers, perfect for birdwatching and walking. You can also cross to **Skokholm Island** from Martins Haven (boats June–Aug Mon 10am; £10; booking essential on ☎0646/601636), a couple of miles south of Skomer and far smaller, more rugged and remote, noted for its warm red cliffs of sandstone. Britain's first bird observatory was founded here as far back as the seventeenth century, and there is still a huge number of petrels, gulls, puffins, oystercatchers and rare Manx shearwaters. The trip includes a guided tour by the island's warden. The final boat trips head out even further, to the tiny oupost of **Grassholm Island**, over five miles west of Skomer (boats June–Sept landing trip on Mon, round trip on Fri, evening trip on Thurs; £19 to land, £16 otherwise; ☎0646/601636), an unforgettable experience, largely due to the sixty thousand or so screaming gannets – the second largest colony in the world – who call it home. All of these trips can be booked at the National Park information centres. Accommodation is also available on Skomer and Skokholm – see below for details.

Back on the mainland, the coast path continues round to **Musselwick Sands**, a beautiful and unspoilt beach less than half a mile from the village of Marloes (can be dangerous at high tide). Further north along the peninsula is the narrow **St Bride's Haven**, at the end of the lane that peters out by the tiny chapel of St Bride, whose cemetery is on the way to the beach, a tiny, but beautiful inlet, well sheltered from the winds. There are some good rock pools around the beach.

Practicalities

For **accommodation**, the cheapest option in Dale is the *Eaton Hall* guesthouse (☎0646/636293; ②), at the northern end of the village; more pricy is the *Post House Hotel* in the middle of Dale (☎0646/636201; ④), a dependable choice. Marloes village is well stocked for B&Bs: pick from the *East End* guesthouse (☎0646/636365; ②), the *Foxes Inn* (☎0646/636527; ②) or *Greenacre* (☎0646/636400; ②). The **youth hostel** at Runwayskiln (March–Oct; ☎0646/636667) consists of a series of converted farm buildings overlooking the northern end of Marloes Sands. **Camping** is possible at *Greenacre* (see above), near the youth hostel at Runwayskiln (☎0646/636257), or at *West Hook Farm* (☎0646/636424) near Martins Haven, who can also provide a hearty breakfast. To stay on Skokholm (fully catered) and Skomer (self-catering), contact the *Dyfed Wildlife Trust* (☎0437/765462). **Food** and **drink** are available at the *Post House Hotel* in Dale, and at the *Foxes Inn* in Marloes.

From Little Haven to Solva

Altogether flatter and more easily walked by tourists, the coast north of **LITTLE HAVEN** can be disappointingly blighted by tacky seaside developments. Little Haven village is the exception – a picturesque old fishing village and coal port that descends in steep streets to a sheltered stony beach, extremely popular with divers and swimmers in summer. **Accommodation** in the village centres on the inexpensive *Little Haven Hotel* (☎0437/781285; ②) or *Burton House* (☎0437/781426; ②), and you can **camp** at *Howelston Farm* (☎0437/781253) in the middle of the village. The most noteworthy place to **eat** here is the redoubtable *Swan Inn* by the harbour, with bar snacks available each day, and an excellent restaurant, specializing in local seafood between Wednesday and Saturday (☎0437/781256).

Quite different from Little Haven are the garish charms of neighbouring **BROAD HAVEN**, a mass of fun pubs and caravan parks above a wide, popular beach fringed by some remarkably fissured and shattered cliffs. There's a National Park **information office** here (April–Sept daily 9.30am–5pm; ☎0437/781412), the major booking office for trips out to Skokholm, Skomer and Grassholm islands, and the village is also well off for **B&Bs** – try *Glenfield*, 5 Atlantic Drive (☎0437/781502; ②), *Ringstone*, on Haroldstone Hill (☎0437/781051; ③), half a mile north, or the breezy, large *Broad Haven Hotel* (☎0437/781366; ④). The **youth hostel** is next to the National Park office (☎0437/781688; ①), and there's **camping** at the tacky *Broad Haven Holiday Park* (☎0437/781277). *Haven Sports* on Marine Road (☎0437/781354) rent out windsurfing equipment (tuition available) and mountain bikes.

The coast path goes it alone from here, occasionally coinciding with a stray country lane that opens out sublime views through the wind-flattened gorse and trees. Worth seeking out a couple of miles north is the quieter sandy beach at **DRUIDSTON HAVEN**, hemmed in by steep cliffs and reached along small paths at the bottom of the sharply sloping lane from Broad Haven that accelerates down from the clifftop *Druidston Hotel* (☎0437/781221; ③), where decent bar food is available. Just before the hotel, a lane heads inland for a few hundred yards to the tiny hamlet of **DRUIDSTON**, where you can **camp** at *Shortlands* (☎0437/781234).

Nolton Haven and Solva

NOLTON HAVEN, a mile along the coast, is little more than a picturesque cluster of houses and caravans around a sheltered shingle cove. Part of the tracks of long defunct tramway that brought coal down to the jetty from the nearby Trefrane colliery can be seen here. The *Mariners Inn* in Nolton Haven has an excellent, if hardly cheap menu; just inland is the village of Nolton, in the centre of which is *Celtic Corner* in North Nolton Farm (☎0437/710254), with nights of raucous harp-twanging, boozing, local delicacy devouring and even a bit of dancing.

A cliff path and small lane climb out of Nolton Haven, after a half-hour walk descending to the southern end of the vast west-facing **Newgale Sands**, popular with families and surfers alike. The southern end of the beach, away from the main Haverfordwest–St David's road and the tawdry little village of **NEWGALE**, is a better bet for seclusion.

The coast turns west, rising abruptly to spectacular riveted cliffs beyond Newgale, a wilder, somehow more Celtic landscape than that of southern Pembrokeshire. The coast path meets the main A487 again at **SOLVA** (Solfach), a pleasant village of good pubs and restaurants at the head of an inlet that runs down into the sea by the **Gwadn Beach**, on the east side of the river. Above the beach is the **Gribin Headland**, a good viewpoint over the rippled coast and sweeping curve of bay, with scant remains of two Iron Age settlements still visible.

In Solva, most of the B&Bs are in the upper village en route to St David's, including *The Manse*, 47 High St (☎0437/721533; ②), and, down in the lower village, *Llys Aber*, 27 Main St (☎0437/721657; ②), and the *Old Printing House*, Main St (☎0437/720944; ③). There's **camping** just outside Solva on the St David's road, at *Llanungarfach* (☎0437/721202). In the centre of the village, *Le Papillon Rouge* (☎0437/720802) serves good-value lunches and pricier but excellent evening meals with imaginative use of local seafood and meats, and vegetarians are very well catered for. The *Cambrian Hotel* is dependable enough for a drink, although geared heavily to undiscriminating tourists.

St David's

ST DAVID'S (Tyddewi) is one of the most enchanting spots in Britain. This miniature city clusters around the foot of its purple- and gold-flecked cathedral at the very western point of Wales in bleak, treeless countryside; spiritually, it is the centre of Welsh ecclesiasticism, totally independent from Canterbury.

Traditionally founded by the Welsh patron saint himself in 550 AD, the see of St David's has drawn pilgrims for a millennium and a half – William the Conqueror included – and by 1120, Pope Calixtus II decreed that two journeys to St David's was the spiritual equivalent of one to Rome. The surrounding city – in reality, never much more than a large village – grew up in the shadow cast by the cathedral, and St David's today still relies on the imported wealth of newcomers to the area, attracted by its savage beauty, together with the spending power of numerous visitors.

Arrival and information

From the bus terminus situated in New Street, the friendly and efficient **tourist office** (Easter–Oct daily 9.30am–5.30pm; ☎0437/720392) is just a short walk away in City Hall on the High Street. As a National Park office, they can only book local accommodation, but they also hold information on the annual **classical music festival** held at the end of May in the cathedral, as well as the regular **craft fairs** taking place in the Cathedral Hall. Local boat companies organize trips to the outlying islands: *St David's Adventure Days*, 28a High St (☎0437/721611), book a tour (£8) to Ramsey Island (see p.158), as well as running kayaking, abseiling, mountain biking, rock climbing, windsurfing and orienteering expeditions; *Thousand Island Expeditions*, Cross Square (☎0437/721686), run all-day trips through some terrifyingly turbulent seas to Grassholm, Skomer, Skokholm, and Smalls lighthouse, as well as a frightening tour through the immense waves that rise towards the tidal peak around Ramsey: an absolute soaking is guaranteed.

Apart from the adventure centres, **bike rental** is available from *St David's Cycle Hire*, just off the High Street at Digby's End, New Street (☎0437/720057 or 720354).

Accommodation

There are numerous places to **stay** on the St David's peninsula, with prices fairly high in season at the larger hotels, but coming down dramatically for the rest of the year. Campsites abound in and around the city. For accommodation on Ramsey Island, see p.158.

HOTELS AND GUESTHOUSES

Alandale, 43 Nun St (☎0437/720333). Small and friendly, if rather costly guesthouse in the middle of town. ④.

Mr & Mrs Davies, Upper Treginnis, near St David's (☎0437/720234). A comfortable farmhouse B&B a mile to the southwest of the town, above the valley of the River Alun. Tent pitches also available. ②.

Old Cross, Cross Square (☎0437/720387). Comfortable, creaky hotel with decent-sized rooms and a good restaurant. Closed Nov–Feb. ④.

Pen Albro, 18 Goat St (☎0437/721865). Cheery B&B next to the *Farmers Arms*, St David's liveliest (and only) night spot. ③.

Ramsey House, Lower Moo (☎0437/720321). Excellent small hotel on the road to Porth Clais, with superb Welsh cuisine. ③.

St Non's, Goat St (☎0437/720239). Rambling old-fashioned country hotel near the River Alun. ④.

Whitesands Bay, Whitesands (☎0437/720403). Family-oriented beach hotel with outdoor pool, above the very popular beach. ④.

Y Glennydd, 51 Nun St (☎0437/720576). Town centre B&B place in a converted Victorian house. ②.

HOSTELS AND CAMPSITES

Caerfai Farm, Caerfai Bay (☎0437/720548). Best campsite near St David's, a fifteen-minute walk from the city. Closed Oct–April.

Lleithyr Farm, Whitesands Bay (☎0437/720245). Campsite and caravan park just off the B4583, half a mile short of Whitesands Bay.

Llaethdy youth hostel, Llaethdy (☎0437/720345). Large and popular hostel, two miles northwest of St David's near Whitesands Bay. ①.

Rhosson Farm, St Justinians (☎0437/720335). Popular year-round campsite, handy for the boats out to Ramsey Island.

Twr-y-Felin Hostel, Caerfai Road, St David's (☎0437/720391). Wonderful outdoor activity centre, lively and friendly, with a wide range of sporting pursuits alongside decent hostel accommodation.

The Town

The main road from Haverfordwest enters St David's inauspiciously, past a petrol station and a ragbag of hotels. Becoming the High Street, the road courses down to Cross Square, a triangular city centrepiece around a **Celtic cross**, and continues under the thirteenth-century **Tower Gate**, which forms the entrance to the serene **Cathedral Close**, backed by a windswept landscape of distant farms and knobbly rock, a heathland almost devoid of trees.

The cathedral lies down to the right, hidden in a hollow by the River Alun. This apparent modesty is explained by reasons of defence, as a towering cathedral, visible from the sea on all sides, would have been vulnerable. On the other side of the babbling Alun lie the ruins of the Bishop's Palace. New Street heads north past the enjoyable **Oceanarium** (daily 10am–6pm; Oct–March closes 4pm; £2.25), complete with a shark tank overlooked by a viewing gallery. Running parallel to New Street is Nun Street, where number 41 has been turned into an exquisite small commercial art gallery, **Oriel yr Albion**; watercolours of the fearsome local coast washed by the unique clarity of Pembrokeshire light are the highlights of the work on sale.

The cathedral

Approached down the Thirty-nine Articles (or steps) that run from beyond the powerfully solid **Tower Gate** – the only remaining medieval gate of four – the gold and purple stone cathedral's 125-foot tower has clocks on only three sides (the people of the northern part of the parish couldn't raise enough money for one to be constructed facing them), and is topped by pert golden pinnacles that seem to glow a different colour from the rest of the building. You enter the **cathedral** through a porch in the south side of the low twelfth-century nave, although the line of the former higher roof can be clearly seen outside of the tower. The most striking feature of the nave is the intricate latticed oak **roof**, built to hide sixteenth-century emergency restoration work, when the nave was in danger of collapse. The nave floor still has a discernible slope and the support buttresses inserted in the northern aisle of the nave look incongruously new and temporary.

At the end of the nave, an elaborate **rood screen** was constructed under the orders of fourteenth-century Bishop Gower, who envisaged it as his own tomb. Behind the rood screen and the organ, the choir sits directly under the magnificently bold and bright lantern ceiling of the tower, another addition by Gower. The round-headed arch over the organ was built in Norman times, contrasting with the other three underpinning the tower, which are pointed and date from the rebuilding work that took place in the 1220s. At the back of the right-hand choir stalls is a unique **monarch's stall**, complete with royal crest, for, unlike any other British cathedral, the Queen is an automatic member of the St David's cathedral Chapter. Behind the left-hand choir stalls, the **north transept** contains the tomb of St Caradoc, with two pierced quatrefoils, in which it is believed people would insert diseased limbs in the hope of a cure. Off the north transept, steps from St Thomas' chapel lead up to the Chapter Library.

Separating the choir and the presbytery is a finely traced, rare **Parclose screen**. The back wall of the **presbytery** was once the eastern extremity of the cathedral, as can be seen from the two lines of windows. The upper row has been left intact, while the lower three were blocked up and filled with delicate gold mosaics in the nineteenth century, surrounded by over-fussy stonework. The colourful fifteenth-century roof, a deceptively simple repeating medieval pattern, was extensively restored by Gilbert Scott in the mid-nineteenth century. At the back of the presbytery, around the altar, the **sanctuary** has a few fragmented fifteenth-century tiles still in place. On the south side is a beautifully carved sedilla, a seat for the priest and deacon celebrating mass. To its right are thirteenth-century tombs of two bishops, Iorwerth (1215–31) and Anselm de la Grace (1231–47), and on the other side of the sanctuary is the disappointingly plain thirteenth-century tomb of St David, largely destroyed in the Reformation.

Behind the filled-in lancets at the back of the presbytery altar is the Perpendicular **Bishop Vaughan's chapel**, whose statue occupies the niche on the left of the altar. On the right is an effigy of Giraldus Cambrensis, his mitre placed not on his head, but at his feet – a reminder that he never attained the status of bishop for which he was evidently desperate. Behind the chapel is the ambulatory, off which the simple **Lady Chapel**, over-burdened with sentimental Edwardian stained glass, leads. Either side of the Lady Chapel are tombs in wall niches: the one on the left was originally believed to have been for Bishop Beck (1280–96), the builder of St David's Bishop's Palace, but now houses Bishop Owen (1897–1926), whose devoted service to the Church in Wales and the Welsh nation is symbolized by the roaring dragon above him.

The Bishop's Palace

From the cathedral, a path leads over the tiny, clear River Alun to the splendid **Bishops' Palace** (April–Oct daily 9.30am–6.30pm; Nov–March Mon–Sat 9.30am–4pm, Sun 2–4pm; CADW; £1.50), built by Bishops Beck and Gower around the turn of the fourteenth century. The huge central quadrangle is fringed by a neat jigsaw of ruined buildings in extraordinarily rich colours: the distinctive green, red, purple and grey tints of volcanic ash, sandstone and many other types of stone. The **arched parapets** that run along the top of most of the walls were a favourite feature of Gower, who did more than any of his predecessors or successors to transform the palace into an architectural and political powerhouse. Two ruined but still impressive halls – the **Bishops' Hall** and the enormous **Great Hall**, with its glorious rose window – lie off the main quadrangle, above and around a myriad of rooms adorned by some eerily eroded corbels. Underneath the Great Hall are dank vaults containing an interesting exhibition about the palace and the indulgent lifestyles of its occupants. The destruction of the palace is largely due to Bishop Barlow (1536–48), who supposedly stripped the buildings of their lead roofs to provide dowries for his five daughters' marriages to bishops.

Eating and drinking

Cartref, Cross Square (☎0437/720422). Enjoyable, swish restaurant with a menu of well-cooked local dishes. Open March–Dec. Moderate.

Cawl a Chan evenings at St David's rugby club, out on the road to Whitesands Bay. Weekly summer (Thurs) nights of raucous singing, beer and Welsh broth – snacks and entertainment for only £3. Details from the tourist office (see p.154).

City Inn, New St. Large and relaxed hotel bar with a selection of home-cooked Indian delicacies. Inexpensive.

Dyfed Café, Cross Square. Cheap and cheery café serving good value cholesterol-laden lunches and dinners to eat in or take away. Open Easter–Sept Mon–Sat noon–2pm and 6–10pm. Inexpensive.

Farmers Arms, Goat St. The city's only pub. Young, lively and very friendly; especially enjoyable on the terrace overlooking the cathedral on a summer's evening.

Fosters Bistro, 51 Nun St (☎0437/720576). Small restaurant with a menu of local dishes and international favourites. Open April–Oct. Moderate.

La Patisserie, Nun St. Daytime bakery with some local delicacies.

St David's Peninsula

Surrounded on three sides by inlets, coves and rocky stacks, St David's is an easy base for some excellent walking around the headland of the same name. A mile due south, accessed along the signposted lane from the main Haverfordwest road just near the school, popular **Caerfai Bay** provides a sandy gash in the purple sandstone cliffs, rock from which was used in the construction of the cathedral. To the immediate west is the craggy indentation of **St Non's Bay**, reached from St David's down the tiny rhododendron-flooded lane, signposted to the *Warpool Court Hotel*, that leads off Goat Street. Saint Non reputedly gave birth to Saint David at this spot during a tumultuous storm around 500 AD, when a spring opened up between Non's feet, and despite the crashing thunder all around, an eerily calm light filtered down on to the scene.

St Non's received pilgrims for centuries, resulting in the foundation of a tiny chapel in the pre-Norman age, whose successor's thirteenth-century ruins now lie in a field to the right of the car park, beyond the sadly dingy well and coy shrine where the nation's patron saint is said to have been born. The 1934 **chapel**, built in front of the austere 1929 **Retreat House** (details of stays and courses from Father Timothy on ☎0437/720224), was constructed in simple Pembrokeshire style from the rocks of ruined houses, which, in turn, had been built from the stone of ancient, abandoned churches.

The road from St David's to St Non's branches at the *St Non's Hotel*, where Catherine Street becomes a winding lane that leads a mile down the tiny valley of the River Alun to its mouth at **PORTH CLAIS**. Supposedly the place at which Saint David was baptized, Porth Clais was the city's main harbour, the spruced-up remains of which can still be seen at the bottom of the turquoise river creek. Today, commercial traffic has long gone, replaced by a boaties' haven.

Running due west out of St David's, Goat Street ducks past the ruins of the Bishop's Palace and over the rocky plateau for two miles to the harbour at **ST JUSTINIANS**, little more than a lifeboat station, car park and ticket hut for the boats over to Ramsey Island, which leave here at great regularity during the summer. As well as the tours based in St David's itself (see above), *Ramsey Island Pleasure Cruises* (☎0437/720285) operate trips to Ramsey.

Under the extremely able stewardship of the RSPB since 1992, **Ramsey Island** itself, a dual-humped plateau less than two miles long, is quite enchanting. Birds of prey circle the skies above the island, whose feathered population is better known for the tens of thousands of sea birds that noisily crowd the sheer cliffs on the island's western side. On the beaches, seals laze sloppily below the deer paths beaten out by a herd of red deer. Accommodation – B&B, self-catering and camping barn – is also available on the island (☎0437/781234).

Thousand Island Expeditions boats for Ramsey depart not from St Justinians, but instead from **Whitesands Bay** (Porth Mawr), two miles to the north and reached from St David's via the B4583 off the Fishguard road (see "Arrival and information", p.154). Campsites and cafés line the shore, one of the most popular in all Pembrokeshire, and as Whitesands faces west, surfing is good. Far less crowded, and spectacularly beautiful, is **Porthmelgan**, a narrow slip of cove reached by a fifteen-minute walk northwest along the coast path from Whitesands car park. **St David's Head**, a thin spit of rock and cliff juts out into the ocean, less than a mile to the west. Rising behind Whitesands and Porthmelgan, the gnarled crag of **Carnllidi** tops a pastoral patchwork of fields. Although it's a difficult climb, the rewards are manifold: unparalleled views over St David's Head, the tumps of Ramsey Island and down to the little city itself.

From St David's to Fishguard

The north-facing coast that forms the very southern tip of Cardigan Bay is noticeably less commercialized and far more Welsh than the touristy coasts of south and mid-Pembrokeshire. From the crags and cairns above St David's Head, the coast path perches precariously on the cliffs, where only the thousands of sea birds have access. The first point of contact with the sea for humans is the black sand beach at **Abereiddi**, half a mile short of the quieter sands of **Traeth Llyfn**.

Although the major income from this part of west Pembrokeshire is now tourism, the stumpy remains of old mines, quarries and ports at Abereiddi and **Porthgain** bear witness to the slate and granite industries that once employed hundreds. Industry dies down towards **Trevine** and up to the more remote beaches and inlets that punctuate the coast as it climbs up to the splendid knuckle of **Strumble Head**. To the east is **Carregwastad Point**, the site of the last invasion of Britain in 1797. The event is also remembered in **Fishguard**, where local soldiers tricked the invading French into unconditional surrender at the Royal Oak Inn in Upper Fishguard's neat little centre. Immediately either side of the upper town lie **Goodwick**, where ferries leave for Ireland, and cutely picturesque **Lower Fishguard**, most famous as the set for the glitzy 1971 movie version of *Under Milk Wood*, with the immortal coupling of Richard Burton and Elizabeth Taylor.

Abereiddi to Abercastle

A quiet lane leaves St David's and runs parallel to the coast across the rocky Pembrokeshire plateau, where the few trees have been blasted into spooky shapes by the relentless gusts off the Irish Sea. A small lane turns left five miles from St David's and tumbles down into the bleak hamlet of **ABEREIDDI**, at the head of its stony, black sand beach. You can find tiny fossilized animals in the shale on the beach, which can become extremely crowded in mid-summer. Above the beach are remains of workers' huts, industrial units and a tramway that once climbed over the hill to Porthgain, all part of the village's slate quarry that closed in 1904. Beyond the ruins, the old quarry was blasted for safety, producing an inland lagoon where the sea water, combined with the minerals, has turned a violent shade of bright blue, but is unfortunately not suitable for swimming in. Near Abereiddi is the homely and welcoming *Cwmwdig Water Guesthouse* (☎0348/831434; ③), tucked between the two lanes from Llanrihan and Croes-goch. A mile along the lane to Croes-goch is *Bank House Farm* (☎0348/831305; ②).

Following the coast path past the Blue Lagoon brings you down to **Traeth Llyfn**, about half a mile away; car drivers can take the track through Barry Island Farm half way down the lane between Llanrihan and Porthgain. Traeth Llyfn is sandier and more peaceful than the beach at Abereiddi, although heed the warnings that currents are deceptively strong and can be perilous for mediocre swimmers.

The lane parallel to the coast passes the hamlet of **CWMWDIG WATER** and leads to tiny **LLANRIHAN**, from where a left-hand turn descends over a mile or so to the rambling village green of **PORTHGAIN**, a fascinating old port that grew up around its slate works, the stumpy remains of which, together with an old brickworks, lime kiln and eerie ruins of workers' cottages, are huddled around the tiny quay. It also has the best pub in the county: the marvellous *Sloop Inn*, an eighteenth-century stone house with excellent beer, good food and numerous wall-mounted photographs of the old port in its sepia heyday. For pricier fare, the *Harbour Lights* (☎0348/831549) has a far-flung reputation for well-cooked local seafood and vegetables.

Two miles further east, where the lane intersects with the coast for the only time, is **Aber Draw**, a small and rugged beach just short of the village of **TREVINE** (Trefin). The natural rock chair in the middle of the village used to be employed as the seat of a mock-mayor, elected annually from amongst the villagers. Trevine is well serviced for **B&Bs**: in the middle of the village is *Maes y Graig*, 18 Ffordd y Felin (☎0348/831359; ②), and *Cranog* (☎0348/831392; ②). There's a YHA **youth hostel** in the old school on Ffordd-y-Avon (March–Oct; ☎0348/831414; ①), and for **camping**, a central site in town is the *Prendergast Holiday Park* (☎0348/831368). The *Ship Inn* is good for food.

The coastal lane continues east to **ABERCASTLE**, past the 4500-year-old **Carreg Samson** cromlech (burial chamber), topped by a sixteen-foot capstone, at Longhouse. Abercastle's harbour, once used for the export of limestone and coal, is now an attractive and popular spot, just above a muddy beach. From Abercastle, one of the best parts of the coast path zigzags east along the wild, vertiginous cliffs to the point at **Trwyn Llwynog**, about two miles away. For **camping** right above the coast path, there's the informal *Carnachen Llwyd* farm one-and-a-half miles east of Abercastle (☎0348/831250).

Mathry to Carregwastad Point

Deserted lanes and a beautiful stretch of coast path meander around the coast from Abercastle to the secluded bay at **Aber Mawr**, two miles directly north of the inland village of **MATHRY**, where the ancient *Farmers Arms* (☎0348/831284; ③) does great B&B and excellent food and drink. In the wooded valley above Aber Mawr, the *New Mill* (☎034 85/637; ②) at Tregwynt, near St Nicholas, is popular with coast path walkers. **Bike rental** is available from *Preseli Mountain Bikes* (☎0348/837709), at Parcynole Fach on the road between Mathry and St Nicholas.

Two miles east of the village of Mathry is **CASTLEMORRIS**, to the north of which is **Llangloffan Farm** (May–Sept Mon–Sat 10am–12.30pm, April & Oct Mon, Wed, Thurs & Sat 10am–12.30pm), whose homespun cheesemaking process is demonstrated to visitors. From Aber Mawr, the coast rises up and meanders for seven or eight miles past treeless heights, cairns and dangerous rocks of **STRUMBLE HEAD**, the closest Welsh mainland point to Ireland, jutting defiantly out into the Irish Sea. A footbridge from near the car park leads over the churning waters on to the grassy stump of **Ynys Meicel**, topped by its 1908 **light-**

house (April–Sept Mon–Sat 1–4pm). A **youth hostel** shelters under the 600-foot Garn Fawr, two miles south of Strumble Head at **PWLL DERI** (March–Oct; ☎034 85/233), where YHA members can also camp; nearby, there's a campsite at *Fferm Tresinwen* (☎034 85/238), a mile short of Strumble Head. For great lunches, *Penny's Pantry* at Pwll Deri, near the youth hostel, is a wholesome, cheap café.

The gorse-clad headland that peaks at Strumble Head is known as **Pen Caer**, an area that was the location for a bizarre attempt by a rabble of Franco-Irish soldiers to conquer Britain in 1797. **Trehowel Farm**, between Strumble Head and the village of **LLANWNDA**, was seized as the headquarters of the would-be conquerors. Apparently the farm was stocked up with food and drink for an imminent wedding and the soldiers set to guzzling with gusto, rapidly becoming too drunk to threaten a doormouse. They attacked the church at Llanwnda, and only managed to steal the silverware. A mile north of Llanwnda is **Carregwastad Point**, the landing place of the motley rebels, now marked by a headstone.

Fishguard

The coast road runs around the bay, along The Parrog and past the 900-yard East Breakwater, before climbing sharply up Gas Works Hill into the hilltop town of **FISHGUARD** (Abergwaun), occupying its own lofty headland. This is an enjoyably attractive town in its own right, with good views from its easy coast walk, but, unfortunately, is seldom seen as anything more than a brief stopping-off place to the ferries, which leave regularly for Rosslare in Ireland from the suburb of **GOODWICK** (Wdig).

The road from Goodwick becomes West Street, which meets up by the town hall with the High Street and Main Street, and it's along these three streets that most of the town's shops, banks, pubs and restaurants lie. Near the town hall is the **Royal Oak Inn**, the scene of the Franco-Irish surrender in 1797 (see above). The hapless forces arrived to negotiate a ceasefire, which was turned by the assembled British into an unconditional surrender. Mementoes of the event can be seen in the pub. Part of the invaders' low morale – apart from the drunken farces in which they'd become embroiled – is said to have been sparked off by the sight of a hundred local women marching towards them. The troops mistook their stovepipe hats and red flannel dresses for the outfit of a British Infantry troop and instantly capitulated. Even if that is not true, it is an undisputed fact that 47-year old cobbler Jemima Nicholas, the "Welsh Heroine", single-handedly captured fourteen French soldiers. Her grave can be seen next to the uninspiring Victorian **parish church**, St Mary's, behind the pub.

Main Street winds northeast before plummeting down around the coast towards **LOWER FISHGUARD**, a cluster of old-fashioned holiday cottages around a muddy, thriving pleasure-boat port – a total contrast to the vast operation on the other side of the town at Goodwick, where the ferries leave for Ireland. Views from Lower Fishguard over the town headland and to the port breakwater are superb.

Practicalities

Fishguard's **tourist office** (April–Sept daily 10am–5.30pm; ☎0348/873484) is in the old town, at the bottom of Hamilton Street on Main Street, and local books, together with information on Ireland, can be found in the *Seaways* bookshop on West Street. **Buses** stop by the town hall in the central Market Square.

The road arrives in the unprepossessing surroundings of Goodwick, where the **ferries** leave daily for Rosslare in Ireland (☎0348/872881); see p.6. The **train station** is next to the ferry terminal on Quay Road.

Accommodation is plentiful and cheap, with most places well used to visitors coming and going at odd times for the ferries. Next to the port is the faded elegance of the *Fishguard Bay Hotel* on Quay Road (☎0348/873571; ③). Up in Fishguard proper is the *Hamilton Guesthouse*, 21–23 Hamilton St, off Main Street (☎0348/873834; ②), and, down in Lower Fishguard, the *Hotel Plas Glyn-y-Mel* (☎0348/872296; ④). There are plenty of places for **food** and **drink**: *Bennetts Navy Tavern* on the High Street is a nautical theme pub selling inexpensive all-day bar meals, the *Happy Fryer* on West Street flogs chips, burgers and pizza, or, for simple drinking, try the earthy and beery *Fishguard Arms* on Main Street and, tucked behind, the staunchly traditional *Cambrian Arms* on Hamilton Street. Down in Lower Fishguard, the eccentric *Ship Inn* is unmissable, with good food and lots of interesting clutter all over the walls and ceiling.

Mynydd Preseli

In a county celebrated for some of the most magnificent coastal scenery in Britain, Pembrokeshire's interior is frequently overlooked. The **Mynydd Preseli** (Preseli Hills) occupy a triangle of land in the north of the county, roughly bounded by the coast in the north, the B4313 to the west and the A478 to the east, and flecked with prehistoric remains. After miles of seabird-swirling coastline, the rickety walled lanes and gloomy bare hills come as a refreshing change.

From Fishguard, the Gwaun River wriggles southeast through the lush Gwaun valley, peddled furiously by the tourist board as a "step back in time", as locals apparently still stick to the pre-1752 Julian calendar and celebrate New Year in the middle of January. Whatever mysticism the valley might have tends to get lost in the trample of those searching for it.

Buses are rare around here – apart from the main road through Dinas, Newport and Eglwyswrw, and only an occasional vehicle delves deep into the hills. A far better bet is **bike rental** – see below.

Newport

The A487 runs east–west through **NEWPORT** (Trefdraeth) above the estuary of the Nyfer River, a pristine little town, a good base for seeing the Mynydd Preseli and a lively place bustling with cafés, restaurants and pubs. To the south of the main street, small roads wind up to the ruins of the privately owned castle and the imposing **church of St Mary**, complete with a rare Norman cushion-type font. Running south from the main street are Long Street and Lower St Mary's Street, which both head down to the southern shore of the estuary. Newport's best beach is on the other side of the estuary, reached along the Feidr Pen-y-bont, the next junction after Lower St Mary's Street.

Framing the rear of the town is the looming hill of **Carn Ingli**, an easy two-hour walk from Newport. On the northeastern slope are a set of Iron Age hut circles, the former site of a camp, believed to have been the home of St Brychan. Breathtaking views from the summit easily stretch from Strumble Head over to the left, past the nodule of Dinas Head and towards Cardiganshire.

Newport's cheerful **tourist office** (April–Sept Mon–Sat 10am–5.30pm; ☎0239/820912) is in a car park on Long Street, and you can rent a **bike** from *Gwaun Valley Mountain Bikes*, Tyriet Cilgwyn, just south of Newport (☎0239/820905).

Accommodation can be found at *2 Springhill*, Parrog Road (☎0239/820626; ②), and the genteel and pleasant *Cnapan Country House* in East Street (☎0239/820575; ③). Great-value farmhouse B&Bs outside town are *Erw Lon Farm* near Pontfaen, in the Gwaun Valley (☎0348/881297; ②), and *Penygraig* in Puncheston (☎0348/881277; ②), four miles south of Pontfaen. The *Morawelon* **campsite** is on the shore just west of Newport at Parrog (☎0239/820565). Outlets for **food** and **drink** are particularly plentiful in Newport: on the main Bridge Street, there are good food-serving pubs – the *Royal Oak* (with vegetarian dishes), the *Llwyngwair Arms* and the *Llew Awr*.

Nevern

A mile or so from Newport along the forested valley of the Nyfer is **NEVERN**, whose ruined and overgrown **castle** is a thirteenth-century replacement of a Norman construction, itself the successor of an earlier Welsh fortress. The village straggles down into the valley, where you'll find **St Brynach's church**, named after a fifth-century Irish holy man who is said to have spent much of his time on Carn Ingli, occasionally in the contemplative company of St David himself. The church is pretty enough – housing the Maglocunus Stone, believed to be fifth-century and inscribed in the ancient script of Ogham as well as Latin – if dwarfed by the contents of its churchyard: an astounding thirteen-foot tenth-century Celtic cross and a yew tree which oozes sap that bears an uncanny resemblance to blood. Legend has it that it will continue to "bleed" until a Welsh lord of the manor is reinstated in the village castle – unlikely, given its tumbledown state. There's a **campsite** four miles northeast of Nevern on the road to Moylgrove at *Trereffith Farm* (☎023 986/207), beautifully sited above the coast path.

Into the hills

Two miles southeast of Nevern, just north of the A487, **Castell Henllys** (April–Oct daily 10am–5pm; £2.50) is an over-restored Iron Age hillfort that has had an assortment of huts, crafts and crops grafted on to it to show a supposed Iron Age village as it would have looked. Far more satisfying are the numerous wild and abandoned clumps of stones and ditchwork that mark the site of other old forts – nearby **Castell Mawr** and **Castell Llwyd**, for instance, sandwiched between the A487 and the Nyfer River, a mile to the south of Henllys.

At **TEMPLE BAR**, two miles east of Newport, a lane leads south off the A487 signposted to **Pentre Ifan**, a further couple of miles into the hills. This vast cromlech, with its sixteen-foot arrowhead topstone precariously balanced on large stone legs, dates back over 4000 years as a burial place. The views from here are superb, situated as it is on the cusp of the stark, eerie mountains of Preseli and the pastoral rolls of countryside to the east.

Walking the Preseli range is easy, as the hills are scarcely steep and the views over the sheep-dotted slopes to the distant azure of the sea are soul-lifting. Due south of Pentre Ifan, the hamlet of **ROSEBUSH** is a good base for the Preselis, with a caravan park, shop, signposted mountain and reservoir walks, the low-key **Preseli Visitor Centre**, with the usual leaflets and walking tour guides and an excellent restaurant and quirky pub, the *Old Post Office*. The bizarre nineteenth-century Klondike atmosphere of Rosebush – together with its corrugated iron pub – is partially explained by the fact that it was built as a would-be Victorian spa on the arrival of the railway.

The *Old Post Office* (☎0437/765171; ②) is a reasonably priced place to **stay**; for food, the corrugated iron *Tafarn Sinc* serves good snacks, and the good-value bistro at the *Old Post Office* (☎0437/532205) includes an extensive veggie and vegan menu.

The B4329 continues south towards Haverfordwest, with a right turn after two miles signposted for **Llys-y-frân**, a 187-acre reservoir and surrounding country park. The modern visitor centre contains a surprisingly upmarket restaurant and useful shop, as well as details of local walks. A mile to the west, just off the B4329, is the hamlet of **Poll Tax**!

travel details

Trains

Carmarthen to: Cardiff (6 daily; 1hr 40min); Ferryside (11 daily; 10min); Fishguard Harbour (1 daily; 55min); Haverfordwest (10 daily; 40min); Kidwelly (10 daily; 15min); Llanelli (hourly; 25min); London (2 daily; 4hr 30min); Milford Haven (hourly; 1hr); Narberth (8 daily; 25min); Pembroke (8 daily; 1hr 10min); Swansea (hourly; 45min); Tenby (8 daily; 45min); Whitland (hourly; 15min).

Fishguard Harbour to: Cardiff (2 daily; 2hr 20min); Swansea (2 daily; 1hr 30min).

Haverfordwest to: Cardiff (7 daily; 2hr 30min); Carmarthen (12 daily; 40min); Milford Haven (11 daily; 20min); Swansea (10 daily; 1hr 30min).

Llanelli to: Cardiff (6 daily; 1hr 20min); Carmarthen (hourly; 25min); Llandeilo (5 daily Mon–Sat; 40min); Llandovery (5 daily Mon–Sat; 1hr); Llandrindod Wells (5 daily Mon–Sat; 1hr 45min); Llanwrtyd Wells (5 daily Mon–Sat; 1hr 25min); Pembrey & Burry Port (hourly; 5min); Shrewsbury (5 daily Mon–Sat; 3hr 30min); Swansea (hourly; 20min).

Tenby to: Cardiff (2 daily; 2hr 35min); Carmarthen (8 daily; 45min); Lamphey (8 daily; 17min); Narberth (8 daily; 20min); Pembroke & Pembroke Dock (8 daily; 20 & 25min); Penally (8 daily; 2min); Swansea (8 daily; 1hr 35min); Whitland (8 daily; 30min).

Whitland to: Cardiff (11 daily; 2hr); Carmarthen (hourly; 15min); Haverfordwest (10 daily; 25min); Milford Haven (10 daily; 40min); Narberth (8 daily; 10min); Pembroke (8 daily; 50min); Swansea (hourly; 1hr); Tenby (8 daily; 30min).

Buses

Carmarthen to: Aberaeron (5 daily Mon–Sat; 1hr 40min); Aberystwyth (3 daily Mon–Sat; 2hr 35min); Cardigan (hourly Mon–Sat; 1hr 30min); Cenarth (10 daily Mon–Sat; 1hr 5min); Drefach Felindre (7 daily Mon–Sat; 50min); Haverfordwest (7 daily Mon–Sat; 55min); Kidwelly (4 daily Mon–Sat; 25min); Lampeter (6 daily Mon–Sat; 1hr 10min); Laugharne (hourly Mon–Sat; 35min); Llanarthney (4 daily Mon–Sat; 30min); Llandeilo (hourly Mon–Sat; 35min); Llandovery (6 daily Mon–Sat; 1hr 15min); Llansteffan (5 daily Mon–Sat; 20min); Manorbier (4 daily Mon–Sat; 1hr 25min); Nantgaredig (hourly Mon–Sat; 20min); Narberth (6 daily Mon–Sat; 40min); Newcastle Emlyn (hourly Mon–Sat; 1hr); New Quay (4 daily Mon–Sat; 1hr 30min); Pembrey (4 daily Mon–Sat; 30min); Pembroke (5 daily Mon–Sat; 1hr 40min); Pendine (hourly Mon–Sat; 50min); Saundersfoot (4 daily Mon–Sat; 45min); Swansea (hourly Mon–Sat; 1hr 30min); Tenby (5 daily Mon–Sat; 1hr); Trelech (6 daily Mon–Sat; 45min).

Fishguard to: Cardigan (hourly Mon–Sat; 50min); Haverfordwest (hourly Mon–Sat; 45min); St David's (7 daily Mon–Sat; 50min); Trefin (7 daily Mon–Sat; 35min).

Haverfordwest to: Broad Haven (5 daily Mon–Sat; 15min); Cardigan (hourly Mon–Sat; 1hr 40min); Carmarthen (7 daily Mon–Sat; 55min); Dale (2 buses Tues & Fri; 35min); Fishguard (hourly Mon–Sat; 45min); Manorbier (hourly Mon–Sat; 1hr 10min); Marloes (Tues & Fri 1 bus; 35min); Narberth (6 daily Mon–Sat; 15min); Newgale (hourly Mon–Sat; 20min); Newport, Dyfed (hourly Mon–Sat; 1hr 10min); Pembroke (hourly Mon–Sat; 50min); St David's (hourly Mon–Sat; 50min); Solva (hourly Mon–Sat; 40min); Tenby (hourly Mon–Sat; 1hr 25min).

Llandeilo to: Carmarthen (hourly Mon–Sat; 35min); Llandovery (8 daily Mon–Sat; 35min); Talley (Tues & Fri 1 daily; 20min).

Milford Haven to: Dale (school service; 25min); Marloes (school service; 40min); Pembroke (hourly Mon–Sat; 40min).

Pembroke to: Bosherston (3 daily Mon–Fri; 1hr); Carmarthen (4 daily Mon–Sat; 1hr 40min); Castlemartin (3 daily Mon–Sat; 30min); Freshwater East (2 daily Mon–Fri; 10min); Haverfordwest (hourly Mon–Sat; 50min); Manorbier (hourly Mon–Sat; 20min); Milford Haven (hourly Mon–Sat; 40min); Pembroke Dock (numerous; 10min); Saundersfoot (2 daily Mon–Sat; 50min); Stackpole (2 daily Mon–Fri; 50min); Tenby (hourly Mon–Sat; 40min).

Pembroke Dock to: Carew (5 daily Mon–Sat; 10min); Saundersfoot (5 daily Mon–Sat; 45min); Tenby (5 daily Mon–Sat; 1hr).

Tenby to: Amroth (hourly Mon–Sat; 40min); Carew (7 daily; 35min); Carmarthen (5 daily Mon–Sat; 1hr); Haverfordwest (hourly Mon–Sat; 1hr 25min); Manorbier (hourly Mon–Sat; 20min); Narberth (4 daily Mon–Sat; 55min); Pembroke (hourly Mon–Sat; 40min); Pembroke Dock (5 daily Mon–Sat; 1hr); St Florence (hourly Mon–Sat; 12min); Saundersfoot (every 30min; 15min).

CHAPTER THREE

POWYS

The only county in Wales with no coastline, **Powys** occupies a quarter of the country from the fringes of the Glamorgan valleys south of the Brecon Beacons, through the sparsely populated lakelands of Radnorshire and up to the open moorland of the Berwyn Mountains. The county shares all of its eastern border with England, with fingers of rural Shropshire and Herefordshire poking into the Welsh landscape. Powys has only been a county since local government reorganization in 1974, but its name harks back to a fifth-century Welsh kingdom. The modern county is an amalgamation of three old ones: Brecknockshire, centred around Brecon and the Beacons, Radnorshire and Montgomeryshire.

By far the most popular attraction in the county is **Brecon Beacons National Park** at the southern end of Powys, and stretching from the moody heights of the Black Mountain in the west, through the gentler Beacons themselves, and out to the English border beyond the confusingly named Black Mountains. The main centres within the Beacons are Abergavenny (see *Southeast Wales*, p.56), in the far southeast, and the small city of **Brecon**, a curious mix of traditional market town, army garrison and often very pretty tourist centre.

The bleaker part of the Beacons lies to the west, around the raw peaks of the **Black Mountain** and **Fforest Fawr**. A few roads cut through the glowering countryside, connecting popular attractions such as the immense **Dan-yr-ogof caves**, opera prima donna Adelina Patti's gilded home and theatre at nearby **Craig-y-nos** and the caves and waterfalls around the popular walking centre of **Ystradfellte**. Walkers are equally well catered for in settlements like **Crickhowell** and **Talgarth**, small towns set in quiet river valleys.

At the northern corner of the National Park, the border town of **Hay-on-Wye** draws in thousands to see the town's dozens of bookshops, housed in warehouses, the old castle and outdoor yards. West of Hay, the peaks of the **Mynydd Eppynt** now form a vast training ground for the British army, on the other side of which lie the old spa towns of Radnorshire – earthy **Llanwrtyd Wells**, moribund **Llangammarch Wells**, the gritty centre of **Builth Wells** and twee **Llandrindod Wells**. The countryside to the north, crossed by spectacular mountain roads such as the **Abergwesyn Pass** from Llanwrtyd, is barely populated and beautiful – quiet, occasionally harsh country, dotted with ancient churches and introspective villages, from the border towns of **Presteigne** and **Knighton**, home of the flourishing **Offa's Dyke path** industry, to inland centres like **Rhayader**, the nearest centre of population for the grandiose reservoirs of the **Elan Valley**.

Montgomeryshire is the northern portion of Powys, similarly underpopulated and remote as its two southern siblings. In common with most of mid Wales, country towns such as the beautiful **Llanidloes** has a healthy stock of old hippies amongst its population, resulting in a greater-than-expected presence of health food shops, healing groups and arts activity. To the west, the inhospitable mountain of **Plynlimon** is flecked with boggy heathland and gloomy reservoirs,

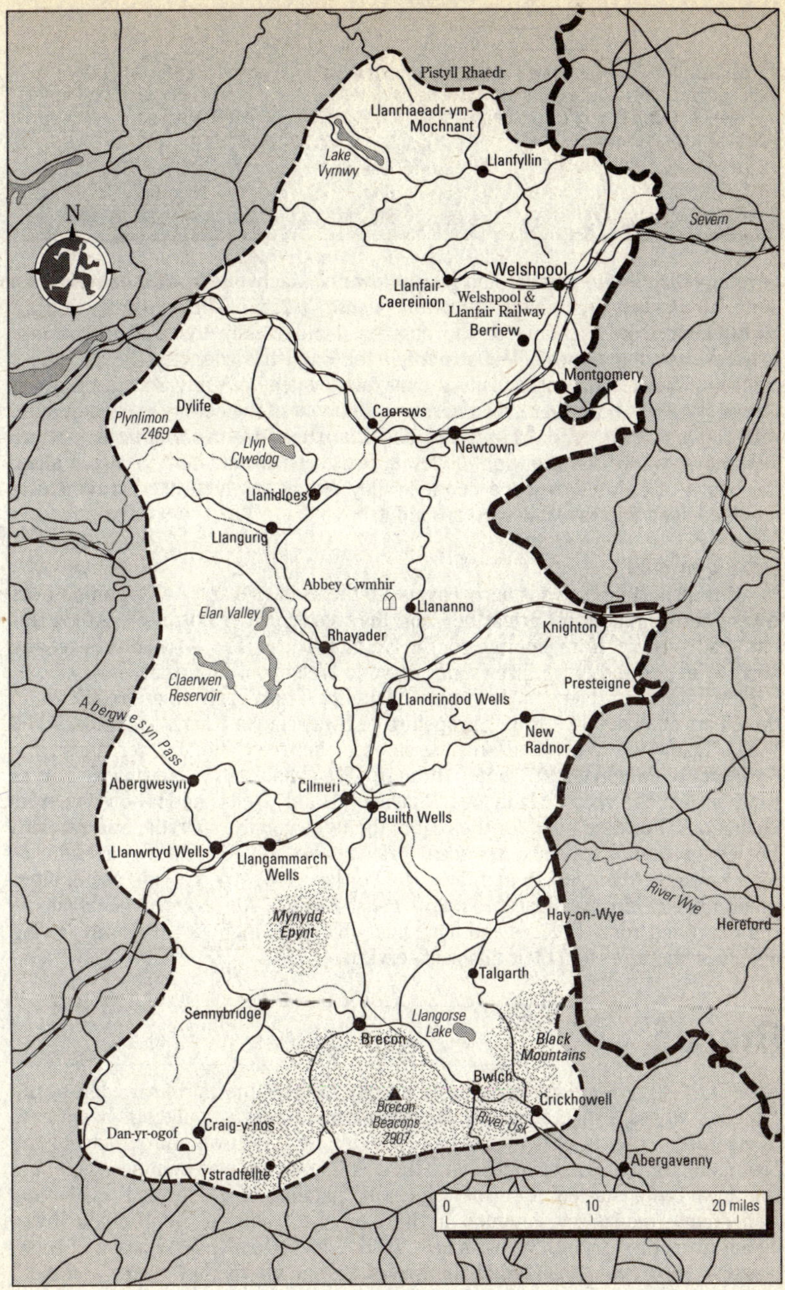

Pistyll Rhaedr
Llanrhaeadr-ym-Mochnant
Lake Vyrnwy
Llanfyllin
Severn
N
Welshpool
Llanfair-Caereinion
Welshpool & Llanfair Railway
Berriew
Montgomery
Dylife
Plynlimon 2469
Caersws
Newtown
Llyn Clwedog
Llanidloes
Llangurig
Abbey Cwmhir
Llananno
Elan Valley
Rhayader
Knighton
Claerwen Reservoir
Presteigne
Llandrindod Wells
Abergwesyn Pass
New Radnor
Abergwesyn
Cilmeri
Builth Wells
Llanwrtyd Wells
Llangammarch Wells
River Wye
Hay-on-Wye
Hereford
Mynydd Epynt
Talgarth
Sennybridge
Llangorse Lake
Brecon
Black Mountains
Bwlch
Brecon Beacons 2907
Crickhowell
River Usk
Craig-y-nos
Dan-yr-ogof
Ystradfellte
Abergavenny
0
10
20 miles

ACCOMMODATION PRICE CODES

Throughout this guide, hotel and B&B accommodation is priced on a scale of ① to ⑨. Category ① only applies to youth hostels; for the rest, the number indicates the **lowest price** you could expect to pay per night for a **double room in high season**. The prices indicated by the codes are as follows:

① under £20/$32	④ £40–50/$64–80	⑦ £70–80/$112–128
② £20–30/$32–48	⑤ £50–60/$80–96	⑧ £80–100/$128–160
③ £30–40/$48–64	⑥ £60–70/$96–112	⑨ over £100/$160

beyond which is the popular and hearty town of Machynlleth, stranded out on a limb of Powys (see *The Cambrian Coast*, p.223). The eastern side of Montgomeryshire is home to the anglicized old county town, **Montgomery**, between the robust town of **Welshpool** on the English border, and the charmless centre of **Newtown**, worth visiting only for devotees of early socialist **Robert Owen**, who was born there. The northern segment of the county is even quieter, with regional centres like **Llanfyllin** and **Llanrhaeadr-ym-mochnant** that are little more than villages, leaving the few crowds seen around here to cluster along the banks of **Lake Vyrnwy**, a flooded-valley reservoir which has harmoniously moulded itself into the landscape around it.

Getting around

Road transport in Powys is fairly easy, with the swift A40 and A438 running from Gwent and England to Carmarthen and the west. Further north, the A44 heads into Radnorshire from Leominster in Herefordshire. The A458 heads off the north Wales-bound A5 at Shrewsbury down to Welshpool and Montgomeryshire.

Public transport takes more forward planning. **Train** services are restricted to the Heart of Wales line from Shropshire to Swansea via Knighton, Llandrindod Wells, Llanwrtyd Wells and smaller stops in between and, further north, the Shrewsbury–Machynlleth route through Welshpool and Newtown. Larger centres such as Brecon, Llanidloes, Rhayader, Builth Wells and Hay-on-Wye have no stations. For them, and for the rest of the huge county, sporadic **bus** services (including school and post services) provide the only access. Towns such as Abergavenny, Machynlleth and, over the border, Oswestry, provide useful intersection points. An excellent free map – *Powys Bus and Rail Guide* – is obtainable from libraries, tourist offices and main post offices throughout the county, giving details of operators and their different services.

Brecon

BRECON (Aberhonddu) is a sturdy county town at the northern edge of the Beacons, whose proliferation of well-proportioned Georgian buildings bears testimony to the town's past importance, but it's for the town's proximity to the National Park that most people come here. A Roman fort was built near here, but the town only started to grow with the building of a Norman castle and Benedictine monastery, founded in 1093 on the banks of the Honddu River, which gives the town its Welsh name. To the dual strands of military and ecclesiastical importance was added the status of regional market centre and cloth weaving town. In the seventeenth-century Civil War, the townsfolk unequivocally demonstrated their neutrality between the forces of Parliament and the Crown by demolishing most of the castle and large sections of the town walls, dissipating the appeal for either side of seizing their town.

Today, many fairweather walkers base themselves here and explore the well waymarked hills to the south of the town, including Pen y Fan, the highest, most challenging peak in south Wales. Brecon is also a good base for sedentary tourists, with its appealing jumble of Georgian, Victorian and occasionally Tudor architecture, and a good social life.

Information and accommodation

The **tourist office** (April–Sept daily 10am–6pm, Oct–March Mon–Sat 9.30am–5.30pm; ☎0874/625692) and **National Park office** (Easter–Oct daily 9.30am–5.30pm) share the same building in the Lion Yard car park off Lion Street, next to the cattle market. The tourist office includes a bureau de change and holds details of local bus services, which leave from The Bulwark, and also provides details of the town's annual **jazz festival** over the long weekend in mid-August.

Accommodation

Brecon is a compact town with much **accommodation** to suit all pockets, and Llanfaes, across the river from the main town, has plenty of smaller hotels and B&Bs on its main street. Be warned, though, that accommodation in Brecon can be tricky to come by during the jazz festival.

HOTELS AND GUESTHOUSES

Beacons Guest House, 16 Bridge St, Llanfaes (☎0874/623339). Rambling converted town house in an excellent position. Good, cheap evening meals also available. ③.

Castle Hotel, Castle Square (☎0874/624611). Large and sumptuous hotel built into the castle ruins, overlooking the Usk. ⑤.

Lansdowne Hotel, 39 The Watton (☎0874/623321). Classy town centre hotel in a handsome Georgian corner house. ④.

Llanfaes Guest House, Llanfaes (☎0874/611115). Exclusively lesbian and gay retreat in a pleasant Georgian town house. Please phone for details. ③.

Paris Guest House, 28 The Watton (☎0874/624205). Smart Georgian house converted into a low-key, friendly town centre hotel. ③.

Tirbach Guest House, 13 Alexandra Rd (☎0874/624551). Small and pleasant B&B behind the cattle market. ②.

Wellington Hotel, The Bulwark (☎0874/625225). Imposing old coaching inn that dominates the town's main square. ④.

HOSTELS, CAMPING AND BUNKHOUSE

Brynich Caravan and Camping Park, Brynich (☎0874/623325). Situated a mile east of town, just off the A40, overlooking the town and the river.

Cantref Bunkhouse, Cantref, near Llanfrynach (☎0874/86223). Overlooking the Cynrig River, two miles southeast of Brecon. Dormitory-style accommodation with kitchen and showers. Also takes campers, who can pitch tents in the grounds. ①.

Llwyn-y-Celyn youth hostel, Libanus (☎0874/624261). Isolated farmhouse hostel, seven miles southwest of Brecon just off the A470 and main bus route to Merthyr. ①.

Ty'n-y-Caeau youth hostel, Groesfford (☎087 486/270). The nearest YHA youth hostel to Brecon, just over two miles east of the town. Reached via the path (Slwch Lane) from

Cerrigcochion Road in Brecon or a mile walk from bus stops at either Cefn Brynich lock (Brecon–Abergavenny buses) or Troedyrharn Farm (Brecon–Hereford buses). ①.

The Town

Buses decant their passengers in **The Bulwark**, Brecon's imposing central square, flanked by the solid red sixteenth-century tower of the otherwise unremarkable **St Mary's church**, an assortment of old-fashioned shop frontages and the elegant Georgian portico of the **Wellington Hotel**.

At the junction of The Bulwark and Glamorgan Street is the neo-Grecian frontage of the **Brecknock Museum** (Mon–Sat 10am–1pm & 2–5pm; April–Sept also Sun; free), where a display of local trades includes a recreated smithy and a collection of agricultural implements unique to the area. More interesting are the walk-through history of Wales and a nineteenth-century assize court, last used in 1971, and preserved in all its ponderous splendour, overseen by the high judge's throne as if judgements came from no less than God himself. Back near the entrance is a collection, dating back as far as four hundred years, of painstakingly carved Welsh lovespoons that were betrothal gifts for courting Welsh lovers.

Running east from The Bulwark is **The Watton**, overlooked by the foreboding frontage of the South Wales Borderers' **barracks**, opposite which is its **museum** (April–Sept Mon–Sat 9am–1pm & 2–5pm; Oct–March Mon–Fri 9am–1pm & 2–5pm; £1), packed with mementoes from the regiment's three-hundred-year existence. Amongst the gung-ho bravado, most noticeable are the tales of the 1879 Zulu War when 140 Welsh soldiers defended against an attack by 4000 Zulu warriors. From here, a series of small streets runs down to the northern terminus of the **Monmouth and Brecon Canal**, where afternoon cruises aboard the *Dragonfly* (☎0831/685222) ease their way out of town for an enjoyably relaxed round trip. The Watton continues to the A40 bypass roundabout and the unlikely home of the **Welsh Whisky Visitor Centre** (Mon–Fri 10am–5pm; May–Sept also Sat 10am–5pm, Sun 11.30am–3.30pm; £2.50), where you'll find Welsh gin, whisky and even *Taffski* vodka, a little-known commodity and considerably better than you might think. The two main whiskies (or *chwisgi*) are a robust standard *Sŵn-y-Mor*, or "sound of the sea", and a fine malt called the *Prince of Wales*. The visitor centre takes you through the history of the nation's whisky production, which reputedly dates back to the fourth century AD and a monastic distillery on Bardsey Island on the Llŷn Peninsula. Needless to say, a few samples are thrown in with the entry fee, and you can buy the end result.

North and west of The Bulwark are a cluttered grid of streets, packed in with Georgian and Victorian buildings. The High Street Inferior is the main route northwest, passing the **Sarah Siddons** pub, converted from the 1755 birthplace of the great actress. High Street Inferior quickly comes to a car-congested crossroads. Straight ahead, Ship Street descends down to the **River Usk**, the bridge crossing the Usk next to the point where the smaller Honddu River flows in from the north. Over the Usk, the southern suburb of **Llanfaes** is best known for its Dominican **friary**, whose ruined thirteenth-century church is now the centrepiece of **Christ College** school, on the immediate western side of the Usk.

From the town centre crossroads, High Street Superior goes north, past the long **Market Hall**, home of a twice-weekly produce market (Tues & Fri) and, on the third Saturday of each month, an excellent **craft market**. The road becomes The Struet, running alongside the rushing waters of the Honddu. Off to the left,

Priory Hill and, a few yards further on, a footpath (signposted Public Conveniences) climb up to the stark grey buildings of the monastery settlement, centred on the **cathedral**, or Priory Church of St John the Baptist. The building's dumpy external appearance belies its lofty interior, graced with a few Norman features intact from the eleventh-century priory that was built here on the site of a probable earlier Celtic church. The hulking Norman font sits at the western end of the nave, near the entrance and the unusual stone cresset, a large boulder indented with thirty scoops in which to place torches. Of the many family monuments in the nave, the most interesting is the **Games monument** (1555), in the southern aisle, made up from three oak beds and depicting an unknown woman whose hands remain intact in prayer, but whose arms and nose have been unceremoniously hacked off. The fine vaulting in the elegant choir is the nineteenth-century work of prolific restorationist Gilbert Scott, who worked on St Asaph and St David's cathedrals, and designed St Pancras Station in London.

Between the cathedral and the River Usk, the few remains of the town's **castle** are moulded into the walls of the *Castle Hotel*. The end result is a powerful, if bizarre, amalgam that looks its best from along **The Promenade** by the River Usk, reached from the town centre side of the river bridge. In high summer, motor and row boats can be rented along the river bank.

Eating and drinking

As an important regional centre first and foremost, Brecon has always been well served for **food** and **drink**. It's a lively and cosmopolitan town, although some of the pubs in the near vicinity of the barracks are definitely worth avoiding.

Restaurants and cafés

Beacons Guest House, 16 Bridge St, Llanfaes (☎0874/623339). Open to non-residents for excellent lunches, teas and evening meals, many inspired by local produce and traditional Welsh recipes. Inexpensive.

Brecon Tandoori, Glamorgan St (☎0874/624653). Traditional curry house just along from the old Shire Hall, behind The Bulwark. Inexpensive.

Castle Hotel, Castle Square (☎0874/624611). Worth investigating for the good-value fixed dinner menu in this enjoyable restaurant in the town's smartest hotel. Moderate.

Coracle Café, High St Inferior. Friendly place providing a solid daytime menu of snacks and hearty meals. Inexpensive.

La Belle Pizza, 1 Church Lane (☎0874/625685). Unexceptional but dependable pizza takeaway joint, open late every night.

Watergate Fish Bar, Ship St. Brightly lit traditional chip shop, almost on the bridge itself. Includes tables to eat in. Inexpensive.

Pubs

Boars Head, Ship St. Two very different bars: the front is basic and the best place to meet locals, whereas the back bar is loud and resembles a youth club.

Bull's Head, The Struet. Small and cheery locals' pub, with views over the Honddu River and towards the cathedral. Good-value food.

Gremlin Hotel, The Watton. Ancient pub with an informal atmosphere and great selection of bar snacks and larger meals (not Sun and Mon eves). Inexpensive.

Old Cognac, High St Inferior. No-nonsense town pub, offering cholesterol-packed lunchtime food. Inexpensive.

Sarah Siddons, High St Inferior. Named after the famous actress, born here when the pub was known as the *Shoulder of Mutton*. A replica of Gainsborough's aloof portrait of her now forms the pub sign. A busy, popular pub.

Saxon's, The Bulwark. Bar and club above an ironmonger's shop. Open for late-night drinking (small entry fee is payable) on Thursday, Friday and Saturday nights, when it can get a little rough.

Wellington Hotel, The Bulwark. Surprisingly unstuffy hotel bar, a frequent venue for live music, especially jazz.

Activities and entertainment

Just off the A470 (turn off at Libanus), five miles southwest of the town, the **Brecon Beacons Mountain Centre** (daily March–June & Sept–Oct 10.30am–5pm; July–August 10am–6pm; Nov–Feb 10.30am–4.30pm; ☎0874/623366) sits on a windy ridge, amongst gorse heathland, overlooking some of the most inspiring scenery in the Beacons. As well as an excellent café, there are interesting displays on the flora, fauna, geology and history of the area, together with a well-stocked shop of maps, books and walking gear. Waymarked walks, both locally around the lofty heath and across the river valley to the more challenging peaks of Corn Du and Pen y Fan, lead away from the centre. Buses leave Brecon for Merthyr, with a stop at Libanus school, from where it is a one-mile uphill walk along the lane next to the church up to the centre.

The town is well served for sports and recreational facilities: the old-fashioned *Coliseum* **cinema** is on Wheat Street (☎0874/622501), near the central crossroads, and there's an indoor **swimming pool** a mile northeast of the centre on the Cerrigcochion Road at Penlan (☎0874/633677). *Kevin Walker Mountain Activities*, 74 Beacons Park (☎0874/625111), organize hillwalking, survival courses, caving, rock-climbing and abseiling trips. For **bike rental**, there's the *Crickhowell Adventure Gear* shop, 21 Ship St (☎0874/611586). They also organize cycling adventure tours.

The Brecon Beacons

With the lowest profile of Wales' three National Parks, the **Brecon Beacons** are the destination of thousands of urban walkers largely from the industrial areas of south Wales and the West Midlands of England. Spongy hills of heather and rock tumble and climb around river valleys that lie between sandstone and limestone uplands, peppered with glass-like lakes and villages that seem to have been hewn from one rock. Known for their vivid quality of light, the hills of the Beacons disappear and re-emerge from hazy blankets of cloud, with shafts of sun sharpening lush green fields out of a dullened patchwork.

The National Park straddles Powys from west to east, covering 520 square miles. Most remote is the area at the far western side, where the vast, open terrain of **Fforest Fawr** and the **Black Mountain** form miles of tufted moorland and bleak, often dangerous peaks in the north, tumbling down to a region of porous limestone in the south. Here is a rocky terrain of rivers, deep caves and spluttering waterfalls, especially around the village of **Ystradfellte** and in the chasms of the **Dan-yr-ogof caves**.

East of Brecon, the series of interlocked peaks known as the **Black Mountains** stretch all the way to the English border, offering the region's most varied scenery, with the wide valley of the River Usk, home to the main settlement of **Crickhowell** and the beautiful double castle at **Tretower**, alongside almost impossibly green hills. Lying underneath the northern bluff of the mountains is the pleasant border town of **Hay-on-Wye**, at the point where the mountainous Brecon Beacons dissolve into the softer contours of Radnorshire.

Black Mountain

The most westerly expanse of upland in the National Park is known as the **Black Mountain** (Mynydd Ddu), rising between the A4069 and A4067, eight miles south of Llandovery (see p.126). Although the mountain is named in the singular, it covers an unpopulated range of barren, smooth-humped peaks that break suddenly at rocky escarpments towering over quiet streams and glacial lakes. This area provides the most challenging and exhilarating walking in south Wales and has long been popular with trippers from the valleys, just a few miles south. Paths cross the wet, wild landscape from Dan-yr-ogof in the east, from the soaring ruins of **Carreg Cennen Castle** (see p.125), just short of Llandeilo in the west, from Tyhwnt, near Ystradgynlais, in the south and, in the north, from the hamlet of **LLANDDEUSANT**, seven miles south of Llandovery, home to a rugged, simple YHA **youth hostel** (☎05 504/634 or 619; ①). The best walks from Llanddeusant run along wooded gulches and moorland bluffs to the twin glacial lakes of **Llyn y Fan Fach** and **Llyn y Fan Fawr**. Llyn y Fan Fach features in one of Wales' most oft-told myths of a beautiful maiden, together with her herd of magic cattle, who rose from the lake to marry a local farmer. The maiden's father had sanctioned the union only on the condition that if the farmer struck his daughter three times, she would return to the lake. Such occasions inadvertently occurred, the final blow being either when he slammed a gate and hit her or when he shook her at a funeral for laughing. The maiden silently left the man and, with her cattle, disappeared beneath the lake's icy waters once more. The round trip from Llanddeusant to both the lakes is around ten miles, and provides often bleak and lonely walking through valleys cut between purple hills, slashed with tumbling streams. This is classic glacial scenery: occasional mounds and moraines of rock debris indicate the force of the ice pushing through the valleys. Such heaps sometimes grew to a size large enough to form a natural dam, building up a lake, such as Llyn y Fan Fach, in its wake.

From Llyn y Fan Fach, a precarious path leads around the top of the escarpment, following the ridge to **Fan Brycheiniog** (2630ft), above the glassy black waters of Llyn y Fan Fawr. A remote path heads from here to the cross-moor road, two miles away.

The Fforest Fawr

Covering a vast expanse of hilly landscape between the Black Mountain and the central Beacons southwest of Brecon, **Fforest Fawr** (Great Forest) seems something of a misnomer for an area of largely unforested sandstone hills dropping down to a porous limestone belt in the south. The "forest" tag refers more to the old definition of a forest as land used as a hunting ground.

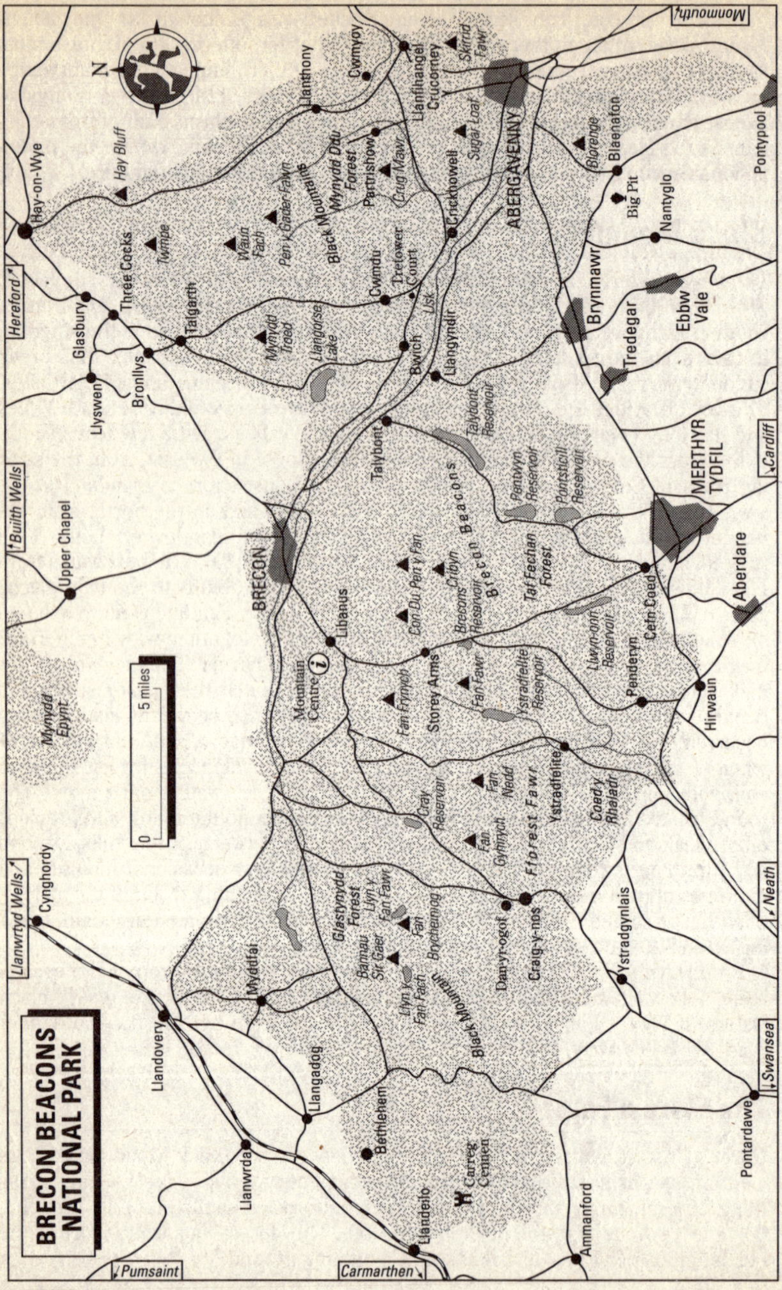
BRECON BEACONS NATIONAL PARK
N
0
5 miles
Pumsaint
Carmarthen
Llanwrtyd Wells
Builth Wells
Hereford
Monmouth
Cardiff
Neath
Swansea
Llandeilo
Llanwrda
Llandovery
Cynghordy
Llangadog
Bethlehem
Carreg Cennen
Ammanford
Myddfai
Black Mountain
Llyn y Fan Fach
Bannau Sir Gaer
Fan Brycheiniog
Llyn y Fan Fawr
Glastynydd Forest
Danyr-ogof
Craig-y-nos
Ystradgynlais
Pontardawe
Fan Gyhirych
Fforest Fawr
Fan Nedd
Cray Reservoir
Ystradfellte
Coed y Rhaeadr
Mynydd Epynt
Mountain Centre
Fan Frynych
Storey Arms
Fan Fawr
Ystradfellte Reservoir
Libanus
Brecons Reservoir
Corn Du
Pen y Fan
Cribyn
Brecon Beacons
Taf Fechan Forest
Llwyn-onn Reservoir
Penderyn
Cefn Coed
Hirwaun
Aberdare
BRECON
Upper Chapel
Talybont
Pentwyn Reservoir
Pontsticill Reservoir
MERTHYR TYDFIL
Llysweh
Bronllys
Glasbury
Talgarth
Three Cocks
Hay-on-Wye
Hay Bluff
Twmpa
Waun Fach
Pen y Gader-Fawr
Black Mountains
Mynydd Troed
Llangorse Lake
Cwmdu
Tretower Court
Bwlch
Usk
Llangynidr
Talybont Reservoir
Tredegar
Ebbw Vale
Brynmawr
Nantyglo
Big Pit
Blaenafon
Blorenge
Pontypool
Crickhowell
ABERGAVENNY
Partrishow
Crug Mawr
Mynydd Ddu Forest
Sugar Loaf
Llanthony
Llanfihangel Crucorney
Cwmyoy
Skirrid Fawr

The hills rise up to the south of the A40 west of Brecon, with the A4067 Sennybridge–Ystradgynlais road piercing the western side of the range and the A470 Brecon–Merthyr road defining the Fforest's eastern limit. Between the two, a twisting mountain road rises up out of the fertile valley of the Senni River three miles south of Sennybridge, straining up to cross the bleak plateau towards the top of Fforest Fawr and decending into the limestone crags around the hamlet of **YSTRADFELLTE**, little more than a handful of houses, a church and a pub. It is, however, a phenomenally popular centre for walking, as a result of the dazzling countryside on its doorstep. Lush, deep ravines – a total contrast to the barren mountains immediately to the north – carve their way through the limestone ridge south of the village, with great pavements of bone-white rock littering fields next to cradling potholes, disappearing rivers and crashing waterfalls. As a classic limestone landscape, the Ystradfellte district is recognized as one of the most impressive in the British Isles.

A mile south of Ystradfellte, the River Mellte tumbles into the dark mouth of the **Porth-yr-ogof** (White Horse Cave), emerging into daylight a few hundred yards further south. A signposted path heads south from the Porth-yr-ogof car park and into the green gorge of the River Mellte. After little more than a mile, the first of three waterfalls is reached at **Sgwd Clun-Gwyn** (White Meadow Fall), where the river crashes fifty feet over two huge, angular steps of rock before hurtling down course for a few hundred yards to the other two falls, the impressive **Sgwd Isaf Clun-Gwyn** (Lower White Meadow Fall) and, around the wooded corner, the **Sgwd y Pannwr** (Fall of the Fuller). These are formed at the edge of the limestone escarpment, where the southerly millstone grit is beginning to appear, and were created when the river broke the upper hard surface and eroded the lower limestone shales. The path continues through the foliage to the confluence of the rivers Mellte and Hepste, half a mile further on. A quarter of a mile along the Hepste is arguably the most impressive, and certainly the most popular, of the area's falls, the **Sgwd yr Eira** (Fall of Snow), whose rock below the main tumble has eroded back six feet, allowing people to walk directly behind a dramatic twenty-foot curtain of water. A shorter two-mile walk to Sgwd yr Eira leads from the village of **PENDERYN**, off the A4059 three miles north of Hirwaun, through which regular buses from Aberdare pass. There's a cosy **youth hostel** (☎0639/720301; ①) at **TAI'R HEOL**, half a mile south of Ystradfellte and just a short walk from Porth-yr-ogof.

Dan-yr-ogof Showcaves and Craig-y-nos

Six miles of upland forest and squelchy moor lie between Ystradfellte and the **Dan-yr-ogof Showcaves** (April–Oct daily 10am–4pm; Nov–March phone for details; ☎0639/730284 or 730693; £4.95), off the A4067 to the west. Only discovered in 1912, they claim to form the largest system of subterranean caverns in Western Europe, and, although relentless marketing has turned them into something of an overdone theme park, the caverns are truly awe-inspiring in their size.

A path to the first series of caves, reached around the hideously kitsch park of plastic dinosaurs, leads through a warren of caverns, framed by eerie stalactites and frothy limestone deposits spewing, frozen, over the crags and walls. Highlight of the bewildering subterranean trip is the **Dan-yr-ogof** cave itself, the longest showcave in Britain. Even better is the trip along the path through the downbeat recreated Iron Age "village", which leads to the opening of a series of caves that culminate in the **Cathedral Cave**. En route, the visitor passes through a winding succession of spookily lit caverns, where water cascades relentlessly down the walls and crusts of thin stalactites, looking like spun pasta squeezed through the rock, hang above. Light and sound come together in the final cave, the 150-foot-long, 70-foot-high Cathedral, in the shape of a swelling classical soundtrack and dancing light show that succeeds, almost despite its inherent tawdriness, in impressing the visitor. The third cave to see is reached along a fearful path behind the dinosaur park, clinging precariously to a cliff edge. **Bone Cave** was known to be inhabited by prehistoric tribes, so the owners have fenced off an assortment of dressed-up mannequins in the cave for an accompanying *son-et-lumière* show that makes Iron Age woman look like a reject from *Miss Selfridge*.

By the main car park for the complex is the Dan-yr-ogof **trekking centre**, which arranges horse rides, and also has a **hotel** (☎0639/730284 or 730693; ③), and **campsite**. Unless you want to get an early start on the caves, or are using it as a base for walking, there's little here to make you stay.

A quarter of a mile south of the cave complex is the spiky shape of the nineteenth-century **Craig-y-nos Castle** (tours Easter–Sept daily; ☎0639/730205; £1.75), a grand folly built in 1842 and fancifully extended from 1878, when it was bought by Adelina Patti, the celebrated Italo-American opera singer. She turned the place into a Disneyesque castle, even adding a gaudy, scaled-down version of the Drury Lane opera house for performances. Small tours take in the theatre, together with Sunday lunches, occasional opera recitals in the theatre and regular evenings of Welsh food, wine and entertainment in the theatre and Banqueting Hall. The grounds have been turned over to the **Craig-y-nos Country Park** (unrestricted entry), whose car park and information centre is the starting point for signposted and leafleted walks around a forty-acre landscaped site along the banks of the young River Tawe.

The central Beacons

Far more popular for walking and pony trekking than the wet and wild Black Mountain and Fforest Fawr, the **central Beacons**, grouped around the two highest peaks in the National Park, are easily accessible from Brecon, just six miles to the north. This is classic old red sandstone country: sweeping peaks rising up out of glacial scoops of land. Although the peaks never reach 3000 feet, the terrain is unmistakably, and dramatically, mountainous.

Pen y Fan (2907ft) is the highest peak in the Beacons, indeed in all south Wales. Together with **Corn Du** (2863ft), half a mile to the west, they form the most popular ascents in the park, particularly along the well-trampled muddy red path that starts from Pont ar Daf, half a mile south of Storey Arms on the A470 midway between Brecon and Merthyr Tydfil. This is the most direct route from a road, where a comparatively easy five-mile round trip gradually climbs up the southern flank of the two peaks. A longer and generally quieter route leads up to the two peaks from the "Gap" route, the pre-nineteenth-century (and possibly Roman) main road that winds its way north from the Neuadd reservoirs, through the only natural break in the sandstone ridge of the central Beacons to the bottom of the lane that eventually joins the main street in Llanfaes, Brecon, as Bailihelig Road. Although the old road is no longer accessible for cars, car parks at either end open out onto the track for an eight-mile round-trip ascent up Pen y Fan and Corn Du from the east.

The Black Mountains

The easternmost section of the National Park is the area around the **Black Mountains**, not to be confused with its singular namesake forty miles west. Far quieter than the central belt of the Brecon Beacons, the Black Mountains combine some of the awesome remoteness of Fforest Fawr with the dry terrain and excellent walking of the central Beacons.

The wide valley of the River Usk divides the central Beacons from the Black Mountains, whose sandstone range rises to better defined individual peaks than can be found in the western end of the National Park. The only exception to the unremitting sandstone is an isolated outcrop of limestone, long divorced from the southern belt, that peaks due north of Crickhowell at Pen Cerrig-calch (2302ft).

The Black Mountains have the feeling, unlike the Black Mountain or Fforest Fawr, of a landscape only partly tamed by human habitation. Tiny villages, isolated churches and delightful lanes are folded into the undulating green landscape. The most popular and rewarding areas to walk are in the east of the mountains, along the lane past Llanthony Priory (see p.62) and along the southern band of peaks, easily reached from Abergavenny (see p.56) and Crickhowell, notably Pen Cerrig-celch, Table Mountain and the Sugar Loaf. The mass of rippling hills in the centre and to the north are less easy to reach, although a couple of good paths cross the contours.

Llangorse, Talybont, Talgarth and Bronllys

Sheltering in the western lee of the Black Mountains, a mile from the pristine village of **LLANGORSE** (Llangors), the reed-shored **Llangorse Lake** (Llyn Syfaddan) washes its way around a low contour in the mountains, and was noted for its miraculous properties (blood-red water, groaning sounds and mythical lost city) in medieval times, but it's a rather more pedestrian affair today. A popular outdoor recreational centre, the lake hosts rowing, canoeing, fishing, windsurfing and yachting, as well as mountain bike and caravan rental and the *Lakeside* **campsite** (☎087 484/226). There is the mediocre *Lakeside* bar and restaurant by the lake, but you'd be better off ambling into the village to sample the excellent food at the *Castle Inn*. The friendly *Red Lion* (☎087 484/238; ③), on the corner of the lane leading down to the lake, does B&B.

The wide, fertile vale of the Usk flows south of Llangorse, passing alongside the Monmouth and Brecon Canal, sitting on a shored-up bank of land above tidy little **TALYBONT-ON-USK**, a village top-heavy with bridges that reveal much about transport history: a disused rail bridge cuts across the main street near an aqueduct that carries a canal over the Caerfanell River, a tributary of the Usk dammed to form the reservoir two miles away. A few yards up the canal is a classic example of an old swingbridge, and another lane heads south from the village to the 323-acre **reservoir**, built to supply water to Newport, and crowded in by steep, conifer-forested hillsides. The lane continues up onto the rocky hillsides, past the waterfalls on the Nant Bwrefwr and beyond to the isolated and hauntingly beautiful **Neuadd reservoirs** in the north, a good starting point for walks to the summits of Pen y Fan and Corn Du along the old "Gap" road (see opposite), or, to the south, the busier and more popular **Pentwyn** and **Pontsticill** (aka Taf Fechan) **reservoirs**. Car parks, snack bars and signposted forest walks form the bulk of most people's experience of these latter two reservoirs, although two eastbound paths at either end of the Pontsticill reservoir enable escape from this in favour of a fairly steep climb up the rocky slopes for wonderful views over the lakes. The hamlet of **PONTSTICILL**, behind the dam at the southern end of the lower lake, is only three miles north of urban Merthyr Tydfil (see p.74). Below the settlement, the tiny **Brecon Mountain Railway** (Easter–Oct mostly daily; ☎0685/722988) shuttles passengers along a two mile section of track on the eastern bank of the reservoir and down to Pant, just north of Merthyr.

Regular Brecon–Crickhowell buses stop at Talybont, where **bike rental** is available from the *Talybont Venture Centre* in the Old Shop (☎087 487/458). Amongst the village pubs, the *White Hart* is enjoyably basic and the *Star* (☎087 487/635; ③) more inspired in its choice of food, jazz and theme nights, ranges of beer and good B&B.

The town of **TALGARTH**, five miles north of Llangorse, is a low-key large village built around its unusual town hall and the brooding bulk of **St Gwendoline's church** tower, built in the fourteenth century but harking back to Talgarth's position as a defence centre against the Norman invasion. The *Tower Hotel*, The Square (☎0874/711253; ③), is the town's focal centre for eating, drinking and B&B. Between Talgarth and the neighbouring village of **BRONLLYS** is **Bronllys Castle**, of which only a large twelfth-century cylindrical tower remains. You can climb to the top and sample some stunning views up the Llynfi River valley and beyond to the light-washed peaks of the Black Mountains. Three miles south of Talgarth, the hamlet of **PENGENFFORDD** is a brilliant base for walks in the mountains, including up to the nearby vast Iron Age hillfort of **Castell Dinas**, whose 2500-year-old ditches and grass ramparts sit 1500 feet up in a magnificent position under an outlying crop of the mountain range, commanding views far down the valley of the Rhian-goll. The site's combined practicality for shelter, defence and settlement were used again when a medieval castle was built to complement Tretower at the other end of the valley, but a few isolated bits of rubble are all that remain. The *Castle Inn* (☎0874/711353; ③), a popular base for walkers for its B&B, food and drink, sits at its base on the main road.

Tretower

Rising out of the valley floor, dominating the view from both the A40 and A479 mountain road, the solid round tower of the **castle and court** (April–Oct daily 9.30am–6pm; Nov-March Mon–Sat 9.30am–4pm, Sun 2–4pm; CADW; £1.80) at **TRETOWER** (Tre-tŵr), was built to guard the valley pass. The bleak thirteenth-century round tower replaced an earlier Norman fortification, and in the late fourteenth century, a comparatively luxurious manor house was built a couple of hundred yards away over a sheep-filled field, gradually being expanded more over the ensuing years. In the summer, Shakespeare and contemporary plays are acted out in the inspirational surroundings of the court (details ☎0874/730279). The court has been fully restored, with its family rooms and ostentatious beam-ceilinged Great Hall facing in on the central cobbled courtyard and square sandstone gatehouse. With much of the work still underway, exposed plaster and beams give a good insight into late medieval building methods. An open-air gallery and wall walk enable the visitor to view the site on the upper level. An enjoyable self-guided Walkman tour takes the visitor around the site.

Crickhowell

One of the liveliest bases in the Black Mountains, **CRICKHOWELL** (Crucywel), on the northern shore of the wide and shallow Usk, has a grand seventeenth-century **bridge** with thirteen arches visible from the eastern end and only twelve from the west, spawning many a local myth. Bridge Street rises from the river and up to the uninspiring mound of the ruined **castle** and the wide **High Street**. New Road runs parallel to Bridge Street from the river, passing the steeple of the town's fourteenth-century **church of St Edmund**. There really isn't that much to see in the town, but its spectacular northern backdrop is **Table Mountain** (1481ft), whose brown cone presides over the rolling green fields below. The best access is along the path past The Wern off Llanbedr Road, and at the summit there are remains of the 2500-year-old hillfort (*crug*) of Hywel, from which the town, tumbling down the slopes below into the Usk Valley, takes its name. Views over the river valley and southern peaks of the Black Mountains are amongst the best in the area. Many walkers follow the route to the north from Table Mountain, climbing two miles up to the plateau-topped limestone hump of **Pen Cerrig-calch** (2302ft).

Crickhowell has many facilities in quite a compact space. The **tourist office** (April–Oct daily 9am–1pm & 2–5pm; ☎0837/812105) is in Beaufort Chambers on Beaufort Street. **Accommodation** is abundant, with the grandiose coaching inn, the *Bear Hotel* on Beaufort Street (☎0873/810408; ④), and the *Dragon* on the High Street (☎0873/810362; ③); for cheaper B&B, try *Glan-nant* (☎0873/810631; ②), opposite the *White Hart Inn* on Brecon Road. There's also the town centre *Riverside Park* **campsite** on New Road (☎0873/810397). Lying under Table Mountain near the delightful village of Llanbedr – on the lane from Crickhowell where the turn for Llanbedr goes off – is *Perth-y-pia* (☎0873/810050), an outdoor centre offering excellent hostel accommodation (①), together with B&B (②) and home-cooked evening meals, and it's handily close to the *Red Lion* pub.

There's no shortage of places to **eat** and **drink** back in Crickhowell: for lunch, there are daytime snacks at the *Corner House* tea room on Beaufort Street, or the the *Cheese Press* on the High Street. Evening food is almost universally available in the town's pubs: the *Bear Hotel* (see above) wins legions of awards for its delectable, pricier-than-average bar and restaurant food; the local delicacies on offer in the *White Hart* on Brecon Road are cheaper, and there's the similar but staid *Six Bells* on New Road. Hearty, if pricy Welsh cuisine is available at *Tŷ Croeso* (☎0873/810573), across the Usk a mile west of Crickhowell at The Dardy, near Llangattock. Down by the town bridge, the *Britannia* is Crickhowell's liveliest pub if you're just after a drink, with pool, games and the youngest clientele.

The *Crickhowell Mountain Gear* shop, next to the market cross at 1 High Street (☎0873/810020), sells all of the predictable caving and walking paraphernalia, offering a **bike rental** service as well, for which it's best to phone in advance. *Perth-y-pia*, two miles north of Crickhowell just outside Llanbedr (see above), co-ordinate numerous outdoor activities, including bike rental, sailing, windsurfing, mountaineering, caving and even archery and hang-gliding.

Hay-on-Wye

The sleepy border town of **HAY-ON-WYE** (Y Gelli), at the northern tip of the Brecon Beacons, is known to most people for one thing – books. Hay saw its first second-hand bookshop open in 1961 and has since become a bibliophile's paradise, with just about every spare inch given over to the trade, including the old cinema, houses, shops and even the ramshackle stone castle. There are now over twenty bookstores here, the largest containing around half a million tomes.

Hay, as a border town full of non-local folk, has little indigenous feel, although its setting amongst soft mountains, together with its creaky little streets, maintain an unhurried charm. It's a fascinating place to visit, bursting alive in the summer with riverside parties, travelling fairs and a vast shifting population. In the last week of May, all fashionable London literary life decamps to Hay for the **Hay Literary Festival**, held in venues around the town. The atmosphere at this time is superb, although accommodation gets booked up well in advance. At any time of the year, the area surrounding Hay makes staying in the town a sensible option. One of the most awesome mountain roads in south Wales south of the town climbs up into the Black Mountains and under the glorious viewpoint at Hay Bluff before descending into the Gospel Pass (see p.62) and Vale of Ewyas (see p.60). This is wonderful walking country, although the little ribbon of road laid seemingly casually across the springy moor can get horribly congested in high summer.

Arrival and information

Buses stop in the functional car park off Oxford Road next to the cheery official **tourist office** (daily Easter–Oct 10am–1pm & 2–5pm; Nov–Easter 11am–1pm & 2–4pm; ☎0497/820144), housed in a grim craft centre. They can recommend from the plentiful local accommodation, which gets booked up long in advance for the festival. **Bike rental** is available from *Price's* at Dan-y-Garth at Cusop (☎0497/820286), a mile south of the town (actually over the border in England). There's a **laundry** in Oxford Terrace, behind the castle.

Accommodation

Belmont House, Belmont Rd (☎0497/820718). Classy guesthouse on the continuation of Broad Street. ②.

Brookfield House, Brook St (☎0497/820518). Small, friendly B&B off Lion Street. ②.

Cwmdulais House, Heol-y-dwr (☎0497/820640). Cheerful B&B on the back road behind Lion Street. ②.

Old Black Lion, Lion St (☎0497/820841). Captivating thirteenth-century inn, which favours candlelight in the evenings. Excellent accommodation. ③.

Old Post Office, Llanigon (☎0497/820008). A wonderful seventeenth-century vegetarian B&B two miles south of Hay. They also rent out bikes and are well placed for local walks, including the Offa's Dyke path (see p.192). ②.

Radnors End campsite (☎0497/820780 or 820233). Five minutes' walk from town, across the Wye bridge and on the road to Clyro. A beautiful setting overlooking Hay, with showers and washing machine on site.

Seven Stars, Broad St (☎0497/820886). Popular town pub near the clock tower, with a good range of bedrooms. ③.

Swan Hotel, Church St (☎0497/821188). Lively nineteenth-century coaching inn at the southern entrance to the town, with en suite rooms. ④.

The Town

Don't come to Hay if you don't enjoy books, as they are the chief concern of this small market town. The best bookshop to start sampling the spirit of the town is up the gated track towards the castle opposite the Oxford Road car park, where you'll find Richard Booth's self-styled **independent tourist information centre** and **Five Star bookshop**, with racks of overspill books under canopied covers outside, together with honesty boxes for payment. The shop itself specializes in an unlikely mix of sci-fi, horror, leisure and tourism, including many a tract containing the Thoughts of King Richard. Here – or from the official tourist office

– you can pick up the invaluable free *Hay-on-Wye Booksellers & Printsellers* leaflet, detailing all of the town's literary concerns. Just beyond the *Five Star* bookshop is the **castle**, a fire-damaged Jacobean mansion built into the walls of a thirteenth-century fortress, and owned – like just about everything in Hay – by Richard Booth. The ruling monarch lives in part of the castle, affected by fires in 1939 and 1978, although his wife runs the *Castle Bookshop*, a very sedate collection of fine art, antiquarian and photography books – in another part of the mansion.

A small bookshop-lined alleyway leads from the gated track to Castle Street, where **H.R. Grant and Son** at no. 6 and **Castle Street Books** at no. 23 are the best in town for contemporary and historical guides and maps, the former selling works pertaining to nineteenth-century diarist Reverend Kilvert and his winsome diaries. Beyond the colonnaded **Buttermarket** at the top end of Castle Street, **Richard Booth's Bookshop**, 44 Lion St, is the largest shop in Hay, a huge, draughty warehouse of almost unlimited browsing potential. Lion Street dips down to Broad Street at the clock tower near **Y Gelli Auctions** (☎0497/821179), with regular sales of books, maps and prints. Further along tree-lined Broad Street is **West House Books**, best for Celtic and women's works.

RICHARD BOOTH AND THE HAY BOOK BUSINESS

Richard Booth, whose family originates in the area, opened the first of his Hay-on-Wye second-hand bookshops in 1961. Since then, he has built an astonishing empire and attracted other booksellers to the town, turning it into the greatest market of used books in the world. There are now over twenty such shops in the minuscule town, the largest of which – Booth's own flagship – contains around half a million volumes.

Whereas so many mid Welsh and border towns have seen populations ebb away over the past fifty years, Hay is booming on the strength of its bibliophilic connections. Booth views this transformation of a hitherto ordinary little market town as a prototype for reviving an agrarian economy, depending on local initiatives and unusual specialisms instead of handouts from vast statutory or multinational corporations. He is unequivocal in his condemnation of bulky government organizations such as the Wales Tourist Board and the Development Board for Rural Wales, which, he asserts, have done little to stem the flow of jobs and people out of the region but which have succeeded instead in lining the pockets of a chosen few. This healthy distaste for hefty bureaucracy, coupled with Hay's geographical location slap on the Wales–England border and Booth's own self-promotional skills, led him to declare Hay independent of the UK in 1977, with himself, naturally as King. He appoints his own ministers and offers "official" government scrolls, passports and car stickers to bewitched visitors. Although such a proclamation of UDI carries no weight officially, most of the people of Hay seem to have rallied behind King Richard and are delighted with the publicity, and visitors, that the town's continuing profile attracts.

King Richard continues to take his self-appointed role seriously, pumping out a series of tracts and pamphlets on subjects dear to his heart, from the predictable rallying cries against supermarket developments to criticism of the town's high-profile annual literary festival, founded on the basis of Hay's bibliophilic reputation. Amongst the egotism and occasional self-righteousness, Booth hits many targets accurately, and his criticism of the homogenization and consequent decline of rural communities due to crass actions by government and big business is a theme to which many have subsequently been drawn.

A road passes over the River Wye and climbs the hill towards **CLYRO**, little more than a mile away. Sheltering behind the busy A438, the village is home to a couple of small commercial art galleries trading on the strength of Clyro's connections with nineteenth-century wandering parson, Francis Kilvert. Although he was vicar of Clyro for only seven years (1865–72), the village, its idyllic surroundings and its precisely recorded inhabitants, featured prominently in his published diaries, drawing a steady trickle of pilgrims to see the place ever since.

Eating and drinking

Blue Boar, Castle St. Tasteful wood-panelled bar on the corner with Oxford Road. Excellent beer and reasonable summer food. Inexpensive.

Granary, Broad St (☎0497/820790). Unpretentious bistro, excellent for vegetarian food and local produce. Moderate.

Kilvert Court Inn, Bull Ring. Warm and friendly locals' pub, with a limited but cheap bar menu. Live music most Thursdays and occasionally at the weekend. Inexpensive.

Old Black Lion, Lion St (☎0497/820841). Beautiful, olde-worlde pub that avoids any element of kitsch. Superb meals in the bar, or more robust fare in the pricier restaurant. Inexpensive.

Pinnochio's, Broad St (☎0497/821166). Relaxed and popular Italian restaurant, with a delightfully convivial atmsophere on a warm summer's evening. Moderate.

Swan Hotel, Church St. Good downstairs bar, popular for its pool tables and games machines. Hearty, good value bar snacks also available. Moderate.

Three Cocks Hotel, Three Cocks (☎049 74/215). Five miles southwest of Hay on the A438, this stuffy hotel has a tasty Belgian restaurant on the ground floor. Expensive.

Three Tuns, Broad Street. Timewarped pub with a dusty, flagstoned bar filled with disorganized mounds of memorabilia. Go easy on the lethal draught local cider.

The Wells towns

Straddling the old border of Brecknockshire and Radnorshire, around fifteen miles north of Brecon, are the four spa towns of mid-Wales, strung out along the Heart of Wales rail line and the main A483. Up until the eighteenth century, all were obscure villages, but then came the great craze for spas, and anywhere with a decent supply of apparently healing water joined in on the act. Royalty and nobility spearheaded the fashion, with spas such as Llandrindod gaining a reputation for licentiousness and a general air of lawless reverie. Come the arrival of the railways, the four Welsh spas became the domain of everyone, although each had its own clientele and appealed to different social groups. The westernmost, **Llanwrtyd Wells** was a popular haunt of the Welsh middle classes in the nineteenth century, locked in mountainous countryside at the foot of the eerily bleak **Mynydd Eppynt** range. From here, the River Irfon winds up into the mountains towards the hamlet of **Abergwesyn**, from which a narrow road climbs up, before dropping down into Tregaron (see p.213). Four miles east along the river, the waters of tiny, nondescript **Llangammarch Wells** contain barium chloride, a popular Victorian remedy for rheumatism and heart problems.

East of here, the larger town of **Builth Wells** is best known nowadays as the home of the huge Royal Welsh Showground, but far prettier – although considerably more twee and anglicized – is **Llandrindod Wells** to the north, whose spa is the only one of the four in any state of decent repair. There are some excellent and fairly gentle walks around Llandrindod, as well as some beautiful, isolated churches – notably, at **Cefnllys** and **Disserth**.

Llanwrtyd Wells and around

Of the four spa towns, **LLANWRTYD WELLS** is the most appealing. It's friendlier, more Welsh, more unspoiled and in more beautiful surroundings than the other three. This was the spa to which the Welsh – farmers of Dyfed alongside the Nonconformist middle classes from Glamorgan – came to great *eisteddfodau* in the valley of the Irfon. The town – claiming the somewhat dubious title of Britain's smallest – shows obvious signs of its Victorian heyday, especially in the tall nineteenth-century town houses that line the streets.

Main Street runs through the town, crossing the turbulent Irfon River just below the town's main square. On the opposite side of the main road, a lane winds for half a mile along the river to the *Dolecoed Hotel*, built near the original sulphurous spring. Although the distinctive aroma had been noted in the area for centuries, it was truly "discovered" in 1732 by the local priest, Theophilus Evans, who drank from an evil-smelling spring after seeing a rudely healthy frog pop out of it. The spring, named **Ffynon Droellwyd** (Stinking Well), can still be sniffed out in the fields beyond the hotel, now erupting around a dome-shaped extension behind the neat red-and-white spa buildings, in the process of restoration.

Back in Llanwrtyd Wells proper, the A483 crests over a hill immediately north of the town, descending to the **Cambrian Woollen Mill** (Mon–Fri 8.30am–4.30pm; £3), a fairly unrewarding factory tour through the process of Welsh tweed production. There is a shop (free entry) on site, also open at weekends.

Practicalities

Llanwrtyd's **tourist office** is just south of the town centre in Dolwen Fields, off the Cefngorwydd road (Easter–Oct daily 10am–5pm). **Accommodation** includes the *Neuadd Arms* in the main square (☎059 13/236; ③), which also rents out **bikes**, the solidly Victorian *Belle Vue Hotel* a few yards away (☎059 13/237; ③), and the cheaper *Cerdyn Villa*, Station Rd (☎059 13/635; ②). Both the *Neuadd Arms* and the *Belle Vue* provide cheap, hearty food. The *Drovers' Rest* café, by the river bridge, serves wholesome traditional Welsh dishes during the day.

The **Neuadd Arms** (☎059 13/236) pub is the base for a wide range of bizarre and entertaining annual events, including a Man versus Horse race, a Drovers' Walk, a town festival in the first week of August, walking expeditions, a snorkelling competition in a local bog, a beer festival in November and a New Year's Eve torchlight procession through the town.

Mynydd Eppynt and Llangammarch Wells

The gorgeous scenery around the town of Llanwrtyd Wells is one of its biggest attractions, nowhere more evident than in the country to the south, where the remote **Crychan Forest** and the doleful mountains of the **Mynydd Eppynt** make up the northern outcrops of the Brecon Beacons, most dramatically along the roads that snake their way across the moors from the towns of Garth and Builth. The bulk of the Eppynt has been appropriated by the British Army, as is painfully obvious from the number of red flags flying stiffly, signs warning you not to stop or touch anything and, saddest of all, the spooky **Drovers Arms**, midway between Garth and Upper Chapel on the B4519, once a welcome and cheerful respite for those droving cattle across the mountains and now a boarded-up, hostile, blank wreck.

The B4519 descends dramatically from the Eppynt above a beautifully isolated valley, the **Cwm Graig Ddu**, from where the views over scores of miles of soft farmland and rippling hills are overpowering. At the bottom of the hill, a lane forks left, soon to join the River Irfon that winds to **LLANGAMMARCH WELLS**, where it meets the Cammarch River. A mile before entering the village is the exquisite black-and-white timbered **Lake Hotel** (☎059 12/202; ⑤), the home of the now defunct barium well that attracted Lloyd George and foreign heads of governments searching for cures, and probably the best reason to come here. The village is excellent for fishing, but singularly dull otherwise.

Abergwesyn and the Pass

Although the drovers' roads and inns across the Mynydd Eppynt are now forbidden territory, the most spectacular of the drovers' routes is thankfully still open. The lane from Llanwrtyd meets up with another road from Beulah at the riverside hamlet of **ABERGWESYN**. From here, a quite magnificent winding thread of a road – the **Abergwesyn Pass** – climbs up alongside the dwindling river, leaving it at the perilous **Devil's Staircase** and pushing up through dense conifer forests to wide, sparse valleys where no sign of human habitation can be seen as far as the eye can travel. Sheep graze unhurriedly by – and on – the road, framed by craggy peaks, bubbling waterfalls and blotches of gorse and heather. At the little bridge over the tiny Tywi River, a track heads south past an isolated, gas-lit **youth hostel** (☎0222/231370; ①) at **DOLGOCH**. On the other side of the river, a new road channels past the thick forest on to Llyn Brianne (see p.128), a couple of miles further on. This is as remote a walking holiday as can be had in Wales – paths lead from Dolgoch, through the forests and hillsides to the tiny chapel at **SOAR-Y-MYNYDD** and beyond, over the mountains to the next hostel at Tŷ'n-y-cornel (☎0222/231370; ①), five strenuous miles from Dolgoch.

From Dolgoch, the Abergwesyn Pass continues over the massive, wide terrain, before dropping down along the rounded valley of the Berwyn River and into Tregaron (see p.213). Although the entire Llanwrtyd–Tregaron route is less than twenty miles in length, it takes a good hour to negotiate the twisting, narrow road safely. The old drovers, driving their cattle to Shrewsbury or Hereford, would have taken a good day or two over the same stretch.

Builth Wells and around

Very much the spa of the Welsh working classes, **BUILTH WELLS** (Llanfair ym Muallt) still caters to its locals. An earthy agricultural town that has little to detain you, it's a useful centre for transport, cheap accommodation and entertainment, and can make a reasonable base for exploring the area around.

The most pleasant area in Builth is the verdant stretch along the Wye, below the architecturally undistinguished High Street, where you'll find the multi-purpose **Wyeside Arts Centre** (☎0982/552555), converted out of the town's Victorian Assembly Rooms right by the Wye bridge. On the other side of the river, Builth's major modern source of prosperity, the **Royal Welsh Showground** (☎0982/553683), hosts numerous agricultural events, together with monthly flea markets and occasional specialized collectors' fairs. The massive **Royal Welsh Show**, a giant coming together of all matters agricultural, takes place in mid-July.

Practicalities

Builth Road **train station** is nearly three miles north of the town and inaccessible by public transport. **Buses** depart from the car park alongside the river bridge, in which the **tourist office** (Easter–Oct daily 10am–6pm; Nov–Easter Mon–Sat 10am–5pm; ☎0982/553307) is to be found.

Accommodation comes cheap: the *White Horse* on the High Street (☎0982/553171; ③) is the liveliest pub in town, and, at the top of the High Street, *The Owls* B&B (☎0982/552518; ②) has an excellent reputation. There are numerous cheap daytime cafés, and pubs such as the *Lion Hotel* on Broad Street, near the bridge, and the *White Horse* (which also hosts regular live music and quizzes) that provide decent evening **food**.

Cilmeri

In the centre of **CILMERI**, an unassuming village that straggles along the main A483 road and rail line between Builth and Llanwrtyd, the *Prince Llywelyn* pub seems incongruously placed as a reminder of Welsh martyrdom in a fairly anglicized corner of eastern Wales. A hundred yards further up the main road towards Llanwrtyd and all becomes clear when you catch sight of a large, pointed granite boulder on a small hillock, said to be the spot at which, in December 1282, Llywelyn ap Gruffydd ("the Last"), was killed by English troops as he was escaping from the abortive Battle of Builth, four miles away. On realizing who they had killed, it is said that the English soldiers hacked off Llywelyn's head, whereupon it was despatched to London and paraded victoriously through the city's streets. The English tablet by the monument calls Llywelyn "our prince". Its Welsh equivalent, tellingly, describes him as "ein llyw olaf" – our last leader. Semantics aside, you are unlikely ever to see the monument without someone's fresh flowers adorning it.

Llandrindod Wells and around

If anything can sum a town up so succinctly, it is the shiny new plaque at **LLANDRINDOD WELLS** (Llandrindod) train station, commemorating the 1990 "Revictorianization of Llandrindod station". The town has not been slow to follow suit, peddling itself as Wales' most upmarket Victorian inland resort as if the very life of the town depended upon it.

It was the railway that made Llandrindod, arriving in 1864 and bringing carriages full of well-to-do Victorians to the fledgling spa. Llandrindod blossomed, new hotels were built, neat parks were laid out and the town came to rival many of the more fashionable spas and resorts over the border. Even now, after faintly gloomy Builth, the town can seem like a salty breath of fresh air. Its fine nineteenth-century buildings have been swabbed and sandblasted, ornate cast-iron railings restored, and the spa brought back to some kind of life. There is plenty of accommodation in the town, a good range of things to do and the surrounding countryside – like all of mid-Wales – offers an endless variety of excellent walks.

Arrival, information and getting around

The **train station** (enquiries ☎0597/822053) is in the heart of town, between the High Street and Station Crescent. **Buses** also depart from outside the train station. The **tourist office** on Temple Street (April–Oct daily 10am–1pm &

2–6pm; Nov–March Mon–Fri 9am–1pm & 2–5pm; ☎0597/822600) holds details of the different local bus companies, their routes and times, and will also recommend and book accommodation. For a wider view of festivals and gigs in the area, consult the posters in *Van's Good Food Shop*, sheltering behind a brilliant red frontage that looks more like a gaudy Victorian traction engine, on Middleton Street, connecting Station Crescent and Spa Road. The town's largest annual event is, no surprise, August's **Victorian Festival**, which culminates in a firework extravaganza over the town lake. The longer-established annual town **eisteddfod** takes place in early October. **Market day** is Friday. **Bike rental** is from the *Greenstiles Bike Shed* (☎0597/824594), behind the station on the High Street.

Accommodation

As the major tourist centre for the past 130 years in all of mid-Wales, Llandrindod is well served for hotels, B&Bs, restaurants and cafés, even if its strait-laced past is reflected in the notable lack of pubs.

Brynllys Guest House, High St (☎0597/823190). Smart and reasonable town centre B&B, near the station and all amenities. ②.

Disserth Farm, Disserth (☎059 789/277). Campsite in a beautiful riverside setting, next to the delightful village church of Disserth, a few miles south of Llandrindod.

Greylands, High St (☎0597/822253). Next door to the *Brynllys*, in another tall Victorian redbrick house. ②.

Griffin Lodge Hotel, Temple St (☎0597/832432). Cheerful hotel in a sturdy Victorian house. ③.

Kincoed Hotel, Temple St (☎0597/822656). Well-appointed old town centre hotel, opposite *Kwik Save* supermarket. ③.

Metropole Hotel, Temple St (☎0597/822881). Elegant and large old spa hotel, the centrepiece of the town. Refined dining room, open to non-residents. ⑤.

Rhydithon, Dyffryn Rd (☎0597/822624). One of the smartest and friendliest guest houses in town, just off the High Street. ②.

The Town

Llandrindod's Victorian opulence is still very much in evidence in the town's grandiose public buildings, especially the lavishly restored **spa pavilion** inside the pleasant **Rock Park**, with its trickling streams and well-manicured glens. European Union regulations prohibit the use of the Llandrindod spa taps in the café inside, and if you're desperate to taste the waters, you'll have to settle for a chalybeate fountain outside that spouts the stuff. A walk from the pavilion leads to **"Lovers' Leap"**, a recreated bit of Victorian nonsense that's just a fake cliff with mediocre views over the river. The architecture around the park entrance is Llandrindod at its most confidently Victorian, with large, elaborately carved terracotta frontages and expansive gabling, and the **High Street** runs from here to the town centre, containing good record, antiques, books and junk shops.

Behind the tourist office on Temple Street, you'll find the small town **museum** (April–Sept daily 10am–12.30pm & 2–4.30pm; Oct–March Mon–Fri 10am–12.30pm & 2–4.30pm & Sat 10–12.30pm, closed Wed; free), where the exhibition is largely dedicated to excavated remains from the Roman fort at Castellcollen, a mile northwest of Llandrindod; kitsch Victoriana makes up the bulk of the rest of the collection, including a large group of dolls. Next to the museum is a glutinous **grotto**, a nineteenth-century whimsy built by a local doctor.

Spa Road, to the west of Temple Street, passes **Lear's Magical Lantern Theatre** (April–Sept Mon–Sat 10am–8pm; Oct–March closes 6pm; £1.20), a personal, highly idiosyncratic collection of slides, moving pictures, cinematographs and a recreated 1904 lanternist's projection room. Further up Spa Road, towards the *Commodore* hotel is a small left turn, leading down to the **Grand Pavilion**, home of tea dances and other genteel pursuits.

Eating and drinking

Aspidistra, Station Crescent. Decent daytime café, serving cheap and wholesome sandwiches and snacks. Inexpensive.

Dillraj, Emporium Buildings, Temple St (☎0597/823843). Extremely classy Indian restaurant, opposite the tourist office. Moderate.

Franky's, Temple St (☎0597/823727). Garish cellar bar-cum-bistro, compensated for by the good range of reasonable pizzas. Inexpensive.

Llanerch Inn, Llanerch Lane. Central Llandrindod's only pub, but an excellent one at that. It's a cosy sixteenth-century inn that predates most of the surrounding town, with lots of pub games and a solid menu of good-value, well-cooked classics. Inexpensive.

Stredders, Park Crescent (☎0597/822186). Popular vegetarian restaurant near the rail bridge south of the station. Inexpensive.

Cefnllys

One of the most popular walks from Llandrindod heads east from the town, along Cefnllys Road, though some beautiful wooden pockets to the banks of the River Ithon at **CEFNLLYS**, just under two miles away. A car park by the river leads on to **Shaky Bridge**, whose name dates from when just two planks of wood connected the two banks – a more solid structure is in evidence today. On the other side of the Ithon, the castle mound rises to the right and you'll see the dumpy witch's hat spire of the thirteenth-century **St Michael's church** ahead. In Victorian times, the rector removed the church roof to persuade the few remaining parishioners to travel into up-and-coming Llandrindod instead for worship. There was an outcry and a collection, and the roof was restored just two years later; photographs in the church show this strange period in its history. Back on the Llandrindod side of the river, **Bailey Einon Wood** is a designated nature reserve running three-quarters of a mile along the river, with some enchanting walks through its open glades.

Disserth

The other outlying former parish of Llandrindod is **DISSERTH**, lying a couple of miles to the south of the town, off the A483 at Howey, where the **church of St Cewydd** lies beside the Ithon in one of its most pastoral stretches. Resembling a fat medieval barn with a squat stone tower attached, the church escaped the restorative zeal of the Victorians, leaving its seventeenth-century wooden box pews intact, many with family names still discernible. The 1687 triple-decker pulpit, looking more like an auctioneer's lectern, is a rare survivor of pre-Victorian days.

Where the lane to Disserth heads west off the A483 at Howey, another lane also climbs up into the **Carneddau Hills**. About two miles after leaving the main road, a number of paths leave the lane and delve south into the rocky terrain, where glacial features like moraines and abandoned blocks of stone litter the landscape.

North and East Radnorshire

Before the reorganization of British counties in 1974, Radnorshire was the most sparsely populated one in England and Wales, and it's still a remote area, especially in the north and east. In the northwest, **Rhayader** is the only settlement of any real size, and although fairly plain to look at, is an excellent base, with some friendly pubs. Most people stay here in order to explore the wild, spartan countryside to the west of the town, a hilly patchwork of waterfalls, bogland, bare peaks and the four interlocking reservoirs of the **Elan Valley**, built at the turn of the century and displaying a grandiose Edwardian solidity.

The countryside to the northeast of Rhayader is slightly tamer, and lanes and bridle paths delve in and around the woods and farms, occasionally brushing through minute settlements like the village of **Abbeycwmhir**, whose name is taken from the deserted Cistercian abbey that sits below in the dank, eerie valley of the Clywedog Brook. The hills roll eastwards towards the English border and some of the most intact parts of **Offa's Dyke**, the eighth-century King of Mercia's border with the Welsh princes. The handsome town of **Knighton**, perched right on the border, is at the centre of the 177-mile path that runs along the dyke and is well geared-up for walkers and cyclists with good accommodation, cheery pubs and cafés. Seven miles south, inches from England, the dignified little town of **Presteigne** contains a few reminders of its former importance as a county capital. The River Lugg flows through Presteigne from the Radnorshire hills, passing the isolated church at **Pilleth**, where Owain Glyndŵr captured Sir Edmund Mortimer, agent of the English king, in 1402.

Rhayader and around

RHAYADER (Rhaeder Gwy, literally "waterfall on the Wye") has boomed this century as mid-Radnorshire's principal base for the spectacular hills and reservoirs of the Elan Valley. Although the waterfall invoked by the town's name virtually disappeared when the town bridge was built in 1780, the Wye still frames the town centre, running in a loop around the western and southern sides. Rhayader was a centre of the mid-nineteenth-century so-called **Rebecca Riots**, when local farmers dressed in women's clothing in order to tear down tollgates that were prohibitively expensive for itinerant and local workers.

Rhayader's handsome four main streets – named North, South, East and West – meet at a small town clock tower. Fifty yards up East Street from the clock tower, there's a tiny **folk museum** (Sat 10am–1pm & 2–5pm; Easter & Whitsun also Mon & Tues 2–5pm; Whitsun to mid-July also Fri 2–5pm; mid-July to Sept also Mon, Wed & Fri 2–5pm; free), good for its examination of the building of the local reservoirs in the Elan Valley, as well as an enjoyably haphazard clutter of agricultural and industrial artefacts from the area.

Practicalities

Buses stop in the main Dark Lane car park, opposite the **tourist office** (April–Oct daily 10am–6pm; ☎0597/810591) that shares its building with a leisure centre. Rhayader has always been well serviced for visitors, and eighteenth-century coaching inns still line the main streets. More modern **accommodation** includes the *Bryncoed* B&B on Dark Lane (☎0597/811082; ②), opposite the tourist office, the *Elan Hotel*, West St (☎0597/810373; ③), or *The Mount*, East St

(☎0597/810585; ②), a friendly B&B and the base for *Clive Powell Mountain Bikes*, from whom you can either rent **bikes** or join one of his organized trips around the tracks of mid-Wales. Alternative bike rental is supplied by the *E.T. James Garage* on East Street (☎0597/810481 or 810396). Almost two miles north-east of the town, off the Abbeycwmhir Road, is the relaxing farmhouse B&B of *Beili Neuadd* (☎0597/810211; ③). There's a municipal **campsite** (☎0597/823737, ext 338) north of the town off the A44, and a **laundry** on East Street.

Despite having a population of less than 2000, there are twelve **pubs** in Rhayader, most offering reasonable pub food. Try the old-fashioned *Cornhill Inn* on West Street, or, over Bridge Street in the small hamlet of **LLANSANTFFRAED CWMDEUDDWR**, usually shortened to Cwmdeuddwr, the tiny, ancient *Triangle*, whose pub toilets are on the other side of the street, and where darts players must stand in a special floor hole for fear of spearing the roof. More upmarket, *The Workhouse* **restaurant** (☎0597/810735), half a mile south on the road to Builth Wells, is good for evening meals.

Elan Valley

Until the last decade of the nineteenth century, the untamed countryside west of Rhayader received few visitors, although the poet Shelley did holiday here: his honeymoon retreat at Nantgwlyllt was amongst the couple of dozen buildings submerged by the waters of the **Elan Valley** reservoirs, a nine-mile-long string of four lakes built between 1892 and 1903 to supply water to the rapidly growing industrial city of Birmingham, 75 miles away; in the 1950s, a supplementary reservoir at **Claerwen**, to the immediate west, was opened. Although the lakes enhance an already beautiful and idyllic part of the world, the colonialist way in which Welsh valleys, villages and farmsteads were seized and flooded to provide water for England is something the tourist boards prefer to gloss over. The natural resentment against this has perhaps been best expressed by poet R.S. Thomas in his soulful elegy *Reservoirs*:

There are places in Wales I don't go:
Reservoirs that are the subconscious
Of a people, troubled far down
With gravestones, chapels, villages even;
The serenity of their expression
Revolts me, it is a pose
For strangers, a watercolour's appeal
To the mass, instead of the poem's
Harsher conditions. There are the hills,
Too; gardens gone under the scum
Of the forests; and the smashed faces
Of the farms with the stone trickle
Of their tears down the hills' side.

The "watercolour's appeal" of the Elan Valley is, nonetheless, extremely strong, not only for the landscape but the profusion of rare plants and birds – red kites especially – in the area. From Rhayader, the B4518 heads southwest four miles to **ELAN** village, off the main road, a curious collection of stone houses built in 1909 to replace the reservoir constructors' village that had grown up on the site. Just below the dam of the first reservoir, **Caban Coch**, the **Elan Valley visitor centre** (mid-March to Oct daily 10am–6pm; free), incorporates a tourist office (☎0597/810898), and a permanent exhibition that is sensitive to the English

Victorian imperialism that built the reservoirs, stressing just how awful conditions were in nineteenth-century Birmingham, how rich the wildlife and flora around the lakes is and even how some of the water is now drunk in Wales. Frequent guided **walks** and even **Landrover safaris** head off from the centre. You can stay at the *Elan Valley Lodge* (☎0597/823298; ②), run by the Radnorshire Wildlife Trust, near the village centre.

From the visitor centre, a road tucks in along the bank of Caban Coch to the **Garreg Ddu** viaduct, where a road winds along the bank for four spectacular miles to the vast, rather chilling 1952 dam on **Claerwen Reservoir**. More remote and less popular than the Elan lakes, Claerwen is a good base for the serious walker, who can follow a path from the far end of the dam and walk the harsh but beautiful eight miles or so across the mountains and past smaller, natural lakes to the monastery of Strata Florida (see p.214). Alternatively, the path that skirts around the northern shore of Claerwen leads across to the lonely **Teifi Pools**, glacial lakes from which the Teifi River springs.

Back at the Garreg Ddu viaduct, a more popular road continues north along the long, glassy finger of **Garreg Ddu** reservoir, before doubling back on itself just below the awesome **Pen-y-garreg** dam and reservoir; if the dam is overflowing, the vast wall of foaming water is mesmerizing. Situated just off the road, above the hairpin bend, is the friendly *Flickering Lamp* hotel (☎0597/810827; ③) and restaurant, which does good food. At the top of Pen-y-garreg lake, it's possible to drive over the final, or more properly the first, dam on the system, at **Craig Goch**. This is the most photographed of all the dams, thanks to its gracious curve, elegant Edwardian arches and neat little green cupola. The lake beyond it is fed by the Elan River, which the road crosses just short of a junction. A bleak, invigorating moorland pass heads west from here to drop into the eerie moonscape of Cwmystwyth (see p.222), while the eastbound road funnels into a beautiful valley back to Rhayader. On the way back, fork off the Elan Valley Road in Rhayader on to the smaller Aberystwyth Road.

Abbeycwmhir

ABBEYCWMHIR (Abaty Cwm Hir) seven miles from Rhayader, takes its name from the abbey whose sombre ruins lie behind the village. Cistercian monks founded the abbey in 1146, planning one of the largest churches in Britain, whose 242-foot nave has only ever been exceeded in length by the cathedrals of Durham, York and Winchester. Destruction by Henry III's troops in 1231 scuppered plans to continue the building, however. The sparse ruins of what they did build – a rocky outline of the floorplan – lie in a conifer-carpeted valley alongside a gloomy green lake, lending weight, if only by atmosphere, to the site's melancholic associations. Llywelyn ap Gruffydd's body, after his head had been carted off to London, was rumoured to have been brought here from Cilmeri in 1282, and a new granite slab, carved with a Celtic sword, lies on the altar to commemorate this last native prince of Wales. It should look incongruous, but somehow it only adds to the eerie presence of the ruins and the village.

Presteigne and around

A tiny, old-fashioned place, whose architecture reeks of its former status as county town, **PRESTEIGNE** (Llanandras) lies snugly between the B4362 town bypass and the River Lugg, the border with England, which flows under the seventeenth-century bridge at the bottom of the handsome Broad Street. Just before the bridge, the solid parish **church of St Andrew** contains Saxon and Norman fragments, as well as a sixteenth-century Flemish tapestry. To the left of the main entrance to the churchyard are twin gravestones that give an insight into the morals of the early nineteenth century. The original stone commemorates one Mary Morgan, who gave birth to a bastard child in 1805, her father persuading her to murder it; he then sat on the jury that condemned her to death. A sickeningly pious inscription records that she was "unenlightened by the sacred truths of Christianity" and "became the victim of sin and shame and was condemned to an ignominious death". Opposite is a later stone erected in repentance by the townsfolk, inscribed "He that is without sin among you, let him first cast a stone at her".

Broad Street heads up to the main crossroads, with the High Street forking west and Hereford Street to the east. On the corner of Hereford and Broad streets is the nineteenth-century Italianate Shire Hall, now the town's tourist office and tiny **museum** (May–Oct Tues & Sat 10.30am–1pm & 2.30–5pm; July–Aug Thurs also; 20p), a beguiling and unpredictable collection of dusty relics from the area's past.

Along the main streets – Hereford Street in particular – there are some enjoyably musty second-hand book and antique shops, and the High Street contains the town's most impressive building, the Jacobean **Radnorshire Arms**, built as a private home for John Bradshaw, a signatory on the death warrant of Charles I, before becoming an inn in 1792.

Practicalities

Buses from Knighton, Kington and Leominster stop outside the *Radnorshire Arms* or just around the corner in Station Road. The **tourist office** (April–Sept daily 10am–6pm; ☎0544/260193) is in the Shire Hall. **Accommodation** spans period luxury at the *Radnorshire Arms* (☎0544/267406; ⑥) to reliable B&Bs opposite at the *Cabin* restaurant (☎0544/267068; ②) or at the antiques shop, 32 High St (☎0544/267731; ②). You can **camp** for £1 at *Beggars Bush Farm* (☎054 76/278), three miles west near Discoed, which also offers farmhouse B&B (②).

Many people "dropped out" here in the 1960s and 1970s, and today it's a centre for folk and traditional music: the August bank holiday sees a **festival**, organized by the excellent free Borders folk/jazz newspaper *Broad Sheep*, take place in Warden Park, while regular music strikes up in the Memorial Hall, the Royal British Legion on Hereford Street and the *Farmer's Inn* on Hereford Street. This is the town's liveliest pub, and serves **food**. Alternatively, eat at the *Cabin* (see above), assorted cafés on the High Street or the old-fashioned *Barley Mow* on Hereford Street.

Old and New Radnor

OLD RADNOR seems cut out of a hillside just off the A44 six miles southwest of Presteigne, and was once the home of King Harold, killed at the Battle of Hastings by William the Conqueror's troops. The site of his castle is down the lane running southeast from the large, very English-looking **church**, overlooking a wooded vale. Inside the church, a massive eighth-century font on four stone feet is the most remarkable legacy. Opposite the church, the rambling fifteenth-century *Harp Inn* (☎054 421/655; ③) has been magnificently restored from its earlier use as a farm cottage.

NEW RADNOR, just over two miles to the west, was built as a small Norman settlement and then planned, in the thirteenth century, to be expanded into a major city and capital of Radnorshire. The project faltered, confirming Wales' antipathy towards large settlements, instead of the more common feature of scattered farmsteads. Today, you enter the village from the A44 to the southeast, past a Victorian steeple erected to honour local dignitary Sir George Cornewall Lewis. This is the only feature of the village that seems to suggest any kind of metropolitan status, as the couple of streets are deathly quiet, lined with a couple of reasonable pubs, the best of which is the surprisingly lively *Eagle* on Broad Street (☎054 421/208; ③). This frequently serves perry, a lethally alcoholic pear drink, and is the base for various local outdoor pursuits, including paragliding.

North of New Radnor, the deep clefted valleys and wooded hillsides of **Radnor Forest** offer some of the region's best walking. The most popular route is along the driveable track that forks north off the A44 just over a mile west of New Radnor, leading into a thick forest and to the rushing cascade of the **Water-break-its-neck** waterfall, at its foaming best in winter.

Knighton

A town that straddles King Offa's eighth-century border as well as the modern Wales–England divide, **KNIGHTON** (Tref-y-clawdd, "the town on the dyke") has come into its own as the most obvious centre for those walking the **Offa's Dyke Path**. Located almost exactly half way along the route, Knighton, although without any specific sights, is a lively, attractive place that easily warrants a stop-off.

So close is Knighton to the border, that the town's **train station** and its accompanying hotel (ironically called the *Central Wales*), are actually in England. From here, Station Road crosses the River Teme into Wales and climbs a couple of hundred yards into the town, joining the pretty Broad Street at Brookside Square. Further up the hill is the town's Victorian alpine-looking clock tower, where

OFFA'S DYKE

George Borrow, in his classic *Wild Wales*, notes that once "it was customary for the English to cut off the ears of every Welshman who was found to the east of the dyke, and for the Welsh to hang every Englishman whom they found to the west of it". Certainly, **Offa's Dyke** has provided a potent symbol of Welsh–English antipathy ever since it was created in the eighth century as a demarcation line by King Offa of Mercia, ruler of the whole of central England. It appears that the dyke was an attempt to thwart Welsh expansionism.

The earthwork – up to 20 feet high and 60 feet wide – made use of natural boundaries like rivers in its run north to south, and is best seen in the sections near Knighton in Radnorshire and Montgomery. Today's England–Wales border crosses the dyke many times, although the basic boundary has changed little since Offa's day. The glorious **long distance footpath**, opened in 1971, runs from Prestatyn on the north Clwyd coast for 177 miles to Sedbury Cliffs, just outside Chepstow in Gwent, and is one of the most rewarding walks in Britain – neither too popular to be unpleasantly crowded, nor too similar in its landscapes. The path is maintained by the *Offa's Dyke Association*, whose headquarters is in the Offa's Dyke centre in Knighton (see opposite).

Broad Street becomes West Street and the steep High Street soars off up to the left, past rickety Tudor buildings and up to the mound of the old **castle**. In West Street, the excellent **Offa's Dyke Centre** also houses the **tourist office** (April–Sept daily 9am–5.30pm; Oct–March Mon–Fri 9am–5pm; ☎0547/528753).

Accommodation is plentiful and geared towards the backpacking market. There's the old-fashioned *Central Wales* hotel (☎0547/520065; ③), next to the station, the basic but cheerful *Red Lion* on West Street (☎0547/528231; ②) and the *Plough Hotel*, on Market Street (☎0547/528041; ③), which also has a **backpacker's caravan** (①) for overnight stays in dorm-style accommodation. For **eating and drinking**, it's hard to beat the comfortable *Horse and Jockey* at the town end of Station Road, which has a vast menu for lunch and early evening, serves huge, tasty pizzas until 11pm and manages to pack in live music and discos as well. You might also find folk and jazz in the *Plough*.

Montgomeryshire

The northern part of Powys is made up of the old county of **Montgomeryshire** (Maldwyn), an area of enormously varying landscapes and few inhabitants. The best base for the spartan and mountainous southwest of the county is the solid little town of **Llanidloes**, less than ten miles north of Rhayader, a base for ageing hippies on the River Severn (Afon Hafren), which arrives in the town after winding through the dense **Hafren Forest** on the bleak slopes of **Plynlimon**.

From Llanidloes, one of Wales' most dramatic roads rises past the chilly shores of the **Llyn Clywedog** reservoir, squeezed into sharp hillsides, and up through the remote hamlets of **Staylittle** and **Dylife**. This stark, uplifting scenery contrasts with the gentler, greener contours that characterize the east of the county, where the muted old county town of **Montgomery**, with its fine Georgian architecture, perches above the border and Offa's Dyke. The Severn runs a few miles to the west, near the impeccable village of **Berriew**, home of the bizarre **Andrew Logan Museum of Sculpture** and below the dank hilltop remains of **Dolforwyn Castle**. Further south, the Severn runs in a muddy channel through drab **Newtown**, good only as a transport interchange and for followers of **Robert Owen**, the pioneer socialist.

In the north of the county, **Welshpool** forms the only major settlement, packed in above the wide flood plain of the Severn. An excellent local museum, the impossibly cute toy rail line that runs to **Llanfair Caereinion**, good pubs and reasonable hotels make the town a fair stop for a day or two. On the southern side of Welshpool is Montgomeryshire's one unmissable sight, the sumptuous **Powis Castle** and its exquisite terraced gardens. The very north of the county is pastoral, deserted and beautiful. The few visitors that there are throng **Lake Vyrnwy** and make their way down the dead-end lane to the **Pistyll Rhaedr** waterfall, leaving the leafy lanes and villages like **Llanfyllin** and **Llanrhaeadr-ym-mochnant** intact for those searching for peace, cheerful pubs and good walking.

Llanidloes and around

Thriving when so many other small market towns seem in danger of atrophying, the secret of success for **LLANIDLOES** seems to be in its adaptability, from rural village to weaving town and, latterly, a centre for artists, craftsfolk and assorted alternative lifestylers. One of mid-Wales' prettiest towns, the four main streets meet at the black and white **market hall**, built on timber stilts in 1600, allowing the market to take place on the cobbles underneath. The market has long since moved, as has the town's wonderfully eclectic **museum** that is in temporary residence in Llanidloes' **library**, though this is likely to change sometime in 1995. Off Longbridge Street is Church Street, which opens out into a yard surrounding the dumpy parish **church of St Idloes**, whose impressive fifteenth-century hammerbeam roof is said to have been poached from Abbey Cwmhir.

From the market hall, Great Oak Street heads west, and Short Bridge Street east down to the River Severn, past two fine nineteenth-century chapels – one Zionist, one Baptist – that stare across the road at each other, seemingly waiting for the other to blink. The town's most historic and attractive thoroughfare is Great Oak Street, a broad, architecturally unified street that runs from the old market hall. Facing each other at the bottom of the street are the **town hall**, home of the tourist office, originally built as a temperance hotel to challenge the boozy **Trewythen Arms** opposite. A plaque on the hotel commemorates Llanidloes as an unlikely-seeming place of industrial and political unrest, when, in April 1839 Chartists stormed the hotel, dragging out and beating up special constables who had been despatched to the town as a futile attempt to suppress the political fervour for change amongst the town's flannel weavers.

Practicalities

Llanidloes is a good base, with friendly pubs and restaurants and plenty of places to stay. China Street curves down to the car park from where all **bus** services operate. The **tourist office**, at the bottom of Great Oak Street (daily 10am–5pm; Oct–Easter Mon–Fri only; ☎0686/412605), has the usual tourist information, and the wholefood *Great Oak* café in Compton's Yard (down the alley alongside *Oxfam* on Great Oak Street) is a source of data on local alternative happenings. One worth investigation is the annual **Fancy Dress Night**, on the first Friday of July, when the pubs open late, the streets are cordoned off and, apparently, virtually the whole town gets kitted out.

Accommodation spans the magnificent eighteenth-century *Trewythen Arms* on Great Oak Street (☎0686/412214; ⑤), the genteel *Unicorn* on Longbridge Street (☎0686/413167; ③), the chintzy *Mount Inn* on China Street (☎0686/412247; ③), and for B&B, the handsome Victorian *Gorphwysfa* on Westgate Street (☎0686/413356; ②). There's B&B and **camping** at *Esgair-maen farmhouse* (☎055 16/272; ②), a couple of miles north near the old mines at Y Fan.

Among the many options for **food**, there's the *Piccola Italia* pizzeria on the Llangurig road, the cheap and hearty *Traveller's Rest* on Longbridge Street or, for a bit of a treat, the *Orchard House* on China Street (☎0686/413700). Most of the **pubs** here serve food, and the lively *Red Lion* on Longbridge Street is best-reputed for meals, while the *Stag* on Great Oak Street, and the *Angel* on the High Street are less touristy than most others.

Llyn Clywedog, Plynlimon, Dylife and Staylittle

Four miles northwest of Llanidloes, the beautiful **Llyn Clywedog reservoir** was built as recently as the 1960s and has settled well into the folds of the Clywedog Valley. At its southern end, this modern concrete dam is Britain's tallest (237ft), towering menacingly over the remnants of the **Bryntail lead mine**, through which a signposted path runs. The roads along the southern shores of Clywedog wind around into the dense plantation of **Hafren Forest**, the only real sign of life and vegetation on the bleak, sodden slopes of **Plynlimon** (Pumlumon Fawr). There is a car park at **RHYD-Y-BENWCH**, in the heart of the forest, from where walking paths fan out, the most popular being a six-mile round trip following the infant River Severn up through the trees, past a waterfall and out to its source, a saturated peat bog on the side of one of the harshest terrains in Wales.

Plynlimon is bleak and difficult walking if you are venturing beyond the fairly well-trodden path to the Severn's source. Water oozes everywhere in this misty wilderness, with four other rivers – the Wye included – rising on its tufted slopes. The rivers Hengwm, Llechwedd-mawr and Rheiddol have been dammed on Plynlimon's western side to form the desolate, black-watered reservoir of **Nant-y-Moch**, reached by road via Ponterwyd (see p.221). There is little sympathetic landscaping here, the lake looking nothing more than the flooded valley that it is.

The hamlet of **STAYLITTLE** (Penfforddlas) – whose English name comes from a village blacksmith who was so quick at shodding horses his smithy became known as Stay-a-little – is above the Clywedog River at the northern end of Llyn Clywedog. Just north of the village, the mountain road to Machynlleth forks left, running past the plunging ravine of the Twymyn River to the north. Old mine workings herald the approach to **DYLIFE**, or "Place of Floods", a lead mining community of around two thousand people in the mid-nineteenth century, with a reputation as a lawless, licentious gambling pit. The mine closed in 1896, and the population has since dwindled to around just twenty, although the population increases when walkers and devotees of good beer and food flock to the old *Star Inn* (☎0650/521345; ③) during the warmer months. Good walks from Dylife include up to Pen-y-crogben, the mine-clad slope that rises to the south of the village, and west to **GLASLYN**, or blue lake, and the reedy shores of **Bugeilyn**. The superb **Glyndŵr's Way** footpath (see below), crosses this patch on its way to Machynlleth. A popular viewpoint on the road two miles west of Dylife has been furnished with a cheery memorial to broadcaster and author **Wynford Vaughan-Thomas** (1908–87), whose outstretched slate hand points out to the dozens of rippling peaks and verdant valleys.

GLYNDWR'S WAY

A fairly new long-distance footpath, **Glyndŵr's Way** weaves its 123 miles through Montgomeryshire and northern Radnorshire countryside well reputed for the solitude that it offers. Running from Knighton in the south, the path climbs up into the remote hills to the northwest before turning south four miles south of Newtown. From here, the path plunges through the pastoral hills and past only occasional settlements towards Abbeycwmhir, where it again turns and heads north towards Llanidloes, Llyn Clywedog, across the mine-scarred mountains around Dylife and down into Machynlleth. The path then heads back inland, along the A489 for a few miles before dipping down into the hills, up over the A470 and across its bleakest stretch: the wet and wild upland moor south of the A458. Through the Dyfnant Forest, Glyndŵr's Way zigzags down to the shores of Lake Vyrnwy, eastwards along the River Vyrnwy and over its last few miles to Welshpool.

Well signposted all the way, Glyndŵr's Way is far quieter than Offa's Dyke path, both in the number of settlements en route and the number of people attempting it. Varied scenery includes barren bog, exhilarating uplands, reservoirs, undulating farmland and sections of river valley walking.

Montgomery and around

The tiny town of **MONTGOMERY** (Trefaldwyn) is Montgomeryshire at its most anglicized. It lies at the base of a **castle** on the Welsh side of Offa's Dyke and the present-day border. The castle was started in 1233 by the English king, Henry III, and today's remains are not on their own worth the steep climb up the lane at the back of the town hall, although the view over the lofty church tower, handsome Georgian streets and the vast green bowl of hills around the town is wonderful. The impressively symmetrical main street – well-named Broad Street – swoops up to the perfect little redbrick **town hall**, crowned by a pert clock tower. The rebuilt tower of Montgomery's parish **church of St Nicholas** dominates the snug proportions of the buildings around it. Largely thirteenth-century, the highlights of its spacious interior include the 1600 monument to local landowner, Sir Richard Herbert, and his wife. Behind them, their eight children have been carved in beatific kneeling positions in archways. One of them was George Herbert, prolific Elizabethan poet and contemporary of John Donne. Equally impressive are the elaborately carved double screen and accompanying loft, believed to have been built from sections removed from a nearby abbey over the border in Cherbury.

Montgomery is near one of the best preserved sections of **Offa's Dyke**, which the long distance footpath shadows either side of the B4386 a mile east of the town. Ditches almost twenty feet high give one of the best indications of the dyke's original look and, to the south of the main road, the England–Wales border still exactly splices the dyke, twelve hundred years after it was built. If you want to **stay** here, the rambling *Dragon Hotel* (☎0686/668359; ④), by the town hall, is dependable, if rather sedate and stuffy. Livelier and younger for **food** and **drink** is *Chequers*, also on Broad Street.

Berriew

North of Montgomery, just five miles southwest of Welshpool, the neat village of **BERRIEW** is more redolent of the black-and-white settlements over the English border than anywhere in Wales, its Tudor houses grouped picturesquely around a small church, the shallow waters of the Rhiw River and the slightly twee *Lion Hotel* (☎0686/640452; ④).

Just over the river bridge, the **Andrew Logan Museum of Sculpture** (May–Sept Wed–Sun noon–6pm; £1) makes for an incongruous attraction in such a setting, with a good selection of the notable British modern sculptor's work. Andrew Logan is the man who inaugurated the great drag-and-grunge ball known as the *Alternative Miss World Contest* in the 1970s, launchpad of the formidable Divine's career, from which astounding costumes and memorabilia form a large chunk of the exhibits at the museum. There's also Logan's oversized horticultural scuplture, including giant lilies encrusted with shattered mirrors and vast metal irises that rise to scrape the roof, as well as his smaller-scale jewellery and model Goddesses that only add to the sublime camp of the exhibition.

Dolforwyn Castle

The A483 continues southwest through the valley, with occasional glimpses of the River Severn and in almost constant proximity to the reed-filled **Montgomery Canal**. Just before the road bridge swings suddenly over to cross them both six miles southwest of Montgomery, there's a small right turn leading up to the *Dolforwyn Hotel* and the gaunt remains of unsignposted **Dolforwyn Castle**.

Described by Jan Morris as "the saddest of all the Welsh castles", this was the very last fortress to be built by a native Welsh prince on his own soil – Llywelyn ap Gruffydd in 1273 – as a direct snub to the English king, Edward I, who had expressly forbidden the project. Llewelyn built his fortress and started to construct a small adjoining town as a Welsh fiefdom to rival the heavily anglicized Welshpool, just up the valley. Dolforwyn only survived for four years in Welsh hands before being overwhelmed after a nine-day siege by the English, and the castle was left slowly to rot. In the past twenty years, the remains have been excavated, and significant portions of the fragile old castle have emerged on the wind-blown hilltop, with its astounding views over the Severn valley, four hundred feet below. The small left turning after the hotel leads down to the entrance to Yew Tree Farm (a muddy track to the right with a black mail box at its entrance), where a public path winds its way up to the lonely ruins. The path circles around the castle and heads north, coming to a stile after a hundred yards or so. Crossing this, and heading diagonally across the field towards the track and another stile, the path brushes past the fragmentary earthwork remains of Llywelyn's lost market town.

Newtown

NEWTOWN (Y Drenewydd), despite its name, was founded in the tenth century around a small castle, growing steadily until its population explosion in the nineteenth century as a centre for weaving and textiles, but today is a dull town, with nothing much to hold you – although you might find yourself making transport connections here, and there is an excellent local theatre, the **Hafren**.

Of Newtown's few sights, the High Street is home to the **W.H. Smith** chain of newsagents, that hosts a small and interesting **museum** about the company and its growth from 1792 (Mon–Sat 9.30am–5.30pm; free). On the other side of Severn Street from the nineteenth-century red terracotta **clock tower** is the house in which early socialist **Robert Owen** was born in 1771, now open as a **Memorial Museum** (Mon–Fri 9.45–11.45am & 2–3.30pm, Sat 10–11.30am; free) that explains this remarkable man's life. The museum's Visitors' Book indicates just how much of a shrine the place has become, with a roll call of socialist politicians and trade unionists scrawling their thanks for Owen's work in its pages. Displays include Owen's own notebooks and ledgers, contemporary paintings of his communities in America and New Lanark, and newspaper records of establishment disdain for his work.

Practicalities

Newtown's **train station** is on the southern edge of the town centre, and a path heads straight up past the ugly Victorian parish church of St David and up Back Lane to the car park that serves both as the **bus station** and as home to the **tourist office** portakabin (Easter–Oct daily 10am–5.30pm; ☎0686/625580). If you have to stay in Newtown, best is the *Plas Canol* guest house, between the station and the town centre on New Road (☎0686/625598; ②). The mock-Jacobean *Pheasant Inn* on Market Street (☎0686/625966; ②) does good B&B, as well as cheap and tasty lunches and real ales. The best traditional food, lunchtimes daily and evenings Thursday to Saturday, is found at the comfortable *Courtyard* on Severn Street. The dowdy but excellent *Merlin's* pizzeria on Parkers Lane, behind the clock tower, is open every night (except Mon) for eat-in and takeaway food.

ROBERT OWEN

Robert Owen (1771–1858) was born in Montgomeryshire in the late eighteenth century, but left Wales to enter the Manchester cotton trade at the age of eighteen and swiftly rose to the position of mill manager. His business acumen was matched by a strong streak of philanthropy towards his subordinates. Fundamentally, he believed in social equality between the classes and was firmly against the concept of competition between individuals. Poverty was something he believed could be eradicated by co-operative methods. Owen recognized the potential of building a model workers' community around the New Lanark mills in Scotland and joined the operation in 1798, swiftly setting up the world's first infant school, an Institution for the Formation of Character and a model welfare state for its people.

Owen's ideas on co-operative living led to his building up the model community of New Harmony in Indiana, USA, which he established between 1824–28, before handing the still struggling project over to his sons. Before long, and without the wisdom of its founder, the idealistic tenets of New Harmony collapsed under the weight of greed, ambition and too many vested interests. Undeterred, Owen, by now back in Britain, was encouraging the formation of the early trade unions and co-operative societies, as well as leading action against the 1834 deportation of the **Tolpuddle Martyrs**, a group of Dorset farm labourers who withdrew their labour in their call for a wage increase. Owen's later years were dogged by controversy, as he lost the support of the few sympathetic sections of the British establishment in his persistent criticism of organized religion. He gained many followers, however, whose generic name gradually changed from Owenites to socialists – the first usage of the term. Owen returned to Newtown in his later years, and died there in 1858.

Welshpool

Three miles from the English border, eastern Montgomeryshire's chief town of **WELSHPOOL** (Y Trallwng) was formerly known as just Pool, its prefix added in 1835 to distinguish it from the English seaside town of Poole in Dorset. It's not a very Welsh place, lying in the anglicized valley of the River Severn (Afon Hafren) and with a history that depended largely upon the patronage of English landlords and kings. The town's new bypass has cleared its streets of excessive traffic, and left a number of well-proportioned roads crowned with some Tudor and many good Georgian and Victorian buildings. But it's for sumptuous **Powis Castle**, one of the greatest Welsh fortresses, that Welshpool is on most people's agenda.

Arrival and accommodation

The pompous neo-Gothic turrets of the old Victorian **train station** sit at the top of Severn Street, which leads down into the town centre. The **tourist office** is at the northern edge of the town in the *Flash Leisure Centre*, Salop Road (daily 10am–6pm; ☎0938/552043), twenty minutes' walk from the central town crossroads. By car, it's just off the bypass at the first Welshpool exit on the road from England.

There is plenty of B&B **accommodation** in town, with a dozen or so along the Salop Road between the town centre and the *Flash Centre*; of them all, Mrs Kaye's *Montgomery House* (☎0938/552693; ②) is the surest bet. Other places include *Severn Farm* on Leighton Road (☎0938/553098; ③), just beyond the Industrial Estate to the east of the station, which will also let you pitch a tent;

Dysserth Hall (☎0938/552153; ③), opposite Powis Castle along a small lane running off the Berenw Road or right at the heart of town at the main crossroads, the traditional, rather upmarket coaching inn, the *Royal Oak* (☎0938/552217; ⑤).

The Town

Arriving at Welshpool's modern **train station** gives a false sense of what to expect from the town, much more attractive than the modern mess around the rail lines would lead you to believe. Two hundred yards along Severn Street, a hump-backed bridge over the much-restored **Montgomery Canal** hides the canal **wharf**, from where gaudily painted boats will chug you up the navigable section for a few miles and a couple of hours (☎0938/553271). There's also an old wharfside warehouse here that has been carefully restored as the **Powysland Museum** (Mon, Tues, Thurs & Fri 11am–1pm & 2–5pm, Sat & Sun 2–5pm; also May–Sept Sat & Sun 10am–1pm; free), an impressively wide collection looking at the local area throughout history. Of special interest is the display about the impact of the Black Death here, when half the town's population died, and Roman remains from the now obliterated local Cistercian abbey of Strata Marcella.

Right at the centre of town are the crossroads, where the Georgian **Royal Oak Hotel** acts as a firm reminder of the junction's importance on the old coaching route. Broad Street is the most architecturally interesting of the streets leading off from here, with the ponderous Victorian town hall and its dominating clock tower overlooking some fine Tudor and Jacobean town houses. Broad Street changes name five times as it rises up the hill towards the tiny Raven Square terminus station of the **Welshpool and Llanfair Light Railway**, half a mile beyond the town hall. The eight-mile narrow gauge rail line (April–Sept daily 10am–4pm; ☎0938/810441) was open for less than thirty years to passengers until its closure in 1931, but now scaled-down engines once more chuff their way along the appropriately modest valleys of the Sylfaen Brook and Banwy neu Einion River to the almost eerily quiet village of **LLANFAIR CAEREINION**, a good daytime base for walks and pub food at the *Goat Hotel*. The post office, opposite the church, stocks free leaflets of some good local circular walks.

Eating and drinking

Welshpool's four main streets are home to most of the town's **eating** and **drinking** establishments. Up Berriew Street are the *Shilam Tandoori* at no. 13 (☎0938/553431; moderate) and the *Silver Fish* takeaway chip shop (daily except Sun). Many of the town's pubs do lunchtime food with some, notably the *Talbot* in the High Street, serving excellent evening meals as well. Cheap and filling breakfasts, lunches and teas are served in the *Buttery*, opposite the town hall on the High Street. Other good pubs for evening entertainment include the small, dark *Mermaid* on the High Street and the *Powys Arms* up Salop Road, which lays on live music, quizzes and karaoke nights.

Powis Castle

In a land of ruined castles, the sheer scale and beauty of **Powis Castle** (April–June, Sept & Oct Wed–Sun 11am–5pm; July–Aug Tues–Sun 11am–5pm; £3.60 gardens and museum; £5.80 castle, gardens and museum; NT), a mile from Welshpool up Park Lane, is the real reason for coming to the town. On the site of an earlier Norman fort, the castle was started in the reign of Edward I by the Gwenwynwyn family; to qualify for the site and the barony of De la Pole, they had to renounce all claims to Welsh princedom. In 1587, Sir Edward Herbert bought the castle and began to transform it into the Elizabethan palace we see today.

Inside, the **Clive Museum** – named after Edward Clive, son of Clive of India, who married into the family in 1784 – forms a lively account of the British in India, through diaries, notes, letters, paintings, tapestries, weapons and jewels, although it is the sumptuous period rooms that impress most, from the vast and kitsch frescoes by Lanscroon above the balustraded staircase to the mahogany bed, brass and enamel toilets and decorative wall hangings of the state bedroom. The elegant Long Gallery has a rich sixteenth-century plasterwork ceiling overlooking winsome busts and marble statuettes of the four elements, placed in between the glowering family portraits.

The **gardens**, designed by Welsh architect William Winde, are spectacular. Dropping down from the castle in four huge stepped terraces, the design has barely changed since the seventeenth century, with a charmingly precise orangery and topiary that looks as if it is shaved daily. Summertime outdoor concerts, frequently with firework finales, take place in the gardens.

Llanfyllin and around

The hills and plains of northern Montgomeryshire conceal a maze of deserted lanes and farm outposts along the contours that swell up towards the north and the foothills of Clwyd's Berwyn Mountains. The only real settlement of any size is **LLANFYLLIN**, a peaceful but friendly hillside town, ten miles northwest of Welshpool in the valley of the River Cain, and the best-equipped place in the area to stay. The High Street is a busy centre of bright pubs, cafés, shops and a weekly Thursday market. Narrow Street forks off from here, climbing to the restored **well of St Myllin**, who has reputedly looked after inhabitants of his town since the sixth century by curing the ailment of any Llanfyllin citizen. From here, views over the town, its unusual plain redbrick church (few churches were built in eighteenth-century Wales), and the looming Berwyn Mountains are delightful.

Llanfyllin has plenty of places to **stay**: the *Cain Valley* on the main High Street (☎0691/648366; ③) is an old coaching inn, and there's B&B at *The Chestnuts* (☎0691/648179; ②). Just west of the town is the splendid *Bodfach Hall* (☎0691/648272; ④), set in luscious grounds. There are two **restaurants** on the High Street: *Seeds* (☎0691/648604), which does a wonderful three-course set dinner menu, and the vegetarian/vegan *Green Oak* (☎0691/648108), open for lunch and evenings in season (Wed & Sat), with occasional live folk and jazz. Alternatively, there's the *Eagle* café, for cheap sit-in food, or good pub food in the back bar of the *Cain Valley*, far less snotty than the posh front area. The *Cross Keys* is the least touristy of the High Street's pubs.

Llanrhaeadr-ym-mochnant, Sycarth and Pistyll Rhaeadr

For a place so near the English border, **LLANRHAEADR-YM-MOCHNANT** is surprisingly Welsh in its language and appearance. The small, low-roofed village, six miles north of Llanfyllin, is best remembered as the serving parish of Bishop William Morgan, who translated the Bible into Welsh in 1588 (see p.323), the single largest event that ensured the survival of the old tongue. The village has two great pubs – the *Three Tuns* and *Wynnstay Arms*, as well as an excellent B&B at *Plas-y-Llan* (☎0691/780236; ③).

Llanrhaeadr lies at the foot of the wild walking country of the southern Berwyn Mountains. A lane from the village courses northwest alongside the Rhaeadr River, through an increasingly rocky valley for four miles, before coming to an abrupt halt at **Pistyll Rhaeadr**, supposedly Wales' highest waterfall at 150 feet. The river tumbles down the crags in two stages, flowing furiously under a natural stone arch that has been christened the Fairy Bridge. When it's quiet, tame chaffinches swoop and settle all around this enchanting spot, although, with the added attraction of a tacky tea room, the charms are a little hard to appreciate amid the tourists on a warm summer Sunday.

The B4396 runs east from Llandrhaeadr, along the Tanat Valley and through the village of **LLANGEDWYN**. A mile or so after the village, few tourists make it up one of the left turns leading to **SYCARTH**, only a mile from the English border, but one of the most Welsh of all shrines; a grass mound marks the site of Owain Glyndŵr's ancestral court, reputedly a palace of nine grand halls. Bard Iolo Goch immortalized this Welsh Shangri-la as a place of "no want, no hunger, no shame / No-one is ever thirsty at Sycarth".

Lake Vyrnwy

A monument to the self-aggrandizement of the Victorian age, **Lake Vyrnwy** (Llyn Efyrnwy) combines its functional role as a water supply for Liverpool with a touch of architectural genius, in the shape of the huge nineteenth-century dam at its southern end and the Disneyesque turreted straining tower which edges out into the icy waters. It's a magnificent spot, and a popular centre for walking and birdwatching, with nature trails. A commemorative stone at the eastern end of the dam arrogantly celebrates "taking and impounding the waters of the Rivers Vyrnwy, Marchnant and Cowny", which flooded a village of 400 inhabitants in the process.

Vyrnwy was the first of the massive reservoirs that mid-Wales came to host, constructed during the 1880s. The village of Llanwddyn was flattened and rebuilt at the eastern end, people receiving compensation of just £5 for losing their homes. The story is told, somewhat apologetically, in the **Vyrnwy Visitor Centre** (daily 11am–6pm; Oct–March Sat & Sun only), which combines with the **tourist office** (same hours; ☎0691/648868) and a Royal Society for the Protection of Birds centre, located in the cluster of buildings on the western side of the dam. Further down the track is the *Bicycle Trade-In Company* (☎069 173/211), who rent out **bikes** and tandems. There are numerous leaflets available on walking, birds and wildlife.

If you want to **stay** near the lake, there's the grand *Lake Vyrnwy Hotel* (☎069 173/692; ⑤), overlooking the waters above the southeastern shore. It's a mite pricy, but if you just want a look, it serves a full afternoon tea in a chintzy lounge overlooking the lake. You'll find cheaper B&B at *Tyn-y-maes* (☎069 173/216; ③), a couple of miles east of the new village of Llanwddyn on the B4393.

travel details

Trains

Knighton to: Crewe (2 daily; 1hr 35min); Llandovery (4 daily; 1hr 40min); Llandrindod Wells (6 daily; 40min); Llanwrtyd Wells (4 daily; 1hr 5min); Shrewsbury (6 daily; 55min); Swansea (4 daily; 3hr 10min).

Llandrindod Wells to: Crewe (2 daily; 2hr 20min); Knighton (6 daily; 40min); Llandovery (4 daily; 1hr); Llanwrtyd Wells (4 daily; 30min); Shrewsbury (4 daily; 1hr 40min); Swansea (4 daily; 2hr 20min).

Welshpool to: Aberystwyth (6 daily; 1hr 30min); Birmingham (7 daily; 1hr 40min); Machynlleth (7 daily; 55min); Newtown (8 daily; 20min); Pwllheli (3 daily; 3hr); Shrewsbury (8 daily; 30min).

Buses

Brecon to: Aberdulais (3 daily; 1hr 5min); Abergavenny (6 daily; 55min); Builth Wells (3 daily Mon–Sat; 40min); Craig-y-nos/Dan-yr-ogof (4 daily; 30min); Crickhowell (6 daily Mon–Sat; 25min); Hay-on-Wye (6 daily Mon–Sat; 45min); Hereford (5 daily Mon–Sat; 1hr 45min); Libanus (6 daily; 8min); Llandovery (2 daily; 40min); Llandrindod Wells (3 daily Mon–Sat; 1hr); Merthyr Tydfil (6 daily; 35min); Newport (5 daily Mon–Sat; 1hr 50min); Pontypool (6 daily Mon–Sat; 1hr 20min); Sennybridge (4 daily; 15min); Swansea (3 daily; 1hr 25min); Talgarth (6 daily Mon–Sat; 25min); Talybont (5 daily Mon–Sat; 15min).

Knighton to: Ludlow (5 daily Mon–Sat; 45min); Newtown (Tues & Thurs 3 buses; 1hr); Presteigne (Tues, Thurs, Fri & Sat 2 daily; 20min).

Llandrindod Wells to: Abbeycwmhir (1 post bus daily Mon–Fri; 2hr); Aberystwyth (Tues, Thurs & Sat 1 bus; 1hr 45min); Brecon (3 daily Mon–Sat; 1hr); Builth Wells (hourly Mon–Sat; 20min); Cardiff (1 daily; 3hr); Disserth (2 daily Mon–Sat; 15min); Elan Village (1 post bus daily Mon–Fri; 35min); Hay-on-Wye (1 daily Mon–Sat; 1hr 10min); Hereford (1 daily Mon–Sat; 2hr); New Radnor (Tues, Wed & Sat 1 daily; 30min); Newtown (3 daily Mon–Sat; 1hr 15min); Rhayader (6 daily; 30min).

Llanfyllin to: Llanwddyn for Lake Vyrnwy (school bus; 20min); Oswestry (4 daily Mon–Sat; 45min).

Llanidloes to: Aberystwyth (1 daily; 1hr 20min); Dylife (1 post bus daily Mon–Sat; 30min); Newtown (8 daily Mon–Sat; 35min); Shrewsbury (4 daily Mon–Sat; 2hr); Welshpool (5 daily Mon–Sat; 1hr 15min).

Llanwrtyd Wells to: Abergwesyn (post bus Mon–Sat; 15min); Builth Wells (2 daily; 45min).

Oswestry (Shropshire) to: Llanfyllin (4 daily Mon–Sat; 45min); Welshpool (5 daily Mon–Sat; 55min).

Shrewsbury (Shropshire) to: Llanidloes (4 daily Mon–Sat; 2hr); Montgomery (3 daily Mon–Sat; 50min); Welshpool (7 daily; 45min).

Welshpool to: Berriew (7 daily Mon–Sat; 15min); Llanidloes (3 daily Mon–Sat; 1hr 15min); Montgomery (school bus; 25min); Newtown (7 daily Mon–Sat; 35min); Oswestry (5 daily Mon–Sat; 55min); Shrewsbury (7 daily Mon–Sat; 45min).

CHAPTER FOUR

THE CAMBRIAN COAST

Cardigan Bay (Bae Ceredigion) takes a huge bite out of the west Wales coast, leaving behind the Pembrokeshire peninsula in the south and the Llŷn peninsula in the north. Between them lies the Cambrian coast, a loosely defined mountain-backed strip stretching from Cardigan in the south to Porthmadog in the north and, for the purposes of this guide, also encompassing the Llŷn.

Before the railway and better roads were built during the nineteenth century, the Cambrian coast was fairly isolated from the rest of Wales, the Cambrian Mountains presenting an awkward barrier from the rest of the country, and only narrow passes and droving routes pushed through the rugged terrain on their way to the markets in England.

Today large sand-fringed sections are peppered with low-key coastal resorts, playing host to largely English Midland families on their summer holidays, although the presence of English-dominated resorts can still create local antipathy in this staunchly nationalistic part of the country. Some foreign settlers do manage to integrate successfully with the local community, but in 1993 threats to raze the property of a dozen or so English-run businesses for offences as minor as refusing to take down the Welsh-only signs in their shop windows illustrated the locals fierce Cymric pride. The Llŷn today still forms a militant hotbed, seven decades after the meeting in Pwllheli that saw the formation of the Welsh nationalist party, Plaid Cymru.

The Cardigan coast starts where the rugged seashore of Pembrokeshire ends, continuing in much the same vein of great cliffs, isolated beaches and swirling seabirds around **Cardigan**, the spirited former county town of Ceredigion (Cardiganshire). The coast breaks at some popular seaside resorts, the best being **Llangranog**, **New Quay** and the robust and cosmopolitan "capital" of mid-Wales, **Aberystwyth**. Inland, the best sights are grouped around two river valleys: the lush and quiet **Teifi** and the dramatic ravines around the **Rheidol**. Along the Teifi, which flows out into the sea at Cardigan, the best bases are the stalwart market towns of **Newcastle Emlyn**, **Tregaron** and **Lampeter**, home also of a branch of the University of Wales. The Rheidol, whose estuary is at Aberystwyth, is great for walks in its own right, using the narrow-gauge railway that climbs out of Aberystwyth to the popular tourist honeypot of **Devil's Bridge**, where three bridges, one on top of the other, span a turbulent chasm of waterfalls.

Although on a western limb of Powys, this chapter includes **Machynlleth**, at the head of the Dyfi estuary to the north and a magical place, the seat of Owain Glyndŵr's putative fifteenth-century Welsh parliament and still a thriving market centre. Just outside the town is the **Centre for Alternative Technology**, an impressive showpiece for community living and renewable energy resources.

The main road continues due north from **Machynlleth**, but trains and the smaller coast road skirt west around **Cadair Idris**, the monumental mountain that dominates the south of **Snowdonia National Park**. Each of its crag-fringed

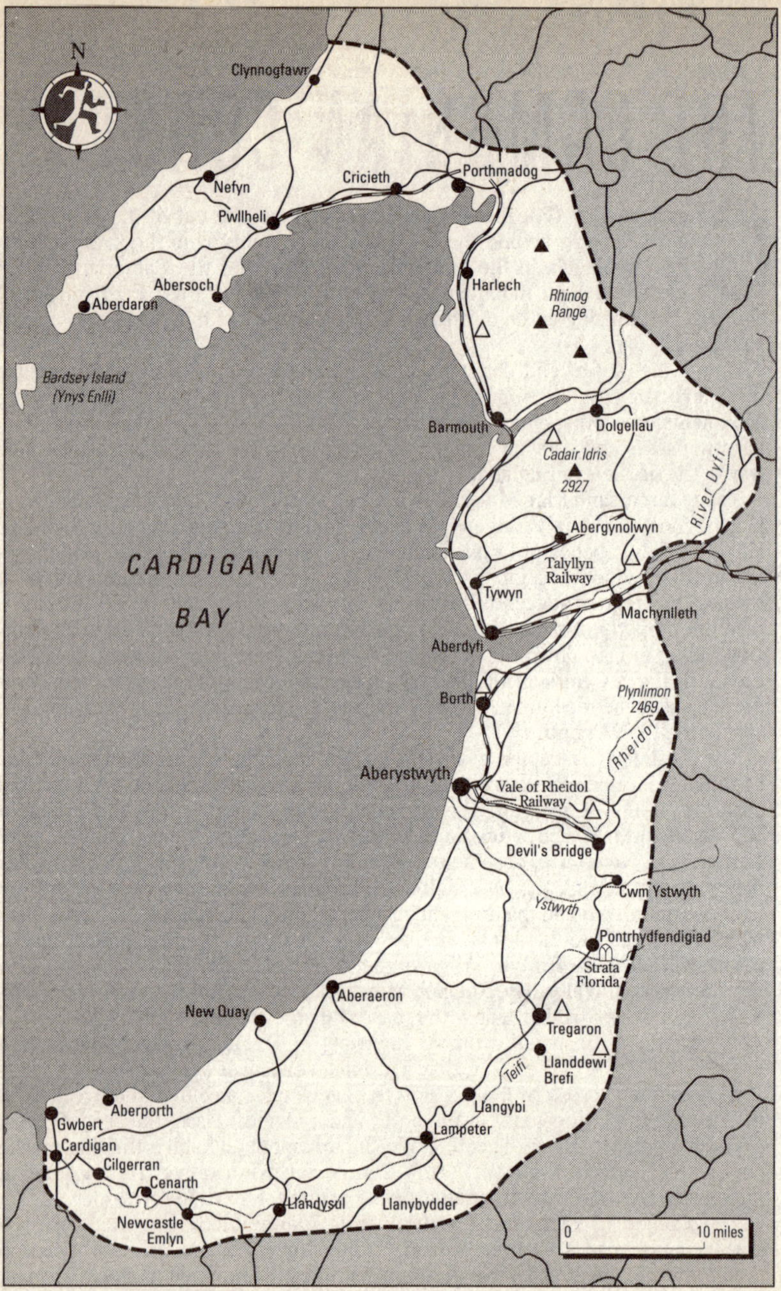
N
Clynnogfawr
Nefyn
Cricieth
Porthmadog
Pwllheli
Abersoch
Aberdaron
Harlech
Rhinog Range
Bardsey Island (Ynys Enlli)
Barmouth
Dolgellau
Cadair Idris
2927
River Dyfi
Abergynolwyn
Talyllyn Railway
CARDIGAN
BAY
Tywyn
Machynlleth
Aberdyfi
Borth
Plynlimon 2469
Rheidol
Aberystwyth
Vale of Rheidol Railway
Devil's Bridge
Cwm Ystwyth
Ystwyth
Pontrhydfendigiad
Strata Florida
Aberaeron
New Quay
Tregaron
Llanddewi Brefi
Teifi
Llangybi
Aberporth
Gwbert
Cardigan
Lampeter
Cilgerran
Cenarth
Llandysul
Llanybydder
Newcastle Emlyn
0
10 miles

ACCOMMODATION PRICE CODES

Throughout this guide, hotel and B&B accommodation is priced on a scale of ① to ⑨. Category ① only applies to youth hostels; for the rest, the number indicates the **lowest price** you could expect to pay per night for a **double room in high season**. The prices indicated by the codes are as follows:

① under £20/$32	④ £40–50/$64–80	⑦ £70–80/$112–128
② £20–30/$32–48	⑤ £50–60/$80–96	⑧ £80–100/$128–160
③ £30–40/$48–64	⑥ £60–70/$96–112	⑨ over £100/$160

faces invites exploration, but it is best approached from the south where the narrow-gauge Talyllyn rail line reaches the tiny settlement of **Abergynolwyn**, a great base for the minor sights of the **Dysynni Valley**. Cadair Idris's northern flank slopes down to the market town of **Dolgellau**, at the head of the scenic Mawddach Estuary, and linked by path to the likeable resort of **Barmouth**. High on its rocky promontory stands the castle at **Harlech**, the southernmost link in Edward I's chain of thirteenth-century castles, overlooking the coast as it sweeps north to the Italianate dream village of **Portmeirion** and the coastal terminus of the wonderful Ffestiniog railway at **Porthmadog**, before turning west along the Llŷn. The Welsh castle at **Cricieth** and the museum devoted to Lloyd George a couple of miles away are the only reasons to pause before Wales ends in a flourish of small coves around **Abersoch** and **Aberdaron**.

Getting around

The most relaxing way to get fairly swiftly to the Cambrian coast is on the mid-Wales **train** line from Shrewsbury in England through to Machynlleth. Here the line splits: one branch runs south to Aberystwyth where you can pick up the Vale of Rheidol line to Devil's Bridge; the other swings north calling at 25 stations in under sixty miles before it terminates at Pwllheli on the Llŷn.

Buses run almost parallel to the trains and also serve inland destinations such as Dolgellau, Minffordd and Abergynolwyn. North of Machynlleth, a coastal service runs as far as Tywyn, where you change to continue to Dolgellau. There's also the express *TrawsCambria* service from Swansea to Bangor through Aberystwyth, Machynlleth, Dolgellau and Porthmadog.

Detailed information on bus and train services as far south as Machynlleth comes in the *Gwynedd Public Transport Guide*, available at tourist offices.

From Cardigan to Aberaeron

The southern section of Ceredigion coastline is enormously popular, combining safe beaches, lively market towns and some great coastal walking. Although some of the larger towns, like **Aberporth** and **Aberaeron** have lost much of their scenic splendour under relentless waves of holiday homes and caravan parks, many of the coast's other settlements manage to cling on to some of the salty charm that makes them so popular: **New Quay** is a delightful town, spread over a hillside overlooking a stone harbour, and smaller coastal settlements such as **Llangranog**, **Penbryn**, **Mwnt** and **Gwbert** maintain a charm that results from a neat juxtaposition of superb countryside and sweeping beaches.

Just inland, at the mouth of the Teifi, is the old county town of **Cardigan**, scarcely thrilling but pretty, cheerful and with an excellent range of pubs, accommodation and entertainment, as well as the focus for quite a large travelling and New Age community.

The main A487 now bypasses Cardigan, on its way parallel to the coast, meeting the sea at Aberaeron. The coastal villages and resorts between Cardigan and Aberaeron are fed by roads that spur off the trunk road. This main road forms the basis of a regular bus service, dipping into the larger seaside villages and towns between Cardigan and Aberystwyth. The frequency of buses rises in the summer, although some of the more remote villages remain inaccessible by public transport.

Cardigan and around

An ancient borough and port until the Teifi Estuary silted up in the last century, **CARDIGAN** (Aberteifi) was founded by the Norman lord Roger de Montgomery around its castle in 1093. The town is at the lowest bridging point of the Teifi Estuary, rising up on the river's northern bank from its medieval bridge, the town's most attractive feature. The castle mound sits at the bridge's town end, with Bridge Street sweeping up a hill around the mound and becoming the picturesque High Street, off which run pavement-less thoroughfares, crammed with a jigsaw of buildings from different eras. The High Street meanders past a good range of pubs, chainstores and interesting local shops to the angular, turreted oddity of the **Guildhall**, with the Welsh flag skewered adamantly to its grey frontage. Through the Guildhall courtyard is the town's **covered market**, a typically eclectic mix of fresh food, some good-quality local craft and second-hand stalls. A couple of hundred yards up Pendre from the Guildhall, Bath House Road dips down to the left and the redoubtable **Theatr Mwldan**, whose imaginative programme of art, theatre, cinema and music, together with a great café and the tourist office, make it an essential stop.

Priory Street leads down the hill from the High Street at the Guildhall, past the council offices and tiny town **museum** (Mon–Fri 10am–5pm; free), mainly concerned with fishing memorabilia. Beyond lies Finch Square, with the bus terminus and some good pubs and cafés.

Practicalities

Cardigan is just beyond the northern end of the Pembrokeshire Coast Path (see p.139), which terminates at Poppit Sands on the other side of the Teifi Estuary. The helpful **tourist office** (Easter fortnight & May–Sept daily 10am–6pm; Easter–April Mon–Sat 10am–5.30pm; Oct–Easter Mon–Sat 9am–5pm; ☎0239/613230) is in the foyer of **Theatr Mwldan** (☎0239/621200), although details of the many local green festivals and meetings are usually posted at the *Hungry Tummy* wholefood café, upstairs in the entrance hall of the market, which has a noticeboard with requests for lift-sharing and accommodation, details of local groups and happenings.

There's plenty of **accommodation**, with numerous B&Bs along the Gwbert Road, off North Road: the *Brynhyfryd* (☎0239/612861; ②), at the town end, and the *Maes-a-Mor* (☎0239/614929; ②), just up in Park Place, are the best. On the High Street, the old-fashioned *Black Lion* pub (☎0239/612532; ③) does good

B&B and evening meals. There's a YHA **youth hostel** (☎0239/612936), four miles away at Poppit Sands, the end of the coast path. Summer buses go there, although in winter they terminate at St Dogmaels, two miles short.

For **eating** and **drinking**, there are a couple of wholefood shops and cafés in Black Lion Mews, a thin strip of lane behind the *Black Lion* pub on the High Street. The café at *Theatr Mwldan* is open every day and for the evenings of performances, and has a cheap range of local dishes and specialities. For more substantial evening food, *Jackets*, 58 North Rd (☎0239/615206), serve pizzas, potatoes, kebabs and pies for eating in, takeaway or a free delivery service within five miles, even to the beach. *Dragon City*, at 49 Pendre (☎0239/612273), is a far better than average Chinese restaurant. The best pub food – lunch and evening – is at the *Eagle*, at the southern end of the town bridge. The *Red Lion* (*Y Llew Coch*), at the bottom of The Pwllhai near Finch Square, is the liveliest town pub, serving great bar snacks at lunchtime until 9.30pm, with a pool room and live rock music – at weekends. The large and friendly *Angel Hotel* on St Mary Street hosts weekend **discos**.

The Ceredigion coast

One of the most popular stretches of coastline in the whole country, the rippled cliffs, expansive beaches and hedged lanes of the Ceredigion coast attract thousands of visitors every year. The Gwbert Road heads out of the neat Cardigan suburbs before descending to the estuary edge and the straggling seaside village of **GWBERT**, worth staying in only if you're searching for a golfing holiday at the local 18-hole course. If that's the case, the functional *Gwbert Hotel* (☎0239/621241; ④), overlooking the sea, is the best bet. From Gwbert, there are some pleasant walks around the coast, past the small **Cardigan Island** and on to the isolated coastal hamlet of **MWNT**, whose exquisite sandy beach, cliffs and tiny, whitewashed fourteenth-century church are all under the custody of the National Trust.

The most popular stopping-off point on this stretch of coast has to be **ABERPORTH**, an elderly resort built around two adjoining bays, neither of which is particularly pretty. The town is well serviced for public transport, accommodation, food and drink, although the neighbouring hamlet of **TRE-SAITH**, a mile to the east, staggering down a tiny valley to the compact beach, is a more rewarding spot, far less like a holiday resort than Aberporth, containing numerous places to stay, including the non-smoking *Iscoed* (☎0239/810030; ②), on the hill down into the village, and the hilltop *Bryn Berwyn* (☎0239/811126; ③). For **food**, try the wholesome *Skippers* restaurant (☎0239/810113) on the shore, who specialize in locally caught seafood. Every Sunday in summer, there are **dinghy races** from the beach. Around the rocks on the right of the beach, another small sandy cove has its own natural after-sea shower in the shape of the River Saith plummeting over the mossy black rocks in a waterfall. At low tide, it's possible to continue around the coast to the wide, sandy **Penbryn Beach**, which can also be reached from **PENBRYN** village, with a 500-yard walk from the car park next to the beach café.

Three miles north of the A487, **LLANGRANOG** is the most attractive village on the Ceredigion coast, wedged in between bracken and gorse-beaten hills. The main streets wind their way to the tiny seafront, well geared up for tourists with a good range of cafés, B&Bs, pubs and sporting activities. The beach can become horribly congested in mid-summer, however, in which case it's better to head around the beach at low tide or over the cliff path to **Cilborth Beach**. The cliff path continues along the glorious NT-owned headland, up to **Ynys Lochtyn** and a couple of remote, sandy beaches. In Llangranog, you can **stay** at the excellent *Ship Inn* (☎0239/654423; ③) or the *Cafe Y Gegin Fach* B&B (☎0239/654642; ②), both on the seafront, or the earthier *Pentre Arms* (☎0239/654345; ②), which also does good food. Between Penbryn and Llangranog is the *Maesglas* caravan park (☎0239/654268), which takes tents.

From Llangranog, you can make walks along the coast path towards New Quay Head, where the prolific seasonal flora swathe the wind-blasted hillsides and cliffs that drop dramatically into clear seas. The cave-walled beach at **CWMTUDU** is glorious, approached along tiny lanes dropping in hairpin bends from above. Bewteen Cwmtudu and the handsome village of **LLWYNDAFYDD** is a complex of self-catering cottages at *Neuadd* (☎0545/560324). In Llwyndafydd itself, just down the lane, the popular *Crown Inn* is deservedly noted for its beers and range of food.

New Quay

Along with Laugharne in Carmarthenshire, **NEW QUAY** (Cei Newydd) lays claim to being the original Llareggub in Dylan Thomas' *Under Milk Wood* (see p.131). Certainly, it has the little tumbling streets, prim Victorian terraces sitting serenely above a cobbled stone harbour, pubs and air of dreamy isolation that Thomas so successfully invoked in his play. In the height of the tourist season, however, the quiet isolation can be hard to find, although even at these times, the town maintains a charm lost in so many of the other Ceredigion resorts. Outside the summer, New Quay is home to one of Wales' most bizarre annual rituals, when every New Year's Eve, virtually the whole town gets kitted out in fancy dress and spends most of the night locked into the numerous pubs and dancing out in the streets.

The main road passes through the upper part of town, with the principal car park at Uplands Square also serving as the dropping-off point for daily buses from Aberystwyth and Cardigan. From here, it's a walk down any of the steep streets to the pretty **harbour**, where a small curving beach is backed by greenery and a higgledy-piggledy line of multi-coloured shops and houses. The sturdy stone quay arcs out from the top of the beach. From here, South John Street winds around to the north, branching into Wellington Place along the northern beach. The beach-front streets comprise the **lower town**, the more traditionally seaside part of New Quay, full of cafés, pubs and beach shops. Acutely inclined streets lead to the upper town, more residential and with some delightful views over the sweeping shoreline below. By the fork is the **tourist office** (April–Sept daily 10am–6pm; ☎0545/560865). On the harbour is the town's **yacht club** (☎0545/560516), who welcome visitors in their activities. The northern beach soon gives way to a rocky headland, **New Quay Head**, where an invigorating path steers along the top of the sheer drops to **Bird Rock**, aptly named for the sheer profusion of sea birds nesting here.

Although there is a singular lack of excitement in New Quay, it is a truly pleasant base for good beaches, walking, eating and drinking. **Accommodation** includes cheap B&Bs at *Elvor*, on George Street (☎0545/560554; ②), the main road to Llanarth, in the upper town, *The Moorings* on Glanmor Terrace (☎0545/560375; ②), and the wonderful *Seahorse Inn* on Margaret Street (☎0545/560736; ③), a little further into town. On the edge of town, overlooking the harbour, is the ugly but luxurious *White House* (☎0545/560968; ③), which has a swimming pool and sauna. There's a **campsite** a mile down the B4342 at *Wern Mill* (☎0545/580699), just outside the grim village of **GILFACHREDA**.

The town contains innumerable cheap, stodgy **cafés**, and the *Mariner's Café*, by the harbour wall, is a sure bet. Most of the **pubs** serve food, the best being the *Black Lion*, tucked up above the harbour and a regular haunt of folk and traditional music, the *Seahorse* (see above) and the traditional, beery *Dolau Inn* on Church Street.

Aberaeron

Although at first glance, **ABERAERON** seems marginally more exciting than New Quay, six miles down the coast, it is almost unique amongst the Ceredigion resorts for being on an unappealing stretch of coastline. Nonetheless, the town, with its pastel-shaded houses encasing a large, calm harbour inlet, is architecturally interesting, with a unity of design unusual in these parts, due to its having been built virtually from scratch in the early nineteenth century by the Reverend Alban Gwynne, who was happy to spend his way through his wife's inheritance by dredging the Aeron Estuary and constructing a formally planned town around it – reputedly from a design by John Nash – as a new port for mid-Wales.

The A487 runs straight through the heart of Aberaeron, down Bridge Street and past the large **Alban Square**, named after the rich rector. On the north side of the town bridge, the grid of streets stretches down to the sea at the Quay Parade, a neat line of ordered, colourful houses on the seafront. At the top of Quay Parade is the **Aeron Express Aerial Ferry** (May–Sept), a bizarre 1980s recreation of a Victorian airborne hand-pulleyed carriage that cranks its way, loaded with a few passengers, over the harbour. An alternative way of crossing the harbour is the shiny new **footbridge**, just up from the aerial ferry, that replaced a 1992 version which collapsed unceremoniously into the water. Right on the harbour, the **Hive on the Quay** (summer daily 9am–5.30pm; winter Mon–Sat only; ☎0545/570445) combines an exhibition of bees with chances to sample honey products, including delicious ice cream.

Quay Parade runs down the side of the seafront past some of the old fisherman's houses and pubs to the fairly interesting **Sea Aquarium** (Easter–Oct 11am–5pm; £2.50) and the **tourist office** (Easter–Sept daily 10am–6pm; Oct–Easter Mon–Sat 10am–5pm; ☎0545/570602), also home to a National Trust shop and displays about the local coastline. The **north beach**, at this end of town, is all stones and rubbish – only marginally better is the town's **south beach** on the other side of the harbour.

For **accommodation**, there are town centre B&Bs at the genteel *Pier Cottage* on Ship Street (☎0545/570132; ③), near the tourist office, and, overlooking the harbour, *Fairview* on Cadwgan Place (☎0545/571472; ②). Along the northern shore, there's a **campsite** at the *Aeron Coast Caravan Park* (☎0545/570349), reached by car off North Road. For **food**, the *Siop Te* on Cadwgan Place is a good all-round day and early evening café, or there's good pub food at the *Black Lion* and the posher *Feathers Royal*, both on Alban Square, or the *Harbourmaster* on Quay Parade. The latter two are the best local bets for live music.

The Teifi Valley

The Teifi is one of Wales' most eulogized rivers – for its rich spawn of fresh fish, its meandering rural charm and the coracles that were a regular feature from pre-Roman times – and flows through some gloriously green and undulating countryside to its estuary at Cardigan. It passes the massive ramparts of **Cilgerran Castle**, and winds its way over the falls at **Cenarth**, before flowing around three sides of another fortress at **Newcastle Emlyn**, and also takes in the proudly Cymric university town of **Lampeter**. Beyond here, the river passes through a different, harsher scenery for eleven miles to **Tregaron**, a town Welsh in its language, feel and flavour, and a good base for nearby **Llanddewi Brefi**, with some spectacular walks up into the Abergwesyn Pass (see p.184) and the reedy bogland of **Cors Caron**. The river's infancy can be seen in the austere town of **Pontrhydfendigaid**, famous for its annual eisteddfod, and the nearby ruins of **Strata Florida Abbey**, beyond which the river emerges from the dark and remote **Teifi Pools**.

Newcastle Emlyn and around

An ancient farming and droving centre, **NEWCASTLE EMLYN** (Castell Newydd Emlyn) still retains a distinctly agricultural feel, particularly on Fridays, the loud and busy market day. The swooping meander of the Teifi River made the site a natural defensive position, first built on by the Normans. The "new" **castle**, of which only a few stone stacks and an archway survive, replaced their fortress in the mid-thirteenth century. Although the ruins aren't impressive, the site, surrounded on three sides by the river flowing through a valley of grazing sheep and rugby fields, is gently uplifting and quintessentially Welsh. The castle is tucked away at the bottom of dead-end Castle Terrace, which peels off the main street by the squat little stone **town hall**, topped by a curiously phallic cupola.

Although there are few other sights in the town there are at least some great pubs, and with its unhurried charm and fabulous scenery, it makes for a good base from which to explore the surrounding area. The town's **tourist office** (Easter–Oct daily 10am–6pm; ☎0239/711333) and the tiny *Attic* **theatre** are both located in the miniature town hall on Bridge Street. Town centre **accommodation** is best at the old-fashioned *Plough* on Emlyn Square (☎0239/710994; ③), and the cheerful *Pelican Inn* on Sycamore Street (☎0239/710606; ②). The latter also does tasty all-day **food**, or other pub grub can be found in the deservedly popular *Bunch of Grapes*, an unexpectedly stylish bar on Bridge Street, hosting live music most Thursdays. Best places for simple drinking are the gnarled old Welsh local, the *Ivy Bush* on Emlyn Square, the *White Hart* on Sycamore Street or the *Bunch of Grapes*.

The area's prolific past as a weaving centre is best seen in the village of **DRE-FACH FELINDRE**, five miles southeast. At the turn of this century, this was at the centre of the wool trade, with 43 working mills in and around the village. Today the National Museum of Wales' **Museum of the Welsh Woollen Industry** (April–Sept daily 10am–5pm; Oct–March Mon–Fri only; £2), housed in a vast Edwardian mill, displays a good use of old photographs, mementoes and weaving looms, which succeed in recounting the history of the industry from domestic beginnings in medieval times.

The B4571 climbs north from Newcastle Emlyn, meeting the A486 after eight miles in the hamlet of **FFOSTRASOL**, annual site of the *Gŵyl Werin y Cnapan* (☎0239/858955), one of the largest **Celtic folk festivals** held anywhere. It takes place in the first or second week of July.

Cilgerran

Back up the Teifi River, just a couple of miles beyond Cardigan, the attractive village of **CILGERRAN** clusters around its wide main street. Behind are the massive ramparts of the **castle** (April–Oct daily 9.30am–6pm; Nov–March closes 4pm; if closed, get the key from the adjoining Castle House; CADW; £1.25), founded in 1100 at a commanding vantage point on a high wooded bluff above the river, then still navigable for sea-going ships. This is the legendary site of the 1109 abduction of Nest (the "Welsh Helen of Troy" according to popular etymology) by a lovestruck Prince Owain of Powys. Her husband, Gerald of Pembroke, escaped by slithering down a toilet waste chute through the castle walls.

The massive dual entry towers still dominate the castle, and the outer walls are some four foot thicker than those facing the inner courtyard. Walkways high on the battlements – not for those suffering vertigo – connect with the other towers. The outer ward, over which a modern path now runs from the entrance, is a good example of the keepless castle evolving throughout the thirteenth century. Any potential attackers would be waylaid instead by the still evident ditch and outer walls and gatehouse, of which only fragmentary remains can be seen. Another ditch and drawbridge pit protect the inner ward underneath the two entry towers. The views over the forested valley towards the pink and grey Georgian fantasy castle of **Coedmore**, on the opposite bank, and towards Cardigan, are inspiring.

A footpath runs down from the castle to the river's edge and the River Teifi **information centre** (April–Sept daily 10am–5pm). Display boards tell the story of the emigrants to America, for whom Cardigan was the last sight of home, and the history of the Teifi valley industries, particularly quarrying, brick making and coracle fishing. Guided **canoe trips** up the river through the wooded valley (☎0239/710391) leave from the quay during the summer months.

Cenarth

A tourist magnet since it was swooped on by nineteenth-century Romantics and artists, **CENARTH**, four miles west of Newcastle Emlyn, is a pleasant spot, but hardly merits the mass interest that it receives. The secret is that the village's main asset, its **waterfalls**, are close to the main road, ideal for lazy visitors. The low but impressive falls are a result of the Teifi being split by rocks, as it tumbles and churns its way over the craggy limestone. The path to the falls runs from opposite the *White Hart* pub and past the **National Coracle Centre** (Easter–Oct Sun–Fri 10.30am–5.30pm; £1), a small museum with displays of original coracles from all over the world, before continuing to a restored seventeenth-century flour mill by the falls' edge.

Lampeter

Eighteen miles from Newcastle Emlyn, **LAMPETER** (Llanbedr Pont Steffan) is the home of possibly the most remote university in Britain. The St David's University College, now a constituent of the University of Wales, was the country's first university college, founded in 1822 by the Bishop of St David's to aid Welsh students who couldn't afford the trip to England to receive a full education. With a healthy student population (albeit one comprised largely of trainee priests and others studying religion), together with large numbers of resident hippies, the small town, with a permanent population of less than 2000, is well geared up for young people and visitors.

There's not a great deal to see in Lampeter, and what you are able to visit is fairly low-key. **Harford Square** forms the hub of the town and is named after the local landowning family who were responsible for the construction of the early nineteenth-century Falcondale Hall, now an opulent hotel, on the northern approach to Lampeter. Around the corner is **Y Galeri**, a showcase for local artists' work, at the back of the *Mulberry Bush* health food shop at 2 Bridge Street.

The main buildings of the **University College** lie off College Street, and include C.B. Cockerell's original stuccoed quadrangle of buildings from 1827, designed as an imitation of an Oxbridge college. The motte of Lampeter's long-vanished **castle**, tucked right underneath the main buildings, forms an incongruous mound amidst such order. The High Street is the most architecturally distinguished part of town, its eighteenth-century coaching inn, the *Black Lion*, dominating the streetscape; you can see its old stables and coach house through an archway. The **Town Hall**, on the other side of the street, contains a minute civic **museum** (Mon–Thurs 9am–1pm & 1.45–4.30pm; free), mainly comprising curly old photographs of the town.

Practicalities

Lampeter makes a good base – it's a lively town, there are frequent gigs and theatre performances and enough pubs and cafés for any visitor. It's also in excellent cycling country, where the surrounding terrain is gentle enough for inexperienced bikers. There are, however, no bike rental places in town, though you might be able to pick up a cheap second-hand cycle from the nameless store next to *Ralph's Bakery* on College Street. There is a **tourist office** of sorts in the Town Hall, open at the same time as the museum (see above), and although they don't book **accommodation**, it's easy to find: noticeboards in the *Mulberry Bush* wholefood shop, 2 Bridge St, contain information about local B&Bs and longer lets. Alternatively, there's a good B&B, *Haul Fan*, 6 Station Terrace (☎0570/422718; ②), behind University College, and hotel accommodation in the *Black Lion* on the High Street (☎0570/422172; ④). The *Castle Hotel* (☎0570/422554; ③) and the *Royal Oak* (☎0570/422453; ②), also on the High Street, do reasonable B&B. There's a **campsite** five miles northeast at *Moorlands*, near Llangybi (☎0570/45543). Just off the B4343, running up the Teifi valley towards Llanddewi Brefi, is one of the area's best farmhouse B&Bs at *Pentre Farm* (☎057 045/313; ③), near Llanfair Clydogau, five miles from Lampeter.

There are plenty of fine places to **eat** in town. *Peppers*, 14 High St, do a wonderful Welsh vegetarian lunch menu, or, at the other end of the cholesterol scale, there's *Lloyds*, an upmarket fish and chip shop and restaurant, in Bridge Street, open until 9pm. Cheap and popular with students is the *Cottage Garden* restaurant, opposite the University on College Street. Also fairly studenty is the friendly *King's Arms* on Bridge Street, a small stone pub with a wide-ranging menu and some very well-kept beer.

Tregaron and around

On the cusp of the lush Teifi Valley and the gloomy moors rising above it, the neat small town of **TREGARON**, ten miles northeast of Lampeter, has a tendency to enchant passing visitors. It feels almost untouched by the late twentieth century, and seems a bastion of the Welsh language and culture in an area that has suffered galloping anglicization over recent decades.

All of the roads in Tregaron lead into the spacious market square, hemmed in by solid eighteenth- and nineteenth-century buildings, of which the most impressive must be the classically symmetrical old drovers' inn, the *Talbot Hotel*. The square and the inn were the very last points of civilization that drovers saw before they headed out of town on the wild Abergwesyn Pass (see p.184), which rises above the town to Llanwrtyd Wells and beyond. The pristine **statue** in the centre of the square is of Henry Richard (1812–88), the founder of the Peace Union, forerunner of the League of Nations and, subsequently, the United Nations. On the corner of the market square and Dewi Road is the *Rhiannon* craft design centre, a wonderful shop stocking jewellery fashioned from Welsh gold and other materials in Celtic designs, as well as goods made of slate and various Welsh-interest books.

The river running through the middle of Tregaron is the Brennig, a babbling tributary of the Teifi, which splits from its mother river a mile south of the town. The Teifi meanders around a wide, flat valley west of Tregaron before flowing through the eerie wetland of **Cors Caron** (Tregaron Bog), two miles north of the town. This is one of the most prodigious areas for wildlife in Wales, a national nature reserve of peat bog, home of marsh grasses, black adders, buzzards and even an occasional red kite. The walkway along the disused rail line alongside the B4343 is open to anyone, but to explore the bog, a permit is needed from the Countryside Council for Wales (☎097 45/671).

Practicalities

Buses depart from the market square, by the Henry Richard statue. There's a small **tourist office** (Mon–Fri 9.30am–5pm; ☎0974/298248) in the council offices in Dewi Road, just off the main square. For **accommodation**, the dingy *Talbot Hotel* on the square (☎0974/298208; ③) is much better for eating and drinking than sleeping. Up the Aberystwyth road are the *Brynawel* B&B (☎0974/298310; ②) and the *Neuaddlas* guesthouse (☎0974/298965; ③). Three miles northeast, along the banks of the Groes, is the remote Blaencaron **youth hostel** (☎0974/298441), perfectly positioned for walks on the towering moorland above the tiny stream.

There are a couple of **cafés** along the road to Aberystwyth, including the cheap and wholesome *Country Kitchen* by the river bridge. Bar meals are served at the *Clwb Rygbi* on the Aberystwyth road and in the *Talbot Arms*. For plain **drinking**, hit *Y Llew Coch* by the river bridge, a young pub with a pool table and bar games.

Llanddewi Brefi

The Dewi Road from Tregaron runs south past a cottage hospital and along the Teifi to the tight little village of **LLANDDEWI BREFI**, whose paint-peeling square and old-fashioned inns lent themselves perfectly as a setting for a recent TV series, *We Are Seven*. The village's present thirteenth-century **church of St**

David is home to one of Wales' most persistent legends. A convocation of 118 Welsh churchmen met here in 519 AD and summoned Dewi Sant (Saint David). As he began to speak, the ground beneath him shuddered ominously and suddenly rose, giving him a natural platform, upon which the church now sits, from where he was able to continue speaking. Part of the church wall consists of two discernible stones with fragmentary Latin inscriptions carved on them. These were broken up by an illiterate eighteenth- or nineteenth-century mason from a single memorial that dated from within a century of David's death – the first recorded mention of the Welsh patron saint. The graveyard has a cool and contemplative atmosphere, and contains a memorial to a local man rejoicing in the name of Ajax Ajax, and inside the church are some interesting stones, one with Ogham inscriptions. Either of the village's two creaky pubs – the *Foelallt Arms* and the ironically-named ancient *New Inn* – are great places to booze away an evening.

Pontrhydfendigaid and Strata Florida

Six miles northeast of Tregaron, the last town on the Teifi is gloomy **PONTRHYDFENDIGAID** ("Bridge near the ford of the Blessed Virgin"), a grey-stoned cluster remarkable only for its annual May eisteddfod in the village pavilion. The infant Teifi flows in from the east, followed by a road that, after a mile, reaches the atmospheric ruins of the mighty **Strata Florida Abbey** (May–Sept 9.30am–6.30pm; £1.50; Oct–April open all times), bucolically located in the *Ystrad Fflur*, the valley of the flowers. This Cistercian abbey was founded in 1164, swiftly growing into a centre for milling, farming, weaving and becoming an important political centre for Wales. In 1238, Llywelyn the Great, originally Prince of Gwynedd, whose conquering exploits throughout the rest of Wales and appeasement of the Marcher lords by marrying off his daughters to them had brought him to the peak of the Welsh feudal pyramid, summoned the lesser Welsh princes to the castle. He was near death, and worried that, should he die, his work of unifying Wales under one ruler would disintegrate, so he commanded the assembled princes to pay homage not just to him (as was now his by right) but also to his son, Dafydd. This plan succeeded until after his death, although Dafydd's role was inglorious and most of the work of regrouping Wales around one standard fell to Llywelyn the Great's grandson and Dafydd's nephew, Llywelyn ap Gruffydd, the Last. The church here was vast – larger than the cathedral at St David's and, although very little survived Henry VIII's Dissolution of the monasteries, the huge Norman west doorway gives some idea of its dimensions. Fragments of one-time side chapels include beautifully tiled medieval floors, and there's also a serene cemetery, but it's really the abbey's position that impresses most, in glorious rural solitude amongst wide open skies and fringed with a scoop of sheep-spattered hills. A sinewy yew tree reputedly shades the spot where Dafydd ap Gwilym, fourteenth-century bard and contemporary of Chaucer, is buried.

Bridle paths running from Strata Florida, or a better lane from near the *Cross Inn* at **Ffair-Rhos**, a mile north of Pontrhydfendigaid, lead off east into the rocky, squelchy moorland that tumbles down to the Claerwen Reservoir (see p.190). Amongst the drenched grass and craggy outcrops are the **Teifi Pools**, a series of sombre lakes where the Teifi River rises for the first time. This is stern, but infinitely rewarding, walking country.

Aberystwyth and around

The liveliest seaside resort in Wales, and capital of the sparsely populated middle of the country, **ABERYSTWYTH** is an essential stop along the Ceredigion coast. With one of the most prestigious colleges of the University of Wales and the National Library both in the town, there are plenty of cultural and entertainment diversions here, as well as an array of Victorian and Edwardian seaside trappings. As a town firmly rooted in all aspects of Welsh culture, it's possibly the most enjoyable and relaxed place to gain the best insight into the nation's psyche.

The precursor of Aberystwyth is the inland village of **Llanbadarn Fawr**, the seat of Wales' oldest bishopric between the sixth and eighth centuries. It grew around the thirteenth-century castle as Llanbadarn, minting its own coins and becoming a major headquarters for Owain Glyndŵr's revolutionaries in the Middle Ages. The *Cymdeithas yr Iaith* (Welsh Language Society) was founded in 1963 and is still located here, and the National Library was begun here in 1907. It was no surprise that, after decades of Liberal domination, the Aberystwyth-dominated Ceredigion and Pembroke North constituency finally plumped for a Plaid Cymru MP in the 1992 election, thus turning the whole west coast – from Anglesey to the bottom of Cardigan Bay – Plaid green on the political map.

The town sits at the mouths of the rivers Rheidol and Ystwyth, both of which flow through picturesque valleys, where hillside forests and remote villages show a few interesting examples of the old quarrying and mining industries. Tourist attractions like **Devil's Bridge** are very popular as the Rheidol line terminates here, although there are numerous other lesser-known beauty spots whose charms require only a little more imagination to discover.

Arrival and information

Aberystwyth's twin **train stations** (one for mainline trains and one for the Vale of Rheidol line) are adjacent to each other on Alexandra Road, a ten-minute walk from the seafront on the southern side of the town centre. **Local buses** stop outside the station, with **long-distance** ones using the bus depot around the corner in Park Avenue. The busy **tourist office** (Easter–Oct daily 10am–6pm; Nov–Easter closes 5pm; ☎0970/612125) is a ten-minute stroll from the station, straight down Terrace Road towards the seafront. Tickets for local events – theatre, cinema, gigs and fairs – are available from the *Welsh Fudge Shop* (☎0970/612721) on Queen's Road.

Accommodation

As in all major seaside towns, there are hundreds of **places to stay**, so beds are generally quite reasonable and easy to find. The tourist office will only give information on accommodation verified by the Wales Tourist Board, so, if desperate, or if the B&Bs they offer are too pricy, there are dozens of cheaper B&Bs in the streets around the station and along South Marine Terrace.

Hotels and guesthouses

Brendan Guest House, 19 Marine Terrace (☎0970/612252). One of the better cheap seafront B&Bs. ②.

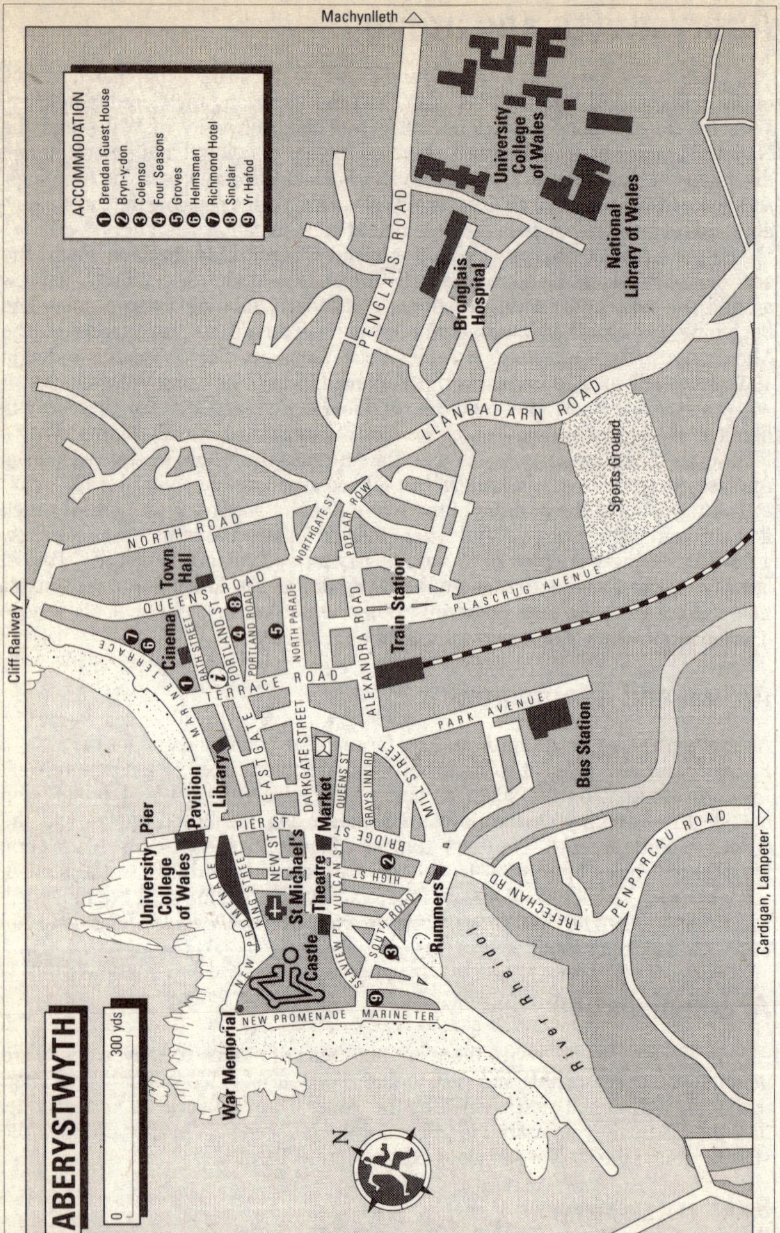
ABERYSTWYTH
0
300 yds
N
ACCOMMODATION
1 Brendan Guest House
2 Bryn-y-don
3 Colenso
4 Four Seasons
5 Groves
6 Helmsman
7 Richmond Hotel
8 Sinclair
9 Yr Hafod
Machynlleth
Cliff Railway
Cardigan, Lampeter
University College of Wales
National Library of Wales
Bronglais Hospital
PENGLAIS ROAD
LLANBADARN ROAD
Sports Ground
NORTH ROAD
NORTHGATE ST
POPLAR ROW
Town Hall
QUEENS ROAD
PLASCRUG AVENUE
Train Station
Cinema
BATH STREET
PORTLAND ST
PORTLAND ROAD
NORTH PARADE
ALEXANDRA ROAD
MARINE TERRACE
TERRACE ROAD
PARK AVENUE
Bus Station
Library
EASTGATE
DARKGATE STREET
QUEENS ST
GRAYS INN RD
MILL STREET
Pavilion
Pier
PIER ST
Market
BRIDGE ST
University College of Wales
NEW PROMENADE
KING STREET
NEW ST
St Michael's
Theatre
VULCAN ST
HIGH ST
SOUTH ROAD
Rummers
TREFECHAN RD
PENPARCAU ROAD
Castle
SEAVIEW PL
War Memorial
NEW PROMENADE
MARINE TER
River Rheidol

Bryn-y-don, 36 Bridge Street (☎0970/612011). Spirited and charming guesthouse, a hundred yards or so up from the station. ②.

Colenso, 11 Rheidol Terrace (☎0970/624876). Long-established harbourside B&B, with a visitors' book dating back to World War I. ②.

Four Seasons, 50–54 Parkland Street (☎0970/612120). Upmarket Victorian town house behind the seafront. ④.

Groves, North Parade (☎0970/617623). Welcoming town centre hotel, also serving evening meals. ③.

Helmsman, 43 Marine Terrace (☎0970/624132). Tall seafront guesthouse in the middle of the curving Promenade. ②.

Richmond, 44–45 Marine Terrace (☎0970/612201). Comfortable, family-run seafront hotel, many of whose rooms have en suite. ③.

Sinclair, 43 Portland Street (☎0970/615158). Small and beautifully designed guesthouse benefiting from the intimacy of its size. ③.

Yr Hafod, 1 South Marine Terrace (☎0970/617579). Compact and cheerful B&B, and the best of the bunch on the seafront south of the castle. ②.

Campsites and self-catering

Aberystwyth Holiday Flats, 9 Northgate Street (☎0970/612878). Self-contained apartments and self-catering.

Glan-y-mor Leisure Park, Clarach Bay (☎0970/828900). The best of the caravan parks in Clarach Bay, on the other side of Constitution Hill, to the north of Aberystwyth. They have caravans for rental and tent pitches.

Midfield, Southgate, Penparcau (☎0970/612542). Campsite just off the A4120 (A487) south of town. Free showers and games area.

University College of Wales, Penglais (☎0970/623757 or 623780). Self-contained flats and B&B (②) available during the student vacations on the Penglais site and also down by the seafront.

The Town

As a seaside resort, Aberystwyth is hard to beat, with two long, gentle bays curving around between two rocky heads: Constitution Hill at the north end of the Promenade and Pen Dinas to the south. The town rises up towards the east from the flat plains in between the two, peaking at Penglais, where the graceful Portland stone buildings of the University gaze over the town.

Constitution Hill (430ft), at the top of the long Promenade, rises sharply away from the rocky beach. It is a favourite jaunt, crowned with a tatty jumble of amenities that includes a café, picnic area, telescopes and an octagonal **camera obscura** (Easter–Oct daily 10am–5.30pm; free), a device popular in the pre-TV era and affording close-up and long-shot views over the town, the surrounding mountains and bays, plus a vista of the hordes of caravans to the north, looking like legions of tanks poised for battle. If you don't fancy the invigorating walk up, you can take the clanking 1896 **cliff railway** (Easter–Oct daily 10am–6pm; 50p) from the grand terminus building at the top of Queen Street, behind the Promenade.

From the bottom of Constitution Hill, the **Promenade** – officially Marine Terrace – arcs away to the south, past ornate benches decorated with dragons, a continuous wall of hotels and guesthouses, a prim bandstand and shingle beach. Terrace Road peels off to the left, almost immediately reaching the **Amgeuddfa**

Ceredigion (Ceredigion Museum) (July–Aug daily 10am–6pm; Easter–June & Sept–Oct Mon–Sat 10am–6pm; Nov–Easter Mon–Sat 10am–5pm; free), atmospherically housed in the ornate Edwardian *Coliseum* music hall. The range of exhibits here is wide, including cosy reconstructed cottages, dairies and a nineteenth-century pharmacy, mementoes of the building as a theatre and cinema and a surprisingly interesting look at the history of weights and measures.

Marine Terrace continues round to the spindly **pier**, beyond which a John Nash-designed turreted sea **villa** dating from 1790 dominates the seafront. It was extended massively in the 1860s as a hotel designed to soak up the anticipated masses arriving on the new rail line, but when the venture failed, the building was sold in 1872 to the fledgling university, who are still here, although the bulk of the departments have long since relocated to Penglais. The Promenade cuts around the front of the building to a rocky headland, where the **castle** ruins (free access) stare blankly out to sea. The thirteenth-century fortress, built by Edward I as part of his conquest of Wales, is more notable for its breezy position than for the buildings themselves, of which the two outer gates are the most impressive remains. South of the castle is the quieter, sandy beach along South Marine Terrace, which peters out by the wide **harbour**, the mouth of the Rheidol River.

A couple of blocks inland from the Promenade, you'll find the terminus of the **Vale of Rheidol railway** (April–Oct; ☎0970/625819) on Alexandra Road, above which is the old restaurant, the fascinating **Aberystwyth Yesterday** exhibition (April–Oct daily 10am–5pm; Nov–March daily 2–5pm; free) is a compulsive ragbag of hundreds of old local photographs, costumes and period furniture.

North Parade meets up with Queen's Road at the bottom of Northgate Street, which winds east, becoming Penglais Road as it climbs the hill towards the **University**'s main campus, and the **National Library of Wales** (Mon–Fri 9.30am–6pm, Sat closes 5pm; free), in a massive white Edwardian building overlooking the town. Temporary exhibitions in the corridors and Gregynog Gallery are invariably excellent, as is the permanent exhibition of **A Nation's Heritage**, giving a well-rounded introduction to the history of the written word and printing in Wales, shown in the absorbing range of old texts, maps, photos, paintings, illuminated manuscripts and the first Bible in Welsh, from 1588. Tickets (☎0970/623816) need to be obtained for entry into the Reading Room, for access to the enormous range of texts, maps, photos and documents, including, as one of the UK's six copyright libraries, copies of every book published in Britain.

Eating, drinking and entertainment

Aberystwyth's cultural and gastronomic life is an ebullient, all-year-round affair, thriving on students in term time, visitors in the summer and a large esoteric-leaning community at all times. As well as a varied range of **pubs** and **restaurants**, this is about the best place to find Welsh **music**, anything from folk to rock, and good for theatre and cinema. For a slice of Edwardian gentility, take afternoon tea in any of the seafront hotels along the Promenade.

Restaurants and cafés

Cornerstone, New St. Youth centre and cheap café, open daytime Tuesday to Thursday, together with Friday and Saturday evenings.

Gannets Bistro, 7 St James Square (☎0970/617164). Small restaurant that manages delicious and imaginative dishes from local farm and sea produce. Closed Tues. Inexpensive.

Gourmet Pizza Company, 11 Pier St (☎0970/617476). Chintzy pink paradise amongst the earthier cafés, with a range of tasty pizzas and pasta dishes. Inexpensive.

Jillybeans, 49 North Parade (☎0970/615374). Wholefood restaurant and gallery, open in the daytime. Inexpensive.

La Bohème, 51 North Parade (☎0970/625707). Animated cellar bar and upstairs restaurant, with an inventive international menu. Moderate.

Royal Pier Tandoori, the Pier (☎0970/624888). Swish, romantic end-of-pier restaurant, with views over the twinkling bay. Serves a good range of curries and a few unusual Indian treats. Moderate.

Y Graig, 34 Pier St (☎0970/611606). Trendy wholefood café with a drinks licence. Great atmosphere, as it's a bit of a focal point for a wide-ranging clientele. Inexpensive.

Pubs

Bay Hotel, Marine Terrace. Student pub with regular discos, open until 1am.

Bear, below the *Marine Hotel*, Marine Terrace. Cellar bar on the seafront, usually packed with students and young people, particularly on Fridays for live Welsh music.

Castle Hotel, South Rd. Harbourside pub, built in the style of an ornate Victorian gin palace. Good bar menu includes vegetarian specialities.

Pier Hotel, Pier St. Endearing old town pub, with the lounge entrance up a tiny side alley.

Rummers, Bridge St, by the River Rheidol bridge. Popular live music pub, particularly good on Thursdays and at the weekend.

Ship and Castle, Vulcan St/High St. Nautical-style bar, with a good range of beer, cider and food. Hosts regular Welsh and Irish folk music, best on Wednesdays.

Weston Vaults, Thespian St/North Parade. Unpretentious and popular with students.

Y Cŵps (Coopers Arms), Llanbadarn Rd. Firmly Welsh local, evident from the green, white and red exterior. Fun and friendly, with regular Welsh folk and jazz nights.

Entertainment

Aberystwyth Arts Centre, the University, Penglais (☎0970/623232). The town's main venue for arthouse cinema, touring theatre, classes, events and wide-ranging temporary exhibitions.

Commodore Cinema, Bath St (☎0970/612421). Screens mainstream current releases.

Theatr y Castell, St Michael's Place/Vulcan St (☎0970/624606). Venue for local amateur productions and a few touring companies.

Listings

Banks All major banks are along Great Darkgate Street and North Parade.

Bike rental *Red Dragon*, Llanbadarn Rd, opposite *Y Cŵps* pub (☎0970/84397).

Books *Siop y Pethe*, North Parade, for a huge array of Welsh-interest books, magazines and music in both Welsh and English. There is also a good bookshop in the University Arts Centre and *Galloways*, Pier St, is the best for a wider range.

Festivals *Friends of the Earth/Greenpeace Festival* takes place annually in June, a *Festival of the Countryside* in late June/early July, a *Traditional Jazz Festival* in early July, a *Music Festival* in late July and a 1920s *Razzamatazz* festival in late October.

Lesbian and Gay Switchboard (Tues 6–8pm; ☎0970/615076).

Post office 8 Great Darkgate St.

Sport *Plascrug Leisure Centre* (☎0970/624579), off the Llanbadarn Rd, has two indoor pools, sauna, solarium, squash and tennis courts, indoor pitches and multigym. The *University Sports Centre* (☎0970/622280) is open to the public in the summer vacation.

The Vale of Rheidol

Inland from Aberystwyth, the Rheidol River winds its way up to a secluded, wooded valley, where occasional old industrial workings have moulded themselves into the contours, rising up past waterfalls and minute villages. It's a glorious route, and by far the best way to see this part of the world is on board one of the trains of the **Vale of Rheidol railway** (see above), a narrow-gauge steam train that wheezes its way along sheer rock faces and up hundreds of feet. It was built in 1902, ostensibly for the valley's lead mines but with a canny eye on its tourist potential as well, and has run ever since.

If you'd rather drive, the easiest way is to take the road that forks off the A44 at Capel Bangor, and hugs the river's edge as far as the **Cwm Rheidol Reservoir**, part of a showpiece hydroelectric scheme. An **information centre** (Easter–Sept daily 11am–4.30pm; Oct daily noon–4pm; free), run by recently privatized electricity generators *Powergen*, explains the scheme's significance. Tickets (£1.50) can also be bought at the centre for a tour of the **power station** itself, with a neighbouring **fish farm** thrown in for good measure.

Slight remains of old lead workings are evident on the banks of the reservoir, although the valley's mining legacy is better seen further along, as the road begins to narrow before finally disappearing into a wood as a mud track. From here, paths rise either side of the river to overlook the burnt orange spoil, vividly coloured water and bright plants, fitted snugly into their green landscape. A sharp path on the south side of the river climbs up to **Rhiwfron** halt on the Rheidol railway, and an even more punishing route from the northern bank scrambles up over the mines for a mile and into the sombre little village of **YSTUMTUEN**, a former lead mining community whose school has been converted into a basic **youth hostel** (☎097 085/693; ①). From here it is also a couple of miles walk into Devil's Bridge.

Devil's Bridge

Folk legend, idyllic beauty and travellers' lore combine at **DEVIL'S BRIDGE** (Pontarfynach), a tiny settlement built solely for the growing visitor trade of the last few hundred years, twelve miles east of Aberystwyth by road (A4120), the narrow-gauge Vale of Rheidol railway or the river itself.

The main attraction here is the Devil's Bridge itself, where the main roads converge and cross the Mynach. This is, in fact, three bridges, one on top of the other, spanning the chasm of the churning River Mynach yards above its confluence with the Rheidol. The road bridge in front of the striking, but distinctly antiquated, *Hafod Arms* hotel (☎097 085/232; ③) is the most modern of the three, dating from 1901. Immediately below it, wedged between the rock faces, are the stone bridge from 1753 and, at the bottom, the original bridge, dating from the eleventh century and reputedly built by the monks of Strata Florida Abbey (see p.214). To see the bridges – and it is worth it, as they make a truly remarkable sight – you have to enter the turnstiles (50p) on either side of the modern road bridge. With your back to the hotel, the right hand side is the shorter route, signposted to the Punch Bowl. Slippery steps lead down to the deep cleft in the rock, where the water pounds and hurtles through the gap crowned by the bridges. The Punch Bowl is the name given to a series of rock bowls scooped by the sheer power of the thundering river, which rushes through past bright, green mossy rocks and saturated lichen.

On the opposite side of the road, the turnstiles open out on to a path that tumbles down into the valley below the bridges, descending ultimately to the crashing **Mynach Falls**. The scenery here is magnificent: sharp, wooded slopes rising away from the frothing river, with distant mountain peaks surfacing on the horizon. A platform overlooks the series of falls, from where a set of steep steps takes you further down to a footbridge dramatically spanning the river at the bottom of the falls. From the platform, and from here, views over the confluence of the two rivers and towards the **Gyfarllwyd Falls** are awesome. Be warned, however, that Devil's Bridge has been a seriously popular day excursion for centuries with no sign of its attraction waning. In order to escape some of the inevitable congestion, it is wisest to come here at the beginning or end of the day, or out of season.

The road towards Aberystwyth from the *Hafod Arms* runs past a few houses and the Devil's Bridge **post office**, where booklets are available detailing other local walks. These are thorough and well worth buying, as they cover the wooded ravines and old lead mines around the Mynach and Rheidol valleys. Just by the post office is the terminus **station** of the Vale of Rheidol railway, a tinpot brown and cream shack. For **camping**, there's a site by the petrol station, just beyond the bridges, or you can at the *Halfway Inn* (☎097 084/631), back along the A4120 towards Aberystwyth, just beyond the spectacularly positioned village of **PISGAH**. Welsh folk, choirs, jazz and special events add to the array of beers and ciders, food and good B&B (③). Nantyronen station, on the Rheidol railway, is less than a mile away, albeit a good five hundred feet lower.

Ponterwyd

The next settlement up from Devil's Bridge on the banks of the Rheidol is **PONTERWYD**, four miles away. Between the bleak moorland of Plynlimon (see p.195) and the rugged mountains to the south, the village grew as a centre of lead mining, and you can now visit an evocative reminder of the local mining trades, the **Llywernog Silver-Lead Mine** (April–Sept daily 10am–6pm; Oct Mon–Sat 10.30am–dusk; £2.95 museum and site, £3.95 including underground tour), a mile west of Ponterwyd. Locally mined lead was rich in silver, making the area particularly ripe for exploitation. Llywernog opened in the 1740s, closing in the early years of this century. In the boom years, towards the latter half of the 1800s, the whole of northern Ceredigion was a mini-Klondike, attracting speculators and opportunists by the trainful. The museum has expanded consistently over the years, and now includes an underground tour around the dark, dank workings of the mine, the chance to pan for "fool's gold" or to dowse for mineral veins. In fact, one of the funniest sections in George Borrow's *Wild Wales* tells of his night in the inn at Ponterwyd – now the *George Borrow Hotel* – when the pompous Englishman met his match in a pugnacious landlord, who, even in 1854 was complaining about the numbers of unimaginative tourists flocking to Devil's Bridge at the expense of neighbouring villages.

The scenery around the old mine is impressive in its barrenness. Afforestation has softened the contours to some extent and affords some wonderful walks amongst the tiny lakes and old mines to the north. A good starting point is the **Bwlch Nant-yr-Arian visitor centre** (Easter–Sept daily 10am–5pm; free), a mile further west from Llywernog, which sits above a magnificent valley scooped out of the wooded hillsides. They stock numerous leaflets about local walks and sights.

The Vale of Ystwyth

The Ystwyth River runs pretty much parallel to the Rheidol, a couple of miles to the south. Four miles south of Devil's Bridge is the drab village of **PONTRHYDYGROES**, once the centre of the local lead mining. The B4343 climbs out of the village and past the delightful country estate of **Hafod**, once the seat of a great house belonging to the wealthy Johnes family. In the late eighteenth century, Thomas Johnes commissioned a mansion here in the Picturesque style, added to by John Nash, amongst others, but in 1807, a terrible fire ravaged the house and its library full of Welsh manuscripts. The replacement sumptuous house was demolished in 1962 as an unsafe ruin, and all that remains is the beautiful estate Johnes landscaped and forested two hundred years ago. The church, off the B4574, is the best place to start the waymarked trails through the estate leading down to the river. Johnes' larch forest, broken by trickling streams, monumental relics and planted glades, tumbles down to the Ystwyth River, less than a mile from the church car park. A bridge spans the river, where paths fan out either way along its banks or up ahead along the tiny valley of the Nant Gau.

Continuing west, a small road grinds up the hill into the bizarre moonscape surrounding **CWMYSTWYTH**, a small, semi-derelict village perched at the bottom of a valley of old lead mines, deserted in the late nineteenth century when the mines were exhausted. As the river shimmers past, the view is one of abandoned shafts, tumbledown cottages, twisted tramways and grey heaps of spoil littering spartan hillsides. The isolated road continues to climb the uninhabited slopes, before dropping down into the Elan Valley (see p.189) and its reservoirs.

The Dyfi Estuary and Valley

Making claims to be "one of the greenest corners of Europe", the **Dyfi Valley** has considerably more chance of substantiating the boast than most places. Beyond the grand scenery of the flat river plain edged in by rolling hills, the area is rife with B&Bs and other businesses started up by idealistic New Agers who have flocked to this corner of Wales since the late 1960s.

Focal point for the valley is the genial town of **Machynlleth**, a candidate for the Welsh capital in the 1950s and site of Owain Glyndŵr's embryonic fifteenth-century Welsh parliament. In the hills to the north, the renowned, self-contained **Centre for Alternative Technology** runs on co-operative lines and makes for one of the most interesting days out in Wales.

The A487 runs to the the south of the Dyfi as it widens towards its vast estuary, and for the most part, the road acts as a demarcation line between the flat lands bordering the estuary and the mountains veering up to the east. The derivation of the name of the roadside village of **Furnace** can be gleaned from the eighteenth-century iron foundry, now open as a museum. Cutting up into the hills above the village is a dead-end track that runs through **Artists' Valley**, so named due to its popularity amongst nineteenth-century landscapists.

The land between the Dyfi Estuary and the sea is a salty seamarsh where the sand dunes are the tallest things to be seen. A national **nature reserve** at **Ynyslas** is the best place to explore the area, or, for safe swimming, head down the coast road into **Borth**, a curious town stretched for nearly two miles along one straight seafront road.

A well co-ordinated network of trains, steam rail lines and buses make getting around the area easy. A **Dyfi Sherpa** ticket (☎0286/679535; £5) combines bus trips, a ride on the Tallylyn steam line and services on a round trip between Machynlleth, Aberdyfi, Tywyn and Corris, and is available from train stations and tourist offices.

Machynlleth and around

Short-listed for Welsh capital in the 1950s and site of Owain Glyndŵr's embryonic fifteenth-century Welsh parliament, **MACHYNLLETH** (pronounced Mah-hun-cthleth) has an air of importance, hardly borne out by its population of a couple of thousand.

It is difficult to imagine a nation's capital consisting essentially of just two intersecting streets, but that is the basis of Machynlleth. The A489 enters the town from the east becoming the wide main street, **Heol Maengwyn**, busiest on Wednesdays when a lively **market** springs up out of nowhere. Heol Maengwyn comes to an end at a T-junction, under the fanciful gaze of an over-fussy **clock tower**, erected in 1873 by local landowner, the Marquess of Londonderry, to commemorate his son and heir's coming of age.

Glyndŵr's partly fifteenth-century **Parliament House** (Easter–Sept daily 10am–5pm, other times by arrangement ☎0654/702827; free) sits halfway along Heol Maengwyn, a modest looking black-and-white fronted building, concealing a large interior. Displays chart the course of Glyndŵr's life, his military campaign, his downfall, and the 1404 parliament in the town, when he controlled almost all of what we now know as Wales and even negotiated international recognition of the sovereign state. The sorriest tales are from 1405 onwards when tactical errors and the sheer brute force of the English forced a swift retreat and an ignominious end to the greatest Welsh uprising. Opposite the Parliament House, a path leads into the landscaped grounds of **Plas Machynlleth**, the elegant seventeenth-century mansion of the Marquess of Londonderry, now municipal offices. Around the corner in Heol Penallt, almost opposite the parish church, is **Y Tabernacl** (Mon–Sat 10am–4pm; free; ☎0654/703355), a beautifully serene old chapel that has been converted into a cultural centre, including the small collection of the **Wales Museum of Modern Art**. It also hosts films, theatre and the annual **Gŵyl Machynlleth** festival in mid to late August, with a combination of classical music, debate, theatre and some folk music.

Practicalities

The **train station** is a five minute walk up the Heol Penallt/Doll from the clock tower. In the old Victorian station building adjoining the modern annex is *Joyrides* (☎0654/703109), a **bike rental** company. Most **buses** leave from the station forecourt. The **tourist office** (daily Easter–Sept 10am–6pm; Oct–Easter closes 5pm; ☎0654/702401) is next to the Glyndŵr Parliament House on Heol Maengwyn.

Accommodation is easily found, including the grand *Wynnstay Arms* (☎0654/702941; ④) on Heol Maengwyn, and the earthier *Glyndŵr Hotel* (☎0654/703989; ②) on Heol Doll, towards the station. B&Bs include the *Llys Maldwyn* on Heol Doll (☎0654/703001; ②), and *Brondre* on the Newtown Road (☎0654/702422; ②), just beyond Heol Maengwyn. There's a **campsite** three miles north near the Centre for Alternative Technology at *Lleyngwern Farm* (☎0654/702492).

OWAIN GLYNDWR

No name is so frequently invoked in Wales as that of Owain Glyndŵr (*c.* 1349–1416), a potent figurehead of Welsh nationalism ever since he rose up against the occupying English in the first few years of the fifteenth century.

Little is known about the man described in Shakespeare's *Henry IV, Part I* as "not in the roll of common men". There seems little doubt that the charismatic Owain fulfilled many of the mystical medieval prophecies about the rising up of the red dragon. He was of aristocratic stock, and had a conventional upbringing, part of it in England of all places. His blue blood furthered his claim as Prince of Wales, being directly descended from the princes of Powys and Cyfeiliog, and as a result of his status, he learned English, studied in London and became a loyal, and distinguished, soldier of the English king, before returning to Wales and marrying.

Wales in the late fourteenth century was a turbulent place. The brutal savaging of Llywelyn the Last and Edward I's stringent policies of subordinating Wales had left a discontented, cowed nation where any signs of rebellion were sure to attract support. Glyndŵr became the focus of the rebellion through a parochial problem: when his neighbour in Glyndyfrdwy, the English Lord of Ruthin, seized some of his land. The courts failed to back Glyndŵr, so, with four thousand supporters and a new declaration that he was Prince of Wales, he attacked Ruthin, and then Denbigh, Rhuddlan, Flint, Hawarden and Oswestry, before encountering an English resistance at Welshpool. Whole swathes of North Wales were however his for the taking. The English king, Henry IV, despatched troops and rapidly drew up a range of severely punitive laws against the Welsh, even outlawing Welsh-language bards and singers. Battles continued to rage, with Glyndŵr capturing Edmund Mortimer, the Earl Marcher, in Pilleth in June 1402. By the end of 1403, he controlled most of Wales.

In 1404, Glyndŵr assembled a parliament of four men from every commot in Wales at Machynlleth, drawing up mutual recognition treaties with France and Spain. At Machynlleth, he was also crowned king of a free Wales. A second parliament in Harlech took place a year later, with Glyndŵr making plans to carve up England and Wales into three as part of an alliance against the English king: Mortimer, would take the south and west of England, Thomas Percy, Earl of Northumberland would have the Midlands and North, and himself Wales and the Marches of England. The English army, however, concentrated with increased vigour on destroying the Welsh uprising, and the Tripartite Indenture was never realized. From then on, Glyndŵr lost battles, ground, castles and was forced into hiding, dying, it is thought, in Herefordshire. The draconian anti-Welsh laws stayed in place until the accession to the English throne of Henry VII, a Welshman, in 1485. Wales became subsumed into English custom and law, and Glyndŵr's uprising becoming an increasingly powerful symbol of frustrated Welsh independence. Even today, the shadowy organization that surfaced in the early 1980s to burn holiday homes of English people and English estate agents dealing in Welsh property has taken the name *Meibion Glyndŵr*, the Sons of Glyndŵr.

There are plenty of **cafés, restaurants** and **pubs** in the town, including a great wholefood shop and café at *Siop y Chwarel*, opposite the post office on Heol Maengwyn. Lunch is good at the otherwise bland *White Lion* on Heol Pentrerhedyn, near the clock tower, but better at the *Wynnstay Arms*, good also for surprisingly reasonable evening meals. Less formal, but very good for food, is the *Dyfi Forester Inn* on Heol Penallt. The *Glyndŵr Arms*, on Heol Doll, has live local music at the weekends, although the liveliest pub is a bikers' haunt, the *Skinners Arms* on Heol Penallt.

Centre for Alternative Technology

Since its foundation in the middle of the oil crisis of 1974, the **Centre for Alternative Technology**, or *Canolfan y Dechnoleg Amgen* (daily 10am–5pm; £2.60; ☎0654/702400), just over two miles north of Machynlleth off the A487, has become one of the biggest attractions in Wales. A former derelict slate quarry, covering seven acres, the centre has over the last twenty years become an entirely self-sufficient community, generating its own power and water from on-site equipment. It's not a museum, but it is open to the public and is a fascinating place to visit, combining earnest education about renewable resources and practices with flashes of pzazz, such as the water-powered cliff rail line that whisks the visitor 197 feet up from the car park. Whole houses have been constructed to showcase energy-saving ideas and the fifty-strong staff – who all live communally and receive identical (very low) wages – are ebullient and helpful in explaining the ideas. There are also organic gardens, beehives, a waterwheel, an adventure playground and numerous hands-on exhibits. The wholefood restaurant, and adjoining bookshop, are excellent. The CAT also run residential **courses** here, their most popular one being a guide to building your own energy-efficient home.

Furnace

As its name suggests, the hamlet of **FURNACE**, six miles southwest of Machynlleth on the A487, grew principally as an industrial centre, firstly around silver refining and then iron smelting during the seventeenth to nineteenth centuries, both of which took place in the **Dyfi Furnace** (May–Sept daily 9.30am–6.30pm; £1.50, Oct–April free access; CADW), a barn-like building constructed to harness the power of the tumbling Einion River with a waterwheel driving the bellows. Inside, you walk around a wall platform and peer into the chasms of the furnace itself below.

The lane on the other side of the river follows the Einion River through a forest and out into the idyllic **Cwm Einion**, known as **Artists' Valley** following its popularity in the last century with landscape painters, including Richard Wilson. From the picnic area and the *Ty'n-y-cwm* tea room, walks head up into the deserted foothills of Plynlimon (see p.195), across the spongy moors and through conifer forests to the remote glacial lakes of **Llyn Conach** and **Llyn Dwfn**, three miles away and five hundred foot further up the slopes.

Ynyslas and Borth

One of the most surprising landscapes in Wales is the sudden plain that appears to the west of the A487. At the heart of it is a raised bog, **Cors Fochno**, which can be seen to the south as you pass along the B4353 or rail line. To the north, the flat landscape meets the formidable sand dunes that line the southern side of the Dyfi Estuary. The road curves round into **YNYSLAS**, an interesting village and entrance to the dramatic estuary-side **nature reserve**, most notable for its birdlife. In winter, wading and sea birds nest among the dunes and mudflats and in summer, some of the most obvious creatures are butterflies flitting around the colourful sand plants growing in the grass. The views here are dramatic: for once, a Welsh view almost uncluttered by mountains, giving far-reaching sights over the sky, estuary and seascape, as well as across the river to the colourful huddle of Aberdyfi (see below). Leaflets and walking ideas can be picked up at the **visitor centre** (April–Sept daily 9am–6pm) in the village.

The B4353 plunges south from Ynyslas, along the sea shore and into **BORTH**, basically one long street stretched out along the seafront for almost two miles, desolate in winter and heaving solid in the summer. As it was solely built for holidaymakers, the only occupants of its austere, washed-out Victorian houses are pubs, restaurants, tacky shops and B&Bs, interspersed with the odd caravan and campsite. The shallow **beach** is good, though, and **B&Bs** are plentiful – try the *Glanmor* (☎0970/871689; ③) or the *Maesteg* (☎0970/871928; ②), both on the High Street. The Edwardian **youth hostel** (☎0970/871498; ①) is at the northern end of the main street, and the *Cambrian coast Holiday Park* (☎0970/871233), just north of the town, is a good **campsite**. Of the annual events, the **Borth Regatta** at the end of September is great fun, with many semi-serious races.

Southern Cadair Idris and the Talyllyn Valley

The southern coastal reaches of Snowdonia National Park are almost entirely dominated by **Cadair Idris** (2930ft), a five-peaked massif standing in isolation, which has some demanding but very rewarding walks. Tennyson claimed never to have seen "anything more awful than the great veil of rain drawn straight over Cader Idris", but catch it on a good day, and the views – occasionally as far as Ireland – are stunning. During the last Ice Age, the heads of glaciers scalloped out two huge cwms from Cadair Idris' distinctive dome, leaving thousand-foot cliffs dropping away on all sides to cool, clear lakes. The largest of these amphitheatres is Cwn Gadiar, the **Chair of Idris**, which takes its name from a giant warrior poet of Welsh legend, although some prefer the notion that Idris' Chair refers to a seat-like rock formation on the summit ridge, where anyone spending the night (another legend maintains just New Year's Eve) will become a poet, go mad or die.

Many favour small-time coastal resorts – like **Aberdyfi** – to mountains, but it is better to press on to **Tywyn** and ride the **Talyllyn Railway**, one of Wales' most popular narrow-gauge lines, running seven miles up the valley to **Abergynolwyn** at the foot of Cadair Idris, a short distance from the dilapidated thirteenth-century **Castell-y-Bere** and the inland cormorant colony at **Craig yr Aderyn**.

The very useful *Dyfi Sherpa*, a summer-only day-ticket (£5), allows a circuit from Tywyn using the Talyllyn Railway to Abergynolwyn, the bus to Machynlleth and the bus or mainline train back to Tywyn. The ticket can also be bought on the bus at Machynlleth.

Aberdyfi

On a blustery winter's day, the battened-down Victorian seafront terraces of **ABERDYFI** can take on the forlorn air of a place where you might expect to find ageing sea captains peering out of every seafront window, binoculars trained on the horizon, and reminiscing on the days when fishing and the coastal trade were more important than pleasure craft. But in the summer, the streets are alive and Aberdyfi turns into an understated and likeable resort, with houses tumbling down the hillside to the shores of the Dyfi Estuary. The sheltering horseshoe of

SNOWDONIA NATIONAL PARK

The oldest and largest of Wales' national parks, **Snowdonia National Park** (Parc Cenedlaethol Eryri) was set out in 1951 over 840 square miles of northwest Wales. Its boundaries brush the north coast near Conwy, stretch south to Cadair Idris and the Dyfi Estuary, and take in 23 miles of superb Cambrian coastal scenery, but the focus of the park is undoubtedly Wales' highest mountain, Eryri, its name derived from either *eryr* (land of eagles) or *eira* (land of snow); since the eagles have long gone, the latter is more appropriate, with winter snows clinging to 3000-foot peaks well into April.

Jagged mountains predominate here, but the harsh lines come tempered by broadleaf lowland woods around calm glacial lakes, waterfalls tumbling from hanging valleys and complex coastal dune systems. However, you won't find total wilderness: twenty-five thousand people live in the park and another twelve million people come here each year to tramp almost 2000 miles of designated paths. In apparent contradiction to its name, the National Park is 75 percent privately owned by the Forestry Commission and National Trust. However, trespass isn't usually a problem as long as you keep to the ancient rights of way that conveniently cross private land where needed. Many of the most popular areas are National Trust land where access is unrestricted.

mountains provides a mild climate for summer crowds drawn by its beach and watersports. Canoes and sailboards can be rented on the beach, but there isn't much else to do here: even swimming is pretty much off limits until the planned sewage pipeline to the treatment station at Tywyn is completed.

In the mid-nineteenth century, the town, with its seamlessly joined eastern neighbour **PENHELIG**, built shallow-draught coastal traders for the inshore fleet, a past remembered in the small **Maritime Museum** (no regular hours; free) by the wharf. Sticking to outdoor pursuits, there's a pleasant coastal walk east to the wooded **Picnic Island** starting at The Green, a manicured lawn in Penhelig. The path follows the inappropriately named Roman Road, a relatively modern path cut into the low coastal cliffs and crossing a couple of short bridges to well-sited rest spots on promontories.

Practicalities

Aberdyfi is served by two equally convenient **train** stations, Penhelig, half a mile east, and Aberdyfi, half a mile west of the **tourist office** at Wharf Gardens (Easter–Oct daily 9am–6pm; ☎0654/767321), near where the #29 **bus** stops.

The best budget **accommodation** here is the friendly *Cartref Guest House*, Penrhos (☎0654/767273; ③), near Aberdyfi train station, which can do meals. Also good is the licensed *Brodawel*, Tywyn Rd (☎0654/767347; closed Jan & Feb; ③), opposite the members-only golf course a mile north of town, or, along the waterfront in town, the *Sea Breeze*, 6 Bodfor Terrace (☎0654/767449; ③), with its own tea shop, and the nearby *Mrs Cross*, 18 Seaview (☎0654/767321; ②). The *Penhelig Arms* (☎0654/767215; ⑥), near Penhelig train station, rates as the best of the pricier places, and serves moderately priced **meals** with an extensive Italian-slanted wine list. For something lighter, try *The Old Coffee Shop*, 13 New St (closed Jan), built into the cliff behind the *Britannia Hotel*, with home-made cakes and good inexpensive lunches. In the evening, *The Dovey Inn* serves the best range of bar meals and, along with the *Britannia*, has the liveliest atmosphere.

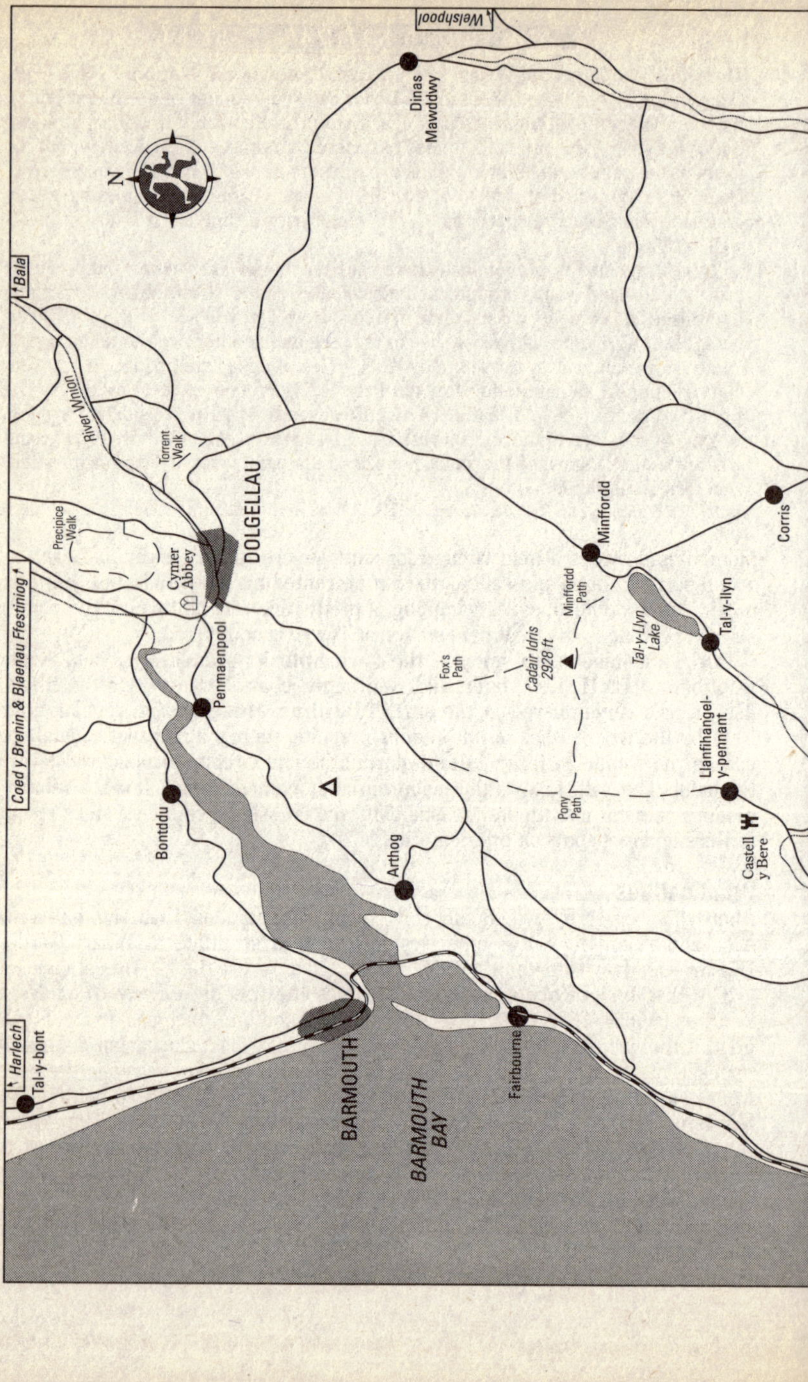
Harlech
Tal-y-bont
BARMOUTH
BARMOUTH BAY
Fairbourne
Bontddu
Arthog
Penmaenpool
Coed y Brenin & Blaenau Ffestiniog
Cymer Abbey
DOLGELLAU
Precipice Walk
Torrent Walk
River Wnion
Bala
N
Dinas Mawddwy
Welshpool
Minffordd
Corris
Minffordd Path
Fox's Path
Cadair Idris 2928 ft
Tal-y-Llyn Lake
Tal-y-llyn
Llanfihangel-y-pennant
Pony Path
Castell y Bere

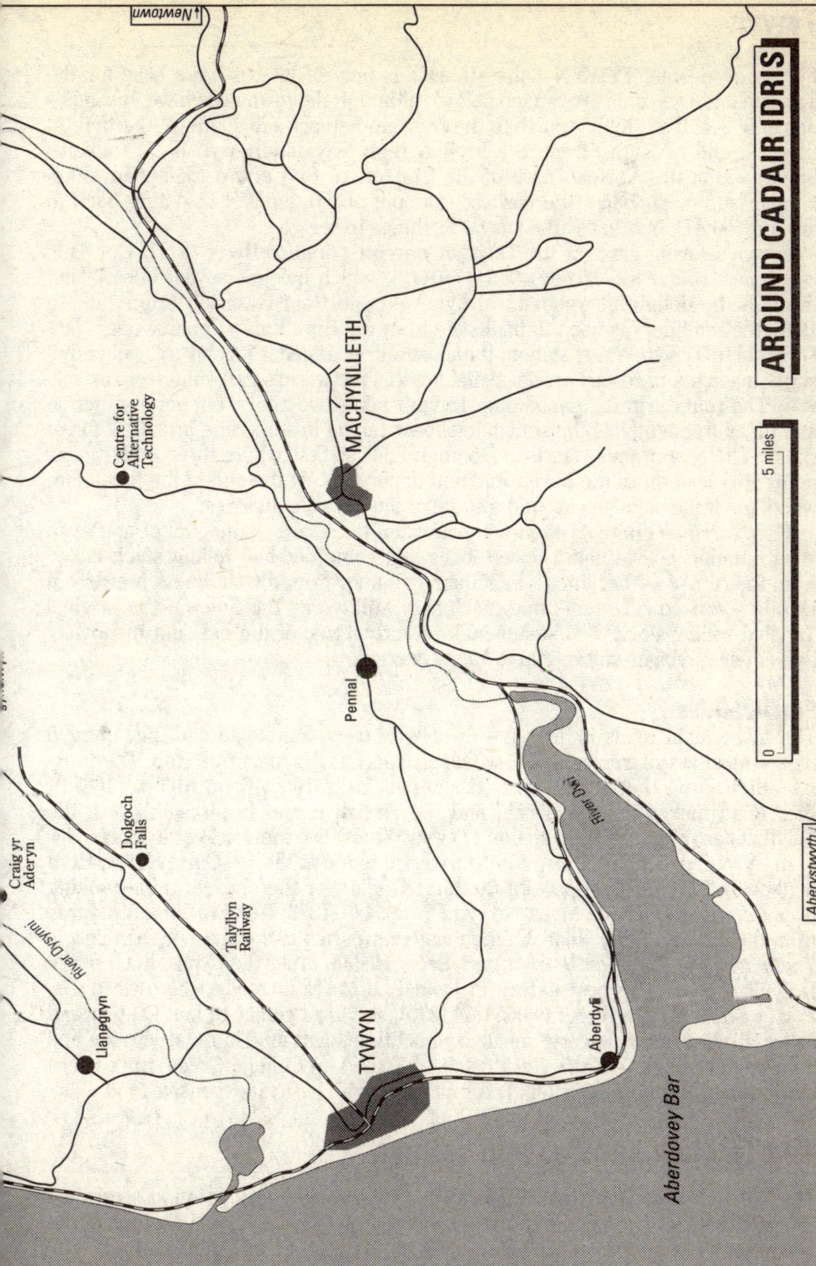
AROUND CADAIR IDRIS
0
5 miles
Newtown
Aberystwyth
MACHYNLLETH
Centre for Alternative Technology
Pennal
River Dyfi
Aberdyfi
Aberdovey Bar
TYWYN
Llanegryn
River Dysynni
Talyllyn Railway
Dolgoch Falls
Craig yr Aderyn

Tywyn

For many people, **TYWYN** ("the strand") is only of interest as a base for the Talyllyn and Dysynni valleys (see below), although the town does have four miles of sandy beach stretching north to the Dysynni Estuary and south to Aberdyfi. At the east end of High Street, the five-foot-high **Ynysmaengwyn** or St Cadfan's Stone, within the Norman nave of the **Church of St Cadfan** (daily 9am–5pm, later in summer), bears the earliest example of written Welsh, dating back to around 650 AD, but that's about as far as things to see go.

Tywyn's saving grace is the **Talyllyn narrow-gauge railway** (April–Oct daily 2–8 trains; round trip £6.80; ☎0654/710472), which belches seven miles inland through the delightful wooded Talyllyn Valley to Nant Gwernol. From 1866 to 1946, the rail line was used to haul slate from the Bryn Eglwys quarry near Nant Gwernol to Tywyn Wharf station, then just four years after its closure, rail enthusiasts managed to restart services, making this the world's first volunteer-run railway. The round trip (at a maximum 15mph) takes two hours, but you can get on and off as frequently as the schedule allows, taking in some fine broadleaf forest walks. The best of these starts at Dôlgogh Falls station, where three trails (maximum 1hr) lead off to the lower, mid and upper falls. At the end of the line, more woodland walks take you around the site of the old slate quarries.

The **Narrow-Gauge Museum** (open when trains are running; 50p) at Tywyn Wharf station boasts half a dozen locos and some odd-ball rolling stock culled from the ruins of other lines – including a shunter from the Guinness brewery in Dublin – but equally venerable machinery still works the line. Of the original Talyllyn rolling-stock, two steam-engines and all five of the oak and mahogany passenger carriages still run up to Nant Gwernol.

Practicalities

The three main roads in Tywyn – the High Street, Pier Road and the Aberdyfi road – meet at the **train station**, which also acts as the main **bus** stop. The **tourist office** is on the High Street (Easter–Oct daily 10am–6pm; ☎0654/710070), Pier Road makes for the beach, and the Aberdyfi road heads south past the Talyllyn narrow-gauge train station (Tywyn Wharf) two hundred yards away.

In Tywyn, decent **accommodation** can be found at the *Ivy Guest House*, High St (☎0654/711058; ②), opposite the tourist office, or the cheaper, non-smoking *Glenydd Guest House*, 2 Maes Newydd (☎0654/711373; ②), two hundred yards from the beach off Pier Road. Of the many **campsites** in the area, the handiest is *Ynysmaengwyn Caravan Park* (April–Sept; ☎0654/710684), a mile out on the Dolgellau road. The best **eating** in town is upstairs at moderately priced *The Proper Gander*, High Street (☎0654/711270), serving a choice of four set teas and cakes all day, and à la carte meals at lunchtimes and on Thursday, Friday and Saturday evenings. *Y Gegin Fach* (☎0654/710229) on College Green, the eastern extension of High Street, is handy for filling up with basic, inexpensive food.

The Talyllyn and Dysynni valleys

The **Talyllyn and Dysynni valleys** form a two-pronged fork pointing southwest towards the sea. The handle is formed by the Talyllyn Valley, which starts at the northeast by Minffordd and is followed by the Dysynni River (Afon Dysynni). The river splits into two at Abergynolwyn, where some ancient geological upheaval forces it to abruptly switch its course north, forming the Dysynni Valley and leaving its original course beside the Talyllyn Railway all but dry. Although a quick tour around the sites won't take more than a day, the area has some good accommodation, making it an ideal choice for a relaxing couple of days exploring.

The Talyllyn Valley is served by the #30 bus, running from Tywyn to Abergynolwyn, continuing to Minffordd (where you can catch #2 to Dolgellau) and Machynlleth. The Talyllyn narrow-gauge railway runs from Tywyn to Abergynolwyn station half a mile short of the village, or to Nant Gwernol, just past the village but off the road. **Accommodation** is scattered throughout the two valleys, but the only **restaurants** are those attached to hotels.

The Talyllyn Valley

From Tywyn, the road up the **Talyllyn Valley** runs parallel to the Talyllyn Railway (see above), meeting it at Dolgoch Falls, the site of some wooded walks and the *Dolgoch Falls Hotel* (March–Oct; ☎0654/782258; ④), where moderately priced meals are available. You'll find cheaper accommodation at the superb farmhouse B&B, *Tan-y-Coed-Uchaf*, half a mile further on (March–Nov; ☎0654/782228; ②), just two miles short of the twin valley's largest settlement, **ABERGYNOLWYN**, comprising a few dozen quarry workers houses, two pubs and the *Riverside Guesthouse and Café*, Cwrt (☎0654/782235; ②), where there are full meals for residents.

The Dysynni Valley branches northwest here, but Talyllyn Valley continues northeast past the basic *Cedris Farm* **campsite** (☎0654/782280), a mile northeast of Abergynolwyn, and two miles further on to **Tal-y-Llyn Lake**. The chief interest here is the fifteenth-century **St Mary's Church** on the southern shores of the lake, a fine example of a small Welsh parish church, unusual because of its chancel arch painted with an alternating grid of red and white roses, separated by grotesque bosses. The church is within a stone's throw of two hotels: the classy, angling-oriented *Tynycornel* (☎0654/782282; ⑧), which has rights to fishing on the lake, a heated outdoor pool, a sauna and an excellent but expensive restaurant open to non-residents; and *Pen-y-Bont* (☎0654/782218; ③), which has inexpensive meals and is also open to non-residents.

From here it's a further two miles northeast to the start of one of the best routes up Cadair Idris (see box overleaf) from **MINFFORDD**, made up of only the *Minffordd Hotel* (March–Dec; ☎0654/761665; ⑥), an eighteenth-century farmhouse and coaching inn, open to non-residents for moderately priced traditional British dinners (Thurs–Sat), and two **campsites**: *Cwmrhwyddfor Farm* (☎0654/761380), half a mile northeast, and *Doleinion* (☎0654/761312), a couple of hundred yards southwest. *Dolffanog Fawr* (☎0654/761247; ②), a seventeenth-century farmhouse B&B, is under a mile to the southeast near the north end of Tal-y-Llyn Lake.

The Dysynni Valley

The Dysynni Valley has more to offer in the way of sights, even though the lack of public transport makes it difficult to get to. A mile and a half northwest of Abergynolwyn, a side road cuts northeast to the hamlet of **LLANFIHANGEL-Y-PENNANT** and the scant ruins of the native Welsh **Castell-y-Bere** (unrestricted access; CADW), a fortress built by Llywelyn ap Iorwerth ("the Great") in 1221 to protect the mountain passes. After being besieged twice in the thirteenth century, this castle – one of the most massive of the Welsh castles – was consigned to

WALKS ON CADAIR IDRIS FROM MINFFORDD

Note: The OS Outdoor Leisure 1:25,000 map of "Cadair Idris/Dovey Forest" is highly recommended for all these walks, although the OS Landranger 1:50,000 "Dolgellau" map will do.

The steepest and most dramatic ascent of Cadair Idris follows the **Minffordd Path** (6 miles; 5hrs; 2900ft ascent), a justifiably popular route that makes a full circuit around the rim of **Cwm Cau**, probably the country's most dramatic mountain cirque.

The path starts just west of the *Minffordd Hotel* at the junction of the A487 and the B4405. From the car park, follow the signs along an avenue of horse chestnuts and up through the woods, heading north. You will reach a fork: take the left path that wheels around the end of Craig Lwyd into Cwm Cau, and before you reach the lake, fork left and climb onto the rim of Cwm Cau, following it round to **Penygadair** (2930ft), the highest point on the massif. Here there's a circular shelter and a tin-roofed hut originally built for dispensing refreshments to thirsty Victorians, and now affording none-too-comfortable protection from wind and rain.

The shortest descent follows the summit plateau northeast, then down to a grassy ridge before ascending gradually to **Mynydd Moel** (2831ft) and a magnificent view down into a cwm containing the waters of Llyn Arran. The descent starts beside the fence, crossed just before the summit, and follows it south all the way to the point below Cwm Cau where the uphill path forked.

On a good day, an **extended route** (9 miles; 7hrs; 2900ft ascent) makes a more pleasurable descent and leaves your knees in better shape for the next day's walk. This follows the ridge around to **Gau Graig** (2240ft), finally dropping off the northernmost of the two spurs and swinging east to the road. Follow the A487 southwest until the old road branches right, then follow this parallel to the main road right back to Minffordd.

seven centuries of obscurity and decay. There's still plenty to poke around, with large slabs of the main towers still standing, but it's primarily a great place just to sit or picnic, with good views to Cadair Idris and **Craig yr Aderyn** (see below). Half a mile northeast of the castle, you pass the ruined **Tyn-y-ddôl** (unrestricted access), once the home of Mary Jones, famed for her 1800 bible-buying walk to Bala (see box, p.277), an event commemorated by a plaque in the remains of the house. Tyn-y-ddôl marks the beginning of a path (10 miles; 7hr; 2900-foot ascent) up Cadair Idris, though a longer and far less exciting one than those described above.

Three miles seaward along the Dysynni Valley road, around thirty breeding pairs of cormorants colonize **Craig yr Aderyn** (Birds' Rock), a 760-foot-high cliff four miles from the coast. As the sea has gradually withdrawn from the valley, the birds have remained loyal to their home, making this Europe's only inland cormorant nesting site. Watch them return in V-formation at dusk from the negligible remnants of an Iron Age fort on top of Craig yr Aderyn reached by an east path (2 miles; 1hr; 750ft ascent) from Llanllŵyda, two miles west of Abergynolwyn. The farmhouse B&B, *Llanllŵyda* (☎0654/782276; ②), lies conveniently by the start of the footpath up Craig yr Aderyn, serves meals and has a simple **campsite**.

A couple of miles further down the valley you meet the coast road (at this stage two miles inland) at **LLANEGRYN**, where the little church on the hill half a mile northwest of the village (open daily) has an unexpectedly beautifully rood screen, probably carved in the fifteenth century, which tradition says was carried overnight from Cymer Abbey (see p.236) after its dissolution. Turn right in the centre of Llanegryn and continue for about half a mile.

Northern Cadair Idris and the Mawddach Estuary

In 1824, Wordsworth found the Mawddach "a sublime estuary", and some years later John Ruskin thought a waterside road he followed here was "the most beautiful walk in the world". Romantic hyperbole perhaps, but these broad tidal flats gouging deep into the heart of the mid-Wales mountains create dramatic backdrops from every angle. With the sun low in the sky and the tide ebbing, the constantly changing course of the river trickles silver through the golden sands.

But the colour of the sands isn't just an illusion: they really do contain gold, though not enough for gold mining company *Rio Tinto Zinc*, who thankfully abandoned their plans to dredge for the stuff in the early Seventies. Spasmodic outbursts of gold fever still occasionally hit the region's main town, **Dolgellau**, but most people are content to come here for some excellent walking up Cadair Idris and along the estuary, or to hit the beaches. The low-key **Fairbourne** and shoddy but relatively alive **Barmouth** are the main lures.

Fairbourne

A small resort on the southern side of the Mawddach Estuary, **FAIRBOURNE** was developed in the late nineteenth century as the country estate of the chairman of *McDougall's* flour company, and sports one of the finest beaches in Wales and great views along the coast and across the estuary. The steam-hauled **Fairbourne Railway** (Easter–Oct 3–6 daily; £3.35 return) is the town's only attraction and makes a pleasant alternative route across the estuary to Barmouth, starting across the road from the **train station** and running a mile to a connecting **passenger ferry** (Easter–Oct; 75p), taking you the rest of the way.

There is little reason not to press on from Fairbourne, but there are many B&Bs here and the comfortable *Fairbourne Hotel* (☎0341/250203; ④) on the main street. With your own transport, a better bet is the non-smoking *Cyfannedd Uchaf Farmhouse* (☎0341/250526; ③), high above the estuary two miles east towards Arthog, then a further two miles south along a narrow road. Excellent meals are available.

Dolgellau

Its distance from England and its historical position in the heartland of Welsh nationalism should make **DOLGELLAU** (pronounced Dol-getl-aye) the Welshest of towns, but the town's architecture draws more from nineteenth-century England, with a dour series of small squares – all with English names – clustering around the solid granite neo-Georgian facades of Eldon Square, built to lure Victorian tourists from across the border to marvel at Cadair Idris and the

Mawddach Estuary. It is a much older town than appearances suggest, lying at the junction of three Roman roads which converged on a now-vanished military outpost. It was here in 1404 that Owain Glyndŵr assembled the last Welsh parliament and later signed an alliance with Charles VI of France for providing troops to fight against Henry IV of England.

In this rural area, seventeenth-century Quakers sought freedom from persecution and built up a small community around Dolgellau. In the 1860s, it became the focus of numerous gold rushes, drawing wave after wave of prospectors to pan the estuary or blast levels into Clogau shale or mudstone sediment under the Coed y Brenin Forest. The quartz veins yielded some gold, but weren't very rich and few made much money. Today, Dolgellau is a fairly dull place, but the town is an excellent base for exploring the surrounding district, in particular some fine lowland walks and a strenuous one up Cadair Idris.

Arrival, Information and accommodation

Dolgellau has no train station but is well served by **buses** from Bala, Barmouth and Machynlleth, which all pull into Eldon Square. A building here houses the **tourist office** (Easter–Oct daily 10am–6pm; Nov–Easter daily except Tues &

WALKS AROUND DOLGELLAU

Note: No map is needed for the first three walks; the OS Outdoor Leisure 1:25,000 map of "Cadair Idris/Dovey Forest" is recommended for the fourth one, although the OS Landranger 1:50,000 "Dolgellau" map will do. If the weather is good and you are well kitted out, this is the one not to be missed.

TORRENT WALK

The most popular walk with the Victorians who came to visit Dolgellau was the attractive lowland beech-woodland **Torrent Walk** (2 miles; 1hr; 100ft ascent), which follows the course of the Clywedog River as it carves its way through the bedrock. Stroll downstream past the cascades to the *Clywedog Tea Garden*, where you can eat home-baked scones in a riverside garden before starting back. Bus #2 can take you the two miles east along the A470, from where you should walk a hundred yards or so down the B4416 to a sign on the left-hand side, marking the beginning of the walk.

PRECIPICE WALK

Nowadays, more people head for the not remotely precipitous **Precipice Walk** (3–4 miles; 2hr; negligible ascent). It's very easy going, simple to follow and has great views to the thousand-foot ramparts of Cadair Idris and along the Mawddach Estuary – catch it in late afternoon or early morning sun if you can. The path makes a circuit around Foel Cynwch, starting three miles north of Dolgellau off the Llanfachreth road just near the Big Bridge. Bus #33 runs three times daily on Tuesdays and Fridays only, from Dolgellau to the car park by the start of the walk. From the car park turn left down a side road then left again up a track following the signs all the way. On the shores of Llyn Cynwch, the path splits. Take the left path along the shores then follow the contour around the bracken- and heather-covered Foel Cynwch back to the lake and return along the approach route. If you don't coincide with the bus, a path beside Cymer Abbey (see p.236) is the next best approach to the Precipice Walk.

Wed 10am–5pm; ☎0341/422888), along with the Quaker Interpretive Centre (see below).

HOTELS AND GUESTHOUSES

Aber Café, Smithfield St (☎0341/422460). Very friendly B&B with rooms above a decent café. ②.

Borthwnog, Bontddu. Small country house on the northern shores of the Mawddach Estuary, with log fires and great meals. It is a mile east of Bontddu and three miles west of Dolgellau on the A496. Catch the #94 Barmouth bus. ⑤.

The Clifton House Hotel, Smithfield Square (☎0341/422554). Good-value hotel built in an ex-police station and jail. The basement cells are used as a restaurant. ③.

Dwy Olwen, Coed y Fronallt, Llanfachreth Rd (☎0341/422822). Peaceful guesthouse in landscaped gardens ten minutes' walk from the centre. Cross the Big Bridge and turn right. ②.

George III Hotel, Penmaenpool (☎0341/422525). Superb seventeenth-century hotel right by the Mawddach Estuary two miles west of Dolgellau (bus #28). Some rooms are in former train station buildings. Top food and drink (see below). ⑧.

Ivy House, Finsbury Square (☎0341/422535). Licensed guesthouse a few yards southeast of Eldon Square with a restaurant and cellar bar. ③.

PENMAENPOOL–MORFA MAWDDACH WALK

Beside the Mawddach Estuary's broad sands, a disused rail line makes for easy going on the **Penmaenpool–Morfa Mawddach Walk** (8 miles one way; 3hr; flat) starting at the car park by the Big Bridge in Dolgellau and passing Penmaenpool on its way to Morfa Mawddach. The first two miles are the least interesting, so it makes sense to catch the #28 bus to the **RSPB Nature Information Centre** (Easter–May Sat & Sun noon–4pm; June to mid-Sept daily 10am–5pm; free) in an old rail signal box at Penmaenpool, just by a wooden toll bridge (daily 8am–11pm; cars 20p, pedestrians 2p) linking the two banks of the estuary. From there the path hugs the estuary bank all the way to Morfa Mawddach, from where you can walk across the bridge to Barmouth (see p.237) or catch the #28 bus back to Dolgellau. Another good scheme is to take the bus to Morfa Mawddach and walk back to Penmaenpool.

PONY PATH

The more ambitious Victorian tourists walked up **Cadair Idris** on the now eroded **Foxes Path** which starts by the *Gwernan Lake Hotel*, two miles southwest of Dolgellau. There is nothing to stop you using it, but the National Park Board sanctioned ascent is by the classic and straightforward **Pony Path** (6–7 miles; 4–5hr; 2500ft ascent), a less demanding and less dramatic approach than the southern one listed from Minffordd (see p.232). The route starts by turning right out of the car park at Ty Nant, a mile further southwest up Cadair Road, then right again at the telephone box following the path to "Cader Idris". Already the views to the craggy flanks of the massif are tremendous, but they disappear as you climb steeply to the col where you turn left on a rocky path to the summit shelter on **Penygadair** (2930ft). The descent is either by the same route or (with some care and considerable efforts to minimize erosion) by taking the first part of the Foxes Path down to Llyn y Gadair. This goes northeast to a grassy plateau then north to a couple of cairns and down. By the lake, forsake the rest of the Foxes Path in favour of a less obvious route heading off from the northwest corner of the lake eventually meeting the Pony Path again. Note that there are no buses up Cadair Road.

Tan-y-Fron, Arran Rd (☎0341/422638). Non-smoking B&B with en suite rooms and associated campsite ten minutes' walk east along Arran Road. Closed Dec & Jan. ③.

Troed-y-Gader, Cader Rd (☎0341/422556). One of the cheapest places around but it is a mile and a half out – past *Ivy House* and left at the *Shell* station. ②.

Tyddynmawr Farmhouse, Islawrdref (☎0341/422331). Eighteenth-century farmhouse on the slopes of Cadair Idris at the foot of the Pony Path under three miles southwest of Dolgellau (no buses). Great value at the low end of this category with all rooms en suite. ③.

HOSTELS AND CAMPSITES

Bryn-y-Gwyn Campsite, Cader Rd (☎0341/422733). A basic tents-only site less than a mile southeast of Dolgellau.

Kings youth hostel, Penmaenpool, four miles west of Dolgellau (☎0341/422392). Large country house a mile up a wooded valley off the #28 Tywyn bus route (last bus around 6pm). This is an ideal base for the Pony Path up Cadair Idris. ①.

Tan-y-Fron Campsite, Arran Rd (☎0341/422638). Well-appointed and reasonably priced camping and caravan site next to B&B.

Vanner Farm (☎0341/422854). Camp and caravan site by Cymer Abbey.

The Town

Today Dolgellau's only central diversion is the **Quaker Interpretive Centre**, in the tourist office (same hours), which uses a series of explanatory panels to tell of the local Quakers' (the Society of Friends) well-recorded sufferings before the 1689 Act of Toleration that put a stop – at least legally – to persecution for their pacifist Nonconformist views, non-attendance at church and non-payment of its tithes. At a trial in Bala in 1679, this last sin earned a group of Friends a prison term, a further encouragement to those thinking of following the two thousand Welsh Quakers who had already fled to the United States and started the Pennsylvania towns of Bangor, Bryn Mawr and others. The building also houses a National Park exhibition.

Prospecting declined after the gold rushes of the late nineteenth century, but the hopeful still occasionally open up an ore vein, the most recent enterprise combining their digging with the three-hour-long **Gold Mining Tour** (April–Oct daily 9.30am–4pm, reduced hours in winter; £9.50; ☎0341/423332). Tours leave from the **Welsh Gold Visitor Centre** (April–Oct daily 9am–7pm, reduced hours in winter; free) at the far end of the car park by the Big Bridge. Be sure to arrive early and grab a front seat in the mini bus for the best view of the Coed y Brenin forest en route to the mine where you alight to be decked out in waterproofs and lamp for the underground experience. On the half-mile walk through the mine you do get to see some of the small workforce operating the milling and separating equipment, but most of the tour is designed with the visitor in mind, with a staged blasting and the opportunity to chip away at the rock for a few minutes. Don't expect to find any nuggets: it usually takes two tons of ore to recover an ounce of metal and the shiny stuff in your rock chips is more than likely iron pyrites (fool's gold). It is fun, but barely justifies the expense.

Long before the Victorian gold frenzy, the Romans had discovered flecks of gold in the Mawddach silt, then thirteenth-century Cistercian monks, based at **Cymer Abbey** (April–late Oct daily 9.30am–6.30pm; late Oct–March Mon–Sat 9.30am–4pm, Sun 2–4pm; CADW; £1, free on Sunday), two miles north of Dolgellau, were given "the right in digging or carrying away metals and treasures free from all secular exaction". The fine location at the head of the Mawddach

Estuary is typical of this austere order, but unfortunately the surrounding caravan site mars the effect of the remaining Gothic slabs. A path beside the abbey makes an alternative approach to the Precipice Walk (see box).

Eating and drinking

AlloAllo, Queen's Square. Awfully named café/bistro serving good coffee and decent light meals behind the tourist office. Inexpensive.

Bwyty Dylanwad Da, Smithfield St (☎0341/422870). The best restaurant in town offers a range of creative fare dished up in simple surroundings. Excellent desserts. Daily in summer, Thurs–Sat evenings in winter but phone first; closed Feb. Moderate.

Fronoleu Farm Restaurant, Tabor (☎0341/422361). Licensed restaurant in eighteenth-century Quaker farmhouse with live harp playing (Tues, Thurs & Sat). A mile east of Dolgellau. Take Arran Road, then branch right after 400 yards. Bar meals also available. Inexpensive to moderate.

George III, Penmaenpool (see hotels). Superb spot for an afternoon drink, an inexpensive bar meal or something gamey from their à la carte menu. Expensive.

Stag Inn, Bridge Street. Straightforward pub with good beer in the town centre.

Tyn-y-Groes Hotel, Glanllwyd (☎0341/40275). Hospitable hotel four miles north of Dolgellau in the Coed y Brenin forest. Good beer washes down fine bar meals or you can opt for the à la carte restaurant. Inexpensive to moderate.

Barmouth and around

The best approach to **BARMOUTH** (Abermo) is from the south, where the Cambrian coast rail line sweeps from Fairbourne over 113 rickety-looking wooden spans across the Mawddach River estuary to the town, lying in the shadow of the cliffs of Dinas Oleu between the shifting sands of the estuary and an endless coastal strand. Descendants of nineteenth-century English Midlands holidaymakers, who fashioned Barmouth as a sea-bathing resort, still come here every summer for the pleasure-beach attractions and sunshine.

Barmouth was once a shipbuilding centre, and although there are now few reminders of the days when two hundred coastal traders were built, the Quay, at the south end of town, still has a maritime air as the departure point for a **passenger ferry** (Easter–Oct; as frequently as custom demands; 75p) to Fairbourne, and several sea angling and sightseeing trips (enquire on quay). In late June each year, the **Three Peaks Race** starts here, and amateur yachties line up for a two-to-three day contest requiring navigating to Caernarfon, the English Lake District and Fort William in Scotland and a run up the highest peak in each country.

The Quay is also where you'll find the **RNLI Lifeboat Museum** (daily 10am–5pm; free), with its workaday exhibition of lifesaving paraphernalia and anecdotes; and the **Tŷ Gwyn Museum** (July–Sept Tues–Sun 10.30am–5pm; free), a medieval tower house where Henry VII's uncle, Jasper Tudor, is thought to have plotted Richard III's downfall. First recorded in a poem around the middle of the fifteenth century, the house was thought to have been destroyed until renovations in the 1980s revealed its identity. It now contains displays on the house and Tudor dynasty, as well as a shipwreck museum.

On the hill behind, the **Tŷ Crwn Roundhouse** (same hours as Tŷ Gwyn) once acted as a lockup for drunken sailors in the eighteenth century, and was reputedly built circular to prevent the devil lurking in any corners and further tempting the incarcerated sailors. It now houses some old photos of Barmouth.

Practicalities

Buses from Harlech and Dolgellau stop in the leisure centre car park by the **train station** and just a few yards from the **tourist office** on Station Road (Easter–Oct daily 10am–6pm; ☎0341/280787).

Barmouth has no shortage of budget **accommodation**, but little in the way of classier places, which you'll find in Harlech and Dolgellau. One of the cheapest and best is the licensed *Sunnybank Guesthouse*, Church St (☎0341/281053; ②), with views of the estuary and hearty inexpensive four-course evening meals. Two other good bets are *Bay View*, 6 Porkington Terrace (☎0341/280284; ②), with more great views and ever-helpful hosts, and *The Gables*, Mynach Rd (☎0341/280553; ②), ten minutes' walk north and particularly welcoming to walkers. There are also a couple of very good licensed seafront hotels on Marine Parade: the *Wavecrest Hotel* at no. 8 (March–Nov; ☎0341/280330; ③), and the *Cranbourne* at no. 9 (☎0341/280202; ③), both serving excellent inexpensive meals. Barmouth also has plenty of places to **camp**. The closest of a long string of sites, and one of the least afflicted with fixed caravans, is *Hendre Mynach*, Lanaber Rd (March–Oct; ☎0341/280262), a mile north of town and just off the beach.

As befits a down-at-heel resort, basic **cafés** are plentiful, though for not much more money you can get mammoth French sticks and pancakes at the inexpensive *Rowleys Licensed Restaurant*, The Quay, and good pizzas next door. Close to The Quay, *The Last Inn* has a cosy **bar** in a former cobbler's shop, with good pub meals. Moderately priced *Brambles*, Church St (summer daily), offers the best-quality food in town, with both British and French à la carte evening meals and very popular Sunday lunches; try also the traditional *Tal y Don* on High St.

WALKS FROM BARMOUTH

The best lowland walk on the Cambrian coast, **Barmouth–Fairbourne Loop** (5 miles; 2–3hr; 300ft ascent) makes a superb loop around Barmouth and Fairbourne, and has fine mountain, estuarine and coastal views all the way. The route can be done with almost no walking at all using the rail line to Fairbourne, the Fairbourne narrow-gauge railway and the ferry across the mouth of the estuary, but walking allows for variation. The route first crosses the rail bridge (30p toll) to Morfa Mawddach station, follows the lane to the main road, crosses it onto a footpath that loops around the back of a small wooded hill to Pant Einion Hall, then follows another lane back to the main road near Fairbourne. Turn north for 400 yards, then left down the main street of Fairbourne to the sea, walk north along the beach and you can catch the ferry back to Barmouth. Any desired extension to the walk is best done from Morfa Mawddach, where the route described meets the Penmaenpool–Morfa Mawddach Walk (see p.235). Follow it for a mile to Arthog to a small road and a mesh of paths leading up past waterfalls to the beautiful **Cregennan Lakes** (NT).

The **Panorama Walk** (10min) is more famous, but apart from the fine estuary view, its chief quality is its brevity, the viewpoint being only yards away from the nearest road. By taking in **Dinas Oleu** (Fortress of Light), which became the National Trust's first property in 1895, it can be turned into a decent walk (3 miles; 2hr; 400ft ascent). Essentially the route follows Gloddfa Road opposite *Woolworths* on the High Street onto the exposed clifftops, where there is a map of the reserve. Go through the metal gate and follow the path past Frenchman's Grave to a road where you turn left to the Panorama Viewpoint. Return by the same route.

Ardudwy

North of Barmouth, the coast opens out to a narrow coastal plain running a dozen miles towards Snowdonia and flanked by the heather-covered slopes of the Rhinog Mountains, five miles inland. This is **Ardudwy**, a land which Giraldus Cambrensis described as "the rudest and roughest of all the Welsh districts", a contention hard to reconcile with a fertile strip used as a fattening ground for black Welsh cattle on their way to the English markets, and now tamed by caravan sites and golf courses.

No modern road crosses the Rhinogs to the east, but until the early nineteenth-century building of coach roads, the existence of two mountain passes (see box overleaf) made this a strategic and populous area, as the number of minor Neolithic burial chambers and small Iron and Bronze Age forts demonstrate. Further up the coast, the small town of **Harlech** was built as one link in Edward I's chain of magnificent fortresses and is the only town of any importance in the region, apart from **Llanbedr**, from where a road runs west to the camping resort on Shell Island, and another rises east, splitting into two delightful remote valleys.

Bus #38 services the coast from Barmouth to Harlech, then inland to Blaenau Ffestiniog with the summer-only #38A running to Llanbedr. The Cambrian coast train line covers the same route to Harlech, from where it makes for Porthmadog.

Llanddwywe and Dyffryn Ardudwy

Two of the most accessible and impressive Neolithic sites in Ardudwy are in the contiguous twin villages of **LLANDDWYWE** and **DYFFRYN ARDUDWY**, five miles north of Barmouth. Turn right opposite the church in Llanddwywe and continue for a mile to get to **Cors-y-Gedol Burial Chamber** (unrestricted entry), a large capstone on deeply embedded uprights. The **Dyffryn Ardudwy Burial Chamber** (unrestricted access, CADW) is more substantial. A path on the left of the Llanddwywe to Cors-y-Gedol road leads north to two more burial chambers and a series of base stones and on to what was once a vast cairn a hundred feet long and up to fifty feet wide. If you are travelling by train, get off at Talybont, walk north to visit the two sites and rejoin the line at Dyffryn Ardudwy, a walk of three miles in all.

Llanbedr and around

LLANBEDR, three miles north of Dyffryn Ardudwy, is home to the **Maes Artro Tourist Village** (Easter–Sept daily 10am–5pm; £1), with its distinctly missable aquarium and Village of Yesteryea . Other than that, its YHA **youth hostel**, Plas Newydd (☎034123/287; ①), right in the centre, makes it a possible place to stay, as do the *Victoria Inn* (☎034123/213; ④) with its beer garden, good bar meals and moderately priced à la carte dinners, and the excellent and moderately priced *Llew Glas Brasserie* (☎034123/555). There's also the reasonably priced but crowded **campsite** (mid-Mar to Oct; ☎034123/217) and restaurant on **Shell Island**, or Mochras (£3 per car), two miles away. A peninsula at anything other than high tide, you reach the island by a tidal causeway, then you can swim, examine the wildflowers or scour the beach for some of the two hundred varieties of shell found here. At low tide you can see a line of rocks in the sand leading out towards Ireland, known as Sarn Badrig (St Patrick's Causeway) and traditionally thought to be the road to a flooded land known as "The Low Hundreds", whose church bells still ring from below the water. Some imagination may be needed to hear this, but you can easily pick out what is probably a glacial lateral moraine, particularly from the top of the Rhinogs, from where it often appears to divide the ocean into two shades of blue.

East of Llanbedr, a narrow road follows the Artro River six miles to the waters of Llyn Cwm Bychan, deep in the heather and angular rocks of the Rhinog range. There's a basic **campsite** at the head of the lake, and paths up to the medieval **Roman Steps** – a medieval packhorse route made of flat slabs cutting through the range – onto Rhinog Fawr (see box). Branching off the Cwm Bychan road, an even narrower and more picturesque road leads to **Cwm Nantcol**, the next valley south, where you can park at the ancient farm of **Maes-y-garnedd** and set off for the walk onto the Rhinogs (see box). There is no public transport up either valley, but on fine days you should get a ride if you try hitching.

Harlech

It's hard to dislike **HARLECH**, three miles north of Llanbedr. Its time-worn castle dramatically clinging to its rocky outcrop alone raises it above its neighbours, and the town cloaking the ridge behind the fortress commands one of Wales' finest views over Cardigan Bay to the Llŷn. There are good beaches nearby, and the town's twisting trail of narrow streets following the ridge harbours places where you can eat and sleep surprisingly well for such a small place.

WALKS ON THE RHINOGS

The northern Rhinogs offer some surprisingly tough walking. At under 2500ft they are not giants, but the large rough gritstone rocks hidden in thick heather make anything but the most well-worn paths hard going and potentially ankle-twisting. The rewards are long views across Cardigan Bay, a good chance of stumbling across a herd of feral goats and a strong sense of achievement. The two walks described here start at the head of different valleys (see "Llanbedr and around"), but share a common summit, that of Rhinog Fawr. Ambitious walkers might try combining the two (10 miles; 7hr; 3700ft), using paths that only approximately follow those marked on the unreliable OS Landranger #124 "Dolgellau" map or the Outdoor Leisure #19 map.

CWM BYCHAN WALK #1

The **Cwm Bychan walk** (5 miles; 3–4hr; 1900ft ascent) starts at the car park in Cwm Bychan, following signs up through a small wood then out onto the open moor and up to the misnamed **Roman Steps**. These guide you up to the pass, Bwlch Tyddiad, giving views east to Bala and beyond. Continue a couple of hundred yards past the large cairn to a smaller one signalling a much less well-defined path leading south and steeply up. Beyond Llyn Du the terrain gets steeper still, and you may have to use your hands to finally reach **Rhinog Fawr** (2362ft). The standard route is then to retrace your steps, but in good weather you can descend the same way you came for a few hundred yards and seek out a line running northwest from the shoulder towards Gloyw Llyn. From there, with some effort, you can pick up a path to the head of Llyn Cwm Bychan.

Arrival, information and accommodation

Harlech's **train** station is on the main A496 under the castle. Most **buses** call both here and on High Street a few yards from the **tourist office**, (Easter–Oct daily 10am–6pm; ☎0766/780658). *Theatr Ardudwy* (☎0766/780667) on the main road occasionally puts on a decent play and has the only cinema in the district.

HOTELS AND GUESTHOUSES

Aris Guesthouse, 4 Pen y Bryn (☎0766/780409). Friendly guesthouse with a great view from just above the village. It is uphill past the *Lion Hotel*, then second left. ③.

Byrdir, High St (☎0766/780316). Good reliable B&B with some en suite rooms, fifty yards from the tourist office. ②.

Castle Cottage (☎0766/780479). Cosy informal hotel with the trappings of a place charging twice as much. Excellent meals and a comfortable bar. ④.

Godre'r Graig (☎0766/780905). B&B very convenient for the station on the other side of the level crossing. ②.

Gwrach Ynys Country Guesthouse, Ynys, Talsarnau, two miles north of Harlech (☎0766/780742). Elegant country house with en suite rooms and good inexpensive home-cooked meals. March–Oct. ③.

Tremeifion, Talsarnau, three miles north of Harlech (☎0766/770491). Luxury one-hundred-percent non-smoking vegetarian guesthouse in three acres of grounds. Turn west towards Soar in Talsarnau. The price is for half-board, including evening meals cooked almost entirely from organic produce. Organic wine also available. ⑥.

Tyddyn-y-Gwynt, two miles above the town (☎0766/780298). Farmhouse run by friendly local people. Take the road past the *Lion Hotel*, straight through at crossroads and left at Bryn Gwyn Cottage. ②.

CWM BYCHAN WALK #2

The second **walk** (6–7 miles; 5–6hr; 2900ft ascent) starts by the farmhouse at the head of Cwm Nantcol and makes a fairly rugged circuit over Rhinog Fawr and Rhinog Fach. Follow the track north from the car park to the house, into the fields and over the stile, then turn northeast and walk gradually towards the base of the rocky southwest ridge, following the white marker posts. Eventually the path turns north to a cairn on the skyline, then east following more cairns up ridge to the summit trig point of **Rhinog Fawr** (2362ft).

To approach Rhinog Fach you first have to make an arduous descent into Bwlch Drws Ardudwy (The Pass of the Door of Ardudwy). In 1773 Thomas Pennant found "the horror of it far exceeding the most gloomy idea that could be conceived of it. The sides seem to have been rent by some mighty convulsion into a thousand precipices". That might be a bit overstated, but describing the route between these precipices is all but impossible. From the summit of Rhinog Fawr head southeast towards a couple of cairns, then with Rhinog Fach ahead of you keep left, descending on whatever looks like it has had the most use. Eventually you'll reach the col, where you cross the stone wall and start on a fairly clear line up **Rhinog Fach** (2236ft). Explore the summit ridge to get the best views either way, then descend to Cwm Nantcol by first walking to a rocky ledge overlooking Llyn Hywel to the south. From here you should be able to see a scrappy path running very steeply down to the lake on the right hand edge of the ledge. You'll have to use your hands at times and there are sections of scree, but you're soon on a clear path that skirts north around the base of Rhinog Fach towards Bwlch Drws Ardudwy. When it reaches the path through the pass, turn left and follow it back to Cwm Nantcol.

HOSTEL AND CAMPSITE

Min y Don, Beach Rd (☎0766/780286). Reasonably priced campsite, only three minutes' walk towards the beach, taking the first right out of the station. Easter–Sept.

Plas Newydd hostel, Plas Newydd (☎034123/287). YHA hostel not in Harlech, but three miles south in Llanbedr. Buses #38 and #94. ①.

The Town

Although blessed with some of the coast's best beaches, it is the substantially complete **castle** (April to late Oct daily 9.30am–6.30pm; late Oct to March Mon–Sat 9.30am–4pm, Sun 11am–4pm; CADW; £2.90), sitting on its 200-foot-high bluff, that is most people's real reason to come to Harlech. Started in 1285 as one of Edward I's Iron Ring of monumental castles (see p.337), it was built of a hard Cambrian rock, known as Harlech grit, hewn from the moat where sheep now peacefully graze. One side of the fortress was originally protected by the sea, now receded and leaving the castle dominating a stretch of duned coastline.

The castle has seen a lot of action in its time: it withheld a siege in 1295, was taken by Owain Glyndŵr in 1404, and the youthful, future Henry VII – the first Welsh king of England and Wales – withstood a seven-year siege at the hands of the Yorkists until 1468, when the castle was again taken. It fell into ruin, but was put back into service for the king during the Civil War, and in March 1647, it was the last Royalist castle to fall.

The first defensive line comprised the three successive pairs of gates and portcullises built between the two massive half-round towers of the **gatehouse**, where an exhibition now outlines the castle's history. Much of the castle's outermost ring has been destroyed, leaving only the twelve-foot-thick curtain walls rising up forty feet to the exposed battlements, and only the towering gatehouse prevents you walking the full circuit. The inner ward was never completed but corbels and inset fireplaces give clues to the original domestic functions.

Outside the castle, a modern equestrian **statue** depicts a scene from *The Mabinogion* recalling a semi-mythical era long before Edward's conquest. The heroic giant and king of the British, Bendigeidfran (Brân the Blessed), ruled the court at Harlech, which needed to ally itself with the Irish. Bendigeidfran's sister Branwen (White Crow) married the king of Ireland and bore him a son, Gwern, but war soon broke out and Gwern was killed. Sorrowful uncle and dead nephew are **The Two Kings** of the sculpture's title.

Eating and drinking

Castle Cottage (☎0766/780479). Limited choice two- and three-course dinner menu featuring the likes of smoked haddock in leek sauce. Very good, informal service and cosy surroundings. Sunday lunch served. Wed–Sat only in winter. Moderate.

Hung Yip, High St. Straightforward but good Chinese meals. Inexpensive.

Lion Hotel. About the liveliest pub in Harlech, with hand-pumped ales and good home-cooked bar meals. Just up from the central crossroads. Inexpensive.

Plâs Café, High St. Licensed place with a good range of food and a great view. Sit in the garden if the weather is fine. Inexpensive.

Yr Ogof (☎0766/780888). Bistro-style place a few yards north of the centre with bentwood chairs and a good-value range of inventive vegetarian and meaty dishes at the bottom end of its price category. Moderate.

Porthmadog and around

Located right at the point where the coast makes a sharp left turn along the south side of the Llŷn, **PORTHMADOG** was once the busiest slate port in north Wales. Nowadays, it's a pleasant enough town to spend a night or two, although it sadly makes little of its situation on the north bank of the vast, mountain-backed estuary. Two things it does make a fuss about are the Italianate folly of Portmeirion, two miles east of the town, and the Ffestiniog Railway that originally carried down slates from Blaenau Ffestiniog through thirteen miles of verdant mountain scenery to Porthmadog-made schooners for export.

Arrival and information

Cambrian coast **trains** pull into the mainline train station at the north end of the High Street; the Ffestiniog station is located down by the harbour, about half a mile to the south. In between the two, *National Express* **buses**, covering the north coast route from Chester, Liverpool and Manchester, stop on Avenue Road outside *The Royal Sportsman Hotel*. Frequent local bus services to Blaenau Ffestiniog, Caernarfon and Pwllheli, and less frequent ones to Beddgelert and Dolgellau stop outside *The Australia Inn* on High Street. Note that Dolgellau buses go inland through Coed-y-Brenin: take the train if you want to stick to the coast.

The helpful **tourist office**, High St (Easter–Oct daily 10am–6pm; Nov–Easter daily except Thurs 10am–5pm; ☎0766/512981), is towards the harbour from the bus stop and across the road from the **Snowdonia Accommodation Booking Office** (summer daily 10am–5pm; ☎0766/513829), which lets rooms throughout north Wales and has a handy bureau de change.

Accommodation

While limited budgets are well catered for, there's not much really decent **accommodation** without pressing on to Cricieth or Harlech, unless you're prepared to lash out for a night at the swanky *Portmeirion Hotel*. The nearest youth hostel is in Blaenau Ffestiniog (see p.290).

Hotels and guesthouses

Camelia, 12 Church St (☎0766/512201). Low-priced non-smoking guesthouse five minutes' walk from the centre, off the A497 Cricieth road. ②.

Mrs Jones, 57 East Avenue (☎0766/513087). Very comfortable guesthouse near the train station. Turn east along Cambria Terrace then right into East Avenue. ②.

Hotel Portmeirion (☎0766/770228). See Portmeirion village (see below) at its best staying in elegant individually designed suites in the hotel or in serviced cottages throughout the village. The more expensive suites will strain your credit, but it is worth asking about deals on low season, mid-week and weekend breaks which can be quite reasonable. Tennis and a heated outdoor pool. ⑧.

The Royal Sportsman, Avenue Rd (☎0766/512015). About the best hotel in the town, near the train station. ④.

Skellerns, 35 Madog St (☎0766/512843). The cheapest guesthouse around, near the Ffestiniog train station two minutes' walk north from the tourist office. ②.

Treforris, Garth Rd (☎0766/512853). Large house overlooking harbour to the west. Take Bank Place off High Street then left onto Garth Road – fifteen minutes in all. ②.

Bunkhouse, self-catering and campsites

Eric's Bunkhouse, two miles north of Porthmadog on the A498 to Beddgelert, opposite *Eric Jones' Café*. Rock climbers' bunkhouse where you can get a mattress for around £2 a night.

Hotel Portmeirion (see above). The hotel also runs fully equipped luxurious self-catering accommodation (two to eight people) let by the week, or half-week in winter. Four-berth cottages cost from £300 to £500 a week.

Tyddyn Llwyn, Black Rock Rd (☎0766/512205). Standard campsite fifteen minutes' walk along the road to Morfa Bychan. Follow Bank Place southwest off High Street. March–Oct.

Tŷ Bricks, Snowdon Street (☎0766/512597). Showerless but the cheapest of local campsites, less than a mile northeast of the centre. March–Sept.

The Town

Porthmadog would never have existed at all without the entrepreneurial ventures of a Lincolnshire MP named William Alexander Madocks, who named the town and its elder brother Tremadog, a mile to the north, after both himself and the Welsh Prince Madog, who some say sailed from the nearby Ynys Fadog (Madog's Island) to North America in 1170. In 1805, Madocks fancied he could get himself some good grazing land by draining a thousand acres of estuarine mud flats here; he bought Ynys Fadog, built an earth embankment, then started on Tremadog. The towns prospered, and between 1808 and 1812, Madocks fought tides and currents to build the mile-long embankment of The Cob, southeast of present-day Porthmadog, enclosing a further 7000 acres of the estuary. The Glaslyn River was rerouted and soon scoured out a deep watercourse close to the north bank, ideal for a slate wharf. This was the first of several which, boosted by the completion of the Blaenau Ffestiniog railway in 1836, spread along a waterfront thick with orderly heaps of slate and the masts of merchant ships. The boomtime has long since slowed, and slate traffic had ceased by the middle of the twentieth century; now only a few dozen pleasure yachts grace the harbour.

The waterfront is still the most interesting place to wander, not least because the last surviving slate shed contains the recently refurbished **Maritime Museum** (June–Sept daily 10am–6pm; £1). Amongst the obligatory ships in glass cases, panels tell of the town's shipbuilding role and its importance in carrying slate around the world.

Just across the harbour, the Ffestiniog railway (see below) begins its ascent, but Porthmadog has a second narrow-gauge line, the far less interesting **Welsh Highland Railway** (Easter & mid-May to Sept 6–8 daily; £1.25), running from just near the train station along a mile of track. Plans are to reopen the route to Beddgelert to Dinas near Caernarfon. At the Ffestiniog railway in the High Street, a small but interesting **museum** (open when trains are running; small donation) presents the history of the line and exhibits some of the original rolling-stock, including horse wagons.

All the sand and water around Porthmadog might leave you hankering for a bit of swimming. **Black Rock Sands**, three miles west, is the best beach, a long swathe of golden sands, not unpleasantly bordered by caravan sites. The #99 bus goes there in summer, or there's a footpath along the coast starting on Lôn Cei

(Quay Lane) at the back of the harbour and continuing past Black Rock Sands to Cricieth.

The Ffestiniog Railway

Without a doubt, the **Ffestiniog Railway** (Easter–Oct 4–10 times daily; Nov–Easter mainly weekends; return to Blaenau Ffestiniog £11.40, single £5.70, less for shorter journeys) ranks as Wales' finest narrow-gauge rail line, twisting and looping up 650 feet from Porthmadog to the slate mines at Blaenau Ffestiniog, thirteen miles away. The gutsy little engines make light of the steep gradients and chug through stunning scenery that ranges from broad estuarine expanses and the deep greens of the Vale of Ffestiniog, only fading to grey on the final approaches to the slate-bound upper terminus at Blaenau Ffestiniog.

When the line opened in 1836, it carried slates from the mines down to the port with the help of gravity, horses riding with the goods, then hauling the empty carriages back up again. Steam had to be introduced to cope with the 100,000 tons of slate a year that Blaenau Ffestiniog was churning out in the late nineteenth century, but the slate roofing market collapsed between the wars and passengers were carried instead, until 1946 when the line was finally abandoned. Most of the tracks and sleepers had disappeared by 1954 when, buoyed by the success of the Talyllyn Railway (see p.230), a bunch of dedicated volunteers began to reconstruct the line, only completing the entire route in 1982.

Leaving Porthmadog, trains cross The Cob then stop at Minffordd, a jumping-off point for the Cambrian coast line and the mile-long walk to Portmeirion (see below). A mile further on, Penrhyn station presents the possibility of a four-mile walk through the woods of Coed Llyn y Garnedd to either the third station, Plas Halt from where it is a short stroll to *The Grapes* pub at Maentwrog (see p.290), or the nearby fourth station at Tan-y-bwlch. Short nature trails spur off from Tan-y-Bwlch as does the longer Vale of Ffestiniog walk (see p.290) which passes Dduallt station by the spiral on its way to Tanygrisiau, the start of the Moelwyn/Cnicht walk (see p.291). You can get on and off as frequently as the timetable allows, and the journey is included in the north and mid-Wales *Rover* and *FlexiRover* tickets (see *Basics*); you must pay £2 each way for bikes, but phone first to confirm. Sit on the right of the carriage to get the best view of the scenery.

Eating and drinking

Blue Anchor, Pen-y-Cei (☎0766/514959). Small harbourside seafood restaurant with good three-course set menu. Moderate.

The Harbour Restaurant, High St, opposite the tourist office (☎0766/512471). Not surprisingly, seafood dominates the menu in this simply decorated but very good restaurant. Open daily in summer, Thurs–Sat in winter. Moderate.

Passage to India Tandoori, 26a Lombard St (☎0766/512144). Highly rated Indian restaurant, especially noted for their Sunday lunchtime buffet. It is across the park west of the High Street. Moderate.

Portmeirion Restaurant (☎0766/770228). Delightful restaurant with views across the Treath Bach sands from the *Portmeirion Hotel*. Inventive modern cuisine employing local game and seafood. Expensive.

The Ship and Cantonese Restaurant, Lombard St (☎0766/512990). Popular pub noted for both its oriental beer and its bar meals, predominantly Thai and Malaysian with some vegetarian. Inexpensive.

Yr Wylan, High St. Filling meals daytime and evening. Inexpensive.

Portmeirion

The other main lure of Porthmadog, apart from the Ffestiniog Railway, is the unique Italianate private village of **PORTMEIRION** (daily 9.30am–5.30pm; £3 in summer, £1.50 in winter), set on a small rocky peninsula in Tremadog Bay, three miles east near Minffordd. You can in fact visit the village by train: both the mainline and Ffestiniog trains, as well as buses #1, #2 and #3 stop in Minffordd, from where it is a 25-minute walk to Portmeirion. You can also walk there from Porthmadog in an hour following the footpath parallel to the Ffestiniog line across The Cob.

Perhaps best known as "The Village" in the Sixties British cult TV series *The Prisoner*, Portmeirion is the brainchild of eccentric architect, Clough Williams-Ellis, and his dream to build an ideal village which enhances rather than blends in with the surroundings, using a "gay, light-opera sort of approach". The result certainly is theatrical: a stage set with a lucky dip of unwanted buildings arranged to distort perspectives and reveal tantalizing glimpses of the sea or the expansive sands left behind.

In the 1920s, Ellis began scouring Britain for a suitable island – he believed only an island could provide the seclusion for his project – but having found nothing he could afford, was gratified to be offered a piece of wilderness five miles from his ancestral home near Porthmadog. A house already on the site was turned into a hotel, the income from it providing funds for Ellis's "Home for Fallen Buildings". Endangered buildings from all over Britain and abroad were broken down, transported and rebuilt, every conceivable style being plundered: a Neoclassical colonnade from Bristol, Siamese figures, a Jacobean town hall, and the Italianate touches, a Campanile and a Pantheon. Ellis designed his village around a Mediterranean piazza, piecing together a scaled-down nest of loggias, grand porticoes and tiny terracotta-roofed houses and painting them in pastels: turquoise, ochre and buff yellows. Continually surprising, with hidden entrances and cherubs popping out of crevices, the ensemble is eclectic, yet never quite inappropriate.

It is just a little tatty these days and badly in need of a lick of paint here and there, but even so, more than three thousand visitors a day come to ogle in summer when it can be a delight, fewer in winter when it is just plain bizarre. Sometimes dismissed as the grandest folly of all, it at least supports Ellis's guiding principle that natural beauty and profitable development needn't be mutually exclusive.

Architectural idealism aside, Portmeirion was always intended to be self-sustaining, much of the finance coming from the opulent waterside *Hotel Portmeirion* (see "Porthmadog Accommodation"). In the evening, when the village is closed to the public, patrons get to see the place at its best: peaceful, even ghostly.

The hotel also takes up many of the cottages (some self-catering) that make up the village, so your time will be spent outside except for viewing a film on Portmeirion, or popping into the shops selling *Prisoner* memorabilia or gaudy Portmeirion pottery. Guests and visitors can eat at the expensive hotel restaurant (see "Porthmadog Eating"), but most will be content with a couple of cafés, or better still, bring a picnic and find a spot on the easy paths that lace the dell and its cloak of exotic forest.

Note that the telephone numbers on some parts of the Llŷn are changing during 1994. Where two numbers are listed, the first is the old one.

The Llŷn

The Llŷn takes its name from an Irish word for peninsula, an apt description for this most westerly part of north Wales, which, until the fifth century, had a significant Irish population. The cliff-and-cove-lined finger of land juts out south and west separating Cardigan and Caernarfon bays, its hills tapering away along the ancient route to Aberdaron where pilgrims sailed for Ynys Enlli (Bardsey Island). Ancestors of those last Irish inhabitants may have been responsible for the numerous hillforts and cromlechs found on the Llŷn, particularly the hut circle of **Tre'r Ceiri** hillfort. But today it is the beaches, not prehistoric remains, that lure people to the south coast family resorts of **Cricieth**, **Pwllheli** and **Abersoch**, and unless you want to rent windsurfers or canoes, it's preferable to make for the much quieter coves punctuating the north coast or press on along the narrow roads that dawdle down towards Aberdaron.

Not even in Snowdonia does it feel more remote than the tip of the Llŷn, and nowhere in Wales is more staunchly Welsh: road signs are still bilingual but the English is frequently defaced; Stryd Fawr is used instead of High Street, and in most local shops you'll only hear Welsh spoken. There are pockets that are being bought up by English second-home owners and other immigrants, many of whom make no attempt to learn the language, and something like twenty percent of all houses on the Llŷn are either holiday homes or weekend retreats. But the peninsula remains defiantly Welsh, and a stronghold of Meibion Glyndŵr, or "Sons of Glendŵr" (see *Contexts*).

The bountiful caravan parks can seem unappealing to campers and often only accept families, but a local ruling allows anyone with a field to run a campsite for one month a year, and through the summer they spring up everywhere. *British Rail* and *National Express* both serve Cricieth and Pwllheli, leaving an extensive network of infrequent buses to cover the rest. Better still, the peninsula's quiet narrow lanes through rolling pastoral land are ideal for cycling, and you can rent bikes in Pwllheli or from *Lanes Cycle Hire* at Ysgubor Fawr, Chwilog (☎0766/810518), midway between Cricieth and Pwllheli.

Cricieth and around

When sea-bathing became the Victorian fashion, English families descended on the sweeping sand and shingle beach at **CRICIETH**, five miles west of Porthmadog. Aided by the rail line, they built the long terraces of guesthouses that grew up behind the beach, which subsequently decayed and were reborn in recent years as retirement homes. These days, beach-bound holidaymakers go further west, leaving a quiet amiable resort which curiously abounds with good places to stay and great restaurants, making it a good touring base for the peninsula and Porthmadog.

There's not much to keep you here, apart from David Lloyd George's childhood home a mile or so to the west at Llanystumdwy (see below), and the battle-

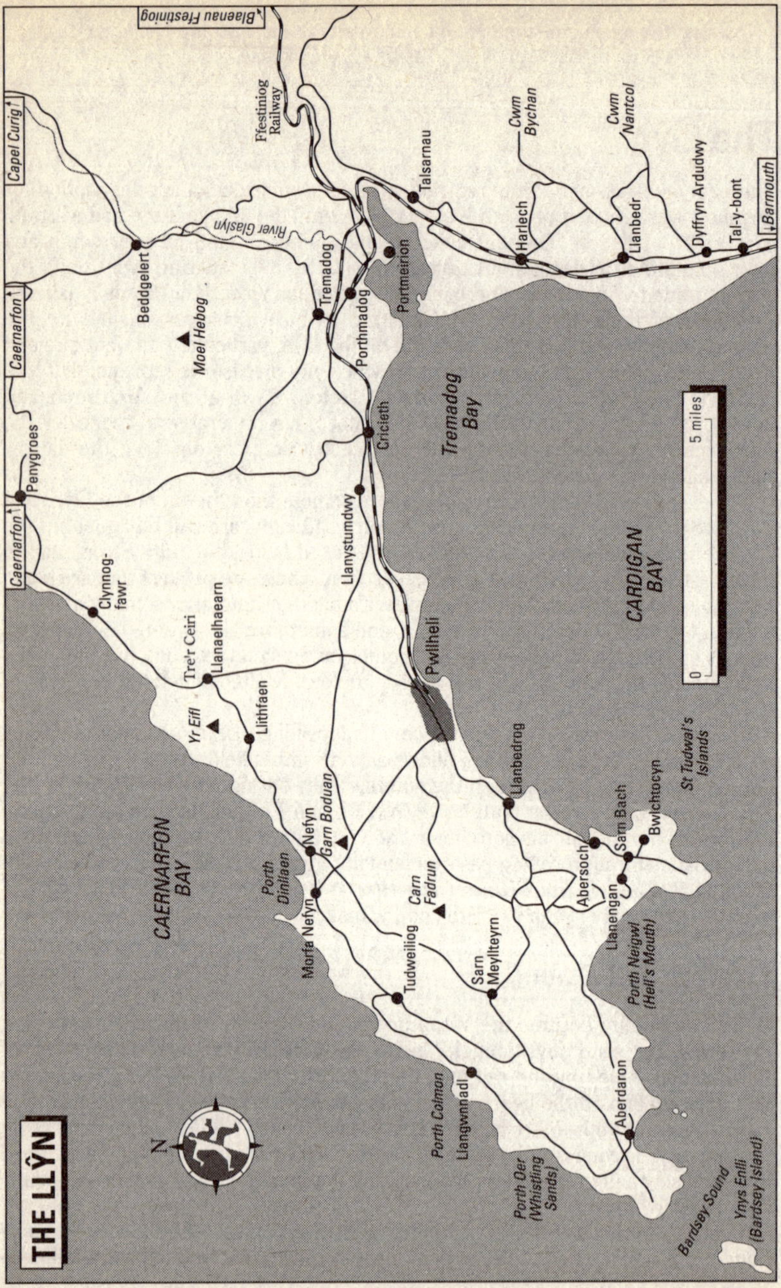
THE LLŶN
N
Capel Curig
Caernarfon
Caernarfon
Penygroes
Blaenau Ffestiniog
Ffestiniog Railway
River Glaslyn
Beddgelert
Moel Hebog
Tremadog
Porthmadog
Portmeirion
Talsarnau
Cwm Bychan
Cwm Nantcol
Harlech
Llanbedr
Dyffryn Ardudwy
Tal-y-bont
Barmouth
Cricieth
Tremadog Bay
5 miles
0
Llanystumdwy
Clynnog-fawr
Tre'r Ceiri
Llanaelhaearn
Yr Eifl
Llithfaen
Pwllheli
CARDIGAN BAY
CAERNARFON BAY
Llanbedrog
St Tudwal's Islands
Nefyn
Garn Boduan
Porth Dinllaen
Morfa Nefyn
Carn Fadrun
Sarn Bach
Bwlchtocyn
Abersoch
Llanengan
Porth Neigwl (Hell's Mouth)
Tudweiliog
Sarn Meyllteyrn
Porth Colmon
Llangwnnadl
Aberdaron
Porth Oer (Whistling Sands)
Bardsey Sound
Ynys Enlli (Bardsey Island)

GIRALDUS CAMBRENSIS & HIS JOURNEY THROUGH WALES

Through his books *The Journey through Wales* and *The Description of Wales*, Norman-Welsh **Giraldus Cambrensis** (Gerald of Wales) has left us with a vivid picture of life in Wales in the twelfth century. Gerald worked his way up the ecclesiastical hierarchy, but failed to achieve his life-long goal, the bishopric of St David's, mainly because of his reformist ideals.

Gerald's influence in Wales made him the first choice when **Baldwin**, the Archbishop of Canterbury, needed someone to accompany him on his 51-day tour around Wales in 1188, preaching the cross and recruiting for a third Crusade that was designed to dislodge the infidel leader Saladin from Jerusalem. Three thousand signed up for the Crusade on Baldwin's circular tour from Hereford in England across south Wales, up the Cambrian coast to Caernarfon, along the north coast and back down the Marches, during which time he said Mass in each of the four cathedrals: Llandaff, St David's, Bangor and St Asaph, the first Archbishop of Canterbury to do so.

During the tour, Gerald amassed much of the material for his books, where he sensitively portrayed the landscape and its people, commenting that "the Welsh generosity and hospitality are the greatest of all virtues", parrying "If they come to a house where there is any sign of affluence and they are in a position to take what they want, there is no limit to their demands". But on the whole, he shows sympathy for the Welsh, coming up with a conclusion that has an oddly contemporary ring: "if only Wales could find the place it deserves in the heart of its rulers, or at least if those put in charge locally would stop behaving so vindictively and submitting the Welsh to such shameful ill-treatment".

worn **Cricieth Castle** (April–Oct daily 9.30am–6.30pm; Nov–March Mon–Sat 9.30am–4pm, Sun 2–4pm; CADW; £1.80), dominating the coastline with what remains of its twin D-towered gatehouse. The castle was started by Llywelyn ap Iorwerth in 1230, but strengthened and finished by Edward I, who took it in 1283, and his successors. During his 1404 rebellion, Owain Glyndŵr grabbed it back, only to raze it and leave little remaining besides a plan of broken walls and the gatehouse. It is a great spot to sit and look over Cardigan Bay to Harlech in the late afternoon, but leave time for the fairly workaday exhibition on Welsh castles and a wonderful animated cartoon based on the twelfth-century Cambrian travels of Giraldus Cambrensis (see box) in the ticket office. If all you want are wonderful views, those from the top neighbouring hill are free and almost as good.

Practicalities

Trains on the Cambrian coast line stop a couple of hundred yards west of Y Maes, the open square at the centre of town. Both *National Express* **buses** from the north Wales coast and frequent local buses from Porthmadog and Pwllheli also stop here. There's no tourist office to help you find **accommodation**, but with so many good choices you shouldn't have any difficulty.

HOTELS AND GUESTHOUSES

Bron Eifion Country House Hotel (☎0766/522385). Beautiful Victorian country house full of carved Oregon pine and set in five acres nearly a mile west of the centre of town. ⑦.

Craig-y-Môr, West Parade (☎0766/522830). Well-appointed rooms, some with excellent sea views. Home-cooked meals for around a tenner. Closed Nov–Feb. ③.

Moelwyn, 27–29 Mona Terrace (☎0766/522500). En suite rooms with sea views and TVs easily justify the price at the top end of the category. Above one of the best restaurants in town. Closed Jan & Feb. ③.

Mynydd Ednyfed, Caernarfon Rd (☎0766/523269). Luxurious country house hotel a mile north on the B4411. Classy moderately priced food too. ⑤.

Preswylfa, 4 Castle Terrace (☎0766/522829). About the cheapest B&B in town, almost opposite the castle. Reductions for two or three nights out of season. Inexpensive home-cooked meals available. Closed Nov–Jan. ②.

The Rhoslyn, Marine Terrace (☎0766/522685). Good simple guesthouse 200 yards west of the castle. ②.

Trefaes Guesthouse, Y Maes (☎0766/523204). Excellent guesthouse where they really take care of you, right at the centre of town. En suite rooms some with views of the castle. ③.

CAMPSITE AND BUNKHOUSE

Mynydd Du (☎0766/522533). Simple campsite a mile towards Porthmadog on the A497. April–Oct.

Tyddyn Morthwyl Farm and Caravan Park, on the Caernarfon road, a mile north of Cricieth (☎0766/522115). Caravan park with bunkhouse in a converted farm building. Book a couple of nights ahead and bring a sleeping bag.

Eating and drinking

For such a small town, good restaurants are surprisingly abundant and offer the best range of eating on the peninsula.

Bron Eifion Country House Hotel (☎0766/522385). Innovative and highly rated cuisine strong on steak and seafood. Open nightly to non-residents. Moderate to expensive.

Bryn Hir Arms, 24 Stryd Fawr. Good pub with beer garden. Wide range of bar meals with a speciality of pizza. Inexpensive.

Cadwalader's, Castle St. Watch the legendary thick rich cream made right in front of you at the original of several *Cadwalader*'s emporia all over north Wales. Inexpensive.

Moelwyn, 27/29 Mona Terrace. French-style meals with superb seafood helped down with something from their comprehensive wine list in airy surroundings. Moderate.

Mynydd Ednyfed, Caernarfon Rd. Tasty and carefully presented food in a country house hotel a mile north of town. Moderate.

Poachers Restaurant, 66 Stryd Fawr (☎0766/522512). French-style restaurant with a three-course dinner for £6 if you eat before 7pm (not Sat). Moderate.

The Prince of Wales, High St. The best pub in town for budget eating. Inexpensive.

Tir-a-Môr, 1–3 Mona Terrace (☎0766/523084). Not strictly an Italian restaurant, but with a large range of Italian-influenced dishes in airy surroundings. It is just downhill from the square in the centre of town. Closed Sunday evening and Monday lunchtime. Moderate.

Llanystumdwy

Though born in Manchester, the Welsh nationalist, social reformer, and British Prime Minister David Lloyd George lived in his mother's home village of **LLANYSTUMDWY**, a mile west of Cricieth, until 1881, when he was nearly eighteen. He grew up in Highgate House, the home of his uncle – the village cobbler – which has now been converted into part of the **Lloyd George Museum** (Easter–Sept Mon–Fri 11am–5pm, Sat & Sun 2–5pm; Oct Mon–Fri 11am–4pm; £2.10). A fairly dull collection of gifts, awards and caskets honouring Lloyd George with the freedom of various cities illustrate the great man's popularity, and the museum's displays are full of anecdotes and little-known facts about him, with explanatory panels and a couple of short films giving a broad sweep of his life.

The video presentations demonstrate some of his talent as a witty and powerful orator, but only hint at the figure described by Churchill as "a man of action, resource and creative energy, [who] stood, when at his zenith, without a rival". Read between the lines to get a sense of the betrayal felt by many Welsh nationalists as his interest turned from the politics of Wales to those of Westminster.

Rustic late nineteenth-century beds and dressers furnish Lloyd George's wooden-floored two-up-two-down house, in a garden laid out much as it would have been in Lloyd George's day. Before ambling through the garden, walk down the path towards the River Dwyfor, beside which Lloyd George is buried under a memorial – a boulder and two simple plaques designed by Portmeirion designer Clough Williams-Ellis (see p.246). Bus #3 runs from Porthmadog and Cricieth, through the village on its way to Pwllheli.

Pwllheli

PWLLHELI (pronounced something like "Pootl-heli") nearly became famous: if Manchester, 120 miles away, had won its bid to host the Olympic Games in 2000, the new marina here was slated as the yachting venue. Occasional races and regattas now keep the boating fraternity happy as the town dejectedly returns to its position as the market town for the peninsula, a role it has maintained since 1355, when it gained its charter. There's little to remind you of the town's age though, as the oldest building only dates back to the early seventeenth century and almost everything else is Victorian. There's really no reason to stop here, but this is the end of the line for buses and trains so you probably will, at least briefly.

Pwllheli's one defining feature is its Welshness. Even in the height of summer, you'll hear far more Welsh spoken here than English and perhaps wish you'd made more of an attempt to learn some. It was at the *Maesgwyn Temperance Hotel* (now a pet shop on Y Maes) during the National Eisteddfod in August 1925 that six people, three from Byddin Ymreolwyr Cymru (the Army of Welsh Home Rulers) and three from Y Mudiad Cymreig (The Welsh Movement) met to form Plaid Cymru. Pwllheli also has one of the few exclusively Welsh-language bookshops in the country, *Llên Llŷn*, Y Maes, owned by writer Alun Jones.

You might as well move on unless you are drawn to the small-thrill roller coasters and heated pools of *Butlin's* **Starcoast World** (daily 10am–10pm, last admission 4pm; summer £5 a day, winter £3), three miles towards Cricieth.

Practicalities

The town spreads out from Y Maes, the central square where *National Express* **buses** pull in and where fairly frequent local buses leave for Aberdaron, Abersoch, Caernarfon, Cricieth and Porthmadog. The **train station**, northern terminus of the Cambrian coast line, stands a few yards to the east, opposite the **tourist office**, Station Square (daily 10am–6pm; Nov–March closes 5pm; ☎0758/613000). You can rent mountain bikes during the summer at £10 a day from *Llŷn Cycle Hire*, Ala Rd (☎0758/612414).

The best of the local **accommodation** is scattered around Pwllheli, but in the centre, try *26 High St* (☎0758/613172; ②), with TVs in all rooms, or four hundred yards away, *Llys Gwyrfai*, 14 West End Parade (☎0758/614877; ③), a comfortable guesthouse with sea views and home-cooked meals. The best place to stay in the vicinity is *Plas Bodegroes* (March–Oct; ☎0758/612363; ⑤), a very comfortable Georgian country house set in parkland at Efailnewydd, two miles northwest of

Pwllheli on the A497, and serving superb meals (see below). Non-smokers are well catered for at *Hen Ficerdy*, Abererch (March–Oct; ☎0758/612162; ③), a former country vicarage with great views of Cardigan Bay, reached by travelling a mile northeast of Pwllheli on the A499, then turning left at the chapel; or try *Gwynfryn Farm*, just over a mile north of Pwllheli (☎0758/612536; ②), a working dairy farm with comfortable B&B rooms, several self-catering units normally let by the week, and a low-cost **campsite** from mid-July to August. The farm is up Goal Street, left of the Salem Chapel, branch left, then straight on until the entrance is signposted on the left. Other campsites include the expensive full-facility *Hendre Caravan Park*, Efailnewydd (March–Oct; ☎0758/613416), a mile northwest on the A497, and the inexpensive *Mathan Uchaf Farm*, Boduan (March–Nov; ☎0758/720487; ③), on a dairy farm three miles north on the A497.

If you have the money, *Plas Bodegroes* (see above; dinner only and closed to non-guests on Mondays; expensive) could present you with the best **eating** you'll experience in Wales. Five smallish courses of innovative, beautifully presented food can be chosen from a limited menu. Don't hope for much change out of £40 for a full meal with wine, but expect to be well pleased. Diners with lighter purses can stay in town and eat moderately priced Italian meals at *Pompei*, 53 Stryd Fawr (☎0758/614944), or anything from mussels in garlic sauce to pizza at the inexpensive *Mariner Bistro* on Station Square.

For **drinking**, Pwllheli's best bets are the *Whitehall*, Goal St, notable for its good beer, and the 400-year-old *Penlan Fawr*, 3 Penlan St, where there's occasional live music, and barbecues in the beer garden in summer. Locals and visitors in the know tend to head for the friendly *Ship Inn*, Bryn-y-Gro, with its very popular summertime beer garden and great, inexpensive pub meals. It is four miles west of Pwllheli in **LLANBEDROG**: turn right at the *Glyn-y-Weddw Arms* on the A499 then continue half a mile through the village.

Abersoch and around

After the distinctly Welsh feel of Pwllheli, **ABERSOCH**, seven miles southwest along the coast, comes as a surprise. This former fishing village pitched in the middle of two golden bays has, over the last century, become a thoroughly anglicized resort, catering largely to comfortably well-off boat owners. The odd foreign entrant to the numerous small-time regattas throughout the summer lends a mildly cosmopolitan air to the place and fuels its haughty opinion of itself.

Such high self-esteem isn't really justified, but at high tide the harbour is attractive, and the long swathe of the beachhut-backed Town Beach is a fine spot even if it is barely visible under the beach towels at busy times. A short walk along the beach shakes off most of the crowds, but a better bet is to make for three-mile-long **Porth Neigwl** (Hell's Mouth), two miles to the southwest, which ranks as one of the country's best surf beaches; you'll need your own gear, and beware of the undertow if you are swimming.

Bus #17a can take you to **LLANENGAN**, a short walk from the beach of Porth Neigwl, where you can also visit the gorgeous twin-aisled fifteenth-century **St Engan's Church** (instructions for obtaining key are inside the porch), with its two altars and two rood screens, integral parts of decoration that have been little changed by the eighteenth- and nineteenth-century reformist zeal that altered most other churches. Llanengan is also home to the *Sun Inn* (see below), a cosy pub serving great bar meals, and with a pleasant beer garden.

Practicalities

Buses from Pwllheli make a loop through the middle of Abersoch passing the **tourist office**, Village Hall, Lôn Gwydryn (Easter to mid-Sept daily 10.30am–5pm; ☎0758/712929). If you are returning to Pwllheli on the #17a, make sure it isn't going to Llangian first. To continue to Aberdaron by bus, you have to take a Pwllheli-bound service as far as Llanbedrog, then catch the #17.

There is no shortage of good **places to stay** in Abersoch, the cheapest being *Trewen*, Lôn Hawen, just off Lôn Sarn Bach (☎0758/712755; ②), the non-smoking *Cadlan*, Lôn Rhoslyn (☎0758 81/2746; ②), next to the *Vaynol Arms*, and the excellent and popular *Tŷ Draw*, Lôn Sarn Bach (☎0758/712647; ②), in extensive grounds half a mile south. *Angorfa Guest House*, Lôn Sarn Bach (closed Dec; ☎0758/712967; ③), is good and very central, as is the *Neigwl Hotel*, Lôn Sarn Bach (☎0758/712363; ⑤), a comfortable hotel with friendly, professional service, and good food. Two and a half miles south of Abersoch, the road through Sarn Bach and Bwlchtocyn goes to the *Porth Tocyn* country house hotel (Easter–Oct; ☎0758/713303; ⑥), with an outdoor pool and great views of Cardigan Bay.

Almost all **campsites** around are family-oriented places, with the exception of the simple *Pant Gwyn Cottage* site (March–Oct; ☎075881/2268) site, a mile south, reached by making a very sharp turn opposite the telephone box in Sarn Bach; and *Penrhyn Terrace* (Easter–Sept; ☎0758/712285), a mile and a half south following signs to Bwlchtocyn and Marchros.

Abersoch isn't over-endowed with **places to eat**, but there is the moderately priced restaurant and inexpensive bar meals at *St Tudwal's Inn* (☎075871/2539). Bar meals are also the mainstay of two very popular pubs in the district, *The Ship* at Llanbedrog (see "Pwllheli") and the *Sun Inn* at Llanengan, an ancient pub a mile or so southwest of Abersoch, serving great food inside or out in their beer garden, a great late afternoon or evening retreat. For more formal eating, head for the moderate *Neigwl Hotel* (see above), which produces consistently good four-course meals in decent quantities, or the moderately priced *Porth Tocyn* (Easter–Oct; see above), where top class cooking is dished up in the form of short-choice five-course meals and a Sunday buffet lunch. For **snacks**, try the afternoon teas and inexpensive light lunches at *Palm Tea Rooms*, Stryd Fawr, or *The Tasty Food Shop*, Lôn Pen Cei, where you can load up on wholefood pasties and quiches. **Drinking** centres on the three pubs mentioned above and the *Vaynol Arms* on Lôn Pen Cei.

You can rent **sailboards** and kayaks on Town Beach by the hour or by the day, and get reasonably priced instruction in both. Alternatively, rent windsurfers, surfboards and wetsuits from *Abersoch Watersports*, Lôn Pont Morgan (☎0758 71/2483) by the harbour. Throughout the summer, **fishing** trips can be organized through the *Craft and Angling Centre*, The Harbour (☎0766/812646).

Aberdaron and around

Travelling through undulating pasture to the small lime-washed fishing village of **ABERDARON**, two miles short of the tip of the Llŷn, you really feel that you are approaching the end of Wales. The village, now comprising just a few dozen houses, was little more than an inn and a church during the millennium from the sixth century, when it was the last stop on a long journey for pilgrims to Ynys Enlli or Bardsey Island (see below), tucked away around the headland. Just back from the water, the fourteenth-century stone *Y Gegin Fawr* (Great Kitchen) served as the pilgrims' final gathering place before the treacherous crossing, and now operates as a café; the twelfth-century **church of St Hywyn** on the cliffs behind the stony beach still serves its original purpose, and was ministered by Wales' greatest living poet, R.S. Thomas, until his retirement in 1978.

Having made your way out here, it's an idea to use this as a base for exploring the narrow lanes at the end of the peninsula leading to the National Trust property around Mynydd Mawr, the hill overlooking Bardsey Sound, and the cliffs of Braich-y-Pwll, two miles west, where pilgrims departed for Bardsey, near the now-ruined chapel and holy well. Alternatively, head two miles north to the clean, safe and secluded bay of Porth Oer, where the white sands whistle when you walk on them. Some #17 buses run to Rhydlios, half a mile from Porth Oer.

Practicalities

Without your own transport, the only way to get to Aberdaron is to catch the #17 **bus** from Pwllheli, though on Sunday you'll have to hitch.

Accommodation is fairly limited. The cheapest option is *Brynmor* (☎0758/760344; ②), overlooking the bay, a hundred yards up the road to Porth Oer; in the village centre, the *Ty Newydd Hotel* (☎0758/760207; ⑤) offers the most comfortable rooms. If you don't mind being a mile or so outside Aberdaron, *Pennant* (☎0758/760810; ②) makes a good base, especially since you can **rent bikes** there: coming from Pwllheli, turn right at the bottom of the hill, right again after 50 yards, then continue straight on until you see the sign. Continuing on the same road for half a mile and forking right, you came to a very good rural non-smoking guesthouse, *Carreg Plas* (☎0758/760308; ③).

The best and quietest **campsite** around is *Mur Melyn* (no phone; open Easter, Whit, July & Aug) just above Porth Oer, two miles north of Aberdaron. Take the B4413 west, fork right then left at Pen-y-Bont house.

For tea and *bara brith* and light meals, head for the **tearooms** at the back of *Hen Blas Crafts* in the middle of the village. For inexpensive bar snacks and moderately priced **meals**, eat at the *Ty Newydd Hotel* (see above).

Ynys Enlli (Bardsey Island)

Bardsey Island or **Ynys Enlli** (The Island of the Currents), two miles off the tip of the Llŷn, has been an important pilgrimage site since the sixth century, when Saint Cadfan set up the first monastery here: three visits were proclaimed equivalent to one pilgrimage to Rome. Legend claims Bardsey as "The Isle of Twenty Thousand Saints" most likely remembering not saints, but vast numbers of pilgrims who came to die at this holy spot. By the twelfth century, Giraldus Cambrensis was already claiming that "the bodies of a vast number of holy men are buried there" and that "no one dies there except in extreme old age, for disease is almost unheard of". Numerous other stories tell of the burial place of Myrddin (Merlin) and the former Bishop of Bangor, Saint Deiniol, but the only hard evidence is the remaining **bell tower** of the thirteenth-century Augustinian Abbey of St Mary and a few Celtic crosses scattered around it. After the Dissolution of the monasteries in 1536, piracy became the focus of the island's economy for over a century, gradually giving way to agriculture and fishing.

Interesting though the abbey ruins and subsequent buildings are, most visitors come here with a view to bird spotting, peering through binoculars at the dozen or so species of nesting seabirds – manx shearwaters, fulmars, guillemots – and hoping for a glimpse of one of the astounding number of vagrants that turn up after being blown off course by storms.

Other than keen birders, few bother to make the journey since **boats** are dependent on tides, winds and a viable load of passengers; contact the Bardsey Island Trust (☎0766/712239) that often runs a Saturday boat from Pwllheli, or Elwyn Evans (☎0758 83/654 or ☎0758/730654), who runs occasional day trips from Porth Meudwy near Aberdaron. There are a few cottages let by the week (phone the Trust on ☎0766/522239), but no other facilities on the island.

The north Llŷn coast

Sprinkled with small coves and sweeping beaches between rocky bluffs, the **north Llŷn coast** is a dramatic contrast to the busier south. It has no settlements of any size, leaving quieter beaches – Porth Ysgadan by Tudweiliog and Traeth Penllech by Llangwnnadl – easily accessible using the #8 bus from Pwllheli and a short walk.

Nefyn

The only settlements of any size on the north coast are a pair of villages overlooking beautiful sweeping bays. **NEFYN** is the larger, but it doesn't have a lot to recommend it. Holidaymakers bring the most trade now, but you can learn about the village's herring-fishing past in the mildly diverting **Maritime Museum** (July & Aug Mon–Fri 10.30am–12.30pm & 2.30–4.30pm; 50p) inside St Mary's Church. The neighbouring village of **MORFA NEFYN**, a mile to the west, and the adjacent shoreline hamlet of **PORTH DINLLAEN** both benefit from having lost the 1839 battle to become the terminus for ferries to Ireland. A single Parliamentary vote swung the decision in favour of Holyhead (see p.359), thus saving the tiny hamlet of Porth Dinllaen from that town's fate, and leaving a pristine sweeping bay and the popular waterside *Tŷ Coch Inn*, a refreshing place after a day on the beach. To get there, walk a mile west along the beach from Morfa Nefyn.

There are a couple of great low-cost **B&Bs** in Morfa Nefyn, a hundred yards towards the beach from the crossroads in the village: *Trigfan*, Lôn Penrhos, (☎0758/720584; ②), or *Nant Môr* (☎0758/720616; ②), a couple of doors down and with en suite rooms. There's also the summer-only *Greenacres* **campsite**, along the road to Nefyn.

Tre'r Ceiri and the Church of St Beuno

By far the most interesting prehistoric remains on the Llŷn are those of **Tre'r Ceiri** or "Town of the Giants" (unrestricted access) hillfort, five miles east of Nefyn. Crowning the entire rounded top of the second highest of the three Yr Eifl mountains, the hillfort is a massive tumble of rocks, mostly formed into the waist-high walls of about 150 dry-stone hut circles, huddling together from the wind and encircled by a rampart twelve feet high in places. Archeological evidence indicates summer habitation here since the Bronze Age, but the huts are probably only a couple of thousand years old. Locals refer to them as *Cytiau Gwyddelod* or Irishmen's Huts, possibly recalling the Irish immigrant population on the Llŷn in the first few centuries AD, when five hundred people lived on this inhospitable site. Today the ruins command a stunning view over the whole peninsula.

The #223 bus passes the base of the main path up, which leads off the B4417 a mile west of Llanaelhaearn, and can be reached by the hourly bus #12 from Pwllheli. The steep path makes for a saddle, then bears right reaching Tre'r Ceiri in under half an hour.

The path to Tre'r Ceiri is also the approach route to the tops of the other two peaks, from where you can look down into Vortigern's valley and the **Nant Gwrtheyrn National Language Centre** (☎0758/750334), in a couple of rows of converted granite quarry cottages. Reached down a narrow track from Llithfaen, three miles east of Nefyn, the centre holds residential courses entirely in Welsh, runs a café and has explanatory leaflets (75p) for its three-mile nature trail.

The last worthwhile stop on the #12 bus route to Caernarfon is **CLYNNOG-FAWR**, where the early sixteenth-century **Church of St Beuno** is built on foundations laid by Saint Beuno in the sixth century. An important stop for pilgrims heading for Ynys Enlli (see above), the present interior still has a spartan monastic interior of whitewash and limestone flags, but also a fine hammerbeam roof with ornamental bosses and a chancel with well-worn misericordes.

travel details

Frequencies for trains are for Monday to Saturday services; Sunday averages 1–3 services.

Trains

Aberdyfi to: Barmouth (8 daily; 30min); Birmingham (6 daily; 3hr); Machynlleth (9 daily; 25min); Porthmadog (8 daily; 1hr 15min); Pwllheli (8 daily; 1hr 40min); Tywyn (8 daily; 5min).

Aberystwyth to: Birmingham (5 daily; 3hr); Borth (9 daily; 12min); Machynlleth (9 daily; 30min); Shrewsbury (6 daily; 2hr); Welshpool (6 daily; 1hr 25min).

Barmouth to: Aberdyfi (9 daily; 30min); Birmingham (6 daily; 3hr 30min); Harlech (8 daily; 25min); Machynlleth (9 daily; 55min); Porthmadog (8 daily, 45min); Pwllheli (8 daily; 1hr 10min).

Cricieth to: Aberdyfi (8 daily; 1hr 25min); Birmingham (5 daily; 4hr 45min); Machynlleth (8 daily; 1hr 50min); Porthmadog (8 daily; 10min); Tywyn (8 daily; 1hr 20min).

Harlech to: Aberdyfi (8 daily; 55min); Barmouth (8 daily; 25min); Birmingham (5 daily; 4hr 15min); Cricieth (8 daily; 30min); Machynlleth (8 daily; 1hr 20min); Porthmadog (8 daily; 20min).

Machynlleth to: Aberdyfi (6 daily; 20min); Aberystwyth (9 daily; 30min); Barmouth (6 daily; 55min); Birmingham (5 daily; 2hr 30min); Dyfi Junction (6 daily; 7min); Harlech (5 daily; 1hr 20min); Pwllheli (5 daily; 2hr); Shrewsbury (6 daily; 1hr 30min); Tywyn (6 daily; 25min); Welshpool (6 daily; 55min).

Porthmadog to: Barmouth (8 daily; 45min); Birmingham (5 daily; 4hr 35min); Blaenau Ffestiniog by Ffestiniog Railway (Easter–Oct 4–10 daily; 1hr); Cricieth (8 daily; 10min); Harlech (8 daily; 20min); Machynlleth (8 daily; 1hr 40min); Pwllheli (8 daily; 25min).

Pwllheli to: Aberdyfi (8 daily; 1hr 40min); Birmingham (5 daily; 5hr); Cricieth (8 daily; 15min); Harlech (8 daily; 45min); Machynlleth (8 daily; 2hr 5min); Porthmadog (8 daily; 25min).

Tywyn to: Aberdyfi (8 daily; 5min); Barmouth (8 daily; 25min); Birmingham (6 daily; 3hr 5min); Cricieth (8 daily; 1hr 20min); Harlech (8 daily; 50min); Machynlleth (8 daily; 30min); Porthmadog (8 daily; 1hr 10min); Pwllheli (8 daily; 1hr 35min).

Buses

Aberaeron to: Aberystwyth (hourly; 40min); Carmarthen (3 daily; 1hr 45min); Lampeter (5 daily; 35min); New Quay (hourly; 20min).

Aberdaron to: Pwllheli (7 daily Mon–Sat; 40min).

Aberdyfi to: Machynlleth (6 daily Mon–Sat; 25min); Tywyn (10 daily Mon–Sat; 10min).

Aberystwyth to: Aberaeron (hourly; 40min); Borth (hourly Mon–Sat; 25min); Caernarfon (5 daily; 2hr 40min); Cardigan (hourly; 2hr); Carmarthen (6 daily; 2hr 35min); Devil's Bridge (2 daily; 40min); Dolgellau (4 daily; 1hr 15min); Lampeter (5 daily; 1hr 25min); Machynlleth (6 daily; 45min); New Quay (hourly; 1hr); Ponterwyd (7 daily Mon–Sat; 30min); Pontrhydfendigaid (3 daily Mon–Sat; 55min); Tregaron (4 daily Mon–Sat; 50min); Ynyslas (11 daily Mon–Sat; 30min).

Barmouth to: Bala (6 daily, 2 Sun in summer; 1hr); Blaenau Ffestiniog (4–6 daily Mon–Sat; 1hr); Dolgellau (14 daily, 2 Sun; 20min); Harlech (9 daily Mon–Sat; 25min).

Cardigan to: Aberaeron (hourly; 1hr 20min); Aberporth (hourly; 55min); Aberystwyth (hourly; 2hr); Carmarthen (hourly Mon–Sat; 1hr 30min); Drefach Felindre (8 daily Mon–Sat; 30min); Fishguard (hourly Mon–Sat; 50min); Haverfordwest (hourly Mon–Sat; 1hr 35min); Newcastle Emlyn (hourly Mon–Sat; 25min); Newport (hourly Mon–Sat; 30min); New Quay (hourly; 1hr).

Cricieth to: Blaenau Ffestiniog (every 30min, 3–4 Sun; 40min); Caernarfon (4 daily Mon–Sat; 45min); Porthmadog (every 30min, 3–4 Sun; 10min); Pwllheli (every 30min, 4 Sun; 20min).

Dolgellau to: Aberystwyth (6 daily, 2 Sun; 1hr 15min); Bala (6 daily, 3 Sun in summer; 35min); Barmouth (14 daily, 2 Sun; 20min); Blaenau Ffestiniog (3 daily Mon–Sat; 50min); Caernarfon (7 daily; 1hr 40min); Cardiff (1 daily; 5hr 50min); Fairbourne (5 daily Mon–Sat; 20min); Llangollen (6 daily, 3 Sun in summer; 1hr 30min); Machynlleth (7 daily, 2 Sun; 35min); Porthmadog (6 daily, 2 Sun; 50min); Tywyn (6 daily Mon–Sat; 50min); Wrexham (6 daily, 1 Sun; 2hr).

Fairbourne to: Dolgellau (5 daily Mon–Sat; 20min); Tywyn (5 daily Mon–Sat; 35min).

Harlech to: Barmouth (9 daily Mon–Sat; 25min); Blaenau Ffestiniog (6 daily Mon–Sat; 35min).

Lampeter to: Aberaeron (5 daily; 35min); Aberystwyth (5 daily; 1hr 25min); Carmarthen (6 daily Mon–Sat; 1hr 10min); Cenarth (10 daily Mon–Sat; 20min); Llanddewi Brefi (4 daily Mon–Sat; 25min); Machynlleth (1 daily; 2hr 25min); Pontrhydfendigaid (Wed & Sat 3 buses; 45min); Tregaron (4 daily Mon–Sat; 30min).

Machynlleth to: Aberdyfi (6 daily Mon–Sat; 25min); Aberystwyth (6 daily, 2 Sun; 40min); Bala (6 daily, 1 Sun; 1hr 20min); Caernarfon (5 daily; 2hr); Cardiff (1 daily; 5hr 15min); Carmarthen (1 daily; 3hr 10min); Corris (10 daily; 12min); Corwen (6 daily, 1 Sun; 2hr 35min); Dolgellau (7 daily, 2 Sun; 35min); Lampeter (1 daily; 2hr 25min); Llangollen (6 daily, 1 Sun; 2hr 55min); Newtown (3 daily Mon–Sat; 1hr 5min); Porthmadog (5 daily, 2 Sun; 1hr 45min); Swansea (1 daily; 4hr); Tywyn (10 daily Mon–Sat; 35–45min); Wrexham (6 daily, 3 Sun in summer; 3hr 20min).

Nefyn to: Pwllheli (11 daily Mon–Sat; 20min).

New Quay to: Aberaeron (hourly; 20min); Aberporth (hourly; 40min); Aberystwyth (hourly; 1hr); Cardigan (hourly; 1hr); Carmarthen (5 daily Mon–Sat; 1hr 40min); Tre-saith (hourly; 35min).

Porthmadog to: Beddgelert (6 daily, 2 Sun in summer; 30min); Blaenau Ffestiniog (every 30min, 3–4 Sun; 30min); Caernarfon (23 daily, 2–3 Sun; 45min); Cardiff (1 daily; 6hr 40min); Cricieth (every 30min, 3–4 Sun; 10min); Dolgellau (6 daily, 2 Sun; 50min); Machynlleth (5 daily, 2 Sun; 1hr 45min); Pwllheli (every 30min, 3 Sun; 40min).

Pwllheli to: Aberdaron (7 daily Mon–Sat; 40min); Abersoch (20 daily Mon–Sat; 15–50min); Blaenau Ffestiniog (every 30min, 3 Sun in summer; 1hr 10min); Caernarfon (roughly hourly, four Sun; 50min); Chester (1 daily; 4hr); Cricieth (every 30min, 3 Sun; 20min); Liverpool (1 daily; 5hr); Llandudno (1 daily; 1hr 25min); Manchester (1 daily; 6hr); Nefyn (11 daily Mon–Sat; 20min); Porthmadog (every 30min, 3 Sun; 40min).

Tywyn to: Abordyfi (10 daily Mon–Sat; 10min); Abergynolwyn (4 daily Mon–Sat; 15min); Corris (4 daily Mon–Sat; 30min); Dolgellau (6 daily Mon–Sat; 50min); Fairbourne (6 daily Mon–Sat; 35min); Machynlleth (10 daily Mon–Sat; 35–45min).

CHAPTER FIVE

THE DEE VALLEY AND SNOWDONIA

Trapped between the brash coastal resorts in the north and the thinly inhabited hill tracts of mid-Wales to the south lies a mountainous strip of land stretching up the Dee Valley and into Snowdonia. Its eastern edge forms part of the Marches, a broad swathe of countryside running the full length of the England–Wales border and notable for its profusion of castles. Though **Chirk Castle** is the only significant, extant Marcher fortress, it remains a potent reminder of the centuries after the Norman conquest of England, when powerful barons fought the Welsh princes for control of these fertile lands. Today they remain pastoral, with the exception of the area around the industrial town of **Wrexham**.

The **Dee Valley** remained more firmly Welsh than the Marches, and three hundred years after the arrival of the Normans was the first big revolt against them. From his base near **Corwen**, Wales' greatest hero, Owain Glyndŵr, attacked the property of a nearby English landowner, sparking a fourteen-year campaign which, at its height, saw Glyndŵr ruling most of Wales by means of Parliaments held on the Cambrian coast (see *The Cambrian Coast*, p.224). Little remains in the valley to commemorate the era, and most people drive through oblivious of its heritage. **Llangollen** is the valley's main draw, with an international folk music festival each July and a broad selection of ruins, rides and rambles to tempt visitors throughout the rest of the year. There's more to detain you here than anywhere east of what is – for most people – north Wales' crowning glory, **Snowdonia**. This tightly packed bundle of soaring cliff faces, jagged peaks and plunging waterfalls measures little more than ten miles by ten, but packs enough mountain paths to keep even the most jaded walking enthusiast happy for weeks. The last Ice Age left a legacy of peaks ringed by cwms – huge hemispherical bites out of the mountainsides – while the ranges were left separated by steep-sided valleys, a challenge for even the most fly-footed climber. Even if lakeside ambles and rides on anti-

ACCOMMODATION PRICE CODES

Throughout this guide, hotel and B&B accommodation is priced on a scale of ① to ⑨. Category ① only applies to youth hostels; for the rest, the number indicates the **lowest price** you could expect to pay per night for a **double room in high season**. The prices indicated by the codes are as follows:

① under £20/$32	④ £40–50/$64–80	⑦ £70–80/$112–128
② £20–30/$32–48	⑤ £50–60/$80–96	⑧ £80–100/$128–160
③ £30–40/$48–64	⑥ £60–70/$96–112	⑨ over £100/$160

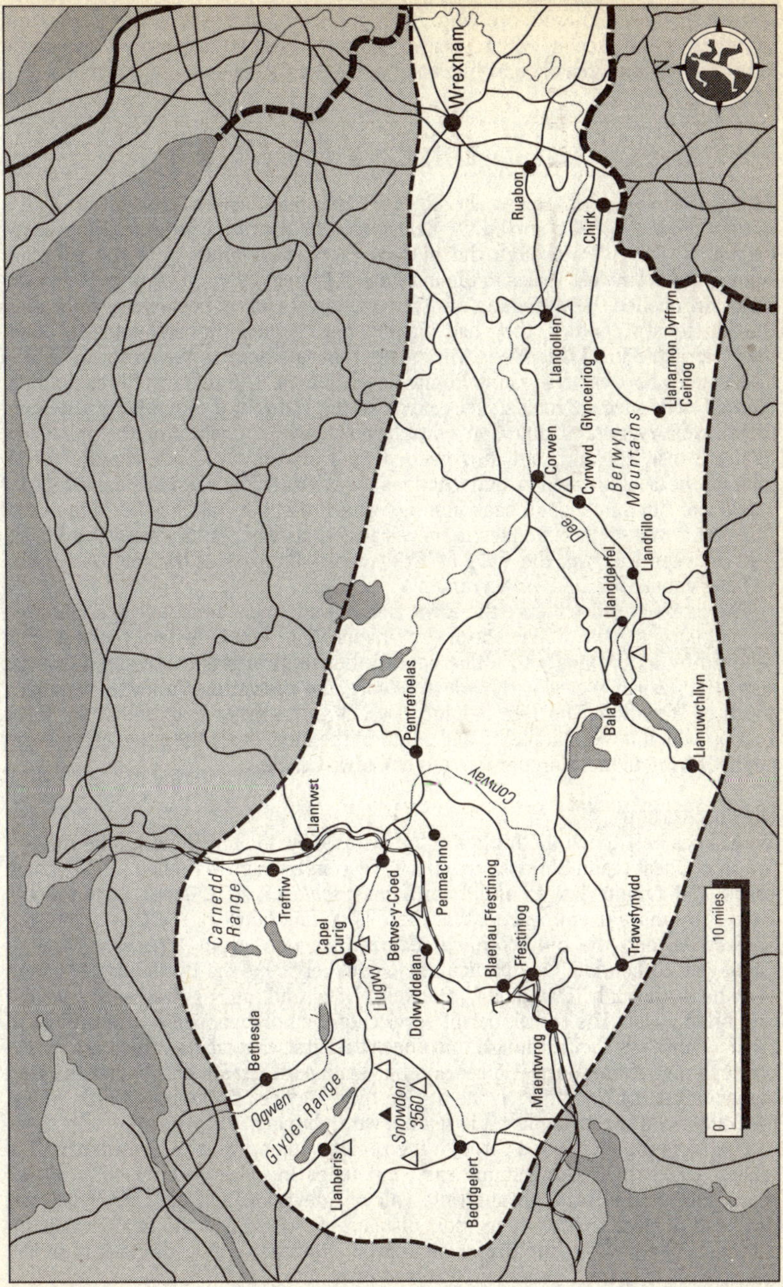

N
Wrexham
Ruabon
Chirk
Llangollen
Llanarmon Dyffryn Ceiriog
Glynceiriog
Corwen
Cynwyd
Berwyn Mountains
Dee
Llandrillo
Llandderfel
Bala
Llanuwchllyn
Pentrefoelas
Conway
Llanrwst
Trefriw
Carnedd Range
Capel Curig
Betws-y-Coed
Penmachno
Llugwy
Dolwyddelan
Blaenau Ffestiniog
Ffestiniog
Trawsfynydd
Bethesda
Ogwen
Glyder Range
Snowdon 3560
Llanberis
Beddgelert
Maentwrog
0
10 miles

quated steam trains are more your style, you can't fail to appreciate the natural grandeur of the scenery which occasionally reveals an atmospheric Welsh castle ruin or decaying piece of quarrying equipment.

THE DEE VALLEY

Llangollen, along with the smaller towns of Bala and Corwen, grew up partly as a market centre, but also served the needs of cattle drovers who used the passage carved by the river through the hills as the easiest route from the fattening grounds of northwest Wales to the markets in England. Long before rail and road transport pushed the dwindling numbers of drovers out of business at the end of the nineteenth century, they had already been joined by early tourists. Most made straight for Llangollen, where the ruins of both a Welsh castle and a Cistercian abbey lent a gaunt Romantic charm to a dramatic gorge naturally blessed with surging rapids. The arrival of the train, in the middle of the nineteenth century, made Llangollen a firm favourite with tourists from the mill towns of northwest England, but also opened up **Corwen** and **Bala**, market towns making the best of the new opportunities for income. The train line closed in the 1960s and Corwen slipped back into its former role, but Bala has become one of Wales' top watersports venues, a mecca for windsurfing and whitewater kayaking. Between the two, the **Vale of Edeyrnion** slumbers at the foot of the fine walking country of the Berwyn range.

The final few miles before the River Dee flows into the sea form an arc around the anglicized town of **Wrexham**. Its unappealing light-industrial tenor is only relieved by its proximity to a fine country house incongruously lodged in what was briefly north Wales' early industrial core, the **Clywedog Valley**. Seven miles south of Wrexham, the Dee is joined by one of its major tributaries, the River Ceiriog which flows, parallel to and south of the Dee, down the peaceful valley of **Glyn Ceiriog** to the Marcher fortress of **Chirk Castle**.

Getting around

Train lines only touch the fringes of the Dee Valley: the line between the English towns of Chester and Shrewsbury cuts a crescent through Wrexham, Ruabon and Chirk, and a minor line from the north coast makes it as far south as Wrexham. **Buses** are more useful, except that there is no link between the Dee Valley and Snowdonia, and the only *National Express* run goes from Wrexham through Llangollen to London. One particularly useful service is the two-hourly #94 from Wrexham through Llangollen, Corwen, Bala and on to Dolgellau on the Cambrian coast. The remainder of services are amply mapped out in the *Clwyd Public Transport Guide*, though this doesn't include timetables, which are available separately from tourist offices and bus stations. *Crosville* buses offer the **Day Rover** ticket (£4.70) valid for one day on their services throughout north Wales, but unless you're moving fast it is seldom worth buying.

The A5 is the main **road** through the region running west to Snowdonia. This makes access to the mountains easy, but tends to force **cyclists** onto quieter roads such as the B4401 through the Vale of Edeyrnion, and the narrow lanes at the head of Glyn Ceiriog. The short distances involved and the heavy traffic on the main roads make **hitching** a viable way of circumventing the lack of public transport linking the Dee Valley to Snowdonia.

Wrexham and the Clwedog Valley

If **WREXHAM** (Wrecsam) is your introduction to Wales, don't be disappointed. It certainly isn't pretty, nor is it characteristically Welsh. George Borrow walked here from Chester in 1854 and observed "its appearance is not Welsh – its inhabitants have neither the look nor the language of Welshmen". At that time it still hadn't been granted its charter, which it earned three years later in recognition of its increasing commercial importance, predominantly in brick and tile manufacture. Industry was not new to the area, the Clywedog Valley (see below), a couple of miles to the south, playing a key role in the early part of the Industrial Revolution and recently being rejuvenated as one of the town's two chief attractions.

The Town

The town's main attraction – apart from the Clywedog Valley – is **St Giles' Church** (Easter–Oct Mon–Fri 10am–4pm; free), its Gothic tower gracefully rising above the kernel of small lanes at the end of Hope Street. Topped off with a steeple in the 1520s, the tower's five distinct levels, stepping up to four hexagonal pinnacles, is replicated at Yale University in the USA in homage to the ancestral home of the college's benefactor, Elihu Yale, whose tomb is here at the base. The engraved stone in the tower wall near Yale's grave came from Yale University, the one it replaced now holding up the replica tower at Yale. The church's spacious interior is mainly of interest for the remains of the late fifteenth-century wall painting of *The Last Judgement* above the entrance to the chancel, and the monument to Mary Myddleton of Chirk Castle by French sculptor Louis Roubiliac. All this is approached through wrought-iron gates installed by the famed Welsh ironworkers Robert and John Davies of Bersham between 1718 and 1724, who also wrought the striking gates at Chirk Castle (see below).

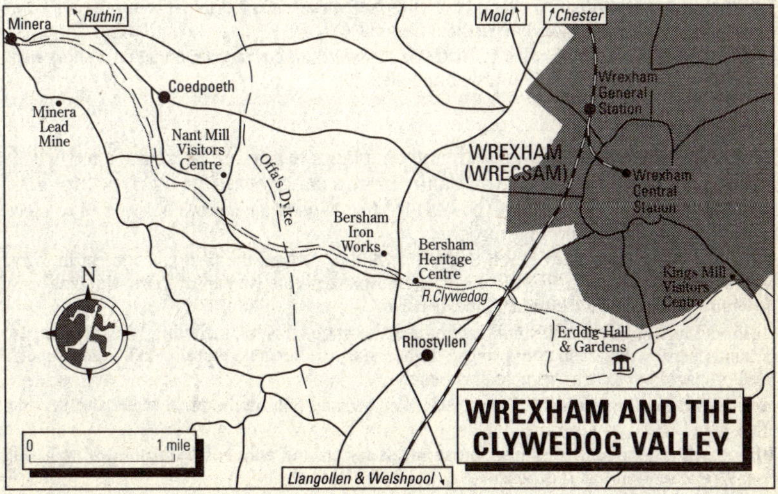

Before heading for the Clywedog Valley or Llangollen, spend twenty minutes in the small but informative **Wrexham Heritage Centre**, 47–49 King St (Mon–Sat 10am–5pm; free), which displays local history, concentrating on the town's nineteenth-century boomtime years.

Practicalities

Wrexham has two **train stations**, half a mile apart. Chester, Chirk and Shrewsbury trains call only at Wrexham General on Mold Road, ten minutes' walk northwest of the centre, while those from Liverpool (change at Bidston on the Wirral line) call at General then at Wrexham Central in Hill Street, right in the middle of town. Part way along Hope Street, King Street branches off left to the **bus station** where *National Express* buses (tickets from *Key Travel*, King St) arrive from Manchester, London or Glasgow and **local buses** leave frequently to Chester, Llangollen and Mold. For information, make for the **tourist office**, Lambpit St (Mon–Sat 10am–5pm; Oct–Easter closes 4pm; ☎0978/292015), reached by turning left where Hope Street takes a turn to the right.

Accommodation

Abbotsfield Priory Hotel, 29 Rhosddu Rd (☎0978/261211). Very comfortable hotel with en suite rooms, converted from an old priory. Follow Regent Street towards Wrexham General, then turn right into Grosvenor Road. ④.

Bodidris Hall, one mile northeast of Llandegla (☎0978/88434). For a little secluded luxury, you can't go far wrong at this largely Tudor place on the moors, ten miles west of Wrexham and a similar distance north of Llangollen on the A5104. ④.

Grove Guesthouse, 36 Chester Rd (☎0978/354288). Reasonably priced guesthouse with a couple of pricier en suite rooms. ③.

Hafod Wen Farm, Bersham, three miles west of Wrexham on the B5426 (☎0978/757343). The best place to camp is at this basic site a mile south of Minera.

Hampson Guesthouse, 6 Chester Rd (☎0978/357665). Budget guesthouse five minutes' walk north of the tourist office. ②.

Lyndhurst Guesthouse, 3 Gerald St (☎0978/290802). Comfortable, central rooms off Grosvenor Road going towards Wrexham General. ③.

Monfa Guesthouse, 65 Ruabon Rd (☎0978/354888). Low-cost accommodation a short walk from the centre on the A5152 towards Llangollen. ②.

Eating and drinking

Wrexham isn't over-endowed with notable places to **eat**, but there are a few worth trying, along with cheap cafés on Bank Street, a narrow passage off Hope Street.

Bumble, 2 Charles St. This café above a gift shop is good for sandwiches as well as more substantial fare. Closed Sun. Inexpensive.

Cloisters Wine Bar, 7–9 Church St (☎0978/290910). About the best place to eat in town, with bistro-style meals during the day in the downstairs café, and an upstairs wine bar open on Thursday to Saturday evenings. Inexpensive.

Golden Lion, High St. Noisy pub serving a wide range of beers, including Wrexham Lager, Britain's earliest lager, first brewed in 1882, using the town's naturally soft water supply. Well-prepared bar meals available. Inexpensive.

Horse and Jockey, Hope St. Characterful low-beamed pub on the main street also serving Wrexham Lager.

Plas Coch, Plas Coch Rd. Three-course meals for around a fiver, fifteen-minutes' walk out past Wrexham General. Inexpensive.

Victorian Tea Rooms, 11 Town Hill, near St Giles' Church. The best place in town for tea and cakes. Inexpensive.

The Clywedog Valley

Forming an arc around the western and southern suburbs of Wrexham, the **Clywedog Valley** was the crucible of industrial success in the northern Welsh borders during the eighteenth century. Iron was the principle activity, but as the Industrial Revolution forged ahead, water power harnessed from the Clywedog became less important, and factories moved closer to their raw materials, leaving the valley barely disturbed. Though a considerable amount of work is still underway, the valley has been turned into a series of attractions linked by the seven-mile-long **Clywedog Trail**. It is all a bit heavy on packaged heritage, but no less interesting for that, and you can see all the sights in one long, varied day. With the exception of Minera and Nant Mill, all the sites are within a couple of miles of the centre of Wrexham, and can be visited without resorting to buses, but the easiest way to see the whole valley is to catch the #10 or #11 which run from Wrexham to Minera, walking right along to King's Mill then catching the #31 the mile or so back into Wrexham. You can also catch the #2B bus to or from the Bersham Heritage Centre and the #37 to Erddig Hall from General Station.

The **Minera Lead Mines** (Easter–Sept Tues–Sun 10am–5pm; 80p), four miles west of Wrexham, is the latest to get the heritage treatment. Currently there isn't a lot to see, but its engine house has been largely rebuilt and awaits a replica beam-engine. Many of the surface workings are still incompletely excavated, but the small museum in the former ore house helps clarify the layout. You get a far better impression from the viewing platform overlooking the hillside which, in the eighteenth century, was covered with mines extracting galena, a silver-and-zinc-rich lead ore from the bottom of shafts over 1200 feet deep.

From the lead mines, a path leads for almost a mile east along the River Clywedog to the wildlife and local history centre at **Nant Mill** (Easter–Oct Tues–Sun 10am–5pm; Nov–Easter Sat & Sun 10am–4pm; free), where you can pick up leaflets for nature trails leading to a very visible section of **Offa's Dyke** (see p.192) in the woods nearby. The Clywedog Trail runs through the wood to **Bersham Ironworks** (Easter–Sept Mon–Fri 10am–5pm, Sat & Sun noon–5pm; £1), established in the seventeenth century for making cannon for Royalists during the Civil War. Cumbrian ironmaster John "Iron-mad" Wilkinson set up business here and, in 1775, patented his new method for horizontally boring out cylinders. This produced the first truly circular, smooth bore, perfect for highly accurate cannon – hundreds were made here for the American Civil and Napoleonic wars – and the production of fine tolerance steam engine cylinders. Engineer James Watt was a big customer: he produced steam engines which made water-powered sites unprofitable and eventually put Bersham out of business. After nearly two centuries of neglect, the remains are now being unearthed, revealing a broad area of mostly knee-high foundations around the centrepiece, the old foundry. This survived largely intact after being turned into a corn mill and still retains the waterwheel that probably drove the foundry bellows. The foundations really only serve to help you visualize the layout, which is better explained inside the old foundry and put in context ten minutes' walk away at the **Bersham Heritage Centre** (Easter–Oct Mon–Fri 10am–5pm, Sat & Sun noon–5pm; Nov–Easter closes 4pm; free), which has a room dedicated to Wilkinson.

Erddig Hall

Despite the closure of the ironworks, coal continued to be mined at Bersham up until 1986. After World War II, coal tunnels were pushed under seventeenth-century **Erddig Hall** (April–Sept daily except Thurs & Fri 11am–5pm; Oct–March "below stairs" and grounds only; full tour £5, "below stairs" and gardens £3.20; NT), adding subsidence to the troubles of an already decaying building. Ever since the mansion was built just south of Wrexham in the late seventeenth century, its owners – all seemingly called Simon or Philip Yorke – maintained a conservative building policy which resulted in near decrepitude. The National Trust took charge in the 1920s and have restored the house to its 1922 appearance and returned the jungle of a garden to its formal eighteenth-century plan.

The house itself isn't distinguished, as eighteenth-century architects James Wyatt and Thomas Hopper were tightly reined when suggesting alterations. The State Rooms upstairs have their share of fine furniture and portraits – including one by Gainsborough of the first Philip Yorke – but any interest really lies in the quarters of the servants, whose lives were fully documented by their unusually benevolent masters. Portraits of the servants painted in the eighteenth- and early nineteenth-centuries are still on display in the Servants' Hall, and each has a verse written by one of the Yorkes, not noted for their poetic prowess, but whose extraordinary devotion to their servants is touching. You can also see the blacksmith's shop, lime yard, stables, laundry, the still-used bakehouse and kitchen.

From Erddig Hall, you can catch the #37 bus back to Wrexham, or walk the two miles back to the town past the *Squire Yorke Inn*, half a mile or so northeast of the Hall. If you have never seen corn being milled and want to, continue along the Trail to **King's Mill Visitor Centre** (Easter–Sept Tues–Sun 10am–5pm; Oct, Feb & March Sat & Sun only; 80p).

Chirk and Glyn Ceiriog

Seven miles south of Wrexham, the busy Dee valley cuts west towards Snowdonia, a great contrast to the valley of the **River Ceiriog**, which runs parallel to the Dee a couple of miles further south, a tranquil stretch that's occasionally – and very optimistically – promoted as the "Little Switzerland of Wales".

Chirk Castle

The valley's entrance is guarded by the massive drum-towered **Chirk Castle** (April–Sept daily except Mon & Sat noon–5pm; Oct Sat & Sun noon–5pm; NT; £4; NT), squatting ominously on a rise half a mile to the west of **CHIRK** (Y Waun). Roger Mortimer began the construction of this Marcher fortress at the behest of Edward I during the thirteenth century, and it eventually fell to the Myddleton family, who have lived here for the past 400 years. The approach to the castle is guarded by a magnificent Baroque gatescreen, the finest work done by the Davies brothers of Bersham, who wrought it between 1712 and 1719. The ebullient floral designs are capped by the Myddleton coat of arms, with a pair of wolves reproduced atop the cage-like gateposts (perhaps a memorial to one of the last wolves in Wales, said to have kept watch over the moat in the 1680s). From the gates, a mile-and-a-half-long avenue of oak leads up to the castle, an austere-looking place, softened only by the mullioned windows. The original plan was probably to mimic Beaumaris castle (see p.352), and building started just a couple of months earlier, but it lacks Beaumaris's purity and symmetry. The east and west walls are both incomplete, stopping at the half-round towers midway along the planned length, and the towers have been cut down to wall level, probably after the Civil War, when taller towers would have been vulnerable to mortar attack. Internal modifications have been no less extensive, leaving a legacy of sumptuous rooms reflecting sixteenth- to nineteenth-century tastes, many returned to their former states after some Victorian meddling by Pugin in the 1840s.

After touring the house, you should try to leave an hour spare to explore the beautiful ornamental gardens or to trace the section of Offa's Dyke that runs across the front of the house, though it was flattened in 1758 for use as a cart track.

Glyn Ceiriog

One thing you won't see from the castle is the Shropshire Union Canal – the Myddletons made sure that they wouldn't have to watch dirty barge-loads of coal drifting across their park by forcing engineer Thomas Telford to build the canal underground. You can see the canal cross the towering 1801 aqueduct seventy feet above the Ceiriog River, which runs beside the road for five miles to the village of **GLYN CEIRIOG**, home to the **Chwarel Wynne Slate Mine** (Easter–Oct daily 10am–5pm; £2.50), a former mine now open to the admission-paying public. The half-hour underground tour and tatty museum are engagingly low-key, but if you are making for Snowdonia, you'd be better to save your money for the more spectacular tours under Blaenau Ffestiniog (see p.289). If you want to stay nearby, there is the *Glyn Valley Hotel* (☎0691/72210; ③) in the centre of the village, and *The Woolpack Inn* (☎0691/72382; ④), just beyond the *Ddol-Hir* (☎0691/718681) **campsite**.

Llanarmon Dyffryn Ceiriog

It's another four miles to the even smaller but more appealing **LLANARMON DYFFRYN CEIRIOG**, a village consisting of nothing but a church, a post office, and some excellent, if pricy, accommodation at either the *West Arms* (☎0691/76665; ⑧), or across the road at the *Hand Hotel* (☎0691/76666; ⑦), both serving very good, but expensive, meals in their restaurants, snacks in the bars and drinks around open fires. If your budget doesn't stretch that far, the non-smoking *Gwynfa* (closed Dec & Jan; ☎0691/76287; ②), and the marginally cheaper *Ty Gwyn* (☎0691/76229; ②), are both good options catering to walkers keen on exploring the Berwyn Range (see p.275) behind. Both serve inexpensive evening meals.

From Llanarmon Dyffryn Ceiriog, you can link up with the walk described on p275, by taking the road heading northwest opposite the church. After five miles, you reach the memorial stone mentioned.

Llangollen and around

LLANGOLLEN, ten miles southwest of Wrexham, is in both setting and character the embodiment of a Welsh town, clasped tightly in the narrow Dee valley between the shoulders of the Berwyn and Eglwyseg mountains. Along the valley's floor, the waters of the River Dee (Afon Dyfrdwy) run down to the town, licking the angled buttresses of the weighty Gothic bridge, which has spanned the river since the fourteenth century. On its south bank, half a dozen streets, their houses harmoniously straggling up the rugged hillsides, are labelled in both Welsh and English, and form the core of the scattered settlement flung out across the low hills.

As the only river crossing point for miles, Llangollen was an important town long before the early Romantics arrived at the end of the eighteenth century, when they were cut off from their European Grand Tours by the Napoleonic Wars. Turner came to paint the swollen river and the Cistercian ruin of **Valle Crucis**, a couple of miles up the valley; John Ruskin found the town "entirely lovely in its gentle wildness"; and writer George Borrow made Llangollen his base for the early part of his 1854 tour detailed in *Wild Wales*. The rich and famous came not just for the scenery, but to visit the celebrated **Ladies of Llangollen**, an eccentric pair of lesbians who became the toast of society from their house, **Plas Newydd**. But by this stage some of the town's rural charm had been eaten up by the works of one of the century's finest engineers, Thomas Telford, squeezing both his **London–Holyhead trunk road** and the **Llangollen Canal** alongside the river. Trips along the canal run either east to his majestic nineteen-span **Pontcysyllte Aqueduct** over the Dee, or west beside the rail line,

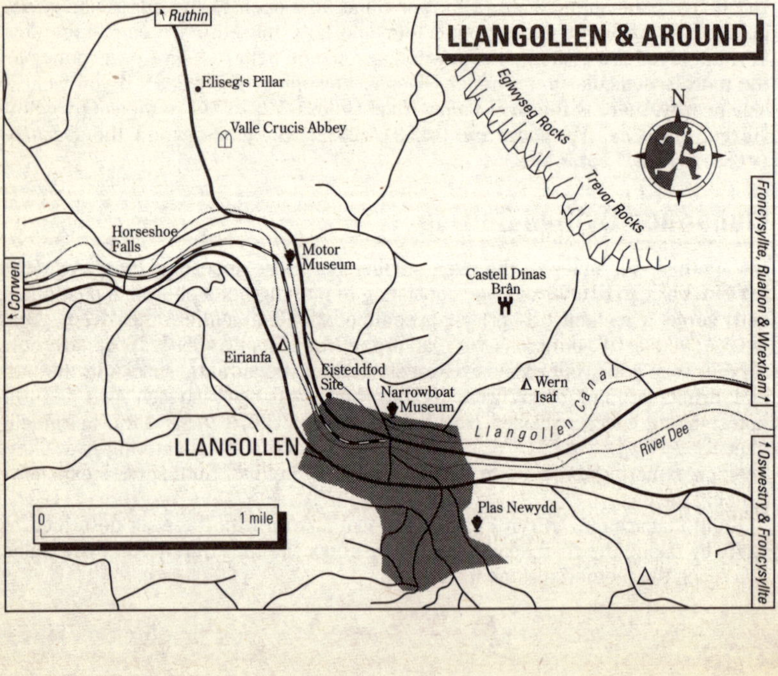

which now operates steam-hauled pleasure trips. If none of this is energetic enough, try the panoramic day-long walk along the limestone escarpment to the north of town (see p.270).

The dozen or so functional-looking streets can seem little different from any other Welsh town, but its rural environs are home to a wealth of historical sites, making this a very popular base throughout the summer, particularly in early July when the town struggles to cope with the thousands of visitors to Wales' celebration of worldwide folk music, the **International Music Eisteddfod** (see p.269).

Arrival, information and getting around

Buses are the only form of public transport to reach Llangollen, with local buses (and the daily Wrexham–London *National Express* service) stopping on Market Street. The nearest **train station** is five miles away at Ruabon, and passed by frequent buses on the Llangollen–Wrexham run. With your own vehicle, the most spectacular way to approach Llangollen is over the 1350-foot Horseshoe Pass (A542) from Ruthin.

The **tourist office** (Easter–Oct daily 9am–6pm; Nov–Easter 9.30am–5pm; ☎0978/860828) is fifty yards from the bridge and less than a hundred yards from the bus stop on Market Street. **Buses** in the immediate locality are very infrequent, so you might as well resign yourself to **walking** everywhere – not unpleasant since Valle Crucis, the most distant sight, is only a mile and a half along the towpath.

For the energetic, **mountain bikes** can be rented from *Llansports*, Abbey Road, just by the bridge (☎0978/860605), for around £15 per day, with all the kit, and a right-of-way route map; you can also take half-hour open **canoe rides** (☎0978/861444) down the rapids below Mile End Mill, half a mile towards Corwen on the A5, for around £5 each including tuition.

Accommodation

Finding **rooms** in Llangollen can be a chore in the middle of summer, especially during the Eisteddfod, though this is alleviated by people letting out one or two bedrooms in the peak period. The tourist office can book you into these as well as ordinary guesthouses. These are dotted all over the valley, though many of the cheaper ones are on Hill Street heading up towards Plas Newydd.

Hotels and guesthouses

Bryn Howel Hotel and Restaurant, Trevor, two miles east off the A539 (☎0978/860331). Country house hotel with gym, sauna, top class moderately priced table d'hôte meals, and expensive à la carte dishes. Some cheaper two-night deals. ⑦.

Cefn-y-Fedw, Garth, Trevor (☎0978/823403). Excellent non-smoking farmhouse B&B five miles from Llangollen. Take the A539 to Trevor then left at the *Australia Arms* and continue straight ahead, following signs for Penycae. Closed Nov–April. ③.

Gales, 18 Bridge St (☎0978/861427). Comfortable guesthouse above a wonderful restaurant. En suite rooms with TV and Laura Ashley decor. ④.

Hafren, Berwyn St (☎0978/860939). Good non-smoking B&B with no supplement for singles, a few steps along the A5 towards Corwen. ③.

Hillcrest, Hill St (☎0978/860208). Convenient, licensed, non-smoking guesthouse serving evening meals on request. ③.

Mrs Lewis, 1 Bodwen Villas, Hill St (☎0978/860882). Bargain B&B close to the centre of town. ②.

Mrs Adams, 2–3 Aberadda Cottages, Hill St (☎0978/860770). One of the cheapest central B&Bs. Non-smoking. ②.

The Old Vicarage, Bryn Howell Lane (☎0978/823018). Country guesthouse by the Dee four miles from Llangollen. Take the A5 east, turn left at *Aqueduct Inn*, then left after the bridge. ②.

The Royal Hotel, Bridge St (☎0978/860331). An excellent nineteenth-century place by the bridge in town. ⑥.

Hostel and campsites

Eirianfa (☎0978/860919). Basic campsite a mile west of the town on the A5.

Llangollen youth hostel, Tyndwr Rd (☎0978/860330). High-standard YHA hostel in a Victorian manor a mile and a half from town – go half a mile along the A5 towards Shrewsbury, right up Birch Hill, then right again. Open all day. ①.

Wern Isaf Farm (☎0978/860632). Simple campsite just under a mile up Wern Road. Turn right over the canal on Wharf Hill.

The Town

Standing in twelve acres of formal gardens, half a mile up Hill Street from the southern end of Castle Street, the two-storied mock-Tudor **Plas Newydd** (April Mon–Sat 10am–5pm, Sun 10am–4pm; May–Sept Mon–Sat 10am–7pm, Sun 10am–5pm; Oct daily 10am–5pm; £1.10) was, for almost fifty years, home to the celebrated **Ladies of Llangollen**. Lady Eleanor Butler and Sarah Ponsonby were a lesbian couple from Anglo-Irish aristocratic backgrounds, who tried to elope together at the end of the eighteenth century. After two botched attempts dressed in men's clothes, they were grudgingly allowed to leave in 1778 with an annual allowance of £280, enough to settle in Llangollen, where they became the country's most celebrated lesbians. Regency society was captivated by their "model friendship" in what Simone de Beauvoir called "a peaceful Eden on the edge of the world". Despite their desire for a "life of sweet and delicious retirement", they didn't seem to mind the constant stream of gentry who called on them. They found the Duke of Wellington a "charming young man, hansom, fashioned tall and elegant" and commemorated his visit by engraving "E.B & S.P." 1814 over the mantlepiece in the Oak Room. Walter Scott was also well received, though he found them "a couple of hazy or crazy old sailors" in manner, and like "two respectable superannuated clergymen" in their mode of dress. Thomas de Quincey humoured the ladies, if only to bend their favour towards his friend Wordsworth, who had displeased them by referring to their house as "a low roofed cot" in an inelegant poem he had composed in the grounds.

Gifts of sculpted wood panelling formed the basis of the riotous friezes of gloomy woodwork that weigh on your every step around the modest black-and-white timbered house, and most of the rooms have been left almost empty, so as not to hide the panelling; only one upper room has been devoted to a few of the ladies' possessions and panels covering their life story.

Llangollen takes its name from the **Church of St Collen** on Bridge Street (May–Sept daily until dusk; free tours at 1pm), dedicated to a sixth-century saint. The interior features a fine fifteenth-century hammerbeam roof said to have come from Valle Crucis (see p.271), but the chief interest is in the graveyard: the triangular railed-off monument to Mary Carryll erected by her mistresses, the Ladies of Llangollen, who are also buried in the churchyard.

THE LLANGOLLEN INTERNATIONAL MUSIC EISTEDDFOD

Llangollen is heaving in summer, but never more so than during the first week of July, when for six days the town explodes into a frenzy of music, dance, poetry and bundles of colour. The **International Music Eisteddfod** comes billed as "the world's greatest folk festival" but unlike the National Eisteddfod (see "Events" in *Basics*), which is a purely Welsh affair, the Llangollen event draws amateur performers from thirty countries, all competing for prizes in their chosen disciplines. Throughout the week, performers present their works at numerous sites around the town, sometimes including Plas Newydd and Valle Crucis. The main venue is on the north bank just west of the Gothic bridge: a much-derided 6000-seat white plastic structure designed to evoke the shape of the traditional marquee which used to be erected on the site each year.

It has been held in more-or-less its present form since 1947, when it was started more or less on a whim by one Harold Tudor. Forty choirs from fourteen countries performed at the first event, and it expanded, drawing praise quickly, from Dylan Thomas, who declared that "the town sang and danced, as though it were right". Today over 12,000 musicians, singers, dancers and choristers from countries around the world descend on this town of 3000 people, further swamped by up to 150,000 visitors. While the whole set-up can seem oppressive, there is an irresistible *joie de vivre* as brightly costumed dancers walk the streets and fill the fish and chip shops.

Unless you are going specifically for the Eisteddfod, the week beginning the first Tuesday of July is probably a good time to stay away. If you come, book early for both accommodation and tickets (☎0978/860236).

On nearby Castle Street is the site of the **European Centre for Traditional and Regional Cultures (ECTARC)** (May–Sept Mon–Fri 10am–5pm, Sat 10am–6pm, Sun 11am–5pm; Oct–April Mon–Sat 10am–5pm, Sun 1–5pm; free), primarily a centre for folk studies. The centre also presents occasional performances and six-monthly displays drawing on each of the twelve EU countries in turn, focusing on such diverse topics as lesser-used languages, ceramics and the effect of tourism on fragile communities.

There's little else to see on the south side of the river so make for the north bank over the bridge which, though widened and strengthened over the years, has spanned the river since the fourteenth century. Below it, the Dee pours through the fingers of shale which make up the unimaginatively dubbed "Town Falls" rapids, an occasional venue for canoe slaloms.

North of the River Dee

Wherever you are in Llangollen, the hills echo to the shrill cry of steam engines easing along the **Llangollen Steam Railway** (April–Oct daily 4–9pm; winter Sat & Sun only; £4.60 return). Shoe-horned into the north side of the valley, it runs from Llangollen's time-warped station to Glyndyfrdwy, near the Horseshoe Falls, and by 1998 will go as far as Corwen. Operating along a restored section of the disused Ruabon-Barmouth line, belching steam engines creep four miles west along the riverbank, hauling ancient carriages which proudly sport the liveries of their erstwhile owners.

The artificial **Horseshoe Falls** are really a crescent-shaped weir built in 1806 to feed water into the Llangollen Canal. This canal was designed as a water supply for the Shropshire Union Canal at Froncysyllte, five miles down the valley, and until the coming of the railway in 1865, was the only means to carry slates from the quarries on the Horseshoe Pass through Llangollen. The small **Llangollen Wharf Canal Museum** on Wharf Hill (Easter–Oct daily 10am–4pm; £1, free for canal tour passengers) admirably explains the construction in the context of Britain's canal building mania at the end of the eighteenth century.

Telford avoided using locks for the first fourteen miles of the canal by building the thousand-foot-long **Pontcysyllte Aqueduct** 126 feet above the Dee, at **FRONCYSYLLTE**, four miles east. It was a bold move for its time, employing long cast-iron troughs supported by stone piers. Diesel-driven narrowboats (summer Sat & Sun noon, also Tues & Thurs in July & Aug; return £5.90, single £4.40) edge their way across on two-hour trips from Llangollen, or you can drive – or walk the towpath – to Froncysyllte on the A542 and take the short ride (45min; £1) across the aqueduct and back, turning a blind eye to the nearby chemical plant.

Castell Dinas Brân

It is the view both ways along the valley which justifies a 45-minute slog up to **Castell Dinas Brân** (Crow's Fortress Castle), perched on a hill eight hundred feet above the town, and reached by a path near the Canal Museum. The lure

A WALK FROM LLANGOLLEN

Note: This walk is not easy to follow without the OS Landranger #117 map.

Climbing up to Dinas Brân, you get a fair idea of what is in store on Llangollen's **Precipice Walk** (14 miles; 7hr; 1800ft ascent), which traces the crest of the wonderful limestone escarpment formed by Trevor and Eglwyseg rocks. One of the most dramatic sections of the Offa's Dyke Path – though not the dyke itself – follows the base of these cliffs, but the tops make a far better walk offering superb views down into the Vale of Llangollen and across the Berwyn Range to the south. Since the eastern half of what is effectively a circuit around Ruabon Mountain is the least interesting part, the walk is described anti-clockwise. Although it is certainly a long walk, the worst of the climbing is quickly over and fine weather makes it a superb outing.

To allow for a visit to **Castell Dinas Brân**, the walk starts by the Canal Museum and follows the signposts up towards the castle ruins. Whether you climb to the castle or skirt the west side of its hill, aim north for a tarmacked road which runs below the escarpment forming part of the Offa's Dyke Path. Turn right and head east along the road following it for three miles, always taking any left turns and keeping the open land of Ruabon Mountain on your left. Half a mile past Hafod Farm turn left to Bryn-Adda following a Public Footpath sign. The route then heads roughly north over dense heather to the forestry plantation at Newtown Mountain and on to the road near Mountain Lodge. Just past the entrance to the lodge, turn west up towards the top of the moor and the head of the valley known as World's End. Follow the southern perimeter of a plantation and pick up the path, which then follows the escarpment south back to Llangollen. The easiest way back is to continue past Dinas Brân to the end of Trevor Rocks, then follow the road down to town.

certainly isn't the few sad vaulted stumps which stand in poor testament to what was once the district's largest and most important Welsh fortress. Built by the ruler of northern Powys, Prince Madog ap Gruffydd Maelor, in the 1230s, the castle rose on the site of an earlier Iron Age fort. Edward I soon took it as part of his first campaign against Llywelyn ap Gruffydd (see p.372), and the castle was left to decay, John Leland, Henry VIII's antiquarian, finding it "all in ruin" in 1540.

Although not much to look at, it is a great place to be when the sun is setting, imagining George Borrow translating seventeenth-century bard Roger Cyffyn:

Gone, gone are thy gates, Dinas Brân on the height!
Thy warders are blood-crows and ravens, I trow;
Now no-one will wend from the field of the fight
To the fortress on high, save the raven and the crow.

Valle Crucis Abbey and Eliseg's Pillar

Following the canal towpath, or the A542, west a mile towards the Horseshoe Falls, you pass Llangollen's **Motor Museum** (Easter–Oct daily 10am–5pm; Nov–Easter Mon–Fri 10am–12.30pm & 1.30–5pm; 80p), a shed full of lovingly restored not-so-vintage cars and vans, but it's more rewarding to follow the road another half-mile to the gaunt remains of **Valle Crucis Abbey** (April to late Oct daily 9.30am–6pm; late Oct to March Mon–Sat 9.30am–4pm, Sun 2–4pm; CADW; £1.50;), in Glyn y Groes (Valley of the Cross). In 1201, Madog ap Gruffydd Maelor of Dinas Brân chose this majestic pastoral setting for one of the last Cistercian foundations in Wales, as well as the first Gothic abbey in Britain. Despite a devastating fire in its first century, and a company of far from pious monks, it survived until the Dissolution in 1535. The church fell into disrepair, after which the monastic buildings, in particular the monks' dormitory, were employed as farm buildings. Later, Turner painted the abbey, imaginatively shifting Dinas Brân a couple of miles west onto the hill behind.

Though less impressive than Tintern Abbey (see p.149), Valle Crucis does greet you with its best side, the largely intact west wall of the church pierced by the frame of a rose window. At the opposite end, the equally complete east wall guards a row of six graves, one of which is said to contain Owain Glyndŵr's resident bard, Iolo Gogh. There are displays on monastic life upstairs, reached by a detour through the mostly ruined cloister and past the weighty vaulting of the chapterhouse.

The cross that gives the valley its name is the eight-foot-tall **Eliseg's Pillar** (unrestricted access; CADW), four hundred yards away by the A542. Erected to a Prince of Powys in the ninth century by his great-grandson, it originally stood 25 feet high but was smashed during the Civil War in the 1640s. The stump remains, but you can now only see half of the full 31 lines glorifying the lineage of the Princes of Powys, which Celtic scholar Edward Lhuyd translated from the remaining pieces in 1696.

Eating and drinking

Though not extensive by city standards, Llangollen boasts a fairly good selection of **restaurants** and no shortage of cafés around town. Outside Eisteddfod week, there's not a great deal of **nightlife**, but local bands do play from time to time.

THOMAS TELFORD (1757–1834)

The English poet Robert Southey dubbed **Thomas Telford** the "Colossus of Roads" in recognition of his pre-eminence as the greatest road builder of his day, if not the greatest ever. Throughout the early years of the nineteenth century, he managed some of the most ambitious and far-reaching engineering projects yet attempted, and there was seldom a public work on which his opinion wasn't sought.

Born in Scotland, he was apprenticed to a stone mason in London where he taught himself engineering architecture, eventually earning himself a position working for the Ellesmere Canal Company, who were planning a canal to link the Severn, Dee and Mersey rivers. His reputation was forged on the **Pontcysyllte Aqueduct**, near Llangollen which, though one of his earliest major projects, was recognised as innovative even before he had completed it as far as Horseshoe Falls, six miles to the west. Though lured away to build the Caledonian Canal in Scotland and St Katherine's Docks in London, he continued to work in Wales, reaching the apotheosis of his road building career by pushing the **London–Holyhead Turnpike** through Snowdonia.

After the 1800 Act of Union between Britain and Ireland, a good road was needed to hasten mail and to transport the new Irish MPs to and from parliament in London. What is now the A5 was shoehorned into the same valley as Telford's Llangollen Canal, then driven right through Snowdonia with its gradient never exceeding 1-in-20. The combination of its near level route and the high quality of its well-drained surface cut hours off the journey time, but the Dublin ferries left from Holyhead on the island of Anglesey separated from the mainland by the Menai Strait. Telford's solution and his greatest achievement was the 580-foot-long **Menai Suspension Bridge**, strung a hundred feet above the strait to allow tall ships to pass under. Though the idea wasn't completely novel, the scale and the balance of grace and function won the plaudits of engineers and admiring visitors from around the world.

Restaurants and cafés

Berwyn Belle (☎0978/860583). Spend two hours on the Llangollen Steam Railway (see above), eating a four-course dinner as it inches its way to Glyndyfrdwy and back. Runs Saturday 7.30pm and Sunday 1pm roughly from May to September and during December. Expensive.

Cedar Tree Restaurant at the *Bryn Howel Hotel*, Trevor (☎0978/860331). An award-winning restaurant serving light three-course table d'hôte meals. Choice of five main courses changed daily, including one vegetarian option. Expensive.

Gales, 18 Bridge St (☎0978/860089). A reason in itself to come to Llangollen. Relax in pews scavenged from old churches while eating large helpings of delicious homemade bistro-style food washed down with a bottle from one of the most extensive wine cellars around. If you don't want to eat here, you can just drink. Closed Sunday. Inexpensive.

The Gallery, 15 Chapel St. Friendly restaurant serving a good range of pizza and pasta dishes. Inexpensive.

Good Taste, 44 Market St. Unlicensed vegetarian place with a wide range of café-style vegetarian meals during the day. Inexpensive.

Jonkers Coffee Shop, 9 Chapel St. A quiet café with books and newspapers to while away the odd half-hour. Inexpensive.

The Woolpack Restaurant, 13 Church St (☎0978/860300). Opposite *Gales* and in direct competition with it, the *Woolpack* does great bistro-style food for just a pound or two more. Moderate.

Pubs

Dee Bar at *The Royal Hotel*, 1 Bridge St. No live music, but very youthful and lively, especially at weekends.

Hand Hotel, 26 Bridge St. Straightforward local pub where you can listen to the male voice choir in full song at 7.30pm on Monday and Friday.

Jenny Jones, Abbey Rd. Good pub with mixed clientele most nights, live country and western music on Wednesday and jazz on Thursday. It is a couple of hundred yards towards Valle Crucis on the A542.

Prince of Wales, Berwyn St. The place to be on Wednesday night if you want to hear local rock.

Wynnstay Arms, 20 Bridge St. This children-welcoming bar is divided into several smaller rooms, and has good beer.

Corwen and around

CORWEN, eight miles west of Llangollen, has many associations with Welsh rebel Owain Glyndŵr, and is the place from where he set out to wrest back all Wales from the English barons (see p.224) in the early fifteenth century. There is precious little to commemorate this fact, only the shape of a dagger incised into a grey-stone lintel of the south porch of the thirteenth-century **church of St Mael and St Julien**, known as **Glyndŵr's Sword**. The Welsh hero, local landowner and scourge of Henry IV is said to have cast the "sword" in anger at the townspeople from atop the hill behind. It actually predates him by half a millennium, but you can still keep his prowess in mind as you follow a path leading up between dry-stone walls from the road to the right of the post office up to the **viewpoint**. Before doing that, take a look around the near-circular churchyard with its well-preserved Celtic cross and gravestone with indentations for penitent's knees. Inside the church, there is a fine Norman font.

In Glyndŵr's time and probably before, Corwen was an important cattle drovers' town. The two main routes out of north Wales – one from Anglesey and the Llŷn peninsula, the other from Ardudwy and Harlech – met here for the final push to the English markets. The arrival of the train killed off the cattle trade but not the town itself, which for a century became an important junction of the Barmouth and Rhyl train lines. Now a fairly quiet market town, it does have a couple of sights nearby, including Capel Rûg (see below). Glyndŵr aficionados will probably be interested in the thirty-foot-high **Owain Glyndŵr's Mount**, on the south bank of the Dee just over three miles east on the road to Llangollen, where he is supposed to have stood on lookout for his enemies. He may well have done so, but the earthworks are more likely to be a Norman motte-and-bailey castle.

Corwen's charms don't really justify stopping overnight, although the *Corwen Court*, London Road (closed Dec–Feb; ☎0490/412854; ②), is a B&B with a difference: converted from a police station and courthouse, the cells are now single rooms, and the doubles are converted from the sergeant's family's quarters. If that doesn't suit, *Powys House Estate*, Bonwm (☎0490/412367; ③), has its own swimming pool and tennis court. It is about a mile east on the A5 to Llangollen.

Buses stop in the centre of Corwen, continuing to Llangollen, Bala, Ruthin and Denbigh. Sadly, there is no useful service to Betws-y-Coed.

Capel Rûg and Eglwys Llangar

Taking its name from the Welsh word for heather, **Capel Rûg** (May–Sept daily except Wed & Thurs 9.30am–6.30pm; ☎0490/412025; CADW; £1.50), a mile west of Corwen on the A494, is one of Wales's best examples of an unmolested seventeenth-century church. Along with the Gwydyr Uchaf Chapel, near Llanrwst (see p.287), it gives a charming insight into worship three hundred years ago, when mass was a private clerical devotion with the congregation kept behind rood screens.

Rûg didn't entirely escape, but much here is as it was built in 1637 by the former privateer and collaborator on William Morgan's Welsh Bible (see p.323), William Salusbury. The plain exterior design gives no hint of the richly decorated interior: wooden angels support a roof patterned with stars and amoebic swirls, and a painting of a skeleton said to represent the transient nature of life and the inevitability of death. Informative displays in the ticket ofice give more details of the building's use.

Your ticket to Capel Rûg also entitles you to an escorted visit from there to another little-changed church, **Eglwys Llangar** (normally locked, phone Capel Rûg for tour times), a mile to the south off the B4401. Parish boundary changes in 1853 made this church redundant, saving its extensive fifteenth-century wall paintings and outsize seventeenth-century figure of death from obliteration.

The Vale of Edeyrnion

If you are not in a hurry to get from Corwen to Bala, take the quiet B4401 along the Dee through the peaceful villages of the Vale of Edeyrnion: Cynwyd, Llandrillo and Llandderfel. None of the villages is particularly interesting, but any can act as a base for walks on the largely undiscovered Berwyn Range to the east (see box), where you can walk all day without seeing a soul.

The road passes a couple of the best country hotels in the area, a simple campsite and a **YHA youth hostel**, *The Old Mill* (☎0490/412814; ①), in the hamlet of Cynwyd, two miles south of Corwen. Walkers who don't fancy the youth hostel might prefer *Fron Gogh Farmhouse and Bunkhouse* a mile and a half south of Cynwyd (☎049084/418), which has B&B (③) as well as a bunkhouse (①), with a bar and moderately priced meals, or the nearest **campsite** *Hendwr Caravan Park* (April–Oct; ☎049083/210), a further half-mile south. This is just one of several which dot the river flats through the valley.

The Berwyns are equally accessible from **LLANDRILLO** where, after a day in the hills, you can luxuriate in the elegant Georgian surroundings of *Tyddyn Llan Country House* (☎049084/264; ⑦) and eat in their expensive restaurant. It is just through the village on the Bala side and serves highly regarded meals. For sheer grandeur, though, you can't beat the hand-painted and intricately carved Victorian interiors of *Palé Hall* (☎06783/285; ⑧), three miles on and just outside Llandderfel, where the ageing Queen once stayed – a great place for a splurge in a mansion which provides bed, breakfast and an excellent dinner. If your budget won't stretch to these kind of prices, there's also the *Bryntirion Inn* (☎06783/205; ③), where you turn off the B4401 to get to *Palé Hall*, which serves moderately priced à la carte evening meals and has free fishing for guests.

In **LLANDDERFEL**, the large stone house at the fork in the road at the far end of the village is *Bronwylfa* (March–Nov; ☎06783/207; ⑤), where you are greeted with tea and *bara brith* (a kind of Welsh fruit loaf). A mile further along the B4401, and only two miles short of Bala, *Melin Meloch* (March–Nov; ☎0678/520101; ③) is partly built from a converted thirteenth-century watermill beside the Dee, and will provide moderately priced communal meals by arrangement.

Bala

The little town of **BALA** (Y Bala), at the northern end of Wales' largest natural lake, **Llyn Tegid** (Bala Lake), is a major watersports centre, and if that's of no interest, there's little point in stopping here. The four-mile-long body of water is perfect for **windsurfing** in particular, with buffeting winds whipping up the valley formed by the Bala geological fault line, which slices thirty miles northeast from the coast, up the Talyllyn Valley, and between the Aran and Arenig mountains flanking the lake.

A WALK ON THE BERWYNS FROM CYNWYD OR LLANDDERFEL

Note: The OS 1:50,000 Landranger #125 map is recommended for this walk.

Henry II's 1165 expeditionary force encamped on the Berwyn Hills until forced to flee back to England from the guerilla tactics of Owain Gwynedd and the Welsh weather. Legend has it that the king beat his retreat along the ancient high-moor trackway, thereafter known as Ffordd Saeson (Englishman's Road). Whether he did or not, the path makes for a good route up onto these lonesome rocky heather-clad outcrops. The **walk** (10 miles; 5–6hr; 2500ft ascent) follows part of Ffordd Saeson starting from Cynwyd beside *Y Llew Glas* (The Blue Lion) pub, passing the YHA youth hostel up through a forest to the deep heather moorland pass of **Bwlch Cynwyd** (1700ft/520m). An alternative to this direct route forks right a hundred yards after the youth hostel and leads past a waterfall and serene lake, before rejoining the main path. From Bwlch Cynwyd, the circular route leads south, but if the skies are clear, the lone summit of **Moel Fferna** (2067ft), a mile or so to the north, makes a rewarding detour. South from Bwlch Cynwyd, follow the path beside the fence for a couple of miles across desolate, somewhat featureless land to the summit of **Pen Bwlch Llandrillo Top** (2037ft), then drop down the other side to an ancient drovers' road. Known locally as the Maid's Path, it was once the harvest-time route for girls heading east from Llandrillo, sometimes as far as Llanarmon Dyffryn Ceiriog, 5 miles from here (see p.265). If you don't have your own transport, walking over the Berwyns from the Vale of Edeyrnion into Glyn Ceiriog is the closest you'll get to experiencing what the drover's life must have been like.

Near where you meet the drovers' road, a much later traveller is commemorated by a stone to "A Wayfarer 1877–1956, a lover of Wales". In the days before knobbly tyres and gas mono-shock suspension systems, one W.M. Robinson rode up here by bicycle, unwittingly laying the groundwork for scores of mountain bikers now following his lead along the bridleways. A metal box nearby contains a book to record your visit.

The cairned summit of **Cadair Bronwen** (2575ft), a mile and a half south of the memorial, is the only place in Wales where you can pick cloudberries (sharp-tasting orange blackberries), otherwise head east for Glyn Ceiriog or west for the Vale of Edeyrnion. After half a mile on the westerly path, a sign points to Llandrillo, while an unsigned path forks right to Cynwyd.

The Town

The narrow town sits slightly back from the lake edge, perhaps to avoid the catastrophe which, according to two legends, drowned the old town which stood where the lake now is. One tells of someone forgetting to put the lid on the well which, during the night, overflowed covering the valley and town. A more entertaining story records the fate of the quasi-legendary prince Tegid Foel, who was warned by a voice that, because of his cruelty to his people, "Vengeance will come". On the birth of his son, he held a banquet at which a hired harpist heard a voice saying "Vengeance has come". A bird led him away onto a hill where he slept, waking to find the town submerged beneath the lake which took the prince's name.

Bala has a role in Welsh history which far outweighs its current status. The district was of only minor importance before the eighteenth century, the Romans having built a fort at the southern end of the lake (not open to the public), and the Normans having erected a motte, now tree-covered and known as **Tomen-y-Bala**, on Heol y Domen off the northern end of the High Street (not normally open to the public). But it was wool – and socks in particular – that brought the town its fame. Until the Industrial Revolution killed the trade, most men and women in the town were involved in knitting, even clothing George III, who wore Bala stockings for his rheumatism. During this period, the people of Bala became noted for their piousness and followed the preachings of Nonconformist ministers Thomas Charles and Michael D. Jones (see box). Charles is buried a mile south in the churchyard at Llanycil; his statue stands outside the Presbyterian church on Tegid Street, and a plaque locates his former home at 68 High Street, in what is now a *Barclays* bank. A nearby plaque records Mary Jones' walk (see box).

The only other thing to do is ride the **Bala Lake Railway** (mid-April to Sept; ☎06784/666; £4.50 return, £3 single), which starts half a mile south of Bala on the other side of the lake and runs for four miles along the route of the former Ruabon–Barmouth standard gauge line, which closed in 1963. It's one of Wales' least interesting narrow-gauge rides, but you can ride the renovated north Wales slate quarry trains down the far side of the lake to Llanuwchllyn. The *Eagles Inn*, ten minutes' walk from Llanuwchllyn station, serves excellent bar meals, and you could even stick around to hear the local male voice choir rehearse in the Village Hall at 7.30pm on Thursdays. Bus #94 runs back to Bala or on to Dolgellau (see p.233).

Practicalities

The best approach to Bala is the A4212 from south of Blaenau Ffestiniog over the wild uplands between the twin peaks of Arenig Fawr and Arenig Fach. Unfortunately, this can't be done by public transport as the only **bus** is the #94, which runs from Llangollen to Dolgellau and usually takes the route through the Vale of Edeyrnion (see above). In Bala, it stops outside the **tourist office**, 28 High St (April–Oct daily 10am–6pm; ☎0678/520367).

Accommodation

Bala has plenty of places to **stay** or you can make the most of the surrounding countryside by staying in the Vale of Edeyrnion (see above), northeast of the town.

THOMAS CHARLES AND MICHAEL D. JONES

During the seventeenth and eighteenth centuries, the religious needs of the Welsh were being poorly met by the established Church. None of the bishops were Welsh, few were resident, and most regarded their positions as stepping stones to higher appointments, and so the preachings of the newly emerging Nonconformists – Quakers, Baptists and later, Calvinist and Wesleyan Methodists – were welcomed by the people. Congregations swelled from the middle of the eighteenth century, but conversion didn't get into full swing until the effects of itinerant religious teachers improved literacy and the strident sermons of native Welsh-speakers fired their enthusiasm. There were already over twice as many chapels as Anglican churches when the chief protagonist of Methodism in Wales, **Thomas Charles**, gave the movement a massive boost through the founding of the British and Foreign Bible Society, a group committed to distributing local-language bibles worldwide.

He had already reprinted Bishop Morgan's 1588 original Welsh translation (see p.323), but was down to his last copy when sixteen-year-old Mary Jones (see p.232), the daughter of a poor weaver from the other side of Cadair Idris, arrived on his doorstep. She had saved money for six years to buy a bible from Thomas Charles and, in 1800, walked the 25 miles to Bala, barefoot some of the way, prompting Charles to found the society.

Despite the rise in Nonconformism, many of the more pious converts sought greater freedom to worship as they pleased, in a land where they felt free; something denied them in Wales by the oppression of both the English church and state. The reformist preacher **Michael D. Jones** came to Bala enlisting recruits for his model colony outside Wales, and accordingly, he helped them found *Y Wladfa*, "The Colony", a Welsh enclave in Chubut Valley, Patagonia: in 1865 he transported 153 Welsh settlers, mostly from Bala, to Argentina, to set up a radical colony where Nonconformism and the Welsh language kept a tight rein. This was the start of a 3000-strong community (and the world's first society to give women the vote), which grew until 1912, when immigration stopped and linguistic assimilation accelerated. Jones stayed in Wales, setting up the Bala-Bangor Theological College and leading campaigns for Welsh causes, and many now regard him as "the father of modern Welsh nationalism".

HOTELS AND GUESTHOUSES

Abercelyn, half a mile south of Bala on the A494 (☎0678/521109). A fine country house worth spending an extra couple of pounds on. ③.

Ye Olde Bull's Head, 78 High St (☎0678/520438). Good-value pub without en suite rooms, but serving decent pub meals. ③.

Plas Teg Guesthouse, Tegid St (☎0678/520268). Handy licensed guesthouse on the street opposite the *White Lion*. ②.

Traian, 95 Tegid St (☎0678/520059). Good-value central guesthouse. ②.

White Lion Royal Hotel, 61 High St (☎0678/520314). In the last century, both Queen Victoria and George Borrow chose the *White Lion*. It is still the best in town, even if the breakfasts are no longer the sumptuous spreads described by Borrow. ⑥.

HOSTELS AND CAMPSITES

The Coach House, Tomen Y Castell on the A494, two miles north of Bala (☎0678/520738). Self-catering bunkhouse with bedding supplied. Meals on request.

Glanllyn, four miles south of Bala at the opposite end of the lake on the A494 (☎06784/227). Campsite where watersports gear can be rented.

Pen-y-Bont, on the B4402 Llandrillo road (☎0678/520549). The nearest campsite, by the outlet of the lake. Open April–Oct.

Plas Rhiwaedog youth hostel, Plas Rhiwaedog, two miles from Bala (☎0678/520215). A seventeenth-century manor house reached by taking the B4402 Llandrillo road then third right after crossing the river. ①.

Eating and drinking

The town has its fair share of decent **restaurants** and **pubs**, including several noteworthy culinary experiences.

Neuadd y Cyfnod, 2 High St (☎0678/521269). This cavernous old school hall has good-value no-nonsense fare. Closed Nov–Easter. Inexpensive.

Plas Gogh, High St (☎0678/520309). Excellent à la carte dinners. Moderate.

The Ship Inn, 30 High St. Good drinking pub with three-course bar meals for around a fiver.

White Lion. Ancient coaching inn and the best place to drink in town, a favourite with both Welsh-speaking locals and rosy-cheeked hill walkers. On a sunny day, their terrace is great for cream teas.

Daytime activities

Slalom kayak fans can make for the **Canolfan Tryweryn** whitewater course below the Arenig mountains, four miles west up the A4212; it wouldn't exist without a 1960s example of England's long-standing habit of flooding Welsh valleys, so that English cities, in this case Liverpool, can have their drinking water.

When water is released (around 200 days a year), it crashes down a mile and a half through the slalom site, the venue for the 1981 World Slalom Championships, and the 1995 Wild Water Racing World Championships, scheduled for August 21–28. Frequent competitions take place on summer weekends, but when the site is free, the centre organizes the only commercial **white-water rafting** trips in Wales (☎0678/521083 to book). It is a fairly steep £7 a pop for a heart-stopping run down the roughest part, but for £120 a group of up to seven can rent a raft and instructor for 2 hours, or about 5 runs.

The only drawback is that you have to pay to get on the lake – £3 for sailing and £2.20 for canoeing or fishing, on top of daily rental fees of around £9 for kayaks up to £17 for sailboards. These are available from a hut on the lakeshore by the *Loch Café* at the southern end of High Street (mainly July & Aug).

SNOWDONIA

What the coal valleys are to the south of the country, the mountains of Snowdonia (Yr Eryri) are to north Wales: the defining feature, not just in their physical form, but in the way they have shaped the communities within them.

To Henry VIII's antiquarian, John Leland, the region seemed "horrible with the sight of bare stones"; now it is widely acclaimed as the most dramatic and alluring of all Welsh scenery, a compact, barren land of tortured ridges dividing glacial valleys, whose sheer faces belie the fact that the tallest peaks only just top three thousand feet. It was to this mountain fastness that Llywelyn ap Gruffydd, the last true Prince of Wales, retreated in 1277 after his first war with Edward I; it was also here that Owain Glyndŵr held on most tenaciously to his dream of regaining the title of Prince of Wales for the Welsh. Centuries later, the English came to remove the mountains; slate barons built huge fortunes from Welsh toil and reshaped the patterns of Snowdonian life forever, as men looking for steady work in the quarries fled the hills and became town dwellers.

From the late eighteenth century, Snowdonia became the focus for the first truly structured approach to geological research. Early proponents of this new science pieced together the glacial evidence – scoured valley walls, scalloped mountain sides and hanging valleys – to come up with the first reliable proof of the last Ice Age and its retreat ten thousand years ago. These pioneers produced the rock type classifications familiar to any students of the discipline: Cambrian rock takes its name from the Roman name for Wales, Ordovician and Silurian rocks from the Celtic tribes, the Ordovices and the Silures.

Botanists found rare alpine flowers, writers produced libraries full of purple prose, and Richard Wilson, Paul Sandby and J.M.W. Turner all came to paint the landscape. Soon, those with the means began flocking here to marvel at the plunging waterfalls and walk the ever-widening paths to the mountain tops. Numbers have increased rapidly since then and thousands of hikers arrive every weekend for some of the country's best walks over steep, exacting and constantly changing terrain.

Recognizing the region's scientific importance, as well as its scenic and recreational appeal Snowdonia became the heartland of Wales's first national park, the **Snowdonia National Park** (Parc Cenedlaethol Eryri, see p.227), an 840-square-mile area which extends south, outside the strict bounds of Snowdonia, to encompass the Rhinogs and Cadair Idris (see p.226). Not surprisingly the **Snowdon** massif (Eryri) is the focus; several of the widely recognized routes up are superb, and you can always take the cog railway up to the summit café from **Llanberis**. But the other mountains are as good or better, often far less busy and giving unsurpassed views of Snowdon. The **Glyders** and **Tryfan** are particular favourites and best tackled from the **Ogwen Valley**.

If you are serious about doing some **walking** – and some of the walks described here are serious, especially in bad weather (Snowdon gets 200 inches of rain a year), you need a good map such as the 1:50,000 OS Landranger #115 or the 1:25,000 OS Outdoor Leisure #17; be sure to phone for local weather forecasts (☎0839/500449; premium rate). Weather reports and walking conditions are often posted on the doors or noticeboards of outdoor shops and tourist offices.

Snowdonia isn't all walking. Small settlements are dotted in the valleys, usually coinciding with some enormous mine or quarry. Foremost among these are **Blaenau Ffestiniog**, the "Slate Capital of North Wales", where two mines open their caverns for underground tours, and **Beddgelert** whose former copper mines are also open to the public. The only place of any size not associated with extracting the earth's wealth is **Betws-y-Coed**, a largely Victorian resort away from the higher peaks, but a springboard for the walkers' hamlets of **Capel Curig** and **Pen-y-Pass**.

Practicalities

Getting to the fringes of Snowdonia is not a problem: mainline **trains** run along the coast to Bangor, while the Conwy Valley line branches at Llandudno Junction penetrating to Betws-y-Coed and on to Blaenau Ffestiniog. Here you can pick up the useful and highly scenic Ffestiniog Railway for Porthmadog. In reverse, this is the best way into the region from the south.

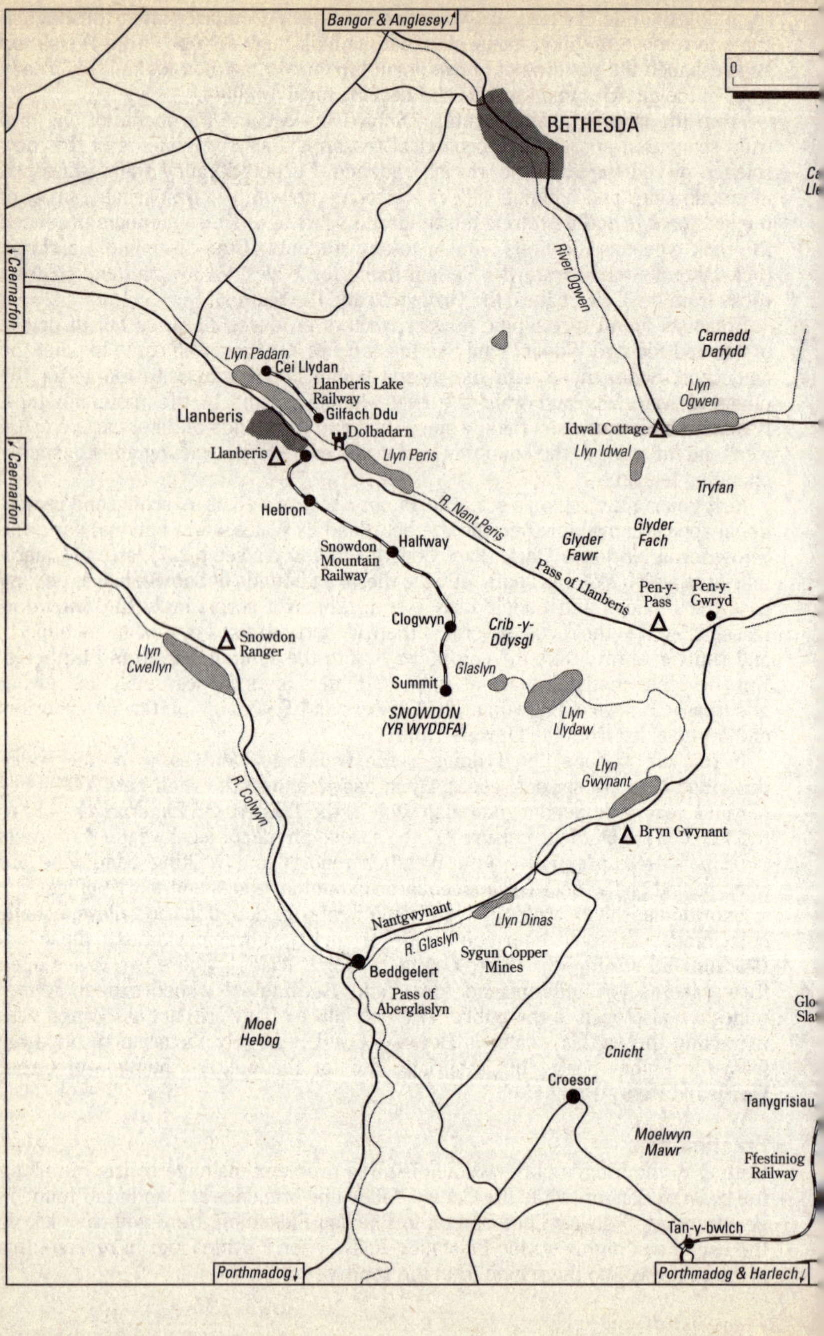
Bangor & Anglesey
BETHESDA
River Ogwen
Caernarfon
Caernarfon
Llyn Padarn
Cei Llydan
Llanberis Lake Railway
Gilfach Ddu
Llanberis
Dolbadarn
Llanberis
Llyn Peris
Hebron
R. Nant Peris
Snowdon Mountain Railway
Halfway
Carnedd Dafydd
Llyn Ogwen
Idwal Cottage
Llyn Idwal
Tryfan
Glyder Fach
Glyder Fawr
Pass of Llanberis
Pen-y-Pass
Pen-y-Gwryd
Clogwyn
Crib -y-Ddysgl
Llyn Cwellyn
Snowdon Ranger
Glaslyn
Summit
SNOWDON (YR WYDDFA)
Llyn Llydaw
Llyn Gwynant
R. Colwyn
Bryn Gwynant
Nantgwynant
Llyn Dinas
R. Glaslyn
Sygun Copper Mines
Beddgelert
Pass of Aberglaslyn
Moel Hebog
Cnicht
Croesor
Tanygrisiau
Moelwyn Mawr
Ffestiniog Railway
Tan-y-bwlch
Porthmadog
Porthmadog & Harlech

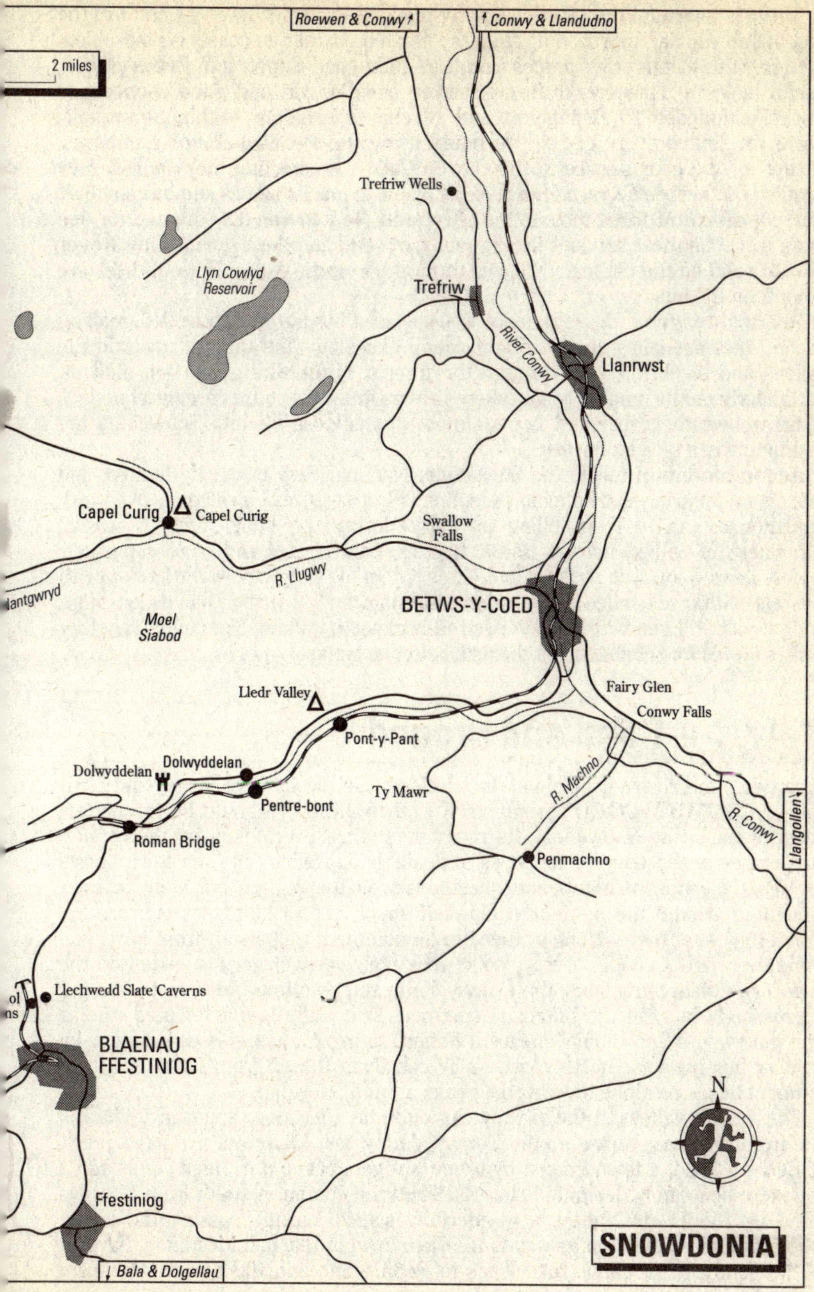
Roewen & Conwy
Conwy & Llandudno
2 miles
Trefriw Wells
Llyn Cowlyd
Reservoir
Trefriw
River Conwy
Llanrwst
Capel Curig
Capel Curig
Swallow
Falls
R. Llugwy
Moel
Siabod
BETWS-Y-COED
Fairy Glen
Conwy Falls
Lledr Valley
Pont-y-Pant
Dolwyddelan
Dolwyddelan
Pentre-bont
Ty Mawr
R. Machno
Roman Bridge
Penmachno
R. Conwy
Llangollen
Llechwedd Slate Caverns
BLAENAU
FFESTINIOG
N
Ffestiniog
SNOWDONIA
Bala & Dolgellau

There is no useful **bus** service linking the Dee Valley to Betws-y-Coed and the rest of Snowdonia. Approaching from the north or Cambrian coasts is no problem though, with half-hourly services from Llandudno and Conwy into Betws-y-Coed, useful buses to Llanberis from Caernarfon and Bangor, and good connections from Porthmadog to Beddgelert and Blaenau Ffestiniog. Within Snowdonia, towns are linked every one to two hours using the so-called *Sherpa* minibuses, except for the poor service in the Ogwen Valley. Routes and times are all fully detailed on the free *Gwynedd timetable* available at tourist offices and bus stations. Current **discount fares** include the **Gwynedd Red Rover** (£3.80) good for one day's travel on most services throughout Gwynedd and the *Crosville* **Day Rover** (£4.70) valid on the company's buses throughout north Wales. Both of these are bought on the bus.

Roads throughout the region are well-surfaced but also well-travelled, making cycling less appealing than it might seem, except for the quieter roads in the valleys and the bridleways through the forests. **Hitchhiking** isn't too difficult, particularly on the smaller roads where drivers know that buses are infrequent. A pack, wet-weather gear and boots almost guarantee a lift into Snowdonia but getting out can be a lot harder.

Accommodation inside the Snowdonia National Park is strictly limited, and most is on the fringes. The main exception is Betws-y-Coed, a village packed with guesthouses, all of them filling up early during the busy summer season. Elsewhere in Snowdonia are B&Bs, hostels, bunkhouses and basic campsites, mostly geared towards walkers and climbers. In all, there are eight **YHA youth hostels** within ten miles of Snowdon's summit, and a further half-dozen other budget places. Even with a medium-sized backpack, walking from one to another makes a welcome change from the usual circular walks.

Betws-y-Coed and around

Sprawled out across a flat plain at the confluence of the Conwy, Llugwy and Lledr valleys, **BETWS-Y-COED** (pronounced Betoos-ah-Coyd) should be the perfect base for exploring Snowdonia. Its riverside setting, overlooked by the conifer-clad slopes of the Gwydyr forest, is undeniably appealing, and the town boasts the best selection of hotels and guesthouses in the region; but after an hour mooching around the outdoor equipment shops and drinking tea you are left wondering what to do. None of the serious mountain walks start from here, and while there are a couple of easy walks (see box) up river gorges leading to the town's two main attractions, the **Conwy Falls** and **Swallow Falls**, these can get depressingly busy in the height of summer. That said, its much-touted role as "the gateway to Snowdonia" means it is hard to avoid. Access is easy, either by train or bus from the north coast, or by car along the A5 from Llangollen, and frequent buses continue towards the peaks around Snowdon.

The quieter valleys in the vicinity can often be a lot more appealing. The rail line from the coast comes up the **Conwy Valley** past **Llanrwst**, five miles north of Betws-y-Coed, a town graced by a fine bridge attributed to Inigo Jones and a couple of beautifully decorated chapels. The train continues south from Betws-y-Coed up the **Lledr Valley**, a wonderfully scenic journey passing the lonely **Dolwyddelan Castle**, on its way to the slate town of Blaenau Ffestiniog. Further to the southeast, a minor road leads to Penmachno and the house of William

Morgan, the translator of the Bible into Welsh. Walkers bound for the high hills will be heading west beside the **Llugwy River** to the mountain centre of Capel Curig and beyond to Llanberis and the Ogwen Valley.

Llanrwst is the largest town in the district and operates as a hub for the local **bus** system. Some services terminate, requiring a change onto buses to Betws-y-Coed and Penmachno or Trefriw, Rowen, Conwy and Llandudno. If you are only planning to stop at Llanrwst and then the coastal resorts, **trains** from the station at the north end of town are faster and more comfortable.

Arrival and accommodation

Betws-y-Coed is arranged in a flat triangle bounded by the Conwy and Llugwy rivers and the A5, which forms the town's main street, running between the Waterloo Bridge in the east and the Pont-y-Pair bridge in the west. The **train station** for services up the Conwy Valley from Llandudno Junction and on to Blaenau Ffestiniog is just a few paces across the grass from the **tourist office**, Royal Oak Stables (Easter–Oct daily 10am–6pm; Nov–Easter daily 10am–1pm & 2–5pm; ☎0690/710426), where displays give a quick overview of conservation work in Snowdonia. All **buses** to Penmachno and some to Llandudno stop at the train station; the remainder of services – to the Ogwen Valley, Llanberis, Conwy and Llandudno – stop outside the post office on Main Street.

Accommodation

The town has plenty of **accommodation**, but has to cope with an even larger numbers of visitors pushing prices up in the summer. Expect to pay a pound or two more than in other towns in Snowdonia and don't be surprised to find the places listed full if you arrive late in the day. There are two nearby **youth hostels**, at Capel Curig and in the Lledr Valley. The closest campsite is *Riverside* (Easter–Oct; ☎0690/710310), right behind the station. Walkers and climbers who want direct access to the mountains need to make for Capel Curig (see p.293) or Llanberis (see p.298).

Bryn Afon Guesthouse, Mill St (☎0690/710403). Popular if fairly standard guesthouse just over the Pont-y-Pair bridge from the main road. ③.

Cae'r Berllan, on the A470 towards Llanrwst (☎0492/640027). Country guesthouse in a sixteenth-century manor almost three miles from Waterloo Bridge. Excellent moderately priced à la carte and set menus available. ④.

The Ferns Guesthouse, Holyhead Rd, a few hundred yards towards Capel Curig (☎0690/710587). Licensed non-smoking guesthouse with all en suite rooms. ③.

Glan Llugwy, on the A5 towards Capel Curig 300 yards beyond Pont-y-Pair (☎0690/710592). One of the cheapest B&Bs, with TVs in rooms. ②.

Henllys Old Courthouse, Old Church Rd (☎0690/710534). Guesthouse converted from a courthouse by the Conwy River, off the A5 opposite the *Midland Bank*. ④.

Pont-y-Pair Hotel, High St (☎0690/710407). Budget hotel right by the bridge of the same name. Popular with mountaineers, partly due to lower winter prices. ②.

Riverside Restaurant, Holyhead Rd (☎0690/710650). The cheapest place of all, above the restaurant a few yards towards Capel Curig from the Pont-y-Pair bridge. Non-smoking. ①.

Swn-y-Dwr, Mill St, just past Bryn Afon (☎0690/710648). Popular, non-smoking guesthouse, over the Pont-y-Pair bridge. ③.

Tan-y-Foel, Capel Garmon (☎0690/710507). The best country guesthouse in the district with extensive views, a heated indoor pool and superb cuisine. Take the A470 towards Llanrwst then turn right after about a mile. Non-smoking. ⑦.

Ty Gwyn, on the A5 (☎0690/7103383). Cosy old coaching inn with wood-beamed rooms, a bar that is hard to leave and some top-notch food. It is half a mile east of the centre just over Waterloo Bridge. There are a couple of cheaper rooms but you'll need to book well ahead. ④.

Ty'n-y-Celyn House, Llanrwst Rd (☎0690/710202). Friendly Victorian guesthouse with en suite rooms overlooking the Llugwy Valley. Cross the suspension bridge behind the station if you're on foot or take the A470 towards Llanrwst. ③.

The Town

The settlement of Betws-y-Coed is first recorded during the fifth or sixth century, when a monastic cell was founded, earning the town its name of "oratory in the forest". Apart from some lead mining, it remained a backwater until 1808, when road improvements brought the Irish Mail this way. As part of the A5 construction, Telford completed the graceful **Waterloo Bridge** (Y Bont Haearn) in 1815, giving quicker access and luring landscape painters David Cox and J.M.W. Turner, who in turn alerted the leisured classes to the town's beauty. Anglers keen to exploit the richly stocked pools came too, but it was the arrival of the train line in 1868 that really lifted its status from coaching station to genteel resort, an air the town vainly tries to maintain. Today the town is mainly a centre for walkers, although there are few sights worth seeking out, the main one being the fourteenth-century **St Michael's church**, most interesting for the twelfth-century font and a carved effigy of an armoured knight, whose inscription identifies him as Gruffydd ap Dafydd Gogh, the grandson of Llywelyn ap Gruffydd's brother, Prince Dafydd.

Just a few paces away, the **Conwy Valley Railway Museum** (Easter–Oct daily 10.30am–5.30pm; £1) is a fairly dull collection of memorabilia and shiny engines, slightly enlivened by a model of a Welsh slate quarry and the opportunity for kids to take a short ride on a miniature train or tram. If internal combustion interests you more than steam, the **Motor Museum** (Easter–Oct daily 10am–6pm; 75p), a couple of hundred yards away behind the tourist office, is a marginally better bet. The half-dozen classic bikes and fifteen cars on display change frequently, but expect the likes of a 1934 Bugatti Straight 8 and a Model T Ford.

Activities

Whether you're a beginner or intermediate climber, courses on **scrambling**, **climbing** and **abseiling** can be arranged by contacting *Snowdonia Guides* (☎0690/710555) through the *Climber and Rambler* shop opposite Pont-y-Pair bridge for £15–£25 a day. Competent but gear-less climbers can also get a day out on some classic routes with a guide, but you'll have to pay around £75 a day.

Mountain bikes can be rented from *Beics Betws* (☎0680/710766) on Church Hill at the top of the road beside the post office, with permits and information on routes through the Gwydyr Forest obtainable from the tourist office.

Eating, drinking and entertainment

For a town so geared to tourism that you can hardly turn around without knocking someone's cream tea onto the floor, there are surprisingly few places to eat other than the pubs. Guesthouses offering meals will often be your best bet.

The Buffet Coach Café, The Old Goods Yard. Basic café with homemade snacks inside (or outside) a 1940s railway carriage at the station. Inexpensive.

Craig Y Dderwen Hotel, by the Waterloo Bridge (☎0690/710293). Hotel good for snacks and cream teas, sandwiches and puddings. Inexpensive.

Dil's Diner, Station Rd. Basic greasy spoon café beside the train station. A great place for breakfast or to fill up after a day in the hills. Inexpensive.

The Fountain, 2 miles east of Betws-y-Coed. Low-key pub with a mixed clientele, but mainly attracting New Age and bohemian types, and just 300 yards short of the Conwy Falls. Live, usually folky, music on Thursdays and Saturdays. Simple meals available. Inexpensive.

Pont-y-Pair Hotel, High St. The low-cost bar meals are nothing to shout about, but it is the liveliest place to drink and serves good beer, as well as offering accommodation. Inexpensive.

Riverside Tearooms, Holyhead Rd. Well-priced pizza, afternoon teas and restaurant meals, with accommodation available above. Inexpensive.

Ty Gwyn, on the A5 (see "Accommodation"). The best place to eat in town, whether you want a tasty pub meal or one of their praiseworthy table d'hôte meals. Menus usually include game and fish from the Conwy, and as well-prepared vegetarian dishes and delectable desserts. Also does accommodation. Inexpensive to moderate.

The Conwy and Swallow Falls

None of the attractions of Betws-y-Coed can compete with getting out to the gorges and waterfalls in the vicinity, and walking is the ideal way to see them (see below). The final gorge section of the River Conwy, a couple of miles above Betws-y-Coed, is one of the most spectacular things to see, the river plunging fifty feet over the **Conwy Falls** into a deep pool. After paying 20p at the *Conwy Falls Café* (reached by the #49 bus four times daily), you can view the falls and the rock steps which once formed part of a more primitive version.

After carving out a mile or so of what kayakers regard as some of north Wales' toughest whitewater, the Conwy negotiates a staircase of drops and enters the **Fairy Glen**, a cleft in a small wood which takes its name from the Welsh fairies, the *Tylwyth Teg*, who are said to be seen hereabouts. A short path comes up here from Beaver Bridge beside the *Fairy Glen Hotel* (closed Dec & Jan; ☎0690/710269; ③), on the A470 to Blaenau Ffestiniog.

The **Swallow Falls** (a mistranslation of *Rhaeadr Ewynnol* or "foaming cataract") are two miles west along the A5 towards Capel Curig. Though the region's most visited sight, it is just a straightforward, pretty waterfall with the occasional mad kayaker scraping down the precipitous rock. Pay your 30p and you can walk down to a series of viewing platforms.

Less than a mile beyond, the road crosses the river passing **Tŷ Hyll** (Easter–Oct daily 9am–5pm; Nov–Easter Mon–Fri variable hours; 50p), known as the "Ugly House" for its chunky appearance. Decked out with period furniture it is also the headquarters of the environmental campaigning group the *Snowdonia National Park Society*, and has a forest full of easy paths to wander in.

Penmachno

The River Machno enters the Conwy just above the Conwy Falls at the end of its short run down through the small village of **PENMACHNO** from the surrounding hills. Two and a half miles beyond the village at the end of a long drive stands the little cottage of **Tŷ Mawr Wybrnant** (April–Sept Wed–Fri & Sun noon–5pm; Oct Fri & Sun noon–4pm; NT; £1.50), where Bishop William Morgan, the man who first translated the Bible into Welsh (see p.323), was born in 1545. Unfortunately the original cottage has been replaced by this mostly seventeenth-

WALKS FROM BETWS-Y-COED

The best two walks from Betws-y-Coed follow narrow river gorges. Neither is circular, so unless you plan to hitch, consult bus timetables first to avoid a long wait for the infrequent services.

The **Conwy Gorge walk** (3 miles; 1hr 15min; descent only) links two of the districts best-known natural attractions, **Fairy Glen** and the **Conwy Falls** (see above), by way of a cool green lane giving glimpses of the river through the woods. The best approach is to forgo the forty-minute walk along the A5 towards Llangollen and take the #49 bus (four times daily) to the *Conwy Falls Café*. After viewing the falls, walk a hundred yards back along the road towards Betws-y-Coed, then follow a path parallel to the river through the trees. After about half an hour, you'll see the gate to Fairy Glen on your left. Returning to the main path, continue to the *Fairy Glen Hotel*, where you can cross the river by Beaver Bridge, turn right and follow a minor road back to town.

The car park on the north side of the Pont-y-Pair bridge marks the beginning of the **Llugwy Valley walk** (6 miles; 2hr 30min; 600ft ascent), a forested path following the twisting and plunging river upstream to Capel Curig. With the A5 running parallel to the river all the way, there are several opportunities to cut short the walk and hitch or wait for the bus back to Betws-y-Coed. Less than a mile from Pont-y-Pair you first reach a ford where the Roman road Sarn Helen crossed the river, then pass the steeply sloping **Miners' Bridge**, which linked miners' homes at Pentre Du on the south side of the river to the lead mines in Llanrwst. The path follows the river on your left for another mile – though path maintenance sometimes means you have to cut up into the pines – to a slightly obscured view of **Swallow Falls**. Detailed maps available from the tourist office show numerous routes back through the Gwydyr Forest or you can continue half a mile to the road bridge by Tŷ Hyll and follow the right bank to Capel Curig, passing the scant remains of the Caer Llugwy, a Roman fort, and a couple more treacherous rapids: The Mincer and Cobdens Falls.

century stone and slate affair, and doesn't even house a copy of the Bible, so few people come here, only those who consider it a shrine to the man who not only furthered Protestantism in Wales but probably saved the language.

The **Penmachno Woollen Mill** (daily 10am–5pm; free) gives visitors the opportunity to learn more about the weaving process, and has half a dozen ageing looms, producing uninspired patterned cloth, used to lure you into their shop.

The Conwy Valley: Llanrwst and Trefriw

Fed by the water of the Machno, Lledr and Llugwy rivers, the Conwy River leaves Betws-y-Coed along its broad pastoral corridor to the sea at Conwy (see p.333) flanked on the left by the bald tops of Snowdonia's northern and eastern bulwark, the Carneddau range. Most of the land on both banks was part of the Gwydyr Estate owned by the Wynne family, who have left their stamp on the valley in the names of two distinctive chapels and the Gwydyr Forest above Betws-y-Coed.

LLANRWST, five miles north of Betws-y-Coed, is the largest and most economically important town in the valley. Not striking, nor especially large, it does have a working town feel and was once the largest wool market in north Wales and a centre for harp manufacture. It still retains its Wednesday and Friday livestock markets, and general one on Tuesday.

Inigo Jones is said to have been born here, and it is for a possible work of the great seventeenth-century architect, the slender hump-backed **Pont Mawr** with its three graceful arches, that the town is now best known. The bridge carried all the cross-river traffic in the area before the building of Telford's bridges at the estuary of the Conwy and upstream at Betws-y-Coed.

Claims that Jones also had a hand in the design for **Gwydyr Chapel** (open daily) are no easier to verify. He was certainly known to landowner Richard Wynne, who in 1633 commissioned the elaborate chapel to be attached to the Church of St Grwst. A riot of alabaster, carved memorials and seventeenth-century brasses set off a huge stone coffin, said to be that of Llywelyn ap Iorwerth ("the Great"). The beautiful rood screen in the main body of the church was salvaged when the former Maenan Abbey, two miles to the north of the town, was dissolved by Henry VIII.

Forty years later Richard Wynne was busy again, half a mile away across the river, building his own private **Gwydyr Uchaf Chapel** (key from adjacent Forestry Commission office, Mon–Fri 8.30am–4pm; CADW; free). The plain exterior is in striking contrast to the unashamedly Baroque interior, with its roof beams cut into angelic figures. The inward-facing pews are unusual, but it is the painted ceiling which is really outstanding, depicting the Creation, the Trinity and the Day of Judgement.

Since it's so close to Betws-y-Coed, few people will want to stay in Llanrwst, but there are decent **rooms** at *Hendy*, Station Rd (☎0492/640322; ②), *Corn-u-Copia*, Main St (☎0492/640275; ②), and at *The Eagles Hotel*, Main St (☎0492/640454; ④), which has over 200 gourmet sandwiches on offer, and serves moderately priced à la carte meals. For lighter **meals**, cross Pont Fawr to the ever-popular *Tu Hwnt i'r Bont Tearooms* (April–Sept) in a fifteenth-century stone cottage next to the bridge, or pick up picnic requisites from the well-stocked delicatessen *Blas ar Fwyd*, 25 Heol Yr Orsaf, at the north end of town.

Judging by all the brochures scattered over north Wales, you would think that the main interest about the small village of **TREFRIW**, two miles north of Llanrwst, is the **Woollen Mills** (Easter–Oct Mon–Fri 10am–5.30pm; free), which demonstrate late-nineteenth-century weaving methods, using power from the stream outside: it isn't. In the second century, the Romans were the first to make a fuss over the iron-rich waters of **Trefriw Wells** (Easter–Oct daily 10am–5.30pm; Nov–Easter Mon–Sat 10am–5pm, Sun noon–5pm; £2.65), a mile and a half to the north of the village, and at the height of the Victorian spa vogue, health-seekers flocked here; but with no town to support it, the wells waned along with the fashion, although they are still there and you can buy the mineral water, liquid and dried, or take a self-guided tour around the Roman bathhouse and the slate bath inside.

The Lledr Valley

The train line up the Conwy Valley from Betws-y-Coed follows the twists of the beautiful Lledr Valley to Blaenau Ffestiniog, the river flowing through deciduous and pine forests that give way to the smooth, grassy slopes of the Moel Siabod before you bore through over two miles of slate – the longest rail tunnel in Wales – to emerge in Blaenau Ffestiniog. Take this trip while you can: the service is endangered by privatization and may close, though the Ffestiniog Railway have expressed an interest in running trains along it.

The A470 runs parallel to the river from Betws-y-Coed to Blaenau Ffestiniog. Five miles south of Betws-y-Coed you come to Pont-y-Pant station, where the Roman road Sarn Helen crosses the river on a clapper bridge and follows the river to Dolwyddelan. The Lledr Valley YHA **youth hostel** (☎06906/202; ①), across the field from the station, is an ideal starting point for a walk up Moel Siabod (see box p.294) and also accommodates **campers** for half the adult rate.

A mile further on is **DOLWYDDELAN**, a village well placed for the southern approach to Moel Siabod and only a mile east of lonely **Dolwyddelan Castle** (April to late Oct daily 9.30am–6.30pm; late Oct to March Mon–Sat 9.30am–4pm, Sun 2–4pm; £1.50; CADW), commanding the head of the valley. Llywelyn ap Iorwerth ("the Great") (see p.372) may well have been born here, since his father was reputedly responsible for its construction at the end of the twelfth century. The strategic site, on the important route from Aberconwy to the north and Ardudwy to the south, was soon turned against him when Edward I took the castle, refortified it and used it to further subdue the Welsh. By the end of the fifteenth century, it had become redundant and lay abandoned, until the Wynnes of Gwydyr treated it to a suitably Victorian reconstruction, complete with the fanciful battlements and a new roof. Today, all it shelters is a small exhibition on native Welsh castles, and gives a panoramic view from its battlements.

If you want to stay around here, the castle custodian runs the nearby *Bryn Tirion Farm B&B* (☎06906/366; ②), a **campsite** and, from October to March, a **bunkhouse** (①), for which you need your own sleeping bag. Back in the centre of Dolwyddelan, *Elen's Castle Hotel* (☎06906/807; ②) has rooms (②) and a bunkhouse (①), and serves inexpensive bar meals. The best **pub** is the cosy and welcoming *Y Gwydyr*, where Sunday lunch is served in summer.

THE WELSH SLATE INDUSTRY

Slate derives its name from the Old French word *esclater*, meaning to split, an apt reflection of its most highly valued quality.

Six hundred million years ago, what is now north Wales lay under the sea, gradually accumulating a thousand-foot-thick layer of fine-grained mud. In the collision zone of converging continental plates, the deposits were subject to immense pressures which caused the massive folding and mountain-building; the shale then metamorphosed into the purplish Cambrian slates of the Penrhyn and Dinorwig quarries (see p.344 and p.300) and the hundred-million-year-younger blue-grey Ordovician slates of Ffestiniog (see p.290).

The Romans recognized the potential of the substance, roofing the houses of Segontium (see p.347) with it, and Edward I used it extensively in his Iron Ring of castles around Snowdonia (see box p.337). But it wasn't until around 1780 that Britain's Industrial Revolution took hold, leading to greater urbanization and a demand for roofing slates. Cities grew; Hamburg was re-roofed with Welsh slate after its fire of 1842, and it is the same material which still gives that rainy-day sheen to interminable rows of new English mill town houses.

By 1898, Welsh quarries – run by the English, like the coal and steel industries of the south – were producing half a million tons of dressed slate a year, almost all of it from Snowdonia. At Penrhyn and Dinorwig, mountains were hacked away in terraces, sometimes rising 2000 feet above sea level, with the teams of workers negotiating with the foreman for the choicest piece of rock and the selling price for what they produced. They often slept through the week in damp dormitories on the mountain, and tuberculosis was common, exacerbated by the slate dust. At Blaenau

Blaenau Ffestiniog and around

As you approach from the Lledr valley, you make your way across a pass lying between the Manod and Moelwyn Mountains until the town of **BLAENAU FFESTINIOG** appears, cowering at the foot of their stark slopes, thickly strewn with discarded heaps of splintered slate that didn't pass muster. Blaenau means "head of the valley", in this case referring to the lush Vale of Ffestiniog, a dramatic contrast to this forbidding place. A bright, sunny day is the time to see the town at its best, but when clouds hunker low in this great cwm and rain sheets the grey roofs, grey walls and grey paving slabs, it can be a terrifically gloomy place.

Thousands of tons of slate per year were once hewn from the labyrinth of underground caverns, but these days only two mines manage to keep ticking over, aided by the good income made from their tours. Sometimes it feels as though little has changed here since the late Sixties, the last time the mines were really profitable. But there has been a massive upheaval: the population has dropped to less than half its 1910 peak of 12,000, unemployment remains high and *Ar Werth* (For Sale) signs have sprouted everywhere. Almost all the Nonconformist chapels are nowadays just discarded shells and prospects are few, though tourism has kept the town alive partly through the two **mine tours**, but mainly because it forms the junction of two of the finest train journeys to be offered in this part of the country: the narrow-gauge **Ffestiniog Railway** which winds up from Porthmadog, and the Lledr Valley rail line to Betws-y-Coed (see above).

Ffestiniog, the seams required mining underground rather than quarrying, but conditions were no better with miners even having to buy their own candles, the only light they had. In spite of this, thousands left their hillside smallholdings for the burgeoning quarry towns. Few workers were allowed to join Undeb Chwarelwyr Gogledd Cymru (The North Wales Quarrymen's Union), and in 1900 the workers in Lord Penrhyn's quarry at Bethesda went out on strike. For three years they stayed out – Britain's longest ever industrial dispute – but failed to win any concessions. Those who got their jobs back were forced to work for even less money as a recession took hold, and although the two World Wars heralded mini-booms as bombed houses were replaced, the industry never recovered its nineteenth-century prosperity, and most quarries and mines closed in the 1950s.

Although slate is now produced worldwide, none beats the quality of north Wales' output. For the 1862 London Exhibition, one skilled craftsman produced a sheet ten feet long, a foot wide and a sixteenth of an inch thick – so thin it could be flexed – firmly establishing Welsh slate as the finest in the world. Millions of tons of it were shipped around the globe during the nineteenth and early twentieth centuries, primarily for use as a cheap and durable roofing material.

The quarries which do survive no longer produce such quantities, and of what is made, much of it is used for other things besides roofing, such as floor tiles, road aggregate or an astonishing array of nasty ashtrays and coasters etched with mountainscapes. More memorable are the roadside fences made from lines of broken, wafer-thin slabs, the beautifully carved slate fire surrounds and mantlepieces occasionally found in pubs and houses, and Westminster Abbey's memorial to Dylan Thomas which is made entirely of Penrhyn slate.

Arrival and accommodation

The **train station** on the High Street serves both the Ffestiniog line from Porthmadog and mainline train services from Betws-y-Coed, and also houses the **tourist office** (April–Oct daily 10am–6pm; ☎0766/830360). **Buses** stop either in the car park around the back or outside *Y Commercial* pub on High Street.

A vast number of Blaenau Ffestiniog's visitors ride the train up from Porthmadog, visit a slate mine and leave, and this is reflected in the limited range of accommodation. There are good **hotels**, like the excellent, welcoming cheapie *Afallon*, Manod Rd (☎0766/830468; ②), almost a mile south of the tourist office, and *Fron Heulog Guesthouse*, (☎0766/831790; ②), half a mile closer to town; for a few extra pounds, you might want to travel the mile or so south on the A470 to *Cae Du*, Manod Rd (☎0766/830847; ③), a seventeenth-century farmhouse down a long drive, or five miles further to *Tyddyn Du*, Gellilydan (☎0766/85281; ③), an old farmhouse with a separate cottage suite and moderately priced evening meals; bus #35 passes nearby. The nearest YHA **youth hostel**, Caerblaidd, Llan Ffestiniog (☎0766/762765; ①), is a mile off the A470 three miles south of Blaenau Ffestiniog (bus #1, #2 or #35) in a large house with magnificent views over to the Moelwyn Mountains.

The town and mines

It is difficult to get a real feeling of what slate means to Blaenau Ffestiniog without a visit to one of the town's two slate mines, a mile or so north of town on the Betws-y-Coed road (bus #140, hourly when the mines are open) both of

WALKS FROM BLAENAU FFESTINIOG

The following two walks can both be done from Blaenau Ffestiniog, but involve a fairly dull first mile easily avoided by catching the Ffestiniog Railway or driving to the reservoir at Tanygrisiau.

The easier walk down into the **Vale of Ffestiniog** (4–5 miles; 2–3hr; descent only) follows the train line to its 360° loop, through sessile oak woods and past several cascades all the way to Tan-y-bwlch. It is easy going, and has some great views south to the Rhinogs (see p.240) and west to the Glaslyn Estuary, and includes a ride back on the train; check the times at Tanygrisiau station and buy your ticket when you start to ensure a place on the return train. From the station, turn right past the Tanygrisiau information centre then take the second left, not the road beside the reservoir but the next one following the footpath signs. Cross the train line, then pass a car park on your left before turning left down a track and skirting behind the powerhouse. The path then sticks closely to the train line, occasionally crossing it. Even when there are several paths you can't go far wrong if you keep the train lines in sight. *The Grapes* pub at Maentwrog, half a mile from Tan-y-bwlch, is a great place to while away the time until the next train (or the one after that).

The second walk, a circuit of the peaks of **Moelwyn Mawr, Moelwyn Fach and Cnicht** (13 miles; 7hr; 4000ft), is tougher, longer and best left for a fine day. Even then, navigation isn't always easy, and you need both the Landranger #115 Snowdon map and the Landranger #124 Dolgellau map (the Outdoor Leisure 1:25,000 maps #17 and #19 are better still). These factors make this group far less which present entertaining and informative insights into the rigours of a miner's life.

The **Llechwedd Slate Caverns** (March–Sept daily 10am–5.15pm; Oct–Feb daily 10am–4.15pm; single tour £4.35, both tours £6.65) are slightly closer to the town and were spectacular enough to be chosen as the setting for the first ever Welsh language film *Y Chwarelwr* (The Quarrymen) in 1935. You can walk around the reconstructed mining village, watch slate being split and visit *The Miners Arms* pub for nothing, but to visit some of the 25 miles of tunnels and sixteen working levels you need to take one of two tours.

The **Miners' Tramway Tour** takes you by a small train a third of a mile along one of the oldest levels. On foot you then make your way through the enormous Cathedral Cave and the open-air Chough's Cavern, – both tilted at 30° to follow the slate's bedding plane – as you are plied with factual stuff about slate mining. The awe-inspiring scale of the place justifies going on the tour even without the tableaux of Victorian miners at work chained high up in the tops of the caverns. On the more dramatic **Deep Mine Tour** you're bundled onto specially designed carriages and lowered drops to one of the deepest parts of the mine down a 1-in-1.8 incline – Britain's steepest underground inclined railway. After donning waterproofs and headgear, you head off into the labyrinth of tunnels guided by an irksome taped spiel of someone pretending to be a Victorian miner that greets you at each cavern. That said, the content is good and biased towards the working and social life of the miners who in winter never saw daylight, taking their breaks in a dank underground shelter known as a *caban*. The long caverns angling back into the gloom become increasingly impressive culminating in one filled by a beautiful opalescent pool.

popular than either Snowdon or the Glyders, but given the right conditions it can be a great walk past masses of old slate workings up onto some respectably lofty tops with panoramic views of southern Snowdonia.

From the station in Tanygrisiau, turn right past the information centre then follow the road as it doubles back north away from the reservoir. After a couple of hundred yards, turn left at a T-junction onto a track up to a car park. Follow the footpath signs past the disused quarries in Cwmorthin, swinging west up to Bwlch-y-Rhosydd (not named on Landranger map), a small plateau strewn with slate waste and long-discarded slate-built workshops. The route from here up **Moelwyn Mawr** (2526ft) starts behind the largest building heading south up an old incline, skirting left around a quarry eventually reaching the northeast ridge route to the summit. From there to **Moelwyn Fach** (2333ft) is straightforward, heading south down a generally easy ridge to Bwlch Stwlan then up the west ridge.

From Moelwyn Fach turn west and follow the ridge to the hamlet of Croesor. If you have transport this makes a good starting point, cutting three miles off the walk since you avoid the stretch from Tanygrisiau to Bwlch-y-Rhosydd and back.

A road to the left of the disused chapel in Croesor leads to a stile from where the route up **Cnicht** (2260ft) is clearly signposted. From this angle, you are looking along the southwest-to-northeast ridge line of the mountain, giving it the triangular shape which earns it its "Matterhorn of Wales" nickname. The climb up is not really difficult, but it is steep in places. A series of almost equally high summits then give way to a shallow descent towards Llyn yr Adar. Just before the lake, a path cuts right and makes a gradual undulating southeast descent back to Bwlch-y-Rhosydd, from where you retrace your steps to Tanygrisiau.

The **Gloddfa Ganol Slate Mine** (mid-July to Aug daily except Sat 10am–5.30pm; Easter to mid-July, Sept & Oct Mon–Fri 10am–5.30pm; £3.25) is slightly further along the same road from Blaenau Ffestiniog and hailed as the world's largest slate mine. The set up in the **main mine** is much like at Llechwedd, though there are no trains. You walk in down a level tunnel and follow taped explanations through fourteen caverns, past mannequins dressed as miners and lamps probing the darker recesses of caverns 240ft deep, but in this case the tour is self-guided allowing you more freedom to amble around and soak up the feel of the place. It is worth saving some time to inspect the workings above ground which are still worked as an open cast quarry. This is visible from windows in either the tame **heritage centre** or one of the **two museums** which surround the pit. The first of these tells some of the history and changing fortunes of Blaenau Ffestiniog, along with examples of the multifarious uses of slate; the second presents a mainly photographic exhibition on the Manod Slate Quarry, two miles east of here, which was requisitioned during World War II for the storage of national treasures. You can't visit the site which is now empty, but the museum tells of the vast chambers which were levelled, strengthened, ventilated and heated before most of the collections of the National and Tate galleries, pieces from the British Museum and, some say, the Crown Jewels were secretly transported here in chocolate delivery vans.

As at Llechwedd, the surface buildings house demonstrations of slate splitting and cutting, but don't let it distract you from the excellent **Quarrymen's Cottages**, a faithful reproduction of a three-cottage terrace, each two-up-two-down decorated in a different period: 1885, World War I and World War II.

You can also dish out for the hour-long **LandRover Tour** (book at the reception; £2.50) which dives into the mountain, climbs up through six levels past the remoter chambers and disgorges you at a wonderful vantage point with views over the vast heaps of discarded slate around Blaenau Ffestiniog.

Both these quarries, as well as all their now-deceased kin, dispatched their dressed and packed product, on the first leg of its journey to the markets around the world, down to Porthmadog, thirteen miles away on the **Ffestiniog Railway** (see p245). Whether you're heading to Porthmadog or just want to ride the train, it is well worth considering doing part of the journey on foot (see box).

About a mile down the track the train stops at Tanygrisiau station, a short walk from the powerhouse for the **Ffestiniog Pumped Storage Power Station** with a mildly diverting **information centre** (Easter–Oct daily 10am–4.30pm; free) and hour-long **guided tours** (hourly on the half-hour; £2) around rows of humming machinery and up to the reservoir in the hills above.

Eating, drinking and entertainment

Good **food** isn't especially abundant in Blaenau Ffestiniog. *Caffi Glen*, south of the tourist office on the High Street, does decent all-day breakfasts and snacks, but for something more substantial you're limited to the moderate, broad-ranging menu at *Myfanwys*, 4 Market Place (☎0766/830059), or the hearty, inexpensive Greek and Italian dishes at *The Firefly* (☎0766/830097), opposite *Caffi Glen*. Most locals flock to *Grapes* (☎0766/85208) at Maentwrog, four miles south down the A496, where there's the moderately priced and gamey *Flambard's* restaurant, but the place is lauded for their gargantuan and inexpensive bar meals. Leave room for the desserts if you can.

The *Wynnes Arms* rates as Blaenau Ffestiniog's best **pub**, a short walk south of *Afallon* guesthouse. About the only other thing to do in the evening is to listen to one of the **male voice choirs** practising. The *Brynthoniaid* choir practises at Ysgol y Moelwyn on Wyne Road near the hospital (Mon & Thurs 7.45pm); *Côr Meibion y Moelwyn* use the Old Salem Chapel in Rhiw, half a mile north of the tourist office on the A470, then left as the road narrows (Tues & Fri 7.30pm).

South of Blaenau Ffestiniog

Blaenau Ffestiniog is surrounded by slate waste on three sides, and the fourth drops away into the bucolic **Vale of Ffestiniog**, best explored using the Ffestiniog Railway (see p.245), or on the walk described in the box (p.290).

Heading south from Blaenau Ffestiniog, the A470 runs through the village of Llan Ffestiniog (Ffestiniog on maps, just Llan locally), three miles away, broadly following what is left of the old Great Western Railway route across the broad open moors of the Migneint to Bala. The only stretch which still operates (though not for passengers) serves the greatest blot on the National Park's landscape, the **Trawsfynydd Nuclear Power Station**, a further four miles south of Blaenau Ffestiniog. It no longer produces electricity, but it will take until 1996 to remove all the fuel, then until 2130 before the area is safely cleared and landscaped.

With the eastern flanks of the Rhinogs (see p.240) on the right, the A470 continues south to Dolgellau (see p.233) through **Coed y Brenin** (The King's Forest). Economics dictate that this vast plantation comprises row upon row of pines but there is the occasional patch of deciduous wood and some fine waterfalls. The best way to see them is to drop in to the **Maesgwn Visitor Centre** (Easter to early Sept daily 10am–5pm; early Sept to Oct daily 11am–4pm; free) and **rent a bike** (£2.50 per hour; ☎0341/40296), or go **orienteering** (50p) on one of three courses.

Capel Curig

Tantalizing glimpses of Wales' highest mountains flash through the forested banks of the Llugwy as you climb west from Betws-y-Coed on the A5. But Snowdon, the mountain which more than any other has become a symbol of north Wales for walkers, mountaineers, botanists and painters alike, eludes you until the final bend before **CAPEL CURIG**, six miles west of Betws-y-Coed, a tiny, scattered village that is a major centre for outdoor enthusiasts. There is scarcely a building which isn't of some use either as inexpensive accommodation, a mountain-gear shop or just a place to replenish the body. Foremost among them is **Plas-y-Brenin: The National Mountaineering Centre**, a quarter of a mile along the A4086 to Llanberis from the town's main road junction, built around a former coaching inn and hotel, and now running nationally renowned residential courses in orienteering, canoeing, skiing and climbing. There are daily mountain weather forecasts in reception. If you're just passing through and don't have your own equipment, the two-hour abseiling, canoeing and dry-slope skiing sessions held during July and August (£7) may be of interest. There is also a state-of-the-art climbing wall open throughout the year (daily 10am–11pm; £2 on weekdays, £3 at weekends), and the opportunity to hear talks or watch slide shows of recent expeditions (usually Mon–Thurs & Sat 8pm; free).

Despite Capel Curig's popularity, the only major walk is up Moel Siabod (see box), but the village acts as a base for the Ogwen Valley (see below) and Snowdon. The road to the valley runs four miles southwest past **DYFFRYN**, the farm written about by Thomas Firbank (see "Books" in *Contexts*), to the *Pen-y-Gwryd Hotel* (see p.305). The A498 continues south to Beddgelert (see p.305), past the best view of the east face of Snowdon, while the A4086 branches west to Llanberis passing Pen-y-Pass (see p.305), the start for the best-known Snowdon walks.

Practicalities

The only **buses** servicing Capel Curig are the #19 which runs between Llandudno and Llanberis via Betws-y-Coed, Capel Curig and Pen-y-Pass, and the #95 which leaves Llanrwst for Betws-y-Coed, Capel Curig and the Ogwen Valley for Bangor. If none of these suit, you can always walk the six miles along the Llugwy River from Betws-y-Coed (see box p.286).

Once here, there are plenty of **places to stay**, though none is especially luxurious. The best is either the *Bron Eryri* (☎06904/240; ③), a comfortable and welcoming B&B half a mile outside the village towards Betws-y-Coed, or the *Bryn Tyrch Hotel* (☎06904/223; ③), also on the A5 but closer to the main road junction. The *Llugwy Guesthouse* (☎06904/218; ②) is on the A4086 towards the adventure centre of **Plas-y-Brenin** (☎06904/214; ②), which has a limited amount of accommodation. The cheapest option in the village is the **YHA youth hostel** (☎06904/225; ①), five hundred yards along the A5 towards Betws-y-Coed. Two and a half miles west down the Ogwen Valley you can stay for a good deal less in the *Williams Barn* bunkhouse and **campsite** (see p.298).

During the day, walkers tend to patronize the *Pinnacle Café*, grafted onto the post office and general store at the main road junction. In the evening they retire to

A WALK FROM CAPEL CURIG

If you approached Capel Curig from the west, you won't have looked twice at the rounded grassy back of **Moel Siabod** (2862ft), but its the challenging east ridge and magnificent summit view of the Snowdon Horseshoe that is adequate compensation.

The mountainous section of the **east ridge walk** (5 miles; 4hr; 2200ft) is circular and brings you back into the Llugwy valley. The route starts from opposite the YHA youth hostel in Capel Curig, crossing the concrete bridge and following the right bank downstream past the falls by *Cobdens Hotel* to the Pont Cyfyng road bridge (30min), an alternative starting point for the walk. Taking the road south, turn right on the second path signposted to Moel Siabod. The path quickly rises out of the valley and keeps to the left of the mountain, past a disused slate quarry and across some boggy land, before the long scramble up the east ridge. Once found, the path is fairly clear, but it weaves around outcrops past places where a moment's inattention could be perilous. The summit is flat and uninteresting, so once you've admired Snowdon, turn northeast and follow the craggy summit ridge which eventually starts to drop across grass to the moors below, soon rejoining your ascent route for the hike back to Pont Cyfyng.

An alternative, if you are prepared to carry all your gear or chance the public transport system to get back to Capel Curig, is to approach the summit by the route described then retrace you steps down the ridge, and descend through a pine forest above Dolwyddelan into the Lledr Valley (see p.287).

the warm and lively bar at the *Bryn Tyrch Hotel* (see above) to swap tales of the day's exploits. The inexpensive **meals** here are huge, and predominantly vegetarian – indeed, this is one of the few establishments in the whole of Snowdonia to make any real attempt to please vegans. Everyone who isn't at the *Bryn Tyrch* is in the sociable bar at the Plas-y-Brenin centre eating cheaper but less imaginative meals, flicking through the mountaineering and canoeing magazines and watching the novices on the floodlit dry ski slope outside.

The Ogwen Valley

Prising apart the Carneddau and Glyder ranges northwest from Capel Curig, the A5 forges through the **Ogwen Valley** to Bethesda, where one of Wales' last surviving slate quarries continues to tear away the end of the Glyders range, only just keeping the tatty town viable.

Coming from the east, you cross the watershed between the Llugwy and Ogwen rivers. To the north, the frequently mist-shrouded Carneddau range glowers across at the Glyders range and its triple-peaked **Tryfan**, arguably Snowdonia's most demanding mountain, which forms a fractured spur out from the main range and blocks your view down the valley. As you approach along the valley, you can pick out the twin monoliths of Adam and Eve that crown Tryfan's summit: the courageous or foolhardly make the jump between them as a point of honour at the end of every ascent. West of Tryfan the road follows a perfect example of a U-shaped valley, carved and smoothed by rocks frozen into the undersides of the glaciers that creaked down **Nant Ffrancon** ten thousand years ago.

The time-compacted moraine left by the retreating ice formed Llyn Ogwen. **IDWAL COTTAGE**, one of the few settlements in the valley and so small it isn't named on maps, is on the western shore and comprises just a mountain rescue centre, a snack bar and a YHA **youth hostel** clustered around the car park. The main reason to come here is to make some of Wales' most demanding and rewarding walks (see box overleaf), or start the easier twenty-minute walk to the magnificent classically formed cirque, **Cwm Idwal**.

The evidence of glacial scouring is so clear here that you wonder why it took geologists so long to work out the process that created these hollowed faces and scored rocks. In 1842, Darwin wrote of his visit with the geologist Alan Sedgewick eleven years earlier recalling that "neither of us saw a trace of the wonderful glacial phenomena all around us". The cwm's scalloped floor traps the beautifully still **Llyn Idwal**, which reflects the precipitous grey cliffs behind, split by the jointed cleft of Twll Du, **The Devil's Kitchen**. Down this channel, a fine watery haze runs off the flanks of **Glyder Fawr** soaking the crevices where early botanists found rare arctic-alpine plants (see *Contexts*) the main reason for designating Cwm Idwal as Wales' first **nature reserve** (NT) in 1954. More common species carpet the reserve in early summer but have to compete with grazing sheep who destroy all but the comparatively luxuriant fenced-off control areas. Geomorphologists pay more attention to the twisted rocks beside the Devil's Kitchen, one of the few places where you can see the downfolded strata of what is known as the Snowdon syncline (see *Contexts*), evidence that the existing mountains sat between two much larger ranges some 300 million years ago. To their left, the smooth inclines of the Idwal Slabs act as nursery slopes for budding rock climbers: good for some half-hearted "bouldering" for the ill-equipped.

An easy well-groomed path leads up to the reserve from the car park, where the café (daily 8.30am–5pm, later on summer weekends) will sell you a nature trail booklet for 60p. A five-minute walk down the valley from the car park, the

WALKS FROM OGWEN: TRYFAN, THE GLYDERS & THE CARNEDDAU

Note: The OS Outdoor Leisure 1:25,000 map of "Snowdonia" is highly recommended for all these walks, though the latter half of the Carneddau walk is omitted. The 1:50,000 Landranger #115 covers the whole area.

THE GLYDERS

The sheer number of good walking paths on the Glyders make it almost impossible for us to choose one definitive circular route. The individual sections of the walk have therefore been defined separately in order to allow the greatest flexibility. All times given are for the ascents: expect to take approximately half the time to get back down.

If you've got the head for it, the **North Ridge of Tryfan** (3002ft) (1 mile; 1hr–1hr 30min; 2000ft ascent) is one of the most rewarding scrambles in the country. It's not as precarious as Snowdonia's Cribgoch, but you get a genuine mountaineering feel as the valley floor drops rapidly away and the views stretch further and further along it. The route starts in the lay-by at the head of Idwal Lake and goes left across rising ground, until you strike a path heading straight up following the crest of the ridge. Anyone who has seen pictures of people jumping the five-foot gap between Adam and Eve, the two chunks of rhyolitic lava which crown this regal mountain, will wonder what the fuss is about until they get up there and see the mountain dropping away on all sides. In theory the leap is trivial, but the consequences of overshooting would be disastrous.

There are two other main routes up Tryfan. The first follows the so-called **Miners' Track** (2 miles; 2hr; 1350ft ascent) from Idwal Cottage, taking the path to Cwm Idwal then, as it bears sharply to the right, keeping straight ahead and making for the gap on the horizon. This is **Bwlch Tryfan**, the col between Tryfan and Glyder Fach, from where the **South Ridge** of Tryan (800 yards; 30min; 650ft ascent) climbs past the Far South Peak to the summit. This last section is an easy scramble. The second route, which is more often used in descent, follows **Heather Terrace** (1.5 miles; 2hr; 2000ft ascent), which keeps to a fault in the rock running diagonally across the east face. The start is the same as for the north ridge, but instead of following the ridge, you cut left, heading south until you arrive between the South and the Far South Peaks. A right turn then starts your scramble for the summit.

GLYDER FACH

The assault on **Glyder Fach** (3260ft) begins at Bwlch Tryfan, reached either by the Miners' Track from Ogwen Cottage or by the south ridge from Tryfan's summit. The trickier route follows **Bristly Ridge** (1000 yards; 40min; 900ft ascent) which isn't marked on OS maps but runs steeply south from the col up past some daunting-looking towers of rock. It isn't that difficult, and saves a long hike southeast along a second section of the **Miners' Track** (1.5 miles; 1hr 30min; 900ft ascent), then west to the summit, a chaotic jumble of huge grey slabs that many people don't bother climbing up, preferring to be photographed on a massive cantilevered rock a few yards away.

road crosses a bridge over the top of **Rhaeadr Ogwen** (Ogwen Falls), which cascades down this step in the valley floor. Before you put your camera away, look under the road bridge, where you'll see a simple mortarless arch of a bridge,

GLYDER FAWR

From Glyder Fach, it is an easy enough stroll to **Glyder Fawr** (3280ft) (1 mile; 40min; 200ft ascent), reached by skirting round the tortured rock formations of **Castell y Gwynt** (The Castle of the Winds) then following a cairn-marked path to the dramatic summit of frost-shattered slabs angled like ancient headstones.

Glyder Fawr is normally approached from Idwal Cottage, following the **Devil's Kitchen Route** (2.5 miles; 3hr; 2300ft ascent) past Idwal Lake, then to the left of the Devil's Kitchen, zigzagging up to a lake-filled plateau. Follow the path to the right of the lake, then where paths cross, turn left for the summit.

A **southern approach** to Glyder Fawr (3 miles; 2hr 30min; 2100ft ascent) leaves from beside the YHA youth hostel at Pen-y-Pass (see p.305), following a "courtesy path" marked by red flashes of paint. It rises steeply behind the hostel heading northwest, but turning north for the summit to avoid straying onto the screes on the flanks of the neighbouring mountain, Esgair Felen.

THE CARNEDDAU RANGE

The appearance of the **Carneddau Range** could hardly be in greater contrast to the jagged edges of the Glyders. These peaceful giants, which present the longest stretch of ground over three thousand feet in England and Wales, form a rounded plateau stretching to the cliffs of Penmaenmawr on the north coast. The sound of a raven in the neighbouring mist-filled cwms, and the occasional wild pony can often be your only company on inclement days, but in fine weather the easy walking and roof-of-the-world views make for a satisfying day out. Though the tops are fairly flat once you're up there, getting to them can be a hard slog. The start from Idwal Cottage is the most strenuous, requiring a long push up the shaley south ridge from the stile beside the road bridge at the foot of Ogwen Lake. If you can, avoid this in favour of a fine **Carneddau loop** (9 miles; 5hr; 3500ft ascent) starting from the lay-by at the head of the lake near Tal y Llyn Ogwen farm, and taking in the range's four mighty southern peaks. The path keeps to the right of the farm, then follows boggy land by a stream towards its source, Ffynnon Lloer, before turning left up the east ridge of **Pen yr Ole Wen** (3212ft), with its magnificent view down into Nant Ffrancon and back to Tryfan. In clear weather, you can see the route running north past Carnedd Fach, past what looks to be a huge artificial mound, to **Carnedd Dafydd** (3425ft). After a short easterly descent, the path skirts the steep Ysgolion Duon cliffs, then climbs over stones to the broad, arched top of **Carnedd Llewelyn** (3491ft), the highest of the Carneddau and surpassed in Wales only by two of Snowdon's peaks, Yr Wyddfa and Crib-y-ddysgl. For little extra effort, enthusiasts can conquer **Yr Elen** (3152ft), a short distance to the northeast, but most will be content with the easterly descent to **Craig yr Ysfa**, a sheer cliff which drops away into **Cwm Eigiau**, a vast amphitheatre to the north. Continuing with care, skirt around the north of Ffynnon Llugwy reservoir and climb to the grassy top of **Penyrhelgi-du** (2733ft), from where there is a steady broad-ridged descent to the road near Helyg. The mile back west to the starting point is best done on the old packhorse route running parallel to the A5, and linked to it occasionally by footpaths.

If you are considering one-way walks, several other possibilities present themselves, the most appealing of which is the full ridge walk from here linking up with the Roman road which links Roewen to Aber (see p.339).

part of the original packhorse route that followed the valley before Telford pushed the Holyhead road through.

Practicalities

Depending on the season and school holidays, two or three **buses** run along the valley daily between Betws-y-Coed and Bangor. They are usually inconveniently timed, but rather than hitch along a fast and busy road, use the footpath parallel to it, following the five-mile-long packhorse route that runs the length of the valley from a track beside the mountain equipment shop in Capel Curig to Idwal Cottage (see above). **Accommodation** in the valley is limited. Two and a half miles west of Capel Curig, the *Williams Barn*, Gwern-y-Gof Isaf Farm (☎06904/276; ①), has a self-catering bunkhouse and **campsite**, and there's the smaller *Gwern Gof Uchaf* campsite, a mile further west, and the *Idwal Cottage* **YHA youth hostel** (☎0248/600225; ①), at the western end of Llyn Ogwen, five miles from Capel Curig. Residents can get meals at the youth hostel, otherwise the valley is self-catering.

Llanberis and around

Mention **LLANBERIS**, ten miles west of Capel Curig, to any mountain enthusiast and **Snowdon** springs to mind. The two seem inseparable, and it's not just the five-mile-long umbilical of the **Snowdon Mountain Railway** (see below), Britain's only rack and pinion railway bonding the town to the summit, nor the popular path running parallel to it (see box, p.302). This is the nearest you'll get in Wales to an alpine climbing village, its single main street thronged with weather-beaten walkers and climbers decked out in Gore-Tex and Fibrepile, high fashion for what is otherwise a dowdy town. Most are Snowdon-bound, others are just making use of abundant budget accommodation and the best facilities this side of Betws-y-Coed.

At the same time Llanberis is very much a Welsh rural community, albeit a depleted one now that slate is no longer being torn from the flanks of Elidir Fawr, the mountain separated from the town by the twin lakes of Llyn Padarn and Llyn Peris. The quarries, which for the best part of two centuries employed up to three thousand men to chisel out the precious slabs, closed in 1969, leaving a vast staircase of sixty-foot-high terraced platforms as a testament to their labours. At much the same time proposals were tabled for a power station to be built on the site of the former quarries. Environmentalists – as often as not the same middle-class English second-home owners who had pushed property prices beyond the means of the local people – were incensed that this fragile spot on the fringes of the national park could be desecrated. The people of Llanberis, still reeling from the closure of the quarries, had no such qualms. In the end both parties were pacified: the project went ahead underground.

With the power station now operating, the jobs are gone and the community struggles on servicing the needs of nearby farms and fitfully coexisting with the ever-growing band of outdoor enthusiasts.

Arrival, information and accommodation

With no train or *National Express* services, the easiest way here is on bus #77 from Bangor, bus #88 from Caernarfon or bus #11, which links those two towns via Llanberis and Beddgelert. All stop near the Power of Wales museum, which doubles up as the town's **tourist office** (daily mid-June to mid-Sept 10am–6pm; April to mid-Sept closes 5pm; ☎0286/870765).

There is plenty of low-cost **accommodation** in or close to town, as well as up at Pen-y-Pass (see p.305). Luxurious places are more scarce, so if you have your own transport and don't mind being a few miles further from the mountain, you might prefer to stay in nearby places listed under Caernarfon (see p.346), or Bangor (see p.341).

Hotels and guesthouses

Dolafon Hotel, High St (☎0286/870933). Comfortable B&B in its own grounds, with en suite rooms. Moderately priced evening meals available. Situated near the junction with the A4086. ③.

Dolbadarn Hotel, High St (☎0286/870277). Former coaching hotel in one of the oldest buildings in the village, which operates its own hiking centre. ④.

The Heights, 74 High St (☎0286/871179). Primarily catering to the walking and climbing set, the *Heights* does B&B in either double rooms or dorms. Climbing wall, good restaurant and lively bar on site. Double rooms ③; eight-bed dorms ②.

Mount Pleasant Hotel, High St (☎0286/870395). Family-run hotel in the centre of town, serving inexpensive evening meals. ③.

Royal Victoria Hotel, opposite the Mountain Railway (☎0286/870253). The town's largest and best hotel. Satellite TV and all mod cons. ⑥.

Hostels, bunkhouses and campsites

Cae Gwyn Campsite, three miles southeast of Llanberis (☎0286/870718). Simple campsite almost opposite Pen y Pass "Park and Ride".

Gallt-y-Glyn Bunkhouse, a mile northwest of Llanberis on the Caernarfon Road (☎0286/870370). A comparatively luxurious bunkhouse with breakfast, pushing the price to the top of this category. Bar-type meals available. Take the #88 bus. ①.

Jesse James' Bunkhouse, Buarth y Clythiau, Penisarwaen (☎0286/870521). Run by a mountain guide, this non-smoking bunkhouse also has bar meals. Take the A4086 two miles towards Caernarfon, turn right onto the B4547 and continue for a mile. ①.

Llwyn Celyn youth hostel, Llwyn Celyn (☎0286/870280). Run-of-the-mill YHA hostel, a 700-yard uphill slog along Capel Goch Road signposted off High Street. ①.

Nant Peris B&B and Bunkhouse, Gwastadnant (☎0286/870356). Use this as a B&B or cut bed costs to the minimum in the bunkhouse. Also has **camping** facilities. It is three miles east of Llanberis, beyond Nant Peris. B&B ②; bunkhouse ①.

Pritchard's Camping, two miles east of Llanberis, opposite the *Vaynol Arms* (☎0286/870494). The closest campsite to Llanberis catering mainly to climbers. Toilets and showers only.

The Town

Scattered remains are all that is left of thirteenth-century **Dolbadarn Castle** (April to late Oct daily 9.30am–6.30pm; £1; unrestricted access in winter; CADW), on a perch between Llyn Peris and Llyn Padarn. Llywelyn ap Iorwerth ("the Great") probably built it to guard the entrance of the Pass of Llanberis, but its construction is undocumented and its circular keep is redolent of a Norman Marcher fort more than a native Welsh castle. There's not a lot to look at, but you can see why both Richard Wilson and Turner came to paint it.

The road opposite the Mountain Railway terminus, at the east end of town, runs past the castle and then left to the grounds of the **Parc Padarn** (Llyn

Padarn Country Park; unrestricted access), where lakeside oak woods are gradually recolonizing the discarded workings of the defunct Dinorwig Slate Quarries. Here, the **Welsh Slate Museum** (Easter–Oct daily 9.30am–5.30pm; £1.50) occupies the former maintenance workshops of what was one of the largest slate quarries in the world. The fifty-foot-diameter water wheel that once powered lineshafts, countershafts and flapping belts operating cutting machines still turns, but no longer drives the machinery; most of the equipment dates back to the early part of this century, as do quite a few of the former quarry workers who demonstrate their skills at turning an inch-thick slab of slate into six, even eight, perfectly smooth slivers. The slate was delivered to the slate-dressing sheds by means of a maze of tramways, cranes and rope lifts, all kept in good order in the fitting and repair shops that are also staffed by former workers keen to demonstrate on the lathes and drill presses. As you pass through, look out for the scales used to calculate the price each rock cutter would have to pay for the rope he needed to extract the diverse types of slate. Some of these are displayed nearby and range from mottled burgundy and bottle green to every shade of grey.

To keep everything in working order, the craftsmen here operate an ageing foundry, producing pieces for the scattered branches of the National Museum of Wales, as well as repairing the rolling stock belonging to the nearby **Llanberis Lake Railway** (March to early Oct 4–11 daily except Sat; £3.60 return). Originally built to transport slate and workers between the Dinorwig quarries and Port Dinorwig on the Menai Straits, this now runs for a tame two miles to Pen-y-llyn along the shores of Lake Padarn. The smoking tank engine takes about forty minutes for the round trip, and although there's nothing much to do at the other end, you can at least catch a different train back. You're really better off just walking around the old slate workings and through the ancient woodlands of Coed Dinorwig slowly, making for the period-furnished **Quarry Hospital** (May–Sept 10am–4.45pm; free), where the resident surgeon patched up gruesome injuries from gunpowder blasts and falling rock.

In 1974, five years after the quarry closed, work began hollowing out the vast underground chambers of the **Dinorwig Pumped Storage Hydro Station**. Designed to help cope with the early-evening increase in the electricity demand when everyone starts to cook dinner it can be wound up to its maximum power output (1800 Megawatts) in ten seconds. This is achieved by letting the contents of the Marchlyn Mawr reservoir rapidly empty through the turbines into Llyn Peris, then when the demand lessens, pumping it up again – a net drain on the national grid. If you can bear the thinly disguised electricity industry advertisement which comes before it, you can take an hour-long minibus tour around the enormous pipework in the depths. For this, you need to call at the **The Power of Wales** museum complex (June to mid-Sept daily 9.30am–6pm; mid-Sept to May 9.30am–6pm; museum £3.50, museum and power station tour £5), by the lake on the A4086 which bypasses the town centre. As well as operating as the town's tourist office the complex has a museum in which the disembodied voice of "Merlin" guides you around some missable tableaux of regional interest.

Eating, drinking and entertainment

The High Street in Llanberis is the best place to **eat**, with a range of pubs and restaurants for all pockets.

Arthur's Café, next to *Dolafon Hotel*. Real Welsh rarebit and bentwood chairs. Inexpensive.

Y Bistro, 43–45 High St (☎0286/871278). The best restaurant for miles around, offering generous two-, three- and four-course set meals from a bilingual menu, all served with canapés on homemade bread. Booking essential. Closed Sun. Expensive.

The Heights, 74 High St. Excellent value meat, vegetarian and vegan meals, and one of the liveliest bars in town. Full of climbers and walkers. Inexpensive.

Pete's Eats, 40 High St. Climbers and walkers flock here for top-value basic meals of gut-splitting proportions and a few more delicate touches. Summer daily to 8pm; winter Mon–Fri till 5pm, Sat & Sun till 8pm. Inexpensive.

Prince of Wales, 38 High St. Ordinary local pub which comes to life on Saturday night when you can join in with the Welsh singing led by the resident electric-organist.

Vaynol Arms, Nant Peris. Two miles east of Llanberis and the only pub before Pen-y-Gwryd, the *Vaynol Arms* serves good beer in a convivial atmosphere. It's usually full of campers from across the road.

Activities

By far the most popular activity around Llanberis is simply getting out on foot. This is principally on Snowdon (see box, p.302) whose vast steep-sided cwms have become the summer playground for rock athletes picking their way up impossibly sheer faces. Those interested in such pursuits should contact *Snowdonia Mountaineering* (☎0286/674481) who run specialized courses in scrambling, climbing and canoeing. If you're looking for something less specialized, *Merlin Water Sports and Activities Centre*, Parc Padarn (☎0286/674481), offer the broadest range of both **watersports** and land-based activities. Half-day or longer courses in canoeing, windsurfing, sailing and climbing are offered from around £18, and the more experienced can rent gear by the hour or day.

As well as being one of the most popular walking routes up Snowdon, the **Llanberis Track** (see Snowdon box) is designated a bridleway, making it, the Snowdon Ranger Path and the Pitt's Head Track to Rhyd-Ddu open for **cyclists**. A voluntary agreement exists restricting access to and from the summit between 10am and 5pm from June to September, but otherwise these paths are open. Unfortunatley, there is no bike rental in Llanberis, but you can rent them in Betws-y-Coed (see p.284).

You can also take a **horse** up onto Snowdon's lower slopes at a cost of around £7 an hour from *The Dolbadarn Pony Trekking Centre*, High Street (☎0286/870277).

Snowdon

The highest British mountain south of the Scottish Grampians, the **Snowdon** massif (3650ft) forms a star of shattered ridges with three major peaks – Crib Goch, Crib-y-ddysgl and Y Lliwedd – and the summit, **Yr Wyddfa**, crowning the lot. If height were its only quality, it would be popular, but Snowdon also sports some of the finest walking and scrambling in the park, and in the winter, the longest season for ice climbers and cramponed walkers. Some hardened outdoor enthusiasts dismiss it as overused, and it certainly can be crowded. A thousand visitors a day press onto the postbox-red carriages of the Snowdon Mountain Railway (see below), while another fifteen hundred pound the well-maintained paths to make this Britain's most-climbed mountain. Opprobrium is chiefly levelled at the train for its mere existence, and at the abominable concrete-bunker summit café for selling the country's highest pint of beer. But at least there's a warm place for walkers to rest, and those unable to walk up have the chance of seeing the mighty **views** over most of north Wales – and even across to Ireland on exceptionally clear days.

WALKS ON SNOWDON

Note: The OS Outdoor Leisure 1:25,000 map of "Snowdonia" is highly recommended for all these walks.

LLANBERIS PATH

The easiest and longest route up Snowdon, the **Llanberis Path** (5 miles to summit; 3hr; 3200ft ascent), following the rail line, is widely scorned by walkers, particularly by the same serious hikers who wouldn't deign to take refreshment at the Halfway Station café (March to late Sept daily; winter Sat & Sun only). To the south of the café, **Clogwyn Du'r Arddu** (The Black Cliff, or "Cloggy" to its friends) frames a small lake. Today, climbers sprint up the face, which caused an early exponent to lament, "No breach seems either possible or desirable along the whole extent of the west buttress. Though there is the faintest of faint hopes for a human fly rather on the left side." The annual Snowdon Race passes the café on the fourth Saturday in July, the barely believable times being posted inside. Continuing up, the path gets steeper to the "Finger Stone" at **Bwlch Glas** (Green Pass) marking the arrival of the Snowdon Ranger Path (see below), and three routes coming up from Pen-y-Pass to join the Llanberis Path for the final ascent to **Yr Wyddfa**.

THE MINER'S TRACK

The **Miners' Track** (4 miles to summit; 2hr 30min; 2400ft ascent) is the easiest of the three routes up from Pen-y-Pass. Leaving the car park, a broad track leads south then west to the former copper mines in Cwm Dyli. Dilapidated remains of the crushing mill perch on the shores of Llyn Llydaw, a mountain tarn-turned-reservoir with one of the worst eyesores in the park, an above-ground pipeline slicing across Snowdon's east face to the power station in Nantgwynant. Skirting around the right of the lake, the path climbs more steeply to the lake-filled Cwm Glaslyn, then again to Upper Glaslyn, from where the measured steps of those ahead warn of the impending switchback ascent to the junction with the Llanberis Path.

PIG TRACK

The stonier **Pig Track** (3.5 miles to summit; 2hr 30min; 2400ft ascent) is really just a variation on the shorter and steeper Miners' Track, leaving from the western end of the Pen-y-Pass car park and climbing up to **Bwlch y Moch** (the Pass of the Pigs), which gives the route its name. Ignore the scramble up to Crib Goch and traverse below the rocky ridge looking down on Llyn Llydaw and those pacing the Miners' Track, content that you're already 500 feet up on them. They'll soon catch up as the two tracks meet just before the zigzag up to the Llanberis Path.

SNOWDON HORSESHOE

Some claim that the **Snowdon Horseshoe** (8 miles round; 5–7hr; 3200ft ascent) is one of the finest ridge walks in Europe. The route makes a full anticlockwise circuit around the three glacier-carved cwms of Upper Glaslyn, Glaslyn and Llydaw. Not to be taken lightly, it includes the knife-edge traverse of **Crib Goch**. Every summer's

There is no longer a tumulus on the top of Snowdon, but the Welsh for the highest point, Yr Wyddfa, means "The Burial Place" – near proof that people have been climbing the mountain for millennia. More recently, early ascents were for botanical or geological reasons – 500-million-year-old fossil shells can be found near the

day, dozens of people find themselves straddling the lip, empty space on both sides, and wishing they weren't there. In winter conditions, an ice-axe and crampons are the minimum requirement. The path follows the Pig Track to Bwlch y Moch, then pitches right for the moderate scramble up to Crib Goch. If you balk at any of this, turn back. If not, wait your turn then painstakingly pick your way along the sensational ridge to **Crib-y-ddysgl** (3494ft), from where it is an easy descent to Bwlch Glas and stiffer ascent to Yr Wyddfa. Having ticked off Wales' two highest tops, turn southwest for a couple of hundred yards to a marker stone where the Watkin Path (see below) drops away to the east. Follow it down to the stretched saddle of **Bwlch-y-Saethau** (Pass of the Arrows), then on to the cairn at Bwlch Ciliau from where the Watkin Path descends to Nantgwynant. Ignore that route, continue straight on up the cliff-lined northwest ridge of **Y Lliwedd** (2930ft), then descend to where you see the scrappy but safe path down to Llyn Llydaw and the Miners' Track.

SNOWDON RANGER PATH

Many of the earliest Snowdon climbers engaged the services of the Snowdon Ranger, who led them up the comparatively long and dull but easy **Snowdon Ranger Path** (4 miles to summit; 3hr; 3100ft ascent), from the Snowdon Ranger YHA hostel (see under Beddgelert) on the shores of Llyn Cwellyn, five miles northwest of Beddgelert. To the left of the hostel, a path leads up a track then ascends, steeply flattening out to cross sometimes boggy grass, eventually skirting to the right of the impressive Clogwyn Du'r Arddu cliffs (see "Snowdon Horseshoe", above). This is another steep ascent which eventually meets the Llanberis Path at Bwlch Glas.

PITT'S HEAD TRACK

The **Pitt's Head Track** (4 miles to summit; 3hr; 2900ft ascent) has two branches, one starting from Pitt's Head Rock, two and a half miles northwest of Beddgelert, the other from the National Park car park in Rhyd-Ddu, a mile beyond that. They join up after less than a mile's walk across stony, walled grazing land, and after crossing a kissing gate continue to the northwest up to the stunning final section along the rim of Cwm Clogwyn and the south ridge of Yr Wyddfa.

WATKIN PATH

The most spectacular of the southern routes up Snowdon, the **Watkin Path** (4 miles to summit; 3hr; 3350ft ascent), begins at Bethania Bridge, three miles northeast of Beddgelert in Nantgwynant. The path starts on a broad track through oaks which narrows before heading past a disused tramway to a series of cataracts. Climbing higher, Cwm Llan opens out into a natural amphitheatre, where the ruins of the South Snowdon Slate Works only temporarily distract you from **Gladstone Rock**, at which in 1892, the 83-year-old Prime Minister and Liberal statesman officially opened the route. A narrower path wheels left around the base of Craig Ddu, then starts the steep ascent past Carnedd Arthur to Bwlch Ciliau, the saddle between Y Lliwedd (see "Snowdon Horseshoe" above) and the true summit (Yr Wyddfa), then turning left for the final climb to the top.

summit from when Snowdon was on the sea bottom – but the Welsh naturalist Thomas Pennant came up here mainly for pleasure, and in 1773, his description of the dawn view from the summit in his *Journey to Snowdon* encouraged many to follow. Some were guided by the Snowdon Ranger from his house on the south side (now a YHA hostel), but the rapidly improving facilities in Llanberis soon shifted the balance in favour of the easier Llanberis track, a route later followed by the railway. This remains one of the most popular routes up, though many prefer the three shorter and steeper ones from the Pen-y-Pass car park at the top of the Llanberis Pass. By far the most dramatic, if also the most dangerous, is the wonderful Snowdon Horseshoe, which calls at all four of the high peaks.

The Snowdon Mountain Railway

The **Snowdon Mountain Railway** (mid-March to Oct 3–18 trains daily; summit return £12.50) was completed in 1896, and seventy-year-old carriages pushed by equally old steam locos still climb to the summit in just under an hour. The three-thousand-foot, one-in-five struggle up the shallowest approach to the top of Snowdon starts at the eastern end of Llanberis opposite the *Royal Victoria Hotel*, and continues to the summit **café** (open when the trains are running to the top) and a post office where you can buy a "Railway Stamp" (10p) to affix to your letter – along with the usual Royal Mail one – thereby entitling you to use the highest post box in the UK and enchant your friends with a "Summit of Snowdon – Copa'r Wyddfa" postmark.

Times, type of locomotive (steam or diesel) and final destination vary with demand and ice conditions at the top, but if it is running, the full steam-pushed round trip takes two and a half hours. To avoid disappointment, buy your tickets early on clear summer days. If you walk up by one of the routes detailed in the Walks on Snowdon box (see p.302), you can still take the train down. Standby tickets back to Llanberis (£5) are sold at the summit, but only if there are seats. Round-trippers get priority.

Legends, painters and poets

From the departure of the Romans until the tenth century, Welsh history comes down to us leavened with equal measures of myth, and populated with the shadowy figures of Arthur, Gwrtheryn (Vortigern) and Myrddin (Merlin). Glastonbury in England lays a powerful, though not incontestable, claim to being the location of Arthur's court and burial place, but his British (as opposed to Anglo-Saxon) blood gives him a firm place in Welsh hearts; and in Wales, Snowdon is always held to be his home. It was on top of Dinas Emrys, the seat of Gwrtheryn's realm at the foot of the south ridge near Beddgelert, that that most potent symbol of Welsh independence, the **Red Dragon**, earned its colours. The Celtic king, Gwrtheryn, was trying to build a fortress to protect himself from the Saxons but each night the earth swallowed the building stones, a phenomenon that Myrddin divined to be due to two dragons sleeping underground: one white, the other red. When woken they engaged in an unending fight which Myrddin pronounced to symbolize the Red Dragon of Wales' perpetual battle with the White Dragon of the Saxons.

Arthur's domain was higher up the mountain. Llyn Llydaw aspires to being the pond where Bedivere threw King Arthur's sword Excalibur, while thirteen hundred feet above, Bwlch-y-Saethau (The Pass of the Arrows) was where a wayward arrow mortally wounded Arthur, while on the point of vanquishing his nephew Modred. The remains of Carnedd Arthur, just below Bwlch Ciliau on the Watkin Path (see below), are claimed as his burial site, but it is probably a fairly modern cairn. Another burial place is that of one of Arthur's victims, Rhita Gawr, whose now-vanished tumulus gave Snowdon's highest point, Yr Wyddfa, its name.

Throughout the eighteenth and nineteenth centuries, anywhere with Arthurian associations proved an irresistible magnet for all manner of writers and painters. Thomas Gray added to both the mystery of the place and its Celtic symbolism in his ode *The Bard*, in which the last Welsh bard hurls himself off the summit while fleeing Edward I's marauding army, but the painter Richard Wilson had already beaten him to the task. His *Snowdon from Llyn Nantlle* had already planted the pre-Romantic seeds from which grew a vast, and still growing, body of work capturing the mountain's changing moods from every conceivable angle.

The Llanberis Pass and Pen-y-Pass

Llanberis is only the start for one of the easiest routes up Snowdon, the Llanberis Pass. For something more challenging you need to grind five miles east up the deepest, narrowest and craggiest of Snowdonia's passes to the youth hostel, café and car park at the settlement of **PEN-Y-PASS**. The Miners', Pig and Horseshoe routes on Snowdon (see p.302) leave from the car park, while a route up Glyder Fawr (see Ogwen box, p.296) follows a "courtesy path" to the west of the hostel.

Frequent year-round *Sherpa* **buses** travel up daily to Pen-y-Pass: the #11 Caernarfon *Sherpa* (5 daily), looping from Caernarfon through Beddgelert, Pen-y-Gwryd and Pen-y-Pass to Llanberis, and the #19 Llandudno *Sherpa* running from there through Betws-y-Coed to Llanberis. From mid-July to August, there is also the #96 Pen-y-Pass shuttle from Llanberis, the recommended approach even if you have a car, since the Pen-y-Pass car park is almost always full and is expensive. Use the "Park and Ride" car park at the bottom of the pass.

The only **accommodation** at Pen-y-Pass is the YHA **youth hostel** (☎0286/870428; ①), which opens at 1pm each day and offers free parking. From here you can walk a mile east to the nearest **pub** with accommodation, the *Pen-y-Gwryd Hotel* (☎0286/870211; March to early Nov daily; winter weekends only; ④), which is used to muddy boots in the bar. Amongst others, the first successful expedition up Mount Everest in 1953 stayed at the hotel while doing final equipment testing, and took time out to sign the ceiling: Edmund Hillary, Chris Bonnington, Doug Scott and Portmeirion designer Clough Williams-Ellis are all there. The Everest team also brought back a piece of the mountain, which now sits in pride of place on the bar. If you stay, expect a congenial though somewhat regimented atmosphere and moderately priced meals.

Beddgelert

Almost all of the prodigious quantity of rain which falls on Snowdon spills down the valleys on its south side: either into the Glaslyn River in Nantgwynant or the Colwyn River in Nant Colwyn. At their confluence, just before they jointly crash down the bony **Aberglaslyn Gorge** towards Porthmadog, the few dozen hard grey houses making up **BEDDGELERT** huddle together in some majestic mountain scenery.

WALKS FROM BEDDGELERT

As you might expect for a village sited at the southern point of the Snowdon massif, there are a couple of ascents of Snowdon starting near Beddgelert, listed in the Snowdon box (see p.302). Otherwise the following walks are the best ones to do from the village.

THE ABERGLASLYN GORGE

An easy walk follows the short but very picturesque **Aberglaslyn Gorge** (4 miles; 2hr 30min; 600ft ascent) returning to the copper mines (see Beddgelert) on a path up Cwm Bychan between Mynydd Sygun and Moel y Dyniewyd. Take the right bank of the river, past Gelert's Grave, crossing over the bridge onto the disused track-bed of the Welsh Highland narrow-gauge rail line. This then hugs the left bank for a mile down to Pont Aberglaslyn, at the bottom of the gorge, an easy path with the more adventurous Fisherman's Path just below it, giving a closer look at the river's course through chutes and channels in sculpted rocks. From the road bridge at Pont Aberglaslyn road bridge – the tidal limit before The Cob was built at Porthmadog (see p.243) – you can retrace your steps, follow the A498 back on the far bank, or head north up Cwm Bychan on a path near the exit of the disused railway tunnel. It is about a two-mile valley walk to the copper mines from where a track follows the left bank of the River Glaslyn to Beddgelert. You can do the walk in reverse by setting off from the top level of the copper mines at the end of the guided tour. Ask the guide for directions.

MOEL HEBOG

From Beddgelert you are unlikely to have missed the lumpish **Moel Hebog** (Bald Hill of the Hawk; 2569ft) to the west of the village. It is the highest point on a fine panoramic **ridge walk** (8miles; 5hr; 2800ft ascent) which also takes in the lesser peaks of Moel Lefn, and Moel yr Ogof (Hill of the Cave), named after a refuge for Owain Glyndŵr when fleeing the English in 1404 after his failed attempt to take Caernarfon Castle. The final forest section can be a bit disorientating, even in good weather, so make sure you have your compass.

Start half a mile northwest of the centre of Beddgelert on the A4085, where Pont Alyn crosses the river to Cwm Cloch Isaf Farm. Follow the signs to a green lane, which soon leads up onto the broad northeast ridge, keeping left of the Y Diffwys cliffs. The summit cairn is joined by two walls, the one to the northwest leading down a steep grassy slope to Bwlch Meillionen, from where you can ascend over rocky ground to Moel yr Ogof, or descend to the right, then skirt left in a probably fruitless attempt to locate the difficult-to-find Glyndŵr's Cave. From the top of Moel yr Ogof, it's a clear route north to Moel Lefn, then down to a cairn from where you can plan your descent. The easiest line is to Bwlch Cwm-trwsgl, near the highest point of the Beddgelert Forest, where a stile over a wire fence leads into the forest. Both OS 1:25,000 "Snowdonia" and 1:50,000 #115 "Snowdon" maps then show a clear, though not always easy-to-follow, route to the Beddgelert Forest Campsite, where you turn right and tramp a mile along the A4085 to Beddgelert.

If you tire of the view from the village, it is easy enough to get out on one of the longer walks described in the box (see above). A shorter and more celebrated excursion takes you four hundred yards south, along the right bank of the Glaslyn, to the spot that gives the village its name, **Gelert's Grave** (*bedd* means burial place), where a railed-off enclosure in a field marks the final resting place of Prince Llywelyn ap Iorwerth's faithful dog, Gelert, who was left in charge of the prince's infant son while he went hunting. On his return, the child was gone and the hound's muzzle was soaked in blood. Jumping to conclusions, the impetuous Llywelyn slew the dog, only to find the child safely asleep beneath it's cot and a dead wolf beside him. Llywelyn hurried to his dog, which licked his hand as it died. Sadly, the story is an all too successful nineteenth-century fabrication, conjured up by a wily local publican to lure punters.

The real source of the name is probably the grave of Celert, a sixth-century British saint who is supposed to have lived hereabouts, possibly near **Dinas Emrys**, a wooded mound a mile up Nantgwynant on the A498, where Vortigern's fort once stood and, legend has it, dragons once fought (see p.304). There's little enough to see now, except for the red-brown stain on the hillside opposite, identifying the **Sygun Copper Mine** (Easter–Sept Mon–Fri 10am–5pm, Sat 10am–4pm, Sun 11am–5pm; Oct–Easter daily 11am–4pm; £3.75), whose ore drew first the Romans, then nineteenth-century prospectors here. The dilapidated remains of what was the valley's prime source of income under a century ago have now been restored and made safe for the cool (9°C) 45-minute guided tour up through the multiple levels of tunnels and galleries, accompanied by the disembodied voice of a miner telling of his life in the mine. After the tour, you are free to potter around the ore-crushing and separation equipment, or ask the guide to point you over the hill towards the foot of the Aberglaslyn Gorge (see above).

Practicalities

Beddgelert sits on two **bus** routes: the #11 Caernarfon *Sherpa* which runs along Nant Colwyn to Beddgelert then up Nantgwynant to Pen-y-Pass and Llanberis; and the #97 to Portmeirion and Porthmadog. All stop near the road bridge over the Colwyn River, the effective centre of town and just a few yards away from the **National Trust Shop and Information Centre** (April–Oct daily 10am–5pm; ☎0766/890293) which is the nearest thing in the village to a tourist office.

Accommodation

Bed and breakfast **accommodation** is abundant. Most of the houses near the bridge and along the Caernarfon road let rooms, though if you're wanting to make an early start on the Snowdon walks you'll find the hostels better sited.

HOTELS AND GUESTHOUSES

Ael-y-Bryn, Caernarfon Rd (☎0766/890310). Central guesthouse with good views and inexpensive home-cooked evening meals. ②.

Beddgelert Antiques and Tea Rooms, Waterloo House (☎0766/890543). Limited accommodation above the restaurant and tea rooms, directly opposite the bridge. ②.

Colwyn (☎0766/890276). Central three-hundred-year-old cottage guesthouse with comfortable en suite rooms. Separate two-person self-catering cottage let by the week also available. ③.

Plas Colwyn (☎0766/890458). Non-smoking guesthouse by the bridge, with inexpensive home-cooked evening meals in licensed restaurant. ②.

Prince Llewelyn (☎0766/890242). Cosy country inn. ③.

Royal Goat Hotel (☎0766/890224). Large central hotel with heavy sports leanings – fishing, horse riding and golf available to guests – and a residents-only bar. ⑦.

Sygun Fawr Country House, three quarters of a mile away off the A498 (☎0766/890258). Partially sixteenth-century house in its own grounds with a sauna and good moderately priced evening meals. Closed Jan. ④.

HOSTELS AND CAMPSITES

Beddgelert Forest Campsite (☎0766/890288). Excellent and reasonably priced campsite a mile out on the Caernarfon road. Here you can brush up your compass work on the site's orienteering course in the forest before testing it on the hills. Open all year.

Bryn Dinas Bunkhouse (☎0766/890234). Fully self-catering bunkhouse, right at the foot of the Watkin Path (see Snowdon box p.302) three miles northeast of Beddgelert on the A498. Bring your own sleeping bag. ①.

Bryn Gwynant YHA youth hostel (☎0766/890251). Beautifully sited hostel in Nantgwynant four miles northeast of Beddgelert on the A498. It also has a campsite where you can use the hostel's facilities for half the adult rate. ①.

Cae Du Camping (☎0766/890595). Simple summer-only site less than ten minutes' walk towards Capel Curig on the A498.

Snowdon Ranger YHA youth hostel (☎0286/650391). Former inn five miles northwest of Beddgelert on the Caernarfon road at the foot of the Snowdon Ranger Path (see Snowdon box p.302). ①.

Eating and drinking

Beddgelert Antiques and Tea Rooms, Waterloo House (☎0766/890543). Attentive service and cosy surroundings make this the best place to spend an evening picking from a gamey menu. Good daytime tea rooms and some accommodation. Moderate.

Lyns, Church St. Decent tea rooms offering substantial daytime meals. Garden seating. Inexpensive.

Prince Llewelyn. Convivial atmosphere around the fire. Good real ales.

Tanronen. Pub on the south side of the bridge, with inexpensive bar meals and decent beer.

travel details

Trains

Betws-y-Coed to: Blaenau Ffestiniog (7 daily, 2 buses Sun; 30min); Llandudno Junction (7 daily, 2 buses Sun; 30min).

Blaenau Ffestiniog to: Betws-y-Coed (5 daily, 2 buses Sun; 30min); Llandudno Junction (7 daily, 2 buses Sun; 1hr); Porthmadog by Ffestiniog Railway (April–Oct 4–10 daily; 1hr).

Wrexham to: Caergwrle (roughly hourly, 4 Sun; 15min); Chester (every 2hr; 18min); Chirk (every 2hr; 12min); Liverpool (roughly hourly, 4 Sun; 1hr 20min); Shrewsbury (every 2hr; 40min).

Buses

Bala to: Aberystwyth (6 daily, 2 Sun; 2hr 5min); Corwen (6 daily, 2 Sun; 25min); Dolgellau (6 daily, 2 Sun; 40min); Llangollen (6 daily, 2 Sun; 45min); Machynlleth (6 daily, 2 Sun; 1hr 25min); Wrexham (6 daily, 2 Sun; 1hr 25min).

Beddgelert to: Caernarfon (5 daily, 1–5 Sun; 30min); Llanberis (5 daily, 1–5 Sun; 55min); Porthmadog (6 daily, 2 Sun in summer; 30min).

Betws-y-Coed to: Bangor (2 daily except Sun; 55min); Capel Curig (7–8 daily, 2–5 Sun; 15min); Conwy (7 daily, 5 Sun; 55min); Llanberis (4–6 daily, 2 Sun; 40min); Llandudno (7 daily, 5 Sun; 1hr 15min); Llanrwst (4 daily except Sun; 10min); Ogwen Valley (3 daily except Sun; 25min); Penmachno (4 daily except Sun; 20min).

Blaenau Ffestiniog to: Barmouth (4–6 daily except Sun; 1hr); Caernarfon (roughly hourly, 4 Sun; 1hr 25min); Cricieth (every 30min, summer 3 Sun; 40min); Harlech (4–6 daily except Sun; 35min); Porthmadog (every 30min, 4 Sun; 30min); Pwllheli (hourly, summer 3 Sun; 1hr 10min).

Capel Curig to: Bangor (2 daily except Sun; 40min); Betws-y-Coed (7–8 daily, 2–5 Sun; 15min); Llanberis (5 daily, 2–5 Sun; 25min); Ogwen (2–3 daily except Sun; 10min).

Corwen to: Aberystwyth (6 daily, 2 Sun; 2hr 25min); Bala (6 daily, 2 Sun; 35min); Dolgellau (6 daily, 2 Sun; 1hr 10min); Llangollen (6 daily, 2 Sun; 20min); Machynlleth (6 daily, 2 Sun; 1hr 45min); Ruthin (every 2hr, not Sun; 30min); Wrexham (6 daily, 2 Sun; 50min).

Llanberis to: Bangor (6 daily except Sun; 40min); Beddgelert (5 daily, 1–5 Sun; 55min); Betws-y-Coed (4–6 daily, 2 Sun; 40min); Caernarfon (every 30min, hourly Sun; 25min); Capel Curig (5 daily, 2–5 Sun; 25min); Conwy (summer 4–6 daily; 1hr 30min); Llandudno (summer 4–6 daily; 1hr 50min).

Llangollen to: Aberystwyth (6 daily, June–Sept also 2 Sun; 2hr 55min); Bala (6 daily, June–Sept also 2 Sun; 55min); Chester (hourly, 6 Sun; 1hr 30min); Corwen (6 daily, June–Sept also 2 Sun; 20min); Dolgellau (6 daily, June–Sept only 2 Sun; 1hr 30min); Machynlleth (6 daily, June–Sept also 2 Sun; 2hr 15min); Wrexham (hourly, 6 Sun; 50min).

Llanrwst to: Betws-y-Coed (4 daily except Sun; 10min); Conwy (hourly, 6 Sun; 35min); Llandudno (hourly, 6 Sun; 1hr); Penmachno (4 daily except Sun; 30min); Rhyl (2 daily except Sun; 1hr 15min).

Ogwen to: Bangor (2 daily except Sun; 30min); Capel Curig (2–3 daily except Sun; 10min).

Wrexham to: Aberystwyth (6 daily, 2 Sun; 3hr 20min); Bala (6 daily, 2 Sun; 1hr 20min); Builth Wells (summer 1 daily; 3hr 30min); Cardiff (summer 1 daily; 5hr 40min); Chester (every 15min, hourly Sun; 40min); Chirk (summer 1 daily; 25min); Corwen (6 daily, 2 Sun; 45min); Dolgellau (6 daily, 2 Sun; 1hr 55min); Llangollen (hourly or better, 7 Sun; 35min); Machynlleth (6 daily, 2 Sun; 2hr 40min); Mold (16 daily except Sun; 1hr); Welshpool (summer 1 daily; 1hr 10min).

CHAPTER SIX

THE NORTH COAST

The **North Coast** encompasses not only the geographical extremities of the country, but takes in an area exhibiting the extremes of the Welsh life. Walking around most of the seaside towns along the eastern section of the coast, only the street signs give any indication that you are in Wales at all: further west, there are places where English is seldom spoken other than to visitors. Those same eastern resorts can be as unashamedly brash as any of their more widely known kin in England, while scattered along the coast, dramatically sited castles work as a superb antidote to low-brow fun-seeking.

In the thirteenth century, the might of English king Edward I all but crushed any aspirations the Welsh princes had, as their armies were forced west towards Anglesey, and Edward set about building the Norman castles which hammered them into subjugation. Towns grew up around Edward's early castles at **Flint** and **Rhuddlan**, but neither had town walls, leaving the mostly ruined structures in isolation. The castles at **Conwy** and **Caernarfon**, however, were surrounded by "bastide" towns, the castle's keepers and town's burghers dependent on one another. Both Conwy and Caernarfon were entirely the preserve of the English, thereby economically and politically marginalizing the Welsh who retreated west, to **Anglesey**, where the English wielded less influence. As a response, Edward sited his final castle at **Beaumaris** to protect the entrance to the **Menai Strait**, the treacherous channel that separates the Isle of **Anglesey** from the mainland. The castle's concentric design was militarily more advanced than either Conwy or Caernarfon, but so complete was the English dominance by this stage that Edward never bothered to complete its construction. Today, Caernarfon is at the heart of one of the most nationalist, Welsh-speaking areas in the country.

The second sweeping change came in the late nineteenth and early twentieth centuries, when the benefits of the Industrial Revolution finally loosened the shackles on English milltown factory workers enough for them to take holidays. Beachfront towns sprang up, catering entirely to the summer visitors who arrived by the trainload to spend one week's annual leave promenading and dancing. The set-up isn't too different today, but the ever-present automobile has all but taken over from the train, caravans are as popular as guesthouses and amusement arcades rule. The stretch of coast from **Rhyl** to **Colwyn Bay** epitomizes this tatty image, the hallmarks of the shabby British seaside resort all too apparent. In contrast, Victorian **Llandudno**, always the posher place to stay, remains a cut above the rest, lying at the foot of the **Great Orme** limestone peninsula.

A few surprises come embedded into this matrix of bingo halls and caravan sites. The allegedly miraculous waters at **Holywell** have attracted the hopeful since the seventh century, while two different species of pilgrims make for either **Prestatyn**, to start the 170-mile Offa's Dyke Path along the English border, or for the National Portrait Gallery's collection at **Bodelwyddan**. To the south of here, the **Vale Of Clwyd** follows a pastoral valley, past Britain's smallest cathedral at **St Asaph**, to a pair of attractive old market towns, **Denbigh** and **Ruthin**.

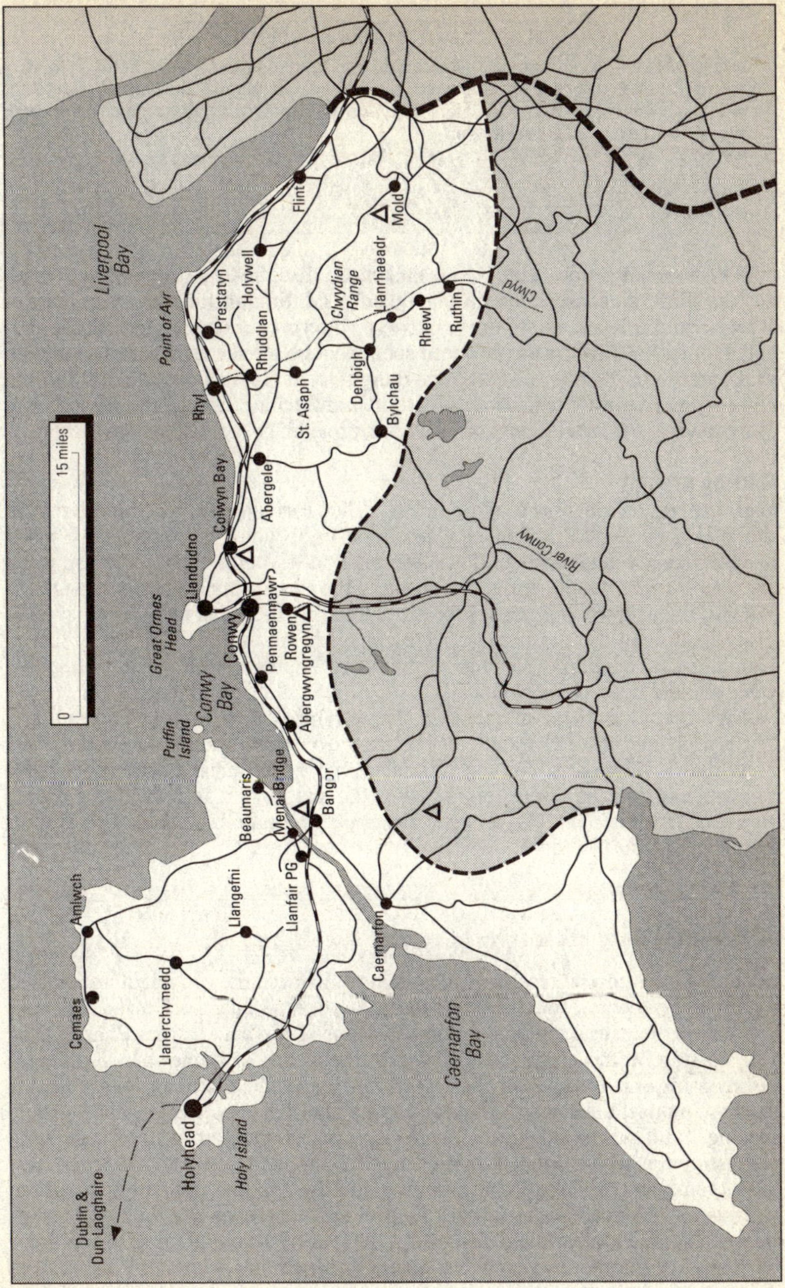

Liverpool Bay
Point of Ayr
Flint
Holywell
Prestatyn
Rhuddlan
Rhyl
Mold
Llanrhaeadr
Clwydian Range
Ruthin
Rhewl
Clwyd
Denbigh
St. Asaph
Bylchau
Abergele
Colwyn Bay
Llandudno
Great Ormes Head
Conwy
Penmaenmawr
Rowen
Abergwyngregyn
River Conwy
Conwy Bay
Puffin Island
Beaumaris
Menai Bridge
Bangor
Llanfair PG
Llangefni
Amlwch
Cemaes
Llanerchymedd
Caernarfon
Caernarfon Bay
Holyhead
Holy Island
Dublin & Dun Laoghaire
0
15 miles

ACCOMMODATION PRICE CODES

Throughout this guide, hotel and B&B accommodation is priced on a scale of ① to ⑨. Category ① only applies to youth hostels; for the rest, the number indicates the **lowest price** you could expect to pay per night for a **double room in high season**. The prices indicated by the codes are as follows:

① under £20/$32	④ £40–50/$64–80	⑦ £70–80/$112–128
② £20–30/$32–48	⑤ £50–60/$80–96	⑧ £80–100/$128–160
③ £30–40/$48–64	⑥ £60–70/$96–112	⑨ over £100/$160

If it is beaches you want, you'll find more discerning swimmers and windsurfers shun the coast of the mainland and head through the university town of **Bangor** to Anglesey, where the southwestern resorts of **Rhosneigr**, **Rhoscolyn** and **Trearddur Bay** are the favoured spots, though for scenery there's a lot to be said for the coast along the extensive dune system of **Newborough** and the sea cliffs around **South Stack**, both great for birdwatching. Lastly, the ferries from **Holyhead**, at the western end of the island, provide the fastest route to Dublin.

Getting around

With the recent conversion of the A55 to a dual carriageway, you can drive from the Welsh border to Bangor or Caernarfon in an hour, bypassing the coastal towns. Unless you take one of the slower alternative routes along the coast, you'll see much more on the **train**, which hugs the coast, linking all the resorts to Bangor, then across to Anglesey for the run to Holyhead and the ferry to Ireland. Travelling along the north coast, then changing onto the Conwy Valley line at Llandudno Junction, provides one of the fastest routes from England to Betws-y-Coed and the heart of Snowdonia.

With the exceptions of *National Express* **bus** services to Holyhead and Caernarfon, and the #X1 *Coastliner* bus from Chester to Caernarfon, which calls at all the major resorts, bus travel is much more piecemeal. Services are fairly frequent and detailed where appropriate in the text, as well as in the encyclopedic *Gwynedd Timetable* and *Clwyd Public Transport Guide*, both available free at tourist offices and bus stations.

Deeside

Making for the coastal resorts or mountains of Snowdonia, you might be tempted to charge headlong through northeastern Clwyd, especially since no sooner have you left the industrial hinterland that spreads over the border from Chester than you seem to hit the north coast. However, the wedge of former mining country between the salt marshes of the Dee Estuary and the Clwydian Range has its share of modest offerings. A thousand years ago this area was heavily forested, making it difficult to defend for the Welsh princes and Norman Marcher lords contesting the Welsh–English border. Castles sprang up on both sides, the best preserved being the Welsh fort at **Ewloe** and the one that put an end to all the skirmishes, the first link in Edward I's Iron Ring of castles at **Flint**. In contrast, there's not much left of the defences at **Mold**, Clwyd's county town, which these days seems to merely watch life tick by. Much the same can be said of understated **Holywell**, an important pilgrimage site for the last thirteen hundred years.

The Dee Estuary lies to the east, its salt-soaked fields supporting huge numbers of waders and **wildfowl**, coming to feed on the sands and mud flats left by retreating tides. Plovers, oystercatchers and Europe's largest concentration of pintails winter here, pushing the population into six figures. The only designated viewing point is the RSPB's **Point of Ayr** site, two miles east of Prestatyn at the head of the estuary, colliery and building site, discouraging all but keen birders.

All of this is easily missed if you follow the A55, which cuts through this corner of Clwyd. The preferable though slower A548 runs parallel to the North Coast train line, sticking to the Dee Estuary, before joining the A55 west of Rhyl (see p.325). Ewloe Castle and Flint are both within striking distance of train stations, but the #X1 *Coastliner* bus from Chester right along the coast to Caernarfon is often equally convenient. Deeside's main **tourist office** (Easter to mid-Oct daily 9.30am–5.30pm; mid-Oct to Easter Fri–Sat 10am–5pm; ☎0244/541597) is in the westbound *Autolodge* service station on the A55, three miles west of Flint.

Mold

Until the boundary rearrangement planned for 1995, **MOLD** (Yr Wyddgrug) continues to be the county town of Clwyd. This tenure doesn't seem to affect the town's largely peaceful character, disrupted only by the Wednesday and Saturday markets. In truth, there's no great reason for a visit, though you may as well stop in on the way to Ewloe Castle, just four miles to the northeast.

The town was founded during the reign of William Rufus, though only a bowling green and a copse of beeches atop a mound mark the site of the motte-and-bailey fortifications on **Bailey Hill**, at the top of the High Street. The fort was built for the local Norman lord, Robert de Montalt, who probably gave the town its English name, essentially the same as the Welsh, meaning "The Mound". The commanding view over the River Alyn (Afon Alun) illustrates the strategic importance of the site, first taken by Owain Gwynedd in 1157 and again in 1199 by Llywelyn the Great, constantly shifting between Welsh and Anglo-Norman control until Edward I's hand came down hard on the region. Relative calm prevailed until a period during the Wars of the Roses, when private armies held sway. In 1465, after a skirmish in the town, local lord Rheinallt ap Gruffydd succeeded in capturing the Mayor of Chester and taking him back to the Tower in Nercwys, where he was presented with a pie containing the rope that would be his noose. A revenge party from Chester attempted to raid the Tower but was locked inside and the place subsequently torched by Rheinallt's men.

Henry VII's assumption of the throne, after his victory at the Battle of Bosworth, stamped some stability on the area. In gratitude for her son's victory, Henry's mother, Margaret Beaufort, commissioned the airy Perpendicular **St Mary's Church** on the site of a thirteenth-century church at the foot of Bailey Hill. The original oak roof carved with Tudor roses has been retained in the north aisle, as has a quatrefoil and animal frieze running below the small clerestory windows, though most of the rest was restored by Gilbert Scott last century.

A window portraying the patron saints of Britain is the town's meagre memorial to its most famous son (at least to English-speakers) and Wales' greatest painter, the eighteenth-century landscapist **Richard Wilson**, whose grave is by the church entrance. Having spent his childhood here, Wilson studied in Italy for six years, where he painted canvases from the Grand Tour, earning a good enough living to support himself back home while he concentrated on the subject for which he is best known: the mountains of Wales, typically dramatic scenes of Cadair Idris or Snowdon, often incorporating Latin elements into the Romantic panoramas. In the decades before John Ruskin's championing of Turner influenced critical taste, Wilson's style went undervalued, and though he co-founded the Royal Academy in 1768 and later won the acclaim of Ruskin, he died a pauper. The story goes that, in return for a few pints, he painted the sign for the *We Three Loggerheads* pub outside the Loggerheads Country Park (see below), the third, undepicted loggerhead being the viewer's.

Since Mold is not notably a Welsh-language stronghold, it seems ironic that it is **Daniel Owen**, a local tailor and nineteenth-century novelist, who should be commemorated by a statue, outside the library. "Not for the wise and learned have I written, but for the common people" is inscribed below the statue and it was his bluntly honest accounts of ordinary life that made him so unpopular with the Methodist leaders of the community. Writing only in Welsh, Owen became the most prominent writer of the late nineteenth century. A room full of his memorabilia should now be back on display in the library, which doubles as the town's small museum (Mon–Fri 9.30am–7pm, Sat 9.30am–12.30pm; free).

There's little else to see in Mold itself, but three miles west on the A494 (bus #B5), **Loggerheads Country Park** offers the pleasures of forest walks and nature trails with views up to the Clwydian Range. You can pick up more information at the visitor centre (summer daily 11am–5pm; winter Mon–Fri 11am–4pm, Sat & Sun 10am–4pm) by the entrance.

Practicalities

Mold has no train station, but the **bus** services from Shotton on the North Coast line from Chester, ten miles away in England, and from Ruthin stop behind the cattle market east of High Street. From there it is a five-minute walk down King Street to Earl Road, where the **tourist office** (April–Sept Mon, Tues, Thurs & Fri 9.30am–7pm, Wed & Sat 9.30am–5pm; ☎0352/759331) is in the town library.

Accommodation isn't plentiful, but close to the centre you have a choice of the classy *Bryn Awel Hotel*, Denbigh Rd (☎0352/758622; ⑤), five minutes' walk north of the church, or *Glendale Lodge* (☎0352/754001; ③), just past *Theatr Clwyd*. The nearest YHA **youth hostel** (March to mid-Dec; no phone, contact the Cardiff office ☎0222/222122; ①) is at Maeshafn, four miles southwest of Mold, a mile and a half down a lane, signposted off the A494 road to Ruthin near Loggerheads Park. You can camp here and use the facilities.

If you can't stretch to the moderately priced table d'hôte **lunches** at *Chez Colette*, 56 High St (☎0352/759225), there are numerous cafés along High Street. *We Three Loggerheads*, opposite Loggerheads Park three miles to the west, is the best of the **pubs** for both meals and drinking, while **entertainment** revolves around the shows at the *Theatr Clwyd* (☎0352/755114), a mile east on the A494.

Ewloe Castle

If only to put Edward I's monstrous castles into perspective, **Ewloe Castle** (unrestricted access; CADW), four miles northeast of Mold, makes an interesting diversion. Tucked in at the end of a wooded glen, it is so cloaked by sycamore and oak that you almost stumble into the ruins. An English stronghold which fell into Welsh hands around 1146, it was being fortified by Owain Gwynedd as an ambush castle when the Battle of Eulo took place in 1157. According to Giraldus Cambrensis, Henry II's "rash enthusiasm" hindered this first assault on Wales, and his push through the wooded pass resulted in the death of many of his men. In gratitude for his own life, the king contributed funds towards the building of Basingwerk Abbey (see p.317).

In 1210 Llywelyn ap Iorwerth ("the Great") built the apsidal Welsh Tower and his grandson, Llywelyn ap Gruffydd ("the Last"), went on to add two wards, protected by a curtain wall and an outer ditch; but while Ewloe was never of great importance, after the completion of Flint Castle in around 1283, it ceased to have any military significance at all.

Until preservation work was begun in the 1920s, local builders had helped themselves to the masonry, leaving just the shell at the head of a valley filled by the ancient woodland of **Wepre Park** (Parc Gwepra). The **visitor centre** (summer daily; winter Sat & Sun) for both park and castle is ten minutes' walk from the castle, and a mile or so from Shotton train station on the North Coast line; walk towards the *Gateway* supermarket then turn left up Wepre Drive.

Flint

If you are travelling on the north coast train line, be sure to take one of the regional services which stop at **FLINT** (Y Fflint) – seven miles north of Mold – and spend the hour between trains in rambling around the yellowish sandstone ruins of **Flint Castle** (unrestricted access; CADW), two minutes' walk over the footbridge from the station. Started in 1277 after the Treaty of Aberconwy, it was the first of Edward I's "Iron Ring" of fortresses (see p.337), standing sentinel over the coastal marshes of the Dee Estuary and the once-important shipping lanes into Chester. The ten-foot-thick pockmarked sandstone walls form a square with drum towers at all except the southeast corner, where a small moat and drawbridge separates the castle from the well-preserved Great Tower or Donjon. Unique in Britain, this was intended as the castle's main accommodation and last place of retreat, and came equipped with its own well. Together with its large grassy outer ward and the adjoining town, the castle formed a unified enclave known as a "bastide" (see p.337). Though Conwy and Caernarfon received the same treatment, Flint can claim to be the first borough in Wales to receive its charter, in September 1284. Until then, towns didn't really exist in essentially rural Wales.

There are few incidents recorded at the castle until 1399, when Richard II was lured here from the safety of Conwy Castle and captured by Henry Bolingbroke, the Duke of Lancaster and future Henry IV. In the scene from Shakespeare's *Richard II*, in response to Bolingbroke's "My gracious Lord, I come but for mine own", the defeated king replies "Your own is yours, and I am yours, and all". Even Richard's favourite greyhound is said to have deserted him at this point.

During the Civil War, Flint remained Royalist until taken in 1647 by General Mytton, who so effectively dismantled it that only six years later it was practically buried in its own ruins. It was in this condition when Celia Fiennes found it on the brief – and generally displeasing – Welsh leg of her journeys around Britain between 1698. She described Flint as "a very ragged place", and things haven't changed much: unless you have come to spot some of the hundred thousand wintering waders on the Dee Estuary, you'll probably want to move on.

Aside from the hourly **trains**, Flint is on the #X1 Chester–Caernarfon *Coastliner* **bus** route, and there are other frequent services to Chester and Holywell, leaving from outside *The Raven* pub, a few yards north from the station along Holywell Street, the main coast road.

Holywell and around

For thirteen hundred years a place of pilgrimage, **HOLYWELL** (Treffynnon), just off the A55 four miles northwest of Flint, comes billed as "The Lourdes of Wales", but with no tacky souvenir stalls, it doesn't really warrant such a comparison. **St Winefride's Well** (daily 10am–5pm; 20p donation) – half a mile from the bus station at the far end of the High Street, then turn right and follow the signs – is the source of all the fuss. The spring was first recorded by the Romans, who used the waters to relieve rheumatism and gout, shedding doubt on the veracity of the legend that takes place around 660 AD. The virtuous Winefride (Gwenfrewi in Welsh) was decapitated here after resisting the amorous advances of Prince Caradoc, and the well is said to have sprung up at the spot where her head fell. When Saint Beuno, her uncle, placed her head beside the body, a combination of prayer and the waters revived her, setting her on track for the rest of her life as an abbess at Gwytherin Convent near Llanrwst.

Richard I and Henry V provided regal patronage, ensuring a steady flow of believers to what became one of the great shrines of Christendom. After the Reformation, pilgrimages – now punishable by death – became more clandestine, and the well became a focal point of resistance to Protestantism. A century and a half later, the Catholic king of England, James II, came here to pray for a son and heir; the eventual answer to his imprecations threatened a Catholic succession and contributed to the overthrow of the House of Stuart.

Pilgrims formerly spent the night praying in the Perpendicular **St Winefride's Chapel** (key from the ticket office; CADW), built around 1500 to enclose three sides of the well. Henry VII's mother, Margaret Beaufort, paid for the construction and earned herself a likeness amongst the roof bosses that depict the life of St Winefride in the ornate, Gothic fan-vaulted crypt that surrounds the well. With the gloom only cut by light from votive candles, she's not that easy to see now.

Though the site's importance is waning, pilgrimages do still take place, mainly on St Winefride's Day, the nearest Sunday to June 22, when a couple of thousand pilgrims are led through the streets behind a relic, part of Winefride's thumb bone. The procession ends by the open side of the crypt where the spring – or at least the outflow of a pump installed after mine working disrupted the spring's source in 1917 – fills a calm pool capacious enough to accommodate the dozens of faithful who dutifully wade through the waters three times in hope of curing their ailments, a rite also associated with the Celtic baptism by triple immersion.

Practicalities

Holywell doesn't have a train station, but a reasonable number of **buses** call at the bus station at the southern end of High Street. There are frequent buses from here to Rhyl, Flint, Chester and Mold, or you can use the #X1 *Coastliner* linking the two nearest train stations – Flint and Prestatyn – passing Basingwerk Abbey a mile away. From the bus station, head a hundred yards down High Street and turn left to get to the **tourist office**, in the library on North St (Mon 10am–

5.30pm, Wed 10am–1pm, Tues, Thurs & Fri 10am–7pm, Sat 9.30am–12.30pm; ☎0352/713157).

The few old pubs and coffee shops probably won't detain you overnight, but if you are **staying**, by far the best bet is the oak-beamed, partly sixteenth-century *Greenhill Farm* (March–Oct; ☎0352/713270; ②), reached by heading northeast from Winefride's Well on the B5121 for a few yards, then taking the second left opposite the *Royal Oak* pub to the farm. *Bryn Beuno Guesthouse*, Whitford St (☎0352/711315; ②), is also convenient: coming uphill from the well, turn right along a small bypass and continue for 300 yards. *The Springfield Hotel* (☎0352/780503; ④), just off the A55 expressway a couple of miles southeast of Holywell, caters mainly to business traffic but does have an indoor pool.

The best-value pub **meals** in town are those available at the *Royal Oak* on the B5121, which is also the best place in town to drink.

Greenfield Valley and Basingwerk Abbey

Trainloads of pilgrims used to arrive at Holywell by a steep branch which once ran off the North Coast line. From St Winefride's Well, a path for a mile along the bed of this train line runs towards the sea past a series of five ponds, the millraces between them providing power for the copper and brass factories whose remains now constitute the **Greenfield Valley Heritage Park**. Most of this area is still being renovated and forms little more than a sideshow as you walk the mile down to **Basingwerk Abbey** (unrestricted access; CADW), where Archbishop Baldwin and Giraldus Cambrensis spent a night on their tour in 1188 (see p.249). Most of the extant slabs of stonework are the remains of domestic buildings used by the abbot and twelve monks of the Savignac order, who lived in the abbey on its founding by Ranulph II, Earl of Chester, in 1131. Sixteen years later the order merged with the Cistercians but went on controlling extensive lands in England and Wales until the Reformation when, in 1537, the abbey was dissolved and its spoils distributed around the region. There's a little more of the history in the visitor centre (Easter–Oct daily 10am–5pm; Nov–Easter Sat & Sun 1–4pm), next to the **Abbey Farm Museum** (Easter–Oct daily 10am–5pm; £1), a preserved working farm where you can feed the animals and amble around reconstructed old farm buildings, many saved from destruction.

With your own transport, it is worth an excursion five miles northwest to **Maen Achwyfan** (the "Stone of Lamentation"; unrestricted access; CADW), Britain's tallest Celtic Cross. Though the shaft, incised with interwoven latticework, is over ten feet high and crowned with a wheel cross, this thousand-year-old cross is little celebrated and stands alone in a field reached by taking the A5026 to the northwest of Holywell, turning right onto the A5151, following the third exit at the first roundabout and turning right at the junction. The #A19 bus runs past the cross from Holywell, but the long wait involved makes the journey less appealing.

The Vale of Clwyd

Separated from the English Marches and Deeside's industrial areas by the soft contours of the broad-backed Clwydian Range, the wide and fertile Vale of Clwyd follows the sandstone course of the barely noticeable River Clwyd (Afon Clywedog), from Corwen on the A5 (see p.273) to the coast near Rhuddlan.

Linked by quiet roads through a patchwork of small farms, three attractive towns of warm-hued stone sit evenly spaced on hillocks above the valley. Few tourists visit them, perhaps because none warrants more than a couple of hours' attention, but together they make a good day's diversion and a link between the north coast and the route up the Dee Valley towards Snowdonia.

Churches loom large in the valley. Britain's smallest cathedral dominates the village-sized city of **St Asaph**, but the building is barely larger than the parish church in the ancient market town of **Ruthin**, thirteen miles to the south. Both these buildings and the ancient village church at **Llanrhaeadr**, midway between them, were modernized in the nineteenth century, but it is the latter which remains the Vale's prime example of medieval ecclesiastical architecture. **Denbigh** is better known for its "hollow crown", the high-walled castle ruin which rings the top of the hill behind the town.

The rail line from Corwen to Rhyl has long since gone, leaving regular **buses** along the A525 between Rhyl and Corwen as the primary transport route.

Ruthin

Though surrounded by modern housing and known primarily as a livestock market town, the centre of **RUTHIN** (Rhuthun), ten miles west of Mold, comprises an attractive knot of half-timbered buildings set between church and castle. It is built on a commanding rise in the Vale of Clwyd, close to lands once held by Owain Glyndŵr, which made it ripe for the first push of his quest for dominion over all of Wales in 1400. The heavily restored red-stone **Ruthin Castle** (not open to public), dating from Edward I's first stint of castle building, was then home to Lord de Grey of Ruthin, a favourite of Henry IV. Coveting a tract of land above Corwen held by Glyndŵr, de Grey used his influence with Henry to have Glyndŵr proclaimed a traitor and was given the land in return. He was thus the first to suffer when Glyndŵr had himself crowned Prince of Wales and with four thousand followers launched an attack on Ruthin on September 20, 1400. The castle itself held but the town was razed, though not until Glyndŵr's men had plundered the goods brought by the English to the town's annual fair. The castle went on to resist the Parliamentarians for eleven weeks during the Civil War, eventually falling to General Mytton in April 1646, after which it was destroyed. It was over three hundred years later until it was partially restored as a hotel in 1963 (see "Practicalities").

Unless you are inclined towards phony medieval banquets, you might as well forget spending any time at the castle in favour of taking a look at the mixed bag of architectural styles around St Peter's Square, the heart of the town's medieval street plan. The northeast corner is dominated by **St Peter's Church** (daily 9am–4pm), approached through a fine pair of 1728 iron gates wrought by the Davies Brothers who also made the gates of St Giles church in Wrexham and Chirk Castle. Impressive though the church gates are, they are upstaged by the ceiling of the north aisle: here, 408 carved black oak panels meet at Tudor Rose bosses. This part of the building dates from the fourteenth century, when it was founded as a collegiate church, but Henry VII reputedly donated the ceiling, possibly from Basingwerk Abbey (see p.317), in gratitude to those who helped him take the English throne. The details can be hard to see, but a switch by the hymn board provides illumination for twenty seconds at a time, and the more intriguing designs – leering and grinning faces – are reproduced on a panel opposite the door. One of the busts on the north wall is of Gabriel Goodman, who in 1574, while Dean of Westminster, re-founded the **grammar school** that had been closed by Henry VIII forty years earlier; it still stands behind the church, next to the Christ's Hospital Almshouses, which Goodman built in 1590 as a gift to the town.

Goodman's birthplace in St Peter's Square, Exmewe Hall, is now occupied by a bank, but outside sits an unimpressive chunk of limestone known as **Maen Huail**, testament to the darker side of King Arthur's character. The less-than-convincing story has Arthur and Huail, brother of a Welsh chieftain called Gildas, fighting over the attentions of a woman. Huail pierced Arthur's thigh, giving him a permanent limp, but promised never to mention Arthur's loss of face. Some time later Huail recognized Arthur dancing, disguised as a woman, and taunted him. Incensed at being found out, Arthur had Huail beheaded on this stone.

Standing isolated on the other side of the square is one of the many half-timbered buildings around the town. Now the *National Westminster* bank, it was built in 1401 as a courthouse and prison and still retains under the eaves a stump of the **gibbet**, last used in 1679 to hang a Franciscan friar.

The most photographed building in Ruthin isn't any of these, but the **Myddleton Arms pub**, built in 1657 in Dutch style and topped by seven dormer windows known as "The Eyes of Ruthin".

WALK TO MOEL FAMAU AND MOEL FENLLI

Walks on **Moel Famau** and **Moel Fenlli** both start from Bwlch-Pen-Barras, a pass four miles east of Ruthin at the top of the B5429, once used for the main turnpike route over the Clwydian Range to Mold. The **Offa's Dyke long-distance path** (though not the Dyke itself) runs along these bald tops (*moel* means "bare mountain"), following the line of a Bronze Age trading route, past the remains of six Iron Age hillforts surrounding the tops and the Jubilee Tower. No public transport comes this way but you can walk two miles up the road from Llanbedr-Dyffryn-Clwyd (bus #B5 from Ruthin) to begin a walk at either of two car parks.

From the first car park, right at the top of Bwlch Pen-Barras, you can make the steep climb southwards to the most impressive of the hillforts on 1800-foot **Moel Fenlli** (1-mile circuit; 30min; 500ft ascent). Excavations here uncovered 35 hut circles within earthworks three-quarters of a mile across. The height from ditch bottom to bank top reaches 35 feet in places, with triple defences on the less easily defended eastern flank.

From the same car park, a broad path leads a mile and a half north to the 1820-foot "Mother Mountain" **Moel Famau** (3-mile circuit; 1–2hr; 650ft ascent), the highest point in the range, topped by the truncated **Jubilee Tower**. The subject of many a disparaging remark when it was built in 1810 to celebrate George III's fifty-year reign, the top of this Egyptian-style structure was never completed. The planned pyramid was to rise to 150 feet but was damaged in a storm in 1862 and only partially repaired in 1970. The ruins may not be much, but on a clear day the views over the Vale of Clwyd as far as Snowdon and Cadair Idris make it all worthwhile.

An alternative approach to Moel Famau leaves a second car park half a mile or so down the eastern side of the pass, from where an easy blue-marked path or slightly harder red path guide you through Corsican pines up the southeastern flank to the tower.

Practicalities

Buses from Denbigh, Corwen and Mold all stop on Market Street, running between St Peter's Square and the **tourist office** (June–Sept daily 10am–5.30pm; Oct–May Mon–Sat 10am–5pm, Sun noon–5pm; ☎0824/703992), 300 yards away inside the *Ruthin Craft Centre*.

Ruthin is well provided with **accommodation**. Top of the range is the luxurious *Ruthin Castle Hotel* (☎0824/702664; ⑧), which has medieval banquets (usually Fri & Sat; £21.50). The *Castle Hotel* (☎0824/702479; ④), a former coaching inn, is on the square. Just around the corner, *Gorffwystfa*, Castle St (☎0824/702748; ②), is the most convenient B&B; there are another couple within ten minutes' walk on the A5105 to Bala, the *Argoed Guesthouse* (☎0824/703407; ③), and *Ye Olde Cross Keys* (☎0824/705281; ③), 200 yards further along. *Eyarth Old Railway Station* (☎0824/703643; ④), out of town on the disused Corwen to Rhyl line, is one of the more comfortable places to stay, and serves reasonably priced meals; take bus #51 to Llanfair Dyffryn Clwyd, from where it's a half-mile walk. You'll also need transport to get to the nearest **campsite** (March–Oct; ☎0824/703178), tucked behind the seventeenth-century *Three Pigeons Inn* in Graigfechan, a mile east on the A494 Mold road, then three miles south on the B5429. The food is also good here.

In Ruthin itself, the best place to **eat** is the moderately priced *Chardonnay Wine Bar*, 1 Upper St (☎0824/705818), or you can get adequate meals in the pubs around the square. Cream teas are served in a wing of the *Ruthin Castle Hotel*.

Llanrhaeadr

Just off the A525, four miles north of Ruthin, **St Dyfnog's Church** seems much too large for the tiny hamlet of **LLANRHAEADR**. In the sixth century Saint Dyfnog established a hermitage here on the site of a healing well, and donations from pilgrims funded the building of the present church in 1533. Typically for the area it has twin aisles and, though heavily restored in 1880, retains many original features, including a glorious carved barrel roof with vineleaf patterns and some outstanding stained glass. Best known is the **Jesse Window** at the east end of the north aisle, depicting the descent of Jesus through the House of Israel from Jesse, the father of King David. This is considered to be one of the finest examples of a Jesse window, drawing you in to the Virgin and Child above the central light, surrounded by 21 of their bearded, ermine-robed ancestors, whose names are recorded in medieval Latin. The window is believed to be original, contemporary with the church, though it was removed and stored in an oak chest during the Civil War, which is when its companion in the south aisle is thought to have been destroyed. Fragments that may have belonged to it were found nearby and pieced together to form the west window in the nineteenth century.

The #51 bus between Ruthin and Denbigh passes every hour throughout the day; or you can **stay** just across the road at the *King's Head Inn* (☎074587/278; ③), a well-preserved sixteenth-century coaching inn with a wide choice of inexpensive food and a low-beamed bar.

Denbigh

The castle ruins that crown its hill strike you from along the valley as you approach **DENBIGH** (Dinbych), eight miles north of Ruthin. Below, the remains of the bastide town tumble down towards the medieval centre, once important for its glove-making, but now just operating Tuesday and Friday markets and servicing the sprawling postwar development on its outskirts.

The market takes place on the broad central section of the High Street, surrounded by a pleasing array of medieval buildings. Thankfully, they haven't been over-restored and, together with the more modern buildings in their midst, help retain a working town atmosphere. *The Old Vaults* pub on the High Street sports a blue and white sign pointing you up Broomhill Lane towards **Denbigh Castle** (May–Sept daily 10am–5pm; unrestricted access in winter; CADW; £1.50). More signs lead up past the crumbling **Burgess Gate**, the former northern entry to the town, to the vast grassy ward of the ruined fortress.

For a long time, the River Clywd (Afon Clywedog) formed the border of England and Wales, guarded here by an unidentified castle built by Dafydd, brother of Llywelyn ap Gruffydd ("the Last"). This probably gave the town its name, meaning "small fort", though it's more imaginatively attributed to John Salusbury, a medieval knight said to have rid the town of a dragon, triumphantly returning with its head to cries of "Dim Dych!" (no more dragon). Dafydd's castle put up strong resistance, but eventually fell, allowing Edward I to erect castles here and at the other key sites of Rhuddlan and Ruthin. By 1282, only the outer defences – the town walls – had been started, under the charge of Henry de Lacy, Earl of Lincoln, who required each of his 63 burgesses to "find a man armed in Denbigh to guard and defend the town". This wasn't enough to repel a Welsh revolt in 1294, which though rapidly suppressed, goaded de Lacy into work on the castle proper, employing many of the concepts already implemented by Edward's architect, James of St George.

The most imposing piece of what remains is the **gatehouse**, its three octagonal towers enclosing an originally vaulted hall, making it one of the finest defensive structures of the era. Entrance is beneath a weathered statue of Edward I in a niche, flanked on the right by the Prison Tower, still showing evidence of five garderobes that discharge into a common cesspit, and the Porter's Lodge Tower on the left. From here, you can walk the only remaining section of the wall, extending as far as the Great Kitchen Tower with its two huge fireplaces. On the far side, the Postern Tower was heavily strengthened after 1294, as were the **town walls** that formed the outer ward branching off at the castle walls. Continue along the short section of wall walk (key from the custodian) down to the **Goblin Tower** from where, at the end of a six-month-long siege in 1646, Charles I threw the castle keys onto the heads of the all-conquering Roundheads.

In 1563, Elizabeth I sold the castle to her favourite Robert Dudley, Earl of Leicester, who in 1579 chose a site just below the castle for the church that he hoped would supplant St Asaph cathedral. It was never completed, but the shell still stands today as **Leicester's Folly**.

Back on High St, a small **local history museum** (Mon, Wed & Fri 9.30am–7pm, Tues & Thurs 9.30am–5.30pm, Sat 9.30am–4pm; free) in the sixteenth-century County Hall, which also contains the local library and tourist office, gives some background history on Denbigh's famous sons. In the sixteenth century, Humphrey Llwyd drew up the first separate map of Wales, published posthumously in 1573. He is commemorated in the **St Marcella's Church**, a mile east of the centre reached from High Street down Vale Street then right along Ruthin Road. Here the cemetery contains the grave of the bard, satirist and playwright Tom o'r Nant or "Tom of the Dingle", who George Borrow casually refers to as "the Welsh Shakespeare". Tom in his autobiography writes, "As soon as I had learned to spell and write a few words I conceived a mighty desire to learn to write; so I went in quest of elderberries to make me ink."

Practicalities

The #51 **bus** along the Vale of Clwyd stops on the High Street, as does the #59/59A to Colwyn Bay via St Asaph and Bodelwyddan. Other buses stop just along from the library, museum and small **tourist office** in Hall Square (Mon, Wed & Fri 9.30am–7pm, Tues & Thurs 9.30am–5.30pm, Sat 9.30am–4pm; ☎0745/816313), where you can pick up some useful handouts detailing town walks. **Accommodation** in the centre is pretty much limited to *The Bull Hotel* (☎0745/812582; ③), just beside the tourist office, and *Cayo Guesthouse*, 74 Vale St (☎0745/812686; ②), a couple of hundred yards down the main St Asaph road. If you have your own transport, you might want to try one of two comfortable country cottage type guesthouses. *Y Berllan Bach* (☎0824/790732; ③) is three miles east at Llandyrnog, at the foot of the Clwydian Range – from the roundabout at the southern end of Denbigh, head east through Llanwfan, past the *Kinmel Arms*, then straight on for another half a mile. *College Farm* (☎0745/70276; ③), at Penial, is three miles southwest of town. The closest **campsite**, *Tyn yr Eithin* (☎0745/813211), is a mile to the north down Vale Street then left along Rhyl Road, by the roundabout.

There are no outstanding **restaurants** in Denbigh, but you can eat well and inexpensively. *The Bull Hotel* provides straightforward bar meals, but for kebabs and other Middle Eastern dishes, visit the inexpensive Kurdish *Kurdoğlu's Castle*, 6 Love Lane (☎0745/815156). Finding a decent place to **drink** is no problem: *The Old Vaults* on High Street is good, or make for Back Row, behind High Street, for the *Y Llew Aur* (The Golden Lion) and *Y Llew Gwyn* (The White Lion).

St Asaph

Five miles north of Denbigh, the cluster of houses centred on a single main street running from a modest church down to the River Elwy (Afon Elwy) ranks as Britain's second smallest city, **ST ASAPH** (Llanelwy). St David's in Pembrokeshire is slightly smaller, but St Asaph boasts the country's smallest **cathedral** (open daily 8am–dusk). It is no bigger than many village churches, standing on a rise above the river with its squat square tower at the crossing of a broad, aisled nave and a well-lit transept.

The town's Welsh name translates as "the church on Elwy River", a title which dates back to the sixth century when Saint Asaph succeeded the cathedral's founder, Saint Kentigern, as abbot in 570, and became its first bishop. Both are commemorated in the easternmost window in the north aisle of the cathedral. There is almost no record of the place from then until 1282 when Edward I's men stormed through and destroyed the church, leaving the incumbent bishop Anian II, whose effigy is in the south aisle, with the task of building the present structure. That too was attacked in 1402 by Owain Glyndŵr, but this time only the woodwork was lost and soon replaced.

From 1601 until his death in 1604, the bishopric was held by **William Morgan** (see box), who was responsible for the translation of the first Welsh-language bible in 1588. An octagonal monument to Morgan, in the churchyard on the south side of the cathedral, also commemorates the work of Morgan and his fellow translators, including William Salusbury and Gabriel Goodman (see p.319).

This is Morgan's only memorial; his grave under the presbytery has been unmarked since Giles Gilbert Scott's substantial restoration in the 1870s.

One thousand Morgan bibles were printed, of which only nineteen remain, one of them displayed in the north transept. The cathedral also has a handsome collection of psalter and prayer books in an alcove in the south transept; Elizabeth I's 1549 copy of *The Book of Common Prayer* only slightly predating Salusbury's New Testament translation of 1567. Tucked into a recess in one of the columns opposite is an exquisite sixteenth-century ivory Madonna, said to have come from the Spanish Armada.

If you ask the cathedral staff, they may let you into the crypt to view the cathedral **treasury**, which alongside its collection of silverware contains a Welsh-Greek-Hebrew dictionary compiled in the nineteenth century by Richard Robert Jones, usually known as Dic Aberdaron, a self-taught scholar who reputedly knew fifteen languages and smatterings of another twenty. The son of a fisherman, he was born in Aberdaron (see p.253) in 1780 and lived more or less as a tramp. His tombstone, in the churchyard of St Mary's Church at the bottom of the High Street, is engraved with a few lines by Ellis Owen which translate as:

A linguist eight times above other linguists – truly he was
A dictionary of every province.
Death took away his fifteen languages.
Below he is now without a language at all.

Practicalities

The A55 runs close by, but without your own transport you must rely on local **buses** only: services up the Vale of Clwyd to Denbigh and Ruthin, and in the other direction to nearby Bodelwyddan, Rhuddlan and Rhyl all stop right outside the cathedral. If you are planning to stay, the best central **rooms** at the *Kentigern Arms* (☎0745/584157; ③), towards the bottom of the High Street, or those at the nicely furnished non-smoking *Chalet*, The Roe (☎0745/584025; ③), quarter of a mile away across the river bridge then right. You'll need little more money to get a plush room at *Plas Elwy*, The Roe (☎0745/582263; ④), further down the same

WILLIAM MORGAN AND THE FIRST WELSH BIBLE

Until 1588 only English bibles had been used in Welsh churches, a fact which rankled Welsh-born preacher William Morgan who insisted that "Religion, if it is not taught in the mother tongue, will lie hidden and unknown". This was the professed reason behind Elizabeth I's demand for a translation, though her subjects' disaffection could be most conveniently controlled through the church. Four clergymen took up the challenge over a period of twenty-five years, but it is Morgan who is remembered: working away in Llanrhaeadr-ym-Mochnant (see p.000), he so neglected his duties that he needed an armed guard to get to his services and was said to preach with a pistol at his side.

The eventual translation was so successful that the Privy Council decreed that a copy should be allocated to every Welsh church. Though it was soon replaced by a translation of the Authorized Version, Morgan's Bible differs little in style from the latest edition used in Welsh services today. More than just a basis for sermons, The Welsh bible (Y Beibl) served to codify the language and set a standard for Welsh prose. Without it the language would probably have divided into several dialects or even followed its brythonic cousin, Cornish, into history.

road; and your own transport to get to the excellent *Fron Haul Farmhouse*, Bodfari (☎0745/710301; ③), five miles southeast of St Asaph. Take the A525 south to Trefnant, turn left at the lights onto the A541 then after two and a half miles turn left onto the B5429. The farm is the first turning on the right after the *Dinorben Arms* in Bodfari.

Sit in for **snacks** and a coffee or collect picnic supplies from the *Farm Shop*, halfway down High Street. For more substantial **meals**, make for the *Kentigern Arms* which, as well as being the most appealing pub, serves inexpensive bar meals and crispy pizzas; or walk across the road to the seventeenth-century former almshouses now operating as St Asaph's best restaurant, the moderately priced *Barrow Alms*, High St (☎0745/582260).

Prestatyn to Colwyn Bay

The twenty-mile stretch of coast from the Point of Ayr, at the end of the Dee Estuary, to Colwyn Bay constitutes the ugliest piece of Welsh coastline. Its entire length is taken up by unceasing caravan parks with barely an arm's length between neighbouring caravans filled by fun-seekers who descend annually from Merseyside and the rest of northern England. Family "amusements" come liberally scattered along the promenades and beachfronts seem designed to keep you off the beaches: a good idea even in the hottest weather since the sea hereabouts is none too clean. While it too has its share of caravan sites, **Prestatyn** is more notable as the starting, or finishing, point of the Offa's Dyke long distance path. **Rhyl** is none too appealing, but is good for budget accommodation and stands two miles to the north of the second of Edward I's castles at **Rhuddlan**, a few miles from the National Portrait Gallery's Welsh outpost at **Bodelwyddan**.

Fortunately the A55 expressway, the #X1 *Coastliner* bus and the North Coast trains can get you through it pretty quickly and on to Llandudno and Conwy beyond. If you feel like entering into the spirit of it all, you can ride an open-top #100 (late May to mid-Sept) from Prestatyn right along to Conwy. If you happen to be passing on July 1, call in to **Abergele**, between Rhyl and Colwyn Bay, where supporters of the Free Wales Army march through the streets in memory of two martyrs-to-the-cause (see p.345).

Prestatyn

PRESTATYN, nine miles northwest of Holywell, is a likeable enough market town, struggling to compete with its neighbours further along the coast by building the **Nova Centre**, a swimming and leisure complex on the beach. Unless you're desperate to try every manner of aquatic activity, then the **Offa's Dyke Information Centre** (Easter–Sept daily 10am–5pm; winter weekends 10am–3pm; if closed enquire in the Nova Centre) next door may prove more interesting, with its interpretive diagram of the 170-mile route of the Offa's Dyke Path to Chepstow (see box on p.192) and a stack of leaflets for walkers. The more committed traditionally start at least ankle-deep in the water, then cross the beach past a stone pillar onto Bastion Road. The path then follows High Street, through the main shopping area, to the *Cross Foxes* pub, from where acorn-marked signs guide you up to the hills behind. The view to Snowdonia, Liverpool and, on a good day, Blackpool, makes up for the fact that you won't come across any earthworks until the path gets south of the Dee, the route planners rightly preferring the Clwydian Ridge to the scrappy industrial towns of Trevor and Ruabon on the dyke's route.

Trains on the North Coast line stop right in the centre of town, close to the bus station, which is served by *National Express* buses, services to Flint, Holywell and Rhyl, and the #100 *Happy Dragon* (late May to mid-Sept). The **tourist office** is in the *Scala* cinema, High St (April–Sept 10am–1pm & 2–6pm; ☎0745/854365).

You'll probably want to continue along the coast, but for those preparing for (or recovering from) the long walk, there are a couple of **B&Bs**. From the station, turn towards the sea, then either right along the main A548 for *Roughsedge House*, 26–28 Marine Rd (☎0745/887359; ②), or left along the A548 to the equally good *Hawarden House*, 13 Victoria Rd (②); *Traeth Ganol*, 41 Beach Rd West (☎0745/853594; ④), is further out, but worth the effort: head for the *Nova Centre*, turn left past it and continue for 100 yards. Both are licensed and serve evening meals. *Nant Mill Farm* (April–Oct; ☎0745/852360) is a simple grassy **campsite** a mile out on the A584 east towards Flint.

Suhail Tandoori (☎0745/856829) serves moderately priced Indian **food** in a converted church near the station on the A548, or try the filled baguettes and lasagne on offer at the inexpensive *Bacchus Café Bistro*, 226 High St (lunches Mon–Sat, dinner Fri & Sat).

Rhyl and around

Anything you can do in **RHYL** (Y Rhyl), three miles west of Prestatyn, you can do better elsewhere. Apart from using it as a base for visits to Rhuddlan and Bodelwyddan, there's almost no reason to stay in this decaying Edwardian resort completely disfigured by amusement arcades. While desperately trying to woo back the punters with EU-funded initiatives, it fails on the most basic of requirements: the town doesn't even sport a decent swimming beach. Most people rightly prefer the lure of the slides and surfing-wave pool of north Wales' most popular tourist attraction, the **Sun Centre** (mid-April to mid-Sept daily 11am–8.30pm or later; £3.50) on the Promenade. There's more watery entertainment 400 yards further west at the **Sea Life Centre** (daily 10am–5pm; £4) with its spanking new tanks full of British coastal aquatic life. Several coastal environments are re-created, but the star attraction is the perspex shark tunnel, where dogfish, basking sharks and various eels leisurely drift all around you until the day's highlight: feeding time. The town's other attraction is bingo halls.

Wellington and Russel roads form the main street, with the **train station** and **bus stops** all close to the **tourist office** (June–Aug Mon–Sat 9am–6pm, Sun 10am–6pm; Sept–May Mon–Fri 9am–5pm, Sat 10am–5pm; ☎0745/355068), in the town hall close to where Wellington Road crosses High Street. Competition has forced **B&B** prices down: two central cheapies are *Gwynfa*, 6 Beechwood Rd (☎0745/353848; ②), off East Parade near the *Sun Centre*; and *Stoneleigh Guesthouse*, 1 Morlan Park (☎0745/336344; ②), off Bath Street, running between East Parade and Russel Road. Moving slightly upmarket it's worth trying *Kilkee Guesthouse*, 50 River St (☎0745/350070; ③), and *Medeor Hotel*, 3 Elwy St (☎0745/354489; ③); both are off the right-hand side of Wellington Road, walking west from the tourist office. Despite the vast number of caravan parks, the nearest **campsite** taking tents is *Henllys Farm Caravan and Campsite* (May–Oct; ☎0745/351208), three or four miles west of Rhyl, between Towyn and Abergele.

Decent **eating** places are almost as abundant as hotels. *Boswell's* on Bodfor Street offers an eclectic range of inexpensive bistro food and a healthy wine and cocktail list, but on a sunny day you are better off at the beachfront *Splash Point*, at the eastern end of Marine Drive along the front. The twenty-minute walk from the centre should build an appetite worthy of the monkfish cutlets or chicken burritos to be eaten in the bar, the conservatory or outside on the patio. The reasonably priced *Indian Garden*, 41 Abbey St (☎0745/35009), comes lauded as the best of the curry restaurants, while pricy *Barratt's*, 167 Vale Rd, the southern continuation of High St (☎0745/344138), tops them all with modern French cuisine in Rhyl's oldest house.

Splash Point rates as the ideal place for a **drink** on a warm afternoon or evening but the beer is equally good at the more central and very lively *Caskey's*, 21 Vale Rd.

Rhuddlan

RHUDDLAN lies on the banks of a tidal reach of the Clwyd River (Afon Clywedog), which finally meets the sea at Rhyl, two miles to the north. The town itself seems little more than an insignificant suburb of Rhyl but for the diamond-shaped ruin of **Rhuddlan Castle** (May–Sept daily 10am–5pm; CADW; £1.50). Constructed by Edward I during his first phase of castle building from 1277 to 1282, it was designed as a garrison and royal residence. The still-impressive castle commands a canalized section of the then strategic river that allowed boats to service the castle and provided water for the huge stone-lined moat around the other three sides. **Gillot's Tower**, by the dockgate, provided protection for the supply ships. The massive towers behind were the work of James of St George, who was responsible for the concentric plan that allowed archers on both outer and inner walls to fire simultaneously. This had become irrelevant by 1648, when Parliament forces took the castle during the Civil War and demolished it.

When Giraldus Cambrensis visited Rhuddlan a hundred years before the construction of Edward's castle, he was put up by David ap Owain, son of Owain Gwynedd, at a castle which once stood on **Twt Hill** (unrestricted access), reached by a footpath to the south of the present castle, now just a low hump in a bow of the river.

Important though the castle was, Rhuddlan earns its position in history as the place where Edward I signed the **Statute of Rhuddlan** on March 19, 1284, consigning Wales to centuries of subjugation by the English that many insist still continues. The ceremony took place on the site of **Parliament House**, on the main street 200 yards to the north: a sign on the building cynically claims that the Statute secured Welsh "judicial rights and independence", despite the fact that Edward laid down the laws by which the Welsh should be governed.

There's no reason to stop here for very long, but if necessary you can eat, drink and sleep at *The New Inn* (☎0745/591305; ④). The frequent #51 bus from Rhyl or from the Vale of Clwyd and Bodelwyddan stops just outside.

Marble Church and Bodelwyddan Castle: the National Portrait Gallery

Barrelling west along the A55 expressway towards the coast, the closest you come to Rhyl is the small village of **BODELWYDDAN**, four miles to the south. There is nothing of interest here, but from miles around you can pick out the slender 202-foot limestone spire of **Marble Church**, a quarter of a mile to the east of Bodelwyddan, standing as a beacon over the flat coastal plain. The finely worked tracery of the spire is the church's most impressive feature; inside, the marble arcades that give the church its nickname are something of a let-down. Local architect John Gibson, the sole pupil of Sir Charles Barry, designed it in the 1850s, his choice of Scottish granite intended to bring to mind the home of Saint Kentigern, the first bishop of nearby St Asaph and, under his alternative name of Saint Mungo, the patron saint of Glasgow.

More samples of Gibson's sculptural work are displayed in the finest art showcase in north Wales, **Bodelwyddan Castle** (July & Aug daily 10am–5pm; mid-April to June, Sept & Oct 10am–5pm, closed Fri; £3.50, gardens £2), set amidst landscaped gardens on its hill, half a mile south of Bodelwyddan. Although crenellated and edged with turrets, the castle is substantially a nineteenth-century country mansion built on the site of a fifteenth-century house, its opulent Victorian interiors re-created during its restoration in the 1980s, after sixty years as a girls' school. Williams Hall, a wing of the building, now houses one of four provincial outposts of the **National Portrait Gallery**, specializing in works contemporary with the castle.

Most of the two hundred paintings, which change every few years, are on the ground floor, approached through the "Watts Hall of Fame". This long corridor was specially decorated in William Morris style to accommodate not only a chair by Morris, but 26 portraits of eminent Victorians by G.F. Watts, among them Millais, Rossetti, Browning and Walter Crane. Leading off the corridor, the Drawing Room serves as sculpture gallery, with a portrait of John Gibson looking down on his own images of Bacchus and Cupid. In the Ladies' Drawing Room opposite, a beautiful Biedermeier sofa outshines paintings of little-celebrated nineteenth-century women around the walls.

Of the three main rooms, it is the Dining Room that stands out. Two sensitive portraits here highlight the Pre-Raphaelite support for social reform: William Holman Hunt's portrayal of the vociferous opponent of slavery and capital punishment Stephen Lushington; and Ford Madox Brown's double portrait of Henry Farell, prime mover in the passing of the 1867 Reform Bill, and suffragette Millicent Garrett. Works by John Singer Sargent and Hubert von Herkamer also adorn the room, which like the others, is furnished with pieces from the Victoria and Albert Museum in London. The table and chairs originally belonged to one Alfred Waterhouse, who designed the superb walnut and boxwood grand piano.

The grand staircase leads from the hall between the two drawing rooms to a more detailed presentation of significant aspects of nineteenth-century portraiture. Portrait photography and works by female artists get generous coverage along with animal painters, Landseer in particular. The top floor is reserved for temporary exhibitions.

Unfortunately the gallery doesn't issue an English leaflet – an incentive to fork out a substantial sum for the full illustrated guide – though the information boards in each room are adequate. By summer 1994, a nasty-sounding adults-only hotel complex will have opened in the castle grounds, though in compensation there will also be an outpost of the National Museum of Wales, concentrating on archeological finds in north Wales.

To get here, catch the #51 bus from Rhyl, Rhuddlan or anywhere in the Vale of Clwyd, bringing you within ten minutes' walk of both the castle and the church; or the #010 from Rhyl (mid-July to Aug) straight to the castle entrance.

Colwyn Bay

The A548 coast road west from Rhyl meets the A55 near the imposing nineteenth-century folly of Gwrych Castle and then continues on to **COLWYN BAY** (Bae Colwyn). Though the hilly setting gives the place more charm than its neighbours, there's no more to it than Rhyl, especially since its Victorian pier has now closed, leaving only an excellent restaurant (see below) and one sight, the **Welsh Mountain Zoo** (daily 9.30am–dusk; £4.75), to coax you off the train. Only the zoo's location high in the woods behind the town gives validity to its name, since the animals come from every continent. Californian sealions and "Chimpanzee World" are touted as the main attractions, or you might just be tempted by the free-flying eagle displays.

Trains stop on the seafront across the road from the **tourist office**, 40 Station Rd (July & Aug daily 9.30am–5.30pm; Sept–June Mon–Sat 9.30am–5pm; ☎0492/530478) from where the zoo is well signposted. Llandudno and Conwy are both close by, offering a better choice of **accommodation**, though you might want to take advantage of the **YHA youth hostel**, Nant-y-Glyn Rd (mid-Feb to Oct; ☎0492/530627; ①), nearly two miles from the station. To get there, turn left at the top of Station Road and Nant-y-Glyn Road is a couple of hundred yards on the left. The *Briar Lea Guesthouse*, 44 Greenfield Rd (☎0492/530052; ②) is more convenient: turn left at the top of Station Road, then it's the third turning on your left. If you do decide to stay for the evening, you could do worse than sample some of the Provençal dishes at moderately priced *Café Niçoise*, 124 Abergele Rd (☎0492/531555; closed all day Sun and Mon lunch), on their two- and three- course *menu touristique*. *Totem*, 2a Erskine Rd, just around the corner from *Café Niçoise*, is a completely different kettle of lentils, serving tasty and inexpensive vegetarian meals during the day (Mon–Sat).

Llandudno

Almost invariably, the wind funnels between the limestone hummocks of the 680-foot **Great Orme** and its southern cousin the Little Orme, which flank the gently curving Victorian frontage of **LLANDUDNO**. But don't let that put you off visiting this archetype of the genteel British seaside town. Set on a low isthmus, it has an undeniably dignified air, its older set of promenading devotees, often huddled in the glassed frontages of once-grand hotels, only slowly being replaced by more rumbustious fun-seekers, something that really needs to be encouraged to save the place from retirement home stagnation.

Llandudno's early history revolves around the Great Orme, where Saint Tudno, who brought Christianity to the region in the sixth century, built the monastic cell that gives the town its name. When the early Victorian copper mines looked to be worked out in the mid-nineteenth century, local landowner Edward Mostyn exploited the growing craze for sea bathing and set about a speculative venture to create a seaside resort for the upper middle classes. Being MP for the constituency, and having the Bishop of Bangor in his pocket, he was able to tease through Parliament an enclosure act giving himself the rights to the land.

Work got under way around 1854 and the resort rapidly gained popularity until the end of the century, when Llandudno had become synonymous with the

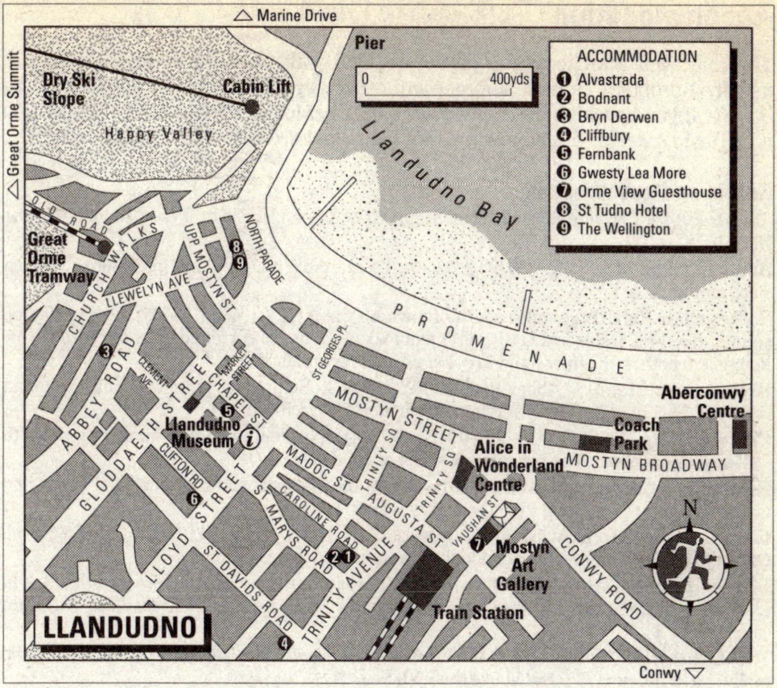

Victorian ideal of a respectable resort, drawing music stars such as Adelia Patti (see p.176) and Jules Rivière, the French conductor who sat in a gilded armchair facing the audience as he waved his bejewelled ivory baton. Mostyn Street, with its wrought-iron and glass verandahs, was said to have some of the finest shops outside London, patronized by the titled guests staying in the hotels: Bismarck, Napoleon III, Disraeli, Gladstone, and Queen Elizabeth of Romania, who stayed here for five weeks in 1890 and is said to have given the town its motto *Hardd, haran, hedd*, meaning "beautiful haven of peace". It may have been just that in 1890, but today it is boisterous, with less-exalted emporia along Mostyn Street and fewer pretensions amongst the hotel owners.

Arrival and information

The **train station** at the corner of Augusta and Vaughan streets is only five minutes' walk down Augusta Street/Madoc Street from the **tourist office**, 1 Chapel St (Easter–Sept daily 9am–6pm; Oct–Easter Mon–Fri 9am–5pm; ☎0492/876413). Direct trains come from Chester, those from Bangor and Betws-y-Coed generally requiring a change at Llandudno Junction. There is no Sunday service. Chapel Street runs parallel to Mostyn Street, where **local buses** from Bangor, Betws-y-Coed, Conwy and Rhyl stop. Less than ten minutes' walk south, *National Express* buses pull in to the **coach park** on Mostyn Broadway.

Accommodation

You may well want to stay a day or so, and with over 700 **hotels**, this is not usually a problem. In high summer and especially bank holidays, booking ahead is wise. If you haven't booked ahead, the best bet for inexpensive accommodation is St David's Road, with almost a dozen high-standard ② and ③ category places.

Hotels and guesthouses

Alvastrada, 24 Caroline Rd (☎0492/878229). Good-value place with TVs in rooms. March–Nov. ②.

Bodnant, 39 St Mary's Rd (☎0492/876936). Comfortable non-smoking guesthouse with en suite rooms. ③.

Bodysgallen Hall, three miles south of town on the A470 (☎0492/584466). One of the top country hotels in Wales in a partly seventeenth-century house surrounded by terraced lawns. Rooms are both in the house and in cottages in the grounds. ⑨.

Bryn Derwen Hotel, 34 Abbey Road (☎0492/876804). Sumptuous hotel with huge Victorian rooms at the foot of the Orme serving terrific meals. March–Nov. ④.

Cliffbury Hotel, 34 St David's Rd (☎0492/877224). Excellent-value non-smoking hotel with well-appointed rooms. The best on this street of good places. ②.

Fernbank, 9 Chapel St (☎0492/877251). One of the cheapest and best equipped of a string of low-cost hotels just along from the tourist office. ②.

Gogarth Abbey Hotel, West Shore (☎0492/876211). Fully fixtured hotel with heated pool. Once the summer home of Alice Liddell of Wonderland fame. ⑦.

Gwesty Leamore Hotel, 40 Lloyd St (☎0492/875552). One of the few guesthouses in Llandudno actually run by Welsh people. Friendly welcome and good facilities including satellite TV. ③.

The Lighthouse, Marine Drive, three miles from Llandudno (☎0492/876819). This place really is a lighthouse, 370 feet above the Irish Sea. ④.

Orme View Guesthouse, 5 Vaughan St (☎0492/870840). Another bargain place just a few steps from the train station above *Baxters Photography*. ②.

St Tudno Hotel, North Parade, just behind the pier (☎0492/874411). Superb, small seafront hotel heaped with accolades including "The Best Hotel Loos in Britain". Excellent meals. ⑦.

The Wellington, 12 North Parade (☎0492/876709). Good-value seafront hotel with views across the bay from the front rooms. Good inexpensive meals available. ③.

Campsite

Dinarth Hall Farm, Dinarth Hall Rd, Rhos-on-Sea, three miles east of Llandudno (☎0492/548203). Take The Promenade east to the roundabout at the bottom of the hill, then follow signs for the B545 to Colwyn Bay, then right at the College buildings. The #13, #14 and #15 buses run frequently.

The Town

No Victorian resort would be complete without its **pier** (open all year; free), and despite the pavilion being destroyed by fire in early 1994, Llandudno's is one of the few remaining in Wales, jutting out into Llandudno Bay with views back to the limestone cliffs of the Great Orme. From the pier, it's a leisurely ten-minute stroll along The Promenade to Vaughan Street and the region's premier contemporary arts centre, the **Mostyn Art Gallery**, 12 Vaughan St (Mon–Sat 10.30am–5pm; free), named after Lady Mostyn, for whom it was built in 1901. The gallery has no permanent collection, but its eight shows a year are usually worth catching, featuring works by artists of international renown with a particular leaning towards the current Welsh arts scene.

If you have kids to entertain, you're better off heading down Charlton Street from the gallery to the **Alice in Wonderland Visitor Centre**, 3–4 Trinity Square (daily 10am–5pm; Nov–March Mon–Sat only; £2). Here you are guided through the "Rabbit Hole", full of fibreglass Mad Hatters and March Hares, a headset relaying instructions and treating you to readings of *Jabberwocky* and the like. Llandudno is where Lewis Carroll first met the inspiration for his books, Alice Liddell, whose parents had a holiday home in what is now the *Gogarth Abbey Hotel*. The only other sight in town is the **Llandudno Museum**, 17–19 Gloddaeth St (Easter–Oct Tues–Sat 10.30am–1pm & 2–5pm; Nov–Easter Tues–Sun 2–5pm; £1.50), which presents local history, focusing on pieces unearthed in the copper mines (see below), Roman artefacts and a rebuilt rural kitchen from Llanberis.

The Great Orme

The top of the **Great Orme** (Pen y Gogarth) ranks as the one spot in north Wales with comparable views to those from the far loftier summits in Snowdonia. In many ways they are superior, combining the seascapes east towards Rhyl and west over the sands of the Conwy Estuary to the shores of Anglesey with the brooding quarry-chewed northern limit of the Carneddau range where Snowdonia crashes into the sea. Take a short walk across the rounded top of the Orme to get away from the crowds around the summit car park and it is easy to find somewhere to admire the view as fulmars wheel on the thermals, but it's less easy to see the feral goats which roam all over the mountain.

Formed about 300 million years ago at the bottom of a tropical sea, this huge lump of carboniferous limestone was subject to some of the same stresses that folded Snowdonia, producing fissures filled by molten mineral-bearing rock. Though there are a few minor Neolithic sites dotted over the hill, it was in the Bronze Age that the settlement really developed, when the people began to smelt the contents of the malachite-rich veins, supplying copper – if current speculation turns out to be true – throughout Europe.

The Romans seemed to ignore the Orme's potential, leaving it to early Christian Celts like Saint Tudno. The Vikings later gave the place its name, which derives from Old Norse meaning "worm" or "sea serpent" – just how it might have appeared in the mist to those approaching by sea. Today it is favoured not just by day-trippers here for the view, but also by botanists drawn by the profusion of maritime species: goldilocks aster, spotted cats-ear and spiked speedwell.

Apart from walking there are three other ways to explore the Orme. Traditionally the most popular is **Marine Drive**, a five-mile circuit right around the base, passing Pen-trwyn, a rock-climbing venue with several of Britain's trickiest limestone routes. Major flooding in the summer of 1993 brought a huge chunk of hillside down onto the Drive, but it is now open once again. You can walk if you wish, or make the anticlockwise circuit from just near Llandudno's pier in your own vehicle. Another road leads up to the cafés and bar at the **Summit Complex** (Easter–Oct daily; Nov–Easter Sat & Sun only; ☎0492/870610), following Old Road from Llandudno. The road up to the summit runs parallel to the route of the vintage, San Francisco-style **Great Orme Tramway** (April–Oct 10am–6pm; Nov–March 10am–4pm; £3 return, £2 single), creaking up from the bottom of Old Road much as it has done since 1902. The third route starts at the base of the pier, close to the start of Marine Drive, where an Italianate colonnade flanks the short road to the **Happy Valley** formal gardens and the **Cabin Lift** (Easter–Oct daily 10am–12.15pm & 1.45–4.30pm, to 5.30pm in July & Aug; £4 return, £3.50 single), which carries you up over the Orme to the Summit Complex, two miles away. At the start it swings over *Ski Llandudno* (daily 10am–10pm), where £10 will get you a couple of hours on the dry slopes (including all equipment), or for a quarter of the price you can make a couple of runs down a 700-yard-long snow-free **Toboggan Run**.

The Great Orme Mines

From the midway station of the tramway it is just a five-minute walk to the long-disused **Great Orme Copper Mines** (March–Oct daily 9am–6pm; reduced hours in Nov; £3.50), though you're better off catching the free bus (until end Sept) from Prince Edward Square in the town or from the Summit car park. The Victorians, who last mined the area, were aware of earlier workings, and until the late 1970s these were assumed to be Roman. Digs in the 1980s, however, uncovered 4000-year-old animal bones which had been used as scrapers up to 200 feet down. This is the only site in Britain where mineral veins were accompanied by dolomitization, a rock-softening process that permitted the use of the simple tools available in the Bronze Age. Ease of extraction led to this becoming the pre-eminent copper mine in Europe, and with more excavations continuing in the off-season, it may well turn out to have been the world's largest.

Hard hats and miner's lamps are provided on the **guided tour**, which, after a poor explanatory video, takes you down through just a small portion of the tunnels. It's enough, though, to get a feel for the cramped working conditions and the dangers of rock fall, and to see one of the three cats thought to have been ritually sacrificed by superstitious miners.

Eating, drinking and entertainment

Llandudno is blessed with the best choice of **restaurants** in north Wales, ranging from budget cafés to one of the most expensive places in the country. Most cluster at the foot of the Great Orme around Mostyn Street, where numerous pubs cater to most tastes.

Around the turn of the century, all the best performers clamoured to play Llandudno but today you're lucky to get anything more than faded stars plying the resorts throughout the summer. However, with the new *North Wales Theatre* (see below) and the **Llandudno October Festival**, things are looking a little rosier. The tourist office can usually give you a good idea of what's on, but we've listed the most promising venues.

Restaurants and cafés

Bartons, St George's Place. An all-you-can-eat pizza and salad bar in the café and a wine bar upstairs later on. Inexpensive.

Bodysgallen Hall, three miles south of town on the A470 (☎0492/584466). Top-notch traditional and modern British fare in one of the best country hotels around. Table d'hôte with a selection of over 300 wines. Very expensive.

Frenchy McCormicks, 149 Mostyn St (☎0492/872020). A corny menu, but great food spanning the Tex-Mex border: pork 'n' beans to chimichangas. Moderate.

The Garden Room Restaurant at the *St Tudno Hotel*, North Parade (☎0492/874411). One of Wales' best restaurants producing French-style meals utilizing fresh Welsh produce where possible. Three-course lunches are only moderately priced but in the evening you get the full five-course extravaganza. Expensive.

Habit Tearooms, 12 Mostyn St. Rich homemade cakes and light lunches are served in this bentwood chair and pot plant setting. Inexpensive.

King's Head, Old Rd. Substantial and tasty bar meals ranging from Welsh rarebit to noisettes of lamb in this low-beamed pub. Inexpensive.

No.1 Wine Bar, 1 Old Rd (☎0492/875424). Simply furnished and imaginative French-styled bistro. Wine served only with meals. Closed all day Sun and Mon lunch. Moderate.

Pinocchio Zorba, 153 Mostyn St (☎0492/860670). Relaxed Greek/Italian place serving well-prepared meze, pizza and pasta. Sunday lunch buffet for a fiver. Inexpensive to moderate.

Richards, 7 Church Walks (☎0492/877924). Basement bistro dishing up solid servings. The goat's cheese salad with plum dressing and their local mullet are particularly good. Seafood-based menu. Moderate.

Bars and pubs

Barton's, George St. Under-thirties frequent the wine bar above this restaurant in the early evening.

Cottage Loaf, Market St. Flag-floored pub built from old ships' timbers on top of an old bakehouse. Popular for lunchtime eating, and drinking all day.

King's Head, Old Rd, by the bottom of the Great Orme Tramway. The oldest pub here and where Edward Mostyn and his surveyor mapped out the town.

London Hotel, 131 Mostyn St (☎0492/876740). Despite the red telephone box inside and the Dick Whittington sign, it is a decent pub with good beer and a family room that turns into a piano bar at night.

Entertainment

Arcadia Theatre in the Aberconwy Centre, ten minutes' walk south of the pier along The Promenade (box office ☎0492/879771). The main venue for has-been entertainers, but it occasionally throws up something of interest.

The Boulevard, corner of Mostyn Broadway and Ty'n y Ffridd Rd. Llandudno's liveliest nightclub, currently rave on Thursdays and over-25s on Wednesday and Friday.

North Wales Theatre (Theatr Gogledd Cymru), The Promenade (☎0492/879771). Spanking new 1500-seat theatre designed to lure touring theatre companies.

The Palladium, Gloddaeth St (☎0492/876244). Llandudno's cinema, showing predominantly mainstream blockbusters.

Conwy and around

Until 1991, traffic ground steadily through **CONWY** making a visit thoroughly unpleasant. Now, with the completion of the bypass tunnel under the Conwy River (Afon Conwy), its approaches tucked behind a landscaped embankment, the town is learning to cope with tranquillity, soon to be dissipated as numbers of visitors increase, drawn by a fine castle and nearly complete belt of town walls. A mad scramble is under way to replace tarmac with cobbles, and to prettify the shopfronts, but for the moment, it remains one of the highlights of the north coast, its setting on the Conwy Estuary, backed by a forested fold of Snowdonia, irresistible to painters and photographers, ever since Englishman Paul Sandby published his *Views of North Wales* in 1776.

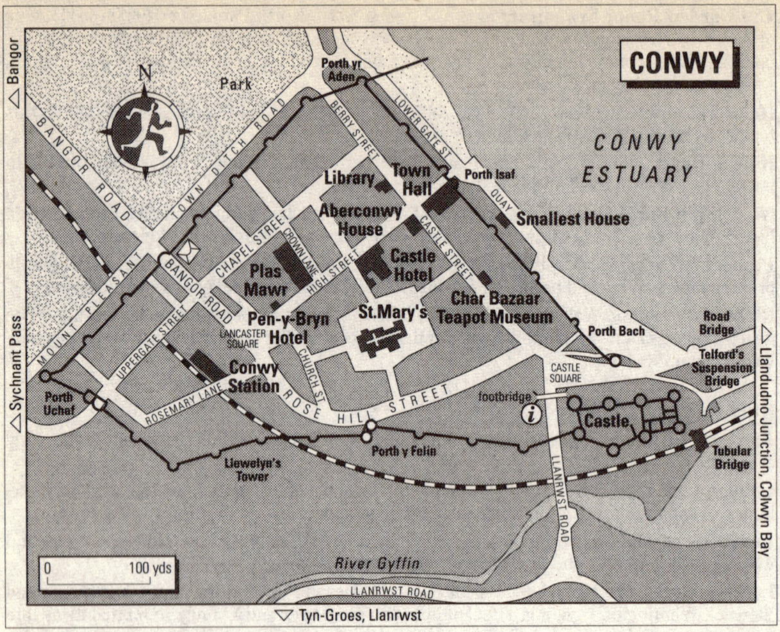

In Sandby's day, the Conwy Estuary still produced a good living for the families who had held mussel-gathering rights on the sands for centuries, a heritage which goes back long before the foundation of the Cistercian monastery of Aberconwy in 1172. The monastery, where Llywelyn ap Iorwerth died in 1240, was on the present site of the parish church of St Mary and All Saints, but a century later was moved eight miles upriver to Maenen, near Llanrwst, to make way for one of the toughest-looking links in Edward I's chain of fortresses.

Apart from a brief siege during the Welsh uprising of 1294, the bulk of events in Conwy's history occurred at the end of the fourteenth century: Richard II stayed at the castle on his return from an ill-timed trip to Ireland in 1399, until lured from safety by Bolingbroke's vassal the Earl of Northumberland. Northumberland swore in the castle's chapel to grant the king safe passage, but Richard was taken to Flint (see p.315) and kept captive, Bolingbroke becoming Henry IV. Just two years later, on Good Friday when the fifteen-strong castle guard were at church, two cousins of Owain Glyndŵr, Gwilym and Rhys ap Tudor, took the castle and razed the town for Glyndŵr's cause. Harry Hotspur, Chief Justice of north Wales, rushed from Denbigh (see p.320) to besiege the occupied fortress, eventually doing a deal: nine Welsh were to be handed over then hanged, drawn and quartered in return for the Tudors' freedom. After this, the castle fell into disuse, and was bought in 1627 for £100 by Charles I's Secretary of State, Lord Conway of Ragley, who then had the task of refortifying it for the Civil War. It held out until 1646, only surrendering to Mytton once the town had been taken. At the restoration of the monarchy in 1665, the castle was stripped of all its iron, wood and lead, and was left substantially as it is today.

Arrival and information

Llandudno Junction, less than a mile across the river to the east, serves as the main **train station** for *Intercity* services from Chester to Holyhead, as well as for trains heading south to Betws-y-Coed and Blaenau Ffestiniog; only slow, regional services stop in Conwy itself. *National Express* **buses** pull up outside the town walls on Town Ditch Road, while local buses to Bangor, Betws-y-Coed and Llandudno use the stops in the centre, mostly on Lancaster Square or Castle Street.

Walking south from either Conwy station or the Lancaster Square bus stops, skip the Conwy Visitor Centre, in favour of the **tourist office** (April–late Oct daily 9.30am–6.30pm; late Oct–March Mon–Sat 9.30am–4pm, Sun 11am–4pm; ☎0492/592248), which shares the same building and hours as the castle ticket office.

Accommodation

Accommodation right in the centre of town is a bit thin, so booking ahead is advisable in summer, especially if you don't have the transport to get to the less central hotels and guesthouses.

Hotels and guesthouses

Carreg y Groes, Garth Road, Glan Conwy (☎0492/580706). Guesthouse set in attractive grounds with all rooms overlooking the River Conwy. Fifteen minutes' drive from Conwy, signposted off the A470. Within easy striking distance of Bodnant Garden. There's no bus from Conwy but #84 runs from Llandudno Junction. ③.

Castle Bank Hotel, Mount Pleasant (☎0492/593888). Licensed, non-smoking hotel with country house atmosphere. Ten minutes' walk from the town centre: turn first left outside the town walls on the Bangor road. Excellent, moderately priced meals. ⑤.

Church House, Llanbedr-y-Cennin, five miles south of Conwy (☎0492/660521). Fine, old two-roomed guesthouse with beautiful views. Get off the #19 or #49 bus in Tal-y-Bont and walk half a mile west. The *Olde Bull Inn* is nearby (see "Eating and drinking"). ③.

Glan Heulog, Llanrwst Rd, on the outskirts of town half a mile towards Llanrwst on the B5106 (☎0492/593845). About the best B&B within easy walking distance of Conwy. ②.

Glyn Uchaf, Conwy Old Road, Capelulo, two miles from town (☎0492/623737). One of the best secluded B&Bs around, backing onto the hills just over Sychnant Pass. Good evening meals. ③.

Gwern Borter Country Manor, Barker's Lane, Roewen (☎0492/650360). Comfortable guesthouse on a Conwy Valley farm, just north of Roewen (bus #19). Pony-trekking available or walks onto the nearby Carneddau range. Meals available. ④.

Gwynedd Guesthouse, 10 Upper Gate St (☎0492/596537). The cheapest central B&B and consequently often full. ②.

Henllys Farm, Llechwedd, a mile and a half outside Conwy (☎0492/593269). Guesthouse on a working farm. Turn up Upper Gate St, bear left along St Agnes Road, follow signs for Llechwedd – *Henllys* is on the right. Meals and single rooms available. April–Nov. ③.

The Old Rectory, Llansantffraid Glan Conwy (☎0492/580611). Georgian-style country house, opulently furnished with antiques, overlooking the Conwy Estuary. Creative, expensive meals available. Closed Jan. ⑦.

Pen-y-Bryn, 28 High St (☎0492/596445). Well-appointed, non-smoking B&B in a central sixteenth-century building above tearooms. ③.

Hostels and campsites

Conwy Touring Park (☎0492/592856). A fully fixtured campsite taking tents, just over a mile south along the B5106 (bus #19). April–Oct.

Roewen youth hostel, Roewen, a mile up a steep hill above the village (☎0492/530627). Simple but superbly set YHA youth hostel on the flanks of the Carneddau range, reached by turning right fifty yards past Roewen's pub. Hourly bus #19 from Conwy in summer. Easter & May–Aug. ①.

The Town

Nowhere in the core of medieval and Victorian buildings is more than two hundred yards from the irregular triangle of protective masonry formed by the town walls. This makes it wonderfully easy to potter around and though you'll get to see everything you want to in a day, you may well want to stay longer.

Conwy Castle

During their incursions along Wales' north coast, Edward I's Anglo-Norman ancestors had all but destroyed the castle at Deganwy, near Llandudno, but maintaining a bridgehead west of the Conwy River had always eluded them. Accordingly, once over the river in 1283, Edward set about establishing another of his bastide towns, the castle relying on the town for its supplies, and the town on the castle for its protection. He chose a strategic knoll at the mouth of the Conwy River and set James of St George to fashion a castle to fit its contours. With the help of 1500 men, James took a mere five years to build **Conwy Castle** (April–late Oct daily 9.30am–6.30pm; late Oct–March Mon–Sat 9.30am–4pm, Sun 11am–4pm; CADW; £2.90), now entered through a separate ticket office and over a modern bridge.

Being overlooked by a low hill, the castle appears less easily defended than others along the coast, but James constructed eight massive towers in a rectangle around the two wards, the inner one separated from the outer by a drawbridge and portcullis, and further protected by turrets atop the four eastern towers, now the preserve of crows. Strolling along the wall-top gallery, you can look down onto something unique in the Iron Ring fortresses, a roofless but largely intact interior. The outer ward's 130-foot-long Great Hall and the King's Apartments are both well preserved, but the only part of the castle to have kept its roof is the **Chapel Tower**, named for the small room built into the wall whose semicircular apse still shows some heavily worn carving. On the floor below, there's a small exhibition on religious life in medieval castles which won't detain you long from exploring the passages.

The rest of the town

Anchored to the castle walls as though a drawbridge, Telford's narrow **suspension bridge** (NT) was part of the 1826 road improvement scheme, prompted by the need for better communications to Ireland after the Act of Union. Contemporary with his far greater effort spanning the Menai Strait (see p.351), Telford's bridge mimics the crenellations of the battlements above – an attempt to compensate for spoiling the view of the castle painted by J.M.W. Turner in 1802–3. The bridge was used until 1958, by which time the demands of modern traffic had inflicted tarmac, signs and street lighting on it. The current restoration job will rid the bridge of these additions, returning it to its original structure by spring 1995, when it will reopen as a footbridge. Similar aesthetic objections were levelled at Stephenson who, when pushing through the London–Holyhead rail line in 1848, built a twin-tubular span which is still in use today.

The approach to the third bridge has created the only breach in the thirty-foot high **town walls** which branch out from the castle into a three-quarter-mile-long circuit, enclosing Conwy's ancient quarter. Inaccessible from the castle they were designed to protect, the walls are punctuated by 21 evenly spaced horseshoe towers, as well as 12 latrines bulging out from the wall-walk. At present, only a third of the distance can be walked, starting from Porth Uchaf on Upper Gate Street – where you get the best combined view of the estuary and the castle – and running down to a spur into the estuary. Here, you come down off the walls by the brightly rigged trawlers, mussel boats and the *Queen Victoria*, which runs **river trips** (Easter–Oct daily; £2.50 for 30min; ☎0492/592284) from the quay, either upriver or around the estuary, depending on the tide. The red-painted lean-to, at the end of the row fronting onto the quay, has justifiable claims to being the **smallest house in Britain** (Easter–June & Sept to mid-Oct daily 10am–6pm; July & Aug daily 10am–9pm; 50p). It is only nine feet high and five wide, the door taking up only a quarter of the frontage, so most will have to duck to get in, though few as much as the last resident and great-grandfather of the present guardian, a six-foot-three fisherman.

THE "IRON RING"

Dotting the north Wales coast, a day's march from each other, Edward I's fearsome **Iron Ring** of colossal fortresses represents Europe's most ambitious and concentrated medieval building project, designed to prevent the recurrence of two massively expensive military campaigns (see "History" in *Contexts*). After Edward's first successful campaign in 1277, he was able to pin down his adversary, **Llywelyn ap Gruffydd** ("the Last") in Snowdonia and on Anglesey. This gave him room and time enough to build the now largely ruined castles at **Flint**, **Rhuddlan**, **Builth Wells** and **Aberystwyth**, as well as to commandeer and upgrade Welsh castles, Edward's first attempt at subjugation.

Llywelyn's second uprising, in 1282, was also ultimately unsuccessful, and Edward, determined not to have to fight a third time for the same land, set about extending his ring of fortifications in an immensely costly display of English might. Together with the Treaty of Rhuddlan in 1284, this saw the Welsh resistance effectively crushed. The castles at **Harlech**, **Caernarfon** and **Conwy**, though nearly contemporary, display a unique progression towards the later, highly evolved concentric design of **Beaumaris**.

All this second batch, including the town walls of Caernarfon and Conwy, were the work of the master military architect of his age, James of St George d'Espéranche, whose work is now recognized with **UN World Heritage Site** status.

Each of the castles was integrated with a **bastide town** – an idea borrowed from Gascony in southwest France, where Edward I was duke – the town and castle mutually reliant on each other for protection and trade. The bastides were always populated with English settlers, the Welsh permitted to enter the town during the day but not to trade and certainly not carrying arms. It wasn't until the eighteenth century that the Welsh would have towns they could truly call their own.

Porth Isaf, the nearby gate in the town walls, leads up Lower High Street to the fourteenth-century timber and stone **Aberconwy House**, Castle St (April–Oct daily except Tues 11am–1pm & 2–5.30pm; NT; £1.80), a former merchant's house, its rooms decked out in styles that recall its past. Medieval architecture enthusiasts should continue along the High Street to **Plas Mawr** at no. 20 (July–Sept daily 10am–5pm; CADW; £1), one of the best-preserved Elizabethan town houses in the country. Restoration should be complete in around 1998, and for the moment only the ground floor is open. The Dutch-style house was built in 1576 for one of the first Welsh people to live in the town, adventurer Robert Wynne, though much of the dressed stonework was replaced during renovations in the 1940s and 1950s. The interior sports more original features, in particular the friezes and superb moulded plaster ceilings depicting fleurs de lis, griffons, owls and rams. The watchtower is one of the town's classic vantage points.

If you find all this history suffocating, light relief is on hand across the road from Aberconwy House at the **Char Bazaar Teapot Museum**, Castle St (April & May daily 10.30am–5.30pm; June–Aug daily 10am–6pm; Sept & Oct daily 10.30am–5pm; £1), which has a thousand mostly pre-1950s pots – Wedgwood and majolica to Bauhaus. Clarice Cliff is particularly well represented amongst the examples of political caricature and lewd innuendo.

Eating and drinking

For a popular tourist town, Conwy has relatively few **restaurants**, and if you want to sample some really excellent pubs, you've got to get a few miles out of town into the Conwy Valley. **Drinking** in town is less rewarding, and nightlife really isn't a feature here.

Restaurants and cafés

Alfredo's Restaurant, Lancaster Square (☎0492/592381). Low-cost pasta dishes and more expensive *secondi piatti* amongst the Chianti bottles. Closed Sun. Moderate.

Austrian Restaurant, Old Conwy Rd, Capelulo, two miles west over Sychnant Pass (☎0492/622170). Worth making a journey for steaming helpings of gulasch and paprika schnitzel. Closed Sun evening and all day Mon. Moderate.

Groes Inn, Tyn-y-Groes, two miles south on the B5106 to Llanrwst (☎0492/650545). The fifteenth-century pub – which claims to be the first licensed house in Wales – serves excellent bar meals. Inexpensive.

Jade Garden, 136 Conwy Rd, Llandudno Junction (☎0492/581432). Highly regarded Cantonese restaurant, a mile east of Conwy. Inexpensive.

Olde Bull Inn, five miles south in Llanbedr-y-Cennin. Quiet haven away from Conwy serving well-prepared bar meals. Inexpensive.

Pen-y-Bryn Tearooms, 28 High St. Small, non-smoking establishment with the best artery-hardening Welsh teas around and delicious lunches. Inexpensive.

River Grill, 8 Berry Street. Café dishing up substantial all-day breakfasts and a range of vegetarian dishes. Inexpensive.

Pubs

Crown Hotel, High St. Decent town pub and a favourite with the locals.

Groes Inn (see above). A great place to sip a late afternoon tipple or knock back a pint or two of the cask ales available.

Liverpool Arms, The Quay. Great on warm evenings for drinking outside on the dock.

Around Conwy

With a marvellous setting and good accommodation either in or immediately around the town, Conwy is the best base for a couple of days exploring the Lower Conwy valley and the coast around its estuary. It's easy to make a day trip to Llandudno (above), and there's a smattering of other attractive diversions within a few miles radius. Thousands come here specifically to see **Bodnant Garden** beside the lower reaches of the Conwy, flowing down from Llanrwst and Betws-y-Coed. The guesthouses and restaurants mentioned below are all listed under Conwy, see above.

Sychnant Pass and Penmaenmawr

The best short walk from Conwy is on to **Conwy Mountain** and the 800-foot Penmaenbach and Alltwen peaks behind, all giving great views right along the coast. Follow a sign up Cadnant Park off the Bangor road just outside the town walls, then take the road around until Mountain Road heads off on the right towards a hillfort on the summit. This group is separated from the foothills of the Carneddau range by the narrow cleft of **Sychnant Pass**, traversed by Old Conwy Road, which ducks away from the sea, making an alternative route west, and rejoins the A55 expressway at Penmaenmawr. Just over the pass, but still only a couple of miles from Conwy, you come to the hamlet of **CAPELULO**, with the *Glyn Uchaf* guesthouse, a couple of good pubs with beer gardens, and *The Austrian Restaurant*. Bus #71 follows Conwy Old Road through Capelulo to Penmaenmawr.

Though you really need the "Snowdon" OS map, Capelulo makes a good starting point for a walk across **Penmaenmawr Mountain**, an important source of stone for axe making from around 3000 BC. Not surprisingly, the area boasts several Neolithic remains, most notably the misnamed **Druid's Circle** (Y Meini Hirion) – marked on the map simply as "Stone Circle" – on the hills behind Penmaenmawr. Of the thirty stones which originally composed the site, only ten survive, but within the ring archeologists found a buried cist containing a food vessel and the cremated remains of a child: possible evidence of a human sacrifice. Folklore has embellished the theme by naming one of the stones, its top scalloped into a cradle shape, the Stone of Sacrifice. Neo-druidic ceremonies still take place here from time to time.

Roewen and Aber Falls

Nine miles west of Conwy on the A55, the *Aber Falls Hotel* (☎0248/680579; ③) signals a side road leading inland to the 100-foot **Aber Falls**. Though a torrent after a storm, it can be little more than a trickle in high summer and in the dead of winter freezes enough to attract ice climbers. The road from the A55 runs a mile through a pretty oakwood valley to a car park at the start of a nature trail. This comprises several footpaths that lead to the falls, two following the valley with its series of cataracts and cascades, the other cutting up into the pine forests and approaching across a scree slope.

The same road off the A55 continues for two more miles, ending on the northern slopes of the bare Carneddau Hills. From here, a path (6 miles; 2–3hr; 600ft ascent) follows the low-level route of both a Bronze Age trackway and subsequent Roman road through the Carneddau range to **Roewen**. For much of the

Roman occupation, this was the most important road in Wales, linking the legion's headquarters in Chester – where some of the sandstone paving originally came from – via the now barely-visible fort at Canovium, located some two miles southeast of Roewen, to Segontium in Caernarfon (see p.345). The only walkable section these days is the stretch from Aber to Roewen which, along the way, passes a burial chamber, evidence of prehistoric field systems, and far too many power pylons.

The path emerges just behind the superbly set YHA **youth hostel** which, together with a post office, the *Tŷ Gwyn* pub and a few houses, comprise the tiny hamlet of **ROEWEN** (or Rowen). The #19 bus links Conwy with Roewen every two hours.

Bodnant Garden

During the months of May and June, the Laburnum Arch flourishes and banks of rhododendrons are in full and glorious bloom all over **Bodnant Garden** (mid-March to Oct daily 10am–5pm; NT; £3.60), one of the finest formal gardens in Britain, located eight miles south of Conwy. Laid out in 1875 around Bodnant Hall (closed to the public) by its then owner, English industrialist Henry Pochin, the garden spreads out over eighty acres of the east of the Conwy Valley. Facing southwest, the bulk of the gardens – themselves divided into an upper terraced garden and lower Pinetum and Wild Garden – catch the late afternoon sun as it sets over the Carneddau range. Though arranged so that shrubs and plants provide a blaze of colour throughout the opening season, autumn is a perfect time to be here, with hydrangeas still in bloom and fruit trees shedding their leaves. The #25 bus runs here from Llandudno every two hours, calling at Llandudno Junction, or it's a two-mile walk from the Tal-y-Cafn train station on the Conwy Valley line.

Bangor and around

After spending a few days travelling through mid-Wales or in the mountains of Snowdonia, **BANGOR** makes a welcome change. It is not big, but as the largest town in Gwynedd and home to **Bangor University**, it passes in these parts for cosmopolitan. The students are the main reason for Bangor's vibrancy, but once they leave for the summer, the place thins out with only a trickle of visitors to replace them.

The presence of a large non-Welsh student population inflames the passions of the more militant nationalists in what is a staunchly Welsh-speaking area. Antagonism between students and locals seldom inflates to anything more than drunken slanging matches, but if you've just arrived from one of the largely English-speaking north coast resorts, you'll notice a dramatic change.

In the nineteenth century, the slate industry and road and rail projects needed to improve communications with Ireland brought some urbanization to Bangor, but for well over a millennium before that, the city was solely noted for its see, founded as a monastic settlement by St Deiniol in 525. At first, St Deiniol only cleared a space in the woods which became known as *Y Cae Onn*, "The Ash Enclosure", only later developing into the present name, a corruption of *bangori*, a type of interwoven hedge which presumably demarcated the monastic lands.

Arrival, information and accommodation

All trains on the North Coast line running between Chester and Holyhead stop at Bangor **train station** located on Station Road, at the bottom of Holyhead Road. From here Deiniol Road, the town's main street, runs along the bottom of the valley to the **tourist office**, (Easter–Sept daily 10am–6pm; ☎0248/352786) to be found inside the foyer of *Theatr Gwynedd*. Garth Road, which follows the valley almost as far as the pier, is effectively the continuation of Deiniol Road but the short spur of Garth Road, opposite the tourist office, is where both *National Express* **buses** and local services to stop.

With its relatively low number of visitors, Bangor doesn't have a huge choice of **places to stay**. Most cheaper accommodation is at the northern end of Garth Road, about twenty minutes' walk from the train station. As usual, many of the better places are out of town and thoroughly inconvenient unless you have your own transport.

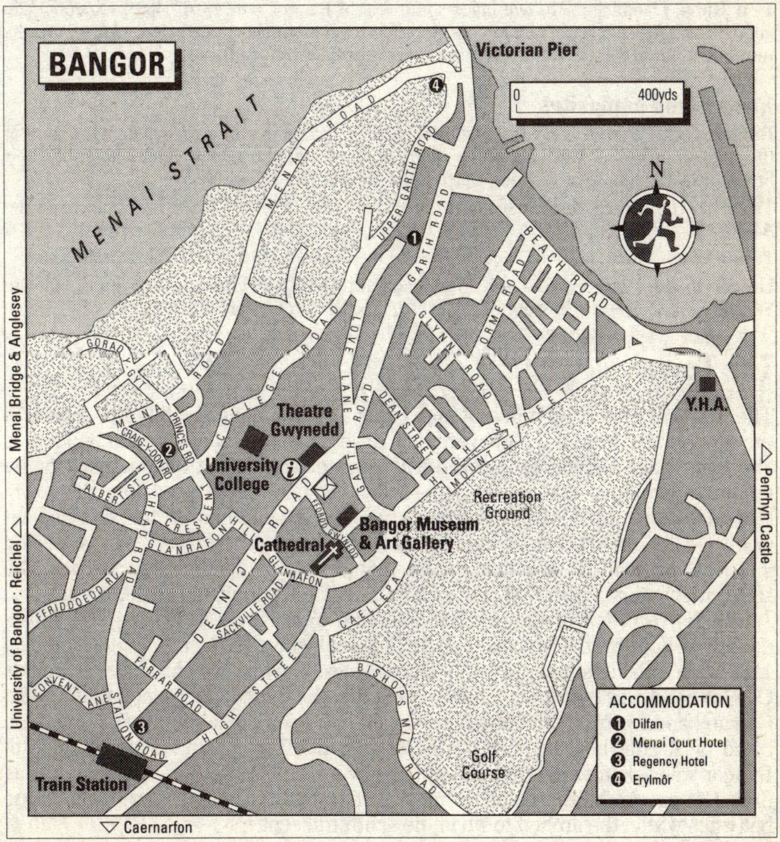

Hotels and guesthouses

Dilfan (☎0248/353030). Marginally the best of a row of three low-cost, serviceable B&Bs. ③.

Eryl Môr Hotel, 2 Upper Garth Rd (☎0248/353789). Quiet, comfortable hotel with front-room views over Bangor's pier and the Menai Strait. ④.

Goetre Isaf Farm, Caernarfon Rd (☎0248/364541). Farmhouse B&B run by folk keen to discuss their own travels. If you arrange it beforehand they may pick you up from the station thereby avoiding a two-mile walk south. Buses #5 and #5a run close by. ②.

Menai Court Hotel, Craig-y-Don Rd (☎0248/354200). Bangor's top hotel with plush decor and well-appointed rooms, some with views of Snowdonia or the Menai Strait. ⑦.

Regency Hotel, Holyhead Rd (☎0248/370819). Excellent value for money opposite the station. ④.

Tros-y-Waen Farm, just off B4547 south of Pentir, six miles south of Bangor towards Llanberis (☎0248/364448). Good-value farmhouse B&B and campsite. ②.

Ty-Mawr Farm, half a mile east of Llanddeiniolen, midway between Bangor and Caernarfon on the B4366 (☎0286/670147). Comfortable B&B on working farm with good home-made food. Self-catering cottages also available. Bus #82 (not Sun) runs infrequently between Bangor and Caernarfon and stops within half a mile. ③.

Tŷ'n Rhos, Llanddeiniolen, five miles southwest of Bangor (☎0248/670489). Exceptionally good farmhouse accommodation, with superb moderately priced four-course meals. Infrequent bus #82 (not Sun) from either Bangor or Caernarfon. ⑤.

Hostels and campsites

Bangor youth hostel, Tan-y-Bryn (☎0248/353516). A large house signposted on the right of the A56, ten minutes' walk east of the centre and reached either by walking along the High Street or taking bus #6 or #7 along Garth Road. Closed Dec & Jan. ①.

Treborth Hall Farm, three miles over the Menai Strait (☎0248/364399). A campsite on the A4080.

Tros-y-Waen Farm, off B4547 south of Pentir (see above). This B&B also has a campsite.

University of Bangor: Reichel, Ffriddoedd Rd (☎0248/372104). In late June and late September and over the Easter holiday, clean, functional rooms are available. ②.

The Town

The university takes up much of upper Bangor, straddling the hill that separates the town centre from the Menai Strait. The shape of the college's main building is almost an exact replica of the **cathedral** (open daily until dusk), which boasts the longest continuous use of any cathedral in Britain, easily predating the town. Nowadays only a blocked-in Norman window gives any hint of the see's ancient origins. Though you won't want to spend a lot of time here, it's worth venturing into the cathedral's spacious white-walled interior, particularly to see the sixteenth-century wooden **Mostyn Christ**, depicted bound and seated on a rock.

Little is recorded of the original cathedral until it was destroyed and subsequently rebuilt by the Normans in 1071. Archbishop Baldwin preached here in 1188 while raising support for the Third Crusade, when his chronicler, Giraldus Cambrensis, was shown a double vault by the high altar containing Owain Gwyned and his brother Cadwaladr. Owain had been posthumously excommunicated by Archbishop Thomas for incest with his first cousin and the Bishop of Bangor was asked to look for an opportunity to remove the body from the cathedral. He was probably reinterred in the churchyard, though many believe the body lies within the arched tomb in the south transept.

The Norman building was heavily damaged by King John in 1211, a second time by Edward I and then again by Owain Glyndŵr, the various reconstructions resulting in the present thirteenth- to fifteenth-century building, heavily restored by Gilbert Scott in 1866. Outside, there's a **bible garden** with a collection of all the biblical trees, shrubs and flowers capable of withstanding the local climate.

Just over the road, the **Bangor Museum and Art Gallery**, Ffordd Gwynedd (Tues–Fri 12.30–4.30pm, Sat 10.30am–4.30pm; free), offers standard regional museum fare, the snippets of local history enlivened by the newly refurbished traditional costume section and the archeology room, containing the most complete Roman sword found in Wales. The most insightful rooms are those devoted to a complete set of furniture from a moderately wealthy Cricieth farm, covering three hundred years of acquisitions from brooding Welsh dressers to fine Italian pieces. Furniture also forms the basis of the museum's homage to Thomas Telford, whose favourite chair sits alongside a model of his bridge complete with the web of chains which were stripped off during strengthening in 1935, when they were found to be heavy and unnecessary. The art gallery downstairs has no permanent collection, its temporary displays concentrating on predominantly Welsh contemporary works.

Heading away from the centre, it is not unreasonable to consider walking out to Telford's bridge. Otherwise, you can get a good look at it from Bangor's pristine **Victorian Pier** (20p), which reaches halfway across to Anglesey. The pier lay derelict for years but has recently been restored and is blessed with just one token amusement pavilion. To get there, either follow Garth Road towards Conwy – a fifteen-minute walk – or work your way down from Upper Bangor along College Road, the latter route allowing a detour across a wooded hill known as Roman Camp. Recent digs here have failed to unearth any evidence at all of Roman occupation, but you do at least get a good view of the strait.

Eating, drinking and entertainment

With the possible exception of Llandudno, Bangor offers the widest selection of **eating** possibilities in north Wales. If you are just grazing or stocking up for a journey there are a number of cheap sandwich and pasta joints along High Street, plus the well-stocked *International Flavours* deli and health food store near the cathedral. For a broad selection of places to eat and drink all within a hundred yards, make for Holyhead Road in Upper Bangor.

Restaurants and cafés

Fat Cat Café Bar, 161 High St. Modern decor and a menu ranging from massive burgers to salmon and broccoli pasta quills help pack this place out with students and locals. Moderate.

Garden, 1 High St (☎0248/362189). Dimly lit Cantonese restaurant serving succulent sesame prawns off a broad but not overwhelming menu. Moderate.

Greek Taverna Politis, 12 Holyhead Rd (☎0248/354991). Souvlaki and stifado favourites and top class Greek salads served either around the fire, in the airy conservatory or outside in the courtyard. Cheaper meals at the bar. Moderate.

Herbs, 30 Mount St. One of the very few vegetarian restaurants around. Daytime only. Inexpensive.

Menai Court Hotel, Craig-y-Don Rd (☎0248/354200). The restaurant of this classy hotel earns the plaudits of foodies for its traditional British and European dishes and its extensive wine list. Expensive.

Pizzeria Trattoria Italia, 6a Holyhead Rd (☎0248/354693). Take out or sit in the *tricolore* surrounds. Also serves meals to go. Inexpensive to moderate.

Tandoori Knight, 10 Holyhead Rd (☎0248/364634). All the usual tandoori dishes in a restaurant that often looks closed when it isn't. Inexpensive.

Pubs, music and nightlife

Belle Vue, Holyhead Rd. The main student pub, right next to the university.

The Octagon, Dean St off High St (☎0248/354977). Bangor's only club, featuring a student night on Wednesday with very cheap happy hours between 8pm and 10pm.

The Skerries, 374 High St. Lively pub with a decent pint, a relatively up-to-date jukebox and a young crowd.

Tafarn Y Glôb, 7 Albert St. If you've tried to learn any of the language you can put it to good use at this traditional local where ordering in Welsh is pretty much *de rigueur*. For a pint of beer try "un peint o cwrw, os gwelwch yn dda".

Theatr Gwynedd, Deiniol Rd (box office ☎0248/351708). Along with its counterpart in Mold, *Theatr Gwynedd* is the most progressive art house in north Wales and is about your only chance of seeing contemporary plays or even slightly off-beat movies.

University Students' Union, Deiniol Rd (☎0248/353709). Fly posters around town almost all point you to the Students' Union, the venue for any touring rock/pop bands. Usually quiet over the summer break.

The Victoria Hotel, Telford St, Menai Bridge. The best bet for local live music, across the water in Menai Bridge (see p.352).

Penrhyn Castle

There can hardly be a more vulgar testament to the Anglo-Welsh landowning gentry's oppression of the rural Welsh than the oddly compelling **Penrhyn Castle** (daily except Tues April–June, Sept & Oct noon–5pm, July & Aug 11am–5pm; £4.40 including 50-min recorded tour, £2 grounds only; NT), two miles east of Bangor, which overlooks Port Penrhyn from its acres of isolating parkland. Built on the backs of slate miners for the benefit of their hated bosses, this monstrous nineteenth-century neo-Norman fancy, with over three hundred rooms dripping with luxurious fittings, was funded by the quarry's huge profits.

The responsibility falls ultimately on sugar plantation owner and anti-abolitionist Richard Pennant, First Baron Penrhyn, who built a port on the north-eastern edge of Bangor in order to ship his Bethesda slate to the world. But it was his self-aggrandizing great-great-nephew George Dawkins who inherited the 40,000-acre estate, added his ancestor's surname to his own, and with the aid of architect Thomas Hopper spent thirteen years from 1827 encasing the neo-Gothic hall in a Norman fortress complete with monumental five-storey keep.

Many would argue that the vulgarity doesn't stop with the owners but runs right through the fabric of the building, with the abundance of carved slate a further slap in the face to the workers. The decoration is glorious nonetheless, and fairly true to the Romanesque, with its deeply cut chevrons, billets and double-cone ornamentation. Hopper even looked to Norman architecture for the design of the furniture but abandoned historical authenticity when it came to installing the central heating system, which piped hot air through ornamental brass ducts at the cost of twenty tons of coal a month.

Everything is on a massive scale and no more so than in the Great Hall with its pair of stained-glass Zodiac windows by Thomas Willement. Three-foot-thick oak doors separate subsequent rooms: the Library, with its full-size slate billiard table, and the oppressive Ebony Room, which leads on to the Grand Staircase. Upstairs, the lightness of the original William Morris wallpaper and drapes around the King's Bed are in marked contrast to the Slate Bed, designed for Queen Victoria but declined by her in favour of the Hopper-designed four-poster in the State Bedroom. The family managed to assemble the country's largest private painting collection. Much of this remains, especially in the two dining rooms, where there's a Gainsborough landscape amongst the family portraits, Canaletto's *The Thames at Westminster* and a Rembrandt portrait.

Once Richard Pennant had built his port he needed some way of getting the slates down to it. His answer was a horse-drawn tramway, which opened in 1801 and remained in use – though using steam engines by this time – until 1962. Gleaming examples of rolling stock from this and the country's other private industrial railways are on display in the **Industrial Railway Museum** (same hours; entry with castle ticket), including Lord Penrhyn's luxurious coach linked to a quarrymen's car. Buses #5 and #7 run frequently from Bangor to the gates from where it is a mile-long walk to the house.

Caernarfon and around

It was in **CAERNARFON** in 1969 that Charles, the current heir to the throne, was invested as Prince of Wales, a ceremony which reaffirmed English sovereignty over Wales in this, one of the most nationalist of Welsh-speaking regions. Since 1282, when the English defeated Llywelyn ap Gruffydd, the last Welsh Prince of Wales, the title has been bestowed on heirs to the English throne, usually in a ceremony held either at Windsor Castle or in Westminster Abbey in London. But in 1911, the machinations of Lloyd George – MP for Caernarfon, Welsh cabinet minister and future Prime Minister – ensured that the investiture of the future King Edward VIII would take place in the centre of his constituency: a paradoxical move for a nationalist considering the symbolic implications.

By the time it was Charles's turn, nationalist activism was on the rise and two of the more militant cadres tried to blow up the Prince's train, succeeding only in killing themselves. That day, July 1, is now commemorated by a march through the streets of Abergele, near where the accident happened, led by their successors *Meibion Glyndŵr*, the Sons of Glendower (see p.383).

This is a town where ardent support for Plaid Cymru guarantees the party a seat in Westminster and where the local dialect is barely intelligible even to other Welsh-speakers. It is also the county town of Gwynedd, a suitable title for what is one of the oldest continuously occupied towns in the country, once the site of the Romans' most westerly legion post. Segontium, on the outskirts of town, was the base of Maximus, the Spanish-born pretender to the imperial throne who was declared Emperor by his British troops in 383 AD, only to undertake an unsuccessful march on Rome.

The remains of Segontium are not especially impressive, but with its magnificent castle and town walls, Caernarfon is an appealing place, especially if you have recently visited the similar setup in Conwy. Apart from the castle, however, there isn't too much to see: you can only walk a small section of the wall and the rest of the town, ripped through by a dual carriageway, has a fairly modern feel. That said, it is well sited on the Menai Strait and has good bus connections to Llanberis and Snowdonia.

Arrival, information and accommodation

With no train station, the hub of Caernarfon's public transport system is Castle Square (Y Maes), right under the walls of the castle, and just a few steps from the **tourist office**, Oriel Pendeitsh, Castle Street (Easter–Oct daily 10am–6pm; Nov–Easter 9.30am–5pm, closed Wed; ☎0286/672232). Both *National Express* and local buses for Bangor, Beddgelert, Blaenau Ffestiniog, Llanberis, Porthmadog and Pwllheli stop on Castle Square.

While there are a number of cheap places close to the centre, Caernarfon isn't so well provided with more upmarket **accommodation**, though the high standard of the farmhouses around about goes some way to redressing the balance. A couple of these – *Ty-Mawr Farm* and *Tŷ'n Rhos* – are in Llanddeiniolen, halfway between Caernarfon and Bangor and detailed in the Bangor section on p.342. The town is well equipped with **campsites**: *Coed Helen* (March–Oct; ☎0286/676770) sits right on the Seiont River just across the footbridge from the foot of the castle, and *Cadnant Valley* (Easter–Oct; ☎0286/673196) is only a little further, at the back of town near the start of the A4086 to Llanberis. The nearest **YHA hostel** is seven miles southeast on the A4085 to Beddgelert (see p.305).

Hotels and guesthouses

The Black Boy Inn, Northgate St (☎0286/673023). Characterful but bathless low-beamed rooms in what is said to be the town's oldest building (bar the castle). Newer en suite accommodation also available. ③.

Gwyn Wylan, 7 North Penrallt (☎0286/672902). Cheap, basic B&B close to town centre. ②.

Isfryn Guesthouse, 11 Church St (☎0286/675628). Good-value B&B in the centre; book ahead in summer. Moderately priced three-course evening meals available. ②.

Pengwern Farm, Saron, three miles southwest of Caernarfon (☎0286/830717). En suite rooms with TVs in a rural setting, with farm-fresh and inexpensive evening meals. Take the A487 south across the river then turn right towards Saron – Pengwern is just over two miles down on the right. Feb–Nov. ③.

Pros Kairon, Victoria Rd (☎0286/676229). Best of the budget places, run by a retired vicar who always gives a generous welcome. Five minutes' walk from the centre towards Segontium, then left up Dinorwig Street. ②.

Seiont Manor, Llanrug, three miles east of Caernarfon on the A4086 (☎0286/673366). Rustic building remodelled into the region's finest hotel, complete with indoor pool, sauna and use of mountain bikes. Superb though pricy French food. ⑨.

Ty Mawr Farmhouse, Saron (☎0286/830091). Top-value farmhouse B&B with evening meals and a choice of traditional, vegetarian or wholefood breakfast. Take the A487 south across the river then turn right towards Saron. Ty Mawr is almost three miles on. ③.

Wallasea Guesthouse, 21 Segontium Terrace (☎0286/673564). Good and very central, overlooking the Seiont. ②.

The Town

In 1283, Edward I started work on **Caernarfon Castle** (April–late Oct daily 9.30am–6.30pm; late Oct–March Mon–Sat 9.30am–4pm, Sun 11am–4pm; CADW; £3.50) the strongest link in his Iron Ring (see p.337), and the decisive hammer-blow to any Welsh aspirations to autonomy. Until Beaumaris Castle was built to guard the other end of the Menai Strait, Caernarfon was the ultimate symbol of both Anglo-Norman military might and political wrangling. With the Welsh already smarting from the loss of their Prince of Wales, Edward is said to have rubbed salt in their wounds by justifying his own infant son's claim to the title declaring the future Edward II "a prince born in Wales who could speak never a word of English". The story is almost certainly apocryphal since, though born at Caernarfon, Edward's son wasn't invested until seven years later.

Edward attempted to appease the Welsh in the building of his castle by paying tribute to aspects of local legend. The Welsh had long associated their town with the eastern capital of the Roman Empire: Caernarfon's old name, Caer Cystennin, was also the name used for Constantinople, and Constantine himself was believed to have been born at Segontium. Edward's architect, James of St George, exploited this connection in the distinctive limestone and sandstone banding and polygonal towers, both reminiscent of the Theodosian walls in present-day Istanbul. The other legend to influence the castle was the medieval *Dream of Macsen Wledig*, in which the eponymous Welsh hero (the Roman legionnaire Maximus) remembers "a fair fortress at the mouth of a river, in a land of high mountains, opposite an island, and a tower of many colours at the fort, and golden eagles on the ramparts". When it came to finishing off the turrets in 1317, Edward III perfected the accuracy of this description by adding eagles – also, ironically, the standard of Owain Gwynedd. These are weathered almost beyond recognition now but the rest of the castle is in an excellent state of repair, thanks largely to Anthony Salvin's nineteenth-century reconstruction, carried out after Richard Wilson and J.M.W. Turner had painted their Romantic images of it.

As a military monument of its time, the castle is supreme. It was taken once, before it was finished, but then withstood two sieges by Owain Glyndŵr with a complement of only 28 men-at-arms. Entering through the **King's Gate**, the castle's strength is immediately apparent. Between the octagonal towers, embrasures and murder-holes face in on no fewer than five gates and six portcullises, and that's once you have crossed the moat, now bridged by an incongruous modern structure. Inside, the huge lawn gives a misleading impression since both the wall dividing the two original wards and all the buildings which filled them crumbled away long ago. The towers are in a much better state, and linked by such a honeycomb of wall-walks and tunnels that a visit can be an exhausting experience. The most striking and tallest of the towers is the King's Tower at the western end, whose three slender turrets adorned with eagle sculptures give the best views of the town. To the south, the Queen's Tower is entirely taken up by the numbingly thorough **Museum of the Royal Welch Fusiliers**, detailing the victories of Wales' oldest regiment, with collections of medals, uniforms and a brass howitzer captured from the Russians at the Battle of the Alma in 1854. Crossing the upper ward from here you pass the site of the original Norman motte, now covered in Dinorwig slate as part of the dais for the investiture of the Prince of Wales. Displays on the most recent ceremony, and others since the pageant was moved here in 1911, are presented in the **Prince of Wales Exhibition** in the Northeast Tower, just beyond the dais.

The castle forms one side of Caernarfon's rectangle of **town walls**, almost as complete as those at Conwy, but less striking, since they've been boxed in by modern buildings. You can only walk a very short section, at the end of Market Street, close to the Chantry of St Mary, the restored fourteenth-century church built into a corner of the town wall on Church Street. Just outside the walls, Victoria Dock is home to a **Maritime Museum** (Easter & June to mid-Sept daily 11am–4pm; 50p) based in and around the *Seiont II* steam dredger, which is gradually being renovated, and the *Nantlys*, the last ferry to ply the Menai Strait.

A ten-minute walk along the A4085 Beddgelert road brings you to the western end of the Roman road from Chester at **Segontium Roman Fort** (March–Sept Mon–Sat 9.30am–6pm, Sun 2–6pm; Oct–Feb Mon–Sat 9.30am–4pm, Sun 2–4pm; CADW; donation). The Romans occupied this five-acre site for three centuries from around 78 AD, though most of the remains are from the final rebuilding after 364 AD. The groundplan is seldom more than shin-high and somewhat baffling, making the museum and displays in the ticket office pretty much essential.

Eating, drinking and entertainment

Caernarfon boasts a number of low-key and likeable **restaurants** which may well be the focus of your evening's entertainment, as there is little else except for a smattering of **pubs**. There is really no organized nightlife, everyone heading ten miles north to Bangor. The *Caernarfon Chronicle*, which comes out on Thursdays, has gig information for both Bangor and Caernarfon.

Restaurants and cafés

The Bakestone, 25 Hole in the Wall St (☎0286/675846). Spartan place with gingham tablecloths. Sit downstairs and you can watch the French food – frog's legs and escargots both available – cooked in front of you. Moderate.

The Black Boy Inn, Northgate St. The best bar meals in town. Inexpensive.

Courteney's, 9 Segontium Terrace (☎0286/677290). Eclectic range of excellent food and good wines served in a small room which is often full, especially at weekends. Closed for Mon & Tues lunches and all day Sun. Moderate.

Rochelle's, 25 Bridge St. Licensed café and restaurant, equally good for lunch, a light dinner or just to relax over a cappuccino in the window seat. Closed all day Sunday & weekday evenings out of season. Inexpensive.

Stone's, 4 Hole in the Wall St (☎0286/671152). Simply decorated brick-walled place serving bistro-style meals ranging from roast pheasant to a choice of four vegetarian dishes. Closed Sun. Moderate.

Pubs

Tafarn Yr Albert, 11 Segontium Terrace. Bustling local where you might catch a Welsh-language band on a Saturday night.

The Black Boy Inn, Northgate St. The closest Caernarfon comes to an old-fashioned British pub, with a choice of two low-beamed bars.

Y Goron Fach, Hole in the Wall St. A good range of cask ales in a friendly setting.

Around Caernarfon

A much-touted but overrated outing is to the **Caernarfon Air Museum** (March–Nov daily 9am–5pm; £3), eight miles south of town at Dinas Dinlle (bus #91), where cases of model airplanes help to fill out a small hangar containing half a dozen examples of the real thing. Better reasons to come out here might be the **scenic flights** over Caernarfon (10min; £15) and Snowdon (25min; £30), or the **Dinas Dinlle** Roman and early British oval hillfort at the south end of the beach. The hill has suffered erosion by the sea, erasing most of the archeological evidence, and has also been damaged by footsteps, so the path to the top is sometimes cordoned off. If it's not, and your visit coincides with low tide, you might be able to see Caer Arianrhod, a row of rocks named after the girl in *The Mabinogion* who gave birth to Lleu Llaw Gyffer, destined to become Lord of Gwynedd.

Anglesey

Signs welcoming you to **Anglesey** (Ynys Môn) announce this to be "Mam Cymru", the Mother of Wales, attesting to the island's former importance as the breadbasket of the region. In the twelfth century Giraldus Cambrensis noted that "When crops have failed in other regions, this island, from its soil and its abundant produce, has been able to supply all Wales", and while feeding their less productive kin in Snowdonia is no longer a priority, the land remains predominantly pastoral, with small fields, stone walls and white houses suggestive of parts of England. Linguistically and politically, though, Anglesey is intensely Welsh. One of the four Plaid Cymru MPs represents the island, which has one of the highest proportions of native speakers, for over seventy percent of whom Welsh is their first language. They at least will understand the lines of one of

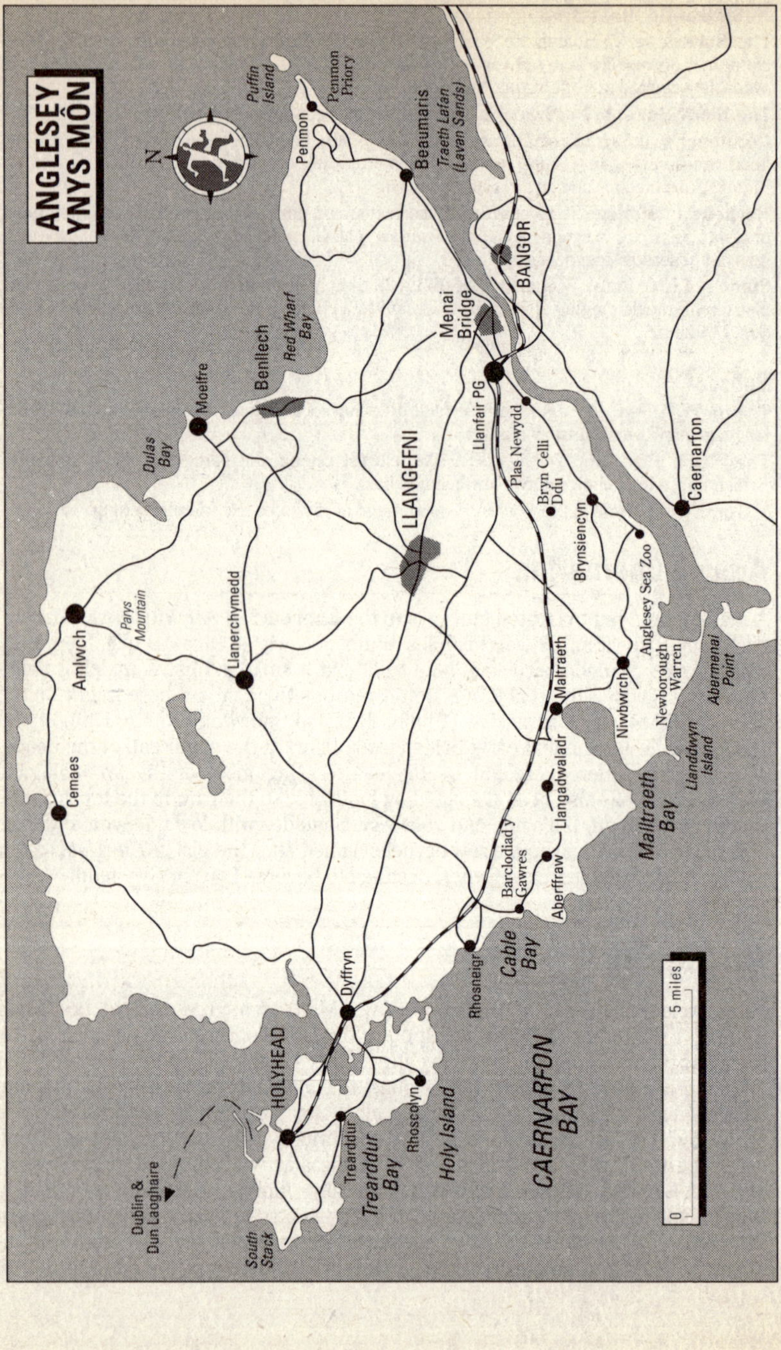
ANGLESEY
YNYS MÔN
N
Puffin Island
Penmon Priory
Penmon
Beaumaris
Traeth Lafan (Lavan Sands)
BANGOR
Menai Bridge
Red Wharf Bay
Benllech
Moelfre
Dulas Bay
Llanfair PG
Plas Newydd
LLANGEFNI
Bryn Celli Ddu
Caernarfon
Brynsiencyn
Anglesey Sea Zoo
Parys Mountain
Amlwch
Llanerchymedd
Maltraeth
Niwbwrch
Newborough Warren
Abermenai Point
Llanddwyn Island
Malltraeth Bay
Llangadwaladr
Barclodiad y Gawres
Aberffraw
Cemaes
Rhosneigr
Cable Bay
Dyffryn
HOLYHEAD
Rhoscolyn
Holy Island
Trearddur
Trearddur Bay
CAERNARFON BAY
Dublin & Dun Laoghaire
South Stack
0
5 miles

Anglesey's most famous poets, Goronwy Owen, whose eulogy on his homeland translates as "All hail to Anglesey/The delight of all regions/Bountiful as a second Eden/Or an ancient paradise". Judging by the numbers who flock to the island's necklace of fine sandy coves and rocky headlands, many agree with Owen, but just as many charge straight through from Bangor to **Holyhead** and the Irish ferries, missing out on Wales' greatest concentration of prehistoric sites and some superb coastal scenery.

The earliest people on Anglesey were Mesolithic hunters who arrived between 8000 and 4000 BC. Around 2500 BC, a new culture developed among the small farming communities, which was responsible for the many henges and stone circles on the island and held sway until the Celts swept across Europe in the seventh century BC, led by their priestly class, the Druids. The Celts established themselves so firmly on Anglesey that it was the last place in Wales to fall to the Romans when under Suetonius Paulinus they crossed the Menai Strait in 61 AD. Tacitus recorded the scene:

> *Women were seen rushing through the ranks of soldiers in wild disorder, dressed in black, with their hair dishevelled and brandishing flaming torches. Their whole appearance resembled the frantic rage of the Furies. The druids were ranged in order, calling down terrible curses. The soldiers, paralysed by this strange spectacle, stood still and offered themselves as a target for wounds. But at last the promptings of the general – and their own rallying of each other – urged them not to be frightened of a mob of women and fanatics. They advanced the standards, cut down all who met them and swallowed them up in their own fires. After this a garrison was placed over the conquered islanders, and the groves sacred to savage rites were cut down.*

The vacuum left by the Roman departure in the fifth century was soon filled by the greatest of all Welsh dynasties, the Princes of Gwynedd, who held court at **Aberffraw**. Initially their authority was localized, but under Rhodri Mawr in the ninth century their influence spread over most of Wales as he defeated the encroaching Vikings, earning thanks from Charlemagne for his efforts. Anglesey again fell to outsiders towards the end of the thirteenth century when Edward I defeated the Welsh princes, sealing the island's fate by building the last of his great castles at Beaumaris.

Getting around the island is easy enough. The train line from Bangor crosses the strait, stopping at the station with the longest name in the world – usually abbreviated to Llanfair PG – before continuing to meet the ferries at Holyhead. The rest of the island is covered by a bus network thoroughly detailed in the free *Gwynedd Timetable*.

Menai Bridge and the approaches

Two bridges – both engineering marvels – link Anglesey to the mainland over the **Menai Strait**, a perilous fourteen-mile-long tidal race that in places narrows to 200 yards, forcing the current up to eight knots as it rushes between Conwy and Caernarfon bays. For centuries before the bridges were built, drovers used these narrows to herd Anglesey-fattened cattle on their way to market in England. Travellers had to wait for low tide to cross Lafan Sands, northeast of Bangor, then find a boat to take them across to Beaumaris, in foggy weather guided only by the sound of church bells. It is no surprise that the Irish MPs, needing transport to Westminster and a faster mail service, pushed for a fixed crossing.

The first permanent connection, in 1826, was Telford's graceful **Menai Suspension Bridge**, the world's first large iron suspension bridge, spanning 579 feet between piers, 100 feet above the water to allow ships to pass. Almost everything about the project was novel, including the process of lifting the first 23-ton cable into place, which involved a pulley system and 150 men kept in time by a fife band. They celebrated their achievement by running across the nine-inch-wide chain from Anglesey to the mainland.

Robert Stephenson also made engineering history with his **Britannia Tubular Bridge** in 1850, which carried trains across the strait in twin wrought-iron tubes. It burnt down in 1970, however, leaving only the limestone piers that now support the twin-deck road and rail bridge to Llanfair PG and Holyhead, bypassing the town of Menai Bridge.

Nestling in the shadow of the older crossing, with a few private islands to break the view across the strait to the mainland, is the town of **MENAI BRIDGE** (Porthaethwy). A short bus ride from Bangor (#53 and #57, not Sun), it's also little more than half an hour's pleasant walk, with views from the bridge over to the fourteenth-century **Church of St Tysilio** (open mid-July to Aug) on Church Island, where the church's patron saint founded his cell around 630 AD. The island can be reached from the town along Belgian Walk, a causeway and waterside promenade built by refugees during World War I.

There's little else to do in Menai Bridge, but if you have children to entertain, take the B5420 two miles northeast of the village to **Pili Palas** (March–Oct 10am–5.30pm; Nov & Dec 11am–3.30pm; £3), a steamy walk-in butterfly house with up to seventy species, some as big as your hand. British butterflies that are becoming less common in the wild are bred here for release, a venture promoted in the educational material available for kids. An aviary and vivarium complete the set-up.

If you plan to **stay** in Menai Bridge, be sure to book ahead at the welcoming *Bwthyn*, 5 Bryn Afon (☎0248/713119; ②), just off Beach Road, the approach to Belgian Walk. The choice of **places to eat** is surprisingly good. Reasonably priced *Jodie's*, Telford Road (☎0248/714864; closed Sun lunch), dishes up refreshingly original wine-bar food in its conservatory and garden; the *Liverpool Arms*, St George's Pier (☎0248/712453; ③), does decent pub food; and both the moderately priced Chinese places – the central *Sunshine*, Wood St (☎0248/712808), and *Jade Village* on the A4080 (☎0248/715409), near *Jodie's* – are highly rated. Another good reason to stay is one of the best live **music** venues in the region, *The Victoria Hotel* on Telford Street, which runs from the bridge into town. Both Welsh- and English-language bands play here, particularly on Wednesdays, ranging from rock through folk and jazz to Cajun.

Beaumaris

The original inhabitants of **BEAUMARIS** (Biwmares) were evicted by Edward I to make way for the construction of his new castle and bastide town, dubbed "beautiful marsh" in an attempt to attract English settlers. Today the place can still seem like the small English outpost Edward intended, with its elegant Georgian terrace along the front (designed by Joseph Hansom, of cab fame) and more English accents than you'll have heard for a while. Many of their owners belong with the flotilla of yachts, an echo of the port's fleet of merchant ships, which disappeared with the completion of the Menai bridges and subsequent growth of Holyhead.

While you can spend an hour or two mooching around, enjoying the views across the Strait from the stumpy pier and the broad swathe of town which backs it, Beaumaris also boasts more sights than the rest of the island put together. This inevitably brings the crowds here in summer.

The Castle

Beaumaris Castle (April to late Oct daily 9.30am–6.30pm; late Oct to March Mon–Sat 9.30am–4pm, Sun 11am–4pm; CADW; £1.50) may never have been built had Madog ap Llywelyn not captured Caernarfon in 1294. When asked to build the new castle, James of St George abandoned the Caernarfon design in favour of the concentric plan he had used for Harlech (see p.240), developing it into a highly evolved symmetrical octagon. Sited on flat land at the edge of town, the castle is denied the domineering majesty of Caernarfon or Harlech, its low outer walls appearing almost welcoming – until, that is, you begin to appreciate the concentric layout of the defences protected by massive towers, a moat linked to the sea and the Moorish-influenced staggered entries through the two gatehouses. Despite over thirty years' work, the project was never quite finished, leaving most of the inner ward empty and the corbels and fireplaces built into the walls never used. You can explore the internal passages in the walls but, unless CADW change their policy, you won't be allowed up onto the low-parapet wall-walk. It's a pity because that's where you get the best idea of the castle's defensive capability, as archers were able to fire simultaneously from the inner and outer defences. Supplies were brought from the sea into the moat to the dock just outside the south gatehouse, protected by **Gunner's Walk**, where the remains of the castle mill can still be seen.

Impressive as they are, none of these defences was able to prevent siege by Owain Glyndŵr, who held the castle for two years from 1403, although during the Civil War they did keep out General Mytton and fifteen hundred Parliamentarian troops until the local Royalists were forced to surrender in 1646. At the restoration the castle was returned to the Bulkeley family, only to be left to fall into ruin before twentieth-century restoration returned some of its glory.

The Town

Almost opposite the castle stands the Jacobean **Beaumaris Courthouse** (Easter & June–Sept Mon–Fri 11am–5.30pm, Sat & Sun 2–5.30pm; May Sat & Sun 2–5.30pm; £1.35, joint ticket for gaol £2.80), built in 1614 and the oldest active court in Britain. It is now used only for the twice-monthly Magistrates Court, but until 1971, when they were moved to Caernarfon, the quarterly Assize Courts were held here. These were traditionally held in English, giving the jury little chance to follow the proceedings and Welsh-speaking defendants none against prosecutors renowned for slapping heavy penalties on relatively minor offences. On session days you can go in to watch the now English-language trials, but won't be able to take the recorded tour or inspect *The Lawsuit*, a plaque in the magistrates' room depicting two farmers pulling the horns and tail of a cow while a lawyer milks it.

Many citizens were transported from the courthouse to the colonies for their misdemeanours; others only made it a couple of blocks to the **Beaumaris Gaol**, Steeple Lane (Easter & June–Sept daily 11am–6pm; £1.55 or joint ticket with courthouse). When it opened in 1829, this was considered a model prison, its facilities including running water and toilets in each cell, an infirmary and eventually heating. Women prisoners did the cooking and were allowed to rock their babies' cradles in the nursery above by means of a pulley system. Advanced perhaps, but nonetheless a gloomy place: witness the windowless punishment cell, the yard for stone-breaking and the treadmill water pump operated by the prisoners. The least fortunate inmates were marched along a first-floor walkway through a door in the outer wall to the gibbet where they were publicly hanged. This was the fate of a certain Richard Rowlands, whose disembodied voice leads the recorded tour of the building and various displays on prison life.

For a more light-hearted half-hour, visit the **Museum of Childhood**, 1 Castle St (Easter–Nov Mon–Sat 10am–5.30pm, Sun noon–5pm; £2.50), which displays over 2000 toys dating from the 1840s to around 1960. Highlights among this hoard of dolls, train sets and piggy banks are the musical instruments, many of them demonstrated by museum staff, and the stereoscopic viewer designed in 1850, showing some of the earliest 3D moving images.

Penmon Priory

One of the earliest monastic sites in Anglesey was on the now uninhabited Puffin Island, four miles northeast of Beaumaris. In Welsh it goes by the name Ynys Seiriol, recalling the sixth-century saint who, on becoming head of the Augustine **Penmon Priory** (unrestricted access; CADW), brought the island community the three-quarters of a mile to Penmon. Saint Seiriol soon became known as the White Saint, not for his unblemished purity, but because his weekly walk to Llanerchymedd to meet Saint Cybi involved journeying with his back to the sun in both directions. Cybi, by contrast, was dubbed the Tawny Saint.

The priory's original wooden buildings were razed by the Danes in the tenth century, but their replacements, the twelfth-century church and the thirteenth-century south range of the cloister, are still standing. Only the church is in good repair, the nave housing an unusual Norman pillar-piscina – a font gouged from the plinth of a pre-Norman cross still used for Sunday services – and a superb zigzag patterned arch. There's more patterned archwork lining the south transept beside the Penmon Cross, moved here to prevent the elements completely scouring off its plait and fret patterns. The church's site was chosen for its proximity to the refreshing waters of **St Seiriol's Well**, which now feeds a calm pool and is reached by either the path behind the church, or another opposite the domed dovecote, built around 1600 to house one thousand pairs of birds.

Three-quarters of a mile beyond the dovecote (80p toll for cars in summer), a short strait separates the easternmost point of Anglesey from **Puffin Island**, now a nesting point for razorbills, guillemots and puffins, all once permissible food during Lent. In summer you can take a cruise around the island from Beaumaris (£2.75). Before retiring to the café, take a walk around the headland or past the quarries, where James of St George cut fossil-ridden limestone for Caernarfon and Beaumaris castles, and Telford and Stephenson found the footings for their bridges. The rock was once part of a single mass that included the Great and Little Ormes, eight miles to the east.

Getting here is no problem, the frequent #57 Bangor–Beaumaris bus continuing to Penmon roughly hourly.

Practicalities

With no trains, long-distance coaches or tourist office, Beaumaris seems poorly served, but it has a regular **bus** service to Bangor (#53 & #57; infrequent on Sun) and no shortage of decent places to eat and stay.

The best of the **hotels** is the ancient and luxurious *Ye Olde Bull's Head Inn*, 18 Castle St (☎0248/810329; ⑦), used as General Mytton's headquarters during the Civil War and, under more peaceful circumstances, by Dr Johnson and Charles Dickens. The *Bishopsgate Hotel*, 54 Castle St (☎0248/810302; closed Jan to mid-Feb; ④), is only a stone's throw away and almost up the same standard. The first of the **B&Bs** to head for is the antique-furnished *Swn-y-Don*, 7 Bulkeley Terrace (☎0248/810794; ③). Otherwise, *Bron Menai* (☎0248/810321; ②), opposite the pier above a café, is good, and – so long as you don't smoke and don't object to an 11pm curfew – then so is *Sea View Guesthouse* (☎0248/810384; ②). The best of the farmhouse B&Bs, and one where you can take Welsh lessons, is *Plas Cichle* (☎0248/810488; ③), two miles away in Llanfaes (#57 bus almost hourly except Sun) – not far from *Kingsbridge*, the nearest **campsite** (☎0248/490636).

There are plenty of daytime cafés serving snacks, and more substantial **restaurants** are also in good supply, the best being *Ye Olde Bull's Head Inn* and *Bishopsgate Hotel* (moderate), both of which also do filling bar meals. At the cheaper end of the scale, budget *Bottles Bistro*, 13 Castle St (☎0248/810623), offers a broad range of bistro perennials, including pizzas, and the inexpensive *Cottage Restaurant*, 10 Castle St (☎0248/810946), serves a varied range of meat and vegetarian dishes in a covered-in verandah.

Llanfair PG and the south coast

Robert Louis Stephenson's "to travel hopefully is a better thing than to arrive" could have been written specifically for **LLANFAIR PG**. You may well have travelled hopefully to this town with the longest place name in Britain, only to find a big wool shop and a small train station bearing the famed sign Llanfairpwllgwyngyllgogerychwyrndrobwlllantysiliogogogoch, which translates as "St Mary's Church in the hollow of white hazel near a rapid whirlpool and the Church of St Tysilio near the red cave". The name was devised by a Menai Bridge tailor in the 1880s, who added to the original first five syllables in an attempt to draw tourists – as indeed it has.

Coming from Bangor, half a mile before the town you'll probably notice the bronze figure atop the 91-foot-high Doric **Marquess of Anglesey's Column**. The apocryphal story has him declaring to Wellington, on having a leg blown off at Waterloo, "Begod, there goes me leg", to which Wellington dryly replied "Begod, so it do". There hadn't been much love lost between them since the Marquess ran off with Wellington's sister-in-law some years previously. Between 10am and 6pm you can climb the 115 steps up to the Marquess (60p) and share his view across the strait to Snowdonia. His replacement leg is on show at Plas Newydd, close to Bryn Celli Ddu: two good reasons to stop off in the town. A further incentive is the **tourist office** by the station (Mon–Sat 9.30am–5.30pm, Sun 10am–5pm; closes 5pm in winter; ☎0248/713177), the only one worth its salt on the island.

Practicalities

There is only a limited range of **accommodation** nearby, but you can't go far wrong at the peaceful *Sarn Faban*, Penmynydd Road, in Llanfair PG (☎0248/712410; ②); follow the road opposite the *Tŷ Gwyn* pub, bear left where the road curves right and it's on the right – half a mile in all. If you're off to Plas Newydd or Bryn Celli Ddu, then *Carreg Goch* (☎0248/430315; ②) is conveniently just a mile beyond them on the A4080. Half a mile southwest of Brynsiencyn on the road to the Sea Zoo, the Georgian *Plas Trefarthen* (☎0248/430379; ③) does inexpensive dinners, while five miles further on at Malltraeth, just off the A4080, you can stay at *Shorelands* (☎0407/840396; ②), a house once lived in by Charles Tunnicliffe (see opposite), and now specializing in birdwatching holidays. Cross the bridge in the village, turn left at the lay-by, then left again in front of the chapel.

Trains continue from Llanfair PG to Rhosneigr and Holyhead, but to visit the **south coast** you'll have to rely on the hourly #42 **bus** that passes through Plas Newydd, Brynsiencyn and Newborough on its way to Llangefni (see p.363). The #42 also branches off as far as Aberffraw, then turns back leaving the #45 as the only bus passing Bryn Celli Ddu and Rhosneigr en route to Holyhead. The #43a runs from Bangor, Menai Bridge and Llanfair PG to Plas Newydd and Sea Zoo.

Bryn Celli Ddu

One of the island's most significant prehistoric sites, **Bryn Celli Ddu** (unrestricted access; CADW), the "Mound of the Dark Chamber", was built by Anglesey's late Neolithic inhabitants four thousand years ago, one and a half miles south. Several seasons of digs have shown it to be an extensive religious site, but today all you can see is a henge and stone circle, later transformed into a passage grave, whose original earthen mound has been replaced by an inept concrete-beam reconstruction. The substantial finds unearthed here – charred bones, arrowheads and spiral-carved stones – are now in the custody of the National Museum in Cardiff. The place is still worth a trip, but be prepared for an hour-long walk from Llanfair PG. Follow the A4080 south for a mile, then cut southwest across farmland, or take the #42 bus for two miles along the A4080, then walk a good half-mile to the right up a signposted side road.

Plas Newydd

Driving or taking the bus from Llanfair PG to Bryn Celli Ddu, you'll pass the approach road to **Plas Newydd** (April–Sept daily except Sat noon–5pm; Oct Fri & Sun noon–5pm; NT; £3.80), a mile and a half south of Llanfair PG. Though now owned by the National Trust, the house remains, as it has been since the eighteenth century, the home of the marquesses of Anglesey. A house had stood on this site since the sixteenth century, but it was the First Marquess's huge profits from Parys Mountain (see p.362) and other ventures that paid for its transformation by James Wyatt and Joseph Potter into a Gothick mansion in the late eighteenth century. Potter designed the pleasing, castellated stable block that almost upstages the modest-looking three-storey house with incongruous Tudor caps on slender octagonal turrets.

Inside, the Gothick Hall with its Potter-designed fan-vaulted ceiling leads to the longest and most finely decorated room in the house, the Music Room, originally the great hall. All available space is covered with oil paintings, including one of the First Marquess and another of Lady Paget, his first wife, both by John Hoppner. Despite the Gothick start, Wyatt was given free rein in the rest of the house, and there's a transition to the Neoclassical on entering the Staircase Hall with its cantilevered staircase and deceptively solid-looking Doric columns, actually just painted wood. Paintings line the stairs and the length of the gallery. Several monarchs and most family members are represented, those of the Sixth Marquess and his sister being the work of Rex Whistler, who spent two years here in the 1930s. You have to get through another half a dozen rooms, including Lady Anglesey's pink and white bedroom and a former kitchen containing a Whistler exhibition, before you get to Whistler's masterwork, in understandably the most popular room in the house. A whole 58-foot long wall of the Rex Whistler Room is consumed by the *trompe l'œil* painting of some imaginary seascape seen from a promenade. Walking along it, your position appears to shift by over a mile as the mountains of Snowdonia and a whimsical composite of elements, culled from Italy as well as Britain, alter their perspective. Portmeirion (see p.246) is there, as are the Round Tower from Windsor Castle and the steeple from St Martin-in-the-Fields in London. Whistler himself appears as a gondolier, and again as a gardener in one of the two right-angled panels at either end, which appear to extend the room further.

A few rooms further on you'll find a **Cavalry Museum**, where the prize exhibit is the world's first articulated leg, all wood, leather and springs, designed for the First Marquess, who lost his leg at Waterloo. All in all, you'll need to allow a couple of hours for a good look around, plus some time to recover in the former milking parlour, now converted into an excellent tiled tea room serving tasty snacks and light meals.

Anglesey Sea Zoo

Facing Caernarfon across the Menai Strait, seven miles southwest of Llanfair PG, **Anglesey Sea Zoo** (March–Oct daily 10am–5pm; Nov–Feb daily 11am–3pm; £3.95), is one of the most absorbing paying attractions on Anglesey. Local sea conditions are simulated in wave tanks, and in shallow pools where plaice and turbot, camouflaged against the shingle bottom, are barely visible from the catwalks above. They haven't entirely got away from glass-sided tanks, but most are large and the contents chosen to depict specific environments: tidal flats, quayside and wrecks amongst them. In keeping with the buildings' previous functions as an oyster hatchery and lobster breeding farm, the zoo uses aquaculture to give the lobsters a much greater chance of survival once released into the wild. In summer, catch the #43a **bus** from Llanfair PG or Plas Newydd; out of season they may pick you up from Brynsiencyn, two miles to the north, if you phone ahead.

Newborough

Three miles southwest of the Sea Zoo, the end of the Menai Strait is marked by Abermenai Point, a huge sand bar backed by the 600-acre **Newborough Warren** (unrestricted access), one of the most important dune areas anywhere in Britain. As its name suggests, rabbits are common here, as are the otherwise rare thick-horned Soay sheep. Since 1948, much of the land has been clad in Corsican and Monterey pine, a commercial operation that also stabilizes the ground, provides cover for red squirrels, goldcrests and warblers, and justifies its designation as **Newborough National Nature Reserve**. Three main walking trails, none more than an hour or two's stroll and all very well marked, weave through the pines to **Llanddwyn Island**. In truth a peninsula of rocky coves and sandy beaches, in summer it can be overrun with kids poking around the ruins of a lighthouse, its keepers' cottages and a thirteenth-century church ruin dedicated to the patron saint of lovers in Wales, St Dwynwen. In the fifth century, after her abortive love affair with a Welsh prince, Maelon, Dwynwen became a nun and requested that hopeful lovers who make a supplication to God in her name should receive divine assistance.

From 1945 until his death in 1979, the estuarine beaches to the north were the haunt of **Charles Tunnicliffe**, who lived a couple of miles away in Malltraeth, and spent much of his days meticulously producing his beautifully detailed wildlife drawings. Birds were always his chief subject, and throughout his fifty-year career he produced thousands of intricate illustrations for other people's works as well as six books of his own, including *Shorelands Summer Diary*, largely researched around Newborough and named after his house in Malltraeth. Examples of his work form a significant part of the *Oriel Ynys Môn* exhibition in Llangefni (see p.363).

Entry to the Newborough Warren section of the reserve is from a free car park down a short track from a roundabout, where the A4080 bends north nine miles southwest of Llanfair PG. The main walk from here is out to Abermenai Point (2 miles), but be careful as rapid tidal changes can quickly cover the broad sandy approach. To get to the reserve's main entrance, continue north along the A4080 for half a mile to the small town of **NEWBOROUGH** (Niwbwrch), then turn left to a second car park (£1.20). The #42 **bus** follows the A4080 past the first car park and through Newborough.

Around Aberffraw

The church in the tiny hamlet of **LLANGADWALADR**, three miles northwest of Newborough, contains the only substantial evidence that this area was once the seat of the great ruling dynasty of the Princes of Gwynedd. From the seventh-century reign of Cadfan until Llywelyn ap Gruffydd's death in 1282, successive leaders controlled northwest Wales, and frequently much of the rest of the country, from this now-quiet corner of Anglesey. When the existing **Llangadwaladr Church** (usually closed except for Sunday mornings) was built during the thirteenth century, a memorial plaque, carved in Latin around 625 AD, was incorporated into an inside wall. It reads "Cadfan the King, wisest and most renowned of all kings". Llangadwaladr village takes its name from Cadwaladr, Cadfan's grandson, who subsequently ruled from **ABERFFRAW**, a mile and a half west (buses #42 & #45), where the coastal heritage centre, **Llys Llewelyn** (Easter–late Sept daily 11am–5.30pm; free), has a few explanatory boards on the court and times of the Princes of Gwynedd and a little information on the flora and fauna of the Anglesey coast.

CABLE BAY (Porth Trecastell), two miles northwest of Aberffraw, has a good sandy beach and the 5000-year-old **Barclodiad y Gawres** burial chamber on a headland. Though superior to Bryn Celli Ddu (see p.356), it is more difficult to see, requiring the key from *The Wayside Café* in **LLANFAELOG** and a torch. Without it, you won't really see the stones carved with chevrons and zig-zag patterns the burial chamber shares with Newgrange and other Boyne Valley sites seventy miles across the water in Ireland. Bus #42 comes as far as Aberffraw but getting further up the coast to Cable Bay and Rhosneigr requires the #45.

Rhosneigr

Two miles further north along the coast, the rambling Edwardian seaside resort of **RHOSNEIGR** is still justifiably popular with English holiday-makers after almost a century of patronage, although space on the beach is these days contested by the dozens of devoted windsurfers who flock here when the wind is right. It is the sort of low-key place you might feel like stopping in for a day or two: if so, you can rent boards and rig from *Surfwind*, Beach Rd (☎0407/810899; £20 a day, £25 for a two-hour beginner's course), or a bike from the *White Gables B&B* on Maelog Lake Road (☎0407/810863; ②), next door but one to the *Cefn Dref* pub.

There's more **accommodation** at *Bryn Maelog* (☎0407/810285; ②), fifty yards down Chelford Close opposite the *Cefn Dref*, at *Minstrel Lodge*, Station Rd (☎0407/810970; ③); and at the **campsite**, *Shoreline Camping*, Station Rd (☎0407/810279), right by the **train station**, a mile north of the clocktower that marks the centre of the town. Amongst the numerous cafés here, the best **place to eat** is *The Honey Pot*, The Square (☎0407/810302; closed Sun in winter), which operates two rooms, one an inexpensive bistro, and the other a moderately priced restaurant.

Holy Island

Holy Island (Ynys Gybi) is blessed with Anglesey's best scenery and cursed with its most unattractive town. The spectacular sea cliffs around South Stack, and the Stone Age and Roman remains on Holyhead Mountain are just a couple of miles from workaday Holyhead, whose ferry routes to Ireland and good transport links mean you'll probably find your way there at some stage.

This hourglass of land adjoins Anglesey's west coast at two points. The 1200-yard-long Stanley Embankment, built by Telford while working on the A5, takes both road and rail directly to the ferry terminal at Holyhead. An alternative route avoids the nasty aluminium smelter outside Holyhead by turning off the A5 onto the B4545 at **VALLEY** (Dyffryn), and crossing the very short Four Mile Bridge, past fine beaches at Rhoscolyn and Trearddur Bay, before reaching Holyhead.

You won't have any trouble getting to Holyhead itself, since trains and a fair number of Anglesey's buses go there. Rhoscolyn and South Stack can be reached from Holyhead by the #40 and the #44 respectively. The #4 bus to Holyhead from Bangor and Llangefni is the only really useful service to Trearddur Bay.

Holyhead

HOLYHEAD (Caergybi) is a town of dilapidated shopfronts and high unemployment, the local council's valiant attempts to brighten its image somehow making it even more depressing. In 1727 Swift found it "scurvy, ill-provided and comfortless", while a century or so later George Borrow called it "a poor, dull, ill-lighted town", and apart from the scurvy and the lighting, little has changed. Fortunately train and ferry timings are reasonably well integrated, so you shouldn't need to spend much time here, and there are a couple of things to see if you do get stuck. The town's Welsh name indicates the site of a Roman fort – an outpost of Segontium – and home of the sixth-century Saint Cybi. Cybi's cell was built in the protection of the Roman walls and is now marked by the partly thirteenth-century **Church of St Cybi** (summer daily 11am–3pm). Both walls and church have undergone substantial reconstruction, the church gaining stained glass by Edward Burne-Jones and William Morris.

From the combined **train station** and *Stena Sealink* terminal, a pedestrian bridge over London Road, past the A5, leads to the *National Express* bus stop on Victoria Road, at the junction with Market Street, which heads up into the shopping area. The less-than-helpful **tourist office**, Marine Square (Easter–Oct daily 10am–6pm; Nov–Easter Mon–Sat 9.30am–5pm; ☎0407/762622), is in a shed by the docks, half a mile away at the end of Victoria Road; a list of B&Bs that accept late arrivals is posted on the door when the office is closed.

The need of these late-arriving ferry passengers has fostered a bunch of poor **B&Bs**, especially those along the A5 into the town, so it's worth searching off the main road. The best place to look is the area around Walthew Avenue, most easily reached by turning left just before the tourist office onto the beachfront Prince of Wales Road – which becomes Beach Road – then left into Walthew Avenue. Try one of several good, basic places: *Glan Ifor* at no. 8 (☎0407/764238; ②), or *Orotavia* at no. 66 (☎0407/760259; ②), or turn right after Orotavia to the very comfortable and welcoming *Yr Hendre*, Porth-y-Felin (☎0407/762929; ③), a former manse where you can get inexpensive evening meals. If an in-house bar and proximity to the ferries are a major consideration the place to go for is *The Marine Hotel* on Marine Square (☎0407/763512; ③), just by the tourist office, where early departures can get a Continental breakfast and save a couple of pounds. Three-quarters of a mile along Beach Road, you'll find the town's comfortable *Boathouse Hotel*, Beach Rd (☎0407/762094; ④), and if you've got your own transport, you could head three miles out of town to the recommended *Tan-y-Cytiau* (☎0407/762763; ③); follow Walthew Avenue away from the sea and follow signs for South Stack.

Fast **food** is the staple diet in Holyhead, but you can still eat well; the budget *Omar Khayyam Tandoori*, 8 Newry St (☎0407/760333), serves the tastiest curries for miles around while the *Boathouse Hotel* concentrates on succulent moderately priced fish and seafood dishes. For its out-of-town setting and good beer, the *Boathouse* is also about the best place to drink. If you prefer the lively weekend pub-hopping scene between the half-dozen bars on Market Street, start at *The Seventy-Nine* at 79 Market St.

Holyhead Mountain and South Stack

The northern half of Holy Island is ranged around the skirts of **Holyhead Mountain** (Mynydd Twr) which rises 700 feet to the west of Holyhead. Its summit is ringed by the remains of the seventeen-acre Iron Age **Caer y Twr** (unrestricted access; CADW), one of the largest sites in north Wales. It seems to have only been used during times of war, as digs haven't unearthed any signs of permanent occupation, just a six-foot-high dry-stone wall enclosure around the ruins of a Roman beacon. In an hour or so you can pick your way up rough tracks from the Holyhead side, but the best approach is by bus #44 or your own transport to the car park at **South Stack** (Ynys Lawd), two miles west of Holyhead. A path (30min) leads from the car park to the top of Holyhead

FERRIES TO IRELAND

Since Sealynx **catamarans** were introduced by *Stena Sealink* (☎0407/766765) in 1993, it's been possible to get from Holyhead to Dun Laoghaire, six miles south of Dublin, in under two hours. The latest sailing times can be checked with any travel agent but at the time of writing were 7am, noon, 5pm, and – at peak periods – 10pm. High-season passenger fares are around £60 return, £10 more expensive than either the *Stena Sealink* **ferries** to Dun Laoghaire (sailings at 2am, 4am, 2.30pm, and at busy times 4.15pm; 3hr 30min) or the *B&I Line* (☎0407/760222) ferries to Dublin (3hr 45min). The latter use a tidal mooring, which occasionally forces changes to their 4am and 3.45pm schedule. There's a shuttle bus from the station to the wharf for foot passengers.

B&I Line generally offer the cheapest **day trips** to Dublin, starting from as little as £8, though this does entail getting the 4am boat. Sealynx day trips are more convenient, shorter and more than twice as expensive.

Mountain, though you'll find most people walking the few yards to the cliff-top RSPB-run **Ellin's Tower Seabird Centre** (Easter–Sept daily 11am–5pm; free). From April until the end of July, binoculars and closed-circuit TV give an unparalleled opportunity to watch up to 3000 birds – razorbills, guillemots and the odd puffin – nesting on the nearby sea-cliffs while ravens and peregrines wheel outside the tower's windows. When the birds have gone, rock climbers picking their way up the same cliff-face replace them as the main interest. A twisting path leads down from the tower to a suspension bridge over the surging waves, once the keeper's only access to the now fully automated pepper-pot lighthouse. Though currently out of bounds, there are plans to open the lighthouse to visitors in the future.

William Stanley, who named Ellin's Tower after his wife, did most of the excavation work on the **Cytiau'r Gwyddelod** hut circles, across the road from the South Stack car park. The name translates as the "huts of the Irish" – a common name for any ancient settlement – but evidence from excavations reveals little more than that the builders were late Neolithic or early Bronze Age people. The visible remains comprise nineteen low stone circles – some up to ten yards across – though there seem to have originally been fifty buildings, formed into eight distinct farmsteads separated by ploughed fields.

Trearddur Bay and Rhoscolyn

At the pinch of the hourglass, a couple of miles south of Holyhead, the scattered settlement of **TREARDDUR BAY** (Bae Trearddur) shambles across low grassy hills, around a deeply indented bay of the same name, punctuated by rocky coves. There's no centre to speak of and the only activities on offer are walking the headlands and swimming, but this is a much more pleasant base than Holyhead. If you can afford it, the best **place to stay** is the *Trearddur Bay Hotel*, Lon Isallt (☎0407/860301; ⑨), overlooking the main bay. On the southern side of the bay, there are some cheaper places along Ravensport Road: the *Seacroft Hotel* (☎0407/860348; ③), and *Highground* (☎0407/860078; ④), which has private beach access. Continue down Ravensport Road for a mile to reach the *Tyn Rhos Campsite* which, though packed with caravans, takes tents as well.

At the southern tip of the island, a mile or so south of Trearddur Bay, a lane runs down to **RHOSCOLYN**, another scattered seaside settlement with a good pub, *The White Eagle*, and accommodation at the *Old Rectory* (☎0407/860214; closed Jan; ④), a Georgian country house with outstanding views of the sea. If you're driving from Holyhead, take the Rhoscolyn road to the right just before Four Mile Bridge, follow it for two miles, then take the narrow road beside the church.

Northern and inland Anglesey

The northern and eastern sides of Anglesey tend to be quieter than the south and west ; the settlements are clustered behind the sheltered coves which, with the odd rocky headland, make up an appealing if seldom dramatic coast. This is primarily family holiday country, though its more thinly spread host of caravan sites make it much less oppressive than the north Welsh coast. None of the resorts is especially notable in its own right but they are well spaced making cycling between them, or even walking the coastal path an ideal way to get around.

Relying on **buses** is possible, though less rewarding. From Holyhead, the #61 runs to Cemaes and Amlwch, where you can pick up the #62 and #63 to Moelfre, Menai Bridge and Bangor. The #32 links Amlwch to Llanerchymedd and Llangefni.

Accommodation is detailed under the appropriate town account, but if you are exploring the coast with your own transport you might want to head inland to stay at one of the farmhouses near Llanerchymedd. Both *Llwydiarth Fawr* (☎0248/470321; ④), a spacious Georgian house on a farm along the B5111, half a mile north of Llanerchymedd, and *Drws y Coed* (☎0248/470473; ③), a mile and a half east on the B5108 to Benllech, are recommended.

Cemaes

Following the A5025 clockwise around the coast, there's nothing to justify stopping until **CEMAES** (Cemais), sandwiched between the ageing Wylfa Nuclear Power Station and a spanking new 24-tower windmill farm. Despite convincing environmental evidence, many locals still support Wylfa, preferring it to the prospect of noise pollution from the wind turbines and high unemployment.

Once the main north coast port, a role since overtaken by Amlwch, Cemaes caters only to the odd trawler, and the boat-loads of yachties drawn by a broad sweep of beach and the most northerly pub in Wales, *The Stag* on High Street, also said to serve the best pub **food** on the coast. The town is the most reliable source of **accommodation** along this coast, with the non-smoking *Tredolphin Guesthouse* (☎0407/710388; ②), 200 yards down Beach Road from *The Stag*, and the *Woburn Hill Hotel*, High St (☎0407/711388; ③), the most central. Best of all, though, is the licensed *Hafod Country House* (☎0407/710500; ③), serving excellent and inexpensive meals: at the roundabout on the A5025, at the top of the High Street, turn inland towards Llanfechell and the house is half a mile along.

Amlwch

AMLWCH, five miles east of Cemaes, would be just another tiny fishing village but for **Parys Mountain** (Mynydd Parys) a mile or so inland, once the world's largest source of copper. The Ordovices, a great Celtic tribe who occupied north Wales in the Neolithic era, probably began to extract the ore, and the Romans certainly made use of it, but it wasn't until the high production levels late in the eighteenth century that pollution became a problem. In the harbour, people noticed that iron hulls of ships didn't corrode, and so began the use of copper sheathing on ships' hulls, further boosting the market for Parys copper. International competition in the early nineteenth century made the business unprofitable, and the town sank back into its role of a fishing port. You can reach the ruined pumping mill on top of Parys Mountain by a path from the car park on the B5111, a mile south of town, just next to the premises of the one company still trying to squeeze a profit from the ravaged heather-and-gorse-clad hulk.

After visiting so many ancient churches in Wales, **Our Lady Star of the Sea**, a couple of hundred yards along the A5025, to the west of the town's Main Street, comes as something of a novelty. Built in the 1930s of reinforced concrete, the great parabolic ribs of what could be a giant toast rack are supposed to represent an upturned boat complete with round portholes.

The handiest **accommodation** in Amlwch is at *Bron Arfor* (☎0407/831493; ②), right by the sea at the end of Ffordd Pen y Bonc, which runs opposite the library; and at the *Dinorben Arms*, High St (☎0407/830358; ③), where you can also get filling pub **food**. Just over a mile south of the centre, some converted farm buildings house the very cheap and friendly *Penmaen Hostel* (☎0407/830887; sleeping bags for rent; ①): it's just a short walk down the lane from Twycerlyn Service Station on the #62 bus route from Bangor.

Moelfre

MOELFRE has a reputation for shipwrecks, though wandering around the peaceful grey-pebbled cove on a sunny day, it seems unlikely. An anchor behind the beach was salvaged from the shipwrecked *Hindlea*, which went down in October 1959, exactly a century after the 2700-ton *Royal Charter* foundered, with the loss of 450 lives and nearly £400,000 worth of gold. The dead are remembered by a memorial stone thirty minutes' walk north along the coastal path that starts at the end of the cove, past a small offshore cormorant colony.

The town's only other point of interest lies a mile west off the A5025, where the Iron Age **Capel Lligwy Hut Group** (unrestricted access; CADW) forms the centrepiece of a site covering three thousand years of human occupation. A five-sided walled enclosure contains the foundations of several circular and rectangular buildings dated to the second and fourth centuries which, along with the hut group on Holy Island, give the best indication of how these people actually lived, rather than how they buried their dead. To the northeast of the main enclosure stands **Capel Lligwy**, a forlorn-looking twelfth-century church, and a short distance to the south is the **Lligwy Burial Chamber** with its 28-ton capstone.

If you want to **stay**, try *Deanfield* (☎0248/410517; ③), 150 yards from the beach on the A5018 south of the village, or the farm **campsite** 500 yards inland from the beach, up the A5018, then down signposted Ystad Nant Bychan.

Llangefni

About the only reason to come to **LLANGEFNI**, five miles west of Llanfair PG, is the *Oriel Ynys Môn* (Tues–Sun 10.30am–5pm; £2, children and students 50p), half a mile along the B5111 from the town (bus #36). This is essentially a tour of the island condensed into one room, its displays, artefacts and reconstructions conveying something of the island's identity, from the pre-Cambrian substrata through copper mining to the arrival of the Irish Packet Steamers. A corner of the room is devoted to the wildlife paintings of Charles Tunnicliffe (see p.357).

It is easy enough to continue onward from Llangefni, since it's on the #4 bus route to Holyhead, Llanfair PG and Bangor; if you're stuck, you can **stay** comfortably a mile west of town at *Argraig* (☎0248/724390; ②) – take the B5420 west then the B4422 south. For a bite to **eat** during the day, there are a number of mainstream cafés on the main street, or try one of the wholefood or home-baked dishes on the blackboard menu at *The Whole Thing*, 5 Field St.

travel details

Trains

Bangor to: Chester (20 daily Mon–Sat, 8 Sun; 1hr 5min); Colwyn Bay (20 daily Mon–Sat, 8 Sun; 25min); Conwy (9 daily Mon–Sat, 2 Sun; 20min); Holyhead (21 daily Mon–Sat, 10 Sun; 30–40min); Llandudno Junction (20 daily Mon–Sat, 8 Sun; 20min); Rhosneigr (8 daily Mon–Sat; 20min); Rhyl (20 daily Mon–Sat, 8 Sun; 35min).

Colwyn Bay to: Bangor (roughly hourly Mon–Sat, 10 Sun; 30min); Chester (40 daily Mon–Sat, 11 Sun; 40–55min); Flint (hourly Mon–Sat, 7 Sun; 35min); Holyhead (7 daily; 55min–1hr 25min); Llandudno (hourly Mon–Sat; 20min); Prestatyn (hourly Mon–Sat, 7 Sun; 20min).

Conwy to: Bangor (7 daily Mon–Sat, 2–3 Sun; 35min); Holyhead (7 daily Mon–Sat, 2–3 Sun; 1hr 15min); Llanfair PG (7 daily Mon–Sat, 2–3 Sun; 40min).

Flint to: Chester (hourly Mon–Sat, 7 Sun; 15min); Colwyn Bay (hourly Mon–Sat, 7 Sun; 35min); Llandudno (hourly Mon–Sat, 7 Sun; 1hr); Llandudno Junction (hourly Mon–Sat, 7 Sun; 40min); Prestatyn (hourly Mon–Sat, 7 Sun; 15min); Rhyl (hourly Mon–Sat, 7 Sun; 20min).

Holyhead to: Bangor (18 daily Mon–Sat, 6 Sun; 30–40min); Chester (18 daily Mon–Sat, 6 Sun; 1hr 25min–1hr 40min); Llandudno Junction (18 daily Mon–Sat, 6 Sun; 1hr); Llanfair PG (8 daily Mon–Sat; 30min); Rhosneigr (8 daily Mon–Sat; 15min).

Llandudno to: Betws-y-Coed (6 daily Mon–Sat, 2 Sun; 30min); Blaenau Ffestiniog (6 daily Mon–Sat, 2 Sun; 1hr 10min); Chester (at least hourly Mon–Sat, 2 Sun; 1hr 10min); Colwyn Bay (at least hourly Mon–Sat, 2 Sun; 20min); Flint (at least hourly Mon–Sat, 2 Sun; 55min); Llandudno Junction (at least hourly Mon–Sat, 2 Sun; 10min); Llanrwst (6 daily Mon–Sat, 2 Sun; 25min); Prestatyn (at least hourly Mon–Sat, 2 Sun; 40min); Rhyl (at least hourly Mon–Sat, 2 Sun; 35min).

Llandudno Junction to: Bangor (24 daily Mon–Sat, 12 Sun; 25min); Betws-y-Coed (6 daily Mon–Sat, 2 Sun; 25min); Blaenau Ffestiniog (6 daily Mon–Sat, 2 Sun; 1hr 5min); Flint (at least hourly Mon–Sat, 10 Sun; 40min); Holyhead (17 daily Mon–Sat, 10 Sun; 45min–1hr); Llandudno (at least hourly Mon–Sat, 5 Sun; 15min); Llanrwst (6 daily Mon–Sat, 2 Sun; 20min); Prestatyn (at least hourly Mon–Sat, 10 Sun; 25min); Rhyl (at least hourly Mon–Sat, 10 Sun; 20min).

Llanfair PG to: Bangor (8 daily Mon–Sat; 10min); Holyhead (8 daily Mon–Sat; 30min); Rhosneigr (8 daily Mon–Sat; 15min).

Prestatyn to: Chester (hourly Mon–Sat, 7 Sun; 30min); Colwyn Bay (hourly Mon–Sat, 7 Sun; 20min); Flint (hourly Mon–Sat, 7 Sun; 15min); Llandudno (hourly Mon–Sat, 7 Sun; 40min); Llandudno Junction (hourly Mon–Sat, 7 Sun; 25min).

Rhosneigr to: Holyhead (8 daily Mon–Sat; 15min); Llanfair PG (8 daily Mon–Sat; 15min).

Rhyl to: Bangor (roughly hourly Mon–Sat, 10 Sun; 40min); Chester (40 daily Mon–Sat, 12 Sun; 40min); Flint (hourly Mon–Sat, 7 Sun; 20min); Holyhead (7 daily; 1hr 10min–1hr 40min); Llandudno (hourly Mon–Sat; 25min); Llandudno Junction (40 daily Mon–Sat, 11 Sun; 20min).

Buses

Bangor to: Beaumaris (roughly hourly Mon–Sat, 2 Sun; 25min); Betws-y-Coed (3 daily Mon–Sat; 55min); Caernarfon (every 30min Mon–Sat, hourly Sun; 40min); Capel Curig (3 daily Mon–Sat; 40min); Cardiff (1 daily; 7hr 45min); Chester (2 daily; 2hr 35min); Dolgellau (1 daily; 2hr); Holyhead (every 30min Mon–Sat, 4 Sun; 1hr 15min); Llanberis (6 daily Mon–Sat; 40min); Llanfair PG (every 30min Mon–Sat, 4 Sun; 15min); Llangefni (every 30min Mon–Sat, 4 Sun; 30min); Machynlleth (1 daily; 2hr 30min); Manchester (2–3 daily; 4hr 10min); Newborough (8 daily Mon–Sat; 35min); Porthmadog (1 daily; 1hr); Trearddur Bay (every 30min Mon–Sat, 4 Sun; 1hr 10min).

Beaumaris to: Bangor (roughly hourly Mon–Sat, 2 Sun; 25min); Menai Bridge (roughly hourly Mon–Sat, 2 Sun; 15min).

Caernarfon to: Bangor (every 15min Mon–Sat, hourly Sun; 25min); Beddgelert (5 daily Mon–Sat, 1–5 Sun; 30min); Blaenau Ffestiniog (roughly hourly Mon–Sat; 1hr 25min); Cardiff (1 daily; 7hr 20min); Cricieth (4 daily Mon–Sat; 40min); Dolgellau (1 daily; 1hr 30min); Liverpool (2–3 daily; 3hr 40min); Llanberis (every 30min Mon–Sat, hourly Sun; 25min); Llandudno (every 30min Mon–Sat, hourly Sun; 1hr 40min); Machynlleth (1 daily; 2hr); Manchester (2–3 daily; 5hr 15min); Porthmadog (23 daily Mon–Sat, 1 Sun; 45min); Pwllheli (23 daily Mon–Sat, 2–3 Sun; 45min).

Conwy to: Bangor (every 30min Mon–Sat, hourly Sun; 45min); Betws-y-Coed (7 daily Mon–Sat, 5 Sun; 55min); Llanberis (4 daily; 1hr 30min); Llanrwst (hourly Mon–Sat, 6 Sun; 35min).

Denbigh to: Corwen (every 30min or better Mon–Sat; 1hr); Rhuddlan (every 30min Mon–Sat, 7 Sun; 30min); Rhyl (every 30min Mon–Sat, 7 Sun; 40min); Ruthin (every 30min or better Mon–Sat; 30min); St Asaph (every 30min Mon–Sat, 7 Sun; 15min).

Flint to: Holywell (every 30min Mon–Sat, Sun every 2hr; 10min); Mold (hourly Mon–Sat; 30min).

Holyhead to: Amlwch (8 daily Mon–Sat, 2 Sun; 50min); Bangor (every 30min Mon–Sat, 4 Sun; 1hr 15min); Cemaes (8 daily Mon–Sat, 2 Sun; 35min); Chester (1 daily; 3hr 30min); Llandudno (1 daily; 1hr 40min); Llanfair PG (every 30min Mon–Sat; 4 Sun; 1hr); Llangefni (every 30min Mon–Sat, 4

Sun; 45min); Menai Bridge (every 30min Mon–Sat, 4 Sun; 1hr 5min).

Llandudno to: Bangor (every 30min, hourly Sun; 1hr); Betws-y-Coed (7 daily, 5 Sun; 1hr 15min); Caernarfon (every 30min, hourly Sun; 1hr 40min); Llanberis (4–6 daily in summer; 1hr 55min); Llanrwst (hourly, 6 Sun; 1hr); Rhyl (every 15–30min, hourly Sun; 1hr 10min).

Llanfair PG to: Bangor (every 30min Mon–Sat, 4 Sun; 15min); Holyhead (every 30min, 4 Sun; 1hr); Llangefni (every 30min, 4 Sun; 15min); Newborough (hourly or better; 20min).

Mold to: Chester (every 30min, hourly Sun; 50min); Ruthin (every 2hr; 45min); Shotton (every 2hr; 35min).

Rhyl to: Llandudno (every 15–30min Mon–Sat, hourly Sun; 1hr 10min); Llanrwst (2 daily Mon–Sat; 1hr 15min); Ruthin (every 2hr Mon–Sat; 1hr 10min); St Asaph (every 30min Mon–Sat; 25min).

Ruthin to: Corwen (every 2hr Mon–Sat; 30min); Denbigh (roughly hourly Mon–Sat; 30min); Mold (every 2hr Mon–Sat; 45min); Rhuddlan (every 2hr Mon–Sat; 1hr); Rhyl (every 2hr Mon–Sat; 1hr 10min); St Asaph (every 2hr Mon–Sat; 45min).

St Asaph to: Corwen (every 30min Mon–Sat; 1hr 15min); Denbigh (every 30min Mon–Sat; 15min); Mold (2 daily Mon–Sat; 1hr 15min); Rhuddlan (every 30min Mon–Sat; 15min); Rhyl (every 30min Mon–Sat; 25min); Ruthin (every 30min Mon–Sat; 45min).

Ferries

Holyhead to: Dublin (2 daily; 3hr 45min); Dun Laoghaire (6–8 daily; catamaran 2hr/ferry 3hr 30min–4hr).

PART THREE

THE CONTEXTS

THE HISTORICAL FRAMEWORK

THE BEGINNINGS

Before the end of the last **Ice Age** around ten thousand years ago, Wales and the rest of Britain formed part of the greater European whole and the early migrant inhabitants eked out a meagre living on the tundra or a better one amongst the oak, beech and hazel forests in the warmer periods. Most lived in the south-east of Britain, but small groups foraged north and west, leaving 250,000-year-old evidence in the form of a human tooth in a cave near Denbigh in north Wales and a hand axe unearthed near Cardiff.

It wasn't until the early part of the **Upper Paleolithic age** that significant communities settled in Wales, those of the Gower Peninsula interring the "Red Lady of Paviland" around 24,000 BC (see p.114). This civilization was far behind those of central France or northern Spain, and remained on Europe's cultural fringe as the melting ice cut Britain off from mainland Europe around 5000 BC. Migrating Mesolithic peoples had already moved north from Central Europe and were followed by **Neolithic colonists**, whose mastery of stone and flint working found its expression in over a hundred and fifty cromlechs (turf-covered chambered tombs) dotted around Wales, primarily Pentre Ifan in Mynydd Preseli (see p.163) and Barclodiad y Gawres on Anglesey (see p.358). Skilled in agriculture and animal husbandry, the Neolithic people also began to clear the lush forests covering Wales below 2000 feet, enclosing fields, constructing defensive ditches around their villages and mining for flint.

The earliest stone circles – more extensive meeting places than cromlechs – were built at this time and continued to spread over the country as the Neolithic period drifted into the **Bronze Age** around 2000 BC. Through their extensive trade networks, the inhabitants of Wales and the rest of Britain gradually adopted new techniques, changing to more sophisticated use of metals and developing a well-organized social structure. The established aristocracy engaged in much tribal warfare, as suggested by large numbers of earthwork forts built in this and the immediately succeeding period – the chief examples being at Holyhead Mountain on Anglesey and the Bulwalks at Chepstow.

THE CELTS

Celtic invaders spreading from their central European homeland settled here in around 600 BC, imparting a great cultural influence. Familiar with Mediterranean civilization through trading routes, they introduced superior methods of metal-working that favoured iron rather than bronze, from which they forged not just weapons but also coins. Gold was used for ornamental works – the first recognizable Welsh art – heavily influenced by the symbolic, patterned **La Tène** style still thought of as quintessentially Celtic.

The Celts are credited with introducing the basis of modern Welsh. The original Celtic tongue was spoken over a wide area, gradually dividing into Goidelic (or Q-Celtic) now spoken in Ireland and Scotland, and **Brythonic** (P-Celtic) spoken in Wales, Cornwall and later exported to Brittany in France. This highly developed language was emblematic of a sophisticated social hierarchy headed by **Druids**, a ritual priesthood with attendant poets, seers and warriors. Through a deep knowledge of ritual, legend and the mechanics of the heavens, the Druids maintained their position between the people and a pantheon of over four thousand gods. Most of these were variations of a handful of chief gods worshipped by the great British tribes: the

Silures and Demetae in the south of Wales, the Cornovii in mid-Wales and the Ordovices and Deceangli in the north. Great though the Celtic technological and artistic achievements were, the people and their pan-European cousins were unable to maintain an organized civic society to match that of their successors, the Romans.

THE ROMANS IN WALES

Life in Wales, unlike that in most of England, was never fully Romanized, the region remaining under legionary control throughout its three-hundred-year occupation. **Julius Caesar** made small cross-channel incursions in 55 and 54 BC kicking off a lengthy but low-level infusion of Roman ideas which filtered across to Wales. This flow swelled a century later when the emperor **Claudius** took the death of the British king Cunobelin (Cynfelyn) as a signal to launch a full-scale invasion in 43 AD which in four years swept across southern England to the frontier of south Wales. Expansionism fomented anti-Roman feeling along the frontier between the Lowland Zone (southern and central England) and the Highland Zone (northern England, Scotland and Wales). Traditionally insular Welsh hill tribes united with their Brythonic cousins in northern England to oppose the Romans, who proceeded to force a wedge between them. The Roman historian **Tacitus** recorded the submission of the Deceangli near Chester, giving us the oldest written mention of a Welsh land. The Romans, held back by troubles at home and with the East Anglian revolt of **Boudicca** (Boadicea), were limited to tentative dabbling in Welsh affairs sending expeditionary forces against the Silures and the toughest nut, the Druid stronghold of Anglesey. The obdurate nature of the Welsh on their back foot kept the Romans at bay until around 75 AD when legionary forts were built at Deva (Chester, England) and Isca Silurium (Caerleon) to act as platforms for incursions west along specially built military roads.

By 78 AD, Wales was under Roman control, its chief fortresses at Deva, Isca Silurium and Segontium (Caernarfon) boasting all the trappings of imperial Roman life: bath houses, temples, mosaics and underfloor heating. Through three centuries of occupation, the Celtic people sustained an independent existence while drawing material comfort from the proximity of Roman cities and auxiliary forts. Elements of Roman life filtered into the Celtic culture: agrarian practices improved, a new religion was partly adopted from the newly Christianized Romans, the language adopted Latin words (*pont* for bridge, *ffenestr* for window) and the prevailing La Tène artistic style took on classical Roman elements.

The Roman Empire was already in decline when **Magnus Maximus** (Macsen Wledig) led a campaign to wrest control of the western empire from Emperor Gratian in 383. Maximus' rule was short lived but Wales was effectively free of direct Roman control by 390.

THE AGE OF THE SAINTS

Historical orthodoxy views the departure of literate Latin historians, skilled stonemasons and an all-powerful army, as heralding the **Dark Ages**. In fact, a civic society probably flourished until a century later, when the collapse of trade routes was hastened by the dramatic spread of Islam around the Mediterranean, and Romanized society gave way to a non-Classical but no less structured form of **Celtic society**.

For the next few centuries, **Teutonic barbarian tribes** were struggling for supremacy in the post-Roman power vacuum in southern and eastern England, having little influence in Wales, where the main dynastic kingdoms set to steer Wales' next seven hundred years were taking root. The confusion that surrounds the early years of these dynasties was further muddied in 1136, when Geoffrey of Monmouth published his *History of The Kings of Britain*, portraying **King Arthur** as a feudal king with his court at Caerleon. Victorian Romantics embellished subsequent histories, making it nearly impossible to extract much truth from this period.

In the fifth century, the **Irish** (Gwyddyl), who had a long tradition of migrating to the Llŷn and parts of mid-Wales, attacked the coast and formed distinct colonies, but were soon expelled from the north by **Cunedda Wledig**, the leader of a Brythonic tribe from near Edinburgh, who went on to found the royal house of Gwynedd, consolidating the Brythonic language and ostensibly naming regions of his kingdom – the modern Ceredigion and Meirionydd – after his sons. In the southwest, the Irish influence was sustained; the kingdom of Dyfed shows clear Irish origins.

These changes took place against a background of increasing religious energy. Between the fifth and the eighth centuries the **Celtic Saints**, ascetic evangelical missionaries, spread the gospel around Ireland and western Britain, promoting the middle-Eastern eremitical tradition of living a reclusive life. Where their message took root, they founded simple churches within a consecrated enclosure, or *llan*, which often took the saint's name, hence Llanberis (Saint Peris), Llandeilo (Saint Teilo) and many others. In south Wales, **Saint David** (Dewi Sant) was the most popular (and subsequently Wales' patron saint), dying around 589 after a miracle-filled life, during which he made a pilgrimage to Jerusalem and established the religious community at St David's, which had become a place of pilgrimage by the twelfth century.

THE WELSH KINGDOMS

Towards the end of the sixth century the **Angles** and **Saxons** in eastern Britain began to entertain designs on the western lands. The inability of the independent western peoples to unify against this threat left the most powerful kingdom, Gwynedd, as the centre of cultural and political resistance, a position it has retained until today. The weaker groups were unable to hold the invaders and after the battle at Dyrham, near Gloucester in 577, the Britons in Cornwall were separated from those in Wales who became similarly cut off from their northern kin in Cumbria after the battle of Chester in 616.

Though still geographically in a state of change, Wales could by now be said to exist. At this point the racial mix in Wales was probably little different from that to the east where Saxon numbers were small, but Wales was held together by the people's resistance to the Saxons. The Welsh started to refer to themselves as **Cymry** (fellow-countrymen), not by the Saxon term used by English-speakers today, which is generally thought to mean either foreigners or Romanized people. The construction of **Offa's Dyke** (Clawdd Offa) – a linear earthwork built in the middle of the eighth century to mark rather than defend the boundary between Wales and the kingdom of Mercia – gave the Welsh a firm eastern border and allowed them to concentrate on a gradual unification of the patchwork of kingdoms as their coasts were being harried by **Norse and Viking invaders**.

Rhodri Mawr (Rhodri the Great) killed the Viking leader off Anglesey, earned himself the formal thanks of the Frankish king Charles the Bald (Charlemagne), and helped the country's rise towards statehood through his unification of most of Wales. By this stage, England had developed into a single powerful kingdom for the first time since the departure of the Romans, and though the various branches of Rhodri's line went on to rule most of Wales down to the late thirteenth century, the princedoms were frequently forced to swear fealty to the English kings. Defensive problems were exacerbated by internecine struggles borne of the practice of partible inheritance that left each of Rhodri's sons with an equal part of Wales to control.

Rhodri's grandson **Hywel Dda** (Hywel the Good) largely reunified the country from Deheubarth, his power base in southwest Wales. He added Powys and Gwynedd to his domain, but his most valuable legacy is his codification, compilation and promulgation of the medieval **Law of Wales** (Cyfraith Hywel Dda) at Whitland (see p.131) around 930. Regional customs were fashioned into a single legal system that was only abandoned under the 1536 Act of Union with England. The laws drew more from the tenets of folk law than state edict: farming was conducted communally, the bard was exempt from menial tasks, a husband did not have unrestricted control over his wife (as was the case in much of Europe), and if a family were destitute they were allowed to retain a cooking pot and their harp.

After Hywel's death in 950, anarchy and internal turmoil reigned until his great-great-grandson, **Gruffydd ap Llywelyn**, seized power in Gwynedd in 1039. He unified all of Wales, taking the coronation of the weak English king, Edward the Confessor, as an opportunity to annex some of the Marches in Mercia. Edward's successor, Harold, wasn't having any of this and killed Gruffydd, heralding a new phase of political fragmentation.

THE ARRIVAL OF THE NORMANS

In 1066, the **Normans** swept across the English Channel, killed Harold, the English king, and stormed England. Though Wales was unable to present a unified opposition to the invaders, the Norman king, William, didn't attempt to conquer Wales. The **Domesday Book** – his masterwork of subjugation commissioned in 1085 to record land ownership as a framework for taxation – indicates that he only nibbled at parts of Powys and Gwynedd. Instead, he installed a huge retinue of barons, the **Lords Marcher**, along the border to bring as much Welsh territory under their own jurisdiction as possible. Despite generations of squabbling, the barons managed to hold onto their privileges until Henry VIII's Act of Union over four hundred years later.

The payment of homage by **Rhys ap Tewdwr** the king of Deheubarth, and **Gruffydd ap Cynan** the king of Gwynedd, kept the Welsh borders safe until the death of William I in 1087. His son William Rufus made three unsuccessful invasions of Wales but finally left it to his Marcher lords (now numbering over 140) to advance from their castles into south Wales, leaving only Powys and Gwynedd independent. A lack of English commitment or resources allowed the Welsh to claw back their territory through years when distinctions between English, Normans and Welsh were beginning to blur. One product of this was the quarter-Welsh Giraldus Cambrensis (see p.249 who left a valuable record of twelfth-century life in Wales and his opinions on Welsh character. "They are quicker witted and more shrewd than any other Western people" he informs us, a quality which helped them form three stable political entities: Powys, Deheubarth and Gwynedd. The latter, led by **Owain Gwynedd** from his capital at Aberffraw on Anglesey, now extended beyond Offa's Dyke and progressively gained hegemony over the other two. Owain Gwynedd's grandson, **Llywelyn ap Iorwerth** (the Great), earned his laurels through shrewd campaigning, progressively incorporating the weaker territories to the south into his kingdom and capturing several Norman castles. Manipulating the favours of the English King John, Llywelyn managed to extend his control over southern Powys before a fearful John led two devastating campaigns into north Wales. Llywelyn was humiliated and forced into recognizing John as his heir should Llywelyn's union with John's illegitimate daughter Joan not produce a son. Channelling a now united Welsh opposition against John, Llywelyn struck back and won some degree of Welsh autonomy. Though Llywelyn was able to engineer the smooth succession of his son Dafydd, the country had only nominal unity and Dafydd's death in 1246 led to a new power struggle.

EDWARD I'S CONQUEST

In 1255, Lleweleyn ap Iorwerth's grandson, **Llywelyn ap Gruffydd** (Llewellyn the Last), won control of Gwynedd. During the next three years he pushed the English out of Gwynedd then out of most of Wales. The English king Henry III was forced to respect Llywelyn's influence and ratified the **Treaty of Montgomery** in 1267, thereby recognizing Llywelyn as "Prince of Wales" in return for his homage. The English monarchy's war with the barons allowed Llywelyn time to politically consolidate his lands which now stretched over all of modern Wales except for Pembrokeshire and parts of the Marches. The tables turned when Edward I succeeded Henry III and began a crusade to unify Britain. Llywelyn had failed to attend Edward's coronation, refused to pay him homage, and at the same time Llywelyn's determination to marry the daughter of Simon de Montfort lost him the support of the south Welsh princes and some Marcher lords. Edward was a skilful tactician and with effective use of sea power had little trouble forcing the already weakened Llywelyn back into Snowdonia. Peace was restored with the **Treaty of Aberconwy** which deprived Llywelyn of almost all his land and stripped him of his financial tributes from the other Welsh princes, but left him with the hollow title of "Prince of Wales".

Edward now set about surrounding Llywelyn's land with castles at Aberystwyth, Builth Wells, Flint and Rhuddlan (see p.337). After a relatively cordial four-year period, Llywelyn's brother Dafydd rose against Edward, inevitably dragging Llywelyn along with him. Edward didn't hesitate and swept through Gwynedd, crushing the revolt and laying the foundations for the remaining castles in his **Iron Ring**, those at Conwy, Caernarfon,

Harlech and Beaumaris. Llywelyn already battered by Edward's force, was captured and executed at Cilmeri (see p.185), after fleeing from the abortive Battle of Builth in 1282. The **Treaty of Rhuddlan** in 1284 set down the terms by which the English monarch was to rule Wales: much of it was given to the Marcher lords who had helped Edward, the rest was divided into administrative and legal districts similar to those in England. Though the treaty is often seen as a symbol of English subjugation, it respected much of Welsh law and provided a basis for civil rights and privileges. Many Welsh were content to accept and exploit Edward's rule for their own benefit, but in 1294 a rebellion led by **Madog ap Llywelyn** gripped Wales and was only halted by Edward's swift and devastating response. Most of the privileges enshrined in the Treaty of Rhuddlan were now rescinded and the Welsh seemed crushed for a century.

OWAIN GLYNDŴR

Throughout the fourteenth century, famine and the Black Death plagued Wales. The Marcher lords appropriated the lands of defaulting debtors and squeezed the last pennies out of their tenants, while royal officials clawed in all the income they could from the towns around the castles. These factors and the pent-up resentment of the English sowed seeds of a rebellion led by the tyrannical but charismatic Welsh hero **Owain Glyndŵr**. Citing his descent from the princes of both Powys and Deheubarth, he declared himself "Prince of Wales" in 1400, and with a crew of local supporters attacked the lands of nearby barons, slaughtering the English. Henry IV misjudged the political climate and imposed restrictions on Welsh land ownership, swelling the general support Glyndŵr needed to take Conwy Castle the following year. By 1404 Glyndŵr, who already had control over most of western Wales and sections of the Marches, took the castles at Harlech and Aberystwyth, summoned a parliament in Machynlleth, and had himself crowned Prince of Wales, with envoys of France, Scotland and Castile in attendance. He then demanded independence for the Welsh Church from Canterbury and set about securing alliances with English noblemen who had grievances with Henry IV. This last ambitious move heralded Glyndŵr's downfall. A succession of defeats saw his allies desert him and by 1408, when the castles at Harlech and Aberystwyth were retaken for the Crown, this last protest against Edward I's English conquest had lost its momentum. Little is known of Glyndŵr's final years, though it is thought he died in 1416, leaving Wales territorially unchanged but the country's national pride at an all-time high.

THE TUDORS AND UNION WITH ENGLAND

During the latter half of the fifteenth century, the succession to the English throne was contested in the **Wars of the Roses** between the houses of York (white rose) and Lancaster (red rose). Welsh allegiance lay broadly with the Lancastrians, who had the support of the ascendant north Welsh Tewdwr (or Tudor) family. Through the early part of the wars, one Henry Tudor lived with his widowed Welsh mother, Margaret Beaufort, at the besieged Harlech castle, escaping to Brittany when Yorkist Richard III took the English throne in 1471. Fourteen years later, Henry returned to Wales, landing at Milford Haven, and defeated Richard at the Battle of Bosworth Field, so becoming **Henry VII** and sealing the Lancastrian ascendancy.

Welsh expectations of the new monarch were high. Henry lived up to some of them, removing many of the restrictions on land ownership imposed at the start of Glyndŵr's uprising, and promoting many Welshmen to high office, but administration remained piecemeal. Control was still shared between the Crown and largely independent Marcher lords until a uniform administrative structure was achieved under Henry VIII.

Wales had been largely controlled by the English monarch since the Treaty of Rhuddlan in 1284, but the **Acts of Union** in 1536 and 1543 fixed English sovereignty over the country. At the same time the Marches were replaced by shires (the equivalent of modern counties), the Welsh laws codified by Hywel Dda were made void and partible inheritance gave way to primogeniture, the eldest son becoming the sole heir. For the first time the Welsh and English enjoyed legal equality, but the break with native traditions wasn't well received. Most of the people remained poor, the gentry became increasingly anglicized, the use of Welsh was proscribed and legal proceedings were held in English (a language few peasants understood). Just as Henry VIII's decision to convert his kingdom from Catholicism to Protestantism was borne more from his desire to divorce his first wife, Catherine of Aragon, than from any religious conviction, it was his need for money not recognition, which brought about the **Dissolution of the monasteries** in 1536. Monastic lands were divided amongst the local gentry, but since Christianity had always been a ritual way of life rather than a philosophical code in Wales, Catholicism was easily replaced by Protestantism. What the Reformation did promote was a more studied approach to religion and learning in general. Under the reign of Elizabeth I, Jesus College was founded in Oxford for Welsh scholars, and the Bible was translated into Welsh for the first time by a team led by Bishop **William Morgan** (see p.323).

With new land ownership laws enshrined in the Acts of Union, the stimulus provided by the Dissolution hastened the emergence of the Anglo-Welsh gentry, a group eager to claim a Welsh pedigree while promoting the English language and the legal system, helping to perpetuate their grasp. Meanwhile, landless peasants continued in poverty, only gaining slightly from the increase in cattle trade with England and the slow development of mining and ore smelting.

THE CIVIL WAR AND THE RISE OF NONCONFORMISM

James I, a direct descendant of the Tudors, came to the throne in 1603 to general popular approval in Wales. Many privileges granted to the Welsh during the Tudor reign came to an end, but the idea of common citizenship was retained, the Council of Wales remaining as a focus for Welsh nationalism. James, fearful of both Catholicism and the new threat of Puritanism – an extreme form of Protestantism – courted a staunchly Anglican Wales and curried the favour of Welsh ministers in the increasingly powerful Parliament. Though weak in Wales, Puritanism was gaining a foothold, especially in the Welsh borders, where William Wroth and Walter Cradock set up Wales' first dissenting church at Llanfaches in Monmouthshire in 1639, to become the spiritual home of Welsh Nonconformism.

The monarchy's relations with the Welsh were strained by **Charles I**, who was forced to levy heavy taxes and recruit troops, but the gentry were mostly loyal to the king at the outbreak of the **Civil War**, which saw the Parliamentary forces installing **Oliver Cromwell** as the leader of the **Commonwealth**. The Puritan support for Parliament didn't go unrewarded and, after Charles' execution, they were rewarded with the livings of numerous parishes and the roots of Puritan Nonconformism spread in Wales. As Cromwell's regime became more oppressive, the Anglican majority became disaffected and welcomed the successful return of the exiled **Charles II**, and the monarchy was restored. Charles replaced many of the clergy in their parishes and passed the Act of Uniformity, requiring adherence to the rites of the Established Church, and so suppressing Nonconformity. The Baptists, Independents and Quakers who made up the bulk of Nonconformists continued to worship in secret, until **James II** passed the **Toleration Act** in 1689, finally allowing open worship, but still banning the employment of dissenters in municipal government; a limitation which remained in force until 1828.

THE RISE OF METHODISM

At the beginning of the **eighteenth century**, Wales was still rural land. The vast majority of its population were illiterate and only scratched a bare living from mountain smallholdings while a few more, working as local administrators, could afford education and decent food. The landowners, though nominally Welsh, shared none of the values of their tenants, showing more interest in their money-spinning pursuits throughout the growing British Empire. Corruption within the Established Church left many parishes without a spiritual leader, the income from tithes being kept by local squires, given free reign by bishops who regarded their rural sees as little more than stepping stones to more lucrative positions.

The propagation of the Nonconformist seed in this fertile soil was less a conscious effort to convert the populace from Anglicanism than to better educate the masses. The late seventeenth century saw a welter of new religious books in Welsh, but with most people still illiterate, religious observance remained an oral tradition. In 1699, the **Society for Promoting Christian Knowledge**, set about establishing schools where the Bible, along with reading, writing and arithmetic, were taught in Welsh as well as English. This met with considerable success amongst the middle classes in anglicized towns, but failed to reach rural areas where children couldn't be spared from farm duties. The next big reformist push came in 1731, when **Griffith Jones** helped organize itinerant teachers to hold reading classes in the evenings and in the quieter winter season, so farmers and their families could attend. Within thirty years, half the Welsh population could read. After Jones's death, **Thomas Charles** of Bala (see p.227) continued his work, establishing Sunday schools and editing the first Welsh Bible to be distributed by the **British and Foreign Bible Society**.

By the middle of the eighteenth century, a receptive and literate populace was ready for three eloquent figures of the **Methodist Revival**, all driven by a strong belief in a resurgent Welsh nation. In contrast to the staid Anglican services, the Methodists held evangelical meetings: **Howel Harris** took his preaching outside or into people's homes, **Daniel Rowlands** converted thousands with his powerful sermons, and **William Williams** became the most important hymn writer in Welsh history.

Until now, Methodism worked within the framework of Anglicanism, but in 1811 the Calvinist Methodists broke away. As the gentry remained with the Established Church, Methodism associated itself with the spiritual and social needs of the masses, becoming a rallying point for the growing sense of disaffection with the traditional rule of the parson and squire. The Chapel became the focus of social life, discouraging folk traditions that brandied them incompatible with the Puritan virtues of thrift and temperance. Political radicalism was also discouraged, perpetuating the stranglehold on parliamentary power exercised by the powerful landed elite, the Williams-Wynn, Morgan and Vaughan families in particular. Only property owners were eligible to vote and few were prepared to challenge established dynasties, even when the rare elections took place.

Human rights became an issue in 1776 with the publication of the American *Declaration of Independence* and a piece by the radical Welsh philosopher, **Richard Price**: *Observations on the Nature of Civil Liberty*. The subsequent calls for a greater degree of democracy – universal suffrage and annual parliaments – increased during the early days of the French Revolution, but little was actually achieved until the next century, when radical Nonconformists were able to exploit the increasing political consciousness of the working class.

WALES AND THE INDUSTRIAL REVOLUTION

Small-scale mining and smelting had taken place in Wales since the Bronze Age, but agriculture remained the mainstay of an economy with a dangerously limited diversity: meat, wool and butter being about the only exports. With the enormous rise in grain prices in the early nineteenth century, Welsh farmers began to diversify and adopted the more advanced English farming practices of crop rotation, fertilizing and stock breeding. Around the same time, acts of Parliament allowed previously common land to be "enclosed", the grazing rights often being assigned to the largest landowner in the district, leaving the previous occupant with few or no rights to its use. This inevitably forced smallholders to migrate to the towns where ever more workers were required to mine the seams and stoke the furnaces, fuelling the **Industrial Revolution**. In the north, **John Wilkinson** started his iron works at Bersham (see p.263) and developed a new method of boring cylinders for steam engines; while in the south, foundries sprang up in the valleys around Merthyr Tydfil, where methods of purifying iron and producing high-quality construction steel were perfected under the eye of English ironmasters. Gradually the undereducated, impoverished Chapel-going Welsh began to be governed by rich, Church-going, English industrial barons.

Improved materials and working methods enabled the exploitation of deeper coal seams, not just to supply the iron smelters but for domestic fuel and to power locomotives and steam ships. As the rich veins of coal deep below the Rhondda valleys were exploited by Welshmen like Walter Coffin and George Insole, south Wales was transformed: rural valleys were ripped apart and quiet hamlets turned into long unplanned rows of back-to-back houses stretching up the valley sides, all roofed in north Wales slate from quarries dug by the Pennant and Assheton-Smith families.

Transportation of huge quantities of coal and steel was crucial for continued economic expansion, and the roads and canals built in the early nineteenth century were displaced around 1850 as the rail boom took hold. Great engineers made their names in Wales: **Thomas Telford** built canal aqueducts and successfully spanned the Menai Strait with one of Britain's earliest suspension bridges; **Isambard Kingdom Brunel** surveyed the Merthyr–Cardiff train line, then pushed his Great Western network almost to Fishguard; and **Robert Stephenson** speeded the passage of trains between London and Holyhead on Anglesey for the Irish ferry connection.

In mining towns, working conditions were atrocious, with men toiling incredibly long hours in dangerous conditions; women and children as young as six worked alongside them, until this was outlawed by the Mines Act in 1842. Pay was low and often in a currency redeemable only at the poorly stocked, expensive company (Truck) shop. The **Anti-Truck Act** of 1831 improved matters, but a combination of rising population, fluctuating prices and growing awareness of the need for political change brought calls for reform. When it came in 1832, the **Reform Bill** fell far short of the demands for universal suffrage by ballot and the removal of property requirement for voters. This swelled the ranks of the reformist Chartist movement, and when a petition with over a million signatures was rejected by Parliament, the **Chartist Riots** (see p.65) broke out in northern England and south Wales. The Newport demonstration was disastrous, the marchers walking straight into a trap laid by troops, who killed over twenty men and captured their leader, **John Frost**. Chartism continued in a weakened form for twenty years, buoyed by the **Rebecca Riots** in 1843, when guerilla tactics put an end to toll-gates on south Welsh turnpikes.

1850 TO WORLD WAR I

During the latter half of the nineteenth century the radical reformist movement and religion slowly became entwined, despite Nonconformist denial of political intentions. Recognizing that their flock didn't share the same rights as Anglicans, the Nonconformists petitioned for **disestablishment** of the Church in Wales and began to politicize their message. In the 1859 election, tenants on large farms (the only ones permitted to vote) were justifiably afraid of voting against their landowners or even abstaining from voting, and the conservative land-owning hegemony held. But as a consequence of the 1867 Reform Act, industrial workers and small tenant farmers got the vote, finally giving a strong working-class element to the electorate, seeing **Henry Richard** elected as Liberal MP for Merthyr Tydfil the following year, the first Welsh member of what soon became the dominant political force. Bringing the ideas of Nonconformity to parliament for the first time, he spoke eloquently on land reform, disestablishment and the preservation of the Welsh language.

The 1872 Secret Ballot Act and 1884 Reform Act, enfranchising farm labourers, further freed up the electoral system and gave working people the chance to air their resentment of tithes extracted by a Church that didn't represent their religious views. Although several bills were tabled in Parliament in the 1890s, the Anglican church was only disestablished in 1920. The Nonconformist Sunday Schools were meanwhile offering the best primary education for the masses, supplemented after **Hugh Owen** pushed through the Welsh Intermediate Education Act in 1885, by a number of secondary schools. Owen was also a prime mover in getting Wales' first tertiary establishment started in Aberystwyth in 1872, soon to be followed by colleges at Cardiff (1883) and Bangor (1884). Until they were federated into the University of Wales in 1893, voluntary contributions garnered by Nonconformist Chapels supported the colleges. The apotheosis of "Chapel power" came in 1881 with the passing of the Welsh Sunday Closing Act, enshrining Nonconformism's three basic tenets: observance of the Sabbath, sobriety and Welshness.

THE RISE IN WELSH CONSCIOUSNESS

During the nineteenth century, Welsh language and culture became weakened, largely through immigration to the coalfields from England. English became the language of commerce and the route to advancement; Welsh being reserved for the home and Chapel life of seventy percent of the population. But Welsh was still being spoken in Nonconformist schools when, in 1846, they were inspected by three English barristers and seven Anglican assistants. The inspectors' report – known as **The Treason of the Blue Books** – declared the standards deplorable, largely due to the use of the Welsh tongue, "the language of slavery". This unfair report did some good in fostering free, elementary education at "Board Schools" after 1870, though the public defence of Welsh that ensued failed to prevent the introduction of the notorious "Welsh Not", effectively a ban on speaking Welsh in school.

As the nineteenth-century Romantic movement took hold throughout Britain, the London-Welsh looked to their heritage. The ancient tales of *The Mabinogion* were translated into English, the **Society for the Utilization of the Welsh Language** was started in 1885, *eisteddfodau* were reintroduced as part of rural life, and the ancient bardic order, the **Gorsedd**, was reinvented. But disestablishment remained the *cause célèbre* of Welsh nationalism which, despite the formation of the **Cymru Fydd** movement in 1886, with its demands for home rule along the lines of Ireland, wasn't generally separatist. Perhaps the greatest advocate of both separatism and Welsh nationalism was **Michael D. Jones**, who helped establish a Welsh homeland in Patagonia and campaigned vociferously against "the English cause" (see p.277).

By 1907 Wales had a national library at Aberystwyth, and a national museum was planned for Cardiff, by now the largest city in Wales and laying claim to being its capital – only officially recognized in 1955.

INDUSTRY AND THE RISE OF TRADE UNIONISM

The rise in Welsh consciousness paralleled the rise in importance of the **trade unions**. The 1850s were a prosperous time in the Welsh coalfields, but by the end of the 1860s the Amalgamated Union of Miners was forced to call a strike (1869–71), which resulted in higher wages. A second strike in 1875 failed and the miners' agent, **William Abraham (Mabon)**, ushered in the notorious "sliding scale" which fixed wage levels according to the selling price of coal. This brought considerable hardship to the valleys, which became insular worlds with strictly ordered social codes and a rich vibrancy borne from the essential dichotomy of the Chapel and the pub. Meanwhile, annual coal production doubled in twenty years to 57 million tons by 1913, when a quarter of a million people were employed. Similarly punitive pay schemes were implemented in the north Wales slate quarries where membership of **Undeb Chwarelwyr Gogledd Cymru** (The North Wales Quarrymen's Union) was all but outlawed by the slate barons. This came to a head in 1900 when the workers at Lord Penrhyn's quarry at Bethesda started Britain's longest ever industrial dispute. It lasted three years but achieved nothing.

From 1885, the vast majority of Welsh MPs were Liberals who helped end the sliding scale in 1902 and brought in an eight-hour day by 1908. The turn of the century heralded the birth of a new political force when **Keir Hardie** became Britain's first Labour MP, for Merthyr Tydfil.

THE TWO WORLD WARS

World War I (1914–18) was a watershed for Welsh society. Seeing parallels with their own nation, the Welsh sympathized with the plight of defenceless European nations and rallied to fight alongside the English and Scots. At home, the state intervened in people's lives more than ever before: agriculture was controlled by the state while food was rationed, and industries, mines and railways were under public control. The need for Welsh food and coal boosted the economy and living standards rose dramatically. Many were proud to be led through the war by Welsh lawyer **David Lloyd George** (see p.250), who rose to the post of Minister of Munitions then of War, becoming Prime Minister by 1916, but by the time conscription was introduced, patriotic fervour had waned. Many miners, reluctant to be slaughtered in the trenches and resentful of massive wartime profits, welcomed the 1917 Bolshevik Revolution, and though Communism never really took hold, the socialist Labour Party was there to catch the postwar fallout.

Similar dramatic changes were taking place in rural areas, where Welsh farming was embracing new machinery and coming out of nearly a century of neglect. High wartime inflation of land prices and the fall in rents forced some landowners to sell off portions of major estates to their tenants in the so-called "green revolution", breaking the dominance of a rural landed gentry.

The boom time of World War I continued for a couple of years after 1918, but soon the depression came. All of Wales' mining and primary production industries suffered, and unemployment reached 27 percent, worse than in England and Scotland, which both weathered the depression better. The **Labour movement** ascended in step with the rise in unemployment, making south Wales its stronghold in Britain. Their stranglehold was challenged by Lloyd George's newly resurgent Liberal Party, but his Westminster-centred politics were no longer trusted in Wales and Labour held firm, seeking to improve workers' conditions: the state of housing was still desperate, and health care and welfare services needed boosting. The Labour party effectively became the hope that had previously been entrusted to the Chapels and later the Liberals.

A new sense of nationalism was emerging, and in 1925, champions of Welsh national autonomy formed **Plaid Genedlaethol Cymru** (Welsh Nationalist Party) under **Saunders Lewis**, its president for ten years. In one of the first modern separatist protests, he joined two other Plaid members and set fire to building materials at an RAF station on the Llŷn, was dismissed from his post and spent his life in literary criticism, becoming one of Wales greatest modern writers. Similar public displays and powerful nationalist rhetoric won over an intellectual majority, but the masses continued to fuel the Labour ascendency in both local and national politics.

Some relief from depression came with rearmament in the lead-up to **World War II**, but by this stage vast numbers had migrated from south Wales to England, leaving the already insular communities banding together in self-reliant groups centred on local Co-ops and welfare halls.

When war became inevitable, the Labour party was committed to halting the Fascist threat along with most of Wales. As a result of the demands of the war, unemployment all but disappeared and the Welsh economy was gradually restructured, more people switching from extractive industries to light manufacturing, a process which continues today.

Plaid Cymru were less enthusiastic about the war, remaining neutral and expressing unease at the large number of English evacuees potentially weakening the fabric of Welsh communities. Their fears were largely ungrounded and the war saw the formation of a Welsh elementary school in Aberystwyth and *Undeb Cymru Fydd*, a committee designed to defend the welfare of Wales.

THE POSTWAR PERIOD

Any hopes for a greater national identity were dashed by the Attlee Labour government from 1945–51, which nationalized transport and utilities with no regard for national boundaries, except for the Wales Gas Board. However, under the direction of Ebbw Vale MP, **Aneurin Bevan**, the postwar Labour government instituted the National Health Service, dramatically improving health care in Wales and the rest of Britain, and providing much-improved council housing.

The nationalized coal industry, now employing less than half the number of twenty years before, was still the most important employer at nationalization, but a gradual process of closing inefficient mines saw the number of pits drop from 212 in 1945 to 11 in 1989, and just one in 1994. Sadly, the same commitment wasn't directed at cleaning up the scars of over a century of mining until after 1966, when one of south Wales' most tragic accidents left a school and 116 children buried under a slag heap at **Aberfan** (see p.74).

In the rural areas, the 1947 Agriculture Act brought some stability to financially precarious hill farmers by stabilizing prices, who were given further protection with the formation of the Farmers' Union of Wales in 1955. A more controversial fillip came from the siting of an aluminium smelter and two nuclear power stations in north Wales; dubious benefits soon eroded by the closure of much of the rural rail system following the Beeching Report in 1963. Despite the switch to light manufacturing and the improved agricultural methods, unemployment in Wales rose to twice the UK average, and women remained greatly under-represented.

After its postwar successes, the Labour party remained in overwhelming control during the 1960s and 1970s, though Plaid Cymru became a serious opposition for the first time, partly due to Labour's reluctance to address nationalist issues. Attlee had thrown out the suggestion of a Welsh Secretary of State in 1946, and not until Plaid Cymru was fielding 20 nationalist candidates in the 1959 election did the Labour manifesto promise a cabinet position for Wales. The position of **Secretary of State for Wales** was finally created in 1964 by the Labour government, led by Harold Wilson, who also created the **Welsh Development Agency** and moved the Royal Mint to south Wales. With Plaid Cymru's appeal considered to be restricted to rural areas, Labour was shocked by the 1966 Carmarthen by-election, when **Gwynfor Evans** became the first Plaid MP. It wasn't until 1974 that Plaid also won in the constituencies of Caernarfon and Merioneth, and suddenly the party was a threat, and Labour was forced to address the question of devolution. By 1978 Labour had tabled the **Wales Act**, promising the country an elected assembly to act as a voice for Wales, but with no power to legislate or raise revenue. In the subsequent **referendum** in 1979, eighty percent of voters opposed the proposition, with even the nationalist stronghold of Gwynedd voting against.

MODERN WALES

In 1979, the Conservative government of **Margaret Thatcher** came to power, achieving an unprecedented 31 percent of Welsh votes. The 1979 referendum effectively sidelined the home-rule issue and Thatcher was able to implement her free market policies with an unstinting commitment to privatizing nationalized industries. With 43 percent of the Welsh workforce as government employees, privatization had a dramatic impact, as employment in the steel industry, manufacturing and construction all plummeted, doubling unemployment in five years. Despite this, the Tories held their share of the vote and, because of changes to constituency boundaries, increased their tally of MPs at the 1983 election, while Labour saw their lowest percentage since 1918.

Vast changes in employment patterns signalled the breakdown of traditional valley communities and the labour movement was weakened by successive anti-union measures. None of this broke the solidarity of south Welsh workers during the year-long **Miners' Strike** (1984–5), after which women took a much greater proportion of the work now transferring out of the valleys onto the south coastal plain. Living standards were still rising and the Welsh were now better off than ever before, but high unemployment and a large rural population meant that average income still lagged behind most areas of England, and despite free medical care, the Welsh remained in poorer health.

During the Eighties, support for Plaid Cymru shifted back to the rural areas, the party holding all three out of four Gwynedd constituencies after the 1987 election. At the same time, general enthusiasm for the Welsh language increased and a steady decline in numbers of Welsh-speakers was reversed. New Welsh-only schools opened even in predominantly English-speaking areas, and in 1982, S4C, the first entirely Welsh-language television channel, started broadcasting.

Although it could be argued that Wales is no more in control of its own destiny than any time in the last seven hundred years, many see hope when Welsh independence is viewed in a European context. With devolution for Scotland within a united Europe still an issue and continuing calls for Catalan and Lombard separation from Spain and Italy respectively, Britain looks ripe for division. But while Scottish independence appears increasingly possible in the long run, Wales' stronger ties with England – the judicial system in particular – look set to thwart any realistic hopes for some time yet.

CHRONOLOGY OF WELSH HISTORY

250,000 BC	Earliest evidence of human existence in Wales.
9–8000 BC	End of last Ice Age.
6000 BC	Rising oceans separate Britain from Europe.
4000 BC	Agriculturalism becomes widespread in Wales.
3000 BC	Arrival of **Bronze Age** settlers from the Iberian Peninsula colonizing Pembrokeshire and Anglesey, while the Gower was settled by people from Brittany and the Loire.
C3rd BC	**Celts** reach the British Isles: the Goidels settle in Ireland, the Brythons in parts of England and Wales.
43 AD	**Romans** begin conquest of Britain.
61	Suetonius Paulinus attacks north Wales and Anglesey.
79	Roman conquest of Wales completed as Agricola kills Druids of Anglesey.
80–100	Caerleon amphitheatre built.
early C4th	Roman departure from Wales.
early C5th	**Cunedda** arrives from Scotland to conquer north Wales.
C5th–6th	**Age of Saints**.
c.500	St Illtud arrives from Ireland, bringing Christianity and founding Llanilltud Fawr monastery.
c.589	Saint David (Dewi Sant) dies.
615	Aethelfrith defeats Welsh at Bangor.
616	Battle of Chester – Wales isolated from rest of Britain.
768	Celtic church accepts some of the practices and customs of the Roman church, including its date for Easter.
c.784	Offa's Dyke (Clawdd Offa) constructed.
844–78	**Rhodri Mawr** rules Gwynedd, later gaining most of the rest of Wales through inheritance and marriage.
C9th–10th	St David's accepts supremacy of Rome.
c.900–50	Hywel Dda rules most of Wales.
C late 10th	Hywel Dda's unified Wales split into four independent principalities.
1039–63	**Gruffydd ap Llywelyn** re-unites Wales.
1066	**Normans** invade Wales.
1067	Chepstow Castle started.
1090	First Norman castle at Cardiff.
1094	Normans repelled from Gwynedd and Dyfed.
1115	Norman bishop installed at St David's.
1143	Cistercians found Hendy-gwyn (Whitland) Abbey.
1180–93	St David's Cathedral built.
1188	Archbishop Baldwin (accompanied by Giraldus Cambrensis) recruits for the Third Crusade.
1196–1240	**Llywelyn ap Iorwerth** (the Great) rules as Prince of Gwynedd and later most of Wales.
1215	English barons force King John into signing Magna Carta. Limited rights for Wales.
1246–82	**Llywelyn ap Gruffydd** (the Last) intermittently rules large parts of Wales.
1267	**Treaty of Montgomery** signed by Henry III, ratifying Llywelyn ap Gruffydd's claim to the title "Prince of Wales".
1270–1320	Tintern Abbey built.
1276–7	**First War of Welsh Independence**.
1277	Llywelyn humiliated by signing **Treaty of Aberconwy**. Edward I begins Aberystwyth, Flint and Rhuddlan castles.
1282–3	**Second War of Welsh Independence**. Llywelyn's brother Dafydd rises up against Edward I.
1283	Caernarfon, Conwy and Harlech castles started.
1284	**Treaty of Rhuddlan** signed by Edward I.
1294	Revolt of Madog ap Llywelyn.
1295	Beaumaris Castle started.
1301	Edward I revives title of "Prince of Wales" and bestows it on his son, Edward II.
1400–12	Third War of Welsh Independence. **Owain Glyndŵr**'s revolt.
1416	Owain Glyndŵr dies in hiding.
1471	Edward IV's Council of Welsh Marches at Ludlow.
1485	Accession of **Henry VII** to throne after landing from exile at Pembroke and beating Richard III at Bosworth.
1536–8	Henry VIII suppresses monasteries.

1536–43	**Acts of Union**: legislation forming the union of Wales and England. Equal rights but with a separate legal and administrative system conducted wholly in English.
1546	First book printed in Welsh: *Yn y Lhyvyr Hwnn*.
1571	Jesus College, Oxford (the Welsh college) founded.
1588	Translation of complete Bible into Welsh, chiefly by **William Morgan**.
1639	First Puritan congregation in Wales convened at Llanfaches, Gwent.
1642	Beginning of Civil War in England.
1644	**Battle of Montgomery**: first battle of Civil War on Welsh territory.
1646	Harlech and Raglan besieged during the Civil War. Harlech, the last Royalist castle, falls in 1647.
1660	Restoration of the monarchy.
1689	Toleration Act passed, allowing open, Nonconformist worship.
1707	Publication of Edward Lhuyd's *Archaeologia Britannica* initiates foundation of Celtic studies.
1743	Establishment of Welsh Calvinistic Methodist Church.
1759	Dowlais Ironworks started, followed by Merthyr Tydfil iron industry.
1782	Beginning of north Wales slate industry with the opening of Pennant's Penrhyn slate quarry at Bethesda.
1789	First **eisteddfod** for 200 years held at Corwen.
1793–4	Cardiff to Merthyr canal built.
1801	First census. Welsh population 587,000.
1811	Separation of Welsh Methodists from Church of England.
1832	Great Reform Act passed in Westminster.
1839	**Chartist** march on Newport fails.
1839–44	**Rebecca Riots** close toll booths on turnpikes.
1841	Taff Vale Railway built.
1845–50	Britannia Tubular Bridge built.
1859	Liberals win major victory in elections; tenants evicted for voting against their Conservative masters; Nonconformist revival.
1865	Michael D. Jones founds Welsh colony in Patagonia.
1872	**University College of Wales** opens in Aberystwyth, followed by Cardiff (1883) and Bangor (1884).
1881	Passing of Welsh Sunday Closing Act.
1884	**Reform Act**. Farm labourers and small tenant farmers get the vote for the first time.
1885	**Welsh Language Society** founded.
1886	Tithe War in north and west Wales.
1893	**University of Wales** established.
1898	Foundation of **South Wales Miners' Federation**.
1900	Britain's first Labour MP, Kier Hardie, elected for Merthyr Tydfil.
1907	Founding of National Museum, Cardiff and National Library, Aberystwyth.
1914–18	World War I.
1916	**David Lloyd George** becomes Prime Minister.
1920	Disestablishment of Church of England in Wales.
1925	*Plaid Genedlaethol Cymru* (Welsh Nationalist Party) formed.
1926	**Miners' strike** and General Strike.
1929–34	Great Depression.
1936	Saunders Lewis and colleagues burn building materials on the Llŷn.
1939–45	World War II.
1951	Minister for Welsh Affairs appointed.
1955	Cardiff declared capital of Wales.
1959	Welsh flag royally accepted as such.
1963	*Cymdeithas yr Iaith Gymraeg* (Welsh Language Society) formed.
1964	James Griffith, first cabinet-level Secretary of State for Wales, appointed.
1966	**Gwynfor Evans**, first Plaid Cymru MP, elected for Carmarthen. Aberfan disaster.
1967	**Welsh Language Act** passed. Limited recognition of Welsh as a formal, legal language.
1974	Local government reorganization, creating eight new counties in Wales.
1979	Referendum on Welsh Assembly. Eighty percent of voters come out against a separate parliament.
1982	Welsh-language TV channel S4C begins broadcasting.
1984–5	**Miners' strike**.
1993	Establishment of the Welsh Language Board.

TWENTIETH-CENTURY WELSH NATIONALISM

If any single event can be said to have given birth to Welsh nationalism in the modern sense, it was a meeting amongst Welsh academics at the 1925 eisteddfod in Pwllheli on the Llŷn peninsula. Led by gifted writer Saunders Lewis, the group metamorphosed into **Plaid Genedlaethol Cymru**, the National Party of Wales.

The Welsh identity had always been culturally rich, but was politically expressed only as part of the great Liberal tradition: in the dying years of the nineteenth century, Welsh Liberal MPs organized themselves into a loose caucus roughly modelled on Parnell's Irish parliamentarians and, although the Welsh group was without the clout or number of the Irish MPs, 25 or 30 MPs voting en bloc was serious enough to be noticed. **David Lloyd George** (1863–1945; Prime Minister 1916–22), fiery Welsh patriot and Liberal premier of Great Britain, had embodied many people's nationalist beliefs, although his espousal of greater independence for Wales came unstuck when, ever the expedient politician, he realized the potential difficulty of translating this ideal into hard votes in the industrialized, anglicized south of Wales. During Lloyd George's premiership, the Irish Free State was established, drawing inevitable comparisons with the Home Rule demands being less stridently articulated in Scotland and Wales. But the Liberal party was in sharp decline, nowhere more markedly than in the industrialized swathe of southern Wales, where the populous and radical mining valleys had deserted the Liberals in favour of new socialist parties. With the urban decline of a steadfast, fiercely pro-Welsh Liberal tradition, and the emergence of the two main parties as class-based warriors at either side of the political spectrum, Welsh nationalism – faced with a persistent slump in the Welsh language – was gradually honed into Saunders Lewis' embryonic political party.

Plaid Cymru – the Genedlaethol was soon dropped – had an inauspicious start electorally, polling a total of 609 votes in its first contest in 1929. The party acted more as a pressure group, focused inevitably on the issue of the decline in the Welsh language and inextricably suffused with a romantic cultural air that had little apparent relevance to party politics. As war loomed over Europe in the latter half of the 1930s, Plaid maintained a controversially pacifist stance, winning few new converts. Most sensationally, in September 1936, Saunders Lewis and two other Plaid luminaries, the Revd Lewis Valentine and D.J. Williams, set fire to the construction hut of a new aerodrome being built on the Llŷn peninsula as part of Britain's build-up to the war. They immediately reported themselves to the nearest police station, attracting huge publicity in the process. Interest in the ensuing trial electrified Wales, causing howls of outrage when the government decided to divert it from sympathetic Caernarfon to the Old Bailey in London. Even recalcitrant nationalist Lloyd George was outspokenly critical of the English decision. The three men were duly imprisoned for nine months, becoming Plaid's first martyrs.

Despite having dwindled throughout the rest of Britain, the prewar Liberal tradition was still strong with the rural majority of Wales, though by the 1951 election, this had become just three parliamentary seats out of thirty-six. The **Labour party** was now the establishment in Wales, winning an average of around 60 percent of votes in elections from 1945 to 1966.

National feelings of loss and powerlessness began to take a hold in postwar Wales as the

Welsh language haemorrhaged from the country. Although Wales consistently voted Labour, the Conservatives, the most fervently unionist of British political parties, were in power for thirteen years from 1951. Labour's 1945–51 administration had tinkered with a few institutions to give them a deliberately Welsh stance, but the Conservatives – winning only six out of 36 Welsh seats in 1951 – had little time for specifically Welsh demands. Two Welsh Labour MPs, Megan Lloyd George, daughter of the great Liberal premier, and S.O. Davies, spearheaded new parliamentary demands for greater Welsh independence, presenting a 1956 petition to Parliament, signed by a quarter of a million people, demanding a Welsh assembly. Massive popular protests against the continued flooding of Welsh valleys and villages to provide water for England shook the Establishment. The 1963 formation of the boisterous *Cymdeithas yr Iaith Gymraeg* (the **Welsh Language Society**) created many headlines and attracted a new youthful breed of cultural and linguistic nationalist to the fold. The ruling Conservatives offered token measures in an attempt to lance the rising boil of nationalism: a part-time Welsh Minister was appointed (although the job was always part of another, more important, ministerial brief), Cardiff was confirmed as capital and the Welsh flag authorized as official. The Labour party, meanwhile, was becoming more distinctively nationalistic, having formed a Welsh Council within the party, from where MPs, trade unionists and ordinary party members began to articulate the need for greater independence. The party stood on a more nationalistic platform than ever before at the **general election of 1964**. As usual, they swept the board in Wales, and finally won throughout the UK as a whole. As promised in their manifesto, the post of **Secretary of State for Wales**, backed by a separate Welsh Office, was created, although with fewer powers than the Scottish equivalent, which had existed since just after the war.

Wales presents a very different proposition from Scotland where early nationalist movements are concerned. Scotland is a far more recent arrival (1707) in the British Union than Wales and still maintains identifiably different education, judicial and legal systems, whereas Wales' are totally subsumed into the English framework. Scotland is also relatively isolated, 400 miles from London, but Wales lies immediately west of English conurbations: Birmingham, Liverpool and Manchester. Nor is Scottish nationalism so wrapped in misty-eyed linguistic pride: Gaelic is so thinly scattered that, unlike in Wales, nationalism has far transcended the language issue. Scottish nationalism has gained acceptance in both urban and rural settings, appealing to fiery socialists in Glasgow as much as well-heeled Tories of Grampian. By contrast, Plaid Cymru's support, with a few occasional exceptions, has always been drawn from the rural, Welsh-language strongholds of the west and north.

Despite these inherent drawbacks, it was Plaid Cymru who scored the first, and most dramatic, strike into Westminster. Veteran Labour MP for Carmarthen, Megan Lloyd George, died just a couple of months after the 1966 general election, precipitating a by-election won by charismatic Plaid president, Gwynfor Evans. For Wales, and for Scotland, two countries with a massive in-built majority for Labour and – for once – under a UK-wide Labour government, the nationalist parties provided a safe (and non-Conservative) repository for protest votes. Plaid Cymru and the Scottish National Party both soared in popularity in the wake of the Carmarthen result. Winnie Ewing, for the SNP, captured Hamilton from Labour in a 1967 by-election. Most dramatically, in the heart of socialist south Wales, Plaid ran the Labour government astonishingly close in two by-elections: in Rhondda West (1967) and Caerphilly (1968), the party saw swings of over 25 percent to cut Labour majorities of over twenty thousand to just a couple of thousand. From humble beginnings, it seemed that Plaid's time had come. Its traditional vote in the north and west was soaring, but, more importantly, they were the only party threatening the dominance of Labour in the English-speaking industrial south. It appeared that the party had finally overcome its single-issue status around the Welsh language, and membership ballooned to forty thousand. Welsh nationalism reached new heights at the time of the Prince of Wales' theatrical 1969 investiture at Caernarfon, a gesture resented by many. The cause also gained its first casualties, when two extremist nationalists blew themselves up at Abergele in Clwyd whilst attempting to lay a bomb on the rail line where Prince Charles was due to travel.

In some ways, this had a detrimental effect on Plaid's cause, wrongly linking extremism with the more moderate and constitutional methods of the party.

Despite this, the **1970 general election** saw Plaid in more robust mood than had ever previously been justified. The astonishing results of the previous few years led them to believe that they could pick up a clutch of Westminster seats. Yet, despite trebling their 1966 tally to 176,000 votes (11 percent of the poll in Wales), they failed to take any new seats and even lost their place in Carmarthen. The new Conservative government checked Plaid's progress, as protest votes could now safely go to the Labour party. Despite that, Plaid polled well in local elections, even taking control of Merthyr borough council. The Labour party, anxiously watching any inroads into their power base that Plaid could make, embarked on another measured programme of vaguely nationalistic proposals. Supporting bilingual road signs (daubing monoglot English signs was a practice of 1970s nationalists), briefly publishing a Welsh Labour party bilingual magazine, *Radical*, and drawing up plans for a watered-down Welsh assembly were hard-fought tenets of the new Labour party, although many traditionalists felt that these were pandering far too much to nationalist sentiment. The second 1974 election returned Gwynfor Evans in Carmarthen to join two other Plaid Cymru MPs elected in the February election. Plaid's parliamentary band of three was dwarfed by the enormous success of the SNP in Scotland, who had succeeded in getting eleven MPs to Westminster. Furthermore, Plaid's earlier success in the industrialized south had evaporated, and they lost their deposits in 26 of the 36 Welsh seats. Once again, they were a party geographically concentrated in the rural outposts of Wales.

The combined strength of the nationalist parties at Westminster, added to the wafer-thin and dwindling parliamentary Labour majority, meant that the political demands of devolution were high on the government's agenda, as they could ill afford to lose the support, and votes, of the SNP and Plaid Cymru MPs. The ruling Labour government dallied with devolutionary proposals, including setting up the **Wales Development Agency**, supporting the new Wales TUC (Trades Union Congress) and devolving the huge responsibilities of the Department of Trade and Industry in Wales to the Welsh Office in Cardiff. As the Labour parliamentary majority became ever thinner, through the government losing a cache of by-elections, the nationalists' demands became more strident. Eventually, the Labour party put forward bills for Scottish and Welsh assemblies, subject to the result of referenda.

The devolution proposals were simple. Both Scotland and Wales were offered national assemblies, or as broadcaster Wynford Vaughan-Thomas put it, "after its long marriage with England, Wales was being offered, if not divorce, at least legal separation". Campaigning by both sides was fervent, but it was obvious from early on that many Welsh people were suspicious of the proposals. A large number of the 80 percent of the country who did not speak Welsh feared that a Welsh assembly would be the preserve of a new "Taffia", a *Cymraeg* elite. Both north and south Walians worried about potential domination by the other. People feared greater bureaucracy, particularly in the wake of the 1974 local government reorganization when a two-tier system of county and district councils had been imposed on Wales. A third tier, with few apparent powers, was not a terribly attractive proposition. On St David's Day 1979, the Welsh people voted and, by a massive margin (just one-fifth of the 59 percent who voted supported the measure), turned down the limited devolution on offer. In Scotland, the proposals also fell, although a slender majority had voted in favour, but not by the margin required in the bill.

The shock waves were great. Weeks later, the Labour government fell and **Margaret Thatcher**'s first Conservative administration was ushered in. Political nationalism seemed to have gone off the boil, and Plaid Cymru were back to just two MPs representing the north-western constituencies of Merionydd and Caernarfon. The early 1980s were dominated by swiftly rising unemployment and a collapse in Britain's manufacturing base. Nowhere was this more evident than in south Wales, where mines and foundries closed and the jobless total soared. Welsh nationalism was suffering an identity crisis, typified by Plaid Cymru's controversial 1981 rewriting of its own constitution to fight for an avowedly "Welsh socialist state", causing some of the more conservative, rural members to quit the party. Basing itself as a republican, left-wing party would, it was believed, bring greater fruit in the populated south. The nationalists suffered by implication from the activities of *Meibion Glyndŵr* (**Sons of Glendower**), a shadowy organization dedicated to firebombing English holiday homes in Wales. Plaid continued to plough a firmly constitutional and peaceful route to national self-determination, but many people assumed that the bombers received covert support amongst the party's ranks.

Gwynfor Evans might well have lost his Carmarthen seat in 1979, but he was single-handedly responsible for the most high-profile activity of Welsh nationalism in the early 1980s. The Conservative party had fought the general election of 1979 on a manifesto that included a commitment to a Welsh-language TV channel. When plans for the new UK Channel 4 were drawn up, this promise had been dropped. The Plaid Cymru president decided to fast until death, if necessary, as a peaceful protest. It did not take long before this action, gaining enormous publicity in the media, forced the Thatcher government to make a U-turn, and **Sianel Pedwar Cymru** (S4C) was born in 1982. Perhaps the Tories realized the political advantage of bringing Welsh nationalism into the legitimate fold, for the Welsh media industry, long accused of a nationalistic bent, dissipated many angry and impassioned arguments for national self-determination. Many of the most heartfelt radicals ended up in prominent positions within Wales' media.

Like so many other political affiliations and ideals in the 1980s, Welsh nationalism underwent something of a sea-change. As the Labour party was routed in the 1983 election, precipitating a rightward slide for the rest of the decade and beyond, Plaid Cymru genuinely began to broaden its base as a radical, multilayered and mature political force with a firmly socialist and internationalist outlook. They developed serious policies on all aspects of Welsh life, from their traditional rallying calls of language and media to sophisticated analyses of economic policy, the Welsh legal framework and the country's role in the European Union and the wider world. But Welsh devolution – if not outright nationalism – has ceased to be the preserve solely of Plaid Cymru. Two of the three UK-wide parties, Labour and, in particular, the Liberal Democrats, inheritors of the great Liberal tradition, have evolved devolutionary strategies for Wales, Scotland and, to a lesser degree, the regions of England. Each party has a semi-autonomous Welsh branch, with its own party conference, election broadcasts and manifesto. Even the Conservatives have continued to devolve more governmental decision making out to the Welsh Office in Cardiff, although this has, ironically, strengthened the nationalist hand. Plaid and the other parties point out that there exists now a huge swathe of government in Wales, overseen by no all-Wales authority, but run instead by unelected bodies, often made up of the government's friends, appointed from Westminster (Parliament) and Whitehall (the civil service). Their call for a Welsh assembly to oversee this vast array of public expenditure is consistently supported by huge majorities in opinion polls.

The Conservatives' two thumping victories in the 1983 and 1987 general elections brought them their largest ever share of Welsh MPs: 14 out of 38 in 1983. This number has fallen ever since, and now Conservative seats in Wales are as patchy as they were in the postwar years. Labour still holds sway as the party of natural government in Wales, commanding over half of the vote, largely on the strength of the sheer weight of population in the southern urban constituencies. The **1992 general election** saw four Plaid Cymru MPs elected to Westminster – their impregnable bastions of Caernarfon and Meirionydd Nant Conwy, together with a tenuous hold on their 1987 gain, Ynys Môn (Anglesey) and, in the biggest surprise anywhere in Britain, vaulting from fourth to first place in Ceredigion and Pembroke North, unseating veteran Welsh-speaking Liberal, Geraint Howells. Despite gaining more seats than they had ever before, they still only polled 8.8 percent of votes in Wales, gaining from their peculiarly tight geographical concentration of support. In the rest of Wales, Plaid reached double-figure percentage points in only five other constituencies and in only one – Gwynfor Evans' old patch of Carmarthen – were they within 25 percent of the winner. With the exception of Carmarthen, it seems that the national party have maximized their parliamentary possibility for the meanwhile.

In many ways, these figures seem to indicate that Welsh nationalism as a political force has reached its modest zenith. However, it should be remembered that the Labour and Liberal Democrat parties are both committed to a considerable programme of real devolution, a possibility likely to be tested in the next few years. Plaid have been gaining council seats all over Wales and are well poised to take their first European parliament seat. Their more sober, less romanticized vision of Welsh nationalism, no longer exclusively based on the language issue, is likely to reap greater rewards, particularly under a Labour government, when they will become the natural repository of protest votes. A taste of this was had in the Pontypridd (1989) and Neath (1991) by-elections, when massive swings from Labour to Plaid Cymru bounced them into second place in a time of Conservative government.

As Plaid Cymru and the opposition British parties plough firmly constitutional paths to devolution or even outright independence, the more extreme nationalist movements, shrouded in anonymity and mystery, have continued to organize. Denouncing Plaid Cymru's leaders as "Westminster apologists", groups like *Meibion Glyndŵr* and the Free Wales Army have run consistent bombing and symbolic vandalism campaigns against offices of state, such as courtrooms and political party headquarters, as well as the more widely known arson campaign against holiday homes in Wales. Since 1979, over two hundred English-owned holiday properties have been torched, a reaction to the lingering death being experienced by many rural Welsh-speaking villages where local people can no longer afford house prices, artificially inflated by their tourist value. Many permanent arrivals who learn the language are made thoroughly welcome, but it is the largely empty properties (up to three-quarters of houses in some villages), filled only occasionally with visitors who make no use of local amenities, that unsurprisingly stir resentment. Other occasional guerrilla tactics include issuing threats to English shop owners and families who, after refusing to display posters in Welsh, were given an ultimatum to leave Wales. Amongst the tightly knit villages of Gwynedd, the police and security services have had great difficulty finding the culprits, although a few cases have come to trial, resulting in prison sentences of up to twelve years. For a visitor, there is almost no chance of coming across anything more than patches of *Meibion Glyndŵr* graffiti, or slogans exhorting *Cymru Rydd!* (Free Wales!). By far the majority of Welsh people disapprove of, and are even ashamed by, the violent methods of the more radical nationalists, although support for their broader aims – a consolidation of the language, control of holiday homes, houses earmarked for local families – is often confirmed in opinion polls.

In contrast to these more hotheaded eruptions, the channels of constitutional and political nationalism have become more sophisticated in recent years. The success of a television channel in both Welsh and English, together with a bold national programme of Welsh-medium schooling, has brought the first upturn in the language ever recorded in Britain's ten-yearly census. Fifteen long years of Conservative government, which neither Wales nor Scotland has ever voted for, has frustrated the Welsh, who feel that the growth in non-elected bodies overseeing their lives (more acute in Wales than anywhere else in the UK) is an affront to their national democracy. Furthermore, as UK politics become less important, Welsh political leaders are looking beyond Westminster to the parliament and executive of the European Union. The EU chose a converted chapel in the centre of Llangollen to host the office of the European Centre for Traditional and Regional Cultures (ECTARC). In 1994, the EU held its inaugural session of the **Council of the Regions**, a forum for the regional components of member states, to which Wales sends three representatives – one Conservative, one Labour and one Plaid Cymru. Plaid's rallying cry of Welsh independence within a Europe of smaller nations and regions may well be setting the agenda in the new millennium.

NATURAL HISTORY OF WALES

A comprehensive account of Wales' landscapes, land use, flora and fauna would take several books to cover; what follows is a general overview of the effects of geology, human activity and climate on the country's flora, fauna and land management.

Wales is covered with a wide array of sites deemed to be of national or international importance, all seemingly with different designations. The three **National Parks** – Snowdonia, the Brecon Beacons and the Pembrokeshire Coast – comprise almost twenty percent of the country, with another couple of percent incorporated into the five **Areas of Outstanding Natural Beauty** (AONB): the Anglesey coast, the Llŷn coast, the Clwydian range, the Gower Peninsula and the Wye Valley. Smaller areas (from a few acres to large chunks of the Cambrian Mountains) with specific habitats like lowland bogs or ancient woodlands are managed as **National Nature Reserves** (NNRs). Most are widely promoted, usually posted with information boards and threaded with easy well-signed walking trails. All NNRs contain **Sites of Special Scientific Interest** (SSSIs; aka triple-SIs), a category including around another 700 locations in Wales singled out for special protection. Most are on private land with no right of access.

It must be remembered that nowhere in Wales is untouched, almost every patch of "wilderness" being partially the product of human intervention, thoroughly mapped, mined and farmed. Nor is anywhere free from pollution: the conurbations of England are too close, nuclear power stations and factories dot the countryside and some of the seas are in a terrible state. That said, several clean air-loving lichen species – found in few other places in Britain – abound in Wales.

GEOLOGY

Geologists puzzled over the forces that shaped the Welsh landscape for centuries before early nineteenth-century geologist **Adam Sedgwick** and his collaborator (and later rival) **Roderick Murchison** began to unravel the secrets. They were able to explain the shattered, contorted and eroded rocks that form the ancient peaks of Snowdonia, but fought bitterly over rock classification. By naming the **Silurian** rock system (400–440 million years ago) after one of Wales' ancient tribes, Murchison started a trend that continued with the naming of the earlier **Ordovician** system (440–500 million years ago), and the **Cambrian** system (500–600 million years ago), given the Roman name for Wales. Anglesey, the Llŷn and Pembrokeshire all have older **pre-Cambrian** rocks, those around St David's some of the most ancient anywhere.

Wales is packed with mountains, and several areas deserve brief coverage. Between 600 and 400 million years ago **Snowdonia** was twice submerged for long periods in some primordial ocean where molten rock from undersea volcanoes cooled to form igneous intrusions in the sedimentary ocean-floor layers. Snowdon, Cadair Idris and the Aran and Arenig mountains are the product of these volcanoes, with fossils close to the summit of Snowdon, supporting the theory of its formation on the sea floor. After Silurian rocks had been laid down, immense lateral pressures forced the layers into concertina-like parallel folds with the sedimentary particles being rearranged at right angles to the pressure, giving today's vertically splitting sheets of **slate**, the classic metamorphosed product of these forces. It is known that the folded strata that rose above the sea bore no resemblance to today's mountains, the cliff face of Lliwedd on Snowdon showing that the summit was at the bottom of one of these great folds between two much higher mountains. One of these is now known as the **Harlech Dome**, a vast rock hump where the softer Silurian rocks on the surface all wore away and the Ordovician layers below were only saved by the volcanic intrusions, principally Snowdon and Cadair Idris. In between the Ordovician rocks wore away exposing the harder Cambrian sand and gritstones of the **Rhinog** range. In the very recent geological past from 80,000–10,000 years ago, these mountains were worked on by the latest series of **Ice Ages**, with glaciers scouring out hemispherical cwms (cirques or corries) divided by angular ridges, then scraping down the valleys, gouging them into U-shapes with waterfalls plunging down their sides.

Snowdonia is linked by the long chain of the **Cambrian Mountains** to the dramatic north-facing scarp slope of the **Brecon Beacons**, south Wales' distinctive east–west range at the head of the south Wales coalfield. Erosion of the ancient Cambrian, Ordovician and Silurian rocks which once covered what is now northern Britain and much of the North Sea washed down great river systems depositing beds of old red sandstone from 350–400 million years ago. These **Devonian** rocks lay in a shallow sea where the molluscs and corals decayed to form carboniferous limestone which in turn was overlaid by more sediment forming millstone grit. Subsequent layers of shale and sandstone were interleaved with decayed vegetable matter forming a band known as **coal measures**, from which the mines once extracted their wealth. The whole lot has since been tilted up in the north, giving a north to south sequence which runs over a steep sandstone ridge (the Brecon Beacons), then down a gentle sandstone dip-slope arriving at the pearl-grey limestone band where any rivers tend to dive underground into **swallow holes**. They reappear as you reach the gritstone often tumbling over waterfalls into the coal valleys.

Erosion still continues today, slowly reshaping the landscape, hastened by the Welsh climate.

LAND SETTLEMENT & USAGE

After the last ice sheet drew back from Wales, the few species which had survived on the ice-free peaks (nunataks) were in a strong position to colonize, producing an open grassland community more than 10,000 years ago. Birch and juniper were amongst the first trees, followed by hazel. Several thousand years later this had developed into a mixed deciduous woodland including oak, elm and some pine, and in wetter areas damp-loving alder and birch. The neolithic tribes began to settle on the upland areas, using their flint axes to clear the mountain slopes of their forests. The discovery of bronze and later iron hastened the process especially since wood charcoal was required for smelting iron ore, and so began the spiralling devastation of Wales' native woodlands. As the domestication of the sheep and goat put paid to any natural regeneration of saplings, more land became available for arable farming. Thin, acidic mountain soils and a damp climate made **oats** – fodder for cattle and horses – about the only viable cereal crop, except in Anglesey which, by the time the Romans arrived in the first century AD, was already recognized as Wales' most important corn-growing land. Cattle rearing was increasingly important on the lusher pastures, and even as late as the twelfth century, Giraldus Cambrensis tells us that "the whole population lives almost entirely of oats and the produce of their herds, milk, cheese and butter."

Giraldus lived at a time when the Normans were pushing into lowland Wales and acting as patrons of the monasteries. Until they were appropriated by Henry VIII in 1536, the seventeen Cistercian houses all kept extensive lands, cleared woods, developed sheep walks and cattle farms. With the Dissolution of the monasteries their lands became part of the great estates which still own large tracts of Wales.

By contrast, the less privileged were still smallholders living simple lives. In the 1770s the travel writer Thomas Pennant noted in his *Tours in Wales* that the ordinary people's houses on the Llŷn were "very mean, made with clay, thatched and destitute of chimneys". The poor state of housing had much to do with the practice of *Tŷ unnos* (literally one-night house), supposedly a right decreed by Hywel Dda, in which building a house of common materials close at hand within twenty-four hours staked your claim on a plot of common land. The practice hadn't completely died out in the 1850s when George Borrow's guide observed "That is a house, sir, built yn yr hen dull in the old fashion, of earth, flags, and wattles and in one night...The custom is not quite dead."

In the eighteenth century, **droving** reached its peak. Welsh black cattle, fattened on Anglesey or the Cambrian Coast, were driven to market in England, avoiding the valley-floor toll roads by taking highland routes that can still be traced. Nights were spent with the cattle corralled in a Halfpenny field next to a lonely homestead heralded by three Scots pines, which operated as an inn. It was a tough journey for men and cattle, but easier than for geese, whose webbed feet were toughened for the long walk with tar and sand.

At home, women ground the corn, aided by mills driven by the same fast-flowing mountain streams that later provided power for textile mills springing up all over the country. The Cistercians had laid the foundations of the **textile industry** for both wool and flannel, but it had generally remained in the cottages with nearly every smallholding keeping a spinning wheel next to their harp. The same sort of damp climate that made Lancashire the centre of the world's cotton industry encouraged the establishment of a textile industry in Ruthin, Denbigh, Newtown, Llandeilo and along the Teifi Valley, but a lack of efficient transport made them uncompetitive.

The next major shift in land use came with a wave of **enclosure acts** from 1760–1820, which effectively removed smallholders from upland common pasture and granted the land to holders of already large estates. With the fashion for grouse shooting taking hold in the middle of the nineteenth century, large tracts of hill country began to be managed as heather moor with frequent controlled fires to encourage new shoots that the grouse fed on. The people were deprived of their livelihood and access to open country was denied to future generations of walkers.

The mountain building processes discussed above have left a broad spectrum of minerals under Wales. **Copper** had been mined with considerable success since the Bronze Age, and was further exploited by the Romans, who dabbled in **gold** extraction. But it wasn't until the latter half of the eighteenth century that mining became big business, with a rapid expansion in both north and south Wales. **Slate** (see p.288) was hewn from deeper mines and higher mountainsides, while the northern ends of the south Wales valleys echoed to the sounds of the ironworks. The fortuitous discovery of iron ore, limestone for smelting and coal for fuelling the furnaces made the valleys the crucible of the iron industry, and iron stayed at the forefront here long after richer ore finds elsewhere.

Originally a service industry, **coal mining** soon took over and shaped the development of south Wales for over a century. Further west, the processing of Cornish **copper** financed the development of Swansea, while Llanelli devoted itself to **tin**.

FLORA

Wales supports 1100 of Britain's 1600 native plants, ferns and other moisture-loving species being specially well represented.

Until five thousand years ago, birch, juniper, hazel, oak and elm covered the mountainsides, but devastating forest clearances and a wetter climate have left only a few pockets of native woodland in the valleys, and they are unable to re-establish themselves as sheep graze on the newly planted saplings. **Pengelli Forest** in Pembrokeshire represents one of Wales' largest blocks of ancient woodland comprising **midland hawthorn** and **sessile oak**, the dominant tree in ancient Welsh forests. Parts of the Severn and lower Wye valleys are well wooded, as is the Teifi Valley where oak, ash and sycamore predominate. Occasionally you still see evidence of **coppicing** – an important and ancient practice common a century ago – where trees are cut close to the base to produce numerous shoots harvested later as small diameter timbers. Under the canopy, **bluebells** and **wood sorrel** are common, and in the autumn look out for the dozens of species of **mushroom**, especially the delicious but elusive **chantrelle**, found mainly under beech trees.

A far greater area of Wales is smothered in gloomy ranks of **conifers** (predominantly sitka spruce), a product of the twentieth-century monoculture ethic. Forbidding to most birds and too shaded and acidic for wildflowers, they are the object of widespread criticism directed towards the Forestry Commission.

Perhaps the most celebrated of all Wales' plants are the **arctic-alpines** that grow away from grazing sheep and goats amongst the high lime-yielding crags and gullies of Snowdonia and the Brecon Beacons, their southernmost limit in Britain. Ever since the ice sheets retreated ten thousand years ago, the warmer weather has forced them towards higher ground, where they cling to small pockets of soil behind rocks. Some get unceremoniously cleaned out by thoughtless climbers trying to push up novel routes, but in the main, their spread hasn't changed since they were discovered by seventeenth-century botanists such as Thomas Johnson and Welshman Edward Lhuyd, who found *Lloydia serotina*, a glacial relic more popularly known as the **Snowdon Lily** (though actually a spiderwort), that looks not unlike a small off-white tulip. In Britain, it is found only around Snowdon and then only rarely seen between late May and early June, when it blooms.

The exemplary habitat for arctic-alpines is widely regarded to be **Cwm Idwal** in the Ogwen Valley, where you may get to see some of the more common species, in particular the handsome **purple saxifrage**, whose tightly clustered flowers often push through the late winter snows, later followed by the starry and mossy saxifrages and spongy pink pads of **moss campion**. The star-shaped yellow flowers of **tormentil** are typical of high grassy slopes, and you may also find **mountain avens**, distinguished by its glossy oak-like leaves, and in June when it blooms by its eight white petals. From June to October, purple heads of **wild thyme** cover the ground providing food for a small beetle unique to Snowdonia.

Sheep prefer the succulent **sheep's fescue**, but competition for the juicier shoots leads to over-grazing and the growth of tough mat-grass which chokes out the **woolly-hair moss**, the **reindeer moss** and the **dwarf willow**, which can otherwise be seen in yellow bloom during June and July. Just below the wind-battered mountain tops you catch the early colonizing species; **alpine meadow grass**, **glacier buttercup**, **mountain sorrel** and **alpine hair grass** among them.

Poor acid soils on the igneous uplands foster the growth of lime-shy purple **heather** – bell, ling, cross-leaved and Scottish are all found – bracken and bilberry which combine with decayed **sphagnum moss** in wetter areas to form peat bogs. Though generally less extensive than upland bogs elsewhere in Britain, the wetlands still support the **bog asphodel** that produces its brilliant yellow spikes in late summer, often in company with the **spotted orchid** and less frequently the tiny **bog orchid**. Insectivorous plants are also found, the **butterwort** (both pale and common varieties) and the **sundew** (long-leaved and round-leaved), which gain nutrients from their poor surroundings by digesting insects trapped on the sticky hairs of their leaves. Limestone uplands such as the Clwydian ridges and parts of the Brecon Beacons are more likely to host less rugged plants, like the **harebell** and the **rock rose**. Streams running off these uplands tumble down narrow valleys hung with ferns and mosses and sometimes scattered with the yellow-flowered **Welsh poppy**.

At sea level, the rivers spawn estuarine "meadows", which in summer are carpeted with bright violet **sea lavender**, followed by a mauve wash of **sea aster** after August. An unusual coastal feature is the dam-formed string of **Bosherton Lakes**, south of Pembroke, where the fresh water supports rafts of white water-lilies. Further west, the Pembrokeshire Coast is a blaze of colour in early summer, with white-flowered **scurvy grass** and **sea campion**, yellow **kidney vetch** and **celandine**, and blue **spring squill**. **Water Crowfoot** is found in fresh water near the coastal footpath, where you can also find the hemispherical lilac heads of **devil's bit scabious**. **Bluebells** and **red campion** cloak Pembrokeshire's islands, while the majority of species mentioned can be found in abundance in Newborough on Anglesey. Here, some of Wales' finest sand dunes are bound by **marram grass**, interspersed with **sea holly**, **sea bindweed** and the odd **marsh helleborine**.

BIRDS

With its long coastline, Wales, as you might expect, abounds in sea birds, and the profusion of islands and its position on the main north–south migratory route make several sites particularly noteworthy. The *Royal Society for the Protection of Birds* (RSPB), Bryn Aderyn, The Bank, Newtown, Powys (☎0686/626678), operates ten sites throughout Wales, half of them on the coast. The islands off the Pembrokeshire Coast are incomparable for sea-bird colonies, the granite pinnacle of **Grassholm** (RSPB), 12 miles offshore, hosting the world's third largest gannet colony with 30,000 pairs. Grassholm can only be visited by prior arrangement after mid-June, but the islands closer to the coast are more accessible (see p.152), **Skokholm** and **Skomer** between them supporting 6000 pairs of **storm petrels** and an internationally significant population of 140,000 pairs of the mainly nocturnal **Manx shearwater**, which spend their winter off the coast of South America. Burrows vacated by the rabbits on the islands also provide nests for puffins, while **razorbills**, **guillemots** (known as elegug in Pembrokeshire) and **kittiwakes** nest on the cliffs. Manx shearwaters are also now colonizing **Ramsey Island**, a few miles north, after the disappearance of the rats that previously deterred burrow-nesting birds, leaving only the rare **chough**, a red-billed, red-legged member of the crow family. A few pairs of choughs are also found on the important migration stopover, **Bardsey Island**, and at the wonderful **South Stack Cliffs** (RSPB) on Anglesey which, especially from May to July, are alive with breeding guillemots, razorbills and puffins. Like much of the coast, **fulmars** and **peregrine falcons** are also present in respectable numbers, as are **cormorants**, which always nest by the sea, except at Craig yr Aderyn, a cliff four miles inland from Tywyn, where the population is in decline.

The mudflats and saltings of Wales' estuaries provide rich pickings for wintering waders. The **Dee Estuary** (RSPB), on the northern border with England, plays host to Europe's largest concentration of **pintail** as well as **oyster catchers**, **knot**, **dunlin**, **redshank** and many others. Numerous terns replace them in the summer months.

Central Wales represents one of Britain's last hopes for reviving the population of **red kites** which, like many other raptors, were traditionally persecuted by gamekeepers and suffered from the use of pesticides which caused thinning of egg shells. The banning of DDT in the 1960s allowed numbers to increase, but there are still only around 100 pairs of these fork-tailed birds left, predominantly in the Elan Valley. However, as with the other persecuted species, the hen harrier, the peregrine falcon and the sparrowhawk, numbers are increasing. Perhaps one day the heights of Snowdonia may again resound to the cry of the eagle which gives the mountains their Welsh name, Eryri.

The high country supports larger populations of **kestrels** hovering motionless before plummeting onto an unsuspecting mouse or vole, and golden-brown **buzzards** gently wheeling on the thermals on the lookout for prey which can be as big as a rabbit. Buzzards and peregrine falcons are as happy picking at carrion, but have to compete with sinister black **ravens** that inhabit the highest ridges and display their crazy acrobatics and often band together to mob the bigger birds.

Acidic heather uplands between one and two thousand feet provide habitats for the black and red **grouse** whose laboured flight is in such contrast to the darting zigzag of its neighbour, the **snipe**. On softer grassland, expect to find the **ring ouzel**, a blackbird with a white cravat, and the **golden plover**, a bird still common but being threatened, like many others, by the spread of conifer forests, which welcome little but woodpigeons and blackbirds.

After the gloomy pines, it is a delight to wander in relict stands of the ancient oak woodlands eyes peeled for tits, redstarts, pied flycatchers, and along the streams the **dipper** and **kingfishers**. On sheltered water you might also find shelduck, Canada geese and three species of swans.

MAMMALS

During the last interglacial period, Wales was warm enough to support hippos and lions but humans, pressed for space by the expanding ice sheets, killed them off, leaving bears and boars which in turn were dispatched by human persecution. Some of the last beaver lodges in Britain dammed the Teifi in the twelfth century, while half a millennium later wolves disappeared from the land. What remains is a restricted range of wild mammals topped up with semi-wild and feral beasts: shy herds of **ponies** on the Carneddau in Snowdonia and on the Brecon Beacons are rounded up annually, deer occasionally stray from captive herds, and the **goats** in Snowdonia (on the Glyderau and the Rhinogau especially) and on the Great Orme at Llandudno are descendants of domesticated escapees. Generally welcomed by farmers, they forage on the precipitous ledges, thereby discouraging sheep from grazing ventures beyond their capabilities. About the only other large land mammal is the soft-fleeced **Soay sheep** at Newborough Warren on Anglesey.

Though widely acknowledged as the scourge of wildlife, the spread of conifer plantations has seen a surge in the population of the elusive cat-sized **pine marten** which thrives in sitka spruce where their diet of squirrels is readily available. Both pine martens and the more common **polecats** are found in Snowdonia, in the ancient woodlands of Pengelli Forest on the slopes of Mynydd Preseli, and in the relict beechwoods of the Brecon Beacons. Polecats also inhabit coastal dunes where they prey on rabbits. **Foxes** are still torn apart by dogs in the name of sport but remain widespread, along with the **brown hare**, **stoat** and **weasel**, though the **badger** is rarer and still the subject of persecution through the cruel sport of badger baiting. **Rabbits** seem to be everywhere, and the north American **grey squirrel** has all but dislodged the native red squirrel from its habitat, though it hangs on around Lake Vyrnwy. Of the smaller beasts, **shrews** and **wood mice** abound, and the island of Skomer has a unique sub-species of **vole**.

Otters almost became extinct in Wales some years back, but a concerted effort on the part of the *Otter Haven Project* has seen their numbers climbing in the Teifi and some of the rivers in Montgomeryshire. They remain an endangered species, and perhaps fortunately are seldom seen but indicate their presence by their droppings.

The waters off the Pembrokeshire Coast around the Marloes Peninsula and Skomer Island have been designated a **marine reserve**, though this doesn't cover the **grey seal** breeding colony on the west coast of Ramsey Island, where each year a couple of hundred white-furred pups are born. Sadly, marine pollution is being increasingly detected in the seals' blubber, a worrying sign too for the **dolphins** and **porpoises** inhabiting the coastline.

FISH, REPTILES & INSECTS

Wales' clean, fast-flowing rivers make ideal conditions for the **brown trout**, a fish managed for sport throughout the country. In Wales, the damming of rivers has seldom cut off spawning grounds, but the fishable limit of the Conwy in particular has been extended by the introduction of a fish ladder around the Conwy Falls. **Salmon** are less common, found mainly in the Usk and the Wye, the only river where it is important as game fish. Along with **roach**, **perch** and other coarse fish, the depths of Bala Lake (Llyn Tegid) claim the unique silver-white **gwyniad**, an Ice Age relic not dissimilar to a small herring, said never to take a lure. Llyn Padarn in Llanberis also notches up a rarity with the freshwater **char**. Conditions for successful fish farming do not exist in Wales, but commercially viable beds of **cockles** still exist on the north coast of the Gower and families still own rights to musseling the sands of the Conwy Estuary.

With Welsh red dragons dying out along with King Arthur, much smaller lizards and two species of snake are all that remains of Wales' reptiles. The poisonous, triangular-headed **adder** is sometimes spotted sunning itself on dry south-facing rocks, but except in early spring when it is roused from hibernation, it frequently slithers away unnoticed. The harmless **grass snake** prefers a wetter environment and is equally shy. Easily mistaken for a snake, the legless **slowworm** is actually a lizard and is common throughout Wales, as are **toads** and **frogs** though the rare **natterjack toad** is only found in a few locations.

As for **butterflies**, southern British species – the common blue and red admiral – are abundant in sheltered spots, but aim for the woodland reserves to be found dotted all over the country to find the **dark green fritillary** and its pearl-bordered and silver-washed kin. South Wales is particularly good with Pengelli Forest home to the rare **white-letter hairstreak** as well as one of Britain's rarest dragonflies, the bright blue **southern damselfly**, and the Gower Peninsula, harbouring populations of **marbled white butterfly** and the **great green bush cricket**, uncommon anywhere else in Wales. Lastly, Snowdonia has the unique and aptly named **rainbow leaf beetle**.

ECOLOGY & THE FUTURE

With the smokestack industries now largely absent from Wales and the valleys mostly devoid of working coal mines, nature (sometimes with the help of schemes to level and replant spoil heaps) is struggling to claw its way back. A verdure inconceivable thirty years ago now cloaks the hillsides, and already the industrial remains are being cherished as cultural heritage; as much a valid part of the "natural" landscape as the mountain backdrops. If you need convincing, climb up to the disused slate workings behind Blaenau Ffestiniog or walk the old ironworks tramways around Blaenavon.

However, in other areas much remains to be done to restore the ecological balance. The increasing commercialization of farming has led not just to the damaging application of pesticides and excessive use of nitrogen-rich fertilizers, but to the wholesale removal of **hedgerows and drystone walls**, ideal habitats for numerous species of flora and fauna. Conservation groups promote the skills needed to lay hedges and build drystone walls, but for every success, another chunk of farmland is paved over with a new by-pass or a meadow is turned over to **conifers**.

The tax incentives which formerly encouraged vast expanses of spruce no longer apply, but economics still favour clear-felling a single species every thirty years or so. The largest forest owner, the Forestry Commission, is keen to shake off its monoculture image and aims to border its forests with a mix of broadleaved trees and conifers of different ages.

Far from being areas where nature is allowed to take its course, the **national parks** can be their own worst enemies, attracting thousands of people a day. Some attempt is being made to control the effects of tourism through path management and the limited promotion of public transport, but this is more than outweighed by the increasingly aggressive promotion of these regions. Paradoxically and for all the wrong reasons, **military zones** – Mynydd Eppynt and most of the Castlemartin peninsula, for example – have become wildlife havens away from the worst effects of human intervention.

Wind farms have become a contentious issue in the mid-Nineties. Initial enthusiasm for this clean energy has waned as local people complain about the constant drone of the generators, and conservationists battle it out over the relative merits of a nuclear power station that will take 130 years to decommission (as well as several millennia for the fissile material to become safe) and several forests of elegant windmills on top of hills. *Friends of the Earth: Cymru* stand firmly in favour of wind power, but have come up against the *Campaign for the Protection of Rural Wales* (CPRW), Tŷ Gwyn, 31 High St, Welshpool, Powys SY21 7JP (☎0938/552525), one of the main independent environment groups, who are pushing for a ban on any new wind farm developments favouring promotion of more efficient power usage.

Offshore, **oil and gas** have been found and exploration continues, while environmental groups campaign for the protection of sensitive areas such as the Dee Estuary, next door to a new gas terminal at the Point of Ayr. One recent controversial idea is the **Usk Barrage** which, if built, will create a freshwater lake on the outskirts of Newport by damming the estuary, thereby forcing otters and other protected species to abandon the river. Eighties-style waterfront development is on the cards if the result of the current public enquiry goes against the alliance of conservation bodies seeking to stop construction of the barrage.

MUSIC IN WALES

For most people, mention of Welsh music conjures up images of miners in badly fitting suits collectively raising the roof of their local chapel, and despite the near obliteration of the mining industry, male voice choirs remain a feature of Welsh rural life, with many choirs opening their practice sessions to the public. But Welsh music extends out into village halls, clubs, festival sites and the pubs, where Saturday nights often resound with impromptu harmonies. In quieter venues, harp players repay their musical debt to ancestors who accompanied the ancient bards (traditional poets and storytellers), while modern folk draws directly from the broader Celtic musical tradition. Exponents of Welsh language rock have traded in their dreams of commercial success for unabashed nationalism expressed through a multiplicity of styles from punk to electro-pop.

What follows is a general overview of the main styles and a run through the stars, both past and present.

FOLK MUSIC

The word "folk" translates into Welsh as *gwerin*, but the Welsh has a much wider meaning than its English counterpart, taking in popular culture as well as folklore. In a Welsh *gwyl werin* (folk festival), you're just as likely to encounter the local rock band as the local dance team, and the whole community will be there – not just committed specialists.

It's often said that the Welsh love singing but ignore their native instrumental music. Welsh folk song has always remained close to the heart of popular culture, with modern folk songwriting acting as the common carrier of political messages and social protest, but traditional Welsh music and dance have had the difficult task of fighting back to life from near-extinction following centuries of political and religious suppression. Unlike their Celtic cousins in Ireland, Scotland and Brittany, folk musicians in Wales have learned their tunes from books and manuscripts rather than from older generations of players, and unlike the Celtic music boom of the 1970s, bands concentrating on Welsh tunes were virtually unknown.

WHERE TO GET INFORMATION

Taplas, the English-language bi-monthly magazine of the folk scene in Wales is the best source for current events. It's based at 182 Broadway, Roath, Cardiff CF2 1QJ (☎0222/499759).

Cymdeithas Ddawns Werin Cymru (Welsh Folk Dance Society), is also a useful source of events information with an annual magazine and a twice-yearly newsletter, both bilingual. The editor is Eiry Hunter, 10 River View Court, Llandaff, Cardiff (☎0222/555055; fax also).

The **South Wales Echo** newpaper carries comprehensive daily listings of events in Gwent and mid- and South Glamorgan (☎0222/583583).

The **Welsh Folk Museum** based at St Fagans, near Cardiff, is a vibrant museum and a vital centre for research and collecting work (☎0222/569441).

Watch out on **posters** for the word *twmpath* – it's the equivalent of a barn dance or ceilidh and is used when Welsh dances are the theme of the night. Calling (dance instructions) could be in Welsh or English, depending on where you are in the country. A *Noson Lwawen*, literally a happy night, is most likely to be found in tourist hotels and usually offers a harpist, perhaps some dancers and a repertoire of Welsh standards.

FESTIVALS

For *eisteddfodau*, see main text, below.

Live At Llantrisant, mid-Glamorgan. Pub weekend staged by Llantrisant Folk Club, with limited space but a great party atmosphere. Late April.

Swansea Shanty Festival, West Glamorgan. Growing every year, the sea song and music take place on and around a tall ship in the marina. Early May.

Mid-Wales Festival, Newtown, Powys. The first big outdoor camping event, with an extensive guest list, has concerts at *Theatr Hafren*, and dances and sessions in most of the town's pubs. Mid-May.

Tredegar House Festival, Newport, Gwent. A laidback and enjoyable weekend at the eighteenth-century country house, good for session players and dancers. Mid-May.

Gwyl Ifan, Cardiff. Welsh for midsummer, the name of a Nantgarw dance is also the title of Wales' biggest and most spectacular dance festival, staged by Cwmni Dawns Werin Canolfan Caerdydd, with hundreds of dancers giving displays in Cardiff city centre, Cardiff Castle and St Fagans Folk Museum. Around June 24.

Gwyl Werin y Cnapan, Ffostrasol, Dyfed. The biggest folk event in Wales, hardly known outside the country, has a powerful line-up of bands from Wales and the rest of the Celtic world. Second weekend in July.

Sesiwn Fawr, Dolgellau, Gwynedd. Events indoors and in the streets. Third weekend in July.

Pontardawe International Festival, West Glamorgan – deservedly one of Britain's flagship folk events, with an ambitious line-up of international performers heading for the Swansea Valley town each year. Clever marketing policies and an excellent craft fair have brought local people pouring in as well as the long-distance festival goers. Third weekend of August.

A number of smaller dance festivals also take place, including **Gwyl Hydref** in Caernarfon on the first weekend of October and **Gwyl Iwerydd** in September 1994 (which will start with a *twmpath* in Fishguard before moving to the night ferry and culminating with dance displays and another *twmpath* in Kilkenny, Ireland!

This general lack of direction has meant that outside influences have had a considerable bearing on groups forming to play Welsh music, despite the common elements in the repertoire. Language has also been more of a divider in Wales than it has been in other Celtic countries; rock and folk are both great pillars of the Welsh language, but English-speakers have not received the same encouragement to explore their own folk culture within the Welsh framework.

The preservation and nurturing of Welsh-language songs, customs and traditions is vitally important, but the folklore of English-speaking Gower and South Pembrokeshire and the rich vein of industrial material from the valleys is actually in much greater danger of disappearing.

HISTORY

The bardic and eisteddfod traditions have always played a key role in Welsh culture. Often the **bard**, who held an elevated position in Welsh society, was the non-performing composer, employing a harper and a *datgeiniad*, whose role was to declaim the bard's words. The first **eisteddfod** appears to have been held in Cardigan in 1176, with contests between bards and poets and between harpers, *crwth*-players (see below) and pipers. Henry VIII's **Act Of Union** in 1536 was designed to anglicize the country by stamping out Welsh culture and language, and the eisteddfod tradition degenerated over the next two centuries.

The rise of **Nonconformist religion** in the eighteenth and nineteenth centuries, with its abhorrence of music, merry-making and dancing, almost sounded the death knell for Welsh traditions already battered by Henry VIII's assault. **Edward Jones**, Bardd y Brenin (Bard to the King), observed sorrowfully in the 1780s that Wales, which used to be one of the happiest of countries "has now become one of the dullest". Folk music only gained some sort of respectability when London-based Welsh people, swept along in a romantic enthusiasm for all things Celtic, revived it at the end of the eighteenth century. As late as the twentieth century, old ladies who knew dance steps would pull the curtains before demonstrating them, in case the neighbours should see.

The **National Eisteddfod Society** was formed in the 1860s and today three major week-long events are held every year – the International Eisteddfod at Llangollen in July, the Royal National Eisteddfod in the first week of August and the Urdd Eisteddfod, Europe's largest youth festival, at the end of May. The National and the Urdd alternate between north and south Wales.

Eisteddfodau have always tended to formalize Welsh culture because competitions need rules, and such parameter-defining is naturally alien to the free evolution of traditional song and music. When Nicholas Bennett was compiling his 1896 book *Alawon Fy Nghwlad*, still one of the most important collections of Welsh tunes, he rejected a great deal of good Welsh dance music because it did not conform to the contemporary high art notion of what Welsh music ought to sound like. Despite this frequently heard criticism, *eisteddfodau* have played a major role in keeping traditional music, song and dance at the heart of national culture.

THE HARP

Historically the most important instrument in the folk repertoire, the **harp** has been played in Wales since at least the eleventh century, although no instruments survive from the period before the 1700s, and little is really known about the intervening years. The only surviving music is the famous manuscript of **Robert ap Huw**, written about 1614 in a strange tablature that has intrigued music scholars: five scales were used, but no-one has yet defined satisfactorily how they should sound. In recent years craftsmen have recreated the *crwth* (a stringed instrument which may have been either plucked or bowed), the *pibgorn* (a reed instrument with a cow's horn for a bell) and the *pibacwd* (the primitive Welsh bagpipe). Some groups have adopted these instruments, but their primitive design and performance means they rarely blend happily with modern instruments.

The simple early harps were ousted in the seventeenth century by the arrival of the **triple harp**, with its complicated string arrangement (two parallel rows sounding the same note, with a row of accidentals between them), giving it a unique, rich sound. The nineteenth-century swing towards classical concert music saw the invasion of the large **chromatic pedal harps** that still dominate today, but the triple, always regarded as the traditional Welsh harp, was kept alive by gipsy musicians who preferred to play something portable.

MUSICIANS

Undoubtedly the most influential player of recent years is the triple harpist **Robin Huw Bowen**, who has revived interest in the instrument with appearances throughout Europe and North America, and has done tremendous work making unpublished mansucripts of Welsh dance music widely available through his own publishing company. In North Wales, the current pacemakers are **Bob Delyn a'r Ebillion**, whose blend of contemporary Welsh and Breton influences veers over into the rock field: they have even won admiration from *Folk Roots* magazine in England.

New bands like **Moniars** are making a strong showing with young audiences in the north, with a raucous electric bass-and-drums approach to Welsh language song; the father of Welsh folk, politician/songwriter **Dafydd Iwan**, remains as hugely popular and prolific as ever with his charismatic performances, and songwriter **Meic Stevens** is still producing good work on the borderlines of folk and acoustic rock. Musician **Tudur Morgan** has been involved in some notable collaborations, including working with Irish musician/producer Donal Lunny on Branwen, a song and music cycle based on the Welsh *Mabinogi* legend.

Singer/harpist **Sian James**, from Llanerfyl in mid-Wales, has produced two albums so far which have won the acclaim of Welsh- and English-speakers alike. One pace-setter among the women is **Julie Murphy**, born in Essex but now a fluent Welsh speaker, whose Welsh-language work alongside Breton-singer **Brigitte Kloareg** in the band **Saith Rhyfeddod** has led to a promising bilingual collaboration with young English hurdy-gurdy expert **Nigel Eaton**. Another quality Welsh-language singer is Cardiff-based **Heather Jones**, who works solo and with fiddlers Mike Lease and Jane Ridout in the trio **Hin Deg**, who blend Welsh song with Welsh/Irish fiddle music.

VENUES

In the Dyfed and Gwynedd heartland of the language, folk music can be heard in many of the same venues that stage rock events. The language is considered more important than musical categories, and the folk club concept is alien to Welsh-speakers, who never saw the need to segregate music that was a natural part of their cultural life. Folk clubs are found in the anglicized areas and only a few of them feature Welsh music. In the south, check for folk in the general programme at the Welsh cultural clubs in the area: Clwb Ifor Bach in Womanby Street, Cardiff (☎0222/232199); Clwb y Bont in Taff Street, Pontypridd, Mid-Glamorgan (☎0443/491424); Clwb Brynmenyn in Brynmenyn, Mid-Glamorgan (☎0656/725323); and Clwb Y Triban, Penallta Road, Ystrad Mynach, Mid-Glamorgan (☎0443/814491).

REGULAR FOLK VENUES IN SOUTH WALES

St Donats Arts Centre (☎0466/792151), in a delightful fourteenth-century Tythe Barn at Atlantic College near Llantwit Major, puts on major folk/roots guests as part of its regular programme.

Llantrisant Folk Club, Cross Keys, High Street, Llantrisant, Mid-Glamorgan (☎0443/226892). International guest list mixed with local sessions centred on Welsh tunes. Weekly, Wednesday.

Penarth Labour Club, Glebe St, Penarth, South Glamorgan. Guitar-oriented, with regular guests. Weekly, Thursday.

Heritage Folk Club, Llantwit Major Rugby Club, South Glamorgan (☎0446/794461). Weekly, Thursday.

The Hostelry, Llantilio Crossenny, Gwent. Beautiful fourteenth-century pub. Weekly, Thursday.

Four Bars Inn, opposite Cardiff Castle. Big name international concerts staged by Taplas magazine. Monthly, Friday.

Pontardawe Folk Club, Ivy Bush Hotel, Brecon Rd, Pontardawe, West Glamorgan. Weekly, Friday.

Boat Inn, Penallt, Gwent. Monthly, last Tuesday.

Halfpenny Golf Club, The Greyhound, Llanrhidian, Gower (☎0792/850803). Weekly, Sunday.

Mullighan's Bar, St Mary St, Cardiff. Irish sessions. Twice weekly, Sunday and Tuesday.

REGULAR FOLK VENUES IN NORTH WALES

ECTARC (the European Centre for Traditional and Regional Cultures) in East St, Llangollen, Clwyd, regularly stages international concerts.

Theatr Clwyd, Mold, Clwyd. Monthly, first Tuesday.

The Bulkeley Arms, Beaumaris, Anglesey. Weekly, Monday.

The London Hotel, Llandudno, Gwynedd. Weekly, Sunday.

The Glangasfor, Rhyl, Clwyd. Weekly, Friday.

The Lex Social Club, Wrexham, Clwyd. Weekly, Thursday.

The Heights, Llanberis, Gwynedd. Weekly, Tuesday.

Y Mount Dinas, Llanwnda, Gwynedd. Weekly, Thursday.

Close harmony songs in three or four parts were a feature of life in mid-Wales, where the *plygain* carol-singing tradition still survives at Christmas. Small parties of carol singers, each with their own repertoire, would sing in church from midnight through until the break of dawn on Christmas morning. The group **Plethyn**, which was formed in the 1970s to adapt this style to traditional and modern Welsh songs, still perform occasionally and member Linda Healey was also involved in the Branwen project.

Wales' busiest band is probably **Calennig**, from Llantrisant in mid-Glamorgan, who blend fiery Welsh dance sets with English-language songs from the Valleys and Gower. They tour regularly in Europe, America and New Zealand and have also helped to popularize Welsh dance with a punchy collection of *twmpath* tunes and up-front calling from **Patricia Carron-Smith**.

From the same town come Welsh-language band **Mabsant**, who have also travelled the world with their own tours in the States and Europe, and British Council tours to the Far

RECORD COMPANIES

Sain, the major Welsh recording company, can boast a good number of folk albums and artists in its catalogue, which is available from Canolfan Sain, Llanddwrog, Gwynedd LL54 5TG (☎0286/831111).

Cwmni Fflach at Llys-y-Coed, Heol Dinbych-y-Pysgod, Aberteifi, Dyfed SA43 3AH (☎0239/614691) is a relative newcomer, with albums by *Mabsant* and *Saith Rhyfeddod* among its folk releases.

Steam Pie, run by Geoff Cripps at 17, The Grove, Pontllanfraith, Gwent (☎0495/222173) has released albums by The Chartists, Huw and Tony Williams, The Milkshakes and other South Wales-based English language artists.

Cob Records at 1–3 Brittania Terrace, Porthmadog, Gwynedd LL49 9NA (☎0766/512170) has an extensive mail order business. The simplest way for international customers to pay is with Visa or Mastercard credit cards.

Menter Osian is a new Celtic music mail order business connected with Gwyl Werin Y Cnapan. They're at Trewerin, Stryd Lincoln, Llandysul, Dyfed SA44 4BU (☎0559/362147). Payments need to be in sterling or Eurocheques; they are not yet equipped to accept credit cards.

RECORDINGS

Aberjaber *Aberjaber* and *Aberdaujaber* (Sain). Two albums by defunct but extremely competent band formed by Cardiff jazz/roots/world musician Peter Stacey, Swansea harpist Delyth Evans and Oxford music graduate Stevie Wishart (Viol and hurdy-gurdy), who experimented with Welsh and original instrumental music.

Ar Log *OIVIV* (Sain). Compilation CD of their last two studio albums.

Robin Huw Bowen *Telyn Berseiniol fy Nghwlad* (Teires). Self-produced CD of dance music and airs for the triple harp.

Calennig Dwr *Glan* (Sain). Rocky Welsh dance sets and songs tinged with Breton and Galician influences.

Cilmeri *Cilmeri* (Sain). Long-defunct but well respected north Wales six-piece, the first band to put a harder Irish-style edge on the music of Wales.

Delyth Evans *Delta* (Sain). Solo album of Celtic harp music by Aberjaber's harpist.

Dafydd Iwan ac Ar Log *Yma O Hyd* (Sain). Compilation CD of two great mid-Eighties albums which celebrated legendary joint tours around Wales by these performers.

Sian James *Distaw* (Sain). Original, modern and traditional songs on harp, keyboard and spine-tingling voice.

Mabsant and Eiry Palfrey *Mabsanta* (Sain). Live show by band and actress celebrating a Welsh Christmas in song and humorous verse.

Y Moniars *I'r Carnifal* (Sain). Debut album from up-front young band.

Tudur Morgan *Branwen* (Sain). Project of songs and music based on the *Mabinogi* legend.

Pedwar Yn Y Bar *Byth Adra* (Sain). Four piece, also now defunct, which arose from the ashes of Cilmeri and added American and other international influences to Welsh music.

Saith Rhyfeddod *Cico Nyth Cacwn* (Fflach). New (1994) album by bagpipers Jonathan Shorland and Ceri Matthews.

Meic Stevens *Er Cof am Blant y Cwm* (Crai). The songwriter's most recent album (1993).

Traditional Plygain parties *Carolau Plygain* (Sain). Few albums are available of Welsh "source" performances, the older generation who handed down their songs, but this Welsh Folk Museum-produced album of Christmas carols from mid-Wales is a gem.

East. Their strength lies in the powerful voice of **Siwsann George**, also a fine solo singer, and soulful sax work from **Steve Whitehead**.

The Hennessys, led by broadcaster, TV personality and songwriter Frank Hennessy, still have a huge and well-deserved middle-of-the-road following in the Cardiff area twenty years after joining the procession of Irish-influenced trios on the folk circuit.

Huw and Tony Williams, from Brynmawr in the Gwent Valleys, are popular names on the British folk club circuit whose following, like other English-language performers, is greater away from home than it is inside Wales. Huw's songwriting – notably songs like "Rosemary's Baby" – has been embraced by Fairport Convention and a string of other big-name performers, but he's best known in Wales for his Eisteddfod-winning clog dancing. Cardiff female trio **The Milkshakes** perform *a cappella* versions of pop hits.

DANCE

Traditional dance in Wales has been revived over the past fifty years after a long period of religious suppression. It plays a big part in the folk culture of Wales, and the top teams are exciting and professional in their approach. Dances written in recent years, often for eisteddfod competitions, have been quickly absorbed into the repertoire. **Cwmni Dawns Werin Canolfan Caerdydd**, Cardiff's official dance team, have taken their spectacular displays to Texas and Japan among the many trips they've made in their first 25 years. Their musicians are recommended for a hearing as well. **Dawnswyr Nantgarw**, from the Taff Vale village that was the source of the country's romantic and raunchy fair dances, have turned Welsh dance into a theatrical art form: concise, perfectly drilled and very showy. **Dawnswyr Gwerin Pen-y-Fai**, from Bridgend, have an adventurous band full of good session players, while Anglesey-based **Ffidl Ffadl** also boast an excellent musician in fiddler **Huw Roberts**, formerly with the early 1980s bands **Cilmeri** and **Pedwar yn y Bar**. **Dawnswyr Brynmawr** also have a capable band who play for *twmpath* dances as **Taro Tant**.

POP MUSIC IN WALES

The lack of international pop artists to emerge from Wales is frequently the subject of debate amongst the country's pop fraternity, and it's often said that because the UK music business is dominated by London-based labels and media, Welsh artists are overlooked.

The response has been twofold; either bands have knocked hard on the door of the English dominated pop establishment, singing in English and playing on the London gig circuit, or they have turned their backs on commerical success, adopting their native tongue to sing in, launching Welsh record labels, and in the process cultivating what is now a thriving Welsh-language music scene.

ENGLISH-LANGUAGE WELSH POP

The biggest, most enduring name in English-language Welsh pop is undoubtedly Sixties sex symbol **Tom Jones**, still pulling crowds around the world. Hailing from Treforest in South Wales, Jones' slick presentation and booming voice has seen him turn his love of Black American soul music into an enduring career. Similarly, Cardiff-born singer **Shirley Bassey**, the daughter of a West Indian seaman, has carved-out a hugely successful career since the mid-Fifties. In 1964 she sang the theme song to the James Bond movie *Goldfinger*, and in 1972 scored a major American hit with "Diamonds Are Forever". Although these days records are rare, she still performs, notably at the opening of the Cardiff International Arena in 1993.

Cardiff musician-turned-record producer **Dave Edmunds**, whose first band Love Sculpture scored a UK hit in 1968, has had his hands on many a hit record since – both as a producer and a solo performer – during the Seventies and Eighties. Classically trained pianist **John Cale**, born in Garnant near Ammanford, went to America in 1963 and found fame with the **Velvet Underground**, one of the most influential avant-garde rock bands of the Sixties. He has since recorded solo and, more recently, has worked with the re-formed Velvet Underground.

Other Sixties successes were **Amen Corner** with their 1968 hit "Bend Me Shape Me". Amen Corner's singer, Andy Fairweather Low, went on to solo fame with the song "Wide Eyed And Legless", a hit in 1975. Swansea's psychedelic-tinged rock outfit **Badfinger** had a brief flirtation with chart success In the late Sixties, whilst at a similar time progressive rockers **Man** courted attention. Man are still going today after over 25 years and thirteen LPs. The rock band **Racing Car** also managed to sustain two hit LPs during the early Seventies, thanks mainly to the success of their single "They Shoot Horses, Don't They?".

In the 1980s, Welsh rock music was personified by Rhyl's rabble-rousing rock fundamentalists **The Alarm**, fronted by Mike Peters, who relaunched his solo career early in 1994. The band rode the stadium-rock wave of the mid-Eighties, their anthemic folk-punk sound bringing huge UK and American success and a career that spanned seven albums in eight years.

Rock ballad singer **Bonnie Tyler** achieved great commercial success from the late Seventies onwards, with a style described as that of a female Rod Stewart. In the mid-Eighties she successfully teamed up with Meatloaf collaborator Jim Steinman. To a lesser extent, the New Romantic synth pop of **Visage** – with the big 1981 UK hit "Fade To Grey" – put a Welsh act in the pop charts, and later in the Eighties, the gentle pop sounds of **Scritti Politti** enjoyed some success. Other notable bands to emerge from Wales in the mid-Eighties were dreamy guitar popsters **The Darling Buds**, fronted by Andrea Lewis, and the whimsical, independently minded **Pooh Sticks**, whose upbeat guitar twang eventually saw them signed to RCA in 1992.

Possibly the most surprising – some would say ludicrous – Welsh success story of the Eighties was Fifties rock 'n' roll impersonator **Shakin' Stevens**. As the name suggests, he mimicked Elvis' rubber-legged dance routine, and by covering old rock 'n' roll standards and writing original songs that sounded like rock 'n' roll standards, he sold millions of records, cashing in on Fifties musical nostalgia.

Most recently, south Wales rock nihilists the **Manic Street Preachers**, a sneering punk-meets-hard-rock band from the small town of Blackwood in the Sirhowy Valley, have been kicking up controversy with inflammatory statements – "I laughed when John Lennon got shot," they screamed on the single "Motown Junk". Released in 1991 on London-based independent Heavenly label, the record saw them courted by the big labels, eventually signing to Sony and producing a string of UK hit singles and the LPs "Generation Terrorists" and "Gold Against The Soul". At the opposite end of the pop spectrum, Wrexham dance band and remixers **K Klass** have been consistently in the UK pop charts and big in the clubs slnce the early Nineties. Their debut LP, "Universal" was released on the EMI-backed Deconstruction label at the end of 1993.

WELSH-LANGUAGE ROCK

Whilst English-language Welsh bands have usually enjoyed success by making their nationality an irrelevance, Welsh-language bands have purposely expounded their strong national identity. Consequently, major commercial success has eluded them. On a positive note, however, it has seen the development of a unique, self-perpetuating Welsh-language pop scene.

The roots of this thriving, youthful and innovative scene owe much to a musical revolution whose shock waves emanated not from Cardiff or Newport, but from London. The **punk** explosion of 1976 kicked over many of rock's statues, partly thanks to the anarchic fervour of London bands like the **Sex Pistols** and **The Clash** (who made it to the South Wales town of Caerphilly on the ill-fated Anarchy Tour in 1976), but also by virtue of its strong DIY ethic.

Just as labels like Rough Trade, Small Wonder and Cherry Red emerged in London, releasing records that major labels wouldn't, **punk bands** in Wales began releasing their own records, though the band **Llygod Ffyrnig** (Savage Mouse), was included on a late 1970s Cherry Red compilatlon, and earned a Melody Maker Single of the Week in 1979. Fellow punks **Trynau Coch** set up their own label, Recordiau Coch, attracting attention from the UK music press in the process.

The punk ethic of the mid- to late Seventies laid the foundations, but it was in the Eighties that the home-grown Welsh-language pop scene really began to consolidate itself. In 1983, Caernarfon punk band **Anhrefn** (Disorder) set up **Recordiau Anhrefn**. The label was responsible for churning out "dodgy compilations of up and coming left-field weirdo Welsh bands", according to Anhrefn's Rhys Mwyn, who now works for Welsh label Crai Records. It was a case of enthusiasm for the burgeoning Welsh-language scene, rather than hit-making.

This enthusiasm is a trademark of the Welsh-language rock scene. In fact, throughout the Eighties any band that couldn't get some sort of record deal would simply press their own vinyl and sell their records at gigs. The market for the music was small, but the bands made up for it with their have-a-go attitude.

The scene was developing nicely, and in the early Eighties, Radio One DJ **John Peel** – the standard-bearer for underground pop in the UK, to many – became aware of the growing number of Welsh-language bands, played their records on air and had bands in for sessions, which proved an important catalyst to new Welsh bands. It also introduced their music to a Europe-wide audience. Peel still features Welsh-language bands broadcasting on Radio One on Friday evening and Saturday afternoon.

By the Nineties, Welsh-language pop music had established a solid infrastructure of bands, labels and venues. One of the most prolific, eclectic and innovative of these labels is Caernarfon-based **Ankst**. Originally started as a part-time venture in 1988, becoming a full-time business in 1990, the label releases Welsh-language pop of varied styles, from the techno-rap of **Llwyrbr Llaethog** to the Fall-style avant-garde rock of **Datblygu** and the eccentric, psychedelic guitar melodies of **Gorky's Zygotic Mynci**, who can claim John Cale as one of thelr biggest fans.

Crai Records, also based in Caernarfon and a subsidary of the more folk-oriented **Sain Records**, is another major promoter of Welsh language pop. The label began life in 1989, and its current roster includes acts as varied as original Welsh punks Anhrefn, the folk roots sound of the cheekily titled band Bob Delyn (see "Musicians", above), the hard-edged weird-pop of **Catstonia** (whose "For Tinkerbell" single was an NME single of the week in early 1994), the Welsh-language releases of ex-Alarm vocalist **Mike Peters** and the London-based black reggae band **One Style**, who apparently have a strong affinity with Wales, despite being based elsewhere.

Other home-grown labels promoting Welsh-language bands include the **Fflach** label in Aberteifi, Dyfed, with their subsidiary Semtex specifically for heavy-rock bands. And in Ty Croes, Gwynedd, there's the **Ofn** label, which originally began in the mid-Eighties to release records by experimental, industrial Welsh-language innovators **Plant Bach Ofnus** (Timed Little Children) and the pop-oriented, electronic music of **Eirin Peryglus** (Perilous Plums).

The grass-roots Welsh **gig circuit** is also healthy, with many bands starting out in thelr local pubs and clubs, always worth frequenting when seeking out up and corning bands. The Student Unions of Treforest Polytechnic or Lampeter, Bangor, Cardiff and Swansea Universities also regularly put on Welsh bands. Other notable venues are *TJs* in Newport, *Sam's Bar* in Cardiff, the *Ship and Castle* in Caernarfon, *Gassy Jacks* in Cardiff, and the *Tivoli* in Buckley, near Mold. Welsh-language pop bands can also be found at the **National Eisteddfod**, although this festival is dominated by more traditional Welsh music.

Welsh-anguage bands have also been forging links in **Europe**. Bands like Anhrefn, U Thant, Fflaps, Ffa Coffi Pawb and Beganifs have all taken Welsh-language pop to an international audience. Prague has been a particularly fertile ground for Welsh pop and rock, and many Welsh-language bands are eager to take their music abroad, without compromising their lyrical stance. Singing in Welsh does not mean that the bands suffer from a parochial attitude: Welsh-language bands are on the march!

ROCK AND FOLK COUNCIL OF WALES (CRAG) AND THE CYTGORD AGENCY

CRAG (Cyngor Roc a Gwerin Cymru) began its first year in 1994, and hcpes to act as a catalyst and co-ordinator of Welsh-language music, with the specific aim of increasing its audience both in Wales and around the world. The emphasis of this fledgling organization – a member of the European Committee of Rock Councils – is to co-operate with musicians to develop their interests and style, to co-ordinate live events across Wales, and to gain more media coverage for Welsh-language bands. CRAG will also be representing Wales at international music conferences around the world. It is a major step towards a higher international profile for Welsh-language pop music. CRAG can be contacted at 8 Rhes Fictoria, Bethesda, Gwynedd (☎0248/600444).

The Cytgord Agency are publishers of the Welsh-language pop magazine **SOTHACH** (☎0248/600578), an extensive guide to new Welsh bands, writton in Welsh. It also publishes a weekly Welsh chart (also in Welsh) of top new Welsh bands, a very useful guide to new bands to watch out for. Address as for CRAG.

WELSH-LANGUAGE RECORD LABEL ADDRESSES

For an update of thooo labclo' activities, contact:

Crai Records, Canolfan Sain, Llandwrog, Caernarfon, Gwynedd (☎0286/831111).

Ankst Records, Gorffwysfa, Heol y Bedyddwyr, **Penyroes**, Caenarfon, Gwynedd (☎0286/881010).

Fflach Records, Llys y Coed, Heol Dinbych y Pysgod, Aberteifi, Dyfed SA43 (☎0239/614691).

Ofn Records, Ein Hoff Le, Llanfaelog, Ty Croes,Gwynedd (☎0407/810742).

SELECTED RELEASES

The following records of English-language Welsh bands should be available through most High Street record shops.

The Alarm – including a live album and a singles collection, The Alarm released seven albums between 1984 and 1991. Here's four recommended LP's.

Declaration (IRS). Debut LP released in 1984, full of catchy rock songs, and establishing a simplistic formula they rarely veered from.

Strength (IRS). Second LP and another big hit, building on their existing style.

Standards (IRS). A compilation of the band's past hits, released in 1990.

Raw (IRS). Last LP, released in 1991, with a Welsh-language version released on Crai Records. The sound of a band ready to split.

Manic Street Preachers

Motown Junk (Heavenly). Essential first single. Total in-your-face punk rock.

Generation Terrorists (Sony). Debut double LP. Rock ballads meets punk ferocity and anti-establishment politics. A great rock record.

Gold Against The Soul (Sony). Second, more mature and darker LP. Straight up-rock with some rousing choruses. "From Despair To Where" – also released as a single – is a classic.

K Klass

Universal (Deconstruction/Parlophone). Debut LP from this Wrexham dance act/remix team, featuring ex-Smiths guitarist Johnny Marr on one track.

WELSH-LANGUAGE BANDS

For Welsh-language music in general, most major towns in Wales have a Welsh Shop (*Siop Gymraeg*), which will often stock an extensive selection of Welsh-language music. Cob Records in Porth Mado (☎0766/512170) and Bangor (☎0248/353020) are also worth checking out.

Ankst Records

Various Artists: "A P Elvis, the Fifth Anniversary Collection". Featuring 15 tracks including tracks from Catatonia, Ian Rush, Ffa Coffi Pawb, Gorky's Zygotic Mynci, Fflaps, Beganifs and Datblygu. A great introduction to modern Welsh-language pop music of all shades.

Gorky's Zygotic Mynci: "Tatay". Debut LP from this young Carmarthen band, loved by John Cale and favourites with the UK music press. A strange but compelling brew of gentle balladeering and noisy guitars.

Various artists: "O'R Gad". Another great Ankst collection, with 18 tracks featuring all the Ankst roster and others.

Crai Records

Distributed by independent record distributors Revolver, and therefore available in most independent stores and mainstream record shops throughout the UK.

Catatonia: "For Tinkerbell". NME single of the week in early 1994, a Welsh-language band attracting attention from the London-based record labels. LP released mid-1994.

Anhrefn: "Rhedeg I Paris". The godfathers of Welsh-language rock, with an LP produced by Sex Pistols producer Dave Goodman. Raw and noisy, as you'd expect.

Anhrefn: "Bwtleg". Live, mono recording from London's Powerhaus, recorded March 1, 1990. Anhrefn in all their gutsy glory. The official bootleg!

Mike Peters: "Back into the System". Comeback single for the ex-Alarm vocalist, joined by all-Welsh band *The Poets*. It sees him taking a more acoustic path than previously.

Ofn Records

Eirin Peryiglus: "Noeth". Electronic dance/pop music, released in 1992.

BOOKS

TRAVEL AND IMPRESSIONS

Dennis Abse, *Journals from the Antheap* (Century Hutchinson). Abse's prose, more accessible than his poetry, succeeds in being wry, serious and provocative at the same time. Much of this volume deals with journeys in his native Wales, which he describes with verve and tongue-in-cheek humour.

George Borrow, *Wild Wales* (Century). Highly entertaining easy-to-read account of the author's walking tour of Wales in 1854, which says as much about Borrow and his ego as it does about Wales and the Welsh, who he treats with benign condescension.

Giraldus Cambrensis, *The Journey through Wales* and *The Description of Wales* (Penguin Classics). Two witty and frank books in one volume, written in Latin by the quarter-Welsh clergyman after his 1188 tour around Wales recruiting for the third Crusade with Archbishop Baldwin of Canterbury. Both superb vehicles for Gerald of Wales' learned ruminations and unreserved opinions, *The Journey* breaks up the seven-week tour "through our rough, remote and inaccessible countryside" with anecdotes and ecclesiastical point scoring, while *The Description* covers rural life and the finer and less praiseworthy aspects of the Welsh character, summing up with "you may never find anyone worse then a bad Welshman, but you will certainly never find anyone better than a good one".

Tony Curtis (ed), *Wales: the Imagined Nation* (Poetry Wales Press). A wonderfully varied selection of essays and wry poetry on a great diversity of topics, including writers such as R. S. Thomas and Dylan Thomas, together with the representation of Plaid Cymru in Welsh and British media, Wales in the movies, images of Welsh women and the country's indigenous theatre. Learned, often funny, and extremely rich.

Daniel Defoe, *A Tour Through the Whole Island of Great Britain* (Penguin). Classic travelogue opening a window onto Britain in the 1720s. Twenty pages on Wales.

Trevor Fishlock, *Talking of Wales – a companion to Wales and the Welsh* and *Wales and the Welsh* (Cassell). Both rather dated now, but often found in secondhand stores. Vivacious outsider's guides to living in Wales from the ex-Welsh correspondent of the London. *Times* newspaper. Both books touch on folklore, humour and politics and paint an engaging picture of a nation perennially trying to define itself.

Jan Morris, *The Matter of Wales* (Penguin). Prolific half-Welsh travel writer Jan Morris immerses herself in the country that she evidently loves. Highly partisan and fiercely nationalistic, the book combs over the origins of the Welsh character and describes the people and places of Wales with precision and affection. A magnificent introduction to a diverse, and occasionally perverse, nation.

H.V. Morton, *In Search of Wales* (o/p). Snapshots of Welsh life in the 1930s. A companion volume to his *In Search of England.*

Thomas Pennant, *A Tour in Wales* (Bridge Books). First published in 1773, the stories from Pennant's horseback tour helped foster the Romantic enthusiasm for Wales' rugged landscapes.

Peter Sager, Wales (Pallas). Not so much a travel guide as a 400-page celebratory essay on Wales and especially its people by a German convert to the cause of all things Welsh. A passionate and fabulously detailed book.

Meic Stephens, *A Most Peculiar People: Quotations about Wales and the Welsh.* A fascinating and varied volume of quotations going back to the century before Christ and up to this decade. As a portrait of the nation, with all of its frustrating idiosyncracies and endearing foibles, it is a superb example. Most tellingly, it is easy to see how the typical English attitude of sneering at the Welsh is rooted way back in history.

Edward Thomas, *Wales* (Oxford University Press). Classic 1905 book, in constant reprint. Lyrical and literary ponderings on the Welsh and harsh put-downs on the English. Thomas' grandolinquent opinions, wrapped and couched in his assured and poetical English, are often maddening, but never dull.

George Thomas, *My Wales*, with photographs by Lord Snowdon (Century). Glossy, ponderous coffee-table tome with selections of other writings and the musings of the ex-House of Commons Speaker as well. Fabulous photographs are the main attraction in a book that's better as a souvenir than as a guide.

HISTORY, SOCIETY AND CULTURE

Leslie Alcock, *Arthur's Britain* (Penguin). Info laden assemblage of all archeological and written evidence on the shadowy centuries after the Roman occupation of Britain.

Janet Davies, *The Welsh Language* (University of Wales Press). The most up-to-date history and assessment of Europe's oldest living language is packed full of readable information, together with plans and maps showing the demographic and geographic spread of Welsh over the ages.

John Davies, *A History of Wales* (Allen Lane). Exhaustive run through Welsh history and culture from the earliest inhabitants to the late 1980s reassessing numerous oft-quoted "facts" along the way. Translated from the original 1990 Welsh edition, it is clearly written and very readable but, at 700 pages, is hardly concise.

Gwynfor Evans, *Land of my Fathers* (Gomer). Plaid Cymru's elder statesman first produced this massive tome in Welsh, translating it into English for publication over twenty years ago. As a thorough and impassioned history, it is hard to beat, although the political viewpoint of the author is always apparent.

Geoffrey of Monmouth, *History of the Kings of Britain* (Penguin). First published in 1136 this is the basis of almost all Arthurian legend. Writers throughout Europe and beyond used Geoffrey's unreliable history as the basis of a complex corpus of myth.

P.H. Jeffery, *Ghosts, Legends and Lore of Wales* (The Old Orchard). Excellent, slim and low-cost, if rambling, introduction to Welsh mythology.

Philip Jenkins, *A History of Modern Wales 1536–1990* (Longman). Magnificently thorough book, placing Welsh history in its British and European contexts. Unbiased and rational appraisal of events and the struggle to preserve Welsh consciousness, with enough detail to make it of valuable academic interest and sufficient good humour to make it easily readable.

J. Graham Jones, *The History of Wales* (University of Wales). The best step forward from our own entry-level history section, this concise, easy-paced overview of Welsh life comes with a welcome bias towards social history.

John Matthews, *A Celtic Reader* (Aquarian). Selections of original texts, scholarly articles and stories on Celtic legend and scholarship. Sections on the Druids, Celtic Britain and The Mabinogion. Assumes a deep interest.

Elizabeth Mavor, *The Ladies of Llangollen* (Penguin). The best of the books on Wales' most notorious and celebrated lesbian couple. This volume traces the ladies' inauspicious beginnings in Ireland, their spectacular elopement and the way that their Llangollen home, Plas Newydd, became a place of pilgrimage for dozens of influential eighteenth-century visitors. A fascinating story lovingly told.

Trefor M. Owen, *The Customs and Traditions of Wales* (University of Wales). Pocket guide to everything from outdoor prayer meetings to the curious Mari Lwyd when men dress as grey mares and snap at all the young girls. Easy to read and fun to dip into.

George Thomas, *Mr Speaker* (Century). The autobiography of Rhondda-born George Thomas, rich toned ex-Speaker of the House of Commons and now sitting in the Lords as Lord Tonypandy. From his humble beginnings, including the forceful discouragement of speaking Welsh at school, Thomas charts his fascinating career and is particularly interesting for his shattering recollections of the Aberfan disaster and, when Secretary of State for Wales, the 1969 investiture of the Prince of Wales at Caernarfon.

Alice Thomas Ellis, *A Welsh Childhood* (Penguin). Wonderfully whimsical reminiscences of growing up in north Wales. Welsh legends and folk tales form a large part of the backdrop, fermenting excitedly in the young imagination of the popular novelist.

Wynford Vaughan-Thomas, *Wales – a History* (Michael Joseph). One of the country's most missed broadcasters and writers, Vaughan-Thomas' masterpiece is this warm and spirited history of Wales. Working chronologically through from the pre-Celtic dawn to the aftermath of the 1979 devolution vote, the book offers perhaps the clearest explanation of the evolution of Welsh culture, with the author's patriotic slant evident throughout.

Jennifer Westwood, *Albion: A Guide to Legendary Britain* (UK Grafton). Highly readable volume on the development of myth in literature.

ART, ARCHITECTURE AND ARCHEOLOGY

Pevsner and others, *The Buildings of Clwyd* and *The Buildings of Powys* (Penguin). Magisterial series covering just about every inhabitable structure. This project was initially a one-man show, but later authors have revised Pevsner's text, inserting newer buildings but generally respecting the founder's personal tone. Volumes of Dyfed, Glamorgan, Gwent and Gwynedd are yet to be published.

T.W. Potter and Catherine Johns, *Roman Britain* (British Museum/University of California). Generously illustrated account of Roman occupation written by the British Museum's own curators.

Wales: Castles and Historic Places (WTD/CADW). General chat and rich colour photos of the major CADW sites around the country.

LITERATURE

Bruce Chatwin, *On the Black Hill* (Picador). This entertaining and finely wrought novel follows the Jones twins' eighty-year tenure of a farm on the Radnorshire border with England. Chatwin casts his sharp eye for detail over both the minutiae of nature and the universal human condition providing a wonderfully gentle angle on Welsh–English antipathy.

Alexander Cordell, *Rape of the Fair Country* (Sphere), *Hosts of Rebecca* (o/p), *Song of the Earth* (o/p). Dramatic historical trilogy in the best-seller tradition partly set in the cottages on the site of the Blaenavon ironworks during the lead up to the Chartist Riots. *This Sweet and Bitter Earth* (Coronet) immortalizes Blaenau Ffestiniog in a lusty slate epic.

John Davies (ed), *The Green Bridge: Stories from Wales* (Seren). Absorbing selection of 25 short stories from a broad spectrum of Welsh authors writing in English during the twentieth century, including Dylan Thomas.

Thomas Firbank, *I Bought a Mountain* (Hodder). One of the few popular books set in north Wales in which Anglo-Canadian Firbank spins an autobiographical yarn of his purchase of most of the Glyder range and subsequent life as a Snowdonian sheep farmer during the 1930s. Generous but patronizing observations about his neighbours and his wife mar an otherwise enjoyable, easy read.

Iris Gower, *Copper Kingdom, Proud Mary, Spinners' Wharf, Black Gold, Fiddler's Ferry, The Oyster Catchers*, the list goes on (all Corgi). Romantic novels by Wales' most popular author.

Glyn Jones, *The Island of Apples* (University of Wales). Set in south Wales and Carmarthen in the early years of the twentieth century, Jones artfully portrays a sensitive valley youth's enthrallment in the glamour of the district's new arrival.

Lewis Jones, *Cwmardy* (Lawrence and Wishart). Longtime favourite socialist novel, written in 1937 and portraying life in a Rhondda valley mining community in the early years of the twentieth century. Followed by its sequel, *We Live*.

Russell Celyn Jones, *Soldiers and Innocents* (Picador). Tale of a soldier who deserts from Northern Ireland, kidnaps his five-year-old son and embarks on a voyage of self-discovery which takes him back to the Welsh mining community.

Richard Llewellyn, *How Green Was My Valley?* (Penguin), *Up into the Singing Mountain* (o/p), *Down where the Moon is Small* (o/p), *Green, Green My Valley Now* (o/p). Vital tetralogy in eloquent and passionate prose following the life of Huw Morgan from his youth in a south Wales mining valley through emigration to the Welsh community in Patagonia and back to 1970s Wales. A best-seller during World War II and still the best introduction to the vast canon of "valleys novels", *How Green was my Valley?* captured a longing for a simple, if tough, life steering clear of cloying sentimentality.

Gwyn and Thomas Jones (transl), *The Mabinogion* (Everyman's). Welsh mythology's classic, these eleven orally developed heroic tales were finally transcribed into the Book of Rhydderch (around 1300–25) and the Red Book of Hergest (1375–1425). Originally translated by Lady Charlotte Guest between 1838–49 at the beginning of the Celtic revival.

Gwyn Thomas, *A Welsh Eye* (Hutchinson). A partly autobiographical, partly anecdotal view of how it feels to grow up in a small Rhondda town full of arcane and idiosyncratic wit and much more.

Dylan Thomas, *Collected Stories* (Dent Everyman). Far better than buying any of the single editions, this book contains all of Thomas' classic prose pieces: *Quite Early One Morning*, which metamorphosed into *Under Milk Wood*, the magical *A Child's Christmas in Wales* and the compulsive, crackling autobiography of *Portrait of the Artist as a Young Dog*. The language still burns bright in a uniquely robust way.

Dylan Thomas, *Under Milk Wood* (Dent Everyman). His most popular play, telling the story of a microcosmic Welsh seaside town over a 24-hour period. Reading it does little justice – far better, instead, to get a tape or record version of the play, and luxuriate in its rich poetry, or, as Thomas himself described it, "prose with blood pressure".

Alice Thomas Ellis (ed), *Wales - an Anthology* (Fontana). A beautiful book, combining poetry, folklore and prose stories rooted in places throughout Wales. All subjects, from rugby and mountain climbing to contemporary descriptions of major events, are included in an enjoyably eclectic mixture of styles. Possibly the best introduction to Welsh writing.

POETRY

John Barnie, *The City* and *The Confirmation* (Gomer Press). One of Wales' best contemporary writers, notable mainly for his mixing of styles from poetry to prose, narration and description. Evocative tales of wartime childhood and stifling parenting, leading to a poignant search for love.

Ruth Bidgood, *Lighting Candles* (Poetry Wales Press). Light, elegiac verse inspired by the Welsh landscape. Her interweaving of climate, scenery and emotion is delicately handled, producing fine, and deceptively robust, pieces that stand up as physical description, spiritual discussion or both.

Gladys Mary Coles, *The Glass Island* (Duckworth). Breathtakingly cool and descriptive poetry, much of which is set in the Berwyn Mountains in Clwyd and the hills of north Wales. Her gently probing technique uses discoveries of random objects or sights to spark off musings about their history and derivation.

Gerard Manley Hopkins, *Collected Works* (Penguin). The religious poetry of this late nineteenth-century Anglo-Catholic still bears scrutiny today. Much of his best work was inspired by Wales – "the loveable west" – and the metre and rhythm of the Welsh language that he strove to learn. Heartfelt and often profoundly sad, with an exquisite ability to marry the grandeur of the landscape with the intensity of his feelings.

David Jones, *The Anathémata* (Faber). Once ranked with Ezra Pound and T.S. Eliot (who once declared him to be the finest poet then working in the English language), Jones has now been relegated to the footnotes of literary Modernism. A pity, because this long poem – a meditation on the history and mythology of Celtic-Christian Britain – is one of the most ambitious and intelligent pieces of writing to come out of Wales. A refreshing change from the emotive lushness of Dylan Thomas.

T. Harri Jones, *Collected Works* (Gomer Press). Jones is one of Wales' most prolific twentieth- century writers, pumping out work firmly rooted in his native country. His passion and nationalism seems occasionally naive, although the *hiraeth* for Wales and its rootedness cannot fail to impress.

Meic Stephens (ed), *Oxford Companion to the Literature of Wales*. A customarily thorough volume of Welsh prose, spanning the centuries from the folk tales of the *Mabinogion* to modern- day writings. A succinct and entertaining collection.

Dylan Thomas, *Collected Poems* (Dent Everyman). Thomas' poetry has always proved less populist than his prose and play writing, largely due to its density and difficulty. Many of his lighter poems resound with perfect metre and precise structure, including classics such as *Do not go gentle into that good night*, a passionate yet calm elegy to his dying father.

R.S. Thomas, *Selected poems 1946–1968* (Bloodaxe). A fierce, reclusive Welsh nationalist, Thomas' poetry tugs at issues such as God (he was an Anglican priest) Wales ("brittle with relices") and the family. His passion shines throughout this book, probably the best overview available of his prolific work.

FOOD AND DRINK

E. Smith Twiddy, *A Little Welsh Cookbook* (Appletree). Slim hardback neatly covering the traditional Welsh staples: *bara brith, cawl,* glamorgan sausages and *laver bread.*

Sarah & Ann Gomar, *Welsh Country Recipes* (Ravette). Despite leaving out some of the traditional dishes this bargain book makes amends with its broad scope of more ambitious Welsh recipes.

The Best Pubs in North Wales (CAMRA). A hundred or so top pubs with the emphasis on good beer, produced by the Campaign for Real Ale.

OTHER GUIDES

William Condry, *Snowdonia* (David & Charles). A personal guided tour around the Snowdonia National Park dipping into geology, natural history and industrial heritage. The best detailed approach to the region.

William Condry, *Wales* (Gomer). As for Snowdonia, but covering the whole country.

David Greenslade, *Welsh Fever: Welsh Activities in the United States and Canada Today* (D. Brown & Sons). Essential companion for anyone searching out Welsh and Celtic roots in North America. Commentary on regions from Quebec to San Diego along with accounts of a hundred individual sites of Welsh or Celtic interest.

Moira K. Stone, *Mid Wales Companion* (Anthony Nelson). Wide-ranging though not terribly detailed look at life in the stretch of Wales from southern and eastern Snowdonia down to the Brecon Beacons. The town guides are perfunctory, and it is better for the examination of history (from transport to art), landscape influences and industry.

WILDLIFE AND THE ENVIRONMENT

D. & R. Aichele, H.W. & A. Schwegler, *Wild Flowers of Britain and Europe* (Hamlyn). Superb full-colour identification guide divided by flower colour and sub-divided by flower form and habitat. Over 900 species covered but not Wales or even UK specific.

Douglas Botting, *Wild Britain: A Traveller's Guide* (Sheldrake). Not much use for species identification but plenty of information on access to the best sites and what to expect when you get there. Excellent photos.

William Condry, *A Welsh Country Diary* (Gomer). Over three hundred brief insights into the intricacies of Welsh country life – from the names of rivers to grass snakes in the garden – seen through the eyes of the longest serving contributor to The Guardian's Country Diary column.

Michael Leach, *The Secret Life of Snowdonia* (Chatto & Windus). Beautifully photographed coffeetable delvings into the least visible natural sights of Snowdonia from feral goats to the Snowdon lily and a close-up of a raven in its nest.

Les Lumsden and Colin Speakman, *The Green Guide to Wales* (o/p). Eco-tourism Cambrian style. A now-dated pocket guide to how to get around Wales with the least damage to the environment and its people. Solid background section on green tourism and good for co-operative and community initiative contacts.

David Saunders, *Where to Watch Birds in Wales* (Helm). Enthusiasts guide to Wales' prime birding locations along with a bird spotting calender and a list of English-Welsh-Scientific bird names. Not an identification guide.

Detef Singer, *Field Guide to Birds of Britain and Northern Europe* (Crowood). Colour-coded sections based on birds' plumage, and 700 beautiful photos back up detailed discussion of behaviour and habitat.

Roger Thomas, *Brecon Beacons National Park - a Countryside Commission Guide* (Webb & Bower). Superb book, going into huge detail on the beginnings and building of the Beacons, as well as the wildlife and flora that you can expect to see there today. Well-written and hugely informative, whilst remaining essentially personal and enthusiastic.

Martin Walters, *Wildlife Travelling Companion: Great Britain and Ireland* (Crowood, £14). One of the best amateur books on the flora and fauna of the British Isles, with a few full-colour pages to aid identification, and region-by-region site guide. Twenty pages specifically on Wales covering South Stack, Newborough Warren, Bardsey, Cadair Idris,

Devils Bridge, St David's Head, Skomer island and more.

Collins Field Guides (Collins). Series of thorough pocket-sized identification guides. Topics include insects, butterflies, wildflowers, mushrooms and toadstools, birds, mammals, reptiles, and fossils.

OUTDOOR PURSUITS

Bob Allen, *On Foot in Snowdonia* (Michael Joseph, hardback £15). Inspirational and superbly photographed guide to the hundred best walks, from easy strolls to hard scrambles, in and around the Snowdonia National Park. Well-drawn maps, faultless instructions and a star rating for each walk help you select your route. An essential guide, perfect but for its weight.

Pete Bursnall, *Mountain Bike Guide: mid-Wales* (Ernest). Easy-to-follow pocket guide to a score of biking routes with hand-drawn maps. Due to be followed by a north Wales edition.

Cicerone Guides, *The Mountains of England and Wales: Wales, The Ridges of Snowdonia; Hill Walking in Snowdonia; Ascent of Snowdon; Welsh Winter Climbs; Scrambles in Snowdonia* and others, various authors (Cicerone). Clearly written pocket guides to the best aspects of Welsh mountain activities.

Constable Guides, *Best walks in Southern Wales, Best Walks in North Wales, Owain Glyndwr's Way, A Guide to Offa's Dyke*, various authors (Constable). More clearly written pocket guides to the best aspects of Welsh mountain activities.

A. J. Drake, *Cambrian Way: A Mountain Connoisseurs Walk* (A. J. Drake). Thorough and detailed lightweight guide to Wales' most demanding long-distance footpath by one of the original proposers of this three-week-long, 274-mile Conwy–Cardiff route along Wales backbone.

Terry Marsh, *The Mountains of Wales* (Hodder & Staughton). A walker's guide to all 183 600-metre peaks in Wales, giving step-by-step descriptions of one or more routes up them all with additional historical references and local knowledge.

Ordnance Survey Pathfinder Guides (Jarrold). Softcover editions for large pockets covering Pembrokeshire and Gower Walks, Snowdonia, Anglesey and the Lleyn Peninsula Walks and Snowdonia Walks with 28 routes in each embellished with useful, if plodding, accounts of sights along the way.

Ordnance Survey National Trail Guides (Jarrold). More large, paperback editions full of instructive step-by-step descriptions and additional side walks from Offa's Dyke North, Offa's Dyke South and Pembrokeshire Coastal Path.

W. A. Poucher, *The Welsh Peaks* (Constable, hardback £9). The classic book on Welsh hill-walking, it is fairly dated now and it is initially awkward to find your way around the 56 routes.

Shirley Toulson, *The Drovers' Roads of Wales with Fay Godwin* (Whittet, £10) and The Drovers' Roads of Wales II: Pembrokeshire and The South with Caroline Forbes (Whittet, £9). A pair of complementary books giving background material along with instructions on how to trace the routes along which Wales' characteristic black cattle were driven to market in England in the eighteenth and nineteenth centuries. The first book covers the northern two-thirds of Wales with superb shots in black-and-white by photography star Fay Godwin, the much more recent second book covers south Wales with more high-quality photos.

Shirley Toulson, *Walking Round Wales: The Giraldus Journey* (Michael Joseph; hardback £15). A very readable guide broken into 30 walks following the route around Wales taken by the twelfth-century clergyman Giraldus Cambrensis and enlivened by his own quirky accounts.

LANGUAGE

Welsh is spoken widely throughout the majority of the country and as a first language in many parts of the west and north. National TV and radio stations broadcast in it, road signs are written in both Welsh and English, Welsh-medium schools are everywhere, books in Welsh are published at a growing rate of around 400 every year, and magazines and newspapers in the old language are mushrooming. The language's survival, and modest resurgence, is a remarkable story, especially considering the fact that the heart of English culture and its language – the most expansionist the world has ever seen – lies right next door.

In the families of Celtic languages, Welsh bears most similarity to largely defunct Cornish and defiant Breton, the language of the northwestern corner of France. Scots and Irish Gaelic, together with defunct Manx, belong to a different branch of Celtic languages, and, although there are occasional similarities, they have little in common.

The language can be traced back to the sixth century. Through Celtic inscriptions on stones, a section of written Welsh in the eighth-century **Lichfield Gospels**, the tenth-century codified laws of Hywel Dda in neat Welsh prose and the twelfth- and thirteenth-century **Mabinogion** folk tales (believed to have been collated from earlier Welsh writings), it can be seen that Welsh was a thriving language in the centuries up to the Norman invasion of 1066. Moreover, the early language is still identifiable and easily comprehensible for any modern-day Welsh speaker.

English domination since the Norman era has been mirrored in the fate of the Welsh tongue. The Norman lords were implanted in castles throughout Wales to subjugate the natives, with official business conducted in their native French. **Edward I** (1272–1307), who conquered Wales in 1284, was politically sensitive to the power of the language to define a nation, and is said to have promised the Welsh a prince, born in their own country who was unable to speak English. This promise was delivered when Edward made his pregnant wife take up residence in Caernarfon castle, enabling the king to hold the new-born infant up as a non-English speaking, Welsh-born prince.

Real linguistic warfare came with the 1536 **Act of Union** under Henry VIII. This stated that "from henceforth no Person or Persons that use the Welsh Speech or Language shall have or enjoy any Manner, Office or Fees within this Realm of England, Wales or other the King's Dominion, upon pain of forfeiting the same Office or Fees, unless he or they use and exercise the English Speech or Language". This only legitimized the growing practice of imposing English lords and churchmen on the restless, but effectively cowed, Welsh. Had it not been for **William Morgan**'s 1588 translation of the Bible into Welsh, it is likely that the language would have died. As it was, bringing written Welsh into the ordinary, everyday arena of the public ultimately ensured its survival.

The fate of the language became inextricably linked with its religious use. Right up until the early part of this century, Welsh was actively, even forcefully, discouraged in educational and governmental establishments, but new and Nonconformist religious movements from the seventeenth century onwards embraced the language. The **Industrial Revolution** brought mine owners and capitalists from England into the rapidly urbanizing southeastern corner of Wales, further diluting the language which was, nonetheless, upheld as the *lingua franca* in the growing numbers of chapels. In the first half of the nineteenth century, it is estimated that over 90 percent of the country's population spoke Welsh, with the remaining 10 percent comprised of those around the English border, in the small pocket of Pembrokeshire long known as "Little England beyond Wales" and the wealthier classes throughout Wales, for whom English was part of their badge of status.

In 1854, **George Borrow** undertook his marathon tour of Wales and noted the state of the native tongue throughout. As a natural linguist, he had mastered Welsh and – in typically pompous declamatory fashion – fired questions at people he encountered as to their proficiency in both Welsh and English. The picture he paints is of poorer people tending to be monoglot Welsh, wealthier people and those near the border bilingual. Discouragement of Welsh continued in many guises, most notably in it being forbidden in schools in the latter half of the last century and in the early years of this one. Anyone caught speaking in Welsh had to wear a "Welsh Not", a piece of wood on a leather strap, known as a cribban, that would only be passed on if someone else was heard using the language. At the end of the school day, the child still wearing the cribban was soundly beaten. There are still older people in Wales who can remember this barbaric practice, and it is hardly surprising that use and proficiency of the language plummeted. Figures are borne out by the official British census, the first of which was undertaken in 1851, when 90 percent of the country are recorded as speaking the language. Every decade, the figures dipped quite spectacularly –49.9 percent in 1901, 37.1 percent in 1921, 28.9 percent in 1951 and 18.9 percent in 1981. Then, in 1991, for the first time ever, the percentage of Welsh speakers rose, still around the one-fifth mark but showing the most marked increase amongst the lower age groups, those most able to ensure its future.

The figure of 20 percent (ie half a million people), usually quoted as the current number of Welsh-speakers in Wales, is best seen in its geographical context. Considering the fact that nearly half of the nation's population live in the anglicized regions of Gwent and around Cardiff, the spread of the language becomes clearer. Although it is unusual to hear it regularly in the border counties, it is commonly understood throughout most of West Glamorgan, Carmarthenshire, the northern half of Pembrokeshire, right around Cardigan Bay up to Caernarfon, the Llŷn Peninsula and Anglesey and in parts of inland Clwyd, Montgomeryshire and Radnorshire. The northwestern corner, centred on Snowdonia, Anglesey and Llŷn are the real strongholds of Welsh, reflected in these areas' political affiliation to Welsh nationalism.

If Welsh is ending the twentieth century on a more upbeat note than could ever have been predicted thirty or so years ago (when it was believed to be dying out), it is largely due to those campaigning to save it. The campaign dates back to the eisteddfod revivalists of the eighteenth century, although movements with a more political aim are a product solely of this century. The formation of **Plaid Cymru**, the Welsh National Party, in 1925 was largely around the issue of language, as, indeed its politics have been ever since. In the early 1960s, concerns about the language reached a zenith in the 1962 radio broadcast entitled *Tynged yr iaith* (the fate of the language) by the Plaid founder-member, Saunders Lewis. This became a rallying cry that resulted in the formation of *Cymdeithas yr iaith Gymraeg* (the **Welsh Language Society**) the following year. One of the most high profile early campaigns was the daubing of monoglot English road signs with their Welsh translations, including any town sign written solely in the anglicized format. As any visitor to Wales sees, nearly all signs are now in both languages. A 1967 Welsh Language Act allowed many forms of hitherto English officialdom to be conducted in either language, stating that Welsh, for the first time in over 400 years, had "equal validity" with English.

Bilingual road signs and tax forms are all well and good, but they could do nothing to stem the linguistic haemorrhage that Wales was threatened with. In the multinational, cross-media world of the late twentieth century, the keys to maintaining and promoting a language were in education and media, particularly television. Following the 1967 act, Welsh medium education blossomed, with bilingual teaching in all primary schools and for at least a year in all secondary schools. Many secondary schools, particularly in areas traditionally associated with the language, had Welsh as a compulsory subject for five years. Increasing numbers of schools all over the land educate their students in all subjects through the Welsh language. These trends have brought little but sneers from the English establishment, profiling loud complaints from numbers of parents, often English immigrants, who object to their children being "forced" to learn a "dead" language. Although there are still periodic rumbles of discontent, most have come round to the well-founded view that a bilingual education actually

WELSH VOCABULARY

Alban Scotland
Amgeuddfa Museum
Ap (ab) Son of
Ar Agor Open
Ar Gau Closed
Ar Werth For Sale
Araf Slow
Bara Bread
Bore Morning
Bore da Good morning
Brecwast Breakfast
Bwrdd Table
Bws Bus
Cân Song
Cenedlaethol National
Crefft Craft
Croeso Welcome
Croglen Rood screen
Cromlech Literally "curved stone", generally used to refer to megalithic burial chambers
Cwm Glacially formed, cliff-backed and often lake-filled bowl in mountains Also called cirque or corrie
Cyhoeddus Public
Cymdeithas Society
Cymraeg Welsh
Cymraes A Welshwoman
Cymreictod Welshness
Cymro A Welshman
Cymru Wales
Cymry The Welsh people
Da Good
Dewi Sant Saint David
Dim No (as an instruction), nothing
Diolch Thank-you
Diwedd End
Druids Priestly class in pre-Roman Celtic culture, often including administrators and judges
Dŵr Water
Dydd Day
Dyn (ion) Man (men)
Eglwys Church
Eisteddfod Festival
Faint? How much?
Gorsaf Station
Gweddol Fair
Gwely Bed
Gwesty Hotel
Hafod Temporary summer house
Hanner Half
Heddiw Today
Heddlu Police
Heno Tonight
Heol Road
Hiraeth Longing, yearning
Hwyl Spirit
Iaith Language
Iawn Fine
Llech Slate
Llety Lodging place, B&B
Llew Lion (often found in pub names)
Lloegr England
Llwybr Path
Llyfr Book
Marchnad Market
Menyw Woman
Mihangel Michael, as in Llanfihangel
Milltir Mile
Neuadd Hall
Neuadd Y Dref Town Hall
Nofio To swim
Nos da Good night
Noson/noswaith Evening
Noswaith dda Good evening
Olaf Last
Os Gwelwch yn Dda Please
Pêl-droed Football
Pentref Village
Plaid Cymru The Party Of Wales
P'nhawn da Good afternoon
Rhiniog Buttress
Sais Englishman
Saesneg English language
Sant Saint
Sarn Causeway
Senedd Parliament
Shwmae Hello
Siop Shop
Sir County, Shire
Stryd Street
Sut ydych chi? (formal) or **Sut ywt ti? (informal)** How are you?
Swyddfa Office
Swyddfa'r Post Post office
Tafarn Pub
Tocyn Ticket
Y, Yr or **'r** The
Yma Here
Ysbyty Hospital
Ysgol School

helps children learn, increasing aptitude for other languages. At the other end of the educational spectrum, Welsh-language courses in the country's universities are growing in popularity and status, meaning that, for pretty much the first time in Wales' history, it is possible to be educated in Welsh from nursery to degree level.

Paralleling Welsh-medium education has been the other modern cornerstone for developing a language, a growth in media. In the mid 1970s, a government report recommended that the putative fourth national TV channel be bilingual in Wales, pulling together (and significantly increasing) periodic Welsh programming on other channels. When plans for Channel 4 were drawn up by the new Conservative administration under Margaret Thatcher in the early 1980s, this recommendation (and her own commitment to uphold this idea) had been dropped. A formidable campaign was launched by *Cymdeithas yr iaith*, culminating in a hunger strike by Plaid Cymru leader, Gwynfor Evans.

WELSH PLACE NAMES

The following list is of the most common words that you will see in town and village names. For a brief guide to pronunciation, see "Alphabet", opposite.

Aber Mouth of a river; confluence of two rivers
Afon River
Bach Small or lesser
Bron Slope of a hill
Bryn Hill
Bwlch Mountain pass
Cadair Stronghold or chair
Caer Fort
Canol Centre
Capel Chapel
Carreg Stone
Cant Hundred
Cartref Home
Castell Castle
Clun Meadow
Clwyd Gate, perch
Coch Red
Coed Forest or woodland
Craig Rock
Cyntaf First
De South
Din (Dinas) Fort
Dros Over
Du Black
Dwyrain East
Fawr Big
Fferm Farm
Ffordd Road
Fforest Forest
Gardd Garden
Glas Blue
Glyn Valley
Gogledd North
Gorllewin West
Gwyn White
Gwyrdd Green
Hen Old
Isaf Lower
Llan Clearing, early church
Lle Place
Llwyd Grey
Llyn Lake
Llys Place or court
Maen Stone
Maes Field
Mawr Great
Melin Mill
Melyn Yellow
Merthyr Burial place of saint
Moel Bare or rounded mountain
Môr Sea
Morfa Coastal marsh
Mynydd Mountain
Nant Valley, stream
Newydd New
Nos Night
Pant Vale
Parc Park
Pen Head or top (as of a valley)
Plas Hall or mansion
Pont Bridge
Porth Port or gateway
Rhiw Hill
Rhyd Ford
Taf Dark
Tomen Mound
Traeth Beach
Tref Town
Tŵr Tower
Tŷ House
Uchaf Uppermost or highest
Uwch Higher
Wrth Near, by
Ynys Island

Margaret Thatcher, ever an astute politican, realized that creating a Welsh martyr could have dangerous ramifications and the government gracelessly capitulated, giving birth to **Sianel Pedwar Cymru** (S4C) in 1982. Together with the Welsh language BBC Radio Cymru, S4C has sponsored and programmed enduringly popular Welsh learners' programmes and given the old language greater space than it has ever enjoyed before. Critics would like to believe that this is a false dawn, but this can easily be dismissed just by touring Wales and seeing the sheer number of Welsh-language classes on offer right across the country, including in some of the most anglicized of border towns. Welsh classes can invariably be found out of Wales too, in language centres across Britain and universities in Europe and North America.

The Welsh language is both one of Wales' key strengths and its key drawbacks in the quest for some sort of national emancipation. There is still suspicion, occasionally bordering on hostility, towards the Welsh-speaking "elite" who are seen to control the media and local government in the country. Welsh nationalism is so defined by the language that Plaid Cymru has nearly always had great difficulty in applying its relevance to those who speak only English, particularly in the urban southeast. Nonetheless, the Welsh language seems to be facing the new millennium in greater heart than could ever have been expected only a few decades ago. The new **Welsh Language Board**, chaired by Lord Dafydd Elis Thomas, the former Plaid Cymru MP, seems robust and confident, although its bite and power have yet to be tested seriously. It is nonsensical to believe that Wales can ever become a primarily monoglot Welsh-speaking nation but it does seem to be developing well as a model bilingual entity, in which there is room for both languages to thrive together.

ALPHABET

Although Welsh words, place names in particular, can appear bewilderingly incomprehensible, the rules of the language are far more strictly adhered to than in English. Thus, mastering the basic constructions and breaking words down into their constituent parts means that pronunciation need not be anywhere near as difficult as first imagined.

The Welsh **alphabet** is similar to the English, although with seven vowels instead of five and a different collection of consonants. As well as the same five vowels (a, e, i, o, u), Welsh also has y and w. Most vowels have two sounds, long and short: a is long as in c**a**r, short as in f**a**t; e long as in br**e**r, short as in p**e**t; i long as in s**ea**, short as an t**i**n; o long as in m**o**re, short as in d**o**g; u roughly like a Welsh i; w long as in s**oo**n, short as in l**oo**k; y long as in s**ea** and short as in b**u**n or p**i**n.

In Welsh **adjoining vowels** are common. Ae, ai, aw, ew, iw, oe, oi, ou, wy and yw are the usual forms and are pronounced as the two separate sounds, with, generally, the stress on the first.

There are no letters j, k, v, x and z in Welsh, except in occasional words appropriated and cymrified from other languages. Additional Welsh consonants are ch, pronounced as in German or as in lo**ch**, dd, pronounced as a hard th as in **th**ose, ff and ph as a soft f as in **f**ive and si as a sh in **sh**oe. The typically Welsh consonant that causes the most problem is the ll, featured in many place names such as **Ll**ango**ll**en. This has no direct parallel in English, although the tl sound in Ben**tl**ey comes close. The proper way to pronounce it is to place the tongue firmly behind the top row of teeth and breathe through it without consciously making a voiced sound. Single Welsh consonants are, for the most part, pronounced in similar ways to English. The exceptions are c and g, always hard as in **c**at and **g**ut (never soft as in ni**c**e or ra**g**e) and f, always pronounced as v as in **v**ine.

A further difficulty for those trying to recognize words is the Welsh system of word **mutation**, where a previous word can affect the beginning of a following one, principally to ease pronunciation. Prepositions commonly mutate the following word, turning an initial B into F or M, an initial C into G or Ngh, a D into Dd or N, F into B or M, G into C or Ngh, Ll into L, M into F, P into B, Mh or Ph, T into Th, D or Nh. Thus, "in Cardiff (Caerdydd)" is "y**ng** **Ngh**aerdydd" (note that the "yn" also mutates to ease pronunciation) and "from Bangor" is "o **M**angor".

WELSH NUMBERS

1 un	13 un-deg-tri	200 dau gant
2 dau (fem. dwy)	20 dau-ddeg	300 tri chant
3 tri (fem. tair)	21 dau-ddeg-un	400 pedwar cant
4 pedwar (fem. pedair)	22 dau-ddeg-dau	500 pum cant
5 pump	30 tri-deg	600 chwe cant
6 chwech	40 pedwar-deg	700 saith cant
7 saith	50 pum-deg	800 wyth cant
8 wyth	60 chwe-deg	900 naw cant
9 naw	70 saith-deg	1,000 mil
10 deg	80 wyth-deg	1,000,000 miliwn
11 un-deg-un	90 naw-deg	
12 un-deg-dau	100 cant	

GLOSSARY OF ARCHITECTURAL TERMS

Aisle Clear space parallel to the nave, usually with lower ceiling than the nave.

Altar Table at which the Eucharist is celebrated, at the east end of the church. When the church is not aligned to the geographical east, the altar end is still referred to as the "east" end.

Ambulatory Passage behind the chancel.

Apse The curved or polygonal east end of a church.

Arcade Row of arches on top of columns or piers, supporting a wall.

Bailey Area enclosed by castle walls.

Barbican Defensive structure built in front of main gate.

Barrel vault Continuous rounded vault, like a semi-cylinder.

Boss A decorative carving at the meeting point of the lines of a vault.

Box pew Form of church seating in which each row is enclosed by high, thin wooden panels.

Buttress Stone support for a wall; some buttresses are wholly attached to the wall, others take the form of a tower with a connecting arch, known as a "flying buttress".

Capital Upper section of a column, usually carved.

Chancel Section of the church where the altar is located.

Choir Area in which the church service is conducted; next to or same as chancel.

Clerestory Upper storey of nave, containing a line of windows.

Corbel Jutting stone support, often carved.

Crenellations Battlements with square indentations.

Crossing The intersection of the nave and the transepts.

Decorated Middle Gothic style, about 1280–1380.

Fan vault Late Gothic form of vaulting, in which the area between walls and ceiling is covered with stone ribs in the shape of an open fan.

Finial Any decorated tip of an architectural feature.

Gallery A raised passageway.

Gargoyle Grotesque exterior carving, usually a decorative form of water spout.

Hammerbeam Type of ceiling in which horizontal beams support vertical pieces that connect to the roof timbers.

Jesse window Stained glass window depicting the descendants from Jesse (the father of David) down to Jesus.

Keep Main structure of a castle.

Lancet Tall, narrow and plain window.

Misericord Carved ledge below a tip-up seat., usually in choir stalls.

Motte Mound on which a castle keep stands.

Mullion Vertical strip between the panes of a window.

Nave The main part of the church to the west of the crossing.

Ogee Double curve; distinctive feature of Decorated style.

Oriel Projecting window.

Palladian Eighteenth-century classical style, adhering to the principles of Andrea Palladio.

Pediment Triangular space above a window or doorway.

Perpendicular Late Gothic style, about 1380–1550.

Pier Massive column, often consisting of several fused smaller columns.

Portico Colonnade, usually supporting a porch to the building.

Rood screen Wooden screen supporting a Crucifix (or rood), separating the choir from the nave; few survived the Reformation.

Rose window Large circular window, divided into vaguely petal-shaped sections.

Stalls Seating for clergy in the choir area of a church.

Tracery Pattern formed by narrow bands of stone in a window or on a wall surface.

Transept Sections of the main body of the church at right angles to the choir and nave.

Vault Arched ceiling.

INDEX

SLEEP EASY
BOOK AHEAD
AUSTRALIA
02 261 1111
CANADA
FREEPHONE 0800 663 5777
DUBLIN
01 301766
LONDON
0171 836 1036
BELFAST
01232 324733
GLASGOW
0141 332 3004
WASHINGTON
0202 783 6161
NEW ZEALAND
09 379 4224
IBN INTERNATIONAL BOOKING NETWORK
Call any of these numbers and your credit card secures a good nights sleep …
in more than 26 countries
up to six months ahead
with immediate confirmation
HOSTELLING INTERNATIONAL
Budget accommodation you can Trust